Social Policy

FOURTH EDITION

Edited by

John Baldock • Lavinia Mitton
Nick Manning • Sarah Vickerstaff

OXFORD
UNIVERSITY PRESS

OXFORD

UNIVERSITY PRESS

Great Clarendon Street, Oxford OX2 6DP

Oxford University Press is a department of the University of Oxford.
It furthers the University's objective of excellence in research, scholarship,
and education by publishing worldwide in

Oxford New York

Auckland   Cape Town   Dar es Salaam   Hong Kong   Karachi
Kuala Lumpur   Madrid   Melbourne   Mexico City   Nairobi
New Delhi   Shanghai   Taipei   Toronto

With offices in

Argentina   Austria   Brazil   Chile   Czech Republic   France   Greece
Guatemala   Hungary   Italy   Japan   Poland   Portugal   Singapore
South Korea   Switzerland   Thailand   Turkey   Ukraine   Vietnam

Oxford is a registered trade mark of Oxford University Press in the
UK and in certain other countries

Published in the United States
by Oxford University Press Inc., New York

British Library Cataloguing in Publication Data

Data available

Library of Congress Cataloging in Publication Data

Data available

Typeset by TNQ Books and Journals Pvt. Ltd.
Printed in Italy
on acid-free paper by
L.E.G.O. S.p.A.—Lavis TN

ISBN 978-0-19-957084-3

1 3 5 7 9 10 8 6 4 2

CONTENTS

DETAILED CONTENTS

Part One The origins, character, and politics of modern social welfare systems

ABOUT THE CONTRIBUTORS

John Baldock is Professor of Social Policy at the University of Kent at Canterbury. His main research and teaching interests concern the ageing of the populations in industrial societies and the provision of care services for older people. He has co-written *The Young, the Old and the State: Social Care Systems in Five Industrial Nations* (with Anneli Anttonen and Jorma Sipilä) (Edward Elgar, 2003). His research and writing has dealt with the maintenance of identity in old age (as part of the ESRC's Growing Older Programme directed by Alan Walker) and a study of how families in Europe combine employment with social care responsibilities (as part of the SOCCARE project funded by the European Commission).

Jochen Clasen is Professor of Comparative Social Research and Director of the Centre of Comparative Research in Social Welfare (CCRSW), University of Sterling. His research interests include comparative social policy, social security policy, and unemployment and employment policy in cross-national contexts. Recent publications include: *Reforming European Welfare States: Germany and the United Kingdom Compared* (Oxford University Press, 2005); *Investigating Welfare State Change: The 'Dependent Variable Problem' in Comparative Analysis* (ed. with N.A. Siegel) (Edward Elgar, 2008); *Comparative Social Policy: Concepts, Theories and Methods* (ed.) (Blackwell, 1999); 'Non-employment and the welfare state: the UK and Germany compared' (with J. Davidson, H. Ganssmann, and A. Mauer), *Journal of European Social Policy* 16(2) 2006; 'Unemployment protection and labour market reform in France and Great Britain in the 1990s: solidarity versus activation?' (with D. Clegg), *Journal of Social Policy* 32(3) 2003; 'Changing principles in European social security' (with W. van Oorschot), *European Journal of Social Security* 4(2) 2002.

Hartley Dean is Professor of Social Policy at the London School of Economics. Before his academic career he worked as a welfare rights worker in one of London's most deprived multicultural neighbourhoods. His principal research interests stem from concerns with poverty and social justice. Among his more recently published books are *Welfare Rights and Social Policy* (Prentice Hall, 2002) and *Understanding Human Need* (The Policy Press, 2010). He is currently co-editor of the *Journal of Social Policy*.

Tina Eadie is a Senior Lecturer in Community Justice in the Division of Community and Criminal Justice at De Montfort University, Leicester. She has been involved in the training of police officers and, having worked in the criminal justice system as both a probation officer and manager, has been a provider of probation training for some twenty years, currently working with Probation Trusts across the Midlands and East of England regions. Her research interests relate to the professionalism and professional development of criminal justice practitioners and she has written a number of book chapters and articles in this area.

Tony Fitzpatrick is a Reader in the School of Sociology and Social Policy at the University of Nottingham, UK. He is the co-editor of the *Journal of Policy and Politics* and his recent books include *Voyage to Utopias*, *Understanding the Environment and Social Policy,* and the second edition of *Welfare Theory*.

Jeremy Kendall is a Senior Lecturer in Social Policy at the School of Social Policy, Sociology and Social Research, University of Kent. His main current research interests include the development of civil society and the third sector policy and practice nationally and internationally, and its relationship to other sectors and forms of socio-economic and political action (the state and the market). This international focus involves an interest both in cross-national comparisons – especially in relation to public policy and social policy – and in the role of European and international institutions in shaping the development of civil society. He is also interested in social policy and the public policy making process more generally. He is a Visiting Fellow at the Personal Social Services Research Unit (PSSRU), LSE Health and Social Care, London School of Economics and Political Science.

Derek Kirton is a Reader in Social Policy and Social Work at the University of Kent. His main research interests rest with childcare policy and practice and particularly the areas of adoption and foster care. This is reflected in his publications, which include *Child Social Work Policy and Practice* (Sage, 2009) and *'Race', Ethnicity and Adoption* (Open University Press, 2000) in addition to numerous journal articles and book chapters. He has led various (both local and national) research projects on foster care and is co-author of a report examining services for adults who have grown up in care.

Mark Liddiard is a Senior Lecturer in Social Policy in the School of Occupational Therapy and Social Work at Curtin University, Perth, Western Australia. He has worked on a wide variety of research projects and has a particular interest in housing policy and homelessness. He is co-author, with Susan Hutson, of *Youth Homelessness: The Construction of a Social Issue* (Macmillan, 1994). He also has a strong research interest in cultural policy and has published on museums, art subsidies, and the impact of the mass media upon public attitudes and policy-makers. His most recent research activities have involved a joint study with RMIT exploring the housing outcomes of young care leavers in Australia, as well as a research project examining the challenges of service delivery for homeless men with complex needs.

Nick Manning is Professor of Social Policy and Sociology at the University of Nottingham, and Director of the Institute of Mental Health. He has conducted research on mental health, social change in Eastern Europe, including social movements, and on employment, poverty and health in Russia. Recent books include: *Una cultura dell'inchiesta: Prove della ricerca e communità terapeutiche* (Giovanni Fioriti Editore, 2007), *Health and Healthcare in the New Russia* (Ashgate, 2009), *International Encyclopaedia of Social Policy* (Routledge, 2010, 3 volumes (paperback edition)).

Lavinia Mitton is a Lecturer in Social Policy at the School of Social Policy, Sociology and Social Research, University of Kent. She teaches on welfare in modern Britain, and poverty, inequality and social security. Her research looks at minority ethnic groups in Britain, in particular Black Africans, and welfare innovations at the local level as they impact on lone parents, migrants and unemployed young people.

Rebecca Morley works part-time as a Lecturer in the School of Sociology and Social Policy at the University of Nottingham. She has taught and researched for many years in the area of men's violence to women. She edited, with Audrey Mullender, the first book in Britain dealing with children and domestic violence, *Children Living with Domestic Violence: Putting Men's Abuse of Women on the Child Care Agenda* (Whiting & Birch, 1994). She completed a study funded by the Economic and Social Research Council's Violence Research Programme on the impact of housing policy on women escaping domestic violence, and was part of a team contracted by the Home Office to evaluate the multi-service project package in the Crime Reduction Programme's Violence Against Women initiative.

Jan Pahl is Emeritus Professor of Social Policy at the School of Social Policy, Sociology and Social Research, University of Kent. Her research interests include the control and allocation of money in the household, financial services and financial exclusion, domestic violence, and health and social care. Her publications include *Private Violence and Public Policy* (Routledge, 1985), *Money* *and Marriage* (Macmillan, 1989), *Invisible Money: Family Finances in the Electronic Economy* (The Policy Press, 1999) and over 70 articles, reports and chapters in books. More recently she has worked as a consultant to the Department of Health to implement the Research Governance Framework in the field of social care and was co-editor of the *Journal of Social Policy.* In 2009 she was elected a member of the Academy of Social Sciences; in 2010 she was given a Lifetime Achievement Award by the Social Policy Association; and in 2011 she was awarded a CBE for services to social science.

Gillian Pascall is Professor Emeritus of Social Policy at the University of Nottingham. She has taught health and health policy, gender and social policy, and international social policy to undergraduate, MA and PhD students. Relationships between welfare states and gender have been at the centre of her research and publications since *Social Policy: A Feminist Analysis* was published in 1986. Research with Professor Anna Kwak at the University of Warsaw on gender after Soviet rule was published as: *Gender Regimes in Transition in Central and Eastern Europe* (The Policy Press, 2005). She is currently completing *Gender Equality in the Welfare State?* also for The Policy Press.

Chris Pickvance is Professor of Urban Studies at the University of Kent. A sociologist by background, his research interests include housing, local government, and urban protest. He is co-editor of *Place, Policy and Politics: Do Localities Matter?* (Unwin Hyman, 1990); *State Restructuring and Local Power: A Comparative Perspective* (Pinter, 1991); and *Environmental and Housing Movements: Grassroots Experience in Hungary, Russia and Estonia* (Avebury, 1997) and is author of *Local Environmental Regulation in Post-Socialism: A Hungarian Case Study* (Ashgate, 2003). His articles have appeared in the journals *Sociology*, the *Sociological Review*, and the *International Journal of Urban and Regional Research*.

Kezia Scales is a doctoral candidate in the School of Sociology and Social Policy at the University of Nottingham, where her research focuses on knowledge translation in services for older people. This work is funded by the Collaboration for Leadership in Applied Health Research and Care for Nottinghamshire, Derbyshire and Lincolnshire. Her previous research has looked at staff and service users' experiences in dementia care and adult inpatient mental health services. She received an MSc in Comparative Social Policy from Oxford University, completing her dissertation on the use of economic and social rights in social policy-making in the United States and United Kingdom. Previously, she worked in communications and development in several public health and social care organisations in the United States. She is currently a member of the *Enquire* editorial team at the University of Nottingham.

Justine Schneider has been Professor of mental health and social care at the University of Nottingham since 2004. She teaches social policy to social work students and conducts applied research across a wide range of topics. She previously worked at the University of Durham and at the Personal Social Services Research Unit, University of Kent.

Sarah Vickerstaff is Professor of Work and Employment at the University of Kent. Her research focuses upon paid work and the life course especially at the beginning and end of working life. She has recently completed a number of projects on older workers and retirement for the Joseph Rowntree Foundation, the Economic and Social Research Council, the Equal Opportunities Commission and the Department for Work and Pensions. Recent publications include: *Work, Health and Well-being: The challenges of Managing Health at Work* (eds S. Vickerstaff, C. Phillipson and R. Wilkie) (The Policy Press, forthcoming 2011); *Encouraging Labour Market Activity Among 60–64 year olds.* (S. Vickerstaff, W. Loretto, J. Billings, P. Brown, L. Mitton, T. Parkin and P. White) (Department for Work and Pensions, *Research Report No. 531*, 2008); *The Future for Older Workers: New Perspectives* (eds W. Loretto, S. Vickerstaff and P. White) (The Policy Press, 2007).

Nicola Yeates is Professor of Social Policy at the Open University, Milton Keynes, UK. She has published extensively in the areas of globalization, migration and social policy. She was section editor ('From welfare state to international welfare') for *The Peter Townsend Reader* (The Policy Press, 2010), co-editor (with Chris Holden) of *The Global Social Policy Reader* (The Policy Press, 2009) and editor of *Understanding Global Social Policy* (The Policy Press, 2008a) (see www.oro.open.ac.uk for a list of recent publications). She is a former Editor of *Global Social Policy: Journal of Public Policy and Social Development* (Sage) and is presently Vice-Chair of the UK Social Policy Association.

ACKNOWLEDGEMENTS

The publishers are grateful for permission to reprint the following copyright material.

Chapter 1
Adapted extract from 'Social data and indicators,' *Social Expenditure*—Reference series under Social Protection under Social and Welfare Statistics from OECD/Stat Extracts, http://stats.oecd.org, accessed on 2005:14, reprinted by permission of the publisher.

Adapted extract from 'The production of social welfare' from *Shifts in the Welfare Mix: Their Impact on Work, Social Services and Welfare Policies: Contributions from Nine European Countries in a Comparative Perspective* by A. Evers and H. Wintersberger, eds, Vienna: European Centre for Social Welfare, Policy and Research, 1988:27, reprinted by permission of the publisher.

Chapter 2
Cartoon 'To the rescue!' from 'The Case for the Insurance Bill' by Rt. Hon. David Lloyd George, reprinted by permission of TUC Library Collections, London Metropolitan University.

Cartoon 'Blair won't let Britain down says Lady Thatcher' reprinted by permission of Anne-Marie Cummings for Michael Cummings, *The Times*, 22 March 1997 (British Cartoon Archive, University of Kent, www.cartoons.ac.uk).

Chapter 5
Cartoon 'Extending working life?' © Jeremy Banx 2005, reprinted by permission of Jeremy Banx.

Cartoon 'Is any job better than no job?' © Jeremy Banx 2005, reprinted by permission of Jeremy Banx.

Chapter 6
Cartoon PC4879, 'Son done for cannabis', © Tom Johnston 1998, first published in the *Mirror* on 6 November 1998, reprinted by permission of the publisher.

Cartoon 'Read with single mother', © David Simonds (PC2156), first published in the *New Statesman* on 6 June 1997, reprinted by permission of David Simonds.

Chapter 7
Extract 'The social and political environment as a 4D web of barriers and opportunities for potential volunteers', © Jeremy Kendall 2009.

Chapter 8
Extract 'A Survey of Public Spending in the UK', Crawford, R., Emmerson, C. and Tetlow, G., Institute of Fiscal Studies, London 2009, reprinted by permission of the publisher.

Extract 'Winners and losers in the CSR 2010', Crawford, R., Institute of Fiscal Studies, London 2010, reprinted by permission of the publisher.

Extract 'Cuts to welfare spending: Take 2' (Spending Review) Brewer, M., Institute of Fiscal Studies, London 2010, reprinted by permission of the publisher.

Chapter 9

Extract originally printed in Deacon, B. 'Global and regional social governance', Nicola Yeates, ed.: *Understanding Global Social Policy*, Bristol: Policy Press 2008, reprinted by permission of the publisher.

Table 'Global social governance and world regional social policy' from Deacon, B., Macovei, M., van Langenhove, L., and Yeates, N. eds (2009) in B. Deacon, L. van Langenhove, M. Macovei and N. Yeates (eds.) *World-Regional Social Policy and Global Governance: New Research and Policy Agendas in Africa, Asia, Europe and Latin America*, Routledge: London, reprinted by permission of the publisher.

Table from Deacon, B. with Hulse, M. and Stubbs, P. (1997) *Global Social Policy: International Organisations and the Future of Welfare*, Sage Publications: London, original source: Deacon and Hulse, 1996:52, reprinted by permission of the publisher.

Table from Deacon, B: 'Global social policy: from neo-liberalism to social democracy', in B. Cantillon and I. Marx (eds.) *International Cooperation in Social Security: How to Cope with Globalisation*, Antwerp: Intersentia, 2005 p.163, reprinted by permission of the publisher.

Chapter 11

Extract from the *Guardian* leader pages, 'GCSEs: Burdens of Success', 26.8.05 p.29, © Guardian News & Media Ltd 2005, reproduced by permission of the publisher.

Cartoon 'GCSEs were easy, A levels were easy, university was easy, getting a job was hard', © Jeremy Banx 2005, reproduced by permission of Jeremy Banx.

Chapter 12

Extract from Acheson (1998), citing Dahlgren and Whitehead (1991) 'Policies and Strategies to Promote Social Equity in Health', Stockholm: Institute for Futures Studies, 2000, The NH Plan: A Plan for Investment, a Plan for Reform. Cm. 4818-1, London: Stationery Office.

'Respiratory tuberculosis: death rates, England and Wales', McKeown (1976: 93) Hodder Arnold, reproduced by permission of the publisher.

Figure 'Health expenditure in relation to GDP', from report OECD Health at a Glance 2009: OECD *Indicators*, OECD Publishing, http://dx.doi.org/10.1787/health_glance-2009-69-en, accessed on 7 February 2011, reprinted by permission of the publisher.

Figure 'Timeline of regulator bodies', Table 17, p.108, from Thorlby, R and Maybin, J, eds. 2010, *A high-performing NHS? A review of progress 1997–2010*, London: The King's Fund (2010), reprinted by permission of publisher.

Chapter 13

Cartoon 'Care home horror' by Colin Wheeler, *Private Eye* issue 1260, p.27, reproduced by kind permission of Private Eye Magazine.

Cartoon 'Grim reaper' by Mike Williams, *Private Eye* issue 1261, p.23, reproduced by kind permission of Private Eye Magazine.

Chapter 16

Cartoon 'Teenagers with labels' by Grizelda from www.CartoonStock.com, reprinted by permission of the publisher.

Extract from 'The Wandsworth Violence Against Women Survey: proportion of 314 women experiencing various forms of men's violence during previous twelve months' (Radford 1987:35),

'Policing male violence: policing men' in *Women, Violence and Social Control* by M. Maynard and J. Hanmer, eds., Macmillan: London, reprinted by permission of the publisher.

Chapter 17

Extract from 'Public social expenditure as % of GDP in selected countries', OECD Publishing, Social and Welfare Statistics, OECD StatExtracs, *Social expenditure*—Aggregated data under Social Protection under Social and Welfare Statistics from OECD. Stat Extracts, http://stats.oecd.org, accessed on 10 February 2011, reproduced by permission of the publisher.

Chapter 18

Table 'Practising Physicians', World Health Statistics 2009, Fact Sheet no. 290 Table 6, http://www.who.int/whosis/whostat/2009/en/index.html, accessed on 7 February 2011.

Table 'Total expenditure on healthcare, percentage of GDP', World Health Statistics 2009, Fact Sheet no. 290 Table 7, http://www.who.int/whosis/whostat/2009/en/index.html, accessed on 7 February 2011.

Chapter 19

Cartoon 'Smiling Through: "Not so much of that Cradle to the Grave's stuff, young 'Erbert. Grandpa's sensitive"' by Josef Lee, Evening Standard 5 October 1944, reproduced by permission of Solo Syndication.

Cartoon 'Self-management of risk' by Sidney Harris, © ScienceCartoonsPlus.com, reproduced by permission of Sidney Harris.

Figure 'Average weekly time spent on chores and childcare' from Legal and General, Report: *The Value of a Parent* 2009, reproduced by permission of the publisher.

Although we have tried to trace and contact copyright holders before publication, in some cases it has not been possible. If contacted we will be pleased to rectify any errors or omissions at the earliest opportunity.

This book is enriched with a number of learning tools to help you navigate the text and reinforce your knowledge of social policy. This guided tour shows you how to get the most out of your textbook package.

Learning outcomes

Each chapter begins with a list of key issues that you can expect to understand after reading the text.

> **Learning outcomes**
>
> At the end of this chapter readers will:
>
> 1 be able to describe how the UK Treasury reviews ar budgets;
>
> 2 understand how public expenditure management objectives and the extent to which these are politic

Boxed features

Throughout the book boxes, tables, figures, and cartoons provide you with extra information or a different perspective on the topic under discussion.

> **Box 9.2 Global social policy**
>
> - Social policy issues are increasingly being perceived to be g
> - Transnational flows of goods, services, capital, ideas, pe around the world.
> - Transnational forms of collective action have emerged.
> - International organizations are tangibly involved in social p

Glossary terms

Key terms appear in blue in the text and are defined in a glossary at the end of the book to aid you in exam revision.

> **cash benefits** where the state provides welfare in the form of money (rather than services in kind) such as unemployment benefits (called Job Seeker's Allowance in the UK), pensions, disability benefits, and a minimum income (Income Support in the UK).
>
> **contracting out** when the public sector contracts the provision of social services to an independent for-profit or not-for-profit organization.

Key legislation

Where relevant, important legislation and policy documents have been listed at the end of the chapter.

> **KEY LEGISLATION**
>
> Child Support Act 1991
>
> Children Act 1989
>
> Civil Partnership Act 2004
>
> Domestic Violence, Crime and Victims Act 2004
>
> Family Law Act 1996

Further reading

Take your learning further by using the suggested reading lists to find the key literature in the field, or more detailed information on a specific topic.

> **FURTHER READING**
>
> **Fraser, D.,** *The Evolution of the British Welfare State: A* 4th edn (Palgrave Macmillan, 2009). An authoritative centuries right up to the present day.
>
> **Finlayson, G.,** *Citizen, State, and Social Welfare in Brita* deals with the contribution of the voluntary sector to
>
> **Glennerster, H.,** *British Social Policy Since 1945,* 3rd ed

Useful websites

The internet is an important source of information on social policy and some useful websites have been selected to complement the themes in each chapter.

> **@ USEFUL WEBSITES**
>
> The Joseph Rowntree Foundation regularly funds resear can be downloaded from: **www.jrf.org.uk**.
>
> Reports and policy documents from the UK Department **http://www.dwp.gov.uk/resourcecentre/policy_st**
>
> The Work Foundation publishes useful evidence-based r benefits and losses of greater flexibility in the labour ma

Essay questions

After reading the chapter, test yourself by answering the essay questions provided.

> **Q ESSAY QUESTIONS**
>
> 1 How do social problems emerge into public attention
> 2 How can citizens influence the kind of social policies t
> 3 To what extent is social policy made exclusively by the
> 4 How can ideology influence the kind of social policies
> 5 What are the principal concepts that make up social p

Online Resource Centre

www.oxfordtextbooks.co.uk/orc/baldock4e/

Social Policy is accompanied by an Online Resource Centre. The resources on this website are free of charge and include:

- Updates on developments in social policy
- An interactive flashcard glossary
- Web links

Introduction to the book

The study of social policy helps us to understand how complex modern societies work, how they are sustained, and how they change. All successful societies must find ways to protect their members from the risks of childhood, old age, disability, and illness and to meet their needs for incomes and shelter. These functions are the core subject matter of social policy. At the same time societies must sustain themselves into the future by transmitting to subsequent generations the knowledge and skills on which they are based and by finding ways to deal with environmental, economic, and political dangers. In studying the institutions that carry out these functions, the academic subject known as 'Social Policy' describes how social systems successfully reproduce themselves. It is also why Social Policy is a multidisciplinary subject. It both uses and contributes to many other disciplines. Similarly an understanding of social policy is a necessary part of the training of professionals who work in key social institutions, such as the health and welfare services, schools, colleges and universities, the civil service, the criminal justice system, and the voluntary sector.

A social policy is always a proactive attempt to change a given social order – to make things different to how they would otherwise have been. In the post-communist era of the new millennium, this often means intervening to modify market forces and to redistribute resources amongst a population. The reasons for these interventions are varied, and they change as the economic, social, and political character of society changes. Social policies have most commonly been associated with the meeting of recognized needs, such as the provision of incomes for the old, sick, and unemployed, or with services such as education and healthcare.

More recently the consequences of globalization, environmental change and crises in the world financial systems have required new social policies to minimize or protect against a growing variety of dangers and forms of social exclusion and disadvantage. This fourth edition of the book has been written at a time when the falling value of sterling, rising food and commodity prices and wage increases at rates lower than inflation are combining to reduce real family incomes at a rate of nearly 5 per cent a year. At the same time, the government has decided it is necessary to lower government borrowing in part by reducing the total cost of public spending on social welfare. Social Policy is increasingly concerned with the study of varieties of financial, social and institutional risks and their management by the state and by international organizations.

What is social policy?

The term 'social policy' is used to refer both to the academic discipline Social Policy and to what it studies—social policies themselves. Part One of this book explores both concepts and shows how they relate to the nature, evolution, and politics of welfare systems. Two fairly conventional definitions provide a starting point:

1 A 'social policy' is defined as a deliberate intervention by the state to redistribute resources amongst its citizens so as to achieve a welfare objective.

2 A 'welfare system' is defined as the range of institutions that together determine the welfare of citizens. Among these are the family and the community networks in which the family exists, the market, the charitable and voluntary sectors, the social services and benefits provided by the state, and, increasingly, international organizations and agreements.

Clearly these two definitions raise further questions, in particular what is meant by 'welfare'. Seeking answers to that question is very much what studying the academic discipline of social policy is about.

The classic justification for a social policy is that it will lead to greater social justice, though that is by no means the classic outcome. And the classic statement of that justification is the Beveridge Report's call for an 'attack upon five giant evils': want, disease, ignorance, squalor, and idleness (Beveridge 1942: 170; the full quotation appears in Chapter 1). This conception of what social justice required formed the basis for the post-war British welfare state. But it does not apply so readily in other times or places. Different societies and different groups within those societies have varied and conflicting views about what is socially just. This means that social policy has become the central task of modern politics: deciding which risks should be tackled through state intervention, and what redistributions should be enforced with the authority of the state.

Beveridge's Report was produced in wartime, and he saw social policy largely in terms of redistribution between whole categories of people: from the employed to the unemployed, from those of working age to those in retirement, and from the healthy to the sick. However, today welfare is often seen in more individualistic terms. State social policies help provide the context in which individuals choose and organize their own lives. This perspective sees individual lives as subject to a whole range of risks, particularly risks of dependency and exclusion. Richard Titmuss, who in 1950 was appointed to what was effectively the first professorship of social policy in Britain (at the London School of Economics and Political Science), distinguished between 'natural dependencies, as in childhood, extreme old age and child-bearing', and 'man-made dependencies' such as the risks of industrial injuries and of unemployment and underemployment (Titmuss 1976: 42–4). He suggested that as economies and societies became more complex and industrialized so the numbers of these man-made risks increased, turning life into something of a lottery unless social insurance and welfare services were developed to meet the new dependencies.

Today many of us are able to live our lives taking for granted the guarantees provided by the welfare state and social policy. It is this context that supports 'institutionalized individualism', a self-centred consumerism which nonetheless depends on a welfare system constructed when people subscribed to more communal values (Beck and Beck-Gernsheim 2002). Social policies are fundamental to the organization of our societies and implicit in the choices we make every day of our lives.

So it is unlikely that you will be neutral, disinterested, or uninterested in the issues of social justice and redistribution described in this book and in the life choices they allow. They are part of what makes social policy an exciting subject; it is relevant to both our values and our lives.

The scale and volume of social policy

The moral and political importance of social policy is also reflected in the sheer scale and number of activities it represents. To study the operation of welfare systems is not to study some marginal aspect of the economy. The 27 nations of the European Union spend an average of 26.9 per cent of their gross national products on 'social protection' (Eurostat 2010: Table 6.3). This amounted in 2006, to between 13,458 euros per person in Luxembourg and less than 2,000 in Bulgaria and Romania with the figure for the UK being 7,500 euros (ibid: Figure 6.14). (Throughout this book technical or specialist terms like **gross national product** and **social protection** are printed in blue when they are first used and a definition is supplied in a glossary at the end of the book.) These levels of expenditure effectively make welfare provision what might be called the largest industry in developed economies. Certainly, organizations such as the National Health Service or the state education system in the UK are substantially larger, in terms of the numbers of people they employ, than most major corporations in the private sector. For example, in 2011–12 the National Health Service planned to spend £105,100 million and employed just over one million people (Cm. 7942, 2010). In contrast, the UK private company with the largest turnover in 2010 was Royal Dutch (Shell), which employed 97,000 people (FT Global 500, 2011). If the number of employees is preferred as the key measure of size, then HSBC, with 295,000 employees in 2010, came closest to the NHS. The production of social welfare is arguably the largest industrial sector found in the richest economies of the world.

What does studying social policy involve?

While the making of social policy may be driven by values and politics, the study of social policy should be informed by evidence. Social research, collecting data about how people live, is central to the traditions of Social Policy as an academic subject, and it has a long history rooted in the work of the early social scientists such as Edwin Chadwick (1800–1890), Friedrich Engels (1820–95), Charles Booth (1840–1916), and Seebohm Rowntree (1871–1954).

Consequently you will find a great deal of empirical data in this book – particularly evidence about how resources are allocated. Studying social policy is an excellent way of getting to know about the real world and how people live in it. In this book much of the material is about the United Kingdom. Social policies are still largely the product of the nation-state, and therefore even a more international approach has to take the form of comparing the detail within one nation with that in another. But, as market forces are increasingly global in their operation, so social polices will have to follow if they are to have any redistributive impact. We have recognized the developing internationalism of social policies in this book by giving some account of what is happening in other countries and by including Chapter 9 on Global Social Policy.

The objectives of the book

1 To provide a comprehensive introduction to the subject matter of Social Policy as it is currently studied in schools, colleges, and universities. It does this by reviewing the key debates and issues, and by setting out some of the basic evidence that is relevant.

2 To provide students with a substantial proportion of the information they will need to prepare for seminars, classes, and presentations, and to write essays. Essay and discussion questions are suggested at the end of each chapter.

3 To provide gateways to the further study of social policy issues. This is done by defining and structuring the core topics, by explaining the meaning of key terms (particularly in the glossary at the end of the book), and by listing a large and accessible literature (in the references at the end of the book and in the guides to further reading at the end of each chapter).

The structure and organization of the book

The chapters are the basic building blocks of the book. It will often be necessary to read a whole chapter to understand an area of welfare needs and the social policy interventions designed to deal with them. Each chapter is an essay within its area. This is because Social Policy, the academic subject, takes the form of sets of interconnected arguments and evidence. There are limits to which particular topics can be taken out of their contexts.

The core chapters are those in Part Four, 'Delivering Welfare'. Here the main ways in which governments intervene to redistribute resources and to provide services are described. All the main organized service areas are found here: social security, education, healthcare, social care (including childcare), housing, and criminal justice. To these we have added the comparative organization of social policy in other countries, especially in Europe.

The chapters found in the other four parts of the book are designed to set the core activities of welfare systems in a broader context. These sections are designed to add background and depth to the accounts in Part Four. Thus readers of the core chapters will often find they are referred to chapters in the other sections for further explanation of the context or related issues.

Part One, The Origins, Character, and Politics of Modern Social Welfare Systems, is designed to introduce the subject of social policy, and to examine the different meanings of terms such as welfare, risk, and social exclusion. Since the Industrial Revolution, the state's responsibility for managing the welfare of its citizens has grown, especially through most of the twentieth century. In the twenty-first century there has been a widespread re-examination of the nature and performance of welfare states, with a halt to rising expenditure. This process has pushed social policy increasingly towards the centre of politics. The social policies of the present are rooted in their historical origins, and in the political conflicts and ideological differences that determine what the state does. Social Policy is rightly called a multidisciplinary subject, and Chapter 3 seeks to provide students with some of the social theory that they need to weigh these arguments.

Part Two, The Social and Economic Context of Social Policy, is designed to give substance to a fundamental truth that is often ignored by students of social policy: that the vast bulk of human needs are not met by the public welfare system but by the market economy and by the family. It is these last two institutions that define the context and the starting point of social policies, and readers of Part Four will often be referred back to these chapters. In Chapters 4, 5, and 6 we have sought to provide much of the fundamental evidence about how the family and the market both meet many needs and produce others. It is also in these chapters, particularly Chapters 5 and 6, that important data about population and demographic change are presented. Later, Chapter 19 complements this discussion by showing that social needs are differentiated with respect to the different ethnic and gendered elements of people's lives, and according to their ages and abilities. These chapters are designed for the non-specialist reader, and any student planning to do a substantial or extended piece of work on a social policy issue should read them.

Part Three, The Financial and Organizational Context of Social Policy, is intended to explain and document how social policies are managed and how they are paid for. The state largely intervenes by using public servants to inspect and provide welfare services, and by making decisions about taxation and expenditure, which allow it to pay for what is provided. Chapter 7 discusses the ways in which welfare services are increasingly delivered through the voluntary and non-governmental sector. Global competition is a key constraint on governments' room for manoeuvre in taxing and spending on social policy, but at the same time a failure to invest in an infrastructure of social welfare eventually hampers a country's competitiveness. These dilemmas are discussed both in the Chapter 9 on global social policy, and in Chapter 3.

Part Five, Consequences and Outcomes of Social Policy, begins with two essays. The first assesses the achievements of social policy in the United Kingdom while the second describes the importance of social policy in distributing welfare across our lives. Both chapters are inevitably speculative and involve judgements about what the evidence means. Broadly, they seek to outline how far social policy has come and where it might be going. Earlier, we described state welfare systems as the largest 'industries' to be found in developed economies. Social Policy, the academic subject, might well be expected to offer an account of whether the resources these industries consume are well spent, of whether they have produced welfare gains, and of how they may develop in the future. Some readers might wish to start their investigation of social policy with these two chapters.

Chapter 20 provides students with help on how to research and then write an assignment on a social policy question.

How to use the book

The book is designed to be used by a student seeking to prepare for a class or seminar discussion, for a presentation or an essay on a social policy topic. The following route is suggested:

1 Chapter headings. If there is a chapter title that broadly covers the topic you are researching, then read all or most of that chapter.

2 Subheadings. At the beginning of each chapter is a list of the subheadings used and these may refer to the particular topic or area you are interested in. If not, consult:

a) the index. This is at the back of the book and lists the pages on which a topic is discussed.

b) the glossary. This is also at the back of the book and defines particular terms. A particular term may occasionally appear in more than one chapter, and be defined slightly differently in each. Because Social Policy is a multi-disciplinary subject and one where argument and differences in emphasis are normal, these differences are usually worth exploring. Please find the multiple terms highlighted in the glossary at the back of the book.

References

Beck, U. and Beck-Gernsheim, E. (2002) *Individualisation: Institutionalised Individualism and its Social and Political Consequences*. London: Sage Publications.

Beveridge, W. (1942) *Social Insurance and Allied Services: A Report by Sir William Beveridge*. Cmd. 6404. London: HMSO.

Cm. 7942 (2010) *The 2010 Spending Review*. London: HMSO.

Eurostat (2010) *Eurostat Yearbook 2010*. Office of Official Publications of the European Communities, Luxembourg: http://epp.eurostat.cec.eu.int

Titmuss, R. M. (1976) *Essays on the Welfare State*, 3rd edn. London: Allen & Unwin.

Part One
The origins, character, and politics of modern social welfare systems

Social policy, social welfare, and the welfare state

John Baldock

Contents

Introduction

There are many, particularly social science, disciplines in which questions to do with social policy and the welfare systems of Britain and other countries are likely to be relevant. This is because spending on social policy is often the largest part of governments' budgets and because welfare services are a large part of the economies of industrial societies. You may be using this book as a student on a social policy programme at university or college; or you may be taking a social policy module as part of professional training in social work or nursing; or because you have chosen a social policy option as part of a course in sociology, economics, politics, or history.

Three terms are central to the subject matter of this book: 'social policy', 'social welfare', and 'the welfare state'. This chapter provides an introduction to the meanings that are attached to these and the debates that surround them.

Learning outcomes

After reading this chapter students will:

1 be able to describe what is meant by key terms used in the study of social policy: social policy, social administration, social welfare, the welfare state, social expenditure;

2 understand the range of objectives that may be contained within social policies: redistribution, the management of risk, reducing social exclusion;

3 be able to distinguish between social policies in terms of intentions, methods, and outcomes;

4 be able to distinguish the ways in which societies meet social needs, particularly the roles of the state, the market, and the household;

5 be able to explain why social policy and welfare services are fundamental to the organization of industrial societies.

Social policy

The phrase 'social policy' generally has two possible meanings. It is used to refer to the academic subject called Social Policy or, more importantly, it means social policies themselves, that is to say the intentions and activities of governments that are broadly social in their nature.

It is not very useful to spend a great deal of time trying to pin down the best definition of social policy. There is no right answer. It is much more helpful simply to look at examples of what are generally called social policies. This book contains a great many such examples, and in that sense our definition of social policy is simply demonstrated in the things that are described in this book. A similar approach was taken by a working party that produced a 'Benchmarking Document' to guide the curriculum for social policy in British universities. Rather than define what social policies are, the working party chose to list the main topics that were commonly studied under that heading, though it admitted that the list would have to change over time (see Box 1.1).

Box 1.1 **Optional units currently found within UK Social Policy degree courses**

Social policy knowledge is typically taught and learnt through a focus upon particular themes, topics or issues within degree courses. [Below is] a list of the topics commonly found within UK Social Policy degree courses. This is neither exhaustive nor prescriptive, and different social policy courses are likely to include various combinations of a number of these, or other relevant topics.

- ageing and social policy
- children and social policy
- crime and criminal justice policy
- community care
- comparative social policy
- disability and social policy
- economics, economic issues, and social policy
- education and social policy
- environmental issues and social policy
- equal opportunity policies and their impacts
- family and social policy
- gender and social policy
- globalization/transnationalization/internationalization and social policy
- health and healthcare services
- history and development of social policy in the UK
- income maintenance and social security policy
- local governance, local welfare institutions, and their policies
- leisure and social policy
- Mixed economies of welfare (voluntary, private, and informal sectors)
- organization, administration, and management in welfare institutions
- philosophy of welfare
- poverty, social exclusion, and social policy
- race, ethnicity, and social policy
- science, technology, and social policy
- service user perspectives and user involvement in the social policy process
- sexuality and social policy
- social care
- social policy and the mass media
- social policy and 'virtual society'
- social research methods
- supranational social policy
- transport and transport policy
- welfare rights and social policy
- work, employment, and labour market policies
- youth, youth work, and associated policies.

(Quality Assurance Agency for Higher Education 2007: Section 2.5)

The classic examples of social policies are the activities of governments in providing money and services to their citizens in five main areas:

- social protection benefits (often known as social security);
- health services;
- education services;
- housing provision and subsidies;
- personal social services.

These five areas form the core of this book, contained in Chapters 10, 11, 12, 13, and 15. They can in part be traced back to a much-quoted paragraph in the Beveridge Report of 1942 (Box 1.2) that outlined five main areas where the state should construct social policy after the war. Beveridge's five did not include personal social services. Rather, he laid great emphasis on policies to maintain full employment, which he believed would make personal intervention in people's lives less necessary. Since Beveridge, as the titles of other chapters in this book show, social policy has come to be defined even more broadly, to include areas of government activity such as arts and culture, the criminal justice system, and environmental policies.

Defining social policy in terms of types of expenditure

The most common way of measuring the amount of social policy in any society is to add up the money spent on it. This is a complex process because in different countries the ways in which social policy is financed varies. International bodies seeking to compare the proportions of resources spent on social policy in different countries have developed increasingly sophisticated ways of ensuring they are comparing like with like. For example, Figure 1.1 shows the share of the gross national product (GNP) of various countries taken up by what the OECD (Organisation for Economic Co-operation and Development) defines as 'social expenditure by broad social policy area' in 2007. There are two parts to each column. The lower shows expenditures made directly by governments, what is called public social expenditure, on cash benefits and services to citizens; such as pensions, unemployment benefits, and health and social care services. The upper part of each column shows spending by non-government organizations on similar benefits and services for citizens. This is called private social expenditure.

The OECD defines social expenditure as:

> The provision by public and private institutions of benefits to . . . households or individuals in order to provide support during circumstances which adversely affect their welfare. . . . Social benefits include cash benefits (e.g. pensions, maternity benefits, social assistance), social services (e.g. medical care, childcare, care for the elderly and disabled), and tax breaks with a social purpose (e.g. tax reductions or credits that favour families with children, or favourable tax treatment of contributions to private health plans). (OECD 2005: 7)

Box 1.2 **William Beveridge's 'five giants'**

The Plan for Social Security is put forward as part of a general programme of *social policy*. It is one part only of an attack upon five giant evils: upon the physical *Want* with which it is directly concerned, upon *Disease* which often causes that Want and brings many other troubles in its train, upon *Ignorance* which no democracy can afford among its citizens, upon the *Squalor* which arises mainly through haphazard distribution of industry and population, and upon the *Idleness* which destroys wealth and corrupts men, whether they are well fed or not, when they are idle.

(Beveridge 1942: 170; emphasis added)

These benefits and services are often called 'social protection'. They exclude direct purchases of goods or services (such as medical or social care) by individuals and families and entirely private insurance or savings contracts which are additional to payments required by governments, and are therefore voluntary.

There are two key aspects to the OECD's definition of social expenditure:

- Social expenditure is the result of explicit government laws or regulations that require the payment of taxes or contributions to meet the costs of adverse circumstances that may affect individuals or households.
- Social expenditure involves a degree of redistribution from the less needy to the more needy. For example, health and pension contributions may be at a fixed rate per person or in proportion to income, but the benefits will depend on how much healthcare is used or how long someone lives. Similarly, tax credits or tax deductions to meet needs such as the costs of childcare or saving for pensions redistribute from those taxpayers who do not have these needs to those who do (though tax deductions are rarely particularly pro-poor in their effects).

Put slightly differently, a distinction is made between three kinds of spending aimed at needs or risks: public social spending, private social spending, and exclusively private spending. Only the first two are the result of social policy. The last form is an entirely voluntary form of spending and consumption. The OECD does not count as social expenditure the spending decisions made quite freely by individuals or families to meet their needs or by private companies that voluntarily provide welfare benefits for their employees.

The important point is that the OECD is defining as 'social' those expenditures made as a result of government policy requiring certain welfare needs to be met. In some countries, such as the UK and Germany, spending on health services is largely by the government or by social insurance funds directly controlled by the government (i.e. public social expenditure), whereas in others, such as the Netherlands and the United States, people are required to contribute to private health insurance funds which then pay for healthcare (i.e. private social expenditure). Similarly, some pension and unemployment benefits are provided directly by the state or from funds it controls, while others are paid for by commercially run funds or by employers but as a result of laws and regulations that require people, usually employees, to be members of such arrangements.

There has been a tendency in the past for some commentators to include only social expenditures made directly by governments and to exclude those that are routed through non-government or private organizations but as a direct consequence of a government policy. This is one of the reasons why social expenditure in the United States has often been understated. The countries shown in Figure 1.1 as having high public social expenditure are generally perceived as having the most generous social policies: Sweden and Denmark, for example. In contrast, countries such as Korea, the United States, and Australia have been portrayed as particularly ungenerous in terms of social benefits. However, if one includes 'private social expenditure', that is if one includes both parts of each column in Figure 1.1, then the very big differences in the public social expenditures of the industrialized nations are adjusted for. France and Belgium become the highest-spending countries, followed closely by Sweden and Denmark, all of them spending about a third of their gross domestic product (GDP) on social protection, while the average across the whole OECD is around a fifth. This is not to suggest that all nations are equally generous, but every form of collective help needs to be taken into account when making comparisons, not just those provided by the state.

As Figure 1.1 shows, in Europe public social spending takes a high proportion of total social spending, accounting for 90 per cent except in the Netherlands, Switzerland, and the UK, where it is closer to 80 per cent. In the United States, in contrast, private social spending constitutes over 30 per cent of total social spending. Across the countries in the OECD tables, the two largest types of social spending, comprising more than half the total, are on incomes for retired people and

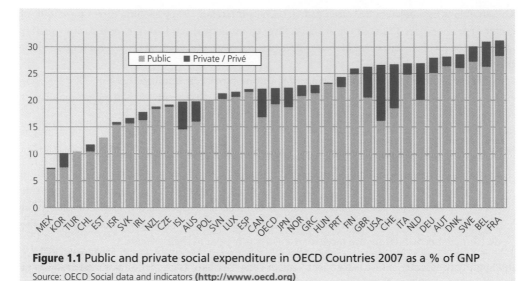

Figure 1.1 Public and private social expenditure in OECD Countries 2007 as a % of GNP

Source: OECD Social data and indicators **(http://www.oecd.org)**

on healthcare. 'With more than 11% of GDP being spent on old age cash benefits and survivor payments, Belgium, Germany, France, Austria, and in particular Italy can be regarded as Pensioner States' (OECD 2005b: 8). The Nordic states—Denmark, Finland, Sweden, Norway, and Iceland—provide social support more evenly between older people and those of working age, though mainly because social spending of all kinds is a larger proportion of their GDPs.

An interesting practical point is that the OECD researchers who compile these widely used social protection statistics choose not to include spending on education, because they argue that governments do not provide education in order to provide support 'during circumstances which adversely affect people's welfare' but rather as a form of investment. Others prefer to regard social investment as a central part of welfare. One of the most influential commentators on social policy, Gøsta Esping-Andersen, has argued that we need a new form of welfare state that is more a 'social investment state' (Esping-Andersen 2002: 26–67) which focuses on children and families because they will provide the welfare of the future. If public expenditure on education is added to Figure 1.1, then both Sweden and Korea would move to significantly higher positions.

Analysing social policy

Although we are suggesting that the careful definitions of social spending used by the OECD provide a good basis for deciding what is included in social policy and what is not, there is no universal agreement as to the definition of a social policy, and it is probably best that this is so. Students of social policy are no more likely to wish for tight boundaries defining their subject than historians would set strict limits on what counts as history, or physicists on what should be included in physics. However, there have developed a number of standard dimensions within which researchers and writers have chosen to analyse the subject matter of social policy. Social policies can be examined in terms of:

1   the intentions and objectives that lie behind individual policies or whole groups of them;

2   the administrative and financial arrangements that are used to deliver policies;

3   the outcomes of policies, particularly in terms of who gains and who loses.

This framework is summarized in Figure 1.2. Over the next few pages we elaborate each of its three parts.

Social policy as intentions and objectives

Sometimes the intentions that inform a social policy or even a whole policy area are fairly clear. For example, in 2001 the British government introduced a new policy to provide an enhanced form of community care called 'Intermediate Care' for older people newly out of hospital or at risk of returning to hospital (see Chapter 13). The policy requires the health service and local government to cooperate in precise ways and to particular deadlines set out in a policy document issued by the Department of Health (DoH 2001a: 49–50). At the same time, the necessary legislation allowing them to work together in these ways was contained in the Health Act 1999.

However, it is more often the case that there are substantial disagreements or uncertainties either within government or between central government and local authorities which lead to vagueness and ambiguity about policy intentions. For example, in 1990 Mrs Thatcher's government issued guidance on its plans to reform community care (DoH 1990) and passed legislation to enable the changes to take place: the NHS and Community Care Act 1990. However, the next decade showed that the intentions had not been clear enough, and local authorities which did not entirely share the government's ambitions were able to find room to do things differently (see Chapter 13). Another example of ambiguous policy goals was the 2005 Education White Paper, 'Higher Standards, Better Schools for All'. A good deal of time was spent by the House of Commons Education and Skills Committee determining exactly what the government's intentions were (HC633-1 2006). White Papers are a key way in which British governments set out their policy goals; but because of disagreements in the cabinet and governing party both principles and detail may be 'fudged', leading to uncertainty rather than a clear policy.

In many areas of social policy, especially where the particular benefits and services have been accumulating over a long period, it is particularly difficult to distinguish what the intentions are now or even what they originally were. They can vary, and involve contradictions. Some goals may be stated clearly, but others remain largely hidden and can only be untangled by looking at the political processes that first created and now sustain social policies and the broader ideologies that influence the key decision-makers. These problems are covered in detail in Chapter 2.

An essential part of the study of social policy is to go beyond the analysis of particular policies and search for common patterns both within one country and comparatively across a number of countries. A number of key common types of intention and objective are suggested by the social policy literature. They are grouped under three headings: redistribution; risk management; and reducing social exclusion.

Redistribution In the Introduction we suggest that redistribution is a defining characteristic of social policy: 'A social policy is defined as a deliberate intervention by the state to redistribute resources amongst its citizens so as to achieve a welfare objective.' There is a sense in which this is always true. No government would intervene through policy if it believed that the existing allocation of resources was satisfactory. So social policy always involves changing what would have been the status quo. However, two kinds of redistribution are particularly important.

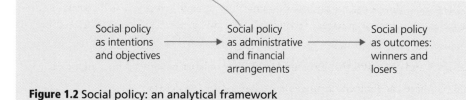

Figure 1.2 Social policy: an analytical framework

First, there is redistribution away from those who have more to those who have less in order to create greater equality along a particular dimension such as income, or access to a key service such as education or healthcare. This is what is sometimes called the 'Robin Hood' function of social policy. This kind of redistribution is essentially driven by ethical and moral considerations to do with fairness and justice. There are many people who believe inequalities of income and wealth beyond a certain point are simply unacceptable and should be corrected through vertical redistribution from the richer to the poorer. There is also growing evidence that the experience of living in a materially unequal society is harmful to people and may lead to ill health and even early death (see Chapter 12). This argument is particularly associated with the work of Richard Wilkinson, who has argued that there are 'psychosocial pathways' between inequality and illness (2000; Wilkinson and Pickett 2010a). More recently Professor Sir Michael Marmot was asked by the Department of Health to conduct a comprehensive review into health inequalities in England; some of the key messages of this review are in Box 1.3.

Secondly, the state may use social policy to redistribute resources because the existing allocation is inefficient. This is a justification in terms of what economists call market failure. Classic examples are the provision of free schooling or of compulsory schemes making people save for old age. Without these interventions, people would not be prepared to pay for enough education to meet the needs of the economy; or, because individuals tend to discount their future needs, they would not save enough for old age. Much of this kind of redistribution may be horizontal redistribution and lifetime redistribution. Through these social policies the state forces people to spend more on education than they otherwise would, by taxing them and spending the money on their behalf. In this way what can happen is that the state redistributes people's incomes across their lifetimes, by taking from them when they are in work so that they may benefit in retirement, sickness, or unemployment. (Chapter 18 explores the degree to which social policies succeed in achieving these sorts of redistribution.)

Box 1.3 Fair Society, Healthy Lives

Reducing health inequalities is a matter of fairness and social justice. In England, the many people who are currently dying prematurely each year as a result of health inequalities would otherwise have enjoyed, in total, between 1.3 and 2.5 million extra years of life.

There is a social gradient in health – the lower a person's social position, the worse his or her health. Action should focus on reducing the gradient in health…

Action to reduce health inequalities will benefit society in many ways. It will have economic benefits in reducing losses from illness associated with health inequalities. These currently account for productivity losses, reduced tax revenue, higher welfare payments and increased treatment costs…

Reducing health inequalities will require action on six policy objectives:

- Give every child the best start in life.
- Enable all children, young people and adults to maximize their capabilities and have control over their lives.
- Create fair employment and good work for all.
- Ensure healthy standard of living for all.
- Create and develop healthy and sustainable places and communities.
- Strengthen the role and impact of ill health prevention.

(Marmot 2010: 9)

The management of risk A powerful way of understanding social policies is to see them as ways in which societies collectively protect themselves from the risks of harm that individuals face in life. Risks are a natural part of the human condition, and they are also the products of our civilization and its technologies. Richard Titmuss distinguished between natural risks or dependencies, such as childhood, sickness, and old age, and man-made risks that are products of our civilization, such as unemployment and industrial injury (Titmuss 1976: 42–4). In the language of the time he defined those upon whom those risks had fallen as being 'in need'. He argued that the social policies of the post-war welfare states were designed to meet certain natural and man-made needs collectively through the mechanism of government. Thus social security systems to provide incomes to the unemployed, the sick, and the retired were set up, as were comprehensive education and healthcare services. In this sense social policy existed to meet social need (see Chapter 4).

More recent social theorists have extended this analysis to point out that, as societies become more complex and interconnected, so these man-made risks increase in number to include the effects of industrial pollution and the negative consequences of technology which may, for example, introduce dangerous particles or drugs into our environment or even accidentally contaminate huge areas, as happened when the explosion at the Chernobyl nuclear power station released radioactive clouds across Europe. The sociologist Ulrich Beck argues we now live in a 'risk society' in which people are confronted with socially and economically created risks that even endanger the survival of the species. He points to 'organized irresponsibility' in which many leading social institutions, including private companies, large government bureaucracies, and the legal system, produce risks of harm or disadvantage against which individuals have little power to protect themselves (Beck 1992). This is an analysis that links the nature of postmodern industrial societies, which are domi-nated by private capital and market interests, to a need for the state to counteract their effects through social policies.

As the pace of change increases and as the risks become more global in nature, so the kinds of policies required changes. Only policy agreements on a world scale will now protect us from some environmental risks. There is also likely to be conflict between different groups seeking to use the state or international agreements to protect themselves. An example of these new, global, and unpredictable risks is the transmission of BSE (bovine spongiform encephalopathy) from cattle to human beings through the food chain. The inquiry into the British government's response showed how the existing divisions between government departments and the broad assumptions about their responsibilities held by civil servants and ministers made it difficult to come up with appropriate 'social policies' to protect the public (House of Commons, 2000).

Social inclusion During the 1990s a growing number of social policies have been justified in terms of their capacity to reduce 'social exclusion'. In 1997 the New Labour government of Tony Blair set up an interdepartmental Social Exclusion Unit to coordinate public policy (**www. socialexclusionunit.gov.uk**). In 1999 the Department for Work and Pensions began the publica-tion of an annual audit of poverty and social exclusion (see for example Cm. 6673, 2005) and in 2006 Tony Blair created a cabinet post specifically to tackle social exclusion. The term social exclusion and its twin, social inclusion, are particularly associated with European Union social initiatives. The Lisbon summit in March 2000 committed member states to promotion of social inclusion through a range of social initiatives (see Box 1.4) and at the Laeken summit a list of indicators that would be applied to all member countries was adopted (a review of progress can be found in Atkinson et al. 2005).

There is ambiguity about what social exclusion actually refers to (for good accounts see Levitas 2000 and Stewart and Hills 2005). It is what is known as a 'contested term'. Some social policy ana-lysts argue that it is just another word for poverty, but one that is preferred in a political context where governments are unwilling to be explicit about the existence of poor people. The European Union, as Box 1.4 shows, links poverty and social exclusion but sees a difference between them.

Box 1.4 Conclusions of the Lisbon European Council meeting 23–4 March 2000

No 32. Promoting social inclusion

The number of people living below the poverty line and in social exclusion in the Union is unacceptable. Steps must be taken to make a decisive impact on the eradication of poverty by setting adequate targets to be agreed by the Council by the end of the year. The High Level Working Party on Social Protection will be involved in this work. The new knowledge-based society offers tremendous potential for reducing social exclusion, both by creating the economic conditions for greater prosperity through higher levels of growth and employment, and by opening up new ways of participating in society. At the same time, it brings a risk of an ever-widening gap between those who have access to the new knowledge, and those who are excluded. To avoid this risk and maximize this new potential, efforts must be made to improve skills, promote wider access to knowledge and opportunity and fight unemployment: the best safeguard against social exclusion is a job. Policies for combating social exclusion should be based on an open method of coordination combining national action plans and a Commission initiative for cooperation in this field to be presented by June 2000.

It suggests that as economies develop, some people become excluded from skills and knowledge and thus become vulnerable to unemployment and poverty. Policies are therefore needed to re-include such people, largely by giving them the skills that will get them into paid work. However, these policies do not always reach the people who need them most. The concept of social exclusion, in the form '*les exclus*' (the excluded), was first used in the context of French social policy debates in the 1970s, where it largely referred to people who slipped through the network of services and benefits designed to help the disadvantaged, particularly the less educated, the disabled, lone parents, and young adults. The exclusion in this sense was exclusion from the social policies of the state, and the danger was that such people would become less committed to central values of a society and thus threaten its stability and solidarity.

The attractiveness of the terms 'social exclusion', as the definition of the problem, and 'social inclusion', as the policy goal that will combat it, is that they combine most of the intentions and objectives that we have already listed as informing social policies.

- Social exclusion is produced when incomes are excessively unequal. The pioneering researcher into poverty, Peter Townsend (1979), showed how families with low incomes cannot participate in the lives of the communities in which they live. They become excluded in part because they cannot pay for the things that make one part of a society: going on holidays; entertaining others in one's home; kitting out their children suitably for sports; or going out with their friends. Providing these people with the ability to re-include themselves in their communities requires vertical redistribution.
- Social exclusion is inefficient. It is an expression of market failure that wastes the potential of people who could work but lack the skills to do so, and it reflects inadequate redistribution to those who are unable to work through youth, illness, or age. It therefore requires horizontal redistribution.
- Social exclusion reflects a failure to tackle the risks that face people in complex societies and it creates new risks, particularly if the excluded become alienated from the wider society. Social policy is therefore required both to tackle the risks that lead to exclusion (for example, unemployment, low skills, illness, low wages, old age) and to prevent the development of new social problems.

Social policy as administrative and financial arrangements

Social policy as social administration In order to deliver the intentions that lie behind social policies in ordered and predictable ways, governments must set up procedures and sometimes organizations to carry them out. A large part of the Beveridge Report (1942) was not about the overall goals but about planning the detailed administrative arrangements that would be required to realize them. In most industrial countries the years 1945–70 witnessed the construction of large government bureaucracies, employing substantial proportions of the workforce and charged with providing the new social security, health, social care, education, and housing policies. In those years in the UK the academic subject now called Social Policy was more often known as Social Administration, and to some extent this reflected that what was of interest was less the social policy intentions themselves but rather the administrative arrangements that would best achieve them. There was broad agreement between political parties about the social policies that were needed. This is sometimes referred to as the 'post-war settlement' or in 1950s Britain as 'Butskellism', a term coined by the *Economist* magazine to highlight the fact that the Tory Chancellor of the Exchequer, Rab Butler, was following very much the same social policy principles as his Labour predecessor, Hugh Gaitskell.

There is, indeed, often more difference between political parties over administrative arrangements than policy goals. Social policies generally use one of three main administrative forms to achieve their goals:

1 **Regulation** This is generally the cheapest way for governments to achieve a social policy goal. Governments pass laws that require individuals and organizations to do, or not to do, particular things: wearing seat belts, observing food hygiene regulations, not selling tobacco to minors. There are likely to be many thousands of government regulations in an industrial society that are intended to achieve broadly social goals. The main advantage from the state's point of view is that regulation is relatively cheap. The cost of compliance falls on the individual or firm rather than on the state. The main cost to the state is some form of inspection and enforcement to ensure that people abide by the regulations.

2 **Services in kind** This administrative method of achieving social goals provides services directly to people, such as healthcare, education, or housing. Governments can set up state organizations to do the job—large public bureaucracies like the National Health Service—or they can delegate the delivery of services to private-for-profit companies or to voluntary organizations (sometimes known as the not-for-profit sector).

3 **Cash benefits** The third fundamental method of achieving social goals is to provide individuals and households with cash either directly or through reductions in the tax they would otherwise have to pay. The cost of cash benefits is the largest area of social policy expenditure in Britain, and has a whole chapter to itself in this book (Chapter 10).

Organizational arrangements can make a great deal of difference to the success of a social policy. For example, in 1998 the British government set out its National Childcare Strategy, designed to make available a nursery school place for every preschool child whose parents wanted one. Provision is by a mixture of local government, voluntary, and for-profit nurseries and approved childminders. Funding is a mixture of central government, through Child Care Tax Credits, local government education and welfare budgets, and direct charges to parents. Current debate about this policy revolves less around its main goals and more around whether the administrative and financial system is the appropriate one to deliver it (Lewis 2003).

Administrative arrangements go wrong in two main ways. First, the detailed rules and procedures that are used to deliver a policy may develop in ways that actually undermine its original intentions. In the case of the National Childcare Strategy, Jane Lewis (2003: 235) concludes that 'the choices parents currently face are determined more by the complex nature of the system that has been created than by the needs of the child. In this crucial sense, the development of childcare in the UK has not been "child-centred"'. Secondly, the organizations involved can develop goals of their own, sometimes as a result of their sheer size, sometimes because particular groups, such as professionals, use them to advance their own interests rather than the policies themselves. These problems, and finding solutions to them, are fundamental to understanding social policy. They have also tended to preoccupy governments. In Britain in the 1980s and 1990s the governments of Margaret Thatcher, John Major, and Tony Blair devoted a great deal of effort to reorganizing welfare bureaucracies and changing the way they are managed. Getting welfare bureaucracies to do what these governments believed they were intended to do involved privatization and contracting out and the setting of precise targets and rewarding their achievement, often referred to as the new managerialism. Privatization dominated the social policy of British governments in the 1980s, new managerialism the 1990s, and after the 2005 election Tony Blair made public sector reform the government's main priority.

Social policy as public finance As Figure 1.1 shows, the social policy activities of governments constitute substantial proportions of the economic output of industrial nations. Both obtaining the money and managing how it is spent are key aspects of social policy.

The two main ways in which social policies are financed are by taxation (the direct taxation of incomes and profits and the indirect taxation of other economic activities) and by social insurance contributions. Paying these taxes and contributions has effects on people's well-being. In this sense taxation policies are also social policies. Governments can recognize this by adjusting taxes and contributions to incomes, for example, through progressive taxes, or by allowing individuals and households exemptions from the payment of tax. In Britain, exemptions are allowed, for example, if one is contributing to a pension scheme, aged over 65, suffering from blindness, or part of a married couple. Up until 1988 allowances were available for those supporting a dependent relative and until 2000 for owner-occupiers paying a mortgage. These, like many other allowances that have existed in the past, have come and gone as governments have sought to adjust revenue and the social policy effects. Increasingly governments are introducing tax credits in order to achieve social policy goals. From April 2003 most parents in Britain have been able to claim a Child Tax Credit, which adds to their income rather than takes away from it. Those in work are eligible for the Working Tax Credit, which provides extra income for workers in low-income households, including those who have a disability. (Chapter 10 provides a more detailed account of these benefits.)

The management of the public finances is a fundamental part of social policy. Two aspects of this management are critical: planning and controlling public expenditure. Delivering services such as healthcare or education requires long-term investment in people and buildings, and advance knowledge of how much is likely to be spent in a particular year. For these reasons planning social policy and planning public expenditure often amount to the same thing. Governments must be able to describe their intended social policies in terms of how much they will cost. Chapter 8 describes how the political and technical aspects of these planning processes have evolved in recent years.

Controlling the amount and pattern of expenditures is similarly central to social policy. In industrial societies the sums involved are so large that preventing waste, inefficiencies, overspending, and underspending requires sophisticated financial management systems. When these fail the consequences can be profound. In 1975 an unexpected rise in inflation meant that public spending outran both planned expenditure and tax receipts to such an extent that a major financial crisis arose. The British Chancellor of the Exchequer at the time, Denis Healey, had to go cap in hand to the International Monetary Fund in order to prevent a collapse in the international value of the pound. The consequences for social policy over the next twenty years were profound as governments gave greater priority to controlling expenditure on social policies, often leading to cuts in previously planned expenditure.

Social policy as outcomes

The proof of the pudding is in the eating. Many analysts of social policy have suggested that the intentions that lie behind policies are less important than what they actually achieve. Richard Titmuss, when seeking to define the academic discipline called 'social policy', headed his list with 'the analysis and description of policy formation and its consequences, intended and unintended' (Titmuss 1968: 22). In much of his research he focused on the evidence of the results of policy interventions, and showed how many policies did not have the outcomes claimed for them, that some achieved almost the opposite of what was intended, and that there were other interventions by governments that had social consequences but were not recognized as social policies.

Clearly it is important, given the substantial proportion of countries' resources redistributed through social policies, that results be carefully monitored. Much of the content of the chapters in this book reports research designed to discover the outcomes of social policies. Chapter 18 is entirely devoted to the question. There is not the space here even to summarize all the issues involved in assessing the consequences of social policy. We shall merely draw attention to one of the more fundamental aspects of the question: the degree to which social policies have been successful in defeating the 'five giant evils' highlighted in William Beveridge's report (see Box 1.2).

As the chapters in this book explain, in the Britain of the first decade of the twenty-first century these 'evils' have been altered and, by most measures, greatly reduced. 'Want', in the sense of grinding poverty, has been almost eliminated by the cash benefits that Beveridge recommended. Poverty is now a matter of relative deprivation (see the discussion of relative poverty in Chapter 4). The consequences of 'disease' have at least been delayed as average life expectancy has been extended. 'Ignorance' has been reduced insofar as people spend longer in full-time education and many more obtain formal qualifications. 'Squalor' in the form of poor-quality homes and large urban slums has been replaced, and 'idleness' has been reduced by a much higher level of participation in paid work.

However, it is more difficult to judge how far these changes have been the outcomes of social policies. It is arguable that they are largely the results of economic growth and improvements in people's material living standards. Figure 1.3 shows how average household income, along with the economy as a whole (measured by GDP) has more than doubled over the last thirty years. Many commentators suggest that it is this economic growth that has been the main engine behind improvements in people's standards of living and which provides the resources that have reduced the severity of Beveridge's 'five giants'.

Earlier in this chapter we suggested that another of the more commonly asserted goals of social policy was to redistribute resources and reduce inequalities, partly so that more people can share in the fruits of economic growth. However, Figure 1.4 shows that inequality, particularly as seen in the incomes of the poorest tenth of households in the United Kingdom, has been stubbornly resistant to social policy. The ONS 2010 *Social Trends* report summarizes the long-run trends:

> During the 1980s there was little change in income in real terms (that is adjusted to remove the effects of inflation) at the bottom of the distribution, while income at the top of the distribution grew strongly. The early 1990s was a period of economic downturn, and there was little real growth in income anywhere in the distribution. Between 1995/96 and 2007/08, income at all three points of the distribution shown in [Figure 1.4] grew by similar amounts in real terms, with median income increasing by a quarter. Thus the income distribution and the extent of inequality have changed considerably over the last three decades. The closer the percentiles are to the median line, the smaller the inequality within the distribution. Inequality grew during the 1980s, was stable during the first half of the 1990s, and then fluctuated slightly between 1994/95 and 2007/08.

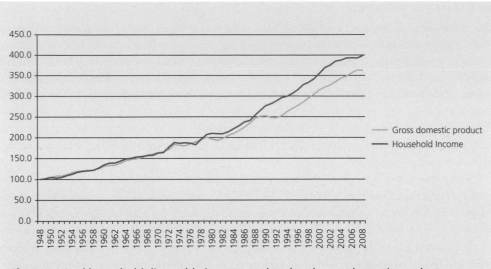

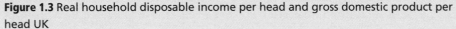

Figure 1.3 Real household disposable income per head and gross domestic product per head UK

Source: ONS (2010: Chart 5.1)

If a reduction in income inequality is a measure of a key outcome of social policy, then it has not been very successful. Chapter 18 includes more discussion of the distributional effects of social policies, including what is known as the **social wage**, the distribution of benefits from public services in kind like healthcare and education.

Social welfare

By focusing on the meaning of the term 'social policy' so far, we have concentrated on the activities of governments and their success or otherwise in achieving social objectives. However, many students of social policy are more interested in what can broadly be called social welfare and which is only partly the product of what governments and policy-makers do. Social welfare is again a term that gains little from being defined very tightly. Writers use it in slightly different ways depending on the issues they wish to cover. Sometimes it refers to very material aspects of well-being such as access to economic resources. At other times it is used to mean less tangible conditions such as contentment, happiness, an absence of threat, and confidence in the future. A whole area of research called 'quality of life studies' seeks to understand and measure what people believe to be the main ingredients of their welfare (see e.g. Baldwin et al. 1990). Social welfare can be thought of in terms of individuals—the concept of individual welfare—but as its name suggests, it is also used on occasion to refer to more collective forms of well-being (collective welfare), such as that of a whole community or nation. The Department for Environment, Food and Rural Affairs publishes annually the results of 68 indicators designed to show how, region by region, England is progressing in terms of health, housing, education, and the environment (see under 'sustainable development' at **www.defra.gov.uk**).

Researchers in social policy are often concerned with how social welfare is produced and sustained, and this work tends to draw attention to the great variety of sources that are involved. A useful and influential way of understanding this complexity is the 'welfare triangle' (Figure 1.5).

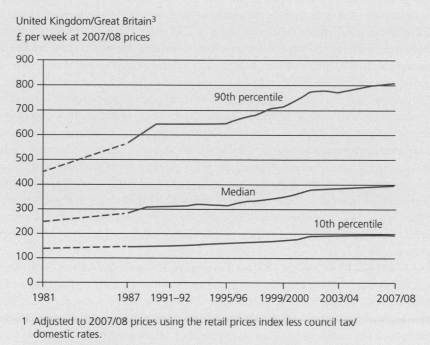

1 Adjusted to 2007/08 prices using the retail prices index less council tax/
   domestic rates.

2 Equivalized household disposable income before deduction of housing
   costs, using OECD equivalization scale. See Appendix, Part 5: Households
   Below Average Income (HBAI), and Equivalization scales for variations in
   source and definition on which the time series is based.

3 Data for 1994/95 to 2001/02 are for Great Britain only.

Figure 1.4 Distribution of real[1] household disposable income[2], UK

Source: ONS (2010: Chart 5.3)

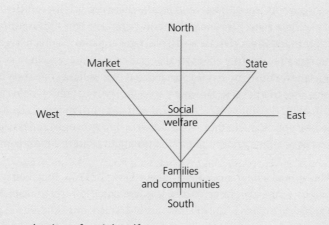

Figure 1.5 The production of social welfare

Source: Adapted from Evers (1988: 27)

The purpose of Figure 1.5 is to illustrate the main sources from which people obtain their welfare or well-being. All of us depend for the quality of our lives, to different degrees, on our links to the market, to the state, and to the families and communities in which we live. Consider for a moment two particularly important measures of social welfare in a society: how it looks after its children and how it looks after its older people. In all societies parents and families are the primary providers of care for children. As the children grow older, so the state, for example in the provision of education, becomes more important. But in some cases where parents cannot or are not there to provide care, the state or the wider community may have to step in. The care of dependent older people can similarly be the product of all three sources. In poor societies, frail older people are usually entirely dependent on the family for income and care. There also is much evidence to show that even in rich societies most personal care for older people is provided by their families. However, assistance is available from the state, in the form of social services. The market too may play a large role, in terms of paid care and the pensions that help finance it. The key point here is that welfare is generally a product of all three sources, or what is called the mixed economy of welfare. It is a matter of history and politics how the actual balance of sources has developed in a particular country.

Imposed on Figure 1.5 are the four points of the compass. This again is merely an illustrative device. But it reminds us that in poor, southern societies the family and community are most important in the production of social welfare. Western countries, particularly the United States, have been associated with a greater use of the market to provide welfare, while Eastern European nations, particularly before the collapse of communism, made greater use of the state. In choosing to develop social policy in a particular area, politicians and administrators always face decisions as to the respective roles of the market, the state, and the family in achieving their goals. For example, this is exactly the basis of the debate about the appropriate funding and provision of university education in Britain.

The welfare state

Defining the welfare state

Societies in which a substantial part of the production of welfare is paid for and provided by the government have been called 'welfare states'. Within the academic subject of social policy there are continuing debates about what is necessary to qualify as a welfare state. Does the United States, for example, provide, through its federal, state, and local welfare provisions, sufficient help to its citizens to be labelled a welfare state? Or should the term be reserved for the Scandinavian countries such as Sweden or Denmark, in which state welfare services constitute a much larger proportion of the economy? Some regard this debate about what actually constitutes a welfare state as sterile, and suggest we should abandon the term and use instead that of a welfare system (Wincott 2003 provides a useful summary of this debate). However, even if a strict definition of 'welfare state' is not necessary from an analytical point of view, the term remains important because of the frequency with which it is used, by politicians, in the media, and by ordinary people, and because, historically, the welfare state was at one time understood as the twentieth century's most complete answer to social need.

In a speech to the annual conference of the Labour Party in 1950, Sam Watson, leader of the Durham coal miners, listed the achievements of the welfare state: 'Poverty has been abolished. Hunger is unknown. The sick are tended. The old folks are cherished, our children are growing up in a land of opportunity' (Hennessy 1992: 423). This turned out to be a rather rosy view, but it captures the confidence of the time in the role of state welfare. It was a conception of its function as setting minimum standards in income, health, housing, and education below which citizens would not be allowed to fall: the idea of the welfare state as a social safety net.

Comparing types of welfare state

Alongside discussion about what counts as a welfare state has been a parallel debate about how welfare states or welfare systems differ from one another. Investigating these differences is fundamental to the comparative study of social policy. Researchers have classified countries in terms of ideologies that inform their welfare policies, the levels and comprehensiveness of benefits they offer their citizens, and the organizational arrangements used to fund and deliver those benefits. This has been called by one commentator 'the welfare modelling business' (Abrahmson 2000). The main object is to understand whether welfare states are becoming more alike or more different, and to analyse whether some types of welfare state are more likely to survive in the context of global economic change. The best-known typology of welfare states is that suggested by Gøsta Esping-Andersen in his important book, *The Three Worlds of Welfare Capitalism* (1990). This divides welfare states into three main types: the neo-liberal (for example the United States), the social democratic (Sweden), and the corporatist (Germany). Esping-Andersen's analysis is described in more detail in Chapter 3.

The development of the welfare state

Sir Robert Walpole, when he was old and poor-sighted, asked his son to read to him, but is reputed to have said, 'Anything but history, for history must be false.' Walpole may have been expressing a view more famously stated by Henry Ford many years later ('History is more or less bunk. It's tradition. We don't want tradition.'), but he was more probably thinking of two problems that all history has to face. First, it inevitably involves selection and simplification. Secondly, the selection process may be biased or inaccurate. For these reasons it is not appropriate in the context of a textbook such as this to attempt a brief summary of the history of welfare states or even of the British welfare state. This would just exaggerate the problems of selection and misrepresentation. There are available some excellent general histories of the welfare state, and some of these are recommended in the guide to further reading at the end of the chapter. Here we limit discussion to highlighting two key themes that may be borne in mind when reading the history of welfare states.

A consequence of industrialization or of political competition?

Two accounts of the evolution of welfare states dominate the literature. Some argue that industrialization and the social needs it generates, particularly unemployment and poverty, make the provision of state welfare more or less inevitable. Classic accounts are found in Rimlinger (1971) and Wilensky (1975). Others argue that state welfare is won through political competition and follows the coming to political power of representatives of the interests of industrial workers or, more recently, other key groups such as women, ethnic minorities, and disabled people. As a result, the scale and comprehensiveness of the welfare state vary between countries depending on their political histories and which groups of citizens win the power to make the state attend to their interests. This historical analysis is represented in various ways by Miliband (1961), Addison (1975), and Gough (1979), and is discussed in Chapter 2.

Most histories of the welfare state give considerable weight to the processes of industrialization. Britain, particularly England, became an industrial and predominantly urban society significantly before most other countries, and many forms of state intervention in the welfare of citizens also appeared there at an early stage (Mathias 2001). There are also substantial similarities in the histories of public welfare across industrial societies, though the pace of development has varied. All developed a version of the Victorian Poor Law in the nineteenth century (Box 1.5), and all exhibited the basic infrastructures of the modern welfare state by around the middle of the twentieth century (Esping-Andersen and Korpi 1987). These issues are also explored in Chapter 2.

Box 1.5 Less eligibility: from the Report of the Poor Law Commissioners, 1834 (the principle of less eligibility that informed the 'New Poor Law' in England from 1834)

The first and most essential of all conditions, a principle which we find universally admitted, even by those whose practice is at variance with it, is, that his situation [that is, the situation of the 'pauper', the recipient of Poor Law relief] on the whole shall not be made really or apparently so eligible as the situation of the independent labourer of the lowest class. Throughout the evidence it is shown, that in proportion as the condition of any pauper class is elevated above the condition of independent labourers, the condition of the independent class is depressed; their industry is impaired, their employment becomes unsteady, and its remuneration in wages is diminished. Such persons, therefore, are under the strongest inducements to quit the less eligible class of labourers and enter the more eligible class of paupers. The converse is the effect when the pauper class is placed in its proper position, below the condition of the independent labourer. Every penny bestowed, that tends to render the condition of the pauper more eligible than that of the independent labourer, is a bounty on indolence and vice . . .

A well-regulated workhouse meets all cases, and appears to be the only means by which the intention of the statute of Elizabeth [of 1601], that all the able-bodied shall be set to work, can be carried into execution.

(Report of the Poor Law Commissioners, 1834)

Conclusion: Has the 'golden age' of the welfare state passed?

It is not yet clear whether the post-Second World War welfare state will turn out to represent a relatively brief stage in the histories of a few countries or whether it will be a permanent and coherent feature of most developed economies. Some dispute there ever was a golden age (Glennerster 2000), but most broadly accept that from the 1940s to the mid-1970s funding for welfare benefits and services in Britain and other European countries grew year by year as a proportion of national income, and the major political parties shared a consensus that the core institutions of the welfare state were a good thing (Lowe 1993). There is even more agreement that since the 1970s the welfare state has been under threat. To some extent this is explained by the coming to power of governments of the 'New Right' (see Chapter 3), such as those of Mrs Thatcher, which did not share the welfare values of the post-war period.

However, a more fundamental argument is that the growth of a global economy requires the driving down of costs in order to compete in economic markets; this has made it very difficult for governments to expand welfare expenditures and has sometimes made it necessary to cut them. Globalization (see Chapter 9) may have brought to an end the golden age of the welfare state. Furthermore, the competitive pressures have been compounded by demographic changes that reduce the number of workers in societies in relation to the non-working young and old, and by the appearance of new risks which are difficult for the established welfare state to deal with.

For two reasons the continuing viability of the existing welfare state edifice is being questioned across all of Europe. The first is simply that the status quo will be difficult to sustain given adverse demographic and financial conditions. The second is that the same status quo seems increasingly out of date and ill suited to meet the great challenges ahead. Our existing systems of social protection may hinder rather than promote employment growth and competitive knowledge-intensive economies. They may also be inadequate in the face of evolving and possibly far more intense social risks and needs. It is against this backdrop that new political entrepreneurs and welfare architects are coming to the fore with calls for major [welfare] regime change (Esping-Andersen 2002: 4).

📖 FURTHER READING

A complete and accessible history of the British welfare state is provided by **Derek Fraser's** *The Evolution of the British Welfare State* in a new edition that takes the story up to 1997 (London: Palgrave Macmillan, 2002). Excellent more recent histories are **Howard Glennerster**'s *British Social Policy Since 1945*, 2nd edn (Oxford: Blackwell, 2000), **Nick Timmins**'s *The Five Giants: A Biography of the Welfare State*, 2nd edn (London: HarperCollins, 2001), and **Rodney Lowe**'s *The Welfare State in Britain since 1945*, 2nd edn (London: Macmillan, 1999). **Pete Alcock**'s *Social Policy in Britain* (2nd edn, London: Palgrave 2006) is a clear introduction to the character of the British welfare state and the ideas that it represents. **Howard Glennerster**'s *Understanding the Finance of Welfare: What Welfare Costs and How to Pay for it* (Bristol: Policy Press, 2003) is an excellent social policy textbook that focuses more on resourcing issues. **Michael Cahill**, *The New Social Policy* (Oxford: Blackwell, 1994) is still an innovative exploration of social policy in communications, arts, transport, and other often neglected areas. **Gøsta Esping-Andersen** is one of the key thinkers about where the welfare state is going, and his and other authors' latest ideas can be explored in *Why We Need a New Welfare State* (Oxford: Oxford University Press, 2002). **John Hills and Kitty Stewart** and others provide a review of what social inclusion policies have achieved across a wide range of dimensions in *A More Equal Society* (Bristol: The Policy Press, 2005). **John Hills**, in the last section of *Inequality and the State* (Oxford: Oxford University Press, 2004), provides an excellent review of the distributional effects of social spending by New Labour. Similar questions, but with a more comparative international stance, are dealt with in *The New Egalitarianism* (**Anthony Giddens and Patrick Diamond**, (eds, Cambridge: The Polity Press, 2005). A good review of New Labour's social policy record is **Polly Toynbee and David Walker**'s *Better or Worse: Has Labour Delivered?* (London: Bloomsbury, 2005). *Comparative Social Policy: Theories and Methods* **Jochen Clasen** (ed.) (Oxford: Blackwell, 1998) is a good introduction to a complex area. *The Young, the Old and the State: Social Care Systems in Five Industrial Countries* **A. Anttonen, J. Baldock, and J. Sipilä** (eds) (Cheltenham: Elgar, 2003) compares how industrial nations look after children and older people. **Vic George and Paul Wilding**, *Globalization and Human Welfare* (Basingstoke: Palgrave, 2002) is an excellent analysis of the concept of globalization itself as well as of the welfare implications for both rich and poor nations.

@ USEFUL WEBSITES

The OECD (Organisation for Economic Co-operation and Development) publishes very useful documents, many dealing with comparative social policy issues, at: **www.oecd.org**.

British Government publications can be explored and accessed from: **www.direct.gov.uk/en/index.htm**. A great many of the publications of the Stationery Office are available at: **www.tso.co.uk**. Perhaps the most useful data source for social policy students is Social Trends online at: **http://www.statistics.gov.uk/StatBase/Product.asp?vlnk=5748**.

Particularly useful government sites for getting up-to-date information about social policy issues are the Department of Health website, **www.doh.gov.uk**, particularly the links to social care issues, and the Treasury website, **www.hm-treasury.gov.uk**, for Government Spending Reviews.

Q   ESSAY QUESTIONS

1 Access the latest issue of *Social Trends* and choose from it five figures or tables that in your view are particularly revealing of the state of social welfare in Britain. Explain your choices.

2 Distinguish between 'public social expenditure' and 'private social expenditure' as defined by the OECD. Suggest reasons for the differences in social expenditure between countries portrayed in Figure 1.1 of this chapter.

3 Suggest an example each of 'a man-made risk', 'a natural risk' and 'an environmental risk' faced by citizens in Britain today. To what extent and in what ways should government seek to manage these risks? Which other institutions should play a part?

4 Find on the web the latest issue of 'Sustainable Development Indicators in Your Pocket' (published by DEFRA and the ONS). Use the information provided in the publication to suggest in which ways social welfare is improving in the UK and in which ways it is not.

5 Identify two important social problems currently facing the population of Britain or another country. Identify ways in which the government might tackle the problems using the mechanisms of regulation, services in kind, and cash benefits. What combination of policies would you recommend to meet each of the social problems?

 ONLINE RESOURCE CENTRE

For additional material and resources, please visit the Online Resource Centre at:
www.oxfordtextbooks.co.uk/orc/baldock4e/.

The history and development of social policy

Lavinia Mitton

Contents

Introduction

It is easy to assume that social policy should be more concerned with how policies should be improved in the present and the future, rather than with the past. Yet a historical perspective enables us to understand the reasons why current social policy has taken the direction it has and can inform public discourse and public policy about urgent contemporary issues, as Berridge (2008) has shown.

The focus of histories of welfare provision in Britain often used to be 'the rise of the welfare state'. However, welfare provision, including state provision, did exist prior to the creation in the 1940s of the classic welfare state. It is also easy to assume that it was inevitable that the state would come to play as large a part in the provision of welfare services as it did in the years immediately after the Second World War (1939–45).

Yet if we stepped back in time we would see developments from a very different standpoint and state provision as far from predestined, for in the early years of the twentieth century welfare was characterized by a large role for voluntary provision, with mutual and friendly societies offering benefits for unemployment, sickness, maternity, and death (Finlayson 1990). Many of the most prestigious hospitals were so-called voluntary hospitals, providing free treatment to the 'deserving poor' but reliant on charitable donations and contribution schemes (Cherry 1996). The historiography of welfare provision is therefore now characterized by an emphasis on the ways in which welfare has been provided not only by the state but instead by a 'mixed economy of welfare', consisting of roles for the state, the voluntary sector, the family, and the market (Harris 2004).

This chapter traces the history of state welfare provision from the mid nineteenth century to the emerging policies of the Conservative–Liberal Democrat coalition before outlining some of the major theories of welfare state development. Inevitably a summary of the history of welfare provision such as in this chapter involves selection and simplification of events. There are, however, many comprehensive textbooks available, some of which are recommended in the guide to further reading at the end of this chapter.

Learning outcomes

By the end of this chapter students should be familiar with:

1 the considerable variety of sources of welfare provision in the past and the present;
2 the key elements of welfare policy since the 1834 New Poor Law;
3 theories of welfare state development;
4 long-standing ideological debates about the proper role for the state in welfare provision.

State intervention in the nineteenth century

The 1834 Poor Law Amendment Act

In the early nineteenth century the majority of people relied on their families, local communities, charity, and philanthropy for welfare support. However, in the course of the following century the extent of state responsibility increased considerably, and this is why this period is the starting point for this chapter. The developing state role was particularly apparent in relation to the administration of the poor law, public health measures, and the provision of education.

Parishes had a responsibility to their poor under the Elizabethan Poor Law. However, the changes of the Industrial Revolution which led to the development of the towns, rapid population growth, and the experience of modern unemployment and the trade cycles caused the costs of poor relief to increase. 'Outdoor relief', a wage subsidy to tide the poor over in difficult times, was regarded as encouraging workers to remain idle, as morally undermining, and contrary to the nineteenth-century principles of thrift and hard work (Frohman 2008). It was said to encourage employers to pay low wages in the knowledge that the parish would supplement the wages of their labourers. It was also argued that the poor law provided a disincentive to population control and encouraged the growth of poverty. These arguments are echoed today in worries about welfare dependency.

In reaction, the New Poor Law of 1834 in England and Wales introduced a national system of poor relief which enforced the principle of 'less eligibility'. (Similar legislation was introduced in Ireland in 1838 and Scotland in 1845.) This new system entailed deterrence by only offering assistance to an able-bodied person if they entered the workhouse, were put to work and submitted to harshness (Harris 2004). The standard of living that awaited them was supposed to be below that of

Box 2.1 **Report of the Royal Commission on the Poor Laws, 1834**

The rationale of the New Poor Law is summarized in the following text:

Throughout the evidence it is shown that in proportion as the condition of any pauper class is elevated above the condition of independent labourers, the condition of the independent class is depressed; their industry is impaired, their employment becomes unsteady, and its remuneration in wages is diminished. Such persons, therefore, are under the strongest inducements to quit the less eligible class of labourers and enter the more eligible class of paupers. The converse is the effect when the pauper class is placed in its proper position, below the condition of the independent labourer. Every penny bestowed that tends to render the condition of the pauper more eligible than that of the independent labourer, is a bounty on indolence and vice.

Source: *Report of the Royal Commission on the Poor Laws*, 1834, XXVII (1834) p.127

the poorest labourer. A distinction was made between the 'deserving' and 'undeserving' poor based on whether their poverty was their own fault. It was (in theory) the workhouse or nothing for those 'undeserving' poor unable to support themselves and their family. The intention was to discourage all but the destitute able-bodied from turning to the Poor Law.

Public health

There was also growth in state intervention in public health. Britain was the first nation to industrialize, a development that had a massive impact at all levels of society. As people moved into towns and cities, overcrowding, unsanitary conditions, and epidemic diseases all followed as clean water, sewerage systems, and refuse disposal were lacking (Evans 1988). Victorian values of individual rights and freedoms were challenged by the results. The cholera epidemic of 1831–2 and the prevalence of typhus provided points of focus for a range of concerns about the conditions of the poor and the consequences of urban growth (Harris 2004). The sanitary movement of the early nineteenth century was led by Edwin Chadwick, whose 1842 *Report on the Sanitary Condition of the Labouring Population of Great Britain* became widely influential. The public health measures recommended cut across individual property-owning rights. Public health became a legitimate concern of government and the 1848 Public Health Act gave powers to local authorities, which, although limited, marked a watershed in the sphere of state responsibility.

Education

During most of the nineteenth century only a minority of children received formal education. Education was mainly a privilege of the aristocracy and the middle classes who could afford the costs of private tuition, fee-paying grammar schools, or perhaps university. There were church-run schools, industrial schools, dame schools, and those provided by charities, but these were not everywhere.

There was much opposition to the extension of the education system from parties with vested interests, such as those who argued that compulsory education was an interference with individual liberties and would prevent children of the labouring classes from learning a trade and from working to contribute to the family income. One of the chief stumbling blocks was the vested interests of religious societies (Harris 2004). There was conflict of opinion over whether the state should pay for schools run by particular religious denominations, or whether schools should have no association with any denomination.

Nevertheless, there was growing pressure for the state to provide schools in areas where none existed and in England the 1870 'Forster' Education Act permitted local authorities to act to improve the attendance of working-class children in schools. The Act allowed voluntary schools to carry on unchanged, but established a system of 'school boards' to build and manage schools in areas where they were needed. The boards were locally elected bodies which drew their funding from the local rates. Most importantly, the Act demonstrated a commitment to provision on a national scale. It did not make elementary education compulsory or free, but it paved the way for both.

Thus, at the end of the nineteenth century the social welfare of the poor depended greatly on whether they paid into a friendly society, lived close to a voluntary hospital or fell within the concern of a particular philanthropic group. There was a patchwork of provision, but many of the poor were not eligible for social welfare.

The beginnings of national insurance

The British tradition was of voluntarism in insurance, in which mutual and friendly societies ran insurance schemes. However, the period after the turn of the nineteenth century saw the beginnings of change. The economic doctrine of laissez-faire gradually gave way to an ideal

---

Box 2.2 **Rowntree's survey of poverty**

When Seebohm Rowntree, a member of the famous confectionery family, studied the conditions of the working class in York at the end of the nineteenth century, he decided what food, housing, and items of clothing he considered the basics of life. Anyone who could not afford these was deemed to be in poverty. Rowntree's subsistence level was equivalent to the rations given to the poor in the local workhouse.

The idea was to challenge the Victorian view that poverty was due to a wasteful life, in which being poor equated to being sinful. Rowntree showed that people were poor because they simply did not earn enough at work or were unable to find work due to illness, injury, or the economic climate of the Victorian free market.

---

which envisaged a role for the state in response to social problems. In the wake of the Boer War (1899 1902), social policies began to be given high priority because of the unexpectedly poor health and physique of those seeking enlistment into the army. This was not a nation that could rule an empire, it was argued. Groundbreaking surveys of poverty by social reformers such as Booth's study of London (1891) and Rowntree's study of York (1901) indicated that poverty might not simply be down to lack of financial management skills. Instead the economics of the free market might be the cause of some poverty. Such surveys demonstrated that up to a third of children were being brought up in great poverty. School and maternal health therefore became a growing concern.

The early years of the twentieth century saw a sharp increase in labour agitation, which, along with growing industrialization, urbanization, and developing trade unionism, was a stimulus to state intervention. In 1900 the Labour Party was formed, posing a potential electoral threat to the Liberals. However, in 1906 the Liberals won a landslide victory. As we have seen, some state welfare was already in existence. So although the Liberal government did not invent state welfare, it did drive it further. In the period from 1906 to the First World War (1914–18) it succeeded, often against considerable opposition, in pushing through a number of social reforms (Hay 1983).

The Liberal reforms

The first reforms were aimed at schoolchildren: school meals provided by the local education authority, and a school medical service that provided for medical examination of children in elementary schools, and promotion of the health of such children. These were significant for being early welfare measures not connected to the Poor Law.

A large number of elderly people preferred to endure poverty than submit to the stigmatizing local Poor Law Board of Guardians. Therefore a non-contributory, means-tested old age pension for the poor paid for entirely by the state was introduced for those aged 70 or over. The new pension was a right, collected by recipients from the local post office, and it was hoped that this would be without the shame of the Poor Law. This measure was notable as it not only marked the development of state welfare separate from the Poor Law, but it was funded out of general taxation and was a national system.

The budget required for welfare measures caused an enormous parliamentary storm, with the House of Lords seeking to overturn what had been decided in the Commons. Lloyd George, the Chancellor, took the 'People's Budget' to the country. After two elections in 1910, and the threat of mass creation of new peers, the Liberals were finally able to get a Bill through Parliament in 1911 that destroyed the Lords' power of veto and in future meant that finance bills bypassed them.

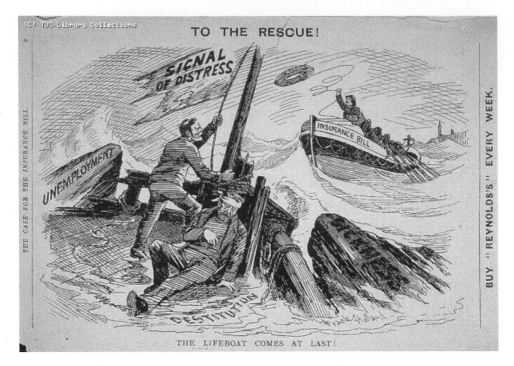

Cartoon 2.1 A view of the 1911 National Insurance Act

Following the constitutional crisis surrounding the adoption of the People's Budget, the government was able to press ahead with further welfare reform.

The 1911 National Insurance Act

One of the most important principles of the British welfare state was introduced by the Liberals, that of social insurance to cover interruption in earnings through ill health or unemployment. Thus, in addition to pensions, another major plank in the Liberals' social welfare programme introduced in 1911 was national health insurance, providing medical care in the shape of a national system of panel doctors, maternity benefit, and sick pay. There was also unemployment insurance for workers in certain industries. Contributions were paid by the employee, the employer, and the state. Contribution and benefit levels were laid down by Parliament, but friendly societies and mutually owned bodies operated the scheme.

The insurance principle was advanced to finance this new welfare because the Liberal government was anxious not to raise income tax and alienate its supporters. The insurance principle was originally met with considerable hostility. Workers resented the compulsory deductions, friendly societies and other insurance companies did not want to lose business, and the British Medical Association objected that doctors who worked for the state system would have low status. The Conservatives argued that the freedom of the individual was undermined by compulsion.

But opposition began to reduce. In fact, it was soon apparent that the main disadvantage of the health insurance scheme was that the scope of the provision was not wide enough, as it covered only working people in some industries, and their dependents only for maternity benefits and the treatment of tuberculosis. It was also argued that since general practitioners were paid a capitation fee—a fee for each patient on their list—there was an incentive to have a long list, to deal with patients cursorily, and not to offer full investigation and treatment.

Neither health nor unemployment insurance were universal in scope, with both favouring the 'deserving' sick and unemployed ('deserving' in that they had previously been in regular employment). But it was clear that the principle of 'individual liberty' was now being challenged by a stronger emphasis on collective welfare rights.

The interwar years

The interwar period saw considerable social and political change in Britain. It saw the decline of the Liberal Party and the rise of the Labour Party, as the vote was widened in 1918 to include all adult men and some women, and in 1928 to include all adults. The interwar years saw prosperity for an expanding middle class contrasting starkly with the poverty, unemployment, hunger, and deprivation of the poorer classes as Britain's previously staple industries such as cotton textiles, coal mining, and shipbuilding went into decline.

Thought was given to health and pensions. The National Health Insurance income limit was raised in 1920, but there were frequent demands for a higher limit and more extensive coverage. Chamberlain, as prime minister, added to this insurance with the Widows, Orphans and Old Age Contributory Pensions Act of 1925. Pensions were paid from age 65 and the widow's benefit was introduced.

However, in the interwar years the problem of unemployment dominated social policy. The unemployment insurance scheme ran into financial difficulty because there were so many long-term unemployed. In 1931 the 'dole' was cut and a means test implemented. Once people had exhausted their entitlement to insurance-based benefits they had to undergo the hated household-based means test for unemployment assistance, which involved enquiries being made into the applicant's savings and circumstances—who lived with whom, who was dependent on whom, and so on.

The reorganization of local government in 1929 meant that the institutions of the Poor Law changed their names, but they were still recognizable. There were criticisms of the legacies of the Poor Law such as the indignities of means-tested payments for those in poverty, because in this era of mass unemployment, being out of work was no longer seen as the unemployed person's fault. The principle of less eligibility was harder to sustain.

The post-war reforms

It was after the Second World War that the British welfare state took its 'classic' form. Yet the school meals, old age pensions and insurance-based social security introduced prior to the war were the forerunners of many of its principles. This path dependency is an important consideration when thinking about the development of the welfare state, as the post-war measures grew out of the situation that existed in 1939. Although they resulted in much consolidation of previously limited and local pre-war coverage, the precise form the 'welfare state' would take was constrained by being based on an existing haphazard collection of measures delivered at central and local levels. For this reason there is an ongoing debate about the extent to which the post-Second World War structures of British welfare were laid down in the reforms introduced prior to 1939 or whether they represented a distinct break with the past.

The Victorian view in which poverty alleviation was largely the province of charitable and philanthropic organizations was swept away with optimism about collectivism. The population rejected the inevitability of mass unemployment. There was a sense of desiring to build a better Britain as the war had brought different classes together serving in the armed forces and Home Guard, sharing refuge in air-raid shelters, food rationing, and caring for evacuated children.

The Labour government's landslide victory in 1945 was very much about creating a new deal for 'the boys back from the front', giving them a sense that their country had been worth fighting for

33

.3 British prime ministers and governments since 1940

ay	1940	Sir Winston Churchill	Coalition
Jly	1945	Clement Attlee	Labour
Oct.	1951	Sir Winston Churchill	Conservative
Apr.	1955	Sir Anthony Eden	Conservative
Jan.	1957	Harold Macmillan	Conservative
Oct.	1963	Sir Alec Douglas-Home	Conservative
Oct.	1964	Harold Wilson	Labour
June	1970	Edward Heath	Conservative
Mar.	1974	Harold Wilson	Labour
Apr.	1976	James Callaghan	Labour
May	1979	Margaret Thatcher	Conservative
Nov.	1990	John Major	Conservative
May	1997	Tony Blair	Labour
June	2007	Gordon Brown	Labour
May	2010	David Cameron	Coalition

and would support and care for them in peacetime by offering them and their families the opportunity for jobs, homes, education, health, and a standard of living of which they could be proud. In the relative social cohesion of the war years they determined that 'never again' should there be a return to the misery of the 1930s (Page 2007). However, Lowe (2005) has argued that the bonds of social solidarity forged during these years were not as strong as have sometimes been assumed. Nevertheless, the slew of post-war reforms showed what was possible in the context of the aftermath of war.

The Beveridge Report

An inquiry had been established in 1941 to propose how best to reorganize state welfare. Beveridge seized the opportunity to redesign the shape of British welfare. His landmark report, entitled *Social Insurance and Allied Services* and published in November 1942, was popular and was used as a propaganda tool. The plans became widely known and became accepted and expected. This blueprint for post-war social security was, however, also the result of longer-term changes since the Victorian period in the attitudes of politicians and the public towards social welfare. Nevertheless, the Beveridge Report symbolized popular hopes and fundamentally altered what was politically possible. The Labour government that took power in 1945 was keen to implement the Beveridge report in full. However, the Conservatives opposed it: they and the Treasury thought it was far too expensive and they warned against plans and promises which they regarded as impossible to fulfil in the future.

The centrepiece was a comprehensive state-run system of compulsory insurance which widened the provisions that some workers had been able to benefit from under the earlier National Insurance scheme. Insurance was popular because benefit would be a right, not given out according to a means test. It was also popular because for the first time the middle class was covered, something that was to become a political asset for it in years to come (Glennerster 2007).

Every worker, by contributing to a scheme of national insurance with a payment deducted through the weekly pay packet, would build up an entitlement to benefits during sickness, unemployment, and widowhood. The scheme would pay pensions at the end of a working life (women over 60, men over 65).

Box 2.4 **William Beveridge (1879–1963)**

Beveridge was a British economist and social reformer, closely associated with the development of the welfare state. He came to prominence during the Liberal government of 1906–14, when he was asked to advise David Lloyd George on old age pensions and national insurance.

In 1941, the government commissioned Beveridge to produce a report into the ways that Britain should be rebuilt after World War Two. He published his report in 1942 and recommended ways in which the government could fight the five 'giant evils' of 'Want', 'Disease', 'Ignorance', 'Squalor', and 'Idleness'.

In 1945, the Labour Party defeated Churchill's Conservative Party in the general election. The new prime minister, Attlee, announced he would introduce the welfare state outlined in the Beveridge Report. A national system of benefits was introduced to provide 'social security' so that the population would be protected 'from the cradle to the grave'. The new system was partly built on the national insurance scheme set up in 1911. People in work still had to make contributions each week, as did employers, but the benefits provided were now much greater.

The other intellectual giant of the era was the economist Keynes. He popularized the notion that a depression could be offset by increasing welfare expenditure to increase demand.

The intention was to set benefits at a level that enabled a man, his wife, and child to survive. A system of Family Allowances (now Child Benefit) for the second child and subsequent children was intended to ensure income security for those with larger families. A further scheme paid money for industrial injuries. There were also to be a marriage grant, a maternity grant and benefit, some specific training grants, and a death grant. The key feature was that people were eligible to receive these benefits and grants because they had contributed. Rich and poor 'paid the stamp' and could claim flat-rate benefits for flat-rate contributions as a right in recognition of the importance of the insurance principle.

Box 2.5 **Beveridge's assumptions**

Although largely a synthesis of ideas that had been around for some time, the Beveridge Report was a blueprint for conquering Want, one of the five giants Beveridge declared should be slain by way of post-war reconstruction.

The 1944 'Butler' Act, which raised the school-leaving age to 15, had already provided free secondary education for all. Alongside these provisions, Beveridge assumed that certain other measures would be in place as well. His thoughts are summarized in the following text:

No satisfactory scheme of social security can be devised except on the following assumptions:

A Children's allowances for children up to the age of 15 or if in full-time education up to the age of 16;

B Comprehensive health and rehabilitation services for prevention and cure of disease and restoration of capacity for work, available to all members of the community;

C Maintenance of employment, that is to say avoidance of mass unemployment.

His endorsement of these ideas greatly influenced social policy, so his importance went beyond social security.

Source: Beveridge, W. (1942). *Social Insurance and the Allied Services*, pp.120–2

For those who had not paid enough contributions there was a second tier of welfare provision, National Assistance, which was a means-tested safety net that finally wound up the remnants of the Poor Law. Beveridge wanted to ensure that there was an acceptable minimum standard of living in Britain below which nobody fell. National Assistance (later to be renamed Supplementary Benefit and later still, Income Support) was meant to be a supplement to the main scheme rather than to be central. Only if extra help was needed was the means test meant to come into play.

Beveridge wrestled with how to strike a balance between a state-provided minimum and incentives for individuals to work and save for themselves, just as policy-makers are still doing today. Beveridge emphasized the limits to state responsibility, which would provide a floor on which individual action could build and be rewarded. Therefore the state pension was set at subsistence level, so as not to discourage working and private pension provision, which he always assumed would supplement the basic pension.

This has been termed the age of the 'classic welfare state' (Lowe 2005) as if the welfare state created in the 1940s formed an ideal. Others have challenged this view (Glennerster 2007), arguing that equality of access to services was not achieved, poverty persisted, and benefits were not adequate.

A period of consensus?

The decades immediately after the Second World War are frequently described as a period when the big political issues of the day had been settled and there was a high degree of overlap in political parties' approaches to social policy (Dutton 1991; Kavanagh 1992; Lowe 1991). It has been argued that the domestic policies of both the Labour and Conservative parties were characterized by substantial agreement in principle about the need for government intervention to ensure economic growth, full employment, and comprehensive welfare services. This turn in politics has been termed 'consensus'. The 'consensus' is said to have consisted of the general acceptance of a capitalist state with a substantial public element, including nationalization of coal, steel, and the railways. There was to be a range of public services including an extensive welfare state and this would be managed

Box 2.6 The creation of the NHS

The National Health Service Act (1946) created a national healthcare system, with visits to doctors, medical treatment, dental, and optical care almost entirely free at the point of use for everyone. The overriding reason for its popularity with the voting public was that it was based on clinical need and not ability to pay. It was funded principally from general taxation, with a small contribution from National Insurance to make contributors feel that they had a right to use the service. It was in principle a model universal social service.

It involved amalgamating the local authority hospitals, which were the successors to the former Poor Law infirmaries, with the voluntary hospitals. The government had in any case had to take over the organization of hospital services during the war, and this paved the way for state takeover of private and charitable hospitals. A general practice service (often called GPs or family doctors) was built on that available under the old National Health Insurance system. Its sponsor was the minister of health, Bevan, who battled with the doctors, who initially refused to join the NHS.

Large hospital bills for those who could barely pay, and suffering and anxiety because of inability to pay for treatment were things of the past. The main changes became operational on 5 July 1948. It was the climax of arguably the most industrious and reforming government of the century.

in such a way as to ensure continually rising living standards and an avoidance of returning to mass unemployment on the interwar scale.

In opposition, the Labour and Conservative parties did not propose any radical changes and when government changed hands there was continuity in social policy. All the governments of the 1950s and 1960s operated within these terms, helped by the fact that the absence of large-scale unemployment meant that many dilemmas for social policy never had to be faced in this period.

However, other historians of the welfare state (Jefferys 1987; Glennerster 2007) emphasize that the social policy legislation of the 1940s was introduced among much controversy, that the Conservative Party felt that it was premature and was unhappy with the form that it took. Conservative critics, both at the time and subsequently, argued that trying to establish an expensive welfare state would cripple the UK economy (Barnett 1986).

The 1964–70 Labour government

The 1964–70 Labour government came to power promising both better economic performance and welfare improvement. However, once in government there was a series of sterling and balance-of-payments crises. Wilson, as prime minister, was repeatedly obliged to revise economic and social strategies. This period was one of adjustment to a new kind of economic environment.

However, the Wilson government did maintain some reforming momentum, even though it did not fulfil all its manifesto promises (Thornton 2006). Among other initiatives it changed National Assistance into Supplementary Benefit, a system which secured many more people an entitlement. Statutory redundancy payments and earnings-related unemployment benefit were introduced. It also promoted the reform of secondary education from the tripartite system, which consisted of grammar, technical, and secondary modern schools, into a comprehensive system.

Despite being thought of as the 'golden age' of the classic welfare state, the 1960s saw the rediscovery of poverty as a social problem. Critics such as Townsend (1957) found large numbers of pensioners in poverty because their pensions were not adequate and they were not claiming the extra means-tested benefits they were entitled to. Flat-rate National Insurance contributory benefits did not entirely prevent poverty as they often failed to provide an income higher than the National Assistance minimum once the cost of rent had been taken into account. Studies such that by Abel Smith and Townsend (1965) also revealed that many people were living below National Assistance level despite being in work (and therefore ineligible for benefits). Further, the idea of basing entitlement on contributions through National Insurance meant that many people, especially women, were excluded from the system. Therefore means-tested National Assistance played a bigger role in alleviating poverty than Beveridge had planned (Glennerster 1998).

Box 2.7 Selectivism and universalism

One of the great themes of social policy debate has been the conflict between universalism and selectivism. Labour was pressed by its supporters to pursue universal benefits that were flat rate. The Conservative policy was one of steering a line between selectivism by means testing on the one hand and unmodified universalism on the other. The unrelenting expansion of means testing, or 'targeting', has led to the increased importance of such benefits. Under New Labour, Tax Credits were devised as near-universal benefits directed at all but the highest-earning families with children, with more benefit going to those on the lowest incomes. The government's policy advisers liked to call this 'progressive universalism'.

The 1970s 'crisis' of the welfare state

The period 1970–9 spans Conservative and Labour periods in power. They can be considered together because both parties were forced to reappraise social spending because of Britain's economic problems—inflation, unemployment, the falling value of the pound on foreign exchange markets, and industrial conflict. Full employment no longer existed. The welfare state was widely perceived to be in crisis in the mid 1970s. The 'consensus', such as it was, was challenged.

As previously mentioned, it had been revealed in the 1960s that National Insurance benefits were not paid at a high enough level to prevent many pensioners and low-paid workers from being poor. In response, the 1970s saw the introduction of a range of means-tested benefits, such as Family Income Supplement, intended to top up the income of the working poor (later renamed Family Credit, and later still Working Tax Credits). Rent Rebates (the forerunner of Housing Benefit) were designed to replace general rent subsidies to council housing tenants with more selective provision. In addition, the real value of state pensions began to be increased. In particular, the basic pension was increased in line with prices or earnings, whichever was greater. Through the link to earnings, pension recipients shared in the increasing prosperity of those in work.

Economic problems

However, both the Conservative government of 1970–4 and the Labour administration of 1974–9 were thrown off course by economic events, as this decade saw the end of automatic steady growth. Oil became hugely more expensive and the oil shocks produced a combination of rapid price inflation and growing unemployment, undermining the tax base from which services were financed.

Measures to boost economic activity and reduce unemployment sucked in extra imports, thereby worsening the trade balance and leading to problematic rises in inflation. The financial markets' loss of confidence meant a sharp slide in the value of sterling, which in turn led to the International Monetary Fund's rescue in 1976. The IMF granted a loan to the British government in return for spending cuts and continued anti-inflation policies. That cuts happened at a time of high unemployment signalled the end of the era of following Keynesian economic policies. Social and economic change also unravelled the founding assumptions of the Beveridge welfare state. Rising life expectancy, rising expectations, and long-term unemployment forced policy-makers to rethink welfare provision.

Governments of both parties turned to prices and incomes policies as an answer to inflation in the 1970s. They tried to agree a 'norm' for annual wage rises with the trades unions. This was difficult, and another feature of the 1970s was the high degree of conflict between governments and trades unions. Wilson's government tried the 'social contract', under which trades unions agreed to pay restraint in return for an enhanced 'social wage' through social policy spending and progressive taxation. These policies managed to keep prices down for a time, but collapsed when powerful groups broke the norm. The 'Winter of Discontent' in 1979 was a key event. A great rash of strikes in crucial public services against the Labour government's income policies destroyed the government's reputation for prudent economic management and its ability to gain the cooperation of the unions.

The welfare state in the 1980s

By the early 1980s economic growth rates in the UK were very low. Unemployment and long-term unemployment increased sharply to levels that were amongst the highest in Europe (Clasen 2003). Mass redundancies, strikes, and industrial conflict were widespread. There was a large decline in the number of (predominantly male) jobs in manufacturing. The government's neo-liberal policies contributed to this economic environment. In the 1980s the gap between the wages of those at the top and those at the bottom widened as the labour market demanded higher skills at one end and

> ## Box 2.8 **Inequality and the welfare state**
>
> The Beveridge scheme was not particularly egalitarian, except inasmuch as the existence of subsistence-level means-tested National Assistance involved some income redistribution (Glennerster 1998). It was post-war full employment that significantly narrowed the gap between rich and poor, until it began to grow again in the 1980s. The Beveridge scheme has been criticized for affirming the subordinate role of women in the family because married women were to depend on their husbands' entitlement to social security, as the National Insurance system was built on the basis that many women stayed at home to bring up their family. Another downside of the National Insurance scheme was that because entitlement to the state pension depended on building up a record of contributions while working, income inequalities during working life were reproduced in retirement. This illustrates how social policy can operate not only to address, but also to create, particular forms of income inequality.
>
> The form the post-war institutions took, and the way they were financed, held some advantages for the middle class. The poorer manual class before the war already had free primary medical care, hospital care on a means-tested basis, and free elementary education. The extension of these to the whole population benefited those on slightly higher incomes but limited their redistributive effect (Le Grand 1982). The inclusion and support of the middle class have been important in sustaining the political appeal of these services (Goodin and Le Grand 1987). However, it is still true that the poor benefited far more from these services as a share of their incomes.

low labour costs at the other (Glennerster 1998). At the same time, relationship breakdown led to more single-parent families receiving benefits. Other labour market problems that emerged in the 1980s were the geographical concentration of worklessness, high rates of inactivity among older workers, a rise in the proportion of households with no one in paid work, and all the related problems of poverty and social exclusion (Clasen 2003).

Politicians were in search of new ideas. On the right, the cost of welfare policies and provisions was held to be intolerable in its toll on the economy. Neo-liberals wanted to 'roll back the state' and reduce the role of the government, with the aim of restoring Britain's international economic competitiveness. Welfare benefits were seen as detrimental to labour market flexibility, as they kept up wages. New Right ideology came to the forefront at this time. It owed much to nineteenth-century liberalism, which cherished economic freedom. Its adherents believed in minimizing the role for the state and particularly in welfare reform, whose budget now dominated public expenditure. Social security benefits were perceived to be undermining incentives to work and leading to a 'dependency culture'. This had echoes of the justification for the 1834 reform of the Poor Law. Free markets were presented as the ideal economic arrangements wherever possible, and state intervention was deemed damaging. Previously fashionable Keynesian economic management was thought to be discredited and irrelevant.

Thatcherism

From 1979 to 1997, Britain was governed by a Conservative Party that was inspired by the New Right—ideas and ideals rooted in economic liberalism combined with social conservatism. Thatcher (1979–90) and Major (1990–7) declared that excessive public expenditure lay at the heart of Britain's economic problems, and the delivery of public services was paternalistic, inefficient, and generally unsatisfactory, thereby justifying the promotion of alternatives. Public service workers came to be condemned as bureaucrats who failed to promote the public's interests. Irrespective of whether welfare spending actually did hamper international competitiveness and create a 'dependency culture', the government believed it did, and acted accordingly to trim the welfare state (Clasen 2003).

Thatcherism promised low taxes, less state intervention, and lower levels of public spending. Thatcher opposed a welfare system that discouraged thrift and bred bureaucracy. This involved, in theory at least, substantial cuts as the government tried to reverse the pattern of incremental growth in welfare spending that had been a feature of the post-war period until then. This goal was manifested in financial management techniques inspired by practice in the private sector and the introduction of market forces. This led to retreat in, for example, pensions and housing. Provision was increasingly residual in nature because the government wanted cost control and was prepared to accept the price of increased economic and social inequality. Some observers accused the government of 'selling off' the welfare state.

Following the haemorrhage of manufacturing jobs in the deindustrialization caused by the 1981–2 recession, the goal of full employment was formally abandoned and priority was instead accorded to keeping inflation low. The power of the trades unions was quashed. They operated in a tighter legal framework, including the requirement for pre-strike ballots; the end of the 'closed shop' (union membership as a precondition of employment in a specific industry); being liable for damages incurred in illegal strikes. They were hardly consulted by the government and their influence waned.

The privatization of formerly state-owned major utilities altered the balance of the mixed economy. Gas, electricity, telephonies, British Airways, and later British Rail were all privatized. In social welfare, the quasi-monopoly which local councils had in the delivery of services came under attack. For example, their traditional role as 'front line' delivery agencies of education, housing, and social care services was challenged.

Welfare state reform in the 1980s

This was a period from which the welfare state emerged substantially changed. The 'marketization' of welfare involved encouraging individuals to finance their own welfare, for example, by saving for their own pension. It also concerned the promotion of linking public and private in welfare provision. This involved a new form of welfare state organization: private commercial or voluntary not-for-profit providers alongside public providers. The assumption was that this process would use competitive pressure to promote greater efficiency and responsiveness to the needs of those using the services. Social policies were devised that encouraged the intermeshing of the 'public' and 'private' in the welfare field, involving new forms of welfare state organization: markets for public services, multiple welfare providers, and new roles for commercial and voluntary providers.

The restructuring process proceeded somewhat differently in different social policy fields: full employment was an early casualty, along with housing investment, but even Thatcher felt that it was prudent to proclaim that the NHS was 'safe in my hands'. Yet the Conservative governments after 1987 engaged in a programme of wholesale restructuring of state welfare. They attempted to increase efficiency and introduce elements of competition within a model of taxpayer funding.

Services were to be 'contracted out' by competitive tender to private or voluntary sector suppliers, rather than employing public sector staff. Central government typically retained regulatory powers and set performance targets for public services which were delivered by a range of separate providers, often operating in competition. The assumption was that this would widen choice and drive down costs. Services from social housing maintenance to refuse collection, from social care to hospital catering, cleaning, and laundry were contracted out to private and voluntary sector agencies. The Thatcherite agenda defined a new role for local authorities: they were to become purchasers in a mixed economy, ensuring a plurality of suppliers across the private and voluntary sectors and moving local authorities away from provider role. These reforms were contentious, especially in circumstances where they did not result in the hoped-for cost savings or led to a poorer quality of service, or pay cuts and job insecurity for workers.

Housing

In housing there were unprecedented cuts in building, maintenance, and subsidization (Maclennan and Gibb 1990). There was also a huge sale to tenants of council housing under a scheme called the 'Right to Buy'. Emphasis was placed on owner-occupation as the solution to individual housing needs, and opportunities for gaining access to social rented housing were in decline (Forrest and Murie 2010). Large reductions in the general subsidy after 1981 were imposed as a way of driving up local authority rent levels. This was also designed to encourage more people to buy their houses and to move social renting towards a more market-related pricing system, with assistance targeted through means-tested Housing Benefit (Clasen 2003).

Social security

Welfare bills were addressed by cutting entitlements in two ways. Insurance-based benefits such as Unemployment Benefit were cut back, with an ever-growing number of individuals pushed on to means-tested support (Clasen 2003). Tighter conditions were imposed on benefits for the unemployed. Over time, income-related benefits became a more important part of the system because the time limit for receipt of contributory benefits was cut, which affected the growing long-term unemployed. Special payments to benefit claimants for specific items were replaced by the Social Fund, which had a more limited budget. A significant saving came in 1980 with the switch to linking the annual uprating of the state retirement pension to price increases rather than the rise in wages, which invariably went up faster. This led to a steady fall in the value of the basic retirement pension relative to earnings (Evans 1998).

The economic liberalism and social conservatism of the Thatcher governments were evident in their reform of support to lone parents. The Child Support Act sought to pursue absent parents to pay child maintenance to their former partner, especially where the lone parent was in receipt of social security benefits. In this way the policy both saved money and promoted social responsibility and the role of the family.

Education

School education was previously financed and administered locally by local education authorities (LEAs), which are departments of local government. Schools were given the opportunity to 'opt out' of LEA control and receive their funding directly from central government. The advantage of this was said to be to introduce some elements of the free market by encouraging a diversity of schools that specialized in certain subjects or carried the values of a certain faith. This would produce competition between schools and enable successful schools to expand.

There was long-running concern about 'standards' in education. The solutions adopted involved greater central control and inspection. The Conservative governments introduced national assessments and, for the first time, a national curriculum that imposed certain obligatory subjects was introduced in 1988 in England and Wales, shifting control from the school to the government. National testing of school pupils, with performance targets, was also introduced in England and Wales as a way for the centre to try to raise and monitor standards. This series of developments that emphasized outcomes measured in targets and performance criteria, rather than processes, reflected a more general trend in government.

The end of the Thatcher period

Towards the end of the Thatcher period an attempt was made to overhaul the system of local authority spending as part of an agenda to weaken local government. Domestic rates (a form of property tax) were replaced by the Community Charge or 'Poll Tax', which was designed to make local authorities more accountable to the electorate and reduce support for parties likely to increase expenditure. It proved to be a big mistake. It was hugely unpopular and voters in reality blamed central government as much as councils for the level of the tax. It led to the end of Thatcher's premiership and defined the limits to which an anti-welfare state strategy could be taken.

Despite cuts in spending on housing and stricter eligibility rules for benefits, the Thatcher revolution was less radical than either its opponents or its supporters claimed: the share of national income going to finance welfare spending in fact remained stationary between the late 1970s and the late 1980s (Glennerster 2007).

The 1990–7 Conservative governments

In his premiership, Major launched an attack on bureaucracy with the 'Citizen's Charter'. A private sector ethos of customer service and choice was promoted, which was thought to result in a service more accountable and sensitive to users (Page 2007). As part of this drive, professional control, such as that held by teachers and doctors, was further undermined. This involved continuing with target setting and performance management as means of trying to raise standards. One policy programme that underwent radical change was health policy.

In the 1970s the NHS was run according to a traditional model of state finance, state provision, and strong trades unions, and health professionals were trusted to run the service. In the 1980s a new style of management was introduced, strengthening the hands of bureaucrats over clinicians (Harrison and Ahmad 2000). How to finance the NHS became an increasingly political issue. Right from the outset, costs had rocketed above those that the wartime planners had anticipated as improvements in medication and medical technology drove up costs and expectations (Cutler 2003). Increasing demand and limited resources meant that by the late 1980s waiting lists were growing, sometimes being over two years for relatively simple procedures (Le Grand and Vizard 1998). Reforms by the Conservatives under Major in response were based on the notion that the NHS would be more cost efficient if market discipline was imposed.

The NHS was therefore overhauled by the far-reaching NHS and Community Care Act (1990) which introduced the so-called 'internal market'. The central innovation was a split between purchaser and provider, which was aimed at bringing about incentives to control costs and make the system more responsive to patients. In establishing the internal market, 'purchasers' (health authorities and some family doctors known as 'GP fundholders') were given budgets with which to buy healthcare from 'providers' (hospitals, and even private providers). NHS hospitals became independent trusts, with their own managements. The internal market improved value for money in the NHS and reduced waiting times. Although the internal market may have been successful at cutting costs, it is less clear whether rewards existed for improving the quality of care (Propper et al. 2008).

New Labour

The task for Labour's final years in opposition before 1997 was to devise a strategy for making Labour electable again. This involved a clear distinction being made between the means and the ends of welfare policy. Thus, from outright repudiation of such policies at the 1983 general election, Labour steadily came to accept the market-led reforms of the previous twenty years. They built on them with a 'what works rather than who does it' approach, 'partnership' with the private sector, regulation of the public sector where markets did not serve public interest, and efforts to increase support for welfare services by 'empowering' service users and involving the public in service planning.

Cartoon 2.2 A view of Thatcher and Blair

When Blair became Labour leader he rejected both right-wing pro-market approaches and traditional Left support for public ownership of state services in favour of a Third Way, in which what mattered was 'what works'. Most strikingly he achieved the replacement of Clause Four of the party constitution, which had called for 'common ownership of the means of production, distribution and exchange.' This signalled a move to the centre ground. Consequently, 'New' Labour was the name given by Blair to his resurgent party, to distinguish it from the discredited policies associated with 'old', weak, divided Labour. New Labour indicated it had no desire to create a socialist society. Instead, it set itself the task of developing a social democratic social policy that worked with, rather than against, global capitalism (Page 2007). While New Labour continued to maintain that the welfare state should be used to tackle opportunity barriers, it no longer espoused that its task was to enhance social solidarity.

Although in opposition the Labour Party criticized the changes the Conservatives made to the welfare state, they did not take apart the reforms of their predecessors, but built on them. This involved: making the control of inflation a priority; giving a greater role to markets, including privatization; flexible labour markets, but with a place for the minimum wage and the 'social chapter' (part of the 1991 Maastricht Treaty on European Union relating to workers' rights and other social issues); lower direct rates of tax; and means testing for some welfare benefits. A 1999 policy document, *Modernising Government*, explained Labour's approach:

> This Government will adopt a pragmatic approach, using competition to deliver improvements. This means looking hard but not dogmatically at what services government can best provide itself, what should be contracted to the private sector, and what should be done in partnership (Prime Minister and Minister for the Cabinet Office, 1999, section 4.5).

This policy was particularly evident with respect to the NHS.

The NHS

Blair at first claimed to have abandoned the Conservatives' reforms that had attempted to establish the internal market in the NHS, but he later attempted a further-reaching agenda to promote choice for patients and competition among providers. New Labour proposed in a 1997 document to hold onto what it felt had worked previously, but to move away from encouraging outright competition to a more collaborative approach (DoH 1997). New Labour's 2000 NHS Plan dismissed the value of competition between hospitals, on the grounds that it resulted in variable standards, and because most local areas lacked competition anyway as they were served by only one or two general hospitals (NHS 2000). But in fact, the main elements of the internal market were retained—the purchasing role of local health authorities (then called Primary Care Trusts) and the provider trusts (Gorsky 2008). Underlying this policy was a recognition of the power of market forces, while attempting to avoid the earlier problems. At the same time, in 2000, Blair pledged to increase NHS spending at a record rate to the European Union average (Klein 2006).

As far as New Labour was concerned, it no longer mattered who provided healthcare on behalf of the NHS, so long as it was free to the patient at point of use and of high quality. For example, a GP surgery for NHS patients run by a private US commercial company opened in 2006 (Dyer 2006). However, despite these developments, the private sector will add only a small contribution to total NHS clinical activity for the foreseeable future.

As well as encouraging a diversity of providers, and in some tension with this policy, a highly centralized process of national targets for acceptable waiting times and quality pervaded the health service (Klein 2006). National standards were put in place in response to 'postcode prescribing', to ensure minimum standards throughout the service for particular client groups. There was also a highly centralized process of audit and performance review (Harrison and Ahmad 2000). Hospital performance was rated, for example.

Welfare reform

Another key part of Blair's New Labour agenda was welfare reform. Certain groups were required to enter work or retraining by participating in the New Deal rather than remain on benefits, although a strong economy creating plenty of jobs helped. A persistent theme in social security policy was the centrality of paid employment, reflected in the phrase 'work for those who can, security for those who cannot' (DSS 1998). The government believed that the social security system must be designed in such a way as to keep the UK ahead in the global economic system. This required flexibility in the labour force, achieved partly by a relatively low replacement ratio.

New Labour's approach to employment policy was known as 'welfare-to-work', based on the belief that work is the surest way out of poverty. This had two strands: first, the 'stick' of compulsion to seek work and increase one's employability; and in return, the 'carrot' of 'making work pay' through relatively low benefits for those out of work, but a national minimum wage, Working Tax Credits, and in-work benefits to top up low wages. New Labour's welfare reforms attempted to create a new contract between the state and the citizen in which more emphasis was placed on responsibilities (to look for work) and less on rights (to benefits).

Another part of the New Labour welfare agenda was to tackle the 'social exclusion' of disadvantaged groups such as the homeless and young adults with troubled lives, who lacked not just income but access to social institutions. There were also area-based initiatives, for instance the Sure Start programme aimed at families with children under 4 in low-income areas. As Chancellor, Brown put 'redistribution by stealth' into effect by increasing benefits to poorer families in work through the system of Tax Credits. He hoped to radically reduce the amount of child and pensioner poverty. Although there was some progress in this area, poverty rates did not fall as fast as the government had hoped.

Devolution

An important policy development affecting governance post 1997 was the increased devolution of some aspects of social policy to England, Wales, and Scotland. The result was policy divergence. Notably the countries went their own way in health policy and education. Yet central government exercised considerable controls over local action in England, a situation dating back to the 1980s when the Conservatives embarked upon a sequence of measures which reduced the status of local government. The New Labour government took measures to revitalize local government. For example, it introduced directly elected mayors of local councils.

As outlined above, the overarching theme of British social policy for the last thirty years has been the encroaching 'marketization' of welfare services. Governments have been interested in market forces and use of the private sector as ways of improving public policy and squeezing out better value for money. The other key motifs of the welfare system were a diversity of autonomous providers at the same time as central regulation and performance targets.

The Conservative–Liberal Democrat coalition

After the 2010 election, the elements of the welfare state that were identified by the incoming Conservative–Liberal Democrat coalition as most needing reform were that too many people were reliant on benefits, too many children left school with insufficient reading and writing skills, and too many people were dissatisfied with their experience of the NHS. The two parties accepted a neo-liberal model of policy as a means of coping with the constraints and opportunities of globalization. Both also accepted the need for reform of public services and for greater value for money.

For the Conservatives, only free enterprise can create the necessary wealth to tackle these problems. According to them, only a partnership of capitalism and government can reach that minority who do not yet share the prosperity of the majority. They argue that everyone will benefit from greater involvement of the voluntary and private sector.

Their other agenda is to devolve power from the centre. Thatcher centralized the country politically. Blair went further, micro-managing public services from the centre through performance targets. But decentralization has found a home with the coalition. Giving away power was the theme of the Conservative's 2010 election manifesto. Cameron was able to forge a coalition with the Liberal Democrats partly because both parties see the state as over-centralized and overbearing. When they hammered out a joint programme for government, the main theme other than austerity was decentralization. Britain is in for a huge shake-up of welfare provision. Three areas are in for particularly deep change: social security, schools, and healthcare.

Social security

Social security is being overhauled. Many fundamental reforms to benefits were announced early on. There is to be a cap on the total benefits a family can claim. A new 12-month time limit on the Employment and Support Allowance (for people whose ability to work is limited by disability or illness) may result in many claimants being moved onto Jobseeker's Allowance and seeing their benefit reduced. It has been widely publicized that Child Benefit will no longer be a universal benefit: it will be withdrawn from families in which one or both parents are higher-rate taxpayers earning more than about £44,000 a year. In the longer term the government plans to introduce one benefit which would replace the current system with a single benefit, to try to simplify the system.

Education

In an approach partly inherited from New Labour, the coalition education policy aims to allow parents more choice. There are proposals for existing schools to be encouraged to switch to academy status. 'Free schools' are to be created, being set up and run by not-for-profit businesses, charities, faith groups, universities, private schools, or parents themselves. These will be able to set pay and conditions for staff, deviate from the national curriculum, decide the length of school days, and so on. The state will pay for premises and provide funding per pupil; poorer children will attract a premium, so that schools are keen to take them on. The injection of choice and competition into the school system could transform it.

The NHS

As radical as the free schools concept is the government's plan for the NHS. The present goal is to give patients more choice, to improve the service by fostering competition. All hospitals are to join the ranks of the foundation trusts, and thus to enjoy greater autonomy. It has been proposed that budgetary control be handed to general practitioners (GPs), grouped in consortia, who are to commission most secondary care. Strategic health authorities and primary care trusts (PCTs), which currently do that job, are to disappear, and patients will have greater freedom to choose their GP. The aim is efficiency: GPs will have an incentive to keep their patients away from costly and unnecessary hospital care. The stakes are enormous, as commissioning involves most of the NHS's budget in England (the changes will not apply in Scotland or Wales).

There are, of course, problems with this programme of reform. The Conservatives' faith that civil society can take on the burdens of the state may not be realistic. Britons dislike services which vary according to the local area in which you live, a so-called 'postcode lottery'. Trades unions will test the government's resolve to drive through cost-cutting changes. Resistance to the coalition's reforms may well be fierce.

Why did welfare states appear?

There are several theories as to why the welfare state emerged, from the view that it was to serve the needs of capitalism by maintaining political stability and providing healthy, educated workers, to the democratic perspective that it arose from the demands of the working class expressed through the ballot box.

The following theories of why welfare states appeared—that welfare state expansion was the result of industrialization, democracy, or as a form of social control—attempt to address the broad reasons for the long-term growth of welfare scope and spending that has been common to all advanced societies in the twentieth century.

Industrialization and the growth of welfare states

Some theories of welfare development make reference to the very basic preconditions for a welfare state, such as industrialization, democratic participation, and a certain level of political mobilization. In these theories the welfare state is an inevitable rational response to the problems of modern society and a capitalist economy. Fraser (2003) is an exponent of this view. The 'logic of industrialization' thesis holds that welfare development is related to problems of industrial development in capitalist societies such as urbanization, poverty, dependence on insecure waged work, the need for a more skilled and more literate workforce, and the recognition of involuntary unemployment. It is based on the evidence of broad similarities between the welfare programmes of Western democracies. In this theory, to demonstrate that state welfare is beneficial to economic growth is sufficient to explain welfare development. In some versions state welfare provision is justified by the idea that as new social needs are uncovered they have to be met, and in others that a healthy and happy workforce will be a more productive one. It is also contended that as economic productivity goes up, so do the resources available for welfare. Variants on the theory include the 'logic of capitalism', which is based on Marxist ideology.

However, this view has been frequently challenged (see Pierson 2006 for a critique). This hypothesis is quite generalized. It is clear that the industrialization thesis fails to explain the precise mechanisms by which concerns about social conditions and needs lead to political action, and it assumes that welfare states are an inevitable by-product of industrialization. Furthermore, the campaign to reform the Old Poor Law took place in a society which was still overwhelmingly agricultural in response to rural poverty (Harris 2004). Industrialization is probably only important in the long run, which we can see by observing the differences in development of welfare in different countries. For this reason these types of theories are more useful for explaining why social policy developed at all, rather than its variations.

The logic of democracy

A second way of understanding the origins of welfare states is to regard their development as a highly political process. There is a body of literature which sees the welfare state as a key achievement of the labour movement. It has been interpreted as taking the step from a basic level of welfare needed by the functional requirements of industrialized economies to a more egalitarian form of social protection. The 'social democratic' welfare state was sought and brought about from the bottom up by those who stood to benefit most—the working class—as a result of struggle between political parties about what social policies they would like to see. This theory has been applied to the British welfare state reforms in the immediate aftermath of the Second World War when, it is argued, the strength of organized labour brought about an institutionalized commitment to universalistic welfare.

A leading exponent of this view was T. H. Marshall. He argued that there was a three-stage development of citizenship from civil to political to socio-economic rights. Civil rights were established in the eighteenth century. Political rights enable citizens to vote and were founded in the nineteenth century. Social rights of citizenship which confer economic welfare and security and enable citizens to share in the standard of living prevailing in society came about in the twentieth century as a result of political mobilization. In the mid 1960s, he summed up 60 or 70 years of 'the story of social policy' with the judgement that social welfare, once confined to 'the helpless and hopeless of the population' (Marshall 1967: 97,182) had been steadily extended to all citizens.

However, this version of history has been challenged by Glennerster (2007) on the grounds that although the NHS was free for the most part as a right of being a citizen, National Insurance benefits were only available to those who had contributed for a minimum period. Harris (2004) also takes issue with this theory, arguing that it assumes the growth of welfare states is rational and even inevitable, that it has not always been associated with notions of social justice, nor have the primary beneficiaries been the working classes. Furthermore, although much scholarship on the history of the welfare state has tended to assume that its expansion has been beneficial, this view has been called into question by other research that argues that some sections of the working class were hostile to state intervention, at least initially (Thane 1984).

Social welfare as social control

The aspects of state welfare which act against the interests of the working class challenge the theory outlined above concerning the influence of labour movements. Another hypothesis suggests that welfare measures were brought in as a response to threats of social disorder. And the purpose of policies was to reinforce work norms (for example, Ginsburg 1979). In this interpretation welfare is seen as the price of industrial and social peace. Modest concessions were granted to the working class to avoid more major reform and preserve the status quo. Once established, welfare policies reinforce the discipline of the market mechanism, for instance as the right to benefit is established through work. Variations of this approach have analysed the interests of business and industry in welfare policy. In extreme cases welfare policy is regarded as a form of social control.

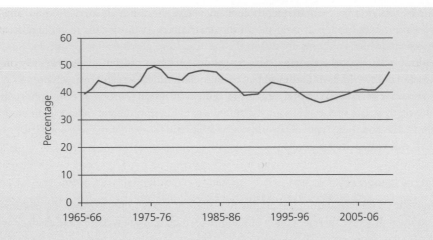

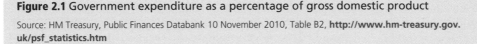

Figure 2.1 Government expenditure as a percentage of gross domestic product

Source: HM Treasury, Public Finances Databank 10 November 2010, Table B2, **http://www.hm-treasury.gov. uk/psf_statistics.htm**

Historians are much less persuaded now as to the reality of any threat of disorder and these explanations cannot account for why welfare states developed beyond the minimum necessary to maintain social order. Nor can it be proven that the new regulative mechanisms headed off more thorough going social change.

The foregoing theories may explain why state welfare exists, but are less useful for explaining the differences in timing between 'pioneer' and 'laggard' states and the different policy mixes in welfare programmes. The following theories are more appropriate to explaining the unevenness in the amount and the pace of the growth in welfare spending by focusing on struggle, debate, and dissent in public debates over social policies.

Pluralism

Pluralist political science is an elaboration of democratic theory, which expects political choice to be determined by the action of individual voters. Pluralist political science focuses on political interest groups in a democracy and how a consensus is achieved. It assumes that individuals are rational actors who recognize their stake in policies. Pluralists expect that political decisions can be explained through the study of participating actors. Thus, pressure groups, civil society organizations, trades unions, administrators, and political parties, their ideologies and the nature of their support, are the focus of study. The state may be dominated by a small group which is able to pursue interests of its own. Considerable attention has been given to the culture of this group. Lowe (2005) has argued that 'pluralism represents the values that were most prevalent in post-war Britain and, on that count alone, has considerable historical validity as an explanation of contemporary decisions' (p. 47).

Pluralist theory tends to treat the state as if it were a passive recipient of the outside pressures upon it. There has been a reaction against this aspect of the theory—'bringing the state back in'. The establishment of the welfare state has involved the creation of a bureaucracy with interests of its own. States are sites where bureaucrats and elected officials may act independently of wider society. The state formulates responses to problems that do not mirror the demands of any particular group. So according to this theory, who benefits from a policy is a different question from why it is instituted. Methods rooted in this theory analyse the workings of the government and bureaucracy in identifying problems, developing solutions, and implementing them. The role of politicians and interest groups is diminished and the importance of bureaucrats and experts expanded.

The administrative explanation exposes a weakness in accounts that focus primarily on social and political variables. But while administrators may take crucial decisions on welfare policy, in the final analysis, larger social forces have determined the policies adopted.

Polity

Pierson (1998) argues that there is a 'new politics' of welfare state retrenchment, unlike the former politics of expansion. Political actors who seek reform must find ways of managing policy to avoid blame for the contraction of services, rather than simply take the credit for the growth of welfare services. Pierson has also emphasized the importance of path dependency as particular systems entrench support for their continuance: welfare policies are likely to have aspects of long-term continuity.

Internal development and maturing of welfare states is seen by Pierson as implying 'permanent austerity', as the cost of commitments entered into in the past under rather different political circumstances is brought home to governments. In analysing the politics of welfare state retrenchment, Pierson identified 'systemic' changes, which are reforms that happen because of the strength of interest groups that support them (Pierson 1994). This applies to services where there is a whole constituency of beneficiaries who will strive to retain their rights. 'Programmatic' changes, on the other hand, do not entrench a particular interest group and are more easily reversed.

A typical argument in the literature links pressures on the welfare state to institutions which either facilitate or constrain policy adaptation and thus lead to change which is path dependent. Pierson finds socio-economic context to be the most important explanation of change to the welfare system, and downplays the role of both individual and collective agency.

This perspective leaves relatively little room for partisan politics and has been criticized as incorporating a degree of 'modern functionalism' (Clasen 2002: 71). Indeed, the link sometimes too readily made between economic or demographic challenges to the welfare state and the government's responses tends to underestimate the role played by the interests and ideas of actors involved in policy-making.

This section has summarized some of the main intellectual theories and schools of thought which have sought to account for the growth of the British welfare state. Since 'grand theories' such as industrialization and Marxism are of limited value in explaining the micro-politics of the policy process, they have been sidelined in recent years by the different set of concerns found in the literature on polity and governance. These offer a more decentred view of the state and analyse the policy process as a complex series of interactions.

As theories have developed they have increased in complexity, specialization, and sophistication. The challenge for the analyst is to strike the right balance between losses in parsimony and gains in explanatory power. Although this chapter has sought to emphasize the ways in which these theories differ from each other, it is also important to recognize that they can complement each other by focusing on different aspects of welfare state development. Politicians have been constrained by the actions of their predecessors and today's policies can be seen as the incremental result of decades of modification and tinkering, which therefore do not reflect any one set of practical concerns or values. Accordingly there is no one ideology that can describe the welfare state, and the criticisms of policy are different in each category of welfare service.

Conclusion: The survival of the welfare state

Social policy has been a component of British politics since the Industrial Revolution. During the twentieth century, particularly immediately following the Second World War, the welfare state grew to form a major part of citizens' relationship with the state. There have been periods of extensive change, and now and then elections have been defining moments, such as Thatcher's 1979 victory. But although changes have often been in the face of vociferous opposition, in reality succeeding governments have rarely dismantled the reforms of their predecessors.

The welfare state has nevertheless been subject to an ongoing process of restructuring. In the early twenty-first century more than ever, governments have had to face the tension between the continuing expansion of the demands of the electorate combined with the difficulty of raising taxes to meet these. To square this circle the contours of the welfare state have been constantly changing and major decisions have been made. For instance, in the traditional understanding of the welfare state in Britain, it was assumed that the state would provide the finance and act as the front-line delivery agency. Now the state also regulates and buys in services. The day-to-day management of welfare services is partly in the public sector and partly in the hands of commercial and not-for-profit voluntary organizations.

In a nutshell, the British welfare system today can be described as mainly publicly financed while moving towards private suppliers in a bid to lower costs. These market-led influences can be divided into, first, a search for efficiency, and secondly, consumer orientation. The desire for efficiency has involved a new role for private sector finance and splitting the role of purchaser and provider of welfare services by contracting out services to a diversity of private and voluntary providers.

Consumer orientation has been achieved by treating service users as 'consumers', offering them choice and involving service users and the public in service planning where choice is not viable. Within the mixed economy of welfare in contemporary Britain, we can observe increasing attempts to give institutions such as hospitals and schools a new autonomy and their own budgetary control whilst simultaneously, and in tension with these developments, the centre has sought to check and regulate services by setting standards and targets but not delivering them directly.

The arrival of Conservative–Liberal Democrat coalition policies means that there will be further blurring of the boundaries of the public sector. Much of the rest of this book discusses how the balance between the government and other welfare providers is changing, bringing about transformation in the 'mixed economy of welfare'.

FURTHER READING

Fraser, D., *The Evolution of the British Welfare State: A History of Social Policy since the Industrial Revolution*, 4th edn (Palgrave Macmillan, 2009). An authoritative account of how the welfare state evolved over two centuries right up to the present day.

Finlayson, G., *Citizen, State, and Social Welfare in Britain 1830–1990* (Clarendon Press, 1994). This book deals with the contribution of the voluntary sector to social welfare within the 'welfare mix'.

Glennerster, H., *British Social Policy Since 1945*, 3rd edn (Wiley-Blackwell, 2007). A lively and readable text on the history of social policy in Britain.

Harris, B., *The Origins of the British Welfare State: Society, State and Social Welfare in England and Wales, 1800–1945*, Illustrated edition (Palgrave Macmillan, 2004). A comprehensive and broad-ranging yet accessible account which challenges the view that present-day welfare arrangements are inevitable.

Lowe, R., *The Welfare State in Britain Since 1945*, 3rd edn (Palgrave Macmillan, 2005). A well-established text that is a full history of the post-war welfare state.

Page, R., *Revisiting the Welfare State* (Open University Press, 2007). An account of the British welfare state since 1940 that re-examines some of the most commonly held assumptions about the post-war welfare state.

Stewart, J., 'The mixed economy of welfare in historical context', in M. Powell, ed., *Understanding the Mixed Economy of Welfare* (Policy Press, 2007). A chapter which stresses how the relationship of the voluntary and charitable sector to the state has altered significantly over the past hundred years.

Timmins, N., *The Five Giants: A Biography of the Welfare State,* Revised edition (HarperCollins, 2001). A lively and detailed account written by a journalist.

@ USEFUL WEBSITES

www.historyandpolicy.org: website of a group of historians demonstrating the relevance of history to contemporary policy-making.

Q ESSAY QUESTIONS

1 Are the principles on which the New Poor Law was based still relevant today?

2 Why were public health, schooling, and child welfare the fields where state intervention came early?

3 Why did the welfare state take the shape it did after the Second World War?

4 With what justification can the Labour Party claim to have established a welfare state between 1945 and 1951?

5 Did the 'classic' welfare state in Britain bring about a fairer society as its creators such as Beveridge hoped; or did it stifle initiative and enterprise, thereby accelerating economic decline?

6 Since the 1980s, has the introduction of greater market discipline into social policy resulted in the dismantling of the welfare state; or has it been effectively restructured to meet new needs?

7 What was 'new' about New Labour?

ONLINE RESOURCE CENTRE

For additional material and resources, please visit the Online Resource Centre at:
www.oxfordtextbooks.co.uk/orc/baldock4e/.

3

Making social policy in a global context

Nick Manning

Contents

Introduction

Government social policy is the mechanism through which modern societies address the social problems of the day. This is not a simple process, since governments share this space with families, markets, and community associations. Governments are also constrained by the historical legacy they inherit (see Chapter 2), their access to resources, and the international pressures on them from financial, legal, and political sources which may be beyond their control. Social policy is thus a fundamentally political process, since the nature of social problems and the preferred solutions to them are disputed by different groups on different grounds. Brief examples will be drawn from around the world, but a more detailed discussion of other countries is presented in Chapter 17.

In this chapter we will look at the nature of social problems, and the ways in which they come to the attention of governments. The nature of political institutions and processes will be described, along with the mechanisms for government action, and the reactions of governments when policy solutions do not work or go wrong. The chapter will then move to a discussion of the different ideologies that are used to debate social problems and their possible social policy solutions. This includes a familiar 'Left–Right' distinction, as well as more recent ideologies arising from new social movements and religious beliefs. Finally there is a discussion of the different pairs of concepts that are frequently deployed in discussions from different ideological points of view, such as needs, rights, justice, and citizenship.

Learning outcomes

This chapter will enable you to:

1 understand the nature of social problems, who sets the agenda for their public discussion, and how governments react to them;

2 understand the way in which governments are structured and the bureaucratic mechanisms used to deal with social issues, including policy failures;

3 understand the general range and structure of social policy ideologies, and the role of ideology in the shaping of social policy arguments;

4 disentangle the specific concepts that are the building blocks within different ideologies and debates within social policy.

What are social problems?

Perhaps the most fruitful distinction with which the sociological imagination works is between 'the personal troubles of milieu' and 'the public issues of social structure'. This distinction is an essential tool of the sociological imagination and a feature of all classic work in social science.

(C. Wright Mills 1959: 8)

A particular difficulty identified by Mills is that of encapsulating and integrating both personal experience and social context. He illustrates this by observing that for any particular individual, unemployment is a personal tragedy, but only when mass unemployment occurs does this multiple experience become a public issue. At what point does this become a social problem? There is no easy answer to this question. The tragedy is experienced individually—indeed, in recent years the unemployed have been increasingly invited to experience their condition individually.

> ### Box 3.1 C. Wright Mills on 'public issues'
>
> A social problem includes three elements:
>   *Size*: it must be an experience shared by the many rather than the few.
>   *Blame*: it cannot be the fault of the individual, but of the social context.
>   *Values*: it will threaten 'cherished social values'.

Is there, then, a natural rate of unemployment, only beyond which a social problem can be said to have emerged?

In moving from personal troubles to public issues there is a further change in addition to mere size. An individual's unemployment can be located within his or her personal biography, and as such can be explained in terms of that biography. In other words, the individual can be seen as the cause, and blame can be attached to them. Yet if this experience expands to be the common experience of many, even the majority of, individuals, Mills argues, we are moving from the realm of biography to the realm of history. As such it becomes difficult to blame individuals for their situation; rather they are subject to more general changes in the social context in which they are embedded.

These two dimensions of size and responsibility are at the heart of any discussion of the nature of social problems, since the term 'social' implies something larger than individual experience, and refers to something more than personal motivation or failure. But there is a third element central to the analysis of social problems. The intersection of biography, history, and social context is not always problematic. What, then, is the distinctive feature of the term 'problem'? Mills's answer here is that we must ask what values are cherished yet threatened or supported in the prevailing era. Social change per se is thus not a problem; it is rather the impact of social change on cherished values. Hence to analyse a social problem is not merely to identify and measure, but also to evaluate (Rubington and Weinberg 2010).

For some social problems, there is a consensus about the cherished social values under threat, and there is little controversy about the call for action—for example, an imminent influenza virus epidemic. In such a case we can get on with the business of identifying the scale of the social condition which constitutes a threat, and the severity of a problem can then be simply read off from a measure of the changing incidence of such conditions. However, for many social issues, there is conflict about the values that are threatened. Whether or not such changing social conditions represent social problems depends on the way they are perceived by different social groups, and the consequent actions and reactions which occur. Thus drug-taking or criminal actions do not of themselves indicate social problems. A crime wave may be merely the result of a change in public tolerance or police practice; a drugs epidemic may be merely the penetration of this practice into previously unaffected groups such as the middle class or schoolchildren. Public reactions, not social conditions, are the key indicator of a social problem.

How do governments react?

Spector and Kitsuse (1977) suggest that social problems are a way of voicing concerns about social issues in the political system in the form of 'grievance claims'. First, a group asserts that a condition exists, and that it is offensive. Second, an official government or other influential agency responds, typically in a routine or ineffectual way. Third, the group restates its original claim, alongside new claims about the unsatisfactory response to stage two. Finally, the group decides to

> **Box 3.2 Spector and Kitsuse on four stages in the 'grievance claims' model**
>
> *First*: a group asserts that a condition exists, and that it is offensive.
> *Second*: an official government or other agency responds, typically in a routine or ineffectual way.
> *Third*: the group restates its claim, alongside new claims about the poor response to stage two.
> *Finally*: the group decides to press for alternatives, ranging from self-help to political change.

press for alternatives to stage two, ranging from self-help activities to serious political change. The claim made (typically to government) is routinely of the form that 'something should be done' about youth unemployment, poverty, obesity, and so on. Whether or not the social conditions themselves, or the claims-making activities surrounding them, are the focus of study, public issues must necessarily be examined in their political context.

However, the conventional study of social problems is peculiarly apolitical. By this I mean that the notion of power is rarely a central focus of analysis, despite the fact that 'grievance claims' are almost always directly or indirectly addressed to the welfare state, usually within one or other government department. What originate as essentially political demands for change are heavily filtered through bureaucratic and professional routines, or if they cannot be assimilated in this way, they rarely get further than stage two in Spector and Kitsuse's model. Townsend (1976) has suggested that:

> bureaucracies have vested interests in defining problems for which they are responsible in forms which show that these problems are of 'manageable' proportions' (p. 307).

Thus, for example, unemployed lone parents or young people attract bureaucratic innovations designed to tackle the individual motivations or skills of the unemployed, but do not suggest that there should be a 'right to work'.

Ryan (1971) has characterized this management of 'grievance claims' about social issues as 'blaming the victim': the second of Mills's trilogy of size, blame, and values. Blaming is frequently implied in official responses to social problems. But this is not done directly. For example, lack of education, poor parenting, lifestyle, and so on are frequently used to direct attention away from government responsibility. A particularly neat strategy is the medicalization of social problems. Examples are not difficult to find: juvenile delinquents, drug addicts, rapists, homosexuals, the depressed and lonely, school truants, the aged, and even the poor on occasions have been 'invited' to undergo some kind of therapy. This accomplishes several objectives simultaneously. It partly attributes responsibility to the victim, yet retains an individualist focus. It draws on a powerful and legitimate source of both expertise and authority, yet diverts claims away from the political arena. Thus it appears that something serious is being attempted by way of solving a social problem. If a medical solution does not work, then at least it appears that one of the most powerful and widely accepted modes of social intervention has been attempted. To the extent that one includes other professions such as social work and law this translation of social problem victims into clients is widespread.

Haines (1979) has suggested that this process amounts to the depoliticization of a social problem by enclosing it in a limited range of legitimate thought and action. In Mills's terms, conflicts of values are reduced to technical issues. Haines suggests that 'the social problem process may be defined as the broad context of conflict and negotiation through which a given social problem develops' (p. 123). The general movement in this process is from 'open' social problems to 'closed' social problems. By 'open' he means that two or more interest groups are contending for the right to define the problem. By 'closed' he means that the political debate is over, and only one definition of the problem now exists. The process of enclosure involves both the limitation of the range of persons and groups who are entitled to define and propose solutions to the problem, and the limitation of the range of perspectives which stand a reasonable chance of being taken seriously as an explanation of the problem and its potential solutions. While in Western society this typically means encapsulation by a scientific world view, the same point can be made with respect to a society in which religious values are pre-eminent, such as Catholic attitudes to birth control, or Islamic attitudes to women.

Who sets the agenda?

Who raises the issues that are to be dealt with through the political processes which permeate the welfare field? The main players include welfare clients, social movements, professionals, bureaucrats and policy networks, and politicians and political parties.

A simple model of the dynamic interplay of these social actors might be to consider the way in which social problems arise in society. When there appears to be a problem, for example the appearance of a new disease such as AIDS or a sharp rise in unemployment, this would normally be brought to the attention of government agencies by professionals such as doctors, social movements, or pressure groups. The latter two groups overlap considerably, and can be thought of as organized associations with the primary aim of changing the direction of state intervention in a particular area, generally through raising an issue on the agenda of public debate. Politicians and government bureaucrats might then be expected to respond to these collectively expressed requests.

Welfare clients such as patients, unemployed workers, and students may also be active in these attempts to change social policies. In this way they are making their voices heard rather than passively accepting existing arrangements. Hirschman (1970) has described the alternatives here in terms of 'exit, voice or loyalty' (Box 3.3). Attempts to change policies are an example of 'voice', when collective or individual disquiet or innovation is expressed in the political arena. Loyalty is the option to support existing policies and welfare arrangements—perhaps the most typical. The final option is to try to escape the situation through individual solutions: for example by setting up a new business rather than expecting government to solve unemployment; or choosing private medicine instead of trying to persuade the government that health policy is wrong.

However, this model of attempts to solve social problems through professional concern, collective action, or individual solutions is too simple to adequately understand political actions in the welfare field. This is for three reasons. First, much social policy is directed not at new social problems, but at ongoing issues of long standing. Second, much debate about policy arises from within government agencies rather than outside them. Third, much state intervention

---

Box 3.3 **Hirschman's 'exit, voice or loyalty'**

Where a person disagrees strongly with a policy, there are only three options:

Exit: leave the situation;
Voice: express dissent and try to change the situation;
Loyalty: change one's own view and learn to accept the situation.

has unanticipated consequences—indeed, not infrequently having little effect or even making matters worse.

Political party debates

The fate of social problems is crucially affected by the views of prevailing political parties. What are the current views of the political parties as to the solution of social problems? In recent years there has been renewed debate about the extent to which governments can and should attempt to solve social problems. In the late twentieth century Labour and Conservative governments had shared a commitment both to the managerial reorganization of social policy and to the requirement that increased resources could only be financed through economic growth. The Left critique of this era was that managerialism further removes the public from democratic participation in social services, and that the only way to find sufficient resources is a policy of redistribution through a progressive tax system. The Right critique also aimed at bringing services and people closer together, but by the simple expedient of encouraging people to provide for themselves. This would simultaneously ease the shortage of resources by forcing the family, the private market, and the voluntary sector to provide more.

With the election of the coalition government in 2010, a new philosophy of the appropriate responsibilities of individual and government was given legitimacy. Despite continuing popular support for the welfare state as the major institution for solving social problems, the Conservative Party in the current coalition government has suggested that the state cannot do everything, and that citizens must try to solve some problems themselves, a notion described by Prime Minister David Cameron as the 'Big Society' (Box 3.4).

The coalition government has been very effective in portraying the New Labour decades as a time in which vast sums were spent in vain; indeed that there has merely been the creation of ever-greater dependency on state expenditure. Of course, much of this debate makes the assumption, on both the Left and the Right, of a value-consensus view of social problems (explored in more detail towards the end of the chapter). The debate is couched in terms of measured social conditions. However, of late the Right has had significant success in also adopting in effect a social constructionist view of social problems. That is to say, in addition to arguments about changing social conditions, the Right has successfully undermined the legitimacy of certain traditional social conditions being accorded social problem status at all. Ten years ago the current levels of unemployment and poverty would have been seen on all sides as disastrous. This is simply not the case now. Moreover, the Right has simultaneously elevated other social conditions to greater social problem status: crime and family morality, for example. I am suggesting

---

Box 3.4 **The Big Society**

'People power' announced by the prime minister and deputy prime minister on 18 May 2010, 12 days after the general election:

- giving communities a greater say over their local planning system;
- creating a new generation of community organizers;
- encouraging volunteering and involvement in social action, including a 'Big Society Day';
- piloting a new National Citizen Service aimed at 16-year-olds;
- supporting mutuals, cooperatives, charities, and social enterprises;
- establishing a Big Society Bank;
- increase access to government-held data through a 'new right to data';
- extending powers and removing restrictions for local government.

here not merely that previously 'closed' social problems (in Haines's terms) are more 'open', but that the Right has become quite conscious of the fact that social problems are socially constructed, and thus may be changed or even 'solved' through effectively managed public debate, rather than concrete action.

However, of course, on many matters there is serious disagreement between the parties over social policy. The British governmental system does enable a determined political party to pursue its policies relatively unchecked. During the New Labour years this resulted in the introduction of market principles into many areas of social policy, the weakening of local government control, and the development of more independent quangos (quasi-autonomous non-governmental organizations) and agencies to undertake government work. Under New Labour the process of policy centralization developed in which a political party could not only pursue particular policies, but a small elite within the party could do so—and sometimes the prime minister alone (Blair 2010). For example, Tony Blair championed the development of faith-based schools, and of course military intervention. Similarly Gordon Brown, from a power base in the Treasury, changed many aspects of social policy, favouring incentives to work, and partnership with industrial and financial organizations.

In this respect the UK is edging closer to US social policy when both public and private social policy expenditure is considered (see Box 3.5).

The ideas that sustain political parties are frequently developed through pressure groups and think tanks who take on the task of thinking the unthinkable as far as future policy options are concerned.

Box 3.5 Public and private social policies in the UK and the United States

Under Gordon Brown's long period as Chancellor of the Exchequer, and subsequently prime minister, a quiet revolution has occurred in British social policy since 1997. The overarching strategy has been to dovetail public social policy efforts with the natural workings of the private market sector. This has happened in two ways. The first was the effort to move unemployed people from welfare dependency to earning their living on the private labour market. This included a range of reforms from tightened benefit conditions (including, notoriously, the restrictions applied to single mothers from 1997), to the payment of benefits through tax incentives (such as tax credits, whereby benefits are paid through the Inland Revenue). Second was the use of private finance raised in the city to fund public investments, the best example being the rebuilding of many hospitals and schools through the PFI (private finance initiative). This was designed to keep public taxes low, by making the costs of these investments appear on the balance sheets of individual health and education trusts. Gordon Brown has thus been able to increase spending considerably, while keeping Britain as one of the lowest-taxed economies in the OECD (Organisation for Economic Co-operation and Development—contains most of the more affluent states in the world).

These changes bring UK social policy closer to the United States. Hacker (2002; Hacker and Pierson 2002) has developed the argument that there is considerable provision, and specific structuring, of social policy through the private market in the United States, such that the US welfare state is more generous and more effective at protecting the poor than is usually recognized. The OECD (2005, Chart 1, p.12) has shown how closely the UK and the United States are matched in their mix of public and private sources of social expenditure. Defining social expenditure as provision by public and private institutions for social purposes that is redistributive or compulsory, the OECD study shows that while the UK and the United States spent 25 and 17 per cent of GNP respectively on social policies twenty-five years ago, this has now converged on 25 per cent in both countries.

For the New Labour government, DEMOS, a non-aligned but radical and innovative think tank was an important influence (the web address, along with those of other similar groups, is listed at the end of this chapter). The current coalition government draws on ideas from the Big Society Network, a looser group of community-oriented activists. In addition, professional associations such as the British Medical Association (BMA), the medical Royal Colleges, and trade union and business groups offer advice or warnings to the government, and may be actively consulted from time to time.

Debates internal to professional and government bureaucracies

Debates about policy changes, however, often arise within those groups of professionals and bureaucrats with responsibility for the area in question, rather than from political parties or pressure groups. The key players here are seen to be a constant set of state functionaries, regardless of which party is in power. Rhodes (1988; Rhodes and Marsh 1992) has proposed that government within the UK can be usefully conceptualized in terms of types of policy network, ranged between two polar types of network: the policy community, and the issue network (see Box 3.6). The continuum between them concerns their relative integration, stability, and exclusiveness. Policy communities, for example legal services, are characterized by relatively tight-knit and stable relationships, continuity of a restricted membership, vertical interdependence based on service delivery, and insulation from other networks, the public, and Parliament. Issue networks, on the other hand, for example local campaigners, typically have a large number of participants, limited interdependence, less stability and continuity, and a more atomistic structure. The Big Society Network is an example. In between these polar types, varying both in stability and in interests, are professional and producer networks, serving professional (for example, doctors) and economic (for example, manufacturers) concerns respectively; and finally there are intergovernmental networks oriented horizontally towards common positions within the structures of government, such as local councillors.

A network is defined primarily in terms of 'resource dependencies', with network interactions chiefly oriented towards resource maximization. However, Rhodes has also included a wider range of factors when considering the way in which policy networks change. Not only are economic considerations relevant, but ideological, knowledge-based, and institutional issues are also identified by him as significant. Thus, although he stresses the effects of changes in party ideology (for example, the Big Society) clearly this could be extended to include a more general consideration of

---

Box 3.6 **Policy networks**

There is a range of networks, depending on how tightly they are integrated:

Policy community: tight-knit and stable relationships, continuity of a restricted membership, vertical interdependence based on service delivery, and insulation from other networks, the public, and Parliament.

Professional/producer/intergovernmental network: these networks are intermediate in terms of how tightly they are organized, and in addition they are focused on different substantive areas, respectively a profession (such as medicine), producers who deliver goods and services (such as the pharmaceutical industry), and government units (such as regional or local government).

Issue network: large number of participants, limited interdependence, less stability and continuity, and a more atomistic structure.

the world views of those individuals who make up the network—their social values, normative assumptions, and so on.

Political institutions and processes

Welfare states are so called because they are part of the nation-state, which continues to be the key to understanding social policy. States as such are a relatively recent invention. Although we think of the United Kingdom as having a very long history, some nation-states, such as Germany and Italy, only emerged in the nineteenth century. States in general have a familiar set of structures and institutions for administering those concerns of their citizens that are considered as legitimately within the public domain. In the welfare area, for example, these might typically include a government department or ministry for dealing with different aspects of healthcare. In the UK this is called the Department of Health, in France and in Russia it is called the Ministry of Health.

The staff of these government departments would typically be full-time career civil servants—an essential component of the modern welfare state. It is the role of these bureaucrats to carry out and implement whatever policies are laid down by the government of the day. For example, where a government, such as the coalition in the UK, plans a new scheme, such as the capping of housing benefit, then civil servants are duty bound to implement this policy.

The right of governments to develop and implement such policies within the state is conferred mainly, although not exclusively, through the process of liberal democracy. This is a mechanism, now very widely diffused throughout the world, for registering the consent of citizens to government action of various sorts, and for making the legal, financial, and military resources available to the government to act. In the field of social policy, financial resources or lack of them are a pre-eminent constraint on government action, but legal arrangements are also of great significance. For example, modern medicine seems to cost more and more each year, partly as the result of the progress of medical science in developing new technology, but also partly as a result of the ageing of the population and the survival of people with significant healthcare needs. Both the medical profession and the public often turn to governments to find the money for this steady expansion of healthcare.

In addition to these resource problems, the rules under which such services operate, many of them inscribed in law, are both a mechanism for government control—through new legislation, for example—and a site for argument and dispute. For example, where a child has become very disruptive in her classroom, there might be a clash between the child's right to education, the parent's obligation to secure that education, the teacher's right to particular conditions of employment, and so on.

One source of such rules in modern states is the existence of a constitution which lays down the structure of government, and the various rules through which it should be set up and should operate. This can be very important indeed for social policy changes and provision. A good example is provided by the United States. After the Declaration of Independence in 1776 at which Jefferson famously declared that 'all men are created equal', the Constitution and the first ten amendments (such as freedom of religious expression) were adopted. There have been more than twenty subsequent amendments to the Constitution, many of which have had profound consequences for social policy. For example, the abolition of slavery, and the right of black Americans to equal access to services such as education, were guaranteed in a series of three amendments (the 13th, 14th, and 15th—see Box 3.7) passed soon after the northern states won the American civil war in 1865.

Britain never rejected or completely neutralized the monarchy, as did the French, the Russians, and the Americans in their revolutions. Without this break, it has been difficult to establish a case

---

Box 3.7 US constitutional amendments

13th   Neither slavery nor involuntary servitude . . . shall exist within the United States.
14th   All persons born or naturalized in the United States . . . are citizens of the United States.
15th   The right of citizens of the United States to vote shall not be denied . . . on account of race, color, or previous condition of servitude.

---

for a written constitution in the UK. This makes it difficult to lodge an appeal to the basic rules which govern British society, for example if there is a case where some feel that there is a fundamental injustice to be corrected. The members of Charter 88, for example, have argued that a written constitution would provide safeguards for citizens against welfare injustices perpetrated by mistake or intent.

Types of government action

The rules and resources which shape political institutions and structures typically give rise to a pattern of government action in the arena of social policy which has been classified by Julian Le Grand (1993) into three mechanisms: direct provision, financial support, and regulation (Box 3.8).

Direct provision is where the state provides both the resources and the rules by which they are to be used. For example, in the UK, health 'insurance' was provided from 1948 to 1994 through the National Health Service directly supplied by the government to citizens who needed healthcare. This approach was felt by British Labour governments for most of the twentieth century to be the most efficient and fairest mechanism for social welfare provision. This entailed either nationalizing existing services, such as the hospitals in 1948, or providing services from scratch, such as local authority housing from the early 1920s, or local authority social work since 1968. Taking these services into public ownership was part of a wider strategy of enlarging direct state provision where capitalism was seen to be inefficient or unfair, and included rail and air transport, steel production, and, for a time, car manufacture.

This policy was tolerated reluctantly by British Conservative governments as an unpleasant but practical necessity. It had been necessary for the development and coordination of the many activities essential to the prosecution of the Second World War, including the Emergency Medical Services. This had amounted in effect to the nationalization of many aspects of the country's production and service provision, and demonstrated that widespread direct state provision could work. Much of the British welfare state set up in the immediate post-war years was typified by this means of direct service provision. There is now, however, decreasing use of direct provision. New Labour, for example, proposed to make schools fully independent of local authority control, and to encourage the development of more faith-based schools. This policy has been expanded by the coalition government's promotion of school academies. This will follow a path already developed in the NHS, which has been broken up into more than four hundred autonomous trusts, each with a structure modelled on private sector companies, run by boards of executive and non-executive directors. In time it is intended that these trusts will operate with full freedom to buy and sell assets and to raise money in private markets. In addition, New Labour's £17 billion hospital building programme was entirely financed through private banks rather than government money, with generous guaranteed rates of return over thirty or forty years.

This change of NHS operations will move it closer to many other services where financial support, but not direct provision, typifies state action. Here the state provides the financial

> **Box 3.8 Types of government action (Le Grand 1993)**
>
> *Mechanism one*: direct provision—state provides both the resources and the rules.
> *Mechanism two*: financial support—state provides the financial resources.
> *Mechanism three*: regulation—state is concerned with the rules only.

resources, but not always the rules for their disbursement. This form of state intervention has often developed in areas where existing private provision is defended through well-organized interests. For example, British governments give people financial help to get privately provided legal services, because lawyers do not wish their service to be nationalized. Housing is also mostly provided by the private sector, but the British and US governments have spent large sums in helping purchasers to acquire cheaper finance for their houses, for example by defraying income tax where income is spent on repaying mortgages. Indeed, this idea of government relief from paying income tax on money spent on services amounts in effect to extensive government spending in terms of 'tax expenditure'.

In many countries, healthcare provision operates in the same way, through the government subsidizing private provision, since doctors have been powerful enough to resist nationalization. The American Medical Association has been notoriously successful in this respect, most recently in portraying President Barack Obama as a socialist for his healthcare reform that extends health coverage to most poor Americans.

Government financial support requires the monitoring of service providers to check that the money is being used in a proper manner. This leads us to consider the third area of state action, regulation. Here the state is concerned more with the rules than the resources necessary for any particular action. In France, for example, the government merely legislates that all citizens should be insured through non-profit independent 'insurance societies' who pay for healthcare. Regulation is a non-market method of state intervention to ensure the delivery of services to, or requisite behaviour from, defined groups or individuals in a manner defined in law or subject to bureaucratic surveillance. Parents are required to ensure that children's education takes place, normally of course at a recognized school. Those children are known to the state, since all births must be registered with the state. The provision of medicines is closely regulated, as they may be dangerous; those of working age seeking income support are required to seek work; all car drivers must take out insurance against the costs of accidents; and so on. What the law requires, and the efficiency or fairness of bureaucratic surveillance, are the subject of sharp dispute from time to time, often organized by pressure groups concerned to secure the well-being of particular groups such as poor, older, or disabled people.

State action also takes place in most countries through lower levels of government. These also have considerable consequences for social policy. In very large countries such as Russia or the United States, the next layer of government structures below the national level is what amounts to 'ministates' within the state. These will have considerable powers of their own, including the ability to raise finance independently from the central state, upon which they will nevertheless usually be partly dependent. In smaller countries—in Europe, for example—these lower tiers of government are likely to have rather less autonomy, and may range from rather loose regional groups to specific counties, as in the UK.

Social provision such as education is often undertaken at these lower levels of government. However, this raises a problem of the relative affluence of different areas, and hence the possibility of social provision varying between citizens of the same country as a result of geographical location. This variation may well be cumulative, so that relative differences are compounded for education, housing, healthcare, employment, and so on. Such regional disadvantages have been termed 'territorial injustice' by Bleddyn Davies (1978).

Local governments also have rules, resources, and different modes of intervention, as we have seen for central government. For example, in the UK, local governments can significantly vary the types of schools provided. They can also vary the level of funding they choose to give to schools, and hence the size of classes, as well as provision of books and equipment and kinds of food. As is the case for central government, these local variations in rules and resources lead to different types of intervention. Some local authorities provide most schooling directly themselves, as in Nottinghamshire, whereas in other areas almost all schools are independently organized, as in Kent.

When policies go wrong: public inquiries

Key political players in the field of social policy may, however, only be revealed at times of change. For example, when policies go badly wrong, there may be an official inquiry to ascertain the exact role that different groups and individuals played. An illustration of this process is given by the long series of public inquiries into cases in which vulnerable children have died in family circumstances where social workers and other professional groups have been unable to help, such as those of Baby P. A similar series of inquiries has examined failures of institutional care in mental hospitals, children's homes, and schools.

In general it has long been recognized, since Merton's succinct essay in 1936, that there can be unintended consequences of 'purposive social action': action over time may not bring about the changes intended (see Box 3.9). He observes that there are a number of reasons why action as intended does not always result in anticipated outcomes. The first two—and the most pervasive—are ignorance and error. The regular discussions in the media of the side effects of new medical technologies, such as drug treatments, are a daily reminder of these problems. This is hardly surprising. However Merton lists additional reasons. An interesting one is his suggestion that a wilful ignorance of the unanticipated can develop as a result of an overwhelming commitment to an intended policy consequence. A good example of this is where a government has made an election manifesto commitment and implements a policy despite worrying concerns that it will not work. Evidence, for example, that the New Labour Sure Start programme for preschool children only improved the performance of already more privileged children, was ignored as the government rolled out the programme right across the UK. Merton also suggests that some policies may be self-contradictory or indeed self-defeating, whereby they generate more problems than they solve. For example, the effects of legalizing soft drugs (which may increase smoking) or banning smoking may generate unanticipated consequences of policies pursued with good intent. The substantial widening of access to UK universities in the last twenty years has inevitably resulted in greater competition in the graduate labour market, and a reduction in the value of a degree to any individual student.

In other circumstances we can see policies being undermined by the resistance of ordinary citizens who either cannot or will not accept the policies. The single largest example was the sudden collapse of the East European welfare states in 1989–91, when citizens gained the confidence to engage in mass defiance of government policies. But specific cases can also be found. For example, when the US federal government decided in the 1960s to force local governments to develop racially integrated schools in the southern states and many northern cities, this led to the active physical resistance by parents of children being 'bussed' between school districts, and to the effective undermining of the policies through 'white flight', where white parents moved house, or moved their children to private schools, in order to avoid the effects of the policies.

Box 3.9 Merton's (1936) unintended consequences of 'purposive social action'

One: ignorance about consequences;

Two: error as to the likely consequences;

Three: wilful ignorance caused by over-commitment to one policy;

Four: self-contradiction, for example expanding higher education while there are low graduate employment prospects;

Five: self-defeating prediction, for example where a future risk is aggravated by current concerns, such as current savings being discouraged by poor future pension prospects.

Ideology and social policy

Social policy, it has been argued so far, is not a neutral or technical matter. There is a great deal of debate within political parties and policy networks, and within the mass media where different private interests have been accused of influencing policy debates. Typically, given the dominance of the state in social policy, social policy ideologies have been analysed through the familiar Left-to-Right framework used as a shorthand for identifying different political ideologies. There are a number of examples of this in the literature (see Box 3.10).

Clearly it is not easy to separate different ideologies cleanly: they tend to shade into each other (Heywood 2003). A major reason for this is that writers have tended to blur the normative ('ought') parts of an ideology with the explanatory ('why and how') parts. Thus two ideological positions might share the same ideals, or end states, but differ over their analysis of the 'why and how' of social policies, and hence the means advocated of attaining common ideals. For example, Marxists and socialists mainly differ over their analysis of how to attain a fairly similar ideal. Even Marx's description of life under communism is expressed in the kind of individualist imagery of personal choice that supporters of the New Right would not disagree with. Perhaps this explains how from time to time social policy analysts have crossed over and changed their ideological position as a result not of changed ideals but of their analysis of how to get to them (see Box 3.11).

Box 3.10 Ideologies of welfare

Wedderburn (1965)
anti-collectivism; citizenship; integrationism; functionalism

Titmuss (1974)
residualism; industrialism; institutionalism

Taylor-Gooby and Dale (1981)
individualism; reformism; structuralism; Marxism

George and Wilding (1994)
New Right; Middle; democratic; Marxism; feminism; Greenism; socialism

Taylor (2007)
Liberalism; Conservatism; Social Democracy; Neo-Liberalism; Third Way; Radical Critics

> ## Box 3.11 **Communist ideals**
>
> Communist society . . . makes it possible for me to do one thing today and another tomorrow, to hunt in the morning, fish in the afternoon, rear cattle in the evening, criticize after dinner, just as I have a mind.
>
> (Marx and Engels 1976)

Fine distinctions between ideologies are therefore difficult to work with, and here we will present a relatively simple three-dimensional view. On the one hand, the Left and the Right can be separated from a middle position. Second, there are a number of new social movements (NSMs) that cut across this traditional political spectrum, such as feminism and environmentalism. Finally, there is a group of beliefs ignored in the studies illustrated in Box 3.10, but possibly more significant than any other for social policy around the world—religious beliefs.

The Left

The Left draws its inspiration either from Marx or from the variety of democratic socialist ideas embedded in the European labour movements of the late nineteenth and early twentieth centuries. In many respects their ideals are quite similar. They are both concerned to harness industrialization (which they do not especially criticize) for the good of all members of society. An egalitarian distribution of goods and services is thus a central concern. The main disagreements between Marxists and other socialists is over means rather than ends. Marxists have been perfectly happy to advocate quite authoritarian means, including a powerful state, to achieve these ends: the Soviet Union was a particularly clear example of this. Other socialists, on the whole, have been concerned to empower ordinary people through democratic parliamentary mechanisms in order to secure their active consent to social policies. Getting the majority of citizens to support policies is critical not merely to retain parliamentary power but to crowd out alternative services, such as private market-based ones. A particularly good example of this approach has been realized in Sweden for much of the post-war period.

The middle

In the middle is a wide range of views united not so much by ends, as was the Left, but by the means for developing social policy, with a much less clear idea of what the ends might be (see Box 3.12). The means they are concerned about are on the whole defined negatively in terms of avoiding the dangers of either too much unregulated capitalism or too much collectivism. This was classically defined by Marshall (1963) in his idea of hyphenated society, by which he meant

> ## Box 3.12 **Muddling through the middle**
>
> The self-transformation of the European social model has never been guided by some grand master plan, from which policy then ensued. The European reform model is replete with contingencies, policy failures, co-ordination and implementation problems and, obviously, shifts in the balance of political and economic power.
>
> Anton Hemerijck, 2002, *The Self-Transformation of the European Social Model(s)*, p. 212

democratic-welfare-capitalism. He argued that in the twentieth century the development of social policy was an essential element in the functioning of modern industrialism, just as the development of civil rights and political rights had been in previous centuries. This is a functionalist model in which the modern welfare state is seen as a pragmatic way of adjusting society to the inevitable market failures that are thrown up by capitalism from time to time. In the early twenty-first century, we should add new problems such as family re-formation and demographic change that need tackling. Much policy-making, from this perspective, is concerned with anxiously avoiding pitfalls that might arise from the unintended consequences of policy intervention, such as undermining work incentives, erecting poverty traps, condoning professional arrogance, missing unrecognized need, or encouraging fraud.

This pragmatic response to social ills as they appear and are recognized has little time for passionate debate about the ideals of social policy. Notions of fairness and balance in social affairs, combined with the support of social institutions such as the family, are the goals of the middle way, anodyne enough for George and Wilding (1994: 73) to observe that 'few would quarrel with Middle Way goals'. In its latest manifestation it has been rebranded the 'Big Society', in which the old divisions between Left and Right will be transcended by civil society, government, and the market as interdependent and equal partners in the provision of welfare, and the challenge for government is to create equilibrium between these three pillars (see Box 3.4). The individual is to be 'pushed' towards self-help, and independent, active citizenship, while business and government must contribute to economic and social cohesion.

The Right

The Right is exceptional in the energy with which it has stated both its ideals and its favoured policy mechanisms. It has made the running in terms of policy debate around the globe, both within nation-states and within the numerous multinational agencies that advise and cajole those states over social policy, such as the World Bank, the International Monetary Fund, and the Organisation for Economic Co-operation and Development. While the Right can trace its ideals at least as far back as Adam Smith in the eighteenth century, its basis can be located in Social Darwinism, which was proposed by Spencer and Sumner in the nineteenth century. Unlike the European roots of socialist ideas, the Right has thus been typically an Anglo-American development; modern exponents such as Murray, Friedson, and Hayek have been based in the United States and the UK.

Social Darwinism drew on Darwin's ideas to suggest that, as in the animal world, social and economic success depended on the fitness of individuals and groups to survive in the brave new world of competitive industrial society. Indeed, it was seen as a useful mechanism for weeding out weakness naturally, and against which there was little point in intervening—intervention, it was thought, might well have highly adverse consequences. This view has reappeared in modified form in writings from the so-called New Right. Their central argument is that society is not perfectible in any particular form. They claim that they do not, therefore, have an ideal society in mind, but argue instead that we should devote our attention to the appropriate means or mechanisms which will allow the maximum chance for any particular pattern of life favoured by an individual or group. Thus freedom from constraint, and the recognition of individuals as paramount judges of their own welfare, are central ideas to the New Right. The key mechanism for ensuring these possibilities is the market; the state should have a substantially reduced role.

New social movements

The previous familiar political spectrum has been extremely important in debates about social policy over the last hundred years. However, since the 1960s a number of new ideologies have come to prominence in social policy discussions and analysis which cannot be located on that single

Left–Right dimension. They are frequently referred to collectively as the new social movements. They share a criticism of the standard Left–Right model that the dimensions are either incomplete or wrong.

There are three sets of values highly pertinent to social policy issues which the traditional ideological division cannot accommodate: feminism, anti-racism, and environmentalism. The first two are discussed by Williams (1989). She argues that while the move away from the traditional study of social administration in the 1970s was made possible by the critical appreciation of the impact on social policy of the social and economic organization of work and production, which informs much left-oriented analysis, such an analysis in relation to work leaves two further themes, of family and nation, unexamined:

> These themes, Work, Family, Nation, which shape welfare policies, reflect the divisions of class, gender, and 'race' respectively. In this picture the welfare state has to be understood as developing within the social relations of imperialism and the social relations of patriarchy, which themselves have changed over time.

> (Williams 1989: xiv)

For social policy writers concerned with gender, such as Pascall (1997) and Daly and Rake (2003), the central questions include those about why women play such a major role in social reproduction, both in the family and as state welfare workers, and how the division of labour in both waged and unwaged work affects their interests. Since social policy is concerned with social reproduction, that is the physical, emotional, ideological, and material processes involved in caring for and sustaining others (both children and adults), feminist writers argue that it is incomprehensible why feminist work should not be at the heart of social policy analysis. As feminist questions and analysis have expanded, they have become entwined with some of the traditional Left–Right debates, such as those about commitment to equality, or the appropriateness of the state or the market for engineering change. Within feminist writing, therefore, we can locate relatively left, middle, or right-wing positions.

Anti-racism reflects the omission of issues of nation from social policy concerns. Within the UK welfare state, welfare services are labour intensive, and black and immigrant workers have played an important role as a reserve of cheap labour: doctors, nurses, cleaners, caterers (Salter 2004). Moreover, welfare services contribute to the reproduction of inequalities in British society. Black children do less well at school and in the youth training and labour markets than their white counterparts. Access to appropriate healthcare and housing has been repeatedly documented as discriminatory against black people. Finally, it can be argued that the welfare state has historically been as much about the maintenance of political stability as about the meeting of social needs, and the presence of black people has been used to justify the frequent revamping of technologies of social control to contain and incorporate a perceived cultural threat. Mechanisms for this have ranged from the pathologizing of black diets, family life, and psychologies to direct policing.

Environmentalism was not central to Williams's 1989 analysis, but is included (along with feminism but not anti-racism) in the 1994 edition of George and Wilding's influential book on welfare ideologies. Green ideology is of two varieties—light green and deep green (Cahill and Fitzpatrick 2002; Fitzpatrick and Cahill 2003). The first is compatible with the current aspirations for most industrial societies, especially the attempt to solve social problems through economic growth. Concern here is that economic and social policies should be sensitive to their effects on animals and the environment. So, within housing there is concern about energy conservation, or within healthcare there is concern about testing drugs on animals, or the development of genetic manipulation without proper ethical and legal controls. Whether these ends are best pursued via market pricing or state intervention is now discussed more extensively by light greens, as their agenda has seeped into the mainstream of Left–Right debate. Deep greens, on the other hand, see the welfare state as little more than an extension of the over-industrialization and over-population that are ruining the planet. There is little debate about social policies per se in deep green ideology.

Other smaller social movements, ranging from more traditional political interest groups to protest groups, have developed, or in some cases renewed and reinvented themselves, within the welfare arena in recent years. For example, action to highlight the needs and rights of disabled people, older people, children, and sufferers from various medical conditions appear from time to time. Some of these groups have developed more extensive ideologies than others, such as the Disability Alliance (Priestley 2003).

Religions

Missed almost universally from these debates over ideologies around welfare issues are the ideas embedded in the major religions of the world. These are important for several reasons. In terms of ideals, religious beliefs affect the functioning of family life, community organization, and the vigour and focus of the voluntary sector. Understanding south-east Asian welfare states, for example, is impossible without appreciating the values embedded in Confucian beliefs, especially about family life. With migration, religious beliefs of all kinds have been transplanted across industrial societies, and understanding and respect for religious belief are important components of discussions about anti-racism and social policy. Second, with the weakening of conventional political ideology, religious ideas have become increasingly central to issues of national and regional identity both in the UK and in other countries. The biggest example would be the resurgence in the Orthodox Church in Russia, and Islam in the central Asian republics; but also within Western Europe. In the Netherlands, for example, we find that religion can be the main organizing principle and structural division in the national society. Without taking into account its religious component, a clear understanding of the Dutch welfare state is impossible.

In addition to ideals, religion affects the structure and functioning of welfare states. Governments around the world are taking steps to forge new relationships with religious movements, often designed to survey and control them (Robins and Lucas 2004). There is comparative evidence from the statistical analysis of Western industrial societies that central government welfare state development is affected by the extent to which Catholicism is predominant in a society (Wilensky 1981). Moreover, insofar as the charitable and voluntary sector is an important component of welfare activity both within a society and in the international aid and relief business, religious inspiration has been an important element in the motivation for and justification of welfare work.

Normative concepts in social policy

Whatever the source of ideologies about social policy, there have emerged a number of middle-range normative concepts in debate and analysis of welfare states that merit discussion and clarification. These will appear in all or most welfare ideologies, and form the building blocks of many debates between proponents of different positions (for example, equality and inequality—see Box 3.15). Although it is difficult to encompass all these ideas in a neat classification, we will present four pairs of concepts that are central to many debates. It is interesting to notice how new social movements take the traditional left-wing position for some items, but very much the right-wing position for others. This confirms that they are in many respects different from the traditional Left–Right dimension, and deserve separate consideration on many issues.

Needs and choice

The first concept is regarded as central to much classic social policy analysis, and discussed in more detail in Chapter 4. Needs are regarded as the main underlying reason for developing social policies by traditional proponents who have occupied the middle ground between the Left and the Right. The needs that should be met have generally been identified as those that alternative institutions such as the market and the family have failed to meet. Thus, where the labour market provides insufficient wages, or none at all, the need for income in order to buy food, clothing, shelter, and so on is identified as a moral imperative that should be met. The difference between Left and Right here centres on the means for meeting this need, and at what level it should be met. The Left has traditionally favoured state provision at levels not too far removed from basic adequacy. The Right has favoured compulsory insurance, or a very meagre state safety net at such low levels that if at all possible people would avoid it (for example the nineteenth-century workhouse).

The identification of needs remains at the heart of ideological differences over welfare. The newer ideologies use the same general argument, but in relation to specific groups such as women, ethnic minorities, disabled people, and older people. Evidence and arguments are assembled to demonstrate that these groups have been left out of provisions for the population in general. In the case of environmentalists, the needs of future generations are a central focus in the concept of sustainability, where current needs should only be met where they do not render the meeting of future needs impossible.

Meeting needs is a complex problem, since needs are difficult to measure unambiguously, and the means of meeting them can have unintended side effects, some of which can render the original effort ineffective. For example, other than very basic needs for water, food, and protection from the weather, many needs are culturally relative. Thus the legitimate types of food, drink, clothing, and shelter that we need vary markedly over time, between regions, between genders, ethnic groups, and so on. This suggests that a closely related concept of choice should be considered in parallel to need. Here the various ideologies differ more sharply than over need. The Right champions the idea that individuals are best helped by being able to exercise choice as a major starting point in arrangements for people's welfare. Since markets are the best way of providing choice, where people have the money to pay, the Right is very supportive of the use of markets and the minimum use of bureaucratic state provision.

The recent New Labour government adopted the rhetoric of choice in relation to health and education provision, such that it blurred this Right–Left distinction. Although it is claimed that this can be delivered outside market mechanisms, feminists argue that women very often do not have access to money or the freedom to spend it as they wish, even in more affluent households. Whatever the mechanism, environmentalists argue that too many of us exercise choices that will damage our own futures, let alone those of our children, through pollution, resource depletion, and genetic manipulation. In other words, choice only works where the consumer has the knowledge and capacity (which usually means money) to make choices.

The empowerment of welfare clients that has been proposed by social policy ideologies concerned with ethnic minorities, disabled people, or elderly people may or may not be accomplished through markets. The Right tends to conflate choice and the market mechanism. In fact, markets are difficult to control, and appear to have side effects that can simultaneously restrict choice. For example, the establishment of quasi-markets for schools may increase choice for some parents initially; but if some schools select the more able pupils, and others slowly run out of pupils and funding and eventually close, parents with children in those schools, or who live near them, may well find their choices severely restricted. Quasi-markets in health may have the same effect; in addition, the costs of preparing complex contracts in health tend to drive up costs, and to lead quickly to producer capture, whereby purchasing is routinized and insulated from real consumer choice.

Rights and obligations

If people have needs that are not being met, the welfare state in principle grants them the right to expect them to be met either directly, by the state, or under its jurisdiction financially or legally. Rights, then, are an intimate part of social policy. However, the meaning of 'rights' varies with the legal context of the welfare state, and de facto with the way in which welfare professionals and bureaucracies work in practice. For example, in Germany welfare rights are legally enshrined, whereas in the UK they are usually not (see Box 3.13).

An important discussion of the relationship between rights and social policy was set out in Marshall's (1963) seminal analysis of the growth of citizenship in the UK. He suggested that the development of rights under the British state had taken place in three stages: in the first, civil rights were recognized in the eighteenth century; in the second, political rights were recognized in the nineteenth century; and in the third, social rights were recognized with the foundation of a mature welfare state in the UK in the twentieth century.

For the ideology of the Right, rights are negative rights about freedom from constraint, particularly interference by the central or local state, and minimal guarantees that social rules, such as those of the market, operate fairly. Although these cost money to police, they are felt to be relatively cheap. By contrast, the rights favoured by the Left, such as positive rights to certain levels of welfare services, are much more expensive to provide. For ideologies associated with the new social movements, rights are about making sure that excluded groups get equal treatment. In this sense they share common ground with the Left. Women, ethnic minorities, future generations, disabled people, and so on have, or should have, the right to a level of service commensurate with their needs. This may mean that in some circumstances they get a level of provision considerably in excess of that typically provided to other citizens.

In recent years obligations have come to be seen as an intimate corollary of welfare rights. Citizens, it has been argued, should be active not merely in their pursuit of rights for themselves but also in their contribution to the social context on which we all, from the richest to the poorest, depend in one form or another. For example, we should not only expect the state to help us if we are poor, but we should expect to take paid work if we can. If we have children, we will be helped through social policy, but we should also strive to be good parents; in state-provided education we should try to achieve our potential. In the health service, we should cooperate with medical staff, and try to get better.

Box 3.13 Social security rights for unemployment in Great Britain and Germany

Jochen Clasen's (1992) study of the comparative erosion of unemployment benefits in Great Britain and in Germany in the 1980s shows how much easier it was for a government to achieve this in Great Britain. Here, with a central ministry responsible for both insurance and means-tested benefits, and no particular legal entitlement for citizens to receive from the insurance system the equivalent of the amounts deposited, the British government was free to reduce unemployment benefits in favour of means-tested assistance.

By contrast, while the German government started to try to make the same kind of fiscal savings by reducing German workers' entitlements, this strategy failed because of three factors. First, unemployment benefits are legally insulated from other pressures on the social security system in a separate agency; second, they are funded by legally separate earmarked contributions; third, there is by law an automatic consolidation of the accumulated fund, which can then be used to retain or finance improvements in benefits for the unemployed.

Such expectations are part of a fundamental aspect of social life: the process of reciprocity. This was a major theme of nineteenth-century social analysis. The spread of industrialization across Europe and America led to the contrast being drawn between the dense network of social relations in traditional communities and the open exchanges typical of industrial market societies. Toennies termed this the move from 'community' to 'society'; Durkheim, from 'organic to mechanical solidarity'; Main, from 'status to contract'. All these writers found the changes wrought by industrialization heightened their consciousness that, as Mauss (1967) described it, when a gift is offered between two parties, this sets up a reciprocal obligation to repay it in some sense, whether in markets, families, or governments. Inability to repay left the recipient with reduced social power and lower status. This is the anthropological source of the stigma so often experienced by welfare recipients, and it alerts us to the complexities that underlie the apparent selflessness of altruism that some have argued as the basis of a good welfare state.

Such obligations, epitomized in the title of a book by Laurence Mead, *Beyond Entitlement* (1986), have increasingly been stressed within right-wing ideology. Active citizenship is not new, however; US President Kennedy, in his inaugural speech in 1960 admonished us, 'Do not ask what your country can do for you, but what you can do for your country.' More recently, the Big Society in the UK has also taken up the idea that we should all feel obliged to return such largesse in some way (see Box 3.4). Thus the New Labour 'welfare to work' scheme obliged benefit claimants to undertake some activity in return for benefit, such as training or community service. The new social movement ideologies also stress such obligations. For example, feminists are concerned that men undertake the obligations of fatherhood, but they are also concerned that typical family obligations have meant obligations for women rather than men, particularly to undertake unpaid social care. Other groups stress the obligations of polluters to pay, or the obligations of able-bodied people to others.

Justice and merit

Meeting needs and fulfilling rights where resources are scarce raise questions of distribution and rationing. What is justice in social distribution? In principle, a just provision of welfare implies the equal meeting of equal needs. However, as we have seen, it can be difficult to determine what needs are when cultural relativities influence judgements. Geographical peculiarities may also lead to territorial injustice. When we have to compare needs for very different services, such as medical intervention and educational provision, the possibilities for relative injustice are compounded. What is the relative welfare effort that should be devoted to education or healthcare? One answer was proposed by John Rawls (1972) (Box 3.14).

Another idea, developed by health economists, is that we should provide services in relation to the quality of life they can subsequently sustain. In healthcare, for example, a medical intervention might be considered as just where it can provide a greater increase in the quality of life for a patient than an equivalent intervention for an alternative patient. This can be refined to take into account the number of years over which the improvement in the quality of life is likely to last. Thus many years of modestly greater quality for a child might be preferable to a few years of a considerable increase in quality for an older person. This idea could be extended, in principle, to the calculation of the relative benefit and costs of different social policies, and hence the ideal just distribution of welfare effort. However, it would be difficult to do these calculations and plan social policy in sufficient detail.

Rawls's conception of justice as equality is really a popular or democratic approach to the rationing of scarce resources, whereas health economists are trying to develop a technical solution. Either way, social justice has been associated most strongly with ideologies of the Left and the new social movements, and arguments in favour of equality achieved through positive policy

Box 3.14 John Rawls's model of justice

Rawls suggests that, in principle, we could plan a society as if we were screened behind a veil of ignorance. What would we choose for ourselves if we did not know what lay in store in our own lives? He argues that we would choose a relatively equal society, without large disparities of wealth and income. The rationalization for this is that it would be the safest way of ensuring that we were unlikely to suffer too much.

However, there are other ways of answering this question. We might choose to risk poverty for the opportunity of greater wealth available to only a few. It can also be argued that a relatively egalitarian society is not, in fact, practicable. Inequality may be inevitable and necessary to motivate or reward the talented, or would otherwise only be possible through a suffocating blanket of state control. The fate of Eastern Europe in the forty years after the Second World War lends support to such a conclusion.

interventions. Equality is a simpler goal than the technical targeting of interventions very precisely where their benefit will be greatest. For the Right, justice is more concerned with civil equality under the law, with an otherwise laissez-faire approach to social planning, in which inequalities could be allowed to arise spontaneously.

Inequality and equality are at the heart of much social policy debate. Inequality is not necessarily incompatible with both justice and merit. If inequality motivated the talents of some for the good of all, would we choose to tolerate inequality from behind the Rawlsian veil? In the absence of detailed social welfare calculations, can we trust professionals such as doctors, planners, social workers, or teachers to provide services to those who need them most? What about functional effects for the whole community? These questions raise a classic issue in social policy: the extent to which policies should strive for equality of outcome or equality of opportunity.

Box 3.15 Equality and inequality are at the heart of social policy

A particularly fundamental issue that runs through most normative social policy concepts is that of inequality. Equality and inequality have been at the heart of most social policy debates throughout the twentieth century. A major issue has been that the welfare state has been seen as a vehicle for egalitarian redistribution, welcomed by the Left and disliked by the Right.

In fact, however, the evidence is complex and not wholly supportive of this assumption. In recent decades, income and health inequalities have grown, while educational and housing inequalities have probably not. However, it is difficult to come to a clear judgement when the units of measurement, such as health or educational needs, and the period of time over which they should be measured, can vary widely. It is also clear that interventions powerful enough to have a significant impact on inequality can have undesirable side effects. Against this view is the observation that too much inequality can also have undesirable side effects, on health needs, educational achievement, crime, and economic productivity (Wilkinson and Pickett 2010). Nevertheless, for mainstream social policy writers the question of the extent of inequality, and what to do to reduce it, continues to be dominant.

Equality of outcome means that after social policy interventions, differences between people in terms of their welfare are less. Their incomes, housing space, educational qualifications might all be more similar than before. This might be possible to achieve through the expansion of some kinds of welfare available to all, for example total income, total healthcare, or total housing. In such cases everyone gains, although at different rates, and this is less likely to cause political controversy. However, other welfare is not expandable in the same way. Education is the classic case. While education is designed to give everyone the skills they need for adult life, it also has a major function of identifying and stratifying people by ability. In this respect it is a positional good (Box 3.16) in that there are only so many top positions, for example in business, medical, legal, or academic life, that can be occupied, just as there are only so many geographical points that can provide a panoramic view. If educational qualifications are expanded, they tend to lose their exclusivity at the same rate—the result of educational inflation.

In reality many kinds of welfare cannot be expanded indefinitely either, and the question arises of who merits access in preference to others. The alternative to equality of outcome is equality of opportunity, whereby we are all given equal support and help, but thereafter inequalities are allowed to multiply as individuals make what they can of their opportunities, and education, employment, income, housing, and so on are distributed according to merit rather than justice. The Left has had a very ambivalent attitude to the question of equality. In principle it has supported equality of outcome, but in practice it has adopted equality of opportunity in its policies. For example, in the 1960s the Labour government removed the strongly symbolic secondary modern–grammar school divide and developed comprehensive secondary education in the state sector as a radical push towards equality in education, yet at the same time left the private ('public') schools in place and rapidly expanded university education for middle-class children. New Labour compromised this principle even further, suggesting that schools should be set free to compete in an educational market outwith local government control.

The Right has also been inconsistent on issues of equality and merit. In principle the Conservative government in the 1980s strongly supported equality of opportunities, but not equality of outcome. Yet in housing it enabled many millions of tenants of state-owned housing to become highly satisfied property owners, and in higher education it engineered such a major expansion of

---

Box 3.16 **Positional goods**

In his book *The Social Limits to Growth* (1977), Fred Hirsch observed that we desire some goods and services that are valuable to us in part because they are not available to everyone. For example, not everyone can enjoy a beautiful countryside view from a commanding height above the potential viewing points of others. While there is a limited technical solution to the problem of mass viewing (as in football stadia and theatres), in the end there will have to be an unequal distribution of the view. He described these goods and services as 'positional goods'.

In social policy, educational achievement is such a good, since part of the function of education is to stratify people, regardless of their objective achievement: only some will get the highest grades, get to the best universities, and develop high-status careers. For some people the attractions of privatized social services (experienced as exclusive and only available to the few) are also in part because they are positional goods. There are many other such goods: traffic-free roads, empty beaches, unpolluted atmosphere, personal autonomy. Hirsch argued that there is a compelling myth that we can all have access to such goods if only economic growth can be sustained at a fast enough pace. This, sadly, is an illusion.

university provision that BA degrees have become widely in reach of working-class children in a more radical manner than ever before. For other ideologies, the relative emphasis on equality of outcome or equality of opportunity has tended to produce disagreements. Light greens, liberal feminists, and the Asian minorities favour equality of opportunities; dark greens, socialist feminists, and the African-Caribbean minorities favour equality of outcomes.

Citizenship and status

In recent social policy analysis, the concepts we have discussed—need, choice, rights, obligations, justice, merit—have been brought together under the term citizenship. Marshall (1963) argued that civil, political, and social rights define the conditions for citizenship to exist. His key observation was that there had been a steady expansion of areas in which citizens had defined rights. Citizens were, Goodin (1988) has argued, gaining membership of a community, and as a result gaining entitlements available to all members of that community. Community membership ensured that needs would be met if possible, but that there would be obligations too. Being a community member was thus the key to welfare citizenship. It implied access to universal services, and a sense of social inclusion.

However, the term 'community', while it might imply relative homogeneity when applied to small groups or pre-industrial societies, is misleading with respect to modern industrial societies. Class stratification, and gender and ethnic differences can multiply within a community, and hence between formally equal citizens (Lewis 2004). Citizenship equality is affected by people's positions in the social and economic structure; hence the term tends to carry quite different meanings for the ideological positions we have considered in this chapter. For the Left, citizenship is about the solidarity expressed through a relatively altruistic welfare state built on the common experience of the Second World War. Participation in the normal life of the community is the mark of the citizen, and indeed has been used by Townsend (1979) as a sociological method of defining poverty as that condition which prevents full social participation. But, for the Right, citizenship is confined to formal equality in law and politics, without any prescribed level of social support. The new social movements have also been critical of defining citizenship as community membership. Lister (1990) points out that membership can mean very different things for men and women, black and white people, able-bodied and non-able-bodied people. Greens have worried that animals have been denied rights to their own welfare, and are thus clearly not regarded as full members of the community.

This critique of citizenship as community membership has highlighted the question of the status of people, and especially whether they are excluded from or included in the life of the community. Max Weber (1947) famously argued that modern societies are stratified not only by social class and by political power, but also by social status, meaning by this the esteem in which people are held. Status can be quite varied within any community, and may systematically exclude certain groups. Where community values celebrate ideals of masculinity, white culture, work, or mobility, those who are unable to embody such values tend to have a lower status or social esteem, and may find themselves excluded from the goods and services commonly available in that community. With the growth of income inequality over the 1990s and 2000s there has been increased concern amongst social policy analysts that large sections of the UK community may have become excluded from the mainstream. While the Left has expressed concern about this process, it has been the new social movements that have been particularly active in challenging the exclusion that results from low status. Feminists have challenged the male domination of public and private values which undervalues women; greens have challenged the celebration of continued economic growth and the dominance of paid work; anti-racists have celebrated ethnic diversity and dignity; and disabled people have affirmed the disabling effects for them of conventional architectural and technological arrangements.

Conclusion: Beyond the nation-state

Social policy is a contested field. Any election in the UK will raise the kind of arguments and issues that we have covered in this chapter. The coalition government's initiatives in areas such as housing benefit, university fees, local government financing, and NHS restructuring, all of which are detailed in the relevant chapters later in the book, are central to social policy. In addition, newly emerging social issues, such as young people's alcohol and drug consumption, neglect of elderly people in care homes, or even the measurement of happiness and well-being are debated through the deployment of the ideologies and concepts we have introduced.

Much of our discussion has been about the politics of welfare at or below the level of the nation-state. The nation-state has only existed for about five hundred years, and much less in many instances. Some observers have wondered whether the nation-state is in decline, and suggested that we should also look at higher levels of organization in order to capture the full range of contemporary and future politics. For example, the European Union has grown in importance for social policy over the last twenty-five years, particularly in relation to issues of social security and employment (see Chapter 17). A growing volume of legislation and legal precedence is accumulating at the European level. Many local authorities now have direct administrative and financial connections to Brussels, and some maintain permanent offices in Brussels to keep abreast of new developments. A parallel development has occurred in voluntary sector organizations which are particularly relevant to social policy. It is likely that the EU will continue to make social policies at the European level.

A further erosion of nation-states can be traced through the development of global institutions which are increasingly moving into the area of social policy, and are widely thought to embody social policy ideas from the United States (see Chapter 9). While the World Health Organization may have always been concerned with social policy, the World Bank and the International Monetary Fund have only recently developed clear views on social policy, particularly in the field of social security in countries which are deemed to require 'structural adjustments' in their public expenditure profile, for example in Eastern Europe, South America, and Africa. Very often an individual country which needs credit from the IMF will have to commit itself to a detailed social security policy, including a strategy for poverty reduction, which in the past was traditionally under the control of the nation-state and its political elite.

For some commentators this represents the 'end of history' as it has traditionally developed, such that in future a global society will develop with an increasing convergence towards one type of (limited) welfare policy. Others disagree, and suggest that with economic growth comes choice over social expenditure, and that there is a parallel regionalization of social politics through which a variety of social policies will continue to evolve. For example, the development of Northern Irish, Welsh, and Scottish assemblies in the UK may lead to greater social policy divergence. The evidence from two hundred years of US federal efforts to integrate American social policies suggests that local autonomy can indeed survive and flourish for long periods of time; and it may therefore be premature to anticipate a decline in the national politics of welfare.

FURTHER READING

Blair, T. (2010) *A Journey*. London: Hutchinson. This book provides a highly engaging insight into the way that social problems and social policy issues were recognized, discussed, and responded to at the heart of government for the last ten years.

Castles, F. G, Leibfried, S., Lewis, J., Obinger, H., and Pierson, C. (2010) *The Oxford Handbook of the Welfare State*. Oxford: Oxford University Press. This is a large collection of original chapters that covers in depth many of the issues raised in this chapter.

Dean, H. (2010) *Understanding Human Need*. Bristol: Policy Press. This discusses the case for the centrality of the concept of need to social policy analysis, and presents a comprehensive discussion of the many ways of classifying it. This is a very accessible, although necessarily more advanced, book.

Fitzpatrick, T. (2005) *New Theories of Welfare*. London: Palgrave Macmillan. This book incorporates new developments in theoretical concepts for analysing social policy.

Rubington, E. and Weinberg, M. (2010) *The Study of Social Problems: Seven Perspectives*. Oxford: Oxford University Press. This is the seventh edition of a key textbook which presents a detailed analysis of seven different models of social problems.

Social Policy Review. This annual, published by the Policy Press, Bristol, on behalf of the British Social Policy Association, includes accessible accounts of recent debates and policy initiatives.

Taylor, G. (2007) *Ideology and Welfare*. London: Palgrave Macmillan. This gives a thorough review of the different ideologies of welfare.

Wilkinson, R. and Pickett, K. (2010) *The Spirit Level. Why Equality is Better for Everyone*. London: Penguin Books. This book argues that inequality lies at the heart of many social problems, and that greater equality would be the best way of underpinning the majority of specific social policy areas.

@ USEFUL WEBSITES

Most websites that discuss the politics of welfare should be used cautiously since they will generally be seeking to advance a particular political or ideological agenda. However, key developments in the politics of welfare are usually first discussed in publications produced by 'think tanks', research units, and pressure groups. Amongst those worth exploring are:

The 'Big Society' (the coalition government's big idea) at: **www.thebigsociety.co.uk**

The Fabian Society at: **www.fabian-society.org.uk.**

Demos, a public services focused think tank at: **www.demos.co.uk**.

The Young Foundation 'brings together insights, innovation and entrepreneurship to meet social needs' at: **www.youngfoundation.org**.

The Fawcett Society, a campaigning research organization focusing on equality between men and women in areas such as pay, pensions, social security, and child support, at: **www.fawcettsociety.org.uk**.

The websites of the main UK political parties such as: **www.conservatives.com**, **www.labour.org.uk**, **www.libdems.org.uk**.

Q **ESSAY QUESTIONS**

1 How do social problems emerge into public attention and affect social policy?

2 How can citizens influence the kind of social policies that their governments plan?

3 To what extent is social policy made exclusively by the nation-state?

4 How can ideology influence the kind of social policies that governments plan?

5 What are the principal concepts that make up social policy ideologies?

6 Will ideologies be more or less important for social policy in the future than in the past?

 ONLINE RESOURCE CENTRE

For additional material and resources, please visit the Online Resource Centre at:
www.oxfordtextbooks.co.uk/orc/baldock4e/.

Part Two
The social and economic context of social policy

4

Social need and patterns of inequality

Mark Liddiard and Lavinia Mitton

Contents

Introduction

The concept of 'social need' lies at the heart of social policy. The recognition and satisfaction of need distinguishes the welfare functions of the state from its other roles and activities. Inseparably linked to the assessments of the nature, effectiveness, and cost of the welfare state are judgements of how far it meets which needs. Yet the concept of 'need' poses difficult conceptual and normative questions. How do we decide which are valid needs and which are not? If some needs are more or less legitimate than others, how do we decide which needs are a priority, and which are not? Are there any needs that are so basic and fundamental that ensuring they are met is central to an individual's rights and an obligation of the state? Even if one can establish a measure of basic needs, to what extent should the meeting of these be the responsibility of the government, or the responsibility of others, such as the family and charity?

Definitions of need, whether they are explicit in policies and eligibility rules, or implicit in the decisions made by welfare providers, are rationing devices: they determine who gets what. People, as individuals and as members of social and interest groups, have radically different ideas about what should be defined as a 'need' and what should not. Often, people's judgements of need are highly subjective and beyond objective agreement. They can pose dilemmas with no best answer, such as when medical professionals, courts, and sometimes politicians are in the unenviable position of deciding on the validity of some people's health needs over others'.

Defining social needs is fundamental to the construction of social policies, and much of the politics of welfare hinges on differing conceptions of needs and evidence of them. If the needs which state welfare, and ultimately state resources, are supposed to be meeting are vague and ill defined, so the arguments in favour of state welfare are weakened. Clarifying social need is more than simply a theoretical debate. It is at the core of the construction and evaluation of social policies, and has real practical significance, particularly for the poorest and most vulnerable in a society.

Learning outcomes

This chapter will provide you with a basic understanding of:

1   the meanings that have been attached to the term 'social need';
2   the relationships between social need, poverty, and inequalities of various kinds;
3   how changes in the demography of a society can also change patterns of social need;
4   the links between social need and social policy.

Defining need

A key characteristic of 'need' is the fact that it can be defined and measured from a variety of perspectives. Jonathan Bradshaw (1972) made this diversity the basis of his taxonomy of social need, in which he outlines four types of need:

- **Normative need**: how an expert or professional identifies a need in the context of a set of professional or expert standards.

    Welfare professionals reach judgements about what may or may not be legitimate need. They are active in the processes which decide whether or not a need exists and, if it does, how this need may best be met within the confines of existing resources. The judgements of welfare professionals, and the bodies of knowledge and standards that they use, are clearly an important feature in defining need.

- **Felt need**: what a person or a group believes they 'need'.

   This conception relies upon the individual's own perception of need, and any discrepancy between their situation and what they believe it ought to be. However, this self-perception is likely to be subjective and may be better described as a 'want'. Felt need is necessarily affected by the knowledge and expectations of the individual, which may be unrealistic. Alternatively, researchers have shown that the poorest sections of society may be only marginally aware of their poverty and the extent of their need.

- **Expressed need**: a felt need that has become a demand.

   Academics have argued that social need can be closely associated with either an effective economic or an effective political demand. Yet it is important to acknowledge that just because people have the power to demand something, this does not necessarily imply that they need it. In this sense, it is important to distinguish between need and demand.

- **Comparative need**: need defined by comparing the differences in people's access to resources.

   This approach recognizes that need is a relative concept, and so any debate about need must take place in the context of a comparison between people. Need may be defined in terms of the average standards found within a community or society, or by comparing the resources available to some in contrast to others who are defined as similarly entitled. A comparative approach has, of course, been most widely employed in the context of debates about poverty.

Bradshaw's taxonomy is very helpful in setting out the range of ways in which need can be approached and understood. A number of authors have developed these ideas further in a number of ways, one of whom was Forder (1974), with his concept of technical need:

- **Technical need**: in simple terms, technical need arises when a new form of provision is invented, or existing provision is made much more effective. This in turn creates a need for a solution that previously did not exist. Once a new invention has occurred, it can then lead to forms of felt, expressed, normative, and comparative need. Advances in medical technology are the most common example of this, and one of the most pertinent illustrations is the development of Viagra, the male anti-impotence pill (Box 4.1).

Box 4.1 **Viagra and the NHS**

The successful development of Viagra for the treatment of male impotency, and the ensuing debate about its availability on the NHS, is an excellent illustration of a *technical need*. The publicity surrounding Viagra has certainly generated a *felt need*. It has also led to more expressed need by legitimizing a request that had previously been highly stigmatized. There has also been a strong element of *comparative need* in this debate—people may have access to it in some countries or parts of countries and not in others. Viagra is available on the NHS only when prescribed to those with specific illnesses or diseases. It is also available to those able and willing to pay for a private consultancy or who obtain it via the internet. The debate here is also much about *normative need*, and about who should be the arbiter of need: government, medical professionals, or consumers?

Questions

- Is it right that Viagra is available on the NHS only to those with specific conditions such as prostate cancer, kidney failure, and diabetes?
- Who should decide the rules that govern the prescription of Viagra on the NHS?

The question remains, however, as to the degree to which it is possible to reach any consensus about need, and whether or not there are any features of need which can be identified as essentially incontestable. Many social theorists have sought to establish basic needs with which all would be likely to agree. The importance of trying to establish a list of basic needs should not be underestimated. If one can establish a concrete and agreed set of basic needs, which really should be met in a society, it may be much easier to add legitimacy to the very existence of welfare states, whose ultimate objective is to meet need.

Attempts to produce a list of human needs have taken a variety of different forms, and one of the first to construct such a list was Maslow (1954), who set out a hierarchy of five basic needs. This hierarchy begins with physiological needs, followed by the need for safety, the need for love and belonging, the need for self-esteem, and, finally, the need for self-actualization. Maslow argued that once the most basic need for survival (physiological need, or the need for air, water, and food) was met, so, in succession, further needs demand attention.

Whilst Maslow's basic human needs are of some theoretical interest, it is immediately apparent that they present real practical difficulties. Not only are they difficult to measure, but they will also vary from individual to individual. Given the fluidity of such needs, it would evidently be impossible to expect state action to ensure that every citizen had them met.

David Harvey (1973) sought to move this debate on by identifying nine categories, goods, and services that people require in order to meet the human needs Maslow had set out:

- food;
- housing;
- medical care;
- education;
- social and environmental services;
- consumer goods;
- recreational opportunities;
- neighbourhood opportunities;
- transport facilities.

The real difficulty with such lists of need, however, comes when considering the relative importance of each of these categories. Clearly, not all forms of need carry equal significance and importance. According to Maslow, only the basic physiological needs are essential for sustaining life, and these must necessarily be met before higher needs. Yet how do we rank the remaining needs? The real problem here is that what we perceive and define as valid and legitimate needs may be little more than subjective judgements, relative to the society and time period in which they are being made. The implication is that, whilst real and important steps may be taken in addressing various agreed needs in society, as social values and ideas about what is essential to living as a full member of society shift, so in turn may the notion of what people legitimately need. In short, the debate about 'need' can be seen to be inherently relative, and heavily influenced by time and social context. Some observers believe that the relative nature of social need means that attempts to measure and order forms of need are essentially misguided and ultimately doomed to failure. They argue that debate about need may ultimately be little more than a political one, in which different political positions succeed or fail in insisting on their particular conception of need.

Can we establish a level of basic needs?

Is it possible to say that there are any basic needs which, once they have been identified, really ought to be met? This is an important question: if one can establish that there are certain basic needs, the meeting of which is essential to being a civilized human being, then this may begin to establish an argument in favour of the welfare state.

A starting point for establishing basic needs is the notion that needs are related to ends: in order to achieve certain ends in life, such as a high level of education, one may have first to fulfil a variety of needs—the need for financial support; the need for childcare; the need for adequate transport; and so on. Indeed, the distinction here is between ultimate needs and intermediate needs. Ultimate needs are the ends to which other activities are directed. In contrast, intermediate needs are not ends in themselves but are rather a means to an end. For instance, we may need something, such as a basic education, in order to fulfil other needs, such as finding a job.

Yet we all have many different ends in sight, and we believe we need different things in order to achieve our ends. We could never say that everyone should have whatever they require in order to fulfil their ends in life—the list of potential needs is infinite. Nonetheless, some writers, particularly Raymond Plant, have made some important progress here by attempting to identify what people need in order to achieve any ends in life at all.

> These needs might be regarded generally as physical well-being and autonomy: an individual would have to be able to function efficiently as a physical entity and have freedom to deliberate and choose between alternatives if he is to pursue any conception of the good. (Plant 1985: 18)

Simplified, Plant's suggestion is that it is possible to identify two basic needs in any society. First, there is a need for physical survival. We obviously cannot hope to achieve anything without physical survival. Secondly, he argues that there is a basic need for autonomy, or freedom. In order to make genuine choices about our paths in life, we need to have autonomy and the freedom to make informed choices. These two basic needs are crucial, argues Plant, because unless they are met, we cannot hope to achieve any ends at all in life.

These arguments seek to derive needs from basic human goals upon which we might all agree. Nonetheless, there do seem to be a number of problems here, not least of which is the question of what rights to survival and autonomy actually justify in practice. Plant, for instance, interprets survival as effectively referring to health. In this sense, one can argue that this justifies the provision of healthcare. However, the level and extent of healthcare being argued for remain very unclear. Does the argument that people need healthcare to ensure survival really extend to saying that they should have as much healthcare as technically possible? If this were the case, it would place unacceptable and unachievable demands upon a health service. In which case, where does one draw the line between what is a justifiable need for healthcare which should be met and what is not? Similarly, in order to guarantee physical survival, one could argue that it is necessary to guarantee an income to ensure subsistence—thus again raising problems concerning what minimum of income is sufficient.

A further and very real problem with Plant's approach concerns the role of the state. Even if one can establish that there are indeed a number of basic needs which can and should be met, it does not simply follow that the state should be the vehicle for meeting these. Presenting a strong and coherent argument for the meeting of certain basic needs may be one thing, but deducing a state obligation—as opposed to those of individuals, families, or charity, for instance—may be a quite different matter.

Need in terms of basic minima

Much social policy debate about need takes place in terms of minima, or basic levels below which some individuals may be defined as being in real need. The difficulty is just how to decide upon the nature of any minimum. For example, some have argued that there is a minimum living standard which applies to all societies, below which one is evidently in need of assistance. Usually based upon various ideas of subsistence, and the very minimum required for survival, this is the notion of absolute poverty. The measurement of absolute poverty generally limits poverty to material deprivation, and seeks to establish a price for the basic necessities in life. Those who are then unable to afford these necessities are deemed to be in absolute poverty, unable to afford to maintain even basic subsistence levels.

Seebohm Rowntree (1871–1954) was one of the first to attempt to define and measure need in this way, and establish a basic minimum income, below which subsistence was not possible. Applying his measure in 1899, Rowntree discovered that a third of the working-class households in York were in absolute poverty—and lacked the minimum income necessary for subsistence. In his third survey of York in 1950, this proportion had dropped to just 1.5 per cent of his total sample, leading some to argue that poverty in the UK had effectively been eradicated.

The concept of 'absolute poverty', however, is not a concrete and objective measure of need. On the contrary, it is very much open to debate and interpretation, and there has been a variety of differing attempts to operationalize this concept, or put it into a form that can be empirically measured. The problem comes in terms of what are defined as the minimum needs necessary for subsistence—do these only refer to physical needs, and the basic need for food, shelter, and good health? Or could we—indeed, should we—include in this approach other needs which may be equally important for becoming a full and involved member of society—access to leisure such as holidays or to sources of cultural enrichment such as concerts or special exhibitions?

Even when focusing exclusively upon nutritional requirements, it is unclear what basic nutritional requirements should be. Different individuals in different occupations, for instance, may have very different nutritional needs. This variety is even more pronounced in the case of other dimensions of need such as housing, clothing, or education.

Official poverty

Despite these difficulties, the idea of need defined in terms of basic minima has proved to be pervasive. Many official definitions of poverty tend to be related in some way to an absolute or subsistence poverty line. In Britain until the 1980s, the government based its estimate of the extent of poverty and need in society on the numbers living at or below benefit levels. Benefits such as Income Support are paid to those who can demonstrate a low income, and are intended to provide a basic minimum income for those experiencing material hardship. Those individuals whose incomes are at or below this level were deemed to be in poverty. Those receiving an income of between 100 and 139 per cent of benefit levels were often defined as on the margins of poverty.

This approach, however, attracted considerable criticism, not least because it implied that every time benefit levels were increased, this paradoxically increased the number of those defined as being in poverty. From 1985 the government chose instead to publish figures on the numbers living below incomes that were 50 per cent of the average adjusted for household type. The number of people living in households with less than 60 per cent of median income is now one of the preferred indicators of poverty for both the UK government and the European Union (see Figure 4.1). In 2008–9, it was estimated that some 13.4 million people were living in British households with below 60 per cent of median income (Palmer 2010). The incidence of income poverty also varies considerably between different groups. A third of working-age disabled adults aged 25 to retirement age live on below 60 per cent of median income (after deducting housing costs), double the rate for non-disabled adults (Palmer 2010).

This has been described as the relative income standard of poverty. Interestingly, the government also modified the way in which it calculated its figures. Originally, it sought to calculate the income for each household member separately. However, this was changed, and all members of a household were assumed to have equal share of the total household income, which is evidently questionable. The result, however, was that this change actually reduced the numbers on low incomes by more than a million people. The problem with such a measure of need, however, is the arbitrary point at which one draws a poverty line.

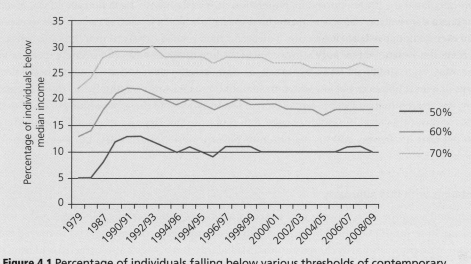

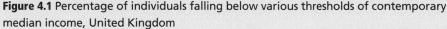

Figure 4.1 Percentage of individuals falling below various thresholds of contemporary median income, United Kingdom

Source: Department for Work and Pensions, 'Households below average income (HBAI) 1994/5–2008/9', Table 3.1tr

Relative poverty

Peter Townsend was a vocal proponent of the idea that poverty must be related to the society in which it may be present. However, he argued that the relative income standard of poverty is arbitrary: it is unclear why the poverty line should be drawn at 50 per cent of average income—70 per cent could have just as much validity. Townsend was therefore keen to establish a more objective and less arbitrary measure of poverty and need, but one which was necessarily relative to wider standards in society. After all, given economic and social change, so standards and expectations may shift, and luxuries may become comforts, and comforts in turn may become necessities. Townsend argued, therefore, that poverty had to be related to and defined by the standards of a particular society at a particular time and, moreover, reflect more than simply material impoverishment. With this in mind, he focused upon the concept of relative deprivation. He suggested that any definition of poverty should include some measure of an individual's ability to participate in social activities which are generally customary in society (see Box 4.2).

With this in mind, Townsend constructed what he described as a deprivation index. This covered some sixty types of household activity relating to diet, clothing, health, recreation, travel, and so on, from which he chose twelve items that he saw as relevant and necessary to the whole of society. He

---

Box 4.2 **Townsend's definition of poverty**

Individuals, families, and groups in the population can be said to be in poverty when they lack the resources to obtain the types of diet, participate in the activities, and have the living conditions and amenities which are customary, or at least widely encouraged or approved, in the societies to which they belong. Their resources are so seriously below those commanded by the average individual or family that they are, in effect, excluded from the ordinary living patterns, customs and activities.

(Townsend 1979)

then calculated the proportion of the population deprived of these. Each household was given a score on a deprivation index, and the more respects in which a household was found to experience deprivation, the higher its score. Townsend then related deprivation to income levels. In particular, he related the average score of households to different levels of income, expressed as a percentage of basic benefit levels. From this, he claimed to have identified a poverty threshold, in terms of a level of income below which the amount of deprivation suddenly increased dramatically—at approximately 150 per cent of benefit levels. Townsend therefore argued that all households without this level of resources were suffering from poverty and in need. Importantly, he also felt that his figures and his definition of poverty were not arbitrary, but were ostensibly objective.

Problems with this approach

Townsend's approach to poverty, and hence to need, was path-breaking. He developed a social measure in terms of household integration into the surrounding community, and so moved measurement on from arbitrarily chosen minimum standards. But his work also attracted criticism, not least from David Piachaud (1981), who makes a number of pertinent points.

Townsend claimed to have found an 'objective' point at which to draw a poverty line, below which deprivation increases very rapidly. In fact, Piachaud argues that a poverty line based on 150 per cent of benefit levels is as arbitrary as any other. Indeed, after examining Townsend's data, Piachaud disputes the suggestion that deprivation starts to rapidly increase below this level of 150 per cent of benefit levels.

It is also not clear why the items employed in Townsend's index have been selected. For instance, it is unclear why not eating cooked meals should necessarily be equated with deprivation, as Townsend claims. After all, some people may prefer to eat sandwiches and salads. This is a crucial point: namely, Townsend does not seek to establish whether scoring high points on his 'deprivation index' is actually a consequence of shortage of money, or a consequence of choice.

Mack and Lansley: breadline Britain

Mack and Lansley (1985; 1991) followed Townsend's social approach to the measurement of need and poverty, defining poverty in relative terms, but attempting to improve the approach in two important ways. First, they sought to clarify whether or not people lacked something by choice, or whether it was a consequence of financial pressure. Secondly, they were concerned about the accusation that any items included in their deprivation index would be necessarily arbitrary. They therefore adopted a consensual approach to poverty, and asked their respondents what they considered to be necessities in contemporary Britain. An item became a necessity if a majority (or more than 50 per cent of the population) classified it as such. On the basis of this deprivation index, they then went on to measure the extent of poverty, which they defined as 'an enforced lack of socially perceived necessities'. Later surveys have used the same method.

The last survey using this 'consensual approach' to measure poverty in Britain (Gordon et al. 2000) came up with some startling and disturbing results:

- In 1983, 14 per cent of households (approximately 7.5 million people) were living in poverty; this had increased to 24 per cent (approximately 14 million people) by 1999.
- Around 9.5 million people in Britain today cannot afford adequate housing, free from damp and adequately heated.
- Some 6.5 million adults go without essential clothing, such as a warm waterproof coat, because of a lack of money.
- About 8 million people cannot afford one or more essential household goods, such as a fridge, a telephone, or carpets for living areas.

It is evident that attempting to establish any measure of need in terms of a basic minimum is fraught with problems. Absolute or subsistence definitions of need and poverty are to a degree arbitrary, or a matter of subjective judgement. In any event, many commentators argue that any attempt to measure deprivation and need must be relative to the standards and expectations of wider society. In other words, the nature of poverty necessarily varies over time, and reflects the contemporary social circumstances in which it is experienced. In this sense, poverty and deprivation are related to social inequality: the poor are those whose incomes or resources are so far short of society's average that they simply do not have an acceptable standard of living. If poverty is measured and gauged in terms of average expectations and average incomes, then reducing poverty and meeting need may actually be impossible without attacking inequality. In the UK, inequality pervades many features of society, most notably in terms of income.

Need and inequality

One of the most significant forms of inequality in the UK is in terms of income distribution. Data on income distribution have been used to chart changing patterns of poverty and need over time. Indeed, according to this measure there has been a considerable increase in the scale of poverty in the UK over the past twenty years or so. In 1979, for instance, 3.3 million people (or 5.9 per cent of the population) were living on below half average incomes after deducting housing costs. By 2008–9 this figure had risen to approximately 9.4 million people, or 15.7 per cent of the population, a worse poverty record than the European Union average (Palmer 2010).

Whilst many industrialized countries experienced moves towards greater income inequality, this grew more rapidly in the UK than in almost any other. Between 1979 and 1995, for instance, incomes for the richest tenth of the population rose by more than 60 per cent, while the real incomes of the poorest tenth showed a fall of 8 per cent, when housing costs were taken into account (Hills 1995). The reasons for these increases in inequality are complex. In particular, they reflect the fact that, during the 1980s, more people became dependent upon state benefits, not least because of increases in unemployment. Yet, simultaneously, the gap widened between the income of those dependent on benefits and the income of that part of the population with earnings. This was a consequence of the fact that, since the early 1980s, benefit levels have generally been linked to prices rather than to income levels. These changes in inequality have affected some social groups more than others.

There are, for instance, important differences between ethnic groups. The incomes of some ethnic minority groups are well below the national average, and a significant percentage of their populations live in areas high in indicators of deprivation. Households where the head of household is from an ethnic minority group are much more likely to appear in the bottom 20 per cent (or quintile) of the income distribution than their white contemporaries. For example, 57 per cent of individuals of Pakistani ethnicity and 72 per cent of individuals of Bangladeshi ethnicity have an income of less than 60 per cent of the median (after deducting housing costs)—three times more than white people and almost twice as many as Indian and black Caribbean people (Palmer 2010). This is, of course, partly related to unemployment and its high incidence amongst some ethnic minority groups. In 2010, for example, black Africans, black Caribbeans, Pakistanis, and Bangladeshis were far more likely to be in a workless household than white people (Palmer 2010).

There are also important differences between men and women here. Whilst men are much more likely to be in the professional and skilled manual groups, women are more likely to be in the skilled and unskilled non-manual groups, reflecting the dominance of women in some occupations such as clerical, retail, and secretarial work, and their importance in some professions such as teaching and medicine. Women have been heavily concentrated in low-paid and low-status employment in the UK, and in 2010 low-paid women were paid around 10 per cent less than low-paid men. High-paid women were paid around 20 per cent less than high-paid men (Palmer 2010).

An important question for social policy concerns the extent to which the welfare state should seek to reduce inequalities (see Box 4.3). Which inequalities are the most damaging in the sense of reducing people's opportunities or in contributing to other needs such as poor health? There is also the risk that welfare allocations, or the taxes necessary to pay for them, may actually have been contributing to forms of inequality.

The welfare state and inequality

It is clear that some households will pay considerably more in taxes than they receive in benefits, while others will benefit more than they are taxed. Overall, one can say that there is some redistribution of income from households on higher incomes to those on lower incomes. In 2008–9, for example, UK households in the bottom quintile group had an average original income (or income derived from various non-governmental sources, such as employment or occupational pensions) of £4,550. Once redistribution through taxes and benefits had occurred, such households were left with a disposable income of £9,760. In other words, on average, these households had gained some £5,210 through redistribution. In contrast, households in the highest quintile group (or the top 20 per cent) had an average original income of £75,720 and a final income of £58,870. In other words, on average, these households had made a net loss of some £16,850 through redistribution (ONS 2010a).

However, the welfare state also has an important redistributional role in terms of welfare services that are provided in kind, rather than as cash benefits; such as the National Health Service, state education, personal social services, and subsidized and social housing. It has been argued that the provision of such services should be considered as a non-monetary form of income, or a social wage, which forms an important addition to cash incomes. However, there has been intense debate about who actually benefits most from the provision of such services. Julian Le Grand, for instance, famously argued that state welfare provision does not in fact enhance redistribution and reduce inequality. Rather, he showed that state welfare services accentuate the divisions between those facing need and those who are comfortably provided for. In the use of transport, education, and possibly healthcare, the better-off consume disproportionately relative to their needs (Le Grand 1982). It has been claimed by some commentators that the welfare state has increasingly been 'captured' by the middle classes.

Box 4.3 **Child poverty**

The New Labour governments made poverty reduction—particularly child poverty—a key element of their policies. This was one of the objectives behind the introduction of benefits such as the Working Tax Credit and the Child Tax Credit. In particular, in 1998 it established a target to reduce the number of children in low-income households by at least a quarter by 2004 and by half by 2010. The challenge was a formidable one. In 1968, just 10 per cent of children lived in households with below half the average income. By 1996 this had risen to a third of all children (over 4.3 million). Nonetheless, the government made some progress, and by 2004 the number of children living in poverty had dropped by approximately 800,000 to 3.5 million, but has risen since then. As a result, the numbers in 2008–9 were back up to the levels of 2002–3 (Palmer 2010). Further, much of the reduction appears to have been a consequence of rising employment and more parents obtaining paid work (Piachaud and Sutherland 2002a). Despite this modest progress, many commentators remain very doubtful as to whether it will be sustained under the coalition government's approach to welfare reform.

In contrast, recent research by Tom Sefton (1997; 2002) has shown that the welfare state did go some way towards tempering the growing income inequalities witnessed in the 1980s. Whilst much attention was devoted to the widening income gap between rich and poor, most calculations failed to take into account the value of welfare services to different groups. In 2000–1 the social wage, or the value in kind of the main state services, such as healthcare and education, was worth an average of £1,700 per person or nearly £4,000 per household. On average, individuals in the bottom two-fifths of income distribution receive around twice the value of benefits in kind as those in the top fifth (Sefton 2002). However, there is considerable variety here between services—higher education, for instance, is certainly worth more to the better-off in society, while subsidized social housing and the personal social services strongly benefit the poor.

That income inequality has increased remains the basic fact. Between 1998–9 and 2008–9, for example, real incomes after deducting housing costs of the richest tenth rose by 37 per cent. Yet the poorest 10 per cent saw a fall of 12 per cent (Palmer 2010). The social wage has helped to offset this growing inequality of cash incomes, although it has still not prevented inequality from rising. Whilst one would anticipate that welfare services would mainly benefit lower-income groups, the surprising reality is that the poorest half of the population receive just 60 per cent of the value of these services. Indeed, only in the context of social housing has there been a clear shift in the distribution of welfare spending towards the poorest individuals and families (Sefton 1997).

Demographic change in the UK

Demographic trends are of fundamental importance for social policy and any debate about social need. Ultimately, demographic changes have a direct impact upon welfare provision, because they alter the size and composition of the population who contribute to and use the services provided by welfare states. One role of those who study and research social policy is to chart and follow demographic trends—both in the short and in the much longer term—and anticipate the needs that different patterns of population change are likely to imply for welfare provision. Demography lies at the heart of social policy because of its close relationship to need and, in turn, demand upon the welfare state.

Knowledge about the size and structure of the population is essential for understanding and anticipating demand for all kinds of welfare service, such as education, healthcare, social security benefits, and pensions. Good data on the demography of a country provide an essential foundation for estimating future needs. Recent demographic changes can also be interpreted as indications of wider social shifts in values and forms of behaviour that may have implications for the needs faced by future governments and taxpayers.

Population structure

Since 1900 the world population has more than trebled—from around 1.6 billion to more than 6.9 billion (Table 4.1). It is estimated that by 2050 world population will be between 7.9 and 10.9 billion. Within this pattern, there are important differences. Less developed areas, for instance, have much lower life expectancies than do more developed regions. Whilst life expectancy at birth is comparatively high in the UK—78 for males, and 82 for females—in some countries life expectancy is almost half this. In Sierra Leone, for example, life expectancy at birth is just 48 for males and 50 for females (WHO 2010).

Europe has also had a considerably slower population growth rate than the world as a whole. Between 1950 and 2001, for instance, the population of Europe rose by less than 33 per cent, compared with an increase of 143 per cent for the population of the world as a whole over the same period. The UK population has similarly experienced a relatively subdued rate of popula-

Table 4.1 World demographic indicators, 2005–10[1]

	Population (millions)[2]	Population density (sq km)[2]	Infant mortality rate[3]	Total fertility rate	Life expectancy at birth (years)[2]	
					Males	Females
Asia	4,167	131	41.5	2.35	67.1	70.8
Africa	1,033	34	82.6	4.61	52.9	55.3
Europe	732	32	7.2	1.50	71.1	79.1
Latin America & Caribbean	587	29	21.8	2.26	70.2	76.7
North America	352	16	5.8	2.4	77.0	81.5
Oceania	36	4	22.8	2.44	74.1	78.9
World	6,909	51	47.3	2.56	65.4	69.8

1 Data are estimates and projections for the period 2005–10, revised in 2008.
2 Data are projections for 2010.
3 Per 1,000 live births
Source: ONS 2010b, Table 1.14.

tion growth. In 1961, the UK population was approximately 53 million and by the 2001 census was under 59 million (see Box 4.4). Change in population is dependent on a number of variables—specifically, the number of births, the number of deaths, and migration in and out of the country.

Box 4.4 **Census 2001**

Since 1801, the UK government has conducted a census every ten years of every household in the country, to collect a variety of important demographic information, which is then used for planning and targeting welfare services and provision. The key findings of the 2001 census included:

- The UK population on the day of the census was 58,789,194—about one million lower than estimates made in 2000.
- For the first time, the number of people over 60 exceeded the number of children aged under 16.
- Those aged 85 and over now make up nearly 2 per cent of the entire population, compared with 0.4 per cent 50 years ago.
- Boys outnumber girls up until the age of 21, but there are fewer men than women in all ages over 21.
- There has been significant regional variation in population change over the past twenty years, with a decline in the population of the north and an increase in the population of the south.

Question

- What are the implications of these findings for the design and delivery of welfare services?

Births and the family

One of the most important factors affecting population structure is the number of live births. The UK has seen a number of changes to fertility patterns. More women are now delaying having their first child, and the average age of mothers for all live births rose from 26.5 in 1977 to 29.4 in 2003 (ONS 2010h). Women are also choosing to have fewer children. There has also been a dramatic increase in the number of births outside marriage. Of live births in Great Britain in 2004, more than 40 per cent occurred outside marriage—more than four times the proportion in 1980 (ONS 2006). However, it is important to remember that 85 per cent of births outside marriage are jointly registered by both parents (ONS 2010c).

The family is a central object of social policy intervention. However, the contemporary family is experiencing a variety of important changes, which in turn attract the attention of social researchers, politicians, and policy-makers. Many of these changes are linked and related in different ways, and have consequences for both the goals and the design of social policies.

Marriage, divorce, and cohabitation

One of the most striking areas of debate has been focused upon the question of marriage and its centrality to modern British society. Whilst politicians regularly proclaim the virtues of marriage, and the benefits of dual parenthood, the contemporary family is now considerably more diverse in its characteristics. Some researchers and politicians have not been slow to attach many of the ills of our modern society to changing family forms. Whilst the main changes involved may be reasonably clear in their nature, what is far from clear are the implications of these for social welfare. A number of developments are notable, one of which has been the declining marriage rate and the corresponding increase in cohabitation.

Marriage may be an institution, but it is one to which growing proportions of the population are hesitant to subscribe. In 2007, for example, there were 193,900 marriages that were the first marriage for at least one party, half the peak of 386,000 in 1970 (ONS 2010d). Not only are fewer people actually marrying, but the average age of people getting married for the first time is increasing. In 2007, for example, the average age for first marriage was 32.0 for men and 29.8 for women, compared with 24.6 for men and 22.6 for women in 1971(ONS 2010d). At the same time, there has been a sharp increase in the number of people cohabiting, together with a shift towards cohabiting for longer periods. For instance, among non-married women aged under 60, the proportion cohabiting more than doubled from 13 per cent in 1986 to 28 per cent in 2001–2 (ONS 2010i).

At the same time as a rise in cohabitation, there has been a dramatic increase in divorce. Since 1971, the divorce rate per thousand of the married population has nearly doubled to 11.2. (ONS 2010e). It is perhaps unsurprising that so many politicians and clergy claim that the concept of marriage in the UK is under threat (see Figure 4.2). The rise in divorce has important and significant implications for social policy, in a number of ways. The complexity of 'reconstituted families' may have important consequences for the meeting of social need in the future. The provision of old age care, for instance, has been the focus of concern. Traditionally a main source of informal care for the elderly has been by younger family members. With the increase in divorce and, in turn, remarriage, it is less clear just how these family responsibilities may or may not be shared out.

Lone parents

A further shift in family form that has provoked concern amongst policy-makers and politicians has been the increase over the past thirty years in the number and proportion of lone-parent families. The UK has one of the highest rates of lone parenthood in the European Union. In 2006, some 24 per cent of all children lived in lone-parent families—more than three times the proportion in 1971—and nine out of ten lone parents are lone mothers (ONS 2007). This high rate of lone parenthood has been viewed by many as being inherently risky, and a number of authors have

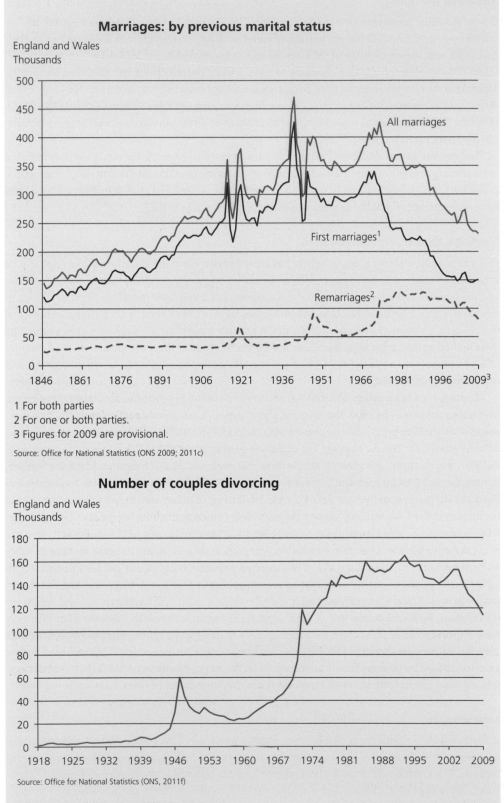

Marriages: by previous marital status

England and Wales
Thousands

All marriages

First marriages[1]

Remarriages[2]

1 For both parties
2 For one or both parties.
3 Figures for 2009 are provisional.

Source: Office for National Statistics (ONS 2009; 2011c)

Number of couples divorcing

England and Wales
Thousands

Source: Office for National Statistics (ONS, 2011f)

Figure 4.2 Trends in marriages and divorces

argued that there is something necessarily advantageous about two-parent households. The high rate of lone parenthood has also led to debates about the provision of benefits to this group. Do their greater needs require higher benefits and more assistance, or will these merely 'reward' lone parenthood? Indeed, the identification of lone parents as somehow being distinct and different from their contemporaries lies at the heart of many arguments about the emergence of an 'underclass' in the UK.

As with all social policy debates, the acknowledgement of demographic change is perhaps less important than the interpretation of such changes, and an assessment of the appropriate response by government. Certainly, many of the debates about lone parents in the UK have only selectively engaged with the demographic evidence. Whilst much is made of the high rate of lone parenthood in the UK by Charles Murray (1990) and others, it is important to clarify a number of points. Lone parenthood, for example, is not necessarily a permanent state. On the contrary, many lone parents go on to form new joint households fairly quickly. Moreover, contrary to the pervasive image of the teenage mother attempting to jump the housing queue, the majority of lone parents are actually divorcees in their 20s or 30s.

In short, the nuclear family is undergoing substantial change in the UK, arising from fewer marriages, more cohabitation, and more extra-marital births; increasing divorce and remarriage; declining fertility and smaller families; and a rise in the proportion of lone parents and reconstituted families. The nuclear family may still be dominant, but it is nonetheless only one possible family form.

Household change

The rise in divorce and the declining fashionability of marriage has led to other changes, all of which are important to social policy. The average size of households in Great Britain has declined since 1961 from 3.1 to just 2.4 people per household in 2009 (ONS 2010b). Of particular significance has been the rise in single-person households. More and more of us, it seems, are living on our own. In 1961, just 14 per cent of households were single-person households. By 2009, this proportion had increased to some 29 per cent (ONS 2010b), and seems set to climb further, as more of us live independently after leaving home and before marriage, as a consequence of divorce or simply as a reflection of the growing proportion of the elderly, many of whom live in 'solo' households. The implications of this development may be profound, not least for housing policy. The growing number of single-person households—who in turn want somewhere to live—has figured strongly in recent debates about inadequate housing supply in the context of rising housing demand. Whilst the population of the UK may have remained reasonably static over the past few decades, it is important to remember that demand for housing can increase within a static population if new and smaller households are forming faster than old ones dissolve (see Table 4.2).

In short, demographic change has a very real and integral relationship with the issue of social need. However, it would be erroneous to assume that one can chart a clear and straightforward relationship between demographic change and the consequent needs faced by society. On the contrary, there may be common acknowledgement of a particular demographic pattern, but very different assessments of the implications for social policy. Nowhere is this more aptly illustrated than in the various debates about an ageing population, and the consequences of this for welfare provision.

Ageing of the population

The population age profile of industrialized societies is changing in important ways, not least of which has been the movement towards what is commonly described as an ageing population. The age structure of the population reflects variation in past births, increases in longevity, and the effects of migration. This is an important debate, reflecting concern about the welfare costs of an expand-

Table 4.2 Households by size, UK (%)

	Percentages				
	1971	1981	1991	2001	2009
One person	18	22	27	29	29
Two people	32	32	34	35	35
Three people	19	17	16	16	16
Four people	17	18	16	14	14
Five people	8	7	5	5	4
Six or more people	6	4	2	2	2
All households (=100%) (millions)	18.6	20.2	22.4	23.8	25.2
Average household size (number of people)	2.9	2.7	2.5	2.4	2.4

Source: ONS (2010b), Table 2.1.

ing dependent population—or the proportion of the population economically supported by those of working age. In other words, this is a crude measure of the number of people economically supported by those of working age—what is known as the dependency ratio. Those people aged under 16 and those over pensionable age are often deemed to represent the dependent population, and, importantly, many countries are experiencing an increase in the proportion of the population above pensionable age. In 1971, for instance, just 12.4 per cent of the UK's population were aged 65 or over, and only 3.9 per cent were aged 75 and over. By 2010, this had increased to some 14.3 per cent and 5.6 per cent respectively (ONS 2010f).

The proportion of the population aged 65 or over is projected to rise further, as the post-Second World War 'baby boomers' reach retirement age. By 2030 it is projected that 18 per cent of the population will be aged over 65 (ONS 2010f). Moreover, there will be a particular increase in the number of very elderly people. Whilst in 2002 there were 388,200 people aged 90 and over in the UK, already by 2009 this number had increased to an estimated 436,600 (ONS 2010g). These developments clearly have profound implications in terms of future need for healthcare, social care, and pensions—and what this is likely to mean for national budgets, taxation, and welfare spending in the near future. Old people are higher users of health services than their younger peers. Health expenditure on those aged over 65, for instance, is approximately four times higher than on those under 65—and can be up to nine times higher for those aged 85 and over (OECD 2006). The stark implication is that a growing proportion of retired people will impose a burden of rising cost upon a shrinking population of working age. This has generated vigorous policy debate in the UK and internationally. Concern about the ability of the country to pay for growing pension costs in the future has led to a variety of reviews and changes to pension provisions in the UK, all of which claim to have at their heart a concern with this demographic trend (see Table 4.3).

Even here, however, where the evidence about demographic change and its relationship to social need appears to be fairly uncontentious, all is not as clear as it initially seems. On the contrary, the impact of the ageing population upon welfare states into the next century may be more complicated than it appears at first. Rather than representing a demographic time bomb, a number of competing points can be made.

Whilst it does seem likely that the ageing population will lead to greater costs in some areas, these are nonetheless likely to be matched by a reduction in other costs, such as childcare. Sefton (1997)

Table 4.3 Population[1] by sex and age, UK (%)

								Thousands	
	Under 16	16–24	25–34	35–44	45–54	55–64	65–74	75 and over	All ages
Males									
1971	7,318	3,730	3,530	3,271	3,354	3,123	1,999	842	27,167
1981	6,439	4,114	4,036	3,409	3,121	2,967	2,264	1,063	27,412
1991	5,976	3,800	4,432	3,950	3,287	2,835	2,272	1,358	27,909
2001	6,077	3,284	4,215	4,382	3,856	3,090	2,308	1,621	28,832
2008	5,898	3,823	3,985	4,533	4,027	3,566	2,447	1,873	30,151
2011	5,949	3,821	4,257	4,303	4,285	3,587	2,623	2,017	30,842
2016	6,128	3,622	4,731	4,043	4,474	3,630	3,032	2,326	31,986
2021	6,411	3,459	4,800	4,334	4,199	4,037	3,127	2,766	33,134
2026	6,489	3,641	4,566	4,800	3,948	4,229	3,201	3,337	34,210
Females									
1971	6,938	3,626	3,441	3,241	3,482	3,465	2,765	1,802	28,761
1981	6,104	3,966	3,975	3,365	3,148	3,240	2,931	2,218	28,946
1991	5,709	3,691	4,466	3,968	3,296	2,971	2,795	2,634	29,530
2001	5,786	3,220	4,260	4,465	3,920	3,186	2,640	2,805	30,281
2008	5,620	3,629	3,916	4,619	4,133	3,706	2,708	2,902	31,232
2011	5,673	3,639	4,128	4,357	4,420	3,743	2,878	2,970	31,807
2016	5,846	3,462	4,526	4,039	4,620	3,798	3,312	3,185	32,787
2021	6,122	3,306	4,606	4,222	4,301	4,254	3,424	3,589	33,824
2026	6,197	3,480	4,395	4,615	3,991	4,455	3,503	4,206	34,841

1 Mid-year estimates for 1971 to 2008; 2008-based projections for 2011 to 2026
Source: ONS (2010b), Table 1.2.

shows that the effect of a smaller child population on education spending has already more than offset the effects of an ageing population on healthcare and personal social services spending. Indeed, those aged over 65 are not necessarily dependent. Far from being economically dependent, the elderly may make a number of important economic contributions to society—in terms of informal and unpaid childcare or care for other elderly people, for instance, and in terms of their important role as consumers of economic goods and services.

Certainly, those aged 85 and over are likely to present a variety of needs in terms of health and social care. However, it is important to acknowledge that they still represent only a very small proportion of the entire population. The fact remains that economic growth could easily meet growing costs here. If current standards of provision are maintained, the cost of maintaining health and social services provision can be met by modest economic growth (Hills 1993). In other words, the issue here is not one of economic necessity, but one of political priority. Who should benefit from increases in economic productivity: existing workers or the retired? Moreover, the costs of an ageing population are not necessarily borne by the state—the movement towards private provision in terms of health and social care, and particularly in terms of pensions, is likely to alleviate some of the projected welfare costs.

Concerns about the demographic ageing of the population also ignore the fact that old age is to an extent a social construct, rather than simply a physical or biological fact. In other words, the current relationship between old age and physical dependency is changing. Old people in the future may be considerably healthier and more active than in the past, because of improvements in diet and lifestyle.

Conclusion: Social need, demographic 'facts', and policy judgements

A logical mind might consider that social policy should be determined by 'social need' and that need should be measured in terms of empirical 'facts' such as changes in the size and structure of a population (demography) and evidence about deprivation (for example, measures of poverty). This chapter has sought to show that there can be no simple links made between facts about need and the necessary social policies. The very words we use to describe demographic change (e.g. 'the ageing population' or 'lone parenthood') involve elements of judgement. All attempts to measure poverty have been criticized for the normative assumptions they inevitably have to make about either minima or the forms of social inclusion and exclusion that count. Therefore, policy cannot follow directly from evidence of need.

FURTHER READING

Bradshaw, J., 'A taxonomy of social need' (*New Society* No. 496, 30 March 1972: 640–3). An important and influential exposition of the different forms that social need might take.

Coleman, D., and Salt, J., *The British Population: Patterns, Trends and Processes* (Oxford: Oxford University Press, 1992). A thorough and comprehensive guide to the many debates surrounding the British population, drawing together a wealth of evidence and argument.

Dorman, P., Flaherty, J., and Veit-Wilson, J., *Poverty: The Facts* (London: Child Poverty Action Group, 2004). The latest edition of a very useful publication, containing a wealth of figures and data on poverty in the UK.

Doyal, L., and Gough, I., *A Theory of Human Need* (Basingstoke: Macmillan, 1991). A considered account of the key issues and dilemmas here, further developing the approach of Raymond Plant to the question of need.

Gordon, D., Adelman, L., Ashworth, K., Bradshaw, J., Levitas, R., Middleton, S., Pantazis, C., Patsios, D., Payne, S., Townsend, P., and Williams, J., *Poverty and Social Exclusion in Britain* (York: Joseph Rowntree Foundation, 2000). A report on the extent and nature of poverty in Britain using the 'consensual method' pioneered by Mack and Lansley.

Gordon, D., Levitas, R., and Pantazis, C. (eds), *Poverty and Social Exclusion in Britain: The Millennium Survey*, (Bristol: The Policy Press, 2006). This reports data from 1999 updating the earlier Breadline Britain surveys.

Levitas, R., *The Inclusive Society? Social Exclusion and New Labour* (London: Palgrave Macmillan, 2005). This challenging book investigates the policies of New Labour and shifts away from defining poverty in terms of income to conceptualizing it in terms of morality and employment.

Lister, R., *Poverty* (Cambridge: Polity Press, 2004).

Palmer, G., Carr, J., and Kenway, P., *Monitoring Poverty and Social Exclusion 2005*. (York: Joseph Rowntree Foundation, 2005). An annual report of indicators of poverty and social exclusion, providing some very useful data which can be followed up on the website: **www.poverty.org.uk**.

Piachaud, D., 'Peter Townsend and the Holy Grail' (*New Society* 57, 10 September 1981: 419–22). An influential challenge to Peter Townsend and the claim that need and poverty can be objectively measured.

Platt, L., *Parallel Lives: Poverty among Ethnic Minority Groups in Britain*. (London: Child Poverty Action Group, 2002). A comprehensive examination of poverty among ethnic minorities in Britain.

Sefton, T., *Recent Changes in the Distribution of the Social Wage*. (London: London School of Economics, 2002). An examination of the 'social wage' in the UK and the distributional impact of welfare spending.

Townsend, P., *Poverty in the United Kingdom* (Harmondsworth: Penguin, 1979). Essential reading for any consideration of poverty in the UK, in which Townsend spells out his 'poverty threshold'.

Townsend, P., and Gordon, D. (eds), *World Poverty: New Policies to Defeat an Old Enemy* (Bristol: The Policy Press, 2002). This collection of essays focuses on policy solutions to poverty in countries such as China and India.

@ USEFUL WEBSITES

There are a wide range of relevant websites on these issues; some of the most useful include:

www.statistics.gov.uk
A rich source of official statistics and data, including online access to the 2001 Census findings and the latest Social Trends.

www.jrf.org.uk
Provides access to a variety of research findings and reports on poverty and other social issues produced by the Joseph Rowntree Foundation.

Q ESSAY QUESTIONS

1 Why is 'social need' an important concept in social policy, but also difficult to define?

2 Outline at least three ways in which researchers have defined and measured poverty. What are the strengths and weaknesses of these approaches?

3 The UK has undergone significant demographic change over the past thirty years or so. What have been the main features of these changes?

4 Why is demographic change important for social policy?

@ ONLINE RESOURCE CENTRE

For additional material and resources, please visit the Online Resource Centre at:
www.oxfordtextbooks.co.uk/orc/baldock4e/.

5

Work and welfare

Sarah Vickerstaff

Contents

Introduction

In this chapter we examine the relationship between paid employment and welfare. We consider the ways in which work has been changing both in terms of the work available and who does it, and what implications this has for the importance of work in people's lives. Different aspects of unemployment are also explored and we go on to investigate both theoretically and practically what the role of government in general should be and how different social policies respond to various employment issues.

Learning outcomes

At the end of this chapter you will have an understanding of:

1   how the world of work has changed in the last fifty years;
2   the impact of gender and age on labour market participation;
3   the reasons why unemployment is seen as a policy problem;
4   the political debates surrounding social policy interventions in employment issues;
5   current policy developments in the UK.

The importance of work to welfare

In 2005 the government commissioned an independent review, 'Is work good for your health and wellbeing?' (Waddell and Burton 2006) which, along with a number of other recent reports, has highlighted the importance of 'good work' to lifelong health and well-being in work and into retirement (see also Black 2008; Marmot 2010). Employment is one of the best defences against poverty, unhappiness, and low self-esteem, which in turn are likely to affect adversely an individual's physical and mental health. As Marmot concluded in his review of health inequalities:

> The relationship between employment and health is close, enduring and multi-dimensional. Being without work is rarely good for one's health, but while 'good work' is linked to positive health outcomes, jobs that are insecure, low-paid and fail to protect employees from stress and danger make people ill. (2010: 68)

In addition to the impacts upon health, paid work outside the home has traditionally been seen as a key mechanism of social integration: a person who 'works' is a full citizen, a useful and 'fully paid up', taxpaying member of society. People who are in paid employment have higher rates of involvement in other social, political, and sporting activities. This is partly a question of money—having the income to enjoy leisure activities—partly a matter of greater social inclusion or greater integration into public life. Thus, although we tend to conflate welfare with the welfare state and its policies, in fact work and employment are more fundamental producers of individual and societal welfare. In the first twenty-five years after the Second World War it was taken for granted in Europe and the United States that a key goal of government policy was the maintenance of full employment. The problem for many societies in Europe today is that there does not seem to be enough work to go round. Since the early 1970s, and especially in the 1980s, with the growth of persistent unemployment, this commitment to full employment, and the belief in its possibility, have been shaken throughout the advanced industrial (or increasingly post-industrial) world. In Britain access to many state-provided welfare measures is conditioned by our work histories and increasingly by our willingness to work if work is available (see Chapter 10).

Unemployment tends to grab the newspaper headlines as *the* key employment issue, but since the 1970s many other developments have been occurring in the world of work. In the UK the growth in the numbers of economically inactive, that is, people of working age who are outside the labour market by reason of caring responsibilities, health issues, or early retirement, have also become a major policy issue. In the labour market the sorts of jobs available and the skills and attributes they require also have been transformed; access to work is changing (who gets what kind of job); and for many people their experience of work, especially in relation to job security and job intensity, has fundamentally altered. In order to consider the connection between work and welfare further we must first look at all of these features of the labour market. We can then go on to review and evaluate some of the policy responses to these issues, and investigate contemporary debates on what to do about unemployment and access to work.

The work available

In the period since the 1960s the UK economy has witnessed a progressive decline in manufacturing industry and hence the number of jobs available in this sector (see Table 5.1). At the same time there has been an increase in service sector and office or white-collar work. This shift from industry to services and the related move from manual to non-manual work have radically changed the pattern of demand in the labour market, especially for some groups:

Table 5.1 Employee jobs by industry[1]

						Percentages	
	1978	1988	1998	2008	2009	Change 1978 to 2008	Change 2008 to 2009
Agriculture and fishing	1.7	1.4	1.3	1.0	1.0	−0.7	—
Energy and water	2.8	1.8	0.8	0.7	0.7	−2.1	—
Manufacturing	28.5	20.7	17.0	10.5	10.0	−18.0	−0.6
Construction	5.7	5.1	4.4	4.8	4.8	−0.8	—
Distribution, hotels and restaurants	19.5	21.3	23.8	23.6	23.5	4.1	−0.1
Transport and communications	6.5	5.9	5.7	5.9	5.8	−0.7	−0.1
Finance and business services	10.5	14.8	18.1	21.4	20.8	10.9	−0.6
Public administration, education and health	21.1	24.5	24.2	26.9	28.1	5.8	1.2
Other services[2]	3.8	4.5	4.7	5.3	5.4	1.5	0.1
All industries (=100%) (millions)	24.3	23.7	24.7	27.2	26.5	2.9	−0.7

1 Data are at June each year and are not seasonally adjusted.
2 Community, social, and personal services including sanitation, dry cleaning, personal care, and recreational, cultural, and sporting activities.
Source: ONS *Social Trends* (2010) 40:49

The transformation of the British economy from a strong manufacturing base to a 'post-industrial' service base has brought with it a collapse in the demand for the labour of unqualified youths. (Ashton 1992: 186–7)

In addition to this shift in the pattern of activity in the economy, technological changes and new standards of customer service have also meant that the skill and competence requirements for jobs have changed.

Twenty years ago, almost all the manual workers in my operation were men and a lot of the work consisted of humping sacks of potatoes around. Today, it's all fiddly work, putting sauce on the bits of chicken for Marks and Sparks, and the assembly line is 90 per cent women. Mostly men don't apply for it—it's part-time and they see it as women's work. (Food factory manager, quoted in Commission on Social Justice 1994: 187)

There is considerable debate about the overall trends in skill requirements for the jobs available in today's economy. Some argue that there is an upward trend in the skill levels required, pointing to the shift from manual to non-manual work and the impact of newer technologies, such as computer applications, whilst others indicate the growth of unskilled service sector jobs which require few skills or personal attributes. Far from the old disciplines of assembly-line work in factories becoming a thing of the past, these work techniques are increasingly being applied to all kinds of other work, for example fast-food restaurants and telephone call-centre workers. (For contrasting views see the arguments in Box 5.1.)

Box 5.1 The McDonaldization thesis versus the knowledge economy

George Ritzer, in a book entitled The *McDonaldization of Society*, has argued that the process typified by the way fast-food restaurants are run is extending into many areas of contemporary life:

First, a McDonaldized world is dominated by homogeneous products. The Big Mac, the Egg McMuffin, and Chicken Nuggets are identical from one time and place to another. Second, technologies like Burger King's conveyor system, as well as the french-fry and soft-drink machines throughout the fast-food industry, are as rigid as many of the technologies in Henry Ford's assembly-line system. Further, work routines in the fast-food restaurant are highly standardized. Even what the workers say to customers is routinized. In addition, the jobs in a fast-food restaurant are deskilled; they take little or no ability. The workers, furthermore, are homogeneous, and the actions of the customers are homogenized by the demands of the fast-food restaurant (for example, don't dare ask for a rare burger). The workers at fast-food restaurants can be seen as a mass of interchangeable workers. Finally, what is consumed and how it is consumed [are] homogenized by McDonaldization. (Ritzer 1993: 155)

An alternative view of how the economy is going is put forward by the proponents of the knowledge economy:

. . . the emerging global knowledge economy . . . highlight[s] the evolution from an economic order in which the clever and organized use of natural resources was sufficient for success . . . to an economy based on knowledge, in which the exploitation of natural resources is not only insufficient but . . . not even necessary (Schwarz, Kelly, and Boyer 1999: 78). In the knowledge economy information and knowledge are key economic resources and 'knowledge workers' need higher levels of education and a commitment to lifelong learning. (OECD 1999)

A major piece of research into the trends in job skills in the UK found evidence for a polarization of skills (for a discussion of this research and the wider debate, see Gallie 1991; 1996; Bradley et al. 2000; Edwards and Wajcman 2005). In other words, the middle ground of semi-skilled jobs is disappearing; instead skilled manual, managerial, and professional jobs are becoming more skilled whilst many of the remaining jobs are becoming more routine and unskilled.

Another feature of the way in which work has been changing is the growth of part-time and other forms of **flexible** or **casual work**. This growth is driven largely by the expansion of the service sector but also by increasing economic competition, leading employers to seek ways to improve efficiency and reduce labour costs. The degree of growth of part-time and flexible work across Europe varies considerably (see O'Reilly and Fagan 1998), depending in large measure on the prevailing context of employment regulation. For example, the UK and the Netherlands have high rates of part-time working, whilst France does not. One thing unites the experience of part-time employment across Europe, however, and that is the fact that it is overwhelmingly women who work part-time. The growth of part-time work is seen as contributing to growing income disparity between the rich and poor in society, which is another feature of the employment landscape in recent years, especially in the United States and Britain (see Box 5.2).

Employment security and labour intensification

These changes in the work available and in access to it raise issues about the experience of work and the impact this has on people's welfare. The growth of flexible and casual work has affected not only the unskilled but also white-collar, managerial, and professional workers. Many people in employment will have seen workforce reductions in their own workplace or have experienced job loss at second hand through friends and relatives. Many men may have had to change their jobs, perhaps losing the occupational identity they believed they would keep for all their working lives. In this context even the employed are likely to feel more insecure about their job prospects. In this respect the changes in the labour market over recent years may have gone some way to making men's patterns of working across the life cycle more like women's: periods of work interspersed with periods of economic inactivity. Such broken career patterns and part-time or casual work

---

Box 5.2 **Case study: the pros and cons of part-time work**

Since part-time employment almost never pays enough to support a family (and perhaps not even a single person), part-time jobs can only be taken by those with another earner in the family—often in practice, women married to men in employment. For this group the tax and benefits system offers a substantial incentive to work part-time . . . For women whose partners are unemployed or earning a low wage topped up by family credit, benefit withdrawal starts at a much lower point; creating effective disincentives for the woman to work.

Thus, it is argued, the rise in part-time working is helping to create a gulf between 'work-rich' families, with more than one job, and 'work-poor' families with no job at all, while offering little or nothing to the unemployed who need a full-time wage. (Hewitt 1996: 44)

Questions:

- Are the reasons why men and women take part-time work the same or different?
- Is the availability of part-time work a good opportunity for women and/or older workers who want to work?
- Why is there much less part-time working in some European countries than in others?

obviously have implications for levels of income, and for any pension entitlement based on years of working service.

Along with a sense of the insecurity of employment, many employees have experienced an intensification of their work. In the public sector, following waves of workforce reduction in the 1980s and 1990s, the 'survivors' (those who have kept their jobs) in areas such as local government or higher education, for example, feel that they are now expected to work harder. The amount of work has increased but the number of people doing it has decreased. In the private sector the introduction of lean production methods has had a similar effect. This sense that people are working harder is borne out by two different measures of work effort: the extent of work, that is, the hours worked, and the intensity of work, that is, how hard people have to work whilst at work (see Green 2001: 56). Average working hours reduced considerably across the twentieth century, but since the 1980s the dispersion of hours has changed: more people work longer hours and more people work for a short number of hours, a pattern obscured by average hours calculations (Green 2001: 58–60). This change in the pattern of work has been noted in publicity about the fact that British fathers have the longest average working hours in Europe. Measures of labour intensity are more difficult to come by, but a range of research reviewed and added to by Green (2001) suggests that many people believe that they have to work harder, if not always longer, than they did in the past. Taken together, these two measures of work effort suggest a number of potentially detrimental effects on the relationship between work and welfare. Labour intensification may well be having an impact on people's levels of stress and overall health, and in some households a long-hours culture may have the effect of putting strain on family relationships.

Participation rates and the dependency ratio

If people spend up to a third of their lives being educated and a third of their lives in retirement, that only leaves a third in work to support the rest . . . Do the maths. It just doesn't add up.

(Alistair Darling, then Secretary of State for Work and Pensions, speech reported in the *Financial Times*, 6 February 2002)

Along with the changes to work already discussed, there has been a trend for the standard patterns of work across the individual's life cycle to change: notably, as the quotation above suggests, people are in paid employment for less time. Young people are staying in education longer (see Chapter 11) and many people, especially men, are retiring earlier. Rather than being a cause for celebration, as working less could perhaps be expected to be, this shortening of working life is seen as a major problem in many European societies. The growing tendency to early retirement, particularly for men in their fifties, has been recognized as an important social trend in Western Europe and the United States. What appears rational and beneficial from the points of view of the individual or the employing organization may be irrational and costly in terms of the collective well-being and health of the whole economy. From a national point of view, early withdrawal from the labour market is seen as a risk and a cost, worsening the dependency ratio, raising public and private pension costs, and threatening additional welfare expenditure over the longer term. There is a tension between individual choice and social benefit (Esping-Andersen 1999). As can be seen in Figure 5.1, many women and men have left the labour market before state pension age (60 and 65 respectively in 2004). The UK government, along with many other European governments, is increasingly trying to encourage older workers to stay in employment for longer.

Employment rates for those over 50 years of age have been increasing in the last few years. In 1950 the average age of retirement for men in the UK was 67.2; by 1990 the average age was 63.5.

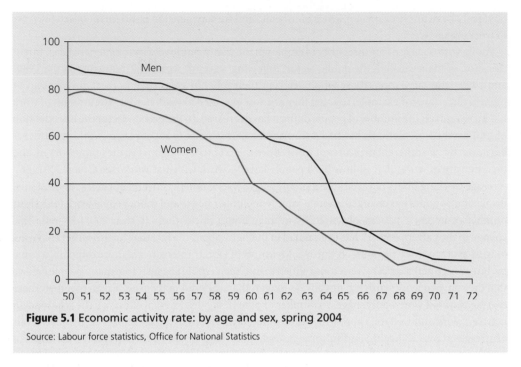

Figure 5.1 Economic activity rate: by age and sex, spring 2004

Source: Labour force statistics, Office for National Statistics

Latest data show that it has risen to 64.6, but there are still concerns about the dependency ratio (see Table 5.2), although, as Table 5.3 indicates, the position in the UK is of less concern than the age imbalance in some other countries. If the number of people of working age reduces in relation to the number of people of retirement age, then fewer people are paying taxes to fund those drawing pensions and making demands upon health and care services.

Cartoon 5.1 Extending working life?

© Jeremy Banks 2005

Table 5.2 Dependency ratio: the number of people of working age for every person of state pension age: projections

2008	2013	2018	2028	2033
3.23	3.19	3.11	3.07	2.78

Source: ONS Statistical Bulletin (2009):
http://www.statistics.gov.uk/pdfdir/pproj1009.pdf

The response from many governments in Europe has been to raise the age at which people are entitled to their state pension. In the UK, women's state pension age has been rising to 65 to match men's, and by 2020 it will be 66 for both men and women, rising to 68 by 2046. In Germany it was agreed in 2007 that there would be a phased rise from 65 to 67, and in France proposals to move from 60 to 62 led to strikes in the autumn of 2010.

Gender and access to work

Although we talk about the period of post-war full employment, this is not really an accurate picture of typical participation rates in the past, as Pamela Meadows reminds us:

> If we take the household as the unit, 50 years ago the head of the household, whether male or female, was likely to be economically active, with other household members other than lodgers and adult or adolescent children likely to be inactive. This model, which had persisted since the industrial revolution, was envisaged by Beveridge as unchanging and still forms the basis of our social security system. However, it does not match present social reality. (1996: 4)

Full employment meant that any man who wanted to find a job had a reasonably good chance of success. As Beveridge had defined it in 1944: 'Full employment . . . means having always more

Table 5.3 Old age dependency ratios*: selected countries 2008 and projected 2035

H	2008	2035
Japan	34	57
Germany	30	53
Sweden	27	40
France	25	42
UK	24	39
Australia	20	36
USA	19	33
Poland	19	38
China	11	30
India	8	14
South Africa	7	12

Source: ONS *Population Trends* (2010): 23
*Old age dependency ratio measures the number of people aged 65 and over for every 100 people aged 15–64.
ONS *Population Trends* (2010), 142:23

vacant jobs than unemployed men' (quoted in Rubery 1997: 63). The male breadwinner model of the family underlay definitions of full employment, and the way in which social security provisions were framed, and also informed employers' and employees' notions of suitable workers for particular jobs. In Britain forty years ago the 'typical worker' (found in many sociological studies of the time) was a man, working full-time in industry in skilled or semi-skilled work. Today the average worker is more likely to be a woman working part-time in a service sector job such as care work or retail.

These facts have profound implications for how we understand 'work', and for the role of public and social policy in responding to labour market problems. As many writers have pointed out, the old view of 'work' as paid employment outside the home in the public sphere served to downgrade the unpaid work which went on, undertaken mainly by women, in the domestic sphere: childcare, cleaning, cooking, etc. (see, for example, the discussion in Glucksmann 1995). Women's access to paid employment outside the home was restricted by domestic responsibilities, especially childcare and the prevalent social belief that women's real place was in the home. One of the most dramatic trends in the labour market since the 1970s has been the steady increase in the numbers of women in paid employment outside the home; in particular, the participation rates of married women have seen very significant rises in most European countries. Table 5.4 gives some indication of these developments. It also begins to reveal another feature of recent labour market changes noted above: as female employment has increased, so male unemployment has grown. This is sometimes referred to as the feminization of work; however, the changes are typically not because of direct substitution (that would be women doing jobs that men once did) but rather because the kinds of job available have changed (see Figure 5.2).

Although many more women are working outside the home, the labour market is still gendered in the sense that typically men and women work in different kinds of jobs, in different sectors. This is also illustrated in Figure 5.2 and Table 5.5. Women are concentrated in service sector jobs, often occupations such as nursing, teaching, catering, and cleaning, which mirror traditional domestic skills and tasks, or in jobs in retail, personal services, and tourism, where

Table 5.4 Employment rates: by sex, UK (percentages)

	Men	Women	All
1971	91.7	56.3	74.7
1975	90.1	59.5	75.5
1980	85.7	60.1	74.4
1985	78.3	60.4	69.8
1990	82.4	67.2	75.0
1995	76.3	65.8	71.2
2000	79.2	69.3	74.4
2005	79.1	70.0	74.7
2009	76.0	69.0	72.7

Note: Data are at Q2 each year and are seasonally adjusted. Men aged 16 to 64 and women aged 16 to 59. See Appendix,
    Part 4: Labour Force Survey
Source: ONS, *Social Trends* (2010) 40: 44

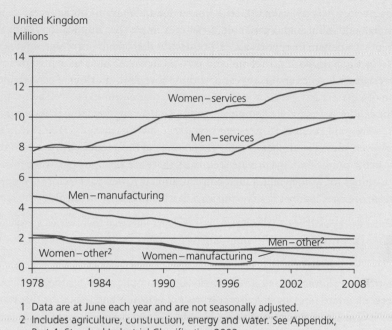

1 Data are at June each year and are not seasonally adjusted.
2 Includes agriculture, construction, energy and water. See Appendix, Part 4: Standard Industrial Classification 2003.
Source: Short- Term Employment Surveys, Office for National Statistics

Figure 5.2 Employee jobs:[1] by sex and industry

ONS *Social Trends* (2009) 39: 43

Table 5.5 All in employment: by sex and occupation, 2009[1]

United Kingdom	Percentages		
	Men	Women	All
Managers and senior officials	19	12	16
Professional	14	13	14
Associate professional and technical	14	16	15
Administrative and secretarial	5	19	11
Skilled trades	18	2	11
Personal service	3	16	9
Sales and customer service	5	11	7
Process, plant and machine operatives	11	2	7
Elementary	12	11	11
All occupations[2] (=100%) (millions)	15.4	13.4	28.8

1 Data are at Q2 and are not seasonally adjusted. People aged 16 and over. See Appendix, Part 4: Labour Force Survey, and Standard Occupational Classification 2000 (SOC2000).
2 Includes people who did not state their occupation.
Source: ONS *Social Trends* (2010) 40:48

women may be in part employed to attract the customers. The distinctions between women's and men's jobs are surprisingly enduring, both in practice and in terms of the career expectations of young women and men. Such a gendered division of labour has implications both for women's and for men's employment opportunities, but also for their relative average wages. This is often referred to by the notions of horizontal and vertical segregation, in which women are concentrated in certain industries and sectors and, within those, at the bottom of career ladders; and by the notion of a gender pay gap, in which women's average earnings are well below those of men. In 2010 the gender pay gap for all employees was 19.8 per cent, meaning that on average women in Britain were paid roughly 80 per cent of average male earnings (ONS 2010). This average figure, however, masks a number of different features of the gender pay issue; for example, the gap is less in the public than the private sector and there are variations between jobs.

Lower earnings for women reflect their concentration in lower-paid sectors of employment and at the bottom of career ladders, but also the ways in which skills are defined:

> In manual work, 'skill' is socially constructed, so that jobs that involve tasks associated with masculine expertise—such as driving—are seen as more skilled than jobs that involve feminine dexterity—such as sewing. (Abbott and Wallace 1997: 195)

Women's relatively lower earning power obviously has implications for their welfare in terms of their current standard of living but also in respect of pensions and hence the threat of poverty in older age. As Ginn and Arber comment:

> Among elderly people, inequality in personal incomes is structured by class and gender, and occupational pensions are the main means by which a disadvantaged position in the labour market during working life is translated into a low income in later life. The concentration of poverty among women in later life is well established. (1993: 47)

The net effect of these changes in the labour market has been to reduce the numbers of traditional 'men's jobs' whilst at the same time increasing the numbers of jobs seen as suitable for women. However, many of the jobs which women are now doing are part-time, poorly paid, and with few prospects of career advancement. Some commentators see these developments as irreversible: 'Men, both the young and the old, may be waiting for the return of an era, which has gone for good' (Balls 1993: 23).

Unemployment and social exclusion

Relatively high rates of unemployment have come to characterize many European economies; however, patterns of unemployment vary considerably in terms of age, race, gender, and geography (see Box 5.3 for the problems of defining unemployment). Unemployment rates are higher for young people, ethnic minorities, and those with no (or poor) educational or training qualifications, and generally higher for men than for women (see Table 5.6 for gender and age variations). In addition, there are regions of exceptionally high unemployment.

Youth unemployment

Young people throughout Europe have been particularly affected by unemployment (see Table 5.7). This has led some commentators to talk about the restructuring of the youth labour market and the prolonging of the transition from school to work (see Chapter 11). As a result, possible responses to youth unemployment have been a major focus for debate and policy reform (see below). The implications of a hard core of long-term unemployed young people have also fuelled the debate about the development of an underclass. A recent definition of the underclass underscores the potential relationship between unemployment and social exclusion:

Box 5.3 **The problems of defining unemployment**

We need to be cautious when looking at unemployment statistics, especially when comparing across countries. Unemployment can be defined for data-gathering purposes in a number of different ways, which have implications for the headline figure of unemployment, and hence public perceptions of the problem. Before April 1998 in the UK the main indicator of unemployment was the government figures based on the claimant count (i.e. those unemployed and claiming benefits). This calculation was much criticized, as it did not include (for example) people on government training schemes. From 1998 the International Labour Office definition is used. This definition of unemployment is accepted as a more workable one for comparative purposes: someone is unemployed if they do not have a job but are available to start work within two weeks and have looked for work in the previous four weeks or have been waiting to start a job. However, even this measure is open to debate. Some people may regard themselves as unemployed even though they may not be officially defined as such, for example someone who was forced to take early retirement but did not wish to give up work, or a disabled person not in work but who would actually like to work if suitable employment were available.

Also, defining someone as unemployed may not be strictly accurate: they may be engaged in work in the informal economy, doing voluntary work, or unpaid caring in the home, thus actually 'working' if not part of the formal economy.

---

a social group or class of people located at the bottom of the class structure who, over time, have become structurally separate and culturally distinct from the regularly employed working class and society in general through processes of social and economic change (particularly de-industrialization) and/or through patterns of cultural behaviour, who are now persistently reliant on state benefits and almost permanently confined to living in poorer conditions and neighbourhoods. (Macdonald 1997: 3–4)

Table 5.6 Unemployment rate by age and gender, UK (percentages)

	16–64	16–17	18–24	25–34	35–49	50–64
All persons						
Sep–Nov 2008	6.3	27.8	14.5	5.6	4.1	3.7
Sep–Nov 2010	8.1	36.6	18.1	7.5	5.6	4.8
Males						
Sep–Nov 2008	6.9	29.7	16.7	5.8	4.3	4.4
Sep–Nov 2010	8.8	39.8	19.7	7.8	6.0	6.0
Females						
Sep–Nov 2008	5.5	25.8	11.8	5.3	3.9	2.7
Sep–Nov 2010	7.2	33.5	16.1	7.1	5.1	3.3

Source: ONS (2010) Labour market statistics

Table 5.7 Youth* unemployment rate, selected European countries, 2009 (percentages)

	Total	Female	Male
Austria	9.0	8.5	9.5
Portugal	19.6	21.4	18.0
Ireland	21.5	16.1	26.5
United Kingdom	17.9	15.2	20.3
Germany	10.5	9.0	12.0
Sweden	24.2	23.7	24.8
Denmark	8.9	7.5	10.1
Czech Republic	12.2	12.9	11.7
Netherlands	6.0	5.4	6.6
Italy	24.9	29.0	22.0
Finland	18.8	16.4	21.3
Lithuania	23.6	15.9	28.8
Spain	33.6	33.7	33.6
France	22.3	21.4	23.0
Greece	24.2	31.8	18.3
EU 27 average	18.3	17.4	19.1

*Aged 15–24
Source: Eurostat (2009)

Many young people only experience unemployment for a short period before going into further education, training, or a job, and therefore we must not assume that unemployment alone causes social exclusion or the basis for an underclass. Nevertheless, in certain countries and certain localities such as Liverpool in England or amongst certain ethnic communities such as blacks in American inner-city ghettos unemployment may be more persistent and intra-generational, leading to the kind of social marginalization implied in definitions of the underclass. (Roberts 1997: 45–7)

Lone parents and unemployment

Another group that has attracted special attention in the debate about unemployment, especially in the United States and the UK, are lone parents. In comparison with other European countries, the UK has a high number of lone-parent households; they are less likely to be in paid employment, and are therefore more likely to be dependent on state benefits.

In America the 'problem' of lone mothers has been seen as a key side effect of earlier welfare systems: income support for lone mothers is thought to have reduced the incentive to marry and to work. Hence, conservative critics have pointed to the growth in the numbers of lone mothers as evidence that the welfare state has contributed to the breakdown of the family and the work ethic. The ability of lone parents to go out to work is obviously dependent upon a range of factors: for example, the accessibility of appropriate and affordable childcare; a supply of jobs that pay sufficient to sustain the household; and the skills and disposition of the individual.

Long-term sickness and disability

There are other reasons for economic inactivity outside unemployment and these vary with age, gender, and domestic circumstances, but another important factor in keeping people out of the labour market is long-term sickness or disability (see Table 5.8). Some 2.7 million people of working age, of whom two-thirds are men, are claiming Incapacity Benefit, a benefit paid to those who are 'incapable' of work. How these men become 'detached' from the labour market has generated considerable academic interest (cf. Alcock et al. 2003), and increasingly this group is the focus of policy attention (Vickerstaff 2006). The reasons for economic inactivity amongst older age groups before state pension age are highly gendered. For men in their fifties, the main factors behind economic inactivity are health afflictions and early retirement. Those suffering from poor health are most likely not to be seeking work and many are on Incapacity Benefit. Those who have retired early are more likely to be financially secure and have chosen to retire from well-paid jobs with an occupational pension. For women, health is a significant factor. However, another main reason for inactivity amongst women over 50 is 'keeping home' or other caring responsibilities, although the numbers giving this reason are declining (Loretto, Vickerstaff and White 2005: 41). Once older workers become unemployed, there is a much greater likelihood that they will become involuntarily, but permanently, detached from the labour market (Ashdown 2000), although there is evidence that significant numbers of these detached workers would like to work if suitable employment was available (NAO 2004: 3).

Table 5.8 Reasons for economic inactivity: by sex and age, 2008[1] (percentages)

	16–24	25–34	35–49	50–59/64	All aged 16–59/64
Men					
Long-term sick or disabled	5	40	62	49	34
Looking after family or home	1	9	16	6	6
Student	82	27	4	—	33
Retired	0	0	1	33	13
Other	10	17	12	9	11
All men (=100%) (millions)[2]	1.2	0.3	0.5	1.3	3.3
Women					
Long-term sick or disabled	3	8	24	41	19
Looking after family or home	23	72	61	27	45
Student	66	10	4	1	22
Retired	0	0	—	14	3
Other	8	8	8	14	9
All women (=100%) (millions)[2]	1.3	0.9	1.4	1.1	4.7

1 Data are at Q2 and are not seasonally adjusted. See Appendix, Part 4: Labour Force Survey.
2 Includes discouraged workers and those who are temporarily sick.
Source: ONS *Social Trends* (2009) 39:59

Explanations of unemployment

There is no single explanation of unemployment, and indeed we should not expect one, as unemployment itself is a varied condition—for example, differences between short-term temporary job loss, long-term unemployment, or 'voluntary' redundancy or early retirement. However, debates about the causes of unemployment are important because they underpin different policy responses. It is generally agreed that the core of recent unemployment is structural: namely that declining employment in some sectors such as manufacturing is not compensated for by employment expansion in other sectors. Unemployment may occur because more jobs are lost than are created or because of constraints on mobility (i.e. the new jobs are located somewhere different from the old jobs), or because people are not prepared or able for a variety of reasons to accept different kinds of work. Another cause of structural unemployment is technological development: advances in process and methods mean that fewer people are required to produce the same level of output as in the past. Thus, both the number of people and the kinds of people in demand in the labour market change.

In relation to policy discussions, we can draw a broad distinction between individualist and structuralist explanations of unemployment, and hence different approaches to its remedy. Neo-liberals see high unemployment as a consequence of the competitiveness of Western economies in comparison with emerging economies in other parts of the world. This competitiveness is seen, in part, as a result of the market distortions created by the welfare state: individuals for a variety of reasons have failed to adapt sufficiently to the new economic circumstances. This may be because they refuse to accept lower wages and change the kind of work they do; because they fail to acquire the new skills needed to get work; or because, in the context of welfare benefits which ameliorate the effects of unemployment, they have lost the incentive to get work. Structuralist explanations, on the other hand, see the unemployed as victims of global economic forces and changes, locked into cycles of social and economic disadvantage beyond their power as individuals to change. All societies in Europe have to wrestle with the issue of unemployment, although the severity of the problem varies from country to country (see Table 5.6).

What can policy do?

There are five main ways in which public policy can have an impact on work and employment. These are:

- broad macroeconomic policy in terms of how the economy is managed and the role of monetary and fiscal policy in encouraging economic growth and development and hence the impact on the demand for labour;
- specific employment regulation such as collective labour laws regarding the conduct of industrial relations and the role of trade unions and individual labour laws regarding aspects such as discrimination and unfair dismissal;
- education and training policies which seek to improve the supply of labour and hence the employability of individuals (see Chapter 11);
- what is often referred to as active labour market policy, which includes job creation or job subsidy policies; and finally,
- welfare and benefit systems which try to ensure a safety net for the inactive, unemployed, or low-paid.

Social policy analysts have traditionally been concerned with the benefit systems, but in practice it is difficult to separate out policy in these different areas, as they inevitably affect each other.

Lying behind policy choices are political views about what government should do and can do. We will consider three different broad approaches to the question of what policy can and should do: the deregulationist or neo-liberal approach; the regulation or social democratic approach, which can take a number of different forms; and the radical alternatives, sometimes thought of as 'green' ideas (see e.g. Esping-Andersen 1996a: 10–21). In practice, as we shall see, real-life policies are sometimes a mixture of these different perspectives.

Deregulation or the neo-liberal approach

A liberal market approach of deregulation and minimal welfare is the approach that broadly characterized the United States and UK in the 1980s and early 1990s.

> The case for a deregulated labour market rests on the belief that regulation—in very broad terms employment protection and minimum wage legislation, plus adequate legal backing for trade unions—renders markets less flexible and less adaptable, thus driving up unemployment. (Philpott 1997a: 12)

Simply put, the belief is that highly paid workers in the first-world economies have priced themselves out of jobs in the face of competition from low-wage economies in other parts of the world. The solution, in part, is to reassert market forces with the aim of depressing wages. The answer to unemployment is to concentrate on restimulating the economy, and free up the labour market so that labour can find its true price. Often combined with this kind of analysis is the argument that the welfare state and its benefit safety net have created a dependency culture in which, even when there is work, people lack the incentives to go out and get it. One approach, advocated, for example, by Charles Murray in the United States, is therefore to withdraw benefits and force people back to work.

These arguments have found their strongest supporters in the United States, where policy has been directed towards the twin aims of creating a lower-wage economy at the bottom end of the labour market and making participation in employment or training a condition of benefit entitlement. The latter approach to unemployment benefits is usually called workfare, and typically carries with it a strong moral undertone:

> Dispute over what can be expected of poor people, not lack of opportunity, is the main reason chronic poverty persists in America. (Mead 1997: 1)

These ideas have travelled from the United States to the UK and were influential in the Conservative and Labour governments of the 1980s and early 1990s. They still inform current policy thinking, as will be seen below. Of course, underlying such policy ideas is the assumption that there are jobs into which people can be forced, and in the US example the expansion of low-paid service sector jobs was considerable up to the most recent recession. In Europe it is not so clear that such a policy could work without some element of government-sponsored job creation.

Regulation or the social democratic approach

A regulation or social democratic approach to unemployment and related employment issues starts from the premise that the difficulties are structural rather than individual, and therefore state intervention of some sort to secure the welfare of disadvantaged groups is legitimate. Thus, policy is expected to combine employment protection measures, such as unfair dismissal legislation and directives on working hours, with social protection for those who are disadvantaged in the labour market. Esping-Andersen (1996a and b) sees Sweden as the archetype of such an approach: comprehensive and universalistic benefit systems combined with active labour market policies designed to create jobs, especially in the public sector, and provide continuing education and training to enable people to take up job opportunities. The problem with such an approach, simply put, is that it is expensive and requires a degree of social consensus that accepts high levels of taxation as the price for a developed welfare system.

In other countries in Europe, a different variant of the social democratic approach has been tried, leading to what Esping-Andersen has characterized as the 'labour reduction route':

> While the Scandinavians have managed the surplus of 'deindustrialized', largely unskilled, masses with retraining and job creation, and the Americans with wage erosion, the continental European nations have opted to subsidize their exit, especially through early retirement. This has arguably produced an 'insider–outsider' divide, with a small, predominantly male, 'insider' workforce enjoying high wages, expensive social rights, and strong job security, combined with a swelling population of 'outsiders' depending either on the male bread-winner's pay or on welfare state transfers. (1996a: 18)

The growth in the number of inactive men, that is, those who are retired and those on invalidity benefits, has been considerable in countries such as Denmark, Germany, and France. Not unsur-prisingly, those most likely either to be forced into early retirement through redundancy or to opt for an early end to work are those whose employment was unskilled and/or poorly paid (OECD 1994: 27–35). As a result, the labour reduction route is liable to increase the dependency of older groups on welfare benefits of one sort or another.

Due to the welfare costs associated with such approaches to the problem of unemployment, social democratic ideas have increasingly come under pressure from the arguments of the neo-liberals. Germany, for example, is now focusing policy effort on encouraging men to work for longer and delay retiring (Spross 2006). However, in most continental European countries the social costs of a deregulation approach as developed in America are seen as too high: unemployment may be reduced, but at the expense of growing poverty and social inequality. Social democratic or regula-tion perspectives have therefore increasingly argued for what Esping-Andersen (1996a: 3) has char-acterized as a 'social investment strategy'. This emphasizes the desirability of moving from passive (income support) benefits to active labour market policies. Thus, in addition to the concern with social security through benefits systems, a regulation approach now typically also puts a premium on so-called 'supply side' measures, that is, policies on education and training designed to make people more employable. In recent debates about the future of the welfare state in Europe, especially in Britain under New Labour, there has been discussion of the possibilities of a 'middle way', that is, a basis for policy that borrows from both neo-liberal and social democratic ideas.

Radical alternatives

Although debate about employment and unemployment policy is dominated by the dispute between deregulation and regulation perspectives, a third set of ideas has increasingly tried to inject radical alternatives into the argument. Such alternatives do not form a coherent whole, but rather come from a number of different perspectives. What unites them is often an anti-state, self-help approach, and for this reason they are sometimes characterized as green ideas.

These ideas revolve around a rejection of continued economic growth as an overarching aim for government policy, or simply see the possibility of a return to post-war 'full employment' as uto-pian (Mayo 1996). Thus, if it will be impossible to find paid employment for everyone, the focus must shift to finding alternatives to work or attempts to share work out more evenly (see also Marsh 1991). This might involve facing the question of why we should continue to see paid em-ployment as a defining characteristic of citizenship or social inclusion. Instead, participation through other activities such as voluntary or community work should rank equally as a contribu-tion to society (see Box 5.4).

Another set of ideas suggests that in the face of continued high unemployment, policy should focus on guaranteed income schemes. This would involve a universal guaranteed income for any-one who fell below an agreed acceptable threshold, whether or not they were in employment (Pixley 1993: 91–4). The Green Party in the UK has advocated a Citizen's Income, which would be an 'un-conditional payment made to each individual as a right of citizenship—like a tax credit paid to

> ## Box 5.4 **Reconceiving work**
>
> But whatever employment levels pertain in the medium term, there are good reasons to recast the utopia from one of full employment to one (sometimes dubbed 'full engagement') which provides access to income and to meaningful work, paid or unpaid as citizens.
>
> First, for the immediate future, the lead export sectors for the UK—such as financial services, tourism, and manufacturing—will remain central to national employment levels and to generating secondary employment and income. However, the evidence of 'jobless' communities is on the rise . . . So, in the face of mass unemployment there is a pressing need for alternative approaches to work within deprived neighbourhoods that meet people's needs and promote self-reliance. At the same time, there is a pressing social and economic need to reverse the low status and conditions of unpaid work, given the increasing stress and personal cost to those doing it.
>
> Second, employment should be seen not as an end in itself, but as a means to achieving a better quality of life. This means distinguishing between forms of work, with the aim of promoting patterns of work that are socially useful and contribute to greater personal autonomy and fulfilment.
>
> (Mayo 1996: 16–17)

everyone whether they're working or not' (Green Party, undated). These ideas are also extended to the idea of a state pension entitlement based on citizenship rather than years of paid employment, a move which would improve the pension entitlement of many older women who typically have broken work histories. Critics of such an idea point both to the cost and to the effect on incentives, arguing that no one would take certain low-paid jobs if they were guaranteed an income regardless of whether they worked or not.

Recent policy initiatives in the UK

Up until the middle of the 1970s full employment was an avowed aim of governments in the UK, and there was a broad political consensus on the role of the welfare state in supporting the unemployed. Since that time, and especially since the early 1980s and the period of Conservative government, the agreement on policy objectives has broken down and policy has moved progressively away from the full employment ideal.

In the 1980s, Conservative governments followed in the footsteps of Republican politicians in the United States in arguing that the welfare state had resulted in perverse incentives, discouraging the unemployed from seeking work and leading to welfare dependency. As a result, policy shifted in a neo-liberal direction, reducing employment protection and the bargaining power of trade unions whilst simultaneously cutting levels of welfare benefits and increasingly moving to a more conditional system of entitlement to benefit.

Changes to social security benefits were focused around two main perceived problems: first, the need to reduce public expenditure, and secondly, to restructure work incentives. Thus, the targets for policy were to reduce the levels of benefit and require the unemployed to demonstrate their availability or willingness to work (see Chapter 10). As Evans summarizes:

> Social security changed from concerns about coverage in the 1970s to concerns about fiscal constraint and labour market incentives. Targeting, economic incentives, and efficiency became the central concerns of policy in the 1980s. (1998: 263)

The Jobseeker's Allowance introduced in 1996 marked the final point of these developments under the Conservative governments of the 1980s and 1990s. This marked the end of insurance-based unemployment benefit, replacing it finally with an allowance that required claimants to demonstrate that they were actively looking for work as a condition of receiving benefit. Critics of these developments viewed them as simply punitive:

> With declining employment prospects for the unskilled, for black people and for working-class youth, who figure disproportionately among the unemployed, the measures introduced by the Jobseeker's Allowance serve only as a form of punishment. (Novak 1997: 106)

The New Labour government of 1997 came to power committed to the reform of the welfare state. However, this was not heralded as a return to the ideas and policies of the 1960s and 1970s. Instead, the new government was keen to develop a new middle way, which took up some of the ideas of the neo-liberals whilst maintaining the social democratic commitment to social justice. This has been developed into the notion of an active welfare system (see Box 5.5). In relation to employment policies and issues this approach has taken three main forms: measures to encourage and subsidize people into or back into work; measures to make work pay; and a range of training policy measures such as Modern Apprenticeships designed to improve the skills of the workforce . We will consider the first two of these in turn.

New Deals

The centrepiece of the New Labour governments' approach was the New Deal, a raft of welfare to work policies announced in the first budget of the new Labour government in 1997. The avowed aim of the policy was to get the long-term unemployed back into work, on the basis that work is the best guarantor of welfare. The original and primary focus of the policy was the young unemployed: 18–24-year-olds who had been claiming Jobseeker's Allowance for six months or more entered a 'gateway' to work, which involved job search and career advice and training before taking up one of four options (see Box 5.6). As Williams (2002: 54) comments:

> The New Deal for Young People contains two new elements which distinguish it from previous programmes of a similar kind (such as Youth Training). The first is that it is client-centred. Rather than places being available on certain schemes and young people being 'slotted into' what is there, the young person's wishes are intended to be the driving force. Each young person has a Personal Adviser (PA) who sees him/her regularly and works intensively to find an option that is right for him/her.

Box 5.5 **An active welfare system**

The provision of benefits for workless people helps to achieve our social goals by increasing incomes and providing security for some of the most disadvantaged people in the country. But it may also reduce the incentive for some people to go out and look for work. The benefits system in the past has been passive in its administration of benefits. It has been content to hand out money without offering people opportunities to get ahead under their own steam. But people in work stand a much better chance of sharing in rising prosperity than those dependent on benefit. We want a welfare system that provides that all-important safety net for those who cannot work. But we want to ensure that in doing so it also provides people with the opportunities they need to fulfil their potential. This is consistent with the generally held view that it is the responsibility of those who are receiving unemployment benefit to be actively seeking work.

(Department for Work and Pensions 2002: 24)

Box 5.6 **New Deal options**

Young people enter a 'gateway' to the four options; this involves a period of one-to-one advice and guidance which may last up to four months. They then move on to one of the following options:

- A job in the private sector: a job subsidy of up to £60 a week for six months will be paid to employers who employ an unemployed young person.
- A job in the voluntary sector: on the same basis as above.
- A place on an environment taskforce: the young person will receive normal benefit plus £20 a week.
- Full-time education and training.

Any young people who refused to take up one of these options had their benefit cut. Gordon Brown (Chancellor of the Exchequer at the time of announcing the policy) said that there would be no fifth option 'to stay at home in bed watching television' (quoted in the *Financial Times*, 26 June 1997). The scheme developed from its beginnings to cover a range of groups including lone parents, the 50+ and the disabled.

> The various New Deals have been claimed by the government as a major success. However, the Government admits that: 'Our welfare to work strategy is proving to be a success for most groups but people claiming incapacity benefit have not shared in that success'. (DWP 2002a: 5)

The New Deal scheme was inevitably controversial: neo-liberals point to the cost of the programme and argue that it produces no new jobs. Critics from the Left argue that it retains too much of the compulsion that characterized the neo-liberal policies which preceded it (see Box 5.7). Whatever one's view, the policy represented a new attempt at a social investment strategy with active labour market intervention in the attempt to reduce unemployment.

The Work Programme

The coalition government elected in 2010 is committed to a major reform of the benefits system and as part of that has announced a new approach to welfare to work policies—the Work Programme, to be introduced from summer 2011. This is alongside the new Universal Credit which will reform and replace current working age benefits and tax credits with a single welfare payment; the expected implementation date for Universal Credit is 2013 (see Box 5.8).

The Work Programme continues in the tradition of the New Deals in the sense that it is mandatory for some benefit recipients and thus continues the trend toward conditionality in benefits, namely that in order to be eligible for out-of-work benefits, claimants must actively be seeking work or work-related support.

Reforming Incapacity Benefit

The number of people receiving Incapacity Benefit (IB) has risen significantly from some 690,000 people in 1979 to a total of 2.6 million adults of working age in 2010 (DWP 2002a: 7; Beatty and Fothergill forthcoming). This is far greater than the combined total of lone parents and unemployed on state benefits. Not surprisingly, government has become increasingly interested in reducing the numbers on IB. Pathways to Work was a new initiative piloted in a number of areas from October 2003. The pathways approach includes more frequent and mandatory work-focused interviews with Personal Advisers, access to rehabilitation services provided by the National Health Service, and a return to work monetary credit when the individual gets a job. From October 2008 IB was

> ### Box 5.7 **Case study: the right to work or the duty to work?**
>
> The underpinning values implied in the New Deal are essentially *moral*. New opportunities are to be provided, the scheme will be client-centred, young people will be offered experience and training that is relevant and meaningful for them, but there will be . . . no fifth option. Those who 'don't want to work' will be made to work by the imposition of financial sanctions.
>
> 'People have got lots of mega problems in their lives, and they aren't terribly bright, and they need to sort themselves out. I feel that the government have not really grasped that. They've not really recognized that you can frighten people into taking jobs but if you've not solved the problems they've got it will emerge again at another point.' (College principal)
>
> 'No one should have to work. I don't want to. If someone wants to live on the dole, why shouldn't they? Most people [who work] do awful jobs they don't like . . . New Deal? Raw deal. They just want to make me do some s——job.' (Davey)
>
> (Williams 2002: 57, 68, 70)
>
> ### Questions:
>
> - Is it right to make schemes such as New Deal effectively compulsory for certain groups?
> - What kinds of unintended effects might arise from making such schemes compulsory?
> - Can society impose a duty to work on its citizens?

replaced by the Employment Support Allowance (ESA) for new claimants and all were eligible for Pathways to Work support. A new medical test the Work Capability Assessment (WCA) was also introduced along with ESA. Early research on the WCA suggests that it is a tougher test of fitness to work than under the IB, with a lower percentage being deemed unfit to work. It is DWP policy to reduce the number of people on incapacity benefits by 1 million by 2016. ESA claimants will also come under the new Work Programme (see Box 5.8).

Making work pay

The second strand of employment policy involves measures designed to make sure that people entering low-paid jobs can afford to work and are no worse off than if they had stayed on benefits. The major measure under New Labour was the introduction in April 1999 of the National Minimum Wage. In addition to this policy innovation, the New Labour governments introduced a number of tax credits to try to ameliorate the effects of in-work poverty. The Working Families Tax Credit and the Disabled Persons Tax Credit were introduced in October 1999 and replaced by the new Working Tax Credit and the Child Tax Credit (McKnight 2005 and see Chapter 12). The coalition government has committed to creating a Universal Credit to replace all these other work related benefits:

> Universal Credit is an integrated working-age credit that will provide a basic allowance with additional elements for children, disability, housing and caring. It will support people both in and out of work, replacing Working Tax Credit, Child Tax Credit, Housing Benefit, Income Support, income-based Jobseeker's Allowance and income-related Employment and Support Allowance...
>
> Universal Credit represents a fundamental change for Britain's welfare system. It will create a leaner but fairer system administered by a single government department delivering support that is integrated and explicitly focused on ensuring that work always pays. It will substantially reduce poverty and, as well as being fairer, the system will also be firmer. The

Box 5.8 **The Work Programme**

This programme replaces all previous New Deals. It is a single integrated package of support providing personalized help for everyone out of work regardless of the benefit they claim.

The Work Programme is the centrepiece of the Government's plans to reform welfare-to-work provision in the UK, and ensure people have the right support as the economy moves out of recession and into recovery. It is designed to contribute to the Government's key aims of fighting poverty, supporting the most vulnerable, and helping people break the cycle of benefit dependency. The Spending Review, published on October 20th, confirmed the Government's commitment to welfare reform, and to the introduction of the Work Programme in the summer of 2011...

In these difficult economic times, we are very aware of the importance of designing a back to work programme that delivers for our customers, for the taxpayer and for our economy. The Work Programme will avoid the failings of previous employment programmes which were inflexible, short term, and failed to support the hardest to reach customers.

Specialist delivery partners from the public, private and voluntary sectors are best placed to identify ways of getting people back to work, so through the Work Programme we will be giving them the freedom to design services that work, free from over-prescription from central government.

Furthermore, many voluntary sector organisations are particularly well placed to deal with specific local customer needs and we want them to play an important part in the successful delivery of the Work Programme...

Customer groups who will receive support under the Work Programme are as follows:

Customer Group	Time of Referral	Basis for Referral
Jobseeker's Allowance customers aged 25+	From 12 months	Mandatory
Jobseeker's Allowance customers aged 18–24	From 9 months	Mandatory
Jobseeker's Allowance customers who have recently moved from Incapacity Benefit	From 3 months	Mandatory
Jobseeker's Allowance customers facing significant disadvantage (e.g. young people with significant barriers, NEETs, ex-offenders)	From 3 months	Mandatory or voluntary depending on circumstance
All Employment and Support Allowance customers	At any time after their Work Capability Assessment	Voluntary
Employment and Support Allowance (income-related) customers who are placed in the Work-Related Activity Group	When customers are expected to be fit for work in 3 months	Mandatory

Source: DWP (2010) *The Work Programme Prospectus*, available at **http://www.dwp.gov.uk/docs/work-prog-prospectus-v2.pdf**

links between benefit payments, earnings and tax will in turn make the system more secure from fraud and error and conditionality will push people to do as much work as is reasonable for them. (DWP 2010: 3)

The idea is to reduce the complexity of the benefit system and thus the cost of its administration, but the policy change also reinforces the conditionality which has come to characterize out-of-work benefits since the late 1980s.

Cartoon 5.2 Is any job better than no job?

© Jeremy Banks 2003

Conclusion

Despite a number of decades of persistent unemployment and widespread popular fears about an emerging 'work-shy', delinquent, and socially marginal underclass, work, or rather employment, seems to be as popular as ever. Most young people want to find a good job, many lone parents would like the opportunity to work, many disabled people feel unfairly excluded from the world of paid employment, and substantial numbers of those forced to take early retirement in the 1990s found other jobs or would have liked to have done so. Employment is still seen by the majority as the ticket to full participation in society. The problem for the UK and other European societies is whether it is possible to produce both high levels of employment and social justice or equality. The US example of a low-wage, low-skills, high-employment economy up until the current recession was impressive in the number of jobs it provided but worrying with respect to the growing ranks of the working poor. This raises the question of whether any job is better for the individual's welfare than no job (see Cartoon 5.2). The Swedish example of a high-wage, high-skills, high-employment economy has looked increasingly unsustainable as competition in the global economy heats up, and countries such as Germany are trying to abandon this route. With the election of the coalition government in 2010, the already existing tendency for the UK to follow a US rather than a Northern European approach to employment and unemployment issues has been magnified. One new issue that is likely to come centre stage of the employment agenda in the coming decade is that of health at work and the extent to which the work currently available is good for health and well-being. This concern is lent further urgency by the ageing population and government's desire to encourage us all to work for longer.

FURTHER READING

McKnight, A. (2005), 'Employment: tackling poverty through "work for those who can"' in **Hills, J. and Stewart, K.,** eds, *A More Equal Society? New Labour, Poverty, Inequality and Social Exclusion* (Bristol: The Policy Press). This chapter in an edited collection provides an interesting overview and review of New Labour policy in the field of employment.

Mooney, G. (2004), 'Exploring the dynamics of work, personal lives and social policy' in **Mooney, G.,** ed., *Work, Personal Lives and Social Policy* (Bristol: The Policy Press and The Open University). This chapter provides an engaging introduction to issues such as how to conceptualize work, the relationship between welfare and work, and recent trends in the world of work.

Beck, U., *The Brave New World of Work* (Cambridge: Polity Press, 2000). A leading social theorist of the last decade argues for a radical rethink of how we conceptualize society. In this book he addresses the implications of the emergence of a risk society for the world of work.

Bradley, H., Erikson, M., Stephenson, C., and Williams, S., *Myths at Work* (Cambridge: Polity Press, 2000). An excellent volume which systematically examines from a critical perspective prevailing popular assumptions about the world of work, for example the increase in non-standard and casual work, the feminization of work, and the need for increased skills amongst today's employees.

Esping-Andersen, G., 'After the golden age? Welfare state dilemmas in a global economy', in **Esping-Andersen,** ed., *Welfare States in Transition: National Adaptations in Global Economies* (London: Sage, 1996). This chapter provides a good review of the problems facing welfare states in the post-full employment period.

Mead, L. M., *From Welfare to Work: Lessons from America* (London: Institute of Economic Affairs, 1997). This book provides an introduction to Mead's work, a leading American thinker on welfare reform along with commentaries from a number of British social policy writers and thinkers, including Frank Field, who was minister for welfare reform for the first fifteen months of the New Labour government in 1997–8.

Philpott, J., ed., *Working for Full Employment* (London: Routledge, 1997). Contributions to this collection examine the nature and consequences of contemporary unemployment and examine different policy responses. A number of contributions compare an Anglo-American deregulation approach with the more European regulation approach.

USEFUL WEBSITES

The Joseph Rowntree Foundation regularly funds research on work and welfare and the most recent reports can be downloaded from: **www.jrf.org.uk**.

Reports and policy documents from the UK Department for Work and Pensions can be found at: **http://www.dwp.gov.uk/resourcecentre/policy_strategy.asp.**

The Work Foundation publishes useful evidence-based reports on aspects of the quality of work lives and the benefits and losses of greater flexibility in the labour market: **www.theworkfoundation.com.**

The Equalities and Human Rights Commission, which oversees discrimination and human rights legislation, has a wealth of information about the employment situation of women, older workers, and ethnic minorities: **http://www.equalityhumanrights.com/.**

The Office for National Statistics (ONS) publishes the annual summary document *Social Trends,* which has a wealth of employment information in it; it is also the gateway for a the labour force survey and a range of information on the labour market and unemployment: **http://www.statistics.gov.uk/default.asp.**

ESSAY QUESTIONS

1 In what ways has the nature of work changed in the last thirty years? Have there been winners and losers as a result of these changes?

2 Should the attempt to provide 'full employment' be a guiding principle of governments' social policy?

3 Why are young people more vulnerable to unemployment?

4 Is there a social duty on everyone who can, to get paid employment?

5 Critically assess the New Deal policies; are they a good response to labour market problems?

@ ONLINE RESOURCE CENTRE

For additional material and resources, please visit the Online Resource Centre at:
www.oxfordtextbooks.co.uk/orc/baldock4e/.

The family and welfare

Jan Pahl

Contents

Introduction

'The family' is a controversial topic. There are some commentators who deplore the changes which are taking place in family life, while others applaud the end of what they see as damaging patterns of family relationships. Some argue that 'family policy' has gone too far and has created a culture of dependency that loads intolerable burdens on the welfare state, while others insist that 'family policy' in Britain has not gone far enough in supporting families and their members in all their diversity. Behind these debates lie deep ideological divides about the proper relationship between the private sphere of the family and the public sphere where social policy is made and implemented.

The situation is complicated by the fact that this chapter is being written at a time of political turmoil. The coalition government, which came to power in May 2010, has made a variety of pronouncements about family policy. At the time of writing it is not certain which of these policies will be implemented, what form the implementation will take, and what the implications will be. Readers of this book will be able to evaluate the impact of recent policy changes on individuals and on families over the coming years.

> ### Learning outcomes
>
> In this chapter we shall be looking at the facts behind the rhetoric. After reading it you should be able to discuss the following questions:
>
> 1 What changes are taking place in the lives of families and their members?
> 2 What part do families, and individuals within families, play in the production of welfare?
> 3 What problems can occur within families and what are the potential solutions?
> 4 What are the principles that underlie family policy and what has been the impact of recent policy changes?

Families and households

Definitions

'Family' and 'household' are important terms for this topic, so we begin with some definitions. The household is a key unit in social policy, since it is the focus of a great many policy interventions. For example, means-tested social security payments are calculated on the basis of household income; council tax is levied on households, not individuals; and many statistics are based on the unit of the household.

One definition of the household is given in *Social Trends*, the annual publication of the Office for National Statistics:

> A household is a person living alone or a group of people who have the address as their only or main residence and who either share one meal a day or share the living accommodation. (ONS 2010)

So households are based on a common place of residence and some sharing of either food or accommodation. Of course, in many cases the 'household' contains a single 'family', but the concept of family is intrinsically much more complicated than the concept of household.

Many definitions have been suggested for the term 'family'. In Britain it seems to be agreed that a married couple and their dependent children constitute a family, but when other social groupings and other cultures are concerned, definitions become less secure. The definitional possibilities can be explored by asking a range of different people whether, in their opinion, the following constitute 'a family':

- one parent and his or her children?
- a cohabiting couple and their children?
- an elderly person and an adult child?
- a lesbian couple and the children of one of them?
- a father living apart from his wife and children but supporting them financially?
- a three-generation household with parents, their adult children, and their grandchildren?

The answers suggest that the idea of the family is essentially subjective, reflecting the norms and values of individuals and cultures with regard to family life; the family has been described as a 'shifting concept' (Hantrais 2004: 3).

However, there do seem to be some characteristics which define a 'family' for most people. These include:

- marriage or a marriage-like relationships between adults;
- the presence of children who are or have been dependent on the adults;
- sharing of resources such as living space, money, and property;
- continuity over time;
- links with other kin.

The official definition of the family, used in all UK government censuses and surveys, is that a family is:

> a married or cohabiting couple, either with or without their never-married children (of any age), including couples with no children or a lone parent together with his or her never-married child or children. (ONS 2010)

However, even this definition might be controversial, since it excludes households which some people would regard as 'families', such as lesbian or gay couples with children, and includes some households which might not be seen as 'families', such as cohabiting couples without children.

A useful distinction has been made between the nuclear family and the extended family. The nuclear family typically consists of one or two adults living together in a household with their dependent children. However, many nuclear families are embedded in larger kin networks, with whom they may from time to time share living space, money, and property, and which may include grandparents, aunts and uncles, cousins, and so on. This larger kin network is described as an extended family, and though it is often described as being characteristic of more traditional societies, it remains an important source of support in Britain.

Another useful distinction is between those who focus on 'the family', a term which implies that there is one, ideal, type of family, and those who focus on 'families', a term which allows for the increasing diversity of family forms. The idea of 'the family' rests on the assumption that the most natural and desirable family is composed of two married parents and their children, with the father as the main breadwinner and the mother as the homemaker, who fits any paid work around her responsibilities for the home and children. The idea of 'families' underlines the point that family life and relationships can take many different forms and that no one type of family should be privileged over the others. For a useful discussion of different forms of family see McCarthy and Edwards (2011:70).

Debates about 'family values'

All the changes taking place in family life throughout Europe and North America have produced fierce debates. On the one hand some people have argued that the 'breakdown of the traditional family' is to blame for a range of social problems, from unemployment and crime to violence and lone-parent families. On the other hand, other people have argued that the 'traditional family' is itself the problem. From this point of view, family violence and lone-parent families are symptoms of inequalities, and even exploitation, within the family, and the changes taking place in family life are to be welcomed rather than deplored.

'Family values' can differ substantially between generations. A study of teenagers showed that their attitudes on gender roles, employment for mothers, family relationships, and sex differed significantly from those held by adults (Phillips 2004). Teenagers were far more accepting of lone parents, with the majority agreeing that one parent is as good as two at bringing up a child. They were less likely to condemn underage sex, and more likely to support the idea of mothers having jobs. However, we cannot be sure whether these attitudes will continue into adult life: in other words, do they reflect the views of people at a particular stage in life, or will they continue into adulthood as part of the increasing liberalization of norms about the family?

These debates reflect profoundly different ideological approaches to families and family life. Since ideology will be a key concept for this chapter, it may be useful to begin with a definition.

> Ideologies are sets of ideas, assumptions and images, by which people make sense of society, which give a clear social identity, and which serve in some way to legitimize power relations in society. (McLennan 1991: 114)

This definition underlines the fact that ideologies not only influence the ways in which individuals think about themselves and their place in the world, but also shape the development of social policy and social action in the broader, political arena. One way of making sense of different ideologies about the family is to consider the theoretical perspectives which underlie them.

Theoretical and policy perspectives on the family

Many theoretical explanations of the social world have been developed within the discipline of sociology. In thinking about families, three theoretical perspectives are particularly relevant.

Three theoretical perspectives

The functionalist analysis of the family was developed by the American sociologists, Parsons and Bales (1956). They suggested that the nuclear family, consisting of a breadwinner/husband and a homemaker/wife, is the type of family which fits most easily with the requirements of industrial society. Lacking close ties to a wider kin network, the nuclear family is able to move from place to place following the demands of the labour market, and generally to perform the functions necessary to the stable continuation of an industrial society.

From this theoretical perspective the modern nuclear family has two main functions: the socialization of children and 'personality stabilization' or 'tension management' for the adults. Parsons and Bales made a clear distinction between the roles of the husband/father and the wife/mother. They saw the father's role as being instrumental, with his employment providing for the economic well-being of the family, while the mother's role was affective, being concerned primarily with the emotional well-being of the family. In Parsons and Bales's analysis the tasks assigned to each sex arose out of biological differences, and in particular out of the mother's responsibility for childbearing and rearing.

Functionalist theories were linked with ideas about modernity, which assume that societies progress towards greater uniformity, leaving behind dysfunctional, or even simply diverse, forms of family life. There was an underlying assumption that the middle-class American family of the 1950s and 1960s was by definition a superior form of the family and one to which other groups should aspire. It was often described as the 'normal' family.

Even though the functionalist perspective is now seen as old-fashioned and ethnocentric, there are ways in which the ideologies which underpinned this work are still powerful. For example, the British Social Attitudes Survey includes a question which asks respondents whether they agree or disagree with the following statement:

A husband's job is to earn the money; a wife's job is to look after the home and family.

Every time that this question is asked there is a minority of people who agree: for example, in 2002, 20 per cent of men and 15 per cent of women said that they agreed with the statement, down from 32 and 26 per cent respectively in 1989 (Crompton, Brockman, and Wiggins 2003: 164). The functionalist perspective on the family is still around. However, a powerful critique of functionalism has been developed by feminists.

Secondly, there is the feminist perspective, which sees the 'normal' or traditional family as essentially unequal. It argues that the dependence of women and children on the male breadwinner creates a damaging power imbalance within the family which is the source of many problems, especially for women and children, and for those who do not fit into traditional family forms. As Charles puts it:

Feminism has developed a critique of 'the family', arguing that it ensures women's dependency on men and their ideological confinement to the domestic sphere and that it institutionalizes heterosexuality and defines other forms of sexuality as deviant. (Charles 2000: 179)

Other feminists have seen the family as the site of a particular type of exploitation:

(Families) are not just random sets of people united by bonds of affection and kinship who live together and share out the jobs that need doing so as to offer each other practical support in a joint endeavour to get along in the world. Rather they are . . . part of a system of labour relations in which men benefit from, and exploit, the work of women—and sometimes of their children and other male relatives too. (Delphy and Leonard 1992: 1)

To sum up, the feminist perspective on the family argues that:

- The traditional family is characterized by inequalities between women and men, and between children and parents, which continue despite the rhetoric of increasing equality.
- These inequalities are translated into inequalities in the allocation of resources, such as money, and in the work done within families, including childcare, domestic work, and caring for dependent members of families.
- These inequalities are maintained by the state, through social and economic policies which assume that families will contain a male breadwinner and a woman who is responsible for childcare and domestic work.
- It would be better if responsibilities and privileges within the family could be shared more equally, and if social policies supported the work which families do, recognizing the variety of forms which families can take.

From the feminist perspective, the increases in cohabitation, in divorce, and in the numbers of lone-parent families are all symptoms of the dissatisfaction which women feel with the traditional form of the family.

Thirdly, there is the New Right perspective, which argues that the changes occurring in family life are evidence of a deterioration which is damaging to all. The rise in births outside marriage, the increase in divorce initiated by women, and the failure of fathers to support their children are all symptoms of what is going wrong. The following quotation may be taken as an example of this perspective:

We also see growing evidence of child homelessness, drug abuse among the young, the physical abuse and neglect of babies and children, high rates of teenage pregnancy and a continuing cycle of broken relationships. As the evidence continues to accumulate, there is one
persistent factor which so often links all this unhappiness. It is the disintegration of the
family. (Kirby 2002: iv)

The Institute of Economic Affairs has been active in setting out the agenda of the New Right in relation to the family, in publications such as those by Morgan (1995 and 2000) and Kirby (2005).
Briefly, the New Right perspective can be summed up as follows:

- The 'normal', and most socially valuable form of the family, consists of a married couple, with
both parents committed to the care of their children, the father through his responsibility for the
family's economic well-being and the mother through her responsibility for the home and
family.
- This form of the family is currently under threat because of demographic and ideological changes
which reflect the influence of feminism, individualism, and a more general moral decay.
- The state has played a part in undermining the normal family, by providing support for other
types of families, by failing to reward marriage, and by tolerating high levels of unemployment
among young males.
- It would be better if more families conformed to the traditional pattern and if social policies were
designed to support marriage, child rearing by mothers, the employment of fathers, and stability
in family life.

The state, politics, and family policy

There have been a number of attempts to produce a definition of family policy. Hantrais and Letablier concluded:

For a social policy to be described as family policy . . . the family would need to be the deliberate target of specific actions, and the measures should be designed so as to have an impact
on family resources and, ultimately, on family structure. (Hantrais and Letablier 1996: 139)

However, definitions of family policy tend to founder against the rocks of national and cultural
differences. In particular, states vary greatly in the extent to which it is seen as appropriate for governments to intervene in family life. Britain never had an explicit family policy until 2003, when the
first Minister for Children, Young People and Families was appointed. By contrast, in Finland,
France, Germany, Greece, Ireland, Italy, Luxembourg, Portugal, and Spain, the constitution recognizes the family as a social institution and undertakes to afford it protection. Some countries, such
as Germany and France, have for many years had a designated Minister for the Family (Hantrais
and Letablier 1996).

There is an ongoing political debate about whether there are particular sorts of families and relationships which the state should encourage or discourage. For example, should social policies
favour marriage over other sorts of relationships or should policies give equal treatment to married
and cohabiting couples, two-parent families and lone-parent families, or heterosexual and same-
sex relationships?

Public statements by politicians reveal much about ways to track changing attitudes and policies
with regard to the family. As an example, let us look at how the Conservative Party changed over the
years with regard to family policy. In the 2001 election the Conservatives explicitly privileged marriage by supporting a tax allowance which did not go to lone parents and which was of particular
help to couples where one of the partners was not earning:

Despite all the evidence that marriage provides the best environment for bringing up children, married couples do not fit into Labour's politically correct agenda. That is why they

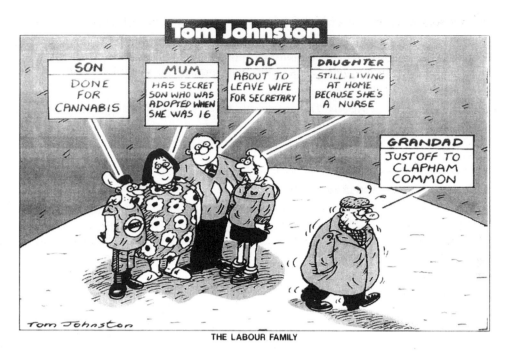

Cartoon 6.1 Tom Johnston (PC4879); first published in the *Mirror* on 6 November 1998

have penalized millions of families by abolishing the Married Couple's Tax Allowance ... We will introduce a new Married Couple's Allowance which will give a tax cut worth £1,000 to many families when they need help most. (Conservative Party 2001)

In 2001 the Conservatives once again lost the election. In the following years they developed a critique of what was called 'Broken Britain'. This term was used to describe a perceived state of social decay, characterized by phenomena such as child neglect, teenage pregnancy, lone-parent families, binge drinking and antisocial behaviour. In the 2010 election campaign, the leader of the Conservatives, David Cameron, promised to 'fix' Broken Britain.

In the 2010 election the Conservatives gained the largest number of seats, but in order to form a government had to enter into a coalition with the Liberal Democrat Party. The narrowness of their win, and the compromises demanded by the coalition, may have led David Cameron to change his stance towards families. In a speech given in December 2010 he was still keen to privilege marriage, but he was also giving support to other types of relationships. He said:

All the evidence shows that the strength and stability of adult relationships are vital to the well-being of children ... I think it's wrong that we are one of the few countries in the world that doesn't recognize marriage in the tax system and I want to see that change. I know that not everyone agrees with this proposal and as part of the coalition agreement we have agreed with the Liberal Democrats that they will abstain on any budget resolutions on transferable tax allowances for married couples. But my view remains that we should recognize and value the commitment people make to one another. And by the way, that's whether it's between a man and a woman, a man and a man, or a woman and another woman. (Cameron 2010)

This last remark represents a tremendous volte-face for the party of conservative values and traditional attitudes to family life.

Demographic trends in family life

Information about the changing patterns of family life comes from a variety of different sources, including the ten-yearly national Census of Population, the General Register Office, which collates certificates for births, marriages, and deaths, and a variety of quantitative and qualitative surveys. The annual review, *Social Trends*, presents a great deal of quantitative data in a very accessible form, and is an essential source of information about all areas of social policy in Britain (ONS 2010). In this chapter it is possible to summarize only a few of the most important trends in family life.

Changes in birth rates and in fertility

First results from the 2001 Census, revealed that the population of the United Kingdom numbered 58,789,194 million (National Statistics Online 2002). It is estimated that this had grown to around 61.8 million by 2010 (ONS 2010). Around one person in every fourteen described themselves as being a member of a minority ethnic group. Census data can be used in a variety of ways to help us understand the changing nature of family life.

The age structure of the population, as shown in a population pyramid, can be a striking way of revealing the life chances of particular individuals and age groups. The population pyramid in Figure 6.1 shows that variations in the number of births and deaths can be quite substantial from one age cohort to another. The bulge in the pyramid in those in their early sixties in 2005 represents the 'baby boom' which followed the Second World War, while the even bigger bulge among people now in their forties and early fifties is a result of the fashion for large families in the 1960s (ONS 2005: 3).

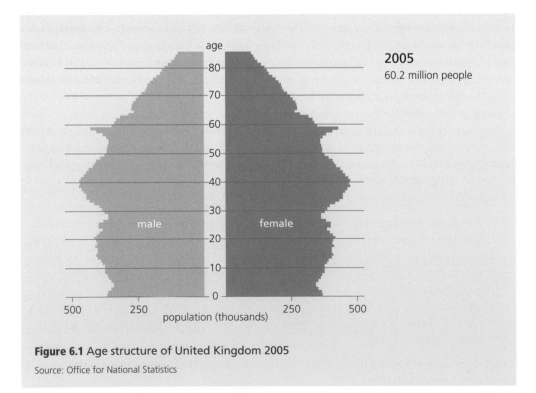

Figure 6.1 Age structure of United Kingdom 2005

Source: Office for National Statistics

Figure 6.1 shows how individual experience can be strongly affected by the age cohort into which a person is born. Those born in the late 1940s, or during the 1960s, will be competing throughout their lives with a larger number of peers for school places, jobs, housing, healthcare, and so on. By contrast, the relatively small cohorts born during the 1930s and the 1970s will face less competition in all these areas. However, when the 'bulge' generations reach old age there will be a relatively small population of working age to support them financially or to care for them. There has been some concern about the effects of these changes in the 'dependency ratio', that is, in the ratio of those who are dependent to those who are economically active.

Changes in households and families

Information about demographic changes is sometimes presented in terms of 'households' and sometimes in terms of 'families'; when using this sort of data it is important to notice which term is being used.

The average size of households in Great Britain has almost halved since the beginning of the twentieth century and in 2001 stood at 2.4 people per household. However, this figure conceals large variations in household type. There has been a decrease in the proportion of 'traditional' family households. So in 1961, 38 per cent of households consisted of married couples with their dependent children, while 26 per cent of all households consisted of couples with no children. However, by 2001 only 23 per cent of households consisted of the 'traditional' family, while couples without children made up 29 per cent of all households (ONS 2005: 20).

One-person households increased from 15 per cent of all households in 1971 to 29 per cent in 2001. This reflects a number of different factors, including the increasing numbers of young people who are financially able to leave the parental home but who delay marriage, the increases in divorce and separation among those who do marry, and the rise in the expectation of life, especially among older women. All these factors make it more likely, and more possible, for individuals to set up homes of their own. It is likely that the number of one-person households will continue to increase.

Turning from households to families, we can see that changes have also taken place in the demography of the family. In particular, there has been an increase in the proportion of lone-parent families, by comparison with other types of families. However, despite the alarms of the New Right, the two-parent family is still very much the norm. Lone-parent families made up 20 per cent of all families in 2001 compared with 7 per cent in 1972, but this still leaves the great majority of children living with both their parents. Most lone-parent families are headed by mothers, and lone fathers continue to be very much in the minority, making up 9 per cent of all lone parents, and in general caring for older children than do lone mothers (ONS 2002: 48).

It is important not to regard being a lone parent as a permanent state. An analysis of the British Household Panel Survey found that in the early 1990s, on average, around 15 per cent of lone mothers per year ceased to be lone parents, usually as a result of forming new partnerships. If such a rate were maintained, half of all lone parents would remain so for only around four years (ONS 1997: 43).

Changes in marriage and divorce

There have been profound changes in the rate of marriage and in the age at which people marry. The marriage rate rose from 1931 to 1971 and then fell dramatically: between 1981 and 1992 the marriage rate per 1,000 of the population fell from 7.1 to 5.4. However, it has been argued that the period from 1950 to 1980 represented an anomaly, in that marriage rates were unusually high, and that rates in the 1990s represented a return to normal. The age at which individuals married rose by about two years between 1961 and 1994, to 28 years for men and 26 years for women, though this figure masks social class differences, in which those of higher social class tend to delay marriage even longer. Similar patterns are found in other European countries, though the United Kingdom has one of the highest marriage rates in the European Union.

There has also been a change towards more cohabitation before marriage, to the extent that this has become the norm, compared with only 7 per cent of those marrying at the beginning of the 1970s (Berthoud and Gershuny 2000: 220). Results from the British Household Panel Survey showed that for the most part cohabitation is a part of the process of getting married and not a substitute for marriage. There has been a parallel rise in the percentage of children born to cohabiting couples; in the majority of cases these births are registered by both parents, who often go on to marry. However, cohabitations are more likely to break up than marriages. So 70 per cent of children born within marriage will live their entire childhood with both parents, but only 36 per cent of children born to a cohabiting couple will live with both parents throughout their childhood (Berthoud and Gershuny 2000: 40).

Attitudes towards cohabitation vary greatly. It has been seen as a threat to marriage, delaying it and creating an environment in which it is devalued (Morgan 2000). In 1973 it was considered so rare, and so embarrassing, that the General Household Survey did not even ask about it (Berthoud and Gershuny 2000: 4). However, surveys show that cohabitation is now becoming accepted as normal and may even be preferred, particularly among younger people. In 2000 the British Social Attitudes Survey asked people whether they agreed with the statement, 'It's all right for a couple to live together without intending to get married'. The proportion agreeing varied from 85 per cent of those aged 12–19, to 69 per cent of those aged over 18, and 35 per cent of those aged over 65 (Phillips 2004: 58; Park et al. 2001).

The British Social Attitudes Survey also casts light on the idea that cohabitation is concentrated among the less educated, less skilled, and unemployed, people sometimes conceptualized as being part of an 'underclass'. In reality the results showed that there was no significant relationship between cohabitation and social class, and that people on benefits were less likely than others to cohabit (Park et al. 2001: 43).

Fewer marriages mean fewer divorces, so there has been a fall in the numbers of couples getting divorced. However, the United Kingdom still has the highest divorce rate in the European Union, and it has been estimated that four out of ten new marriages will end in divorce. In 1994, over one half of all divorces were to couples with children under 16. Wives were much more likely to initiate divorce than husbands. Reasons for the divorce also varied, with women more likely to seek a divorce because of the unreasonable behaviour of their partners, and husbands more likely to cite adultery as the reason for the breakdown of the marriage (Haskey 1996).

The cumulative effect of these changes is that stepfamilies are becoming more common. The children in these families may have two parents and two step-parents, they may move between two different 'homes', and they may have up to eight grandparents. Some of the complexities involved in living in a stepfamily have been described by Ferri and Smith (1998) and Barnes et al. (1998). The evidence suggests that remarriages, and therefore stepfamilies, are at greater risk of breakdown than first marriages (McCarthy and Edwards 2011; 40).

Another important change has been the recognition given to same-sex relationships. Until the Sexual Offences Act 1967, sexual relations between men were illegal. Even after being legalized, lesbian and gay relationships continued to be ignored by the law, which meant, for example, that if one partner died the other might find the house they had shared being sold in order to pay the tax on the estate. The Civil Partnerships Act 2004 allowed people of the same sex to register as 'civil partners' of each other. This gave them the same rights and responsibilities as married people, though without formally being able to say they were 'married'. However, their situation became the same as that of married people with regard to tax and inheritance, employment benefits, state and occupational pensions, and the duty to provide for each other.

Families do not exist in a vacuum, but are profoundly influenced by wider society. Of particular importance are the changes taking place in patterns of employment. These are discussed in Chapter 5, so here we can simply summarize some of the main trends. Over the past twenty years it has become the norm for women to be in employment, even when they are mothers of young children.

> ## Box 6.1 **Recent changes in families and households**
>
> - An increasing trend towards smaller household sizes, so that the average household size in Britain fell from 3.1 people per household in 1961 to 2.4 people in 2009
> - A decrease in the proportion of dependent children living with married parents from 77 per cent in 1997 to 63 per cent in 2009
> - A fall in the number of marriages in England and Wales from 267,961 in 2000 to around 231,500 in 2007
> - A fall in the number of divorces in England and Wales, to around 128,500 in 2007, which was the lowest number of divorces in a single year since 1976
> - A fall in the proportion of babies born to women aged under 25 in England and Wales, from 47 per cent of all births in 1971 to 25 per cent in 2008
> - An increase in babies born before their parents were married, so that in 2007 in England and Wales the average age of women when their first child was born was 27.5 years, compared with an average age at first marriage of 29.8 years
>
> See: ONS 2010.

Increasing education levels and higher qualifications for women have led to increasing levels of attainment in the labour market (Crompton 2003; Crompton et al. 2010). Though discrimination against women persists, it is less prevalent and less severe than it once was. Changes such as these have profound implications for the ways in which families work and care for their members.

The main changes which have taken place in families and households are summarized in Box 6.1.

The production of welfare within families

One theme of this book is that the welfare of individuals is produced, not only by the welfare state, but also by the market and by the family. This next section considers the ways in which families produce welfare for their members.

Types of welfare provided within families

There are four general points which have to be made at the outset. First, for many people the family is a first line of defence against the 'five giant evils' which Beveridge saw as the targets for the welfare state: want, disease, ignorance, squalor, and idleness (Beveridge Report 1942: para. 8). When all goes well, families provide a means of redistributing income from those who earn to those who do not, in order to ensure that individual family members have enough food and clothes, and a roof over their heads. People with minor illnesses and long-term disabilities are usually cared for at home, and home is the place where children are nurtured and where their education begins. Of course, other types of welfare can also be provided within the family, from loving relationships to opportunities for leisure and pleasure of different sorts. However, for the purposes of this chapter the focus will be on the welfare associated with being fed and clothed and housed, and being cared for in childhood and at times of physical dependence.

Secondly, it is important to remember that 'families' do not produce anything: it is the individuals within families who produce, and consume, any welfare which may be created. So in this section we shall have to move the focus from the family itself to the individuals who make up the family. This change of focus reflects a move between disciplines. Traditionally economists have used the household/family as the key unit of analysis, while sociologists have been concerned about the different perspectives of individuals within households: the idea that there can be profound differences between 'the husband's marriage' and 'the wife's marriage' was first introduced by the American feminist sociologist, Bernard (1982).

Thirdly, creating welfare at home is work. This point was made vividly by John Masefield in the following poem:

> To get the whole world out of bed
> And washed, and dressed, and warmed, and fed,
> To work, and back to bed again,
> Believe me, Saul, costs worlds of pain.
>   (Masefield 1946: 61)

Work at home may be unpaid, but it is still work, according to the definition suggested in a sociology textbook:

> Work is the carrying out of tasks, involving the expenditure of mental and physical effort, which have as their objective the production of goods and services catering for human needs. An occupation is work which is done for a regular wage. (Giddens 2006: 741)

One of the concomitants of the development of a welfare state is the move of many sorts of work out of the home: this has particularly affected women, as they have moved into paid work as nurses, social workers, teachers, nannies, and care assistants, doing the sorts of tasks which women in previous generations performed as part of their unpaid family duties.

Fourthly, there is a trade-off between different ways of producing welfare, which relates to the shifting boundaries between paid and unpaid work. A mother who does not have paid employment is able to look after her children herself, cook for the family, and clean the house, and she may produce goods such as soft furnishings and home-made clothes. If the same woman has a full-time job she is likely to have to pay for childcare and to buy more pre-prepared meals; she may employ another woman to clean the house and she will probably buy ready-made soft furnishings and clothes.

In the following pages we shall consider three different types of work, each of which produces welfare for individuals within families; we begin with the work of childcare and with the social policies which are most relevant to the support of children within families.

Childcare and child support

In 2001 there were 12.1 million children aged under 16 in the United Kingdom, with slightly more boys than girls; 10 per cent of children belonged to a minority ethnic group. The majority of children were growing up living with both their parents, but just over 1 million lived in stepfamilies (ONS 2002: 18). Parents do most of the work of childcare, but grandparents also make a significant contribution (Gray 2005).

Having children involves both expense and hard work. One study calculated that a child reaching his or her seventeenth birthday will have cost around £50,000 (Middleton et al. 1997). However, this calculation included only direct costs and did not take account of the lost income of the person who took the prime responsibility for childcare, usually the mother. An estimate of the amount involved concluded that the total could be as high as £202,000 (at 1990 values), of which 40 per cent represented being out of employment during the child's early years, 36 per cent represented working shorter hours in order to fit in with childcare, while 25 per cent represented lower rates of pay because of loss of work experience (Joshi 1992: 121).

There are a number of different reasons why childcare has become an important issue in social policy. The first reason has been concern about the welfare of children, in a society in which many children live in poverty, in which some parents are divorced or separated, and in which a proportion

> **Box 6.2 The Children Act 1989**
>
> The Act rests on the belief that children are generally best looked after within the family with both parents playing a full part and without resort to legal proceedings. That belief is reflected in the:
>
> - concept of parental responsibility;
> - ability of unmarried fathers to share that responsibility by agreement with the mother;
> - local authorities' duty to give support to children and their families.
>
> (Department of Health 1989a: 1)

of parents are failing in their parental responsibilities. For many years the law about caring for, bringing up, and protecting children from abuse had been inconsistent and fragmented. The Children Act 1989 aimed to bring about radical changes and improvements in the law and to provide a single and consistent statement of it.

The Children Act was a long and complex piece of legislation, which was generally welcomed when it came into force. It provided a single and consistent statement of the law that applies to the welfare of children. A guide to the Act and a discussion of the ideologies which are reflected in it were provided by Freeman (1992). He suggested that the Children Act expressed ideologies from both the Right and the Left. On the one hand, it presented the two-parent family as the ideal and warned of the dangers of too much state intervention. On the other hand, it gave new and stronger powers both to local authorities and to children.

The principles which underpinned The Children Act were the basis for its many and complex provisions. The first principle was that the welfare of the child should be paramount.

The second principle was that there should be as little delay as possible in making decisions about the child's future, since delay was likely to prejudice the welfare of the child, because of the uncertainty which this creates, and also because of the damage which delay may do to relationships.

The third principle was incorporated into a checklist which courts should consider in any contested cases. The checklist included such issues as the child's physical, emotional, and educational needs, the likely effect of any change in circumstances, the capacities of the parents to care for the child, and the implications of the child's age, sex, and background. The child's 'background' included his or her religion, racial origin, culture, and language, and this principle reflected the increasingly multicultural nature of the British population.

The fourth principle was concerned with minimal intervention. The Act stated that a court should not make an order 'unless it considers that doing so would be better for the child than making no order at all' (section 1(5)). In this the Act reflected the then Conservative government's suspicion of state interference into family life.

Finally, the Act laid stress on the principle of parental responsibility, marking a shift of emphasis from parental rights to parental responsibilities. The aim seemed to be to stress that parents, rather than the state, have the prime responsibility for children. For further discussion of other responses to child abuse and neglect, see Chapter 14.

The second reason for childcare becoming a focus for social policy has been the rise in the numbers of lone-parent families. This has led to growing concern about the provision of financial support for dependent children. The key issue is whether children living in lone-parent families should be financially supported by the state, through the social security system, by the earnings of the caring parent, usually the mother, or by contributions from the absent parent, usually the father. Compared with other European countries, in Britain a relatively high proportion of lone parents depend on the social security system. Concern about the financial burdens which this laid on the state created the climate of opinion which produced the Child Support Act 1991.

> ## Box 6.3 **The Child Support Act 1991**
>
> The aims of the Child Support Act are to:
>
> - ensure that parents accept financial responsibility for their children whenever they can afford to do so;
> - strike a fair and reasonable balance between 'first' and 'second' families;
> - maintain parents' incentives to take paid work rather than depending on social security.
>
> (Secretary of State for Social Security 1995: 10)

The Child Support Act led to the setting up of the Child Support Agency. This organization undertook to develop a system for ensuring that money would be transferred from the 'absent parent', usually the father, to the 'parent with care', usually the mother. A formula was developed for calculating the amount which should be paid, with an upper limit set at 30 per cent of the absent parent's net income.

From the start the Child Support Agency was criticized from a variety of different positions. Some men's groups considered that the payments to parents with care were set too high and that the formula did not take adequate account of the cost of supporting second families. Some women's groups resented the pressure that was put on women to name the fathers of their children and the failure of the Agency to get fathers to pay what they owed. There was continuing conflict over the extent to which the system benefited the social security budget rather than the children concerned, because fathers' payments would be deducted from mothers' benefit entitlements (Ridge 2005).

At the time of writing this chapter, changes have been announced by the Child Maintenance and Enforcement Commission, which is now responsible for the work of the Child Support Agency. New systems for calculating child maintenance are to be introduced and it will be interesting to see what difference these make to parents claiming maintenance for the children in their care.

Child poverty continues to be a serious issue. Defining poverty can be complicated but a commonly used measure is that it means living in a household with below half the mean income, after housing costs are taken into account. On this basis one-third of children were living in poverty in 1998–9 and the extent of poverty was three times as high as it had been in 1979. This meant that when the Labour government came into power in 1997, 3.4 million children were living in poverty and Britain had the highest proportion of children living in poverty of any European country except Italy (Piachaud and Sutherland 2002).

When the Labour government was elected in 1997 it had a number of aims with regard to family policy. These aims included reducing child poverty, developing provision for childcare, and creating more family-friendly patterns of employment. What policies were introduced to achieve these goals and what was their impact? A useful review has been provided by Williams (2005). There is only space here to summarize the main points.

Reducing child poverty was tackled mainly through tax and benefit changes and through encouraging parents into paid work. These included:

- increasing Child Benefit;
- introducing the Working Tax Credit;
- introducing the Child Tax Credit;
- introducing the Child Trust Fund.

The Child Poverty Action Group calculated that between 1998 and 2005, 600,000 children were lifted out of poverty, but 3.5 million or 28 per cent of all children still lived in poverty (Child Poverty Action Group 2005). An overview of the years from 1997 to 2005 concluded:

Cartoon 6.2 David Simonds (PC2156); first published in the *New Statesman* on 6 June 1997

Child well-being is improving. Educational attainment is higher, child poverty rates are declining steadily and there are some signs that youth crime is decreasing. However, there is cause for concern in other areas. The UK continues to have the highest number of children in workless households in the EU, school exclusions are increasing and homelessness for families with children seems to be going up. (Bradshaw and Mayhew 2005)

The children most likely to continue living in poverty included those from black and ethnic minority families, disabled children, the children of asylum seekers, those whose parents were disabled or in prison, children leaving the care of local authorities, and those living in large families or in households without employment (Preston 2005; Flaherty, Veit-Wilson, and Dornan 2004).

The aim in developing childcare was to provide a free nursery place for every three- and four-year-old. The policies which were introduced included:

- childcare elements in Working Tax Credit and other benefits, paying up to 70 per cent of the costs of childcare (in 2005);
- the National Childcare Strategy. This aimed to increase the amount of good-quality, affordable childcare for children aged 0 to 14. Childcare was to be provided through Sure Start and Children's Centres.

By 2004 there were over 504 Sure Start centres in England offering places to over 400,000 children (HM Treasury 2004). However, demand continued to outstrip supply. The Daycare Trust reported a significant change from 1997, when there was one registered childcare place for every nine children, to 2003, by which date there was one registered place per five children (Daycare Trust 2003).

Creating more family-friendly employment was another area where many new policies were introduced in the years between 1997 and 2010. These included extending maternity leave from six months to a year and introducing paternity leave for fathers, though the latter was unpaid. Other relevant policies included the New Deal, the Parental Leave Directive, the Working Time Directive, and the Part-time Work Directive. The result is that the UK has a greater proportion of women in employment than most European states (for further information see: Hantrais 2004; Wasoff and Dey 2000; Williams 2005; and the relevant websites among those listed at the end of this chapter).

The election of the coalition government in May 2010 changed the direction of family policy. At the time of writing this chapter, a number of cuts have been proposed which will have an impact on the living standards of families. These include:

- a cut of £7 billion in the social security budget, including removing Child Benefit for higher- and middle-income families, which will save £2.5 billion;
- savings of £6 billion produced by cutting jobs in the public sector, which is likely to have an impact on such services as Sure Start and Children's Centres;
- replacement of the Child Tax Credit, paid to mothers, with a Universal Credit, paid to the main earner. This transfer of thousands of pounds per family from mothers to fathers will threaten allocation within household budgets to meet children's needs;
- abolition of the Child Trust Fund.

Readers of this book will be able to assess the impact of these changes on families over the coming years.

Domestic work

Under the heading of domestic work we shall consider such activities as cleaning, preparing meals, washing up, and shopping for food and household necessities. All these activities produce welfare for the members of the household and carrying them out involves an enormous amount of time and effort. It has been calculated that the time spent in productive but unpaid work in the home is equal to the time spent in paid work (Rose 1989: 124). Attempts to estimate the value of domestic work have indicated that including unpaid work in national income would add between a quarter and more than a half to measured income, depending on the methods used for the calculation (Hyman 1994: 63).

When the first path-breaking study of housework was carried out it was initially considered to be a frivolous topic and one not worthy of academic study (Oakley 1974). However, there is now an enormous literature documenting the changing patterns of domestic work. Women still carry the main burden, though there is some evidence of change.

The British Household Panel Survey asked both men and women what share they took of five activities: cleaning, cooking, shopping, laundry, and childcare. From this it was possible to calculate an index of the domestic division of labour. The results showed that:

- women continue to do significantly more domestic work than men;
- there is a tendency for the division of labour to become more equal, especially when the wife moves into full-time paid work or the husband gives up paid work;
- men and women differ in their reports of how much they do, with both partners tending to say they do more than the other (Berthoud and Gershuny 2000).

Despite the importance of domestic work in terms of the welfare it creates, there is very little explicit social policy related to the topic. This probably reflects the fact that until recently domestic work was taken for granted, as something which women did, unpaid, as part of their roles as wives and mothers. Only since 1973 have judges been encouraged to take the unpaid work done at home into account in making the financial settlement when a marriage ends.

However, implicitly the welfare state still tends to assume that women will be responsible for domestic work and childcare. Welfare providers often take for granted that one parent will be free to take children to and from school, to accompany them to the doctor and the dentist, to stay in for the health visitor and the social worker, and to help children with their homework. Women who fail to carry out domestic work and childcare in the way expected of them risk being considered 'bad mothers' by those with responsibility for the welfare of children.

Caring for sick and disabled people

'Caring' is another type of work which was taken for granted until the late twentieth century: it was seen as something that wives and mothers did naturally, as part of their domestic responsibilities. So 'caring about' someone was assumed to involve 'caring for' them, to use the distinction first made by Graham (1983). The word 'carer' came into use during the 1980s, as feminists and pressure groups argued that caring for sick and disabled people was real work and that it reduced the costs of health and social services.

What sorts of people require, and give, care within the family? Besides those with ordinary short-term illnesses, care may be needed because of mental or physical disabilities, or long-term illness, either mental or physical. Most elderly people are fit and well, but there is a tendency for both physical and mental infirmities to increase with age. Care may be given by spouses to each other, by parents to their disabled children, by adult daughters and, less often, adult sons to their parents. Increasingly it is also being recognized that some quite young children provide care for their disabled parents (Becker and Becker 2008; Becker 2007).

In 1985 the General Household Survey asked about caring and produced the first national data about people who give and receive care. Respondents were asked whether they were 'looking after, or providing some regular service for, someone who was sick, elderly or handicapped'. When the results were applied to the whole population it was estimated that there were six million people who were doing some sort of caring for others (Green 1988).

However, the figure of six million has to be treated with some caution. Only about half of these people said that they were the sole or main carer, and only about a fifth spent more than 20 hours per week on caring activities. Nevertheless, this still amounted to a great deal of work done and welfare provided. The study showed that the different sorts of care included:

- personal help with dressing, bathing, toileting, and feeding;
- physical help with activities such as walking, getting in and out of bed, going up and down stairs;
- practical help, such as preparing meals, doing housework or shopping, or doing household repairs and gardening;
- other sorts of help, such as giving medication, changing dressings, taking the person out, or simply keeping him or her company.

The survey showed that needing personal and physical help tended to be associated with very long hours of work for the carer. Some carers, most of them women, were providing a hundred or more hours of care per week, far more than any paid worker would undertake.

Caring is costly in a number of different ways. First, there are costs in terms of lost earnings. The rate of paid employment is lower for all adults providing care. However, the effect is greater for women than men and greatest in the case of a mother caring for a disabled child (Arber and Ginn 1995). Secondly, there are the additional costs of disability. These may include additional heating, when someone is at home all day, adaptations to the house, special equipment, such as wheelchairs and other aids, extra clothes, and bedding, and higher transport costs when a person is unable to use public transport. Thirdly, there are likely to be costs to the carer in terms of stress and strain (Pahl 2006).

Social policy is now beginning to recognize the contribution which carers make to the welfare of individuals within families. In 1985 the Carers (Recognition and Services) Act imposed an obligation on local authorities to assess the needs of carers as well as of those who are cared for. However, the support which carers can expect remains very limited: one study of people looking after a relative with Alzheimer's disease at home found that most carers had less than 16 hours away from caring each week, out of a total of 168 hours in the week (Levin, Moriarty, and Gorbach 1994).

Financial support is provided by the social security system. The rules of eligibility change constantly, but the position at any one time can be checked in the handbooks produced by the Child Poverty Action Group (see for example, Child Poverty Action Group 2010). At the time of writing the main benefits are:

- Disability Living Allowance for people under 65 who have a long-term disability which prevents them taking paid employment.
- Attendance Allowance for people over 65 who need someone to help them with the activities of daily living.
- Carer's Allowance for those who provide care for someone who is receiving the higher rate of the Disability Living Allowance. To qualify for this allowance the carer has to be caring for at least 35 hours per week. At the time of writing the rate was £45.70 per week, so the maximum that anyone could be 'paid' is just over £1.00 per hour: if caring at home is work, it is very badly paid work indeed.
- Disabled Person's Tax Credit, which is an allowance for low-paid workers with a disability. The effect is to top up the wages of those who work for more than 16 hours per week.

Ungerson has written about the many different ways in which care can be paid for (Ungerson 2000; see also Ungerson 2006). These can include:

- caregiver allowances paid through social security and tax systems;
- proper wages paid by the state or state agencies;
- symbolic payments paid by care users to kin, neighbours, and friends;
- paid volunteering paid by voluntary organizations of local authorities;
- routed wages paid via direct payments to care users.

The introduction of policies related to childcare and caring for elderly and disabled people raises many questions about the boundary between public and private spheres. When can, and when should, the state get involved in paying people to do the work by which families create welfare for their members? Are looking after children, doing housework, and caring for sick and disabled people essentially private matters, carried out because people love and care for each other? Is it appropriate for the state to become involved, through social policies focused on the work done within families? And if these issues become a matter of public as well as private concern, what forms should state intervention take, given that historically care and control have tended to advance together? These are likely to be central questions in any discussion of family policy.

Dis-welfares within families

However, families can be sources of disadvantage or 'dis-welfare', as well as of welfare. Many people are ambivalent about their families, even when things are going well, but for some individuals the family becomes the place where they experience inequality, unhappiness, and even danger. In this section we consider three aspects of family life which can create problems for individual family members.

Financial inequalities

Throughout much of social policy the household is regarded as an economic unit. When a man and a woman live together, especially if they are married, it is assumed that they will share the income which enters the household. This assumption underlies the idea of the household means test. Being eligible for a means-tested benefit implies that the income of the household as a whole is below the minimum considered necessary: it is assumed that an individual cannot be poor if he or she lives within a household which has an adequate income.

However, it has become apparent that there can be considerable financial inequalities even within quite affluent families. In particular, women and children have been found living in poverty in households with adequate incomes (Pahl 1989, 1995, and 2005). Most of the research on this topic has focused on married or as-married couples, with or without children, so in this context the word 'family' usually means a nuclear family living together in a household.

There is now a considerable body of research showing that the allocation of money within the household or family has significant implications for the lives of individuals within the household. These differences can be summarized as follows:

- When money is scarce, women tend to get the job of making ends meet, since it is usually they who are responsible for finances in low-income households (see Stocks et al 2007; Miles and Probert 2009).
- Women are likely to bear the brunt of financial cutbacks. When money is short, women are more likely than men to cut back on such things as food, heating, social life, and entertainment (Goode, Callender, and Lister 1998).
- Women are more child and family focused in their spending. Money which is controlled by women is more likely to be spent on children, on food, and on collective expenditure for the household, while men tend to hold more back for their individual use. If the aim is to benefit children, women make more efficient use of household income (Pahl 1989; Middleton et al. 1997).
- Individuals can be poor in households with adequate incomes. This finding has important implications for policy initiatives aimed at the relief of poverty (Pahl 1989; Stocks et al. 2007; Miles and Probert 2009).

Financial inequalities within families often seem to occur when one family member, typically a male breadwinner, uses money as a way of exercising power and of controlling other family members; another source of power and control is violence.

Violence against women within the family

Violence seems to be an enduring characteristic of family life, with women and children being the main victims. Violence against children is considered in Chapter 14. Here we are concerned with violence against women.

Throughout most of history this has been taken for granted, to the extent that in 1792 Judge Buller confirmed that husbands had the right to beat their wives, so long as the stick that was used was not thicker than a man's thumb. What is now described as 'wife abuse' or 'domestic violence' was then considered to be a private matter, lying outside the public domain and not amenable to legislation; it was even a suitable subject for family entertainment, in the form of the Punch and Judy show!

Violence against women became a public issue in the 1970s, largely as a result of the growth of the Women's Movement and the work of feminists in documenting the nature and extent of the problem. The first refuge for abused women was set up in London in 1971, and refuges, or shelters, can now be found in most parts of the world. Male violence within the family has become recognized as a threat to the physical and mental health of women and children and as a major cause of morbidity and mortality. Cross-national studies have shown that violence against women takes very similar forms across the globe, even though the policy responses of governments can be very different (World Health Organization 2005; Pahl, Hasanbegovic, and Yu 2004).

Domestic violence is also a crime. Home Office statistics show that 94 per cent of assailants are men, while women make up the majority of victims. Among murder victims, 47 per cent of women, compared with 12 per cent of men, were killed by their partner or ex-partner. Much domestic violence goes unreported. So in 2008–9, 42 per cent of all violent crimes were reported to the police, compared with 15 per cent of incidents of domestic violence (Home Office 2009).

Box 6.4 The Family Law Act 1996: domestic violence

With regard to domestic violence, the 1996 Family Law Act:

- widened the scope for occupation and non-molestation orders, which now apply to 'associated persons', such as ex-partners, as well as to currently married and cohabiting people;
- increased the rights of courts to attach a power of arrest to court orders;
- simplified the position with regard to the different courts in which cases involving domestic violence can be heard.

A large-scale survey of the general population, carried out in London in 1993, showed that around 30 per cent of women had experienced domestic violence from their partners or ex-partners. Men could also be the victims of domestic violence, though to a lesser extent than women both in terms of frequency and severity. The study showed that most of the violence men experienced occurred in public places; by contrast most violence against women occurred in private (Mooney 2000).

Despite the seriousness of much domestic violence, the appropriate agencies have often been reluctant to provide help for the victims. One problem is that so many different agencies are potentially involved. If a woman has injuries she may need medical and nursing care. She has been the victim of a crime, so the police can be involved and she may have to go to court to get an injunction to prevent her husband from assaulting her again. Many husbands are not deterred by legal action, so she may decide to leave home to protect herself and her children. She may go to a refuge, or to the local authority housing department: if she has dependent children the 1985 Housing Act gives her the right to temporary accommodation. Lacking an income, she is likely to apply to the Benefit Office for income support. There is ample evidence of the ways in which policy-makers and professionals have failed to meet the needs of abused women (Hague and Malos 1998; Mooney 2000).

The law relating to violence in the family was changed and simplified by the Family Law Act 1996. Previously the legal position was quite complicated, with different legislation applying in the case of married and unmarried couples. The 1996 Act consolidated existing legislation and set out the position with regard to the occupation of the family home and the right of individuals to protection against violence.

More recently the Domestic Violence, Crime and Victims Act 2004 gave new powers to the police and courts with regard to offenders, while also improving services to victims. In 2005 the government published a national action plan on domestic violence. It set out the progress made so far, and outlined future proposals to further improve support to victims and bring more perpetrators to justice (Home Office 2005).

Separation and divorce

Unhappy marriages are the root cause of much dis-welfare within families, while separation and divorce tend to create inequalities between the different members of families. When a couple separates the result is typically a reduction in household incomes for women and children and a modest increase in the household incomes of men. The most effective route out of poverty for women in this situation is remarriage, a fact which reflects the greater earning power and job security of men, and the responsibility of women for childcare.

Research on the impact of divorce on children has shown that the children of separated parents are more likely to have behaviour problems, perform less well at school, become sexually active at a younger age, and are more likely to turn to drugs, smoking, and heavy drinking. However, these outcomes may have been a product of the conflict leading up to the separation and of family poverty as well as of parental separation (Rodgers and Pryor 1998). Divorce is associated with a decline in family income, especially for women and children, and low family income is strongly associated with poorer educational attainment in children (Ely et al. 1999).

Current arrangements for divorce stem from the Divorce Reform Act 1969. The main provisions of this Act were:

- The only ground for divorce was the 'irretrievable breakdown' of the marriage.
- Breakdown could be established by reference to one of five 'facts', which included adultery, desertion, unreasonable behaviour, two years' separation if both consented to the divorce, or five years' separation if one partner did not want the divorce.
- Unreasonable behaviour included financial irresponsibility, violence, alcoholism, and constant criticism.

Those who did not want to wait two or five years for a divorce still had to rely on fault-based facts to prove that the marriage had broken down, so bitterness and blame continued to surround divorce proceedings.

At this time legal aid was made available to those who did not have enough money to obtain advice and take the case to court. Since the granting of legal aid was dependent on a means test on individuals, not couples, many wives qualified for legal aid and this made it possible for them to obtain a divorce. After the 1969 Act the divorce rate rose quite sharply, and continued to rise throughout the next twenty years, with about three-quarters of all divorces being granted to women.

Concern over the fact that four in ten marriages were ending in divorce, and that couples were continuing to use fault-based facts to prove breakdown, led to a demand for a new law relating to divorce. This reached the statute book as the Family Law Act 1996.

The Act attempted to send a message that ending a marriage is a serious business. Mediation was not compulsory, unless the courts ordered it because the couple could not agree. The voluntary organization, National Family Mediation, was charged with providing mediation services, but was nevertheless underfunded. In addition, the spouse who had applied for the divorce had to attend an information meeting at the court about financial and other consequences, and then there had to be a three-month 'period of reflection' after the meeting (Bird and Cretney 1997; Lewis and Maclean 1997).

The Family Law Act 1996 ended the concept of fault: the single ground for divorce was that the marriage had broken down. The aim was to make couples think more carefully about getting divorced, but if they decided to go ahead, then the aim was to minimize bitterness and harm to children. The new situation can create clashes of values within families, and between the generations, as they seek to reconcile the changing and sometimes contradictory norms about family life and relationships (Smart 2005).

Box 6.5 **The Family Law Act 1996: divorce**

With regard to divorce, the aims of the Act were:

- to support the institution of marriage;
- to include practical steps to prevent the irretrievable breakdown of marriage;
- to ensure that spouses understand the practical consequences of divorce before taking any irreversible decision;
- to minimize the bitterness and hostility between the parties and reduce trauma for the children;
- to keep to the minimum the costs to the couple and to the taxpayer.

Social policy and families in the future

Patterns of family life and the nature of family policy changed greatly over the second half of the twentieth century. What do demographic trends tell us about the future shape of family life? As we saw earlier in this chapter, family policy reflects strongly held, and often conflicting ideologies. What cultural and ideological forces will shape policy making in the future?

Future trends in family life

Predictions about the future must always be regarded with scepticism. However, demographic trends provide a useful start. In general, these involve taking current patterns and projecting them into the future.

In some respects the future is already unrolling. For example, the population pyramid shown in Figure 6.1 can be used to predict important aspects of the future. The relatively large cohort of babies born during the 1960s will mean a relatively large population of elderly people when these individuals retire from employment in the years around 2030. After that there will be a decline in the numbers of elderly people, and in the population as a whole, because of the low birth rate in the 1970s and 1980s. Changes such as these have implications for social policy, and may have lain behind the government decision to equalize the retirement age for men and women at the age of 65 by the year 2020.

Another view on the future is provided by cultural theorists. Here the focus is on the development of postmodernity, and on the transformations which are said to be taking place in intimate relationships. One approach has been to argue that the focus is shifting 'from institution to relationship', that is from the institution of marriage, with its traditional structures, to the individually chosen relationship, which can be broken when it ceases to satisfy (Giddens 1992). A key concept has been the idea of individualization:

> Individualization means that men and women are released from the gender roles prescribed by industrial society for life in the nuclear family. At the same time, and this aggravates the situation, they find themselves forced, under pain of material disadvantage, to build up a life of their own by way of the labour market, training and mobility, and if need be to pursue this at the cost of their commitments to family, relations and friends. (Beck and Beck-Gernsheim 1995: 6)

Whether or not the cultural theorists will prove to be right in their predictions for the future, it is likely that families will continue to be controversial. The struggle will continue between those who think that change has gone too far and those who think that it has not gone far enough.

European perspectives on family policy

Debates about family policy will increasingly take place in the context of the European Community. However, the different countries involved have very different approaches to family policy (Hantrais 2004).

The tension between policies which support family life and those which encroach on family privacy is revealed in many of the documents which have shaped family policy in Europe. The main treaties of the European Union have not been explicitly concerned with family policy, despite growing pressure that the EU should be concerned with the welfare of families. However, many European initiatives have affected families, most notably in the areas of childcare, working hours, and maternity, paternity, and parental leave. Legislation in these fields has been presented in terms of equal opportunities or health and safety at work. The principle of subsidiarity, according to which actions should be taken at the lowest appropriate administrative level, has inhibited the making of substantive family policy at supranational levels.

Conclusion

Despite a tradition of non-interference in family life in Britain, over the past few years many new policies have been introduced in this field. In general, the Labour government of 1997 to 2010 enacted policies aimed at benefiting children. Many of these reflected a dual concern with raising children out of poverty and getting parents into paid work. They were criticized both for not giving enough support to marriage and to traditional patterns of family life and also for not going far enough in raising children out of poverty.

The coalition government elected in the UK in 2010 is taking a rather different approach to family policy. Cuts are planned in the funds available for the welfare state and these are likely to have a significant impact on families and on services for children. Higher earners will lose Child Benefit, but in general it seems that the cuts will have the greatest impact on the living standards of poor families. It will be important to continue to monitor changes and to assess the impact of new directions in policy on individuals and families.

KEY LEGISLATION

Child Support Act 1991

Children Act 1989

Civil Partnership Act 2004

Domestic Violence, Crime and Victims Act 2004

Family Law Act 1996

FURTHER READING

Crompton, R. Lewis, S., and Lyonette, C. (2010) *Women, Men, Work and Family in Europe* (Basingstoke: Macmillan). Original research from seven European countries.

Hantrais, L. (2004) *Family Policy Matters: Responding to Family Change in Europe* (Bristol: Policy Press). A Europe-wide view on family policy.

McCarthy, J. and Edwards, R. (2011) *Key Concepts in Family Studies* (London: Sage). Definitions, discussion, and suggestions for further reading on some key topics.

Wasoff, F. and Dey, I. (2000) *Family Policy* (Eastbourne: Gildredge Press). A short and readable introduction to debates in family policy.

USEFUL WEBSITES

For information about the National Childcare Strategy go to: **http://www.daycaretrust.org.uk**.

The Child Poverty Action Group website gives information about family living standards and family policy at: **www.cpag.org.uk**.

An account of the work of the Child Support Agency can be found at: **www.csa.gov.uk**.

The Family and Parenting Institute can be found at: **www.familyandparenting.org.uk**.

Gingerbread, the national charity for one parent families, has a useful website at: **http://www.gingerbread.org.uk**.

Women's Aid is the key national charity working to end domestic violence against women and children. For facts, research, and policies see: **http://www.womensaid.org.uk/**.

ESSAY QUESTIONS

1 Why is 'the family' a controversial topic?

2 What are the main changes which have taken place in family policy over the years up to the change of government in 2010?

3 Think about the different forms of welfare provided within families: who mainly provides, and who mainly receives, these different forms of welfare?

4 We know that there are inequalities in the wider society: what sorts of inequalities can exist within families? What policies might reduce these inequalities?

5 What changes do you think will take place within families, and in family life, over the next twenty years?

@ ONLINE RESOURCE CENTRE

For additional material and resources, please visit the Online Resource Centre at:
www.oxfordtextbooks.co.uk/orc/baldock4e/.

Part Three
The financial and organizational context of social policy

7

The voluntary and community sector

Jeremy Kendall

Contents

Introduction

The contributions of the voluntary and community sector (VCS) to social policy—meaning the activities and impacts of organizations between the market and the state—embrace an extraordinarily diverse range of activities. Many of these groups ensure that social needs are highlighted and addressed which would otherwise simply go unrecognized and unmet. From preschool playgroups, hospices, and Age Concern groups well known in many local areas, to Barnardo's and the Child Poverty Action Group on the national stage, and CAFOD and Oxfam internationally, the scope and scale of this sector are remarkable in Britain.

Learning outcomes

At the end of this chapter students should have familiarity with:

1 the size and diverse nature of the voluntary and community sector (VCS) in Britain;
2 the funding of the VCS;
3 government policy towards the VCS;
4 the role of theorists in understanding the important role of civil society organizations as ingredients of social change;
5 how the concept of 'social capital' now exerts a powerful new influence on thinking in this field;
6 how EU institutions are seen as increasingly relevant for shaping policy on the VCS.

The voluntary and community sector

The groups which populate this space are often legally recognized as 'charities': there were 162,414 such bodies registered with these organizations' regulator in England and Wales, the Charity Commission, in December 2010 (Charity Commission 2010). Up until the mid 1990s, dedicated VCS research had focused almost exclusively on such charities. But the aspiration to make international comparisons was associated with the emergence of a broader, more inclusive approach (Kendall and Knapp 1996), which has subsequently been emulated in more recent compilations, including the flagship publication of the National Council for Voluntary Organisations (NCVO), now entitled *The UK Civil Society Almanac* (Clark et al. 2010). Across the whole of Britain, they estimate that around 900,000 'civil society organizations', broadly understood, currently exist, including 600,000 'below the radar' bodies often too small to be registered (see McCabe 2011), 171,000 'general charities', 127,000 sports clubs (most of which are not charitable), 14,000 faith groups—churches, mosques, and the range of sacramental and service activity they organize—4,600 cooperatives, and 1,800 housing associations.

Some campaigning groups have always eschewed charitable status for fear that it will unduly constrain their ability to act politically, and may be constituted as non-charitable unincorporated associations or companies limited by guarantee (as with charities, taking an incorporated form usually makes sense to limit personal liability as economic scale increases). But non-charitable VCS bodies have become more widespread for other reasons too. One example is the 'industrial and provident society' structure, which has long been the format often chosen by the aforementioned housing associations which are now such a prominent part of the field. A new 'community interest company' option brought in under the Labour government has been chosen by some social entrepreneurs, with nearly 3,000 existing by 2010.

At the same time, some groups which the public typically assume are not charities do, in fact, have this status. For example, many private fee-paying independent schools and exclusive hospitals are in this category. The legal position of 'charities' was also changed under the previous government with the implementation of the Charities Act 2006. This partly aimed to rectify some of this confusion by aligning the definition in law more closely with public perceptions and expectations. This is by a combination of definitional widening on one hand, and making demonstrable public benefit a requirement for all registered charities for the first time, with the Charity Commission taking a leading role in implementation (see Box 7.1).

Box 7.1 The Charities Act 2006: a breakthrough in modernizing legislation

This milestone legislation—the most significant legislation on charities for several decades—sought to build public trust and confidence in charities by attempting to create a modern and effective regulatory environment relevant to the needs of charities in the twenty-first century The key provisions of the Act included:

- an updated legal definition of charity:
  - A list of thirteen charitable purposes replaced the 'four heads of charity' established by previous case law over the last 400 years. The new list tries to resemble modern expectations of what causes are, or should be, charitable.
  - All organizations with charitable purposes now have to show that they exist to benefit the public in some way in order to gain and maintain charitable status. This is especially important in the case of religious and educational charities, which, prior to the Act, were simply presumed to exist for public benefit, rather than required to demonstrate this was the case.
- new role and powers of the Charity Commission and a new Charity Tribunal:
  - The Act established the Charity Commission as a 'corporate body' for the first time, with statutory objectives, functions, and duties made explicit and newly defined.
  - The Act created a new independent Charity Tribunal to hear appeals against legal decisions made by the Charity Commission, such as decisions on whether to register a charity.
- new rules affecting the liability of trustees:
  - Most importantly, a new legal form of 'Charitable Incorporated Organization' (CIO) was made available to charities who wish to limit the liability of trustees.
- a more proportionate regulatory framework:
  - The financial threshold for registration was raised, so that very small charities (annual income below £5,000) are no longer required to register.
  - The Commission's regulatory reach was extended to include many previously exempt and excepted charities.
- new rules on charitable fundraising:
  - Most importantly, to promote public confidence in charity fundraising, the Act set a higher standard of transparency for professional charity fundraisers by introducing tighter obligations to make certain statements about their role and how much of the money raised will benefit the cause.

Adapted from NCVO (no date)

However, the involvement of the state in this sector is more extensive than simply making legal structures and frameworks available, with a range of policies developed to promote these organizations collectively evolving in recent years. Historically, public sector officials have often been involved in governance as trustees at the local level, and tax breaks provided for organizations and donors are nationally organized. But flows of funding from both central and sub-national government, and the agendas they promote, are the most visible manifestation of these links. Kendall (2003) suggested that as early as 1995 the state was becoming the most significant funder for this sector, fuelled by flows of funds to support the delivery of social care and housing in particular.

Very significant amounts of public sector funding now support this sector, or at least that part of it which can be reliably captured using existing data sources: according to summary data reported in the *Almanac*, out of £35.5 billion income in 2007–8 to 'general charities', £12.8 billion flowed directly from the state: £9.1 billion from contracts and fees, and £3.7 billion in grants, with the former growing at the expense of the latter as public purchasers increasingly wish to commit providers to the delivery of pre-specified services.

Although most of this finance is tied up with policies specific to particular fields and client groups, a significant amount has sought to foster capacity and infrastructure more generally, particularly with an eye to promoting the sector's overall role in providing public services. This 'horizontal' or 'cross-cutting' agenda was in recent years led from within the state by increasingly high-profile departments and units, culminating in the establishment of an Office for the Third Sector within the Cabinet Office in 2006. This is now known as the Office for Civil Society under the coalition government. Another symbolically important New Labour initiative, the Compact, seeking to underpin and systematize third sector–state relationships from 1998 onwards, has a less certain future: at the time of writing, its main supporting institution, the 'Commission for the Compact' was sacrificed as part of the more general 'bonfire of the quangos' brought in soon after the coalition's election victory. Box 7.2 summarizes some of the types of policy tools now in play in this field in relation to the sector.

Other countries with long track records of liberal democracy also have their own rich traditions of voluntarism and non-profit organization, although the form and shape they take vary dramatically from country to country (Anheier 2005). The range of policy approaches taken by countries and European institutions has also been shown to be remarkably diverse, and there is no simple relationship between policy proactivity and the sector's scope and scale. For example, France has a relatively well developed set of horizontal sector-oriented policy institutions at the national level organized around the concepts of l'économie sociale et solidaire and even has a Compact of sorts. Yet the country has relatively modest levels of associative endeavour, and policy thinking and practices still seem to embody the belief that these organizations' partiality and particularism render them little more than a useful appendage to the powerful, centralized French state (Fraisse 2009). On the other hand, in the Netherlands, where there has been no Compact or centrally driven cross-cutting infrastructure building programme, the sector nevertheless flourishes remarkably as the result of decades of close working between these organizations and the national and sub-national components of the Dutch state (Kendall 2009).

Back in the UK, a uniquely rapidly accelerating degree of policy recognition of these groups had reached such a level by the turn of the millennium that they may be considered to have been collectively 'mainstreamed' in social policy terms under the then Labour government (Kendall 2003, Chapter 3). We must now view this as a prelude to the even greater attention being lavished here under the incumbent coalition. Drivers have included policy-makers' beliefs that voluntary organizations can be more responsive, cost-effective, or responsible than the alternatives, can exhibit greater sensitivity to the needs of socially excluded constituencies, and seem to be central in helping to generate social capital and foster social enterprise (unfamiliar terms to many, and so defined and discussed as we proceed below). Under the coalition, fiscal considerations have been at the forefront in shaping the agenda here, as enhancing the social policy prominence of the sector is seen as

Box 7.2 **Significant national public policy instruments**

Strategic horizontal institutional support involving public sector commitment to building the sector's capacity, profile, and status more generally. Included here would be:

- *strategic grants for infrastructure bodies* seeking to provide the sector with a voice, and represent its shared interests;
- '*capacity builders*', a programme to strengthen the sector's overall capabilities, developed under New Labour but being discontinued under the coalition government;
- the *Compact and allied institutions*, involving annual reviews and action plans geared towards state–third sector partnership, and supported institutionally at Compact Voice (based at NCVO) and the Commission for the Compact (since 2007);
- *volunteer development programmes*, seeking to strengthen volunteering in general, and in recent years, youth volunteering in particular (as epitomized by the 'V' programme).

Direct expenditure by public bodies when third sector organizations are involved in public service delivery, community development, or other sponsored activity. These arrangements were traditionally often quite loosely formulated as *grant* payments in general support of organizational and sectoral activities, and could include current and capital spending. However, in recent years, there has been a tendency to switch to *service level agreements* or *contracts* for recurrent expenditure, whereby specific payments are made for the delivery of services or goods identified in advance; and to encourage social finance to support the capital element of resourcing.

Tax incentives, reliefs, and breaks for donors (individuals, trusts, companies) and third sector organizations themselves. The most clear-cut examples relate to planned or structured giving to charities. Sometimes these are referred to as '*tax expenditures*', because they mean that funds which would otherwise accrue to the public sector purse are retained in the third sector.

National Lottery funds, including the Big Lottery Fund, whose framework is supported by government, but whose processes were designed to be beyond direct government control.

Social finance geared towards building infrastructure in the third sector via capital injections, but unlike traditional grants, explicitly framed as an 'investment' for funders.

- There has been a particular emphasis in recent years on fostering *loan finance*. For example, one of the New Labour government's flagship programmes, *Futurebuilders*, used public funding principally as an 'investment' in an attempt to catalyse wider borrowing for third sector organizations able and willing to 'upscale' their public service delivery roles in particular.

 Other ways of levering 'investment' funds have also been proposed, and have begun to be implemented. New Labour was moving towards a specialist *Wholesale Bank* to undergird more targeted lending—an idea now adopted by the coalition, and now rebranded the '*Big Society Bank*'. Through a range of task forces and initiatives, the government also was increasingly seeking to foster a wider range of other private or public–private hybrid 'investors' to resource these organizations too with new financial instruments. 'Patient capital' schemes, 'social impact bonds', and quasi-equity arrangements were included among the approaches which involve lending on what are presented as favourable and progressive terms for third sector organizations who otherwise would not be able to secure sufficient resources for growth. The 'Big Society' agenda seems likely to add momentum to this aspect of policy.

offering a way to allow the state to rein in its expenditure. The mantra that a more active role from these organizations can take the strain and foster a 'Big Society' as an alternative to 'Big Government' has become a key article of faith of the new government—and as such is to a large degree ideological, despite the claim that it is essentially 'pragmatic'.

We can surmise that some of the motivating pro-VCS beliefs may be well based on evidence and argument, but others are less so, and seem ideologically driven. The extent to which this 'third sector' can and should 'step up' depends upon a range of factors which vary a great deal by policy specialism, with the availability of non-state financial and other resources; and the normative beliefs of those involved concerning whether state downsizing is considered desirable are that it is appropriate for them to substitute for the public sector, are of obvious relevance. These considerations vary greatly between education, health, and social care, for example, and the problem also has an important spatial dimension. This is because the voluntary resources are very far from being evenly distributed across the UK, although existing evidence is very difficult to interpret (see Clark et al. 2010: 28). Nevertheless, rhetorically and ideologically, there is now an unprecedented *general* overarching thrust to foster this sector per se, all against the backdrop of a loss of faith in market and state solutions.

The maturation of civil society studies

Momentum for focusing on this sphere has not just been political or governmental. Many foundational modern social and political theorists were already suggesting the important role of civil society organizations as ingredients in understanding social change. Alexis de Tocqueville, Emile Durkheim, and Georg Frederick Hegel, for example, all attended systematically to this sphere in the context of their own contrasting intellectual approaches. These are still highly relevant to policy and theory today. For example, a market-inclusive approach favoured in parts of the European Commission seems to owe a good deal to Hegelian reasoning. Globally, some of those working with the contemporary concept of 'social capital' (see below) style themselves, or are represented by others, as 'neo Tocquevillean' because of beliefs concerning the social, political, and economic significance of associations.

More generally, from the late twentieth century onwards, influential figures in social science have also referred to these organizations collectively as crucial actors in political and policy processes within the complex, diverse systems of governance which characterize contemporary societies. They have been seen as strengthening societies, but also more problematically potentially providing opportunities for power holders to develop or impose their agendas. For example, Anthony Giddens linked the 'third sector' to the 'third way', with an emphasis on moving away from overreliance on the traditional institutions of either the state or the market. And in looking at deliberative or participatory democracy, Jurgen Habermas systematically brought into focus the contributions of NGOs as a way of surfacing needs emergent in the authentic 'lifeworld', at a distance from both the commodity-oriented market and the bureaucratic state. More critically and darkly, Pierre Bourdieu's framing of social capital emphasized the potential for these organizations to perpetuate disadvantage and inequality; while Michel Foucault's work has served to sensitize analysts to the manipulative and exploitative potential of these and other apparently independent interest groups as part of the 'governmentality' strand of social studies.

In the past twenty years, civil society studies in relation to public welfare services and beyond has taken shape as a recognizable multidisciplinary field of studies in its own right, rather than as a focus of interest dispersed across different thinkers and their home disciplines and interests. At national and international levels, it now has university-based and other research centres; scholarly associations with significant and engaged memberships, and widely read dedicated journals, which serve as vehicles for dissemination alongside other generalized social science media (see websites at the end of this chapter). It involves the application of styles of argument and analytic techniques honed in the traditional social science disciplines, so its embrace includes sociology, economics, political science, and social psychology. But it also offers a space for creative new ways of blending approaches from within and across these disciplines, as well as hosting and interacting with established interdisciplinary bodies of thought. We could think of its relationship with 'social policy' in this way, as well as its connections with 'public administration', 'policy analysis', and 'local government studies', for example.

Definitions and types

An attempt to capture the diversity and variety which characterize this terrain has been made with the label 'a loose and baggy monster' (Kendall and Knapp 1995). Its fluidity and fuzziness have led some commentators to argue that talk of a 'sector' is unhelpful (Kramer 2000). Research has increasingly demonstrated the extent to which resources and people, and even organizations themselves, are often moving across the boundaries which policy-makers and scholars alike have suggested characterize the field (Brandsen et al. 2005; Lewis 2009) Especially in the continental European discourse, some in principle prefer metaphors such as 'space' or 'field', or re-present our subject matter as part of (organized) civil society. Others (including this author) persist in using a specific, settled 'sector' pragmatically as a good enough form of working shorthand for purposes such as statistical mapping, but are willing to recognize that for other purposes, including political and organizational analysis, more attention needs to be devoted to how meanings and coverage have evolved as this has suited political agendas. The very process of constructing, adapting, and shifting the positioning of boundaries, and movement across those evolving boundaries, then comes especially into focus (Brandsen et al. 2005; Billis 2010; Alcock and Kendall 2011).

It may be possible under some circumstances to put into practice more than one definition simultaneously, especially if the analyst is interested in civil society broadly understood (Edwards 2009). Kendall (2009) suggests that for comparative policy analytic purposes, it is appropriate to start with a shared *working* definition to give an initial orientation, and then attend to departures from it in actual existing policy practices.

But for most purposes, researchers have worked with one exclusive or at least dominant approach. If one pragmatically accepts the 'sector' construct, how might this be defined? We have already acknowledged that there is no 'one size fits all', and deciding on inclusions and exclusions is a matter of both political contention and analytic priority: the appropriate formulation depends on the specific purpose of the analyst, against the backdrop of their values and priorities. For example, writers strongly influenced by Marxism would tend to deny the possibility of a durably independent sector flourishing in actual existing capitalist systems (for example, Beckford 1982; Wolch 1990). Another route is neo-elitist, also adopting an anti- or post-positivist epistemology, but now accepting the existence of the sector—albeit with roots as a project of 'construction' pursued in the interests of the powerful. That is, as a political construct flowing from the agendas of special interests, politicians, and allied researchers. The work of Peter Dobkin Hall in the United States and Perri 6 and Diana Leat in the UK have taken this approach (6 and Leat 1997).

However, if we subscribe to a liberal, positivist worldview—involving the claim that there is an organizational terrain 'out there' which can be scientifically 'discovered'—a 'structural operational' definition seems to work well for cartographic purposes (Salamon and Anheier 1997). This defines into the 'non-profit sector' formally organized entities which are constitutionally/legally separate from the state, bound not to distribute surpluses ('profits') to owners, and demonstrably benefiting from some degree of voluntarism (uncoerced giving) of money ('donations') or time ('volunteering').

If we have identified our terrain in this way, it can then be useful to differentiate organizations within it in a number of ways, for heuristic or hypothesis generation and testing purposes. Perhaps the most common distinction made in general policy debates is simply in terms of size, distinguishing large from small organizations, with the latter often assumed to be more rooted in communities, more dependent on volunteers and members (as opposed to paid staff), less 'cosy' with and dependent upon the state, and less 'businesslike' (claims used as both compliments and criticisms). However, empirical studies suggest a much more complex picture, both because the binary size distinction is inadequate (see, for example, Scott 2007; Clarke et al. 2010; Clifford and Backus 2010), and because the links between size, external relationships, human resources, and community embeddedness are much more complex that this (Kendall 2003; Seelos et al. 2010).

Also within the literature 'types' can be distinguished according to their mixing of social functions—such as service provision, advocacy, innovation, 'community building' (or 'community development'), and value-expressive roles. Other taxonomies refer to how leading actors' or constitutional instruments' values, norms, and motivations compare. Contrasts can also be made in terms of arrangements for governance and the distribution of control rights (economic theories, for example, with their attention to non-profit objectives and focus on the identity of controlling stakeholders, have made important contributions here).

Also much used now is the policy field distinction (analogous to the idea of 'industries' in economic life, now tailored to the areas of salience for these groups). For British social policy purposes, these make a good deal of analytic sense. We are usually interested in distinguishing, in decreasing order of economic (but not necessarily social) significance: education and research (if maintained voluntary schools and universities are treated as in scope); social care; development and housing; and health. (Some writers would include the religion-based action mentioned earlier, while others would not—studies in the UK and the United States show that its inclusion or exclusion makes a large difference to the apparent scale and character of the sector.)

The developmental trajectory of sector roles and relations has demonstrably varied significantly from policy field to policy field. For example, the role of the sector and its 'market share' in social housing expanded relatively rapidly long before the recent policy mainstreaming of the sector, while in many areas of social care the expansion of public service delivery beyond 'in house' local authority provision was largely associated with *for*-profit, small business-led growth. These contrasting patterns have evolved as a reflection of variations in the policy legacies, ideologies, and politically constrained national and sub-national government capacities which prevail in each case. The way 'mainstreaming' under current conditions concretely takes shape—and ultimately whether it helps or hinders the sector, and with what consequences—can similarly be expected to vary along these lines, as already noted (Kendall 2003, Chapter 10).

Finally, distinguishing associations according to whether or not they evidence significant trust-building interpersonal, face-to-face interaction was long a common practice in sociological accounts. But it is now increasingly widespread in interdisciplinary circles in the context of renewed interest in the sector as a vehicle for 'civic renewal' or social capital investment (see below). Thus 'secondary associations'—with demonstrably active memberships and apparently vibrant cultures of participation, reciprocity, and networking—are seen as more conducive to economic and political success than 'tertiary associations'—that is, passive, 'armchair', or 'cheque book' membership-based associations (family and friendship circles being the 'primary' form of association). These distinctions, first discussed primarily in the sociological literature, have now had new life breathed into them from across the social sciences as part of the debate on social capital (see below).

The academic nuancing of definitions and typologies is an important part of the knowledge-building process in this field as with other fields of study. But for the purposes of British social policy at the current time, we can ask what the most important basic terms are that the student will typically encounter. Overall, the single formulation which probably has most currency in social policy 'on the ground' in Britain, cutting across these swathes, is probably still simply 'the voluntary sector', sometimes extended to 'the voluntary and community sector', as with our chapter title in this book. This is used to underline the inclusion of small and volunteer-led groups as well as larger organizations, with significant numbers of paid employees. 'Charities' (see above) is also used, especially, of course, when commentators wish to put an accent on that particular legal status and its consequences, or draw attention to issues relating to philanthropy and choice-making in the realm of private giving (Breeze 2010).

'Social enterprise' has also become a new, voguish term (Peattie and Morley 2007). It has been used to encapsulate the notion that this sector and its environs can be an arena for 'charismatic heroes' in social endeavour, a space for enabling management styles distinct from market or state, an appealing route for 'self-reliance at the local level' (Grenier 2009: 185–90).

The interested student of policy also needs to be aware that some parts of the government now favour referring to '(organized) civil society': in particular, the Cabinet Office unit with responsibility here, we have already seen, is now called the 'Office for Civil Society'. Yet, at the same time, many reflective commentators and policy actors believe 'civil society' is a more wide-ranging term, which should not be conflated with 'the sector' either in the UK or indeed elsewhere (cf. Tamas 2010). This is because the wider term may have several meanings and include informal networks and community groups without sufficient structure to be considered a coherent 'sector' (exactly where the boundary with the 'below the radar' groups mentioned earlier lies is somewhat unclear); and for some purposes this formulation is seen even to embrace the private, for-profit sector—the interpretation now adopted in key parts of the European Commission at the EU level.

Theorizing the voluntary sector in the specialist literature

Building on these traditions of thought, a range of frameworks for analysis has been developed and applied in this sphere. For example, in the critical tradition, distinct Marxist and Foucauldian accounts have been developed, casting the sector as an arena for the invidious exertion of power and the imposition of undemocratic agendas on disadvantaged groups. The theoretically elaborated social science here (Wolch 1990; Morison 2000) resonates with longer-standing critiques from the pragmatic left concerning the oppressive, paternalistic, regressive, and socially divisive consequences of relying too much on traditional charity in particular (Gladstone 1979). It is also useful to refer back to our discussion of definitions, which foreshadows the relevance of the two broad epistemic traditions, the positivist 'discoverers' and the political 'constructors'. As governments have become ever more preoccupied with 'performance' measurement, it is pertinent to note that both positivist and constructionist approaches have been in evidence.

Positivist and social constructionist tools have both been used for evaluative purposes in relation to this sector in social policy fields (Kendall and Knapp 1999; Kendall 2003). But most effort in the past two decades has probably gone into attempting to answer two further fundamental questions. First, why do we need a third sector at all in developed market economies? Second, what difference does the third sector make not only in terms of productivity in economic life, but also political performance? This is where 'social capital' has recently come to the fore.

A leading role, at least amongst scholars and networks who self-consciously identify as specialists in the non-profit studies area, has been taken by economic theory. Initially, the discipline acted as an inspiration, but more recently it could be better described as a whipping boy! Indeed, arguably this territory initially achieved critical mass as a significant autonomous multidisciplinary specialist area of knowledge (rather than as low-profile niches within disciplines) in large part thanks to the sharp analytic thinking of US economists in the 1970s and 1980s. Burton A. Weisbrod was one notable pioneer, suggesting that these organizations could be seen as a response to the inabilities of both markets and states to provide collective goods. These are services where benefits cannot be limited purely to paying customers, and in which one person's consumption does not completely exclude that of other people. Most public services have these features at least in part. For example, with healthcare, you benefit from others being vaccinated against contagious diseases; or with education, you also benefit in terms of economic productivity, culture, and social order if your fellow citizens consume this service. Up until that point, the mainstream assumption in orthodox economics was that the market failure associated with public good provision traduced a role for the state, and only the state. But Weisbrod pointed to the extent to which the state could be seen as tending to provide only for the average citizen—leaving minority and specialist public needs unmet, and potentially therefore providing a need for the voluntary sector to meet supramedian demand.

Henry Hansmann was a second leading instigator, with a theory of 'contract failure' pointing out how these organizations typically seemed to be providing under conditions of asymmetric information. Up until this point, economists had reasoned that institutions such as warranties, state regulation, or state ownership and control were the primary ways in which societies protected people with inadequate information from the predations of potential profiteers or 'cowboys'. But Hansmann noticed the significance of non-profits in areas such as care homes, development, and relief and social services. He proceeded to argue that what was characteristic of these situations was that consumers often unable to assess outcomes or adequately surmise output quality due to direct consumer's mental or physiological underdevelopment or frailty, or as a result of the physical distance of the funder from the immediate consumption experience (as with public sector third party funding arrangements or charitable giving overseas). In such situations Hansmann averred that consumers would therefore rationally prefer to purchase from this legal form. It was deemed they could be protected from exploitation by the so called 'non-distribution constraint': since there were no shareholders waiting in the wings, eager to profiteer at funders' and users' expense, givers of donations and vulnerable users could place their trust in non-profit organizations (Hansmann 1987).

Finally, Estelle James and Avner Ben-Ner shifted attention from the demand to the supply side. James pointed to the role of ideologically (including religious and political) motivated entrepreneurs in starting and sustaining such organizations, and Ben-Ner emphasized the extent to which they are often run by a core of enthusiastic high-demand stakeholders who both organize and consume the public service in question. Good examples respectively here are schools and also preschool education (faith schools and parent-run preschool playgroups are widespread in England).

These insights have generated a debate within economics, with wide-ranging elaborations and syntheses, primarily in the United States, but also used to frame analysis of the sector's policy and social roles in Britain (Billis and Glennerster 1998). However, reacting against (catalysed by) the initial 'economistic' lines of reasoning, further more socio-political models have been developed. The criticisms levelled have included these models' a historical character (not a 'problem' in fact for most economists, who tend to privilege predictive power over realism); their claimed failure to recognize patterns of cooperation (rather than substitution) between sectors; their tendency to represent sectoral divisions of labour as reflecting free(-ish), efficient choice and stable demand; and their typical tendency to privilege analysis of the 'service provision' function over others. Better, these critics argue, to see sector outcomes as reflecting some combination of macro political power; and/or to acknowledge the part played by needs rather than wants, and bring in normatively/duty-bound actors rather than sovereign consumers at the micro level.

Prominent here has been the welfare mix approach of Adalbert Evers (1995), bringing in non-instrumental rationalities, and emphasizing the tensions at stake between market-driven, state-driven, and community-driven logics of action. This has been applied most often in the study of social services, and more recently has been adapted to try to accommodate the extent to which hybridity between these competing logics is an important feature in many areas (on the UK, see most recently Billis 2010). Also important has been Salamon and Anheier's social origins framework, borrowing conceptually from Esping-Andersen's welfare regime theory (see Chapter 17). This is more institutionally specific than Evers's account, and has been applied more systematically at an empirical level.

The social origins approach differentiates a small number of logically exclusive categories into which countries' third sector–state relationships can be situated, and stresses the extent to which patterns reflect historical policy legacies. For example, the United States is styled as an archetypal liberal situation, with the scale of the sector large, while government is relatively small, tending to figure less prominently in other countries because of, inter alia, that country's traditional ideological hostility to state action, and prevailing assumptions that 'too much' state will 'crowd out' civil society. In contrast, in Germany the relationship is pictured as representative of the corporatist model, in which both the sector and the state are relatively large, having been pictured as supplementary and interdependent routes for fostering social policy in tandem by policy elites: crowd in, rather than crowd out. Other types proposed are social democratic, wherein a strengthened democratic state has superseded voluntarism, at least in the welfare sphere (for example, Sweden); and the statist, with more modest levels of action from both sectors.

The social origins approach is an attempt to account for how the strategizing of elite political groups at key moments of welfare system design has formatively advantaged, or conversely marginalized, the voluntary sector vis-à-vis the directly owned and controlled state. Although many have welcomed the extent to which it brings historical context back into the modelling of third sector–state relationships, it is certainly controversial, and its assumptions and applications are challenged and debated—not unlike reactions to Esping-Andersen's more general model of social policy relationships, but in a more specific domain. For example, while these authors treat Britain alongside the United States as part of a stable liberal family, this country's complex history of alternating individualistic and collectively oriented political administrations and shifting policy practices suggests a more erratic trajectory. The evidence could be interpreted as suggesting that an unstable hybrid of liberal–social democratic arrangements better captures the essence of the settlement in this country (Kendall 2009).

Social capital

Alongside the approaches outlined above, 'social capital' now exerts a powerful new influence on thinking in this field. This idea is not only concerned with delivering welfare services, but also with more general ties, habits, relationships, and interactions in communities: these function better, it is claimed, when involving trust, reciprocity, stability, and respect. So it also clearly relates closely to the 'functions' of 'community building' or 'community development' suggested earlier, with much longer pedigrees in the British context. What is new about contemporary community-oriented arguments is that relations of trust and norms of reciprocity are presented as not just socially constructive, but economically and politically instrumental. The word 'capital' underlines economic value—while at the same time keeping in play the imagery of citizenship and public-mindedness. Robert Putnam's work is key here, but so too is that of Pierre Bourdieu, who takes a much more sociological approach. He tries to tie the concept in with issues of class and the distribution of opportunity in society by considering social capital alongside other types of capital, including cultural capital and economic capital, of which social capital is considered an amplifier. Our sector is then framed as part of the repertoire of resources which can be and is used to reproduce class inequalities and strengthen political advantage: the reader will note Marxist themes mentioned earlier reasserting themselves.

Less critically, at least in most of the work of Putnam and his acolytes, this sector, and in particular those parts which are 'secondary' (see above) and/or involve volunteers, are seen, then, as extensions now highlighted as a school for fostering civic skills, an arena for rebuilding decayed 'community' values, even 'renewing' democracy itself—while simultaneously strengthening economic performance! No wonder it appeals. But can we really have our cake and eat it? The argument is intensifying, and the evidence base growing, with vibrant rounds of claim and counter-claim (see Kendall 2003: 116–17).

This debate will run and run, but it is certainly increasingly well informed by an array of new research evidence nationally and internationally. There may be a fundamental ontological split between, on the one hand, some influential contributors, such as the economistically oriented sociologist James Coleman and arguably to an extent Putnam himself, especially in his later work, who represent social capital within the ambit of rational choice forms of analysis,and the more sociologically oriented institutionalism of Bourdieu. Other controversial issues include the extent to which interventions from the state—including the basic infrastructure of the welfare state—help or hinder the development of social capital (Rothstein and Stolle 2003); the 'dark' way in which social capital and the trust it engenders can go hand in hand with intolerance of those who are not 'one of us', and even foster corruption (Graeff 2009).

The suggestion that social capital can be differentiated between types seems to be beginning to allow some progress on some of these issues, and may allow non-Marxist analysts, even working close to the Putnam approach, to engage with social policy concerns involving class and socio-economic patterns. In particular, the distinction between bridging social capital which is 'outward looking and encompass[es] people across diverse social cleavages'and bonding social capital which 'reinforces exclusive identities and homogeneous groups' (Putnam 2000) allows for more critical engagement in studying both the positive and the negative effects of associational life (Svendsen and Svendsen 2009). Studying the extent to which voluntary action may or may not be associated with a third resource—linking social capital—which can span asymmetrical power relationships at macro, meso, and micro levels—may further increase the relevance of the concept to analysts concerned with exploitation and oppression in contemporary societies (Halpern 2005).

Volunteerism and voluntary welfare

Voluntarism—taken here to mean voluntary action not directly constrained by state coercion or driven essentially by market imperatives, and also outside the informal sector (see Chapter 6)—is an explicit ingredient in some of the theories encountered above, and implicit in others. Arguably, it should be placed centre stage in any attempt to understand the relationship between this sector and policy (Kendall 2003, chapter 10). **Volunteerism** can be seen as a sub-category, referring specifically to uncoerced giving of time, as opposed to money.

As state engagement with the sector has grown and public funds have flowed, especially into larger organizations, private donations have dwindled in relative terms to become a relatively limited form of support. The was much talk of a 'giving age' in the earlier years of the Labour administration (late 1990s and early 2000s). This was understood primarily in terms of finance—with politicians, the NCVO, and others looking jealously across the Atlantic. Yet in Britain, as elsewhere in Europe, the main way voluntarism is manifested is precisely through volunteerism—unpaid labour—and not through giving money. And while the global *hours* put in by paid workers were demonstrably similar to those of volunteers in the mid 1990s (the last year for which comparative data were available) in terms of *number of people* involved, the latter still vastly outnumber the former. (Most paid workers, even in the voluntary sector, are full time; most voluntary workers contribute less than half a day per week). Moreover, in the key policy field of social care (see Chapter 13), even in 'full-time equivalent' terms, volunteering has remained more important than paid work in the sector—and across all sectors here, there are still many more volunteers than paid employees.

Various definitions for volunteering have been put forward. For example, the then Volunteer Centre UK (later superseded by Volunteering England) encapsulated it as 'any activity which involves spending time, unpaid, doing something which aims to benefit someone (individuals or groups) other than or in addition to close relative or to benefit the environment ... formal volunteering being undertaken by a respondent for, or through a group or organization of some kind' (Lynn and Davies Smith 1991). This definition was reflected in the Compact code of volunteering, so acted as a strategic frame of reference up until very recently (with the Compact now under review, the status of the associated codes in the future is currently unclear). Internationally, the EU, interested in this sphere particularly to the extent it may support learning amongst younger people, has emphasized free will and 'added social value' (European Commission 2004). For its part, the UN definition (used to support the successful International Year of Volunteering in 2001) combines elements emphasizing that the beneficiaries of this activity can include the individual volunteer themselves, as well as others (Paine et al. 2009).

So why do people volunteer? In Titmuss's time (see Chapter 2), we would have alluded to the centrality of altruism fostered by market subordination, to be contrasted with the self-interest thought to characterize paid work (prototypical of markets). But—as our remarks on social capital and the UN definition already hinted—the understanding of volunteering has come on in leaps and bounds, and a much more complex and variegated picture is now in evidence—although it is still arguably possible to discern broad distinctions between apparently more publicly and more privately oriented underpinnings (Powell and Steinberg 2006). Some of the theories reviewed above involve imageries of volunteering too: for example, the relevance of commitment to ideological and political projects is a corollary of James's supply-side theory, while Ben-Ner's synthetic stakeholder approach foregrounds the relevance of control over service quality for their dependents under conditions of uncertainty in groups where those involved in governance are themselves unpaid (the example of parent-run playgroups).

Other recognized motivations for volunteerism which mix altruism and self-interest include deliberate or incidental 'social capital' building (as already discussed: 'making connections' and seeking to demonstrate commitment and trustworthiness); investment in human capital (with advantages for the career-building individual and society in terms of training and experience useful across working life); 'intrinsic' satisfaction from the act of volunteering and the associated processes of relationship building with others; 'extrinsic' satisfaction from the results of volunteering; and the related psychic benefits, or gains in self-esteem and respect (Leete 2006).

Obviously, pro-volunteering state policies and funding programmes may directly or indirectly help or hinder organizations' capacity to recruit and retain volunteers. As part of its thrust to develop policies in this area, the New Labour administration built on their predecessor's (John Major's) 'Making a Difference' programme with initiatives such as Millennium Volunteers. This was then superseded by 'V', epitomizing the administration's particular interest in youth volunteering. It even also built volunteering targets into the Public Service Agreements between spending government departments and the Treasury.

Yet there are numerous other ways in which social policy connects with volunteering. The citizenship surveys undertaken annually in the first years of this century were very valuable in underscoring how volunteering relates to a range of social variables (see Box 7.3). For example, formal education policy and other educative experiences are relevant, because socialization experiences seem to impact on people's basic disposition to volunteer. Attitudes towards volunteering—and the character of opportunities to get involved—seem to be systematically related to ethnicity, gender, and social class; and the nature of paid work and domestic sphere commitments all seem to shape individuals' willingness and ability to get involved as volunteers. Figure 7.1 summarizes how, as a consequence of these and other influences, we can represent people's willingness and ability to commit to volunteer as shaped within a fourfold web of influences and pressures.

> **Box 7.3 Some important correlates of formally organized volunteering according to citizenship survey**
>
> - Socio-economic group (large effect)
> - Education (large effect)
> - Ethnicity (complex effect—huge variation *within* minority ethnic groups, and depending on whether born here or abroad)
> - Religiosity (large effect)
> - Gender (small effect—but masks segmentation effect: caring vs. recreation (cf. Davis Smith 1997)
> - Existing time commitments—mainly paid work but also childcare responsibilities at home as key 'barriers' (or reasons for withdrawal)

Against the backdrop of the 'Big Society' mantra, one of the most striking initiatives taken by the coalition government thus far has been to aggressively promote a 'National Citizen Service' programme. Despite its enthusiasm for youth volunteering, New Labour had hesitated when in office on advancing such a youth citizenship programme per se, not least because of (well grounded) concerns that many voluntary groups would be unwilling to collaborate with a scheme which had, or might potentially have, elements of compulsion. This relates back to definitions: the perceived incompatibility of such a scheme with the core definitions of volunteering nationally and internationally (see above).

The new administration, by contrast, has felt less constrained by such voluntary groups' sensibilities. Certainly, prior to the election the Conservative Party element showed itself to be keen to

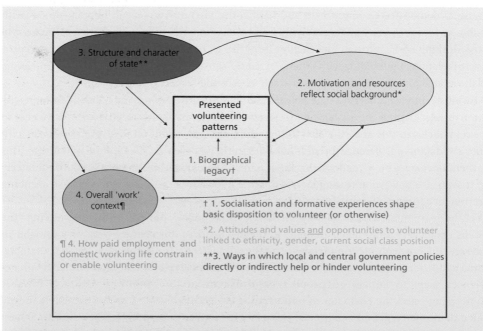

Figure 7.1 The social and political environment as a 4D web of barriers and opportunities for potential volunteers

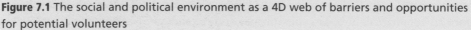

Source: (Kendall 2009)

break away from the assumption that the VCS is especially well placed to support volunteering (as reflected in the organization of 'V', for example). Its pre-election statement on policy revealed its aspiration to see contracted for-profit providers involved as much as possible (Conservative Party 2008). The details of the scheme are shrouded in mystery at the time of writing, although prior to the election the Conservatives seem to have shifted how they presented NCS as involving a heavy stress on coerced participation towards a softer style. A government policy adviser has, however, recently revealed that the coalition is likely to keep the compulsion element prominently available as an option for the future—should insufficient participation materialize, from their perspective, with reliance on voluntary choice. It is also said that the NCS will involve a large-scale youth programme combining a 'residential element, community involvement and social mixing' (Economic and Social Research Council 2010).

Ideologies and ideational frameworks relating to the VCS

It is often claimed that policy support for the VCS should not really be considered a matter of ideology. Under this view, the turn to the VCS is seen as involving a turn away from blind faith in the market or the state, and is promoted as a pragmatic, healthy 'evidence-based' response to the failures of an excessive reliance on those sectors in the promotion of welfare or well-being. It is taken to flow logically from data showing that this sector tends to have a comparative advantage—in terms of cost effectiveness, innovative capacity, community building, and so on—when set against how other sectors tend to 'perform' on these criteria.

There are perhaps three main reasons why this claim can never paint a full picture of recent policy developments. First, if this were the case, the development of policy in this sphere would be a relatively uncontentious matter, with political parties harmoniously responding to the relevant technical, evaluative information in the same way, and with very little or no difference in their policy treatment of this field. Yet while there is a good deal of overlap in the programmes of all the main political parties, there are also very clearly major differences both between and within them. We already saw how this has been manifested when we remarked above on divergences in relation to VCS policy as a whole, and volunteering in particular, between the policies of New Labour and those now being promoted under the coalition.

Second, as Kendall (2003) first showed and we already recognized in the introduction, while these apparent comparative advantages may apply in some situations, they do not apply in others, at least in the British context (see also Macmillan 2010; Jochum 2010). So the suggestion that support for voluntary action simply follows from 'the evidence' is an overgeneralized non sequitur. Narratives to support the sector are now being selectively constructed, integrating supportive evidence and not attending in a sustained way to less comfortable findings, just as narratives in the past have been selectively honed by friends of the market and of the state. Third, and relatedly, these strengths, when they are apparent, anyway often seem to go hand in hand with a raft of problems. We have already acknowledged the 'dark side' of social capital, including that generated by VCS activities. One further useful formulation here is the idea of 'voluntary failure' proposed by Salamon (1987), which recognizes the extent to which reliance on the VCS without appropriate support from the state can involve insufficiency (including under-provision of public goods), particularism (since this sector has neither the universalistic aspirations nor the encompassing capabilities of the state), paternalism (inability to guarantee rights, fostering user dependency), amateurism, and a lack of appropriate accountability structures. Accordingly, the policy choice to enhance support of the VCS tends not to involve straightforward 'win–win' solutions, but a multifaceted political judgement, trading off a range of potential gains and losses with winners and losers across all three sectors.

If both political agreement *and* differences are unavoidably involved in this domain, and assuming that at least *some* of these contrasts involve coherent patterns of guiding ideas, values, and ideologies (rather than merely shapeless ad hoc or opportunistic politicking), how can these facets of the process be modelled? Drawing on Michael Freeden's morphological analysis of political ideologies and Mary Douglas's cultural theory, an attempt can be made to portray the ideological dimension of the evolution of policy in the UK. The former is invaluable because it allows us to conceive of ideology as a fluid, evolving, and restless process rather than as the static end point as portrayed by those who deny the relevance of ideological considerations (Freeden 1996). The latter gives us a parsimonious analytic point of departure for considering ideational possibilities concerning how to work progressively in this sphere, without relying purely on the traditional 'market versus state' two-sector dichotomy (Douglas 1999).

Modelling the ideological dimension demands that we simultaneously attend to two distinctive processes. First,the ideational decontestation which underpins the mainstreaming policies and practices to which we have referred earlier. This embodies the consensual element, where VCS-friendly agendas long gestated within this sector by those groups trying to represent it and foster a favourable environment towards it have increasingly coincided with the institution-building efforts of the state. Those both outside and inside the state have used a permissive, shared language about, and fostered institutions putatively designed to enhance, the 'health', 'capacity', and 'infrastructure' of the VCS. The Compact, while widely criticized for implementation failures at local and national levels (see Zimmeck 2010) did, at least in principle, aspire to institutionalize a three-sector model. It performed a crucial symbolic role here, differentiating a pro-sector environment—involving a conscious three-sector model—from crude two-sector approaches, wherein institutional agendas had been reduced to considerations relating only to market and state.

Second, taking the ideological dimension seriously requires that we explicate contentious elements in the process, particularly by seeking to examine the extent to which competing or conflicting imageries of the VCS may have been in play as policy has evolved in this area in recent decades. These different visions have largely played out within the permissive and vague parameters of decontestation we have mentioned, which constitute the policy mainstream. Agendas have also evolved *outside* the basic mainstream parameters, which could be loosely associated especially with strands of the Marxist thinking mentioned earlier, and have also involved a syndicalist element. But these seem not to have exerted a great deal of direct influence over how policy has actually proceeded (see Kendall 2010).

The three broad approaches within this mainstream discernable from the policy literature and policy debates during Labour's tenure included:

- a consumerist orientation, embracing quasi-market solutions;
- a civil renewal stance, with a premium on hierarchical order, envisioning strengthening the sector's role in the pursuance of security and stability;
- a democratic life revival tendency, most closely connected with support for more fluid and open policy interactions.

We can consider how these linked to specific policy actors in turn. The consumerist approach, promoted with increasing stridency over time by ACEVO, a group representing chief executives (mainly of large service-providing charities) from within the third sector policy community and Alan Milburn when prominent in the government, tended to picture the sector primarily as a source of 'superior performance' comfortable with the challenges of commercialization, strengthened by lessons drawn from business in quasi-market contexts, and as a primary route for the enhancement of user choice. The local-level collective relationships that matter so much to those of a more communitarian disposition are given incidental rather than sustained attention, as are the sector's broad political and educative roles. In political and electoral terms, this fitted with New Labour's drive to improve public services for voters under-stood essentially as increasingly demanding consumers—and only in passing acknowledges features of the sector which do not allow it to be portrayed as part of a 'consumer society'. Rather, the idea has been to use the sector to extend the reality of such a society to socially ex-cluded constituencies.

A consumerist leaning was also implicit in the Treasury's decision, under Gordon Brown, to interpret 'capacity building' (see the introduction) as first and foremost relating to fostering choice in public service delivery (rather than interpreting it more generally as strengthening the sector in other respects). Yet Brown's position in Treasury and later as prime minister was more complex than this: it *also* exhibited strongly dirigiste emphases on control and order. As shown, for example, by the agenda espoused at the Council on Social Action under Brown's leadership, there was a stress on third sector-friendly social roles other than market-style con-sumption. This was partly about citizenship-oriented roles above and beyond public services. But even *within* the context of public service reform, this aspiration for a more pluralistic ap-proach was in evidence. In this view, worries about consumerism as an excessively narrow frame of reference for developing public services were recognized as legitimate, and there was an insistence that traditional hierarchical components, as well as 'co-production' involving dialogue with users, should also play their part in structuring welfare (Council for Social Ac-tion 2008). The more dirigiste order-and-control aspects here were particularly associated with the style of other ministers such as David Blunkett, and some sympathetic high-profile third sector organizations, such as Community Service Volunteers. We can therefore speak in that case of a civil renewal orientation—or more evocatively, civil *order* renewal. Such an ap-proach pictured the state and the third sector as allies coordinating in a relatively regimented style at national and local levels, and involves a preference for predictable, stable hierarchical styles of organization.

Finally, democratic life renewal is a different position again which seemed to be taking shape in the last years of the Labour administration, exhibiting a more open-ended and reflexive style, seeking distance from both markets and hierarchies. It was connected at one level with the 'dia-logic' element of 'co-production' in public services, but went beyond it, with its suggestion that healthiness for civil society requires collective participatory group processes more broadly and generally. That is, a need for the organization of shared, inclusive fora and arenas for delibera-tive debate is emphasized (rather than simply offering discrete opportunities for individual users to exercise voice). This emphasizes voluntary action as predominantly bound up with local empowerment, where this is understood as built around collective communication and deliber-ative processes. There is a strong resonance with locally led 'community development' tradi-tions of organizing (Knight 1993; Community Organising Foundation 2007). Voluntary action here in principle is espoused as precisely avoiding compulsion; and limiting the imposition of well defined a priori rules or centralizing fiat. Its promoters, including David and Ed Miliband (now leader of the Opposition), appeared more comfortable with delegation and reflexive agenda-shaping debate, a position which seems to resonate especially with the priorities of some actors in the 'community sector' policy sub-community. Yet on balance, and despite recent new injections of funds, this appears to have been relatively weakly institutionalized in terms of policy attention and policy effort compared with the consumerist and civil order revival ap-proaches, especially in terms of national-level resource commitments.

Box 7.4 makes an attempt to round off this discussion and connect it more explicitly to the aca-demic discourse, including obvious policy themes but also the ideas associated with the social cap-ital literature. In a stylized but hopefully didactically useful way, it seeks to compare and contrast some of the elements that seem to be encapsulated in each of the three New Labour approaches reviewed. We will return to these models briefly below in our closing remarks on the implications of the new coalition government's agenda.

Box 7.4 **Differentiating the various strands of New Labour third sector thinking**

Ideological orientation	Quasi market consumerist	Civic order renewal	Democratic life revival
Third sector role: policy expectations and ideational emphasis	Principled emphasis on third sector as 'delivering' service providers	Recognition of multiple roles steered decisively through authoritative structures	Fluid on roles, more room for argumentation and contestation within service delivery contexts, and outside them
Envisioned relationship to people in society	Third sector as essentially a quasi-market, or market, participant widening choice to consumers	Grateful 'partner'—third sector strengthens deferential citizen-consumer?	Ally with appropriately democratic state—third sector strengthens challenging citizen?
Prioritized political and economic functioning	Responsive to predetermined needs, preferences emerging in 'consumer society'	High status consultee in shaping of insulated political-technocratic decisions	Co-designer of societal needs and preferences, in necessarily slow and involved process
Approach to trust and relationship with the state	Contracting and trust hand in hand, parcelled and professionally packaged. Contracts should *replace* grants	Advice from sector makes bureaucratic system run better, more trustworthy and better implementer; or faith in state-funded third sector as co-regulator Implicit: space for grants to support these roles	Trust mainly through open ended deliberative processes, suspicious of isomorphic 'contract culture'; space for grants explicit?
Associated interpretation of social capital	Social capital—*a la* Coleman: contractarian rational choice instrumentality, with third sector supplying' appropriable organizations'	Social capital exemplified especially in traditional religious and scientific institutions—cf. the communitarianism of Amatai Etzioni, and Himmelfarb	Social capital—earlier (new institutional) Putnam (cf. Italian regional analysis), with shades of Habermas

Europeanization and the third sector

Like other sectors of society, the third sector is not immune from social, economic, and political processes that cut across national boundaries—despite the fact that core responsibility for policy in this area remains firmly at national and sub-national levels in all developed countries. Cross-national pressures, especially as mediated by the EU institutions, are seen as increasingly relevant for shaping social policy options, both positively and negatively, and in some areas of social policy, analysts have claimed to detect 'convergence'(see Chapter 17). More general internationalization and globalization dynamics may also be less visibly shaping the trajectory of third sector policies (see Kendall 2010b), but we will focus here on European institutions, and the EU in particular.

Within the EU, we have become increasingly aware of the enormous variety that characterizes the scope and role of this sector, with diversity in terms of policy approaches, funding dependencies, and functional and policy field emphases becoming ever more apparent as research has developed. It is perhaps no surprise, then, to report that there is little or no evidence of strong or even weak 'convergence' (for example, with groups of countries following similar pathways) in terms of national cross-cutting policies. Institutional path dependencies, which are especially acute in this area, the culture-specific nature of voluntarism traditions (in terms of meanings and actions), the limited extent to which they can be manipulated by top-down policy tools, and the complex composite nature of policy in terms of national and sub-national elements have tended to lock in established practices, and militate against dramatic deviations from inherited patterns. However, this does not mean that changes associated with transnational institution building have had no impact. Rather, it means that the observable impacts have been confined to sites of policy processing which are believed to be of limited salience and unclear relevance to most VCS actors, or are modest, localized in their effects, and largely incremental in the way they develop.

Three such forms of third sector Europeanization have been stipulated (Kendall 2010b), based upon the theoretical frameworks and empirical materials distilled in the 'Third Sector European Policy' network (Kendall 2009a):

- the process whereby domestic third sector policy communities and the policy architecture they support connect with EU-led actors and institutional pressures;
- the development of an 'organized civil society'-oriented policy discourse and infrastructure in Brussels in proximity to the European Commission, the European Parliament, the European Council, and the European Economic and Social Committee (EESC);
- a multilevel policy process, wherein the various 'policy modes' of the EU institutions (Wallace 2000) are deliberately geared towards policy actors from this sector located at EU, national or subnational level.

Kendall (2009b) shows that in the UK case, the first type of process has tended to develop to only a relatively modest degree compared with other countries, where EU framing and policy orientations are much more significant, even if the forms of these are very different. For example, much more weight is attached to the EU's agenda, albeit for very different reasons, in countries as diverse as Germany, Spain, and the Czech Republic. As far as the second type of process is concerned, while the resources commitments to and possibilities for policy development seem very modest, there is now a range of organizations and arenas in place which have exhibited a good deal of resilience, despite the difficult and complex policy environment they inhabit. For example, within the sector, the Platform of European social NGOs has consolidated a significant position as a European horizontal 'network of networks' which cuts across key European social policy domains (Cullen 2010). This seeks to promote a 'social Europe' which, to use the language introduced above, involves stronger democratic revival and civil order renewal elements and less emphasis on quasi-market consumerism than has been favoured in recent years by the European Commission at a global level. With the public institutions, relatively patterned and settled relationships have been consolidated in relation to the European Parliament and the EESC in particular (see Kendall et al. 2009 for a survey).

As to the third process, progress has been relatively disappointing in engaging this sector, especially as far as the Open Method of Co-ordination has been concerned. This was sold as a policy mode providing unprecedented opportunities for civil society policy engagement by its supporters (De La Porte and Pochet 2003). However, pockets of engagement have emerged, and the European Anti-Poverty Network (EAPN) in particular has had some success in furthering its social exclusion agenda, especially at EU level, inputting relevant expertise and well-honed arguments into this process.

Conclusion: The coalition and the future of the VCS agenda

At the time of writing, a coalition has recently formed the government. Some of the components of its policy approach to this field, as this is evident at the time of writing, are shown in Box 7.5. In general, plaudits for the third sector (now referred to as 'the voluntary sector' or 'civil society sector') are much in evidence—as are high expectations that it can help to define, construct, and defend the 'Big Society'. This term is both vague and unfamiliar, but at the most basic level is simply meant to demarcate the ideological claim that civil society, including voluntary action, can in general really flourish only in the absence of 'Big Government'. This has been equated in this way of thinking with over-bureaucratization, inauthenticity, intrusiveness, and inflexible policy implementation. Accordingly, it is suggested the role of the state should be curtailed and in some fields subjected to draconian cuts, on the assumption that its interventions tend to be inherently counterproductive and are a drain on national resources: Civil society, to the extent possible not funded by the state,

---

Box 7.5 'Big Society' and the third sector policy under the coalition

Some major components:

- Make it easier to set up and run organizations in this sector.
- Make it easier for organizations to deliver public services by initiatives including:

  - 'Red Tape' taskforce;
  - mutuals taskforce;
  - renewal and simplification of the Compact;
  - commissioning Green Paper.

- Localism:

  - legislation intended to devolve power aspires to 'remove barriers to community action and community ownership';
  - four experimental 'vanguard' communities with loosened central control (although now reduced to three, since withdrawal of Liverpool from the scheme).

- National Citizen Service (NCS) for 16-year-olds.
- 'Big Society day' and encouragement of workplace volunteering.
- 'Community organizers'—5,000 to be trained, and become self-funding.
- Big Society Bank, drawing funds from dormant bank accounts and other sources.
- Charity Commission budget cut by 33% in real terms over four-year period.

Public spending context: ultra-deep cuts in public body resource commitments:

- Office for Civil Society (formerly Office for Third Sector) budget to be cut by around 40% to £470m over four years.
- Abolition of third sector-focused quangos—Capacitybuilders, Commission for Compact.
- End of key horizontal funding and loan programmes—Futurebuilders, Change-up, Social Enterprise Investment Fund.
- Cuts in support for 'Strategic Partners' (national voice and representation of the sector).
- Local authority budgets cut:

  - all forms of support for local-level third sector organizations under threat;
  - fears of draconian cuts in grants and loss of contracts;
  - concern that publicly supported community facilities previously offered on favourable terms to voluntary groups will be used for alternative, commercial purposes.

Note: a 'Transition Fund' of £100m to support those most at risk to be delivered by Big Lottery, but this is miniscule compared with the massive scale of planned cuts expected to impact the sector directly or indirectly (local level).
Adapted from Alcock (2011)

can and should step in to 'fill the gap', so the concept's supporters claim. The idea, therefore, seems to be to retain the 'mainstreaming' emphasis of the previous administration in one sense. That sense is that the intention appears to be not to recontest what has been decontested as embodied in the Compact and allied processes. Although the Compact Commission is to be abolished as we noted, it is intended that alternative institutions can and should promote the values that it has sought to espouse. Other aspects of continuity include the NCS plans and the Big Society Bank, versions of which were already planned by New Labour.

In another sense, however, coalition policy does seek to break—and to break violently—with the development of the policy of its predecessors. That is, the newly emphasized assumption that to draw out voluntary welfare's progressive potential, a self-censoring state should contritely take a massive step back, most obviously in relation to finance. While the supporters of the 'Big Society' are often fiscal conservatives who tend to portray this aspect of policy as both necessary and non-ideological 'common sense', such blanket demonization of the state is undoubtedly ideological in character, and is seen as such by many of the VCS's supporters inside the sector, as well as within some of the supporting institutions within the state. The Labour 'ideological composite' we tried to delineate—strong on market consumerism and civil order renewal, and relatively weak on democratic revival priorities—does seem set to be remixed and challenged in new ways as the coalition finds its feet in government. The consumerist has received dramatic further strengthening already. But it is very hard at this early stage to ascertain how the balance will evolve in other respects. For example, on the one hand the NCS policy approach seems likely to be potentially rather regimented and dirigiste in character; yet on the other, some of the rhetoric in relation to 'decentralization' and 'localism' suggests a loosening of control and the potential for real civil society-led social innovation at sub-national levels.

This ever-higher public policy profile—and the greater state proximity in terms of scrutiny it is bringing (even if funding trends may move in the opposite direction)—raises a range of concerns about autonomy, identity, and social functioning. Marxist writers and some influenced by the Foucauldian tradition would tend to read this trend deterministically or fatalistically. For them, this trend is leading, or will necessarily lead, to these organizations' 'incorporation', 'co-option', or 'subordination', whatever the 'surface' claims about making more space for voluntarism to flourish. However, those working from other analytic perspectives are more open to evolving evidence and argument, and consider the issue of how state and third sector can and do co-evolve as an empirical question. As stressed before, there are necessarily severe limits to generalization here because of the sector's diversity in terms of, inter alia, size, substantive policy field, ideologies, and levels and styles of engagement with the state.

We can perhaps highlight two key questions which commentators on policy in the years ahead will need to keep at the forefront of their analysis. First, how do evolving inherited and new voluntary sector policies play out in practice—at the level of front-line implementation—from the perspective of the relevant organizations and their stakeholders—not least, users/beneficiaries and volunteers? Rhetorical acknowledgement has reached, or is close to, saturation point: what matters now is the extent to which claims of policy supportiveness are followed through into concrete practice. Are assertions that these organizations and those involved with them will be given room to breathe and even flourish as government dependence upon them grows going to be easy to keep? Legitimate accountability imperatives as well as less noble political imperatives to intervene and interfere may well undermine such claims, as the late Ralph Dahrendorf anticipated in his analysis of the dangers of greater proximity between the state and the VCS a decade ago. The research to date is mixed on this point—especially in relation to the fractious financial dimension of transactions—and a very close eye will need to be kept on how the process pans out in the years ahead. Second, are relevant policies and front-line practices evolving in a truly balanced way? Are institutions and relations taking shape which respect the range of functions and diversity of roles we have identified? Perhaps the key challenge here is to ensure that the drive to increase the sector's role in public service delivery does not undermine its functioning in other dimensions—including social change-oriented campaigning, and community development contributions.

FURTHER READING

Anheier, H.K. (2005) *Nonprofit Organizations*: *Theory, Management, Policy*, Routledge, London. Stimulating and attractive textbook for relatively advanced students by a leading international comparativist.

Billis, D. and Glennerster, H. (1998) Human services and the voluntary sector: towards a theory of comparative advantage, *Journal of Social Policy*, 27, 1, 79–98. Interesting attempt to draw upon economic and organization theory to interpret the role of the sector in mid 1990s British social policy, with an emphasis on social exclusion. Still relevant today.

Bridge, S., Murtagh, B., and O'Neill, K. (2009) *Understanding the Social Economy and the Third Sector*, Palgrave Macmillan, Basingstoke. A more descriptive and less cerebral account than Anheier's, but useful in drawing together a range of otherwise fragmented materials into a reasonably coherent whole.

Evers, A. and Laville, J.-L. (eds) (2003) *The Third Sector in Europe*, Edward Elgar, Cheltenham. Wide ranging, rich, intriguing—although sometimes polemically anti-American.

Kendall, J. (2003) *The Voluntary Sector: Comparative Perspectives in the UK*, Routledge. Still the most systematic and up-to-date analytical account available on Britain, with a focus on the situation in England. This builds on **Kendall, J. and Knapp. M.** (1996) *The Voluntary Sector in the UK*, MUP (the first systematic attempt to put the UK in comparative context).

Powell, W.W. (ed.) (1987); and **Powell, W.W. and Steinberg, R.** (eds) (2006) *The Nonprofit Sector: A Research Handbook*, Yale University Press, 1st and 2nd edns. Widely regarded as the 'bibles' of research on non-profits in the United States.

Putnam, R. (various) Anyone interested in social capital needs to read Putnam. Moving from the sub-national to the national and international are *Making Democracy Work*, Princeton University Press, 1993; *Bowling Alone*, Schuster & Schuster, 2000; and *Democracies in Flux*, Oxford University Press, 2002, edited collection.

USEFUL WEBSITES

International Society for Third Sector Research. One of the most important examples of a scholarly association which emerged in the late 1980s specifically to promote research in this field. *Voluntas*, the International Journal of Nonprofit Organisation and Voluntary Action, is its house journal: **http://www.istr.org/.**

National Council for Voluntary Organisations: the main coordinating and infrastructure agency for information and policy development within the English voluntary sector, now also heavily involved in much of the new policy architecture. Site can be useful for policy and research materials: **www.ncvo-vol.org.uk.**

National Statistics social capital subsite: a site collating a wide range of material on 'social capital', a good deal of which relates to volunteering, membership of associations, and giving. Established under New Labour, but seems likely to be retained under the coalition government in a similar format: **http://www.ons.gov.uk/about-statistics/user-guidance/sc-guide/index.html.**

Third Sector Research Centre: TSRC was supported to build the evidence base on this sector in the UK (primarily England) over a five-year period from 2008–9 onwards under the previous government, with funding from the (then) Office for the Third Sector, ESRC, and Barrow Cadbury Trust. It offers a wide-ranging and inclusive research programme, and contains a range of materials including policy briefings, research papers, and other publications: **http://www.tsrc.ac.uk/.**

Voluntary Sector Studies Network: the primary UK academic and research association, recently supporting the launch of a new journal in the field, *Voluntary Sector Review*: **www.vssn.org.uk.**

Q ESSAY QUESTIONS

1 Why has political interest in voluntary associations escalated so dramatically in recent years?

2 Is the 'third sector' more efficient and effective than the state?

3 Is the third or voluntary sector important to the design and delivery of welfare?

4 What are the advantages and disadvantages of recent attempts in British policy to rely increasingly on the third sector for welfare?

 ONLINE RESOURCE CENTRE

For additional material and resources, please visit the Online Resource Centre at:
www.oxfordtextbooks.co.uk/orc/baldock4e/.

8

Paying for welfare: public expenditure decision-making

John Baldock

Contents

Introduction

Delivering social policies generally involves spending large amounts of money. The ways in which governments decide how much to spend, and how they control and manage that expenditure, are the central focus of this chapter. At the start of this book (Chapter 1) we defined social policy as the intentions and activities of governments that are broadly social in their nature. We suggested that these social intentions are of three main kinds: the redistribution of resources, usually services or cash, to meet identified needs (for example, the costs of bringing up children); intervention to affect some of the risks to which citizens are exposed (for example, becoming unemployed or ill); and the prevention or reduction of forms of social exclusion (for example, the consequences of poverty or discrimination).This chapter is designed to help students develop an understanding of how public expenditure is managed in order to achieve social policy objectives.

Learning outcomes

At the end of this chapter readers will:

1   be able to describe how the UK Treasury reviews and sets social policy expenditure budgets;
2   understand how public expenditure management involves choices between different objectives and the extent to which these are political choices;
3   understand the meaning of the most important technical terms used in debates about public expenditure;
4   know some of the reasons why levels of expenditure on welfare vary between countries;
5   have explored the key websites providing up-to-date information about social spending by governments.

Why understanding public expenditure decision-making is important

The choices that are involved in the management of public expenditure directly affect our incomes and well-being. As citizens we contribute to the funding of public expenditure when we pay income tax, buy a drink in a pub (paying value added tax (VAT) and excise duty), or fill up with fuel (fuel tax as well as VAT). We are affected as recipients when we attend school, use a university library, or visit a doctor. Most welfare and social programmes depend on public financial support, with government spending money either directly as the provider, or perhaps indirectly as the purchaser of services on behalf of its citizens. The outcomes of social policies that governments pursue and the welfare programmes they provide cannot be properly assessed without considering the effects of the taxes or borrowing used to pay for them. Welfare services are also significantly affected by the methods used to allocate and control spending on them.

The management of public expenditure involves choosing how much to spend on a government's policies and ensuring that the money is properly spent and, as far as possible, achieves the outcomes intended. It is very closely linked to decisions about how to raise the money in the first place, through taxation and borrowing. Taken together, decisions about government spending and taxation are called fiscal policy. Fiscal policy, by taking spending power from taxpayers and by spending money on public services, impacts on the health of the economy more generally. In this sense the management of public expenditure is part of a larger responsibility the government has to manage the economy to the satisfaction of the voters.

Public expenditure decisions are not only economic decisions; they are also decisions about welfare policy. They reveal the intentions and priorities of governments in the very basic sense of how much they are prepared to spend on those intentions and priorities. A policy that is severely underfunded is less of a commitment than one that is adequately financed. The range and types of service provided by governments have changed over time, influenced by factors such as shifting emphases on individualism and collectivism (see also Chapter 3 for the discussion of the ideologies and normative concepts that inform welfare choices), changing needs (e.g. of an ageing population), or new ways of delivering services (e.g. assisted by information technology).

The shift from planning spending increases to planning cuts

During the first ten years of the twenty-first century both the amount of money spent on social policies by the UK government and the proportion of national output that money represented grew significantly. These increases were in part deliberate and planned; they were set out in the Comprehensive Spending Reviews (CSRs) of 2000, 2002, 2004, and 2007. These spending plans sought to fulfil key social policy commitments of the Labour governments of 2001–5 and 2005–10, including a real increase in spending on the NHS, on schools, and the provision of cash benefits that would reduce the proportion of children growing up in poverty. However, when the global recession of 2008–10 sharply reduced the tax income of the government, these planned levels of spending became unsustainable without greatly increased borrowing by the government (see Figure 8.1). The 2010 Spending Review marked a shift from a history of planned increases in spending on social policy to plans for substantial reductions. It committed the UK government to reductions in each of the four financial years from April 2011 to March 2015 so that by the last year, 2014–15, total expenditure would be £81 billion less than if it had been allowed to grow in line with predicted inflation and expected growth in social security payments. The planned reduction in total managed expenditure to £740 billion, if it is achieved, will amount to a 9.9 per cent reduction in real terms, i.e. adjusted for expected inflation (Cm. 7942, 2010: Annex A, para A3: 7).

What makes these plans exceptional is that for most of the period between 1945 and 2011 public expenditure had grown in real terms, particularly driven by increases in spending on the social policy objectives of central and local government. This history of growth is shown in Figure 8.2.

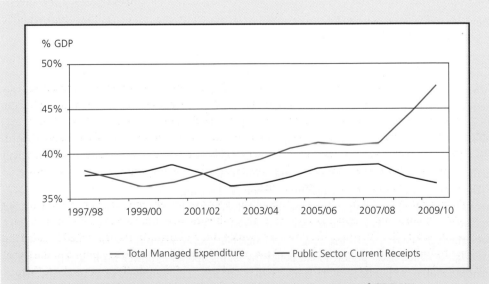

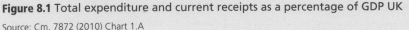

Figure 8.1 Total expenditure and current receipts as a percentage of GDP UK

Source: Cm. 7872 (2010) Chart 1.A

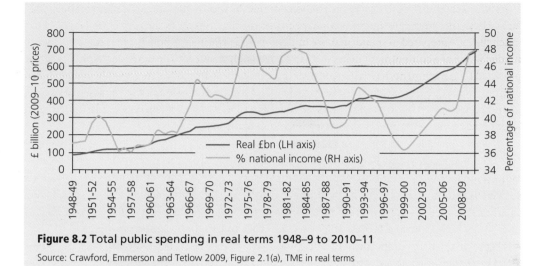

Figure 8.2 Total public spending in real terms 1948–9 to 2010–11

Source: Crawford, Emmerson and Tetlow 2009, Figure 2.1(a), TME in real terms

Because the 2010 Spending Review sought to maintain the increased resourcing of the NHS and schools that had been achieved, it required even sharper reductions in most remaining areas such as local government services, criminal justice and policing, further education colleges and universities, and in capital investment by the public sector. These reductions are summarized in Figure 8.3.

The justification for planning a historically exceptional reduction in most areas of public expenditure was twofold. Firstly, by 2009–10 public expenditure was running at 48 per cent of Gross National Product (GNP), while tax receipts were equivalent to only 37 per cent of GNP, leaving a gap of 11 per cent to be covered by borrowing. The government judged borrowing at this level to be unsustainable in the light of the expected growth of the economy, and defined the shortfall in public finances as a structural deficit that could be tackled only by reducing government expenditure. Secondly, the worldwide banking crisis that began in 2007 had reduced economic growth and tax income while also requiring government to borrow substantial sums to inject capital into British banks that would otherwise have gone bankrupt. While government hopes to recoup the 'investments' in the banks, the abrupt increase in borrowing to support them added to the strain on public finances (Cm. 7942, 2010: paras 1.1–5).

The role of the Treasury

In the United Kingdom, primary responsibility for the management of public expenditure rests with the Chancellor of the Exchequer and the Treasury. Both have a long history in managing the finances of the state. In medieval times the Exchequer was the office within which the King's treasurer guarded and accounted for the royal revenue. The exchequer was literally a chequerboard, used by the treasurer to audit the accounts of local sheriffs who collected and spent money on behalf of the Crown. In 1833 Parliament passed legislation formally creating the Treasury as a ministerial department under the Chancellor of the Exchequer.

While it is Parliament that must vote annually to approve the expenditure of governments, by voting for a Finance Bill, it remains a principle that ministries can only make payments that have been authorized by the Treasury. The process by which this authorization is negotiated is called the spending round, and the announcements of the results of this process are key points in the social policy calendar. An official guide to the spending round is provided on the Treasury website (**http://www.hm-treasury.gov.uk**). Between 1998 and 2009 the round began each November when the Chancellor gave a pre-Budget report designed to provide the economic and policy context for the decisions to be announced in the Budget of the following spring. From 2010 the coalition

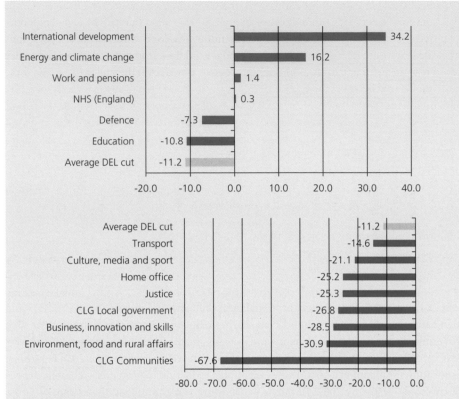

Note: This chart refers only to Departmental Expenditure Limits or DEL spending. It does not include Annually Managed or AME spending, such as social security spending, that is demand-led and cannot be determined in advance. See p.188 for these definitions.

Figure 8.3 Winners and losers in the CSR 2010

Percentage change in real spending 2011–12 to 2014–15
Source: Crawford, IFS 2010, slides 29 and 31

government replaced the pre-Budget Report with a more concise Autumn Statement on the economy. In 2010 the Autumn Statement included a response to the economic and borrowing forecasts of the newly formed independent Office for Budget Responsibility (OBR). It is likely that autumn statements, though less formal than the pre-Budget reports, which were required by statute, will signal the framework for the budget the following year.

Box 8.1 **The Office for Budget Responsibility**

The Office for Budget Responsibility (OBR) is a statutory body set up by an act of parliament in 2010 to make independent assessments of the public finances and the economy. It makes its own forecasts of the growth of the economy and of government income and publishes regular judgements on fiscal policy and forecasts made by the Treasury. It has full access to the data and analysis produced by the Treasury. For each Budget and Pre-Budget Report the OBR confirms whether the government's policy is consistent with a better than 50 per cent chance of achieving the fiscal mandate set by the Chancellor. The OBR makes independent assessments of the public sector balance sheet, including analysing the costs of ageing, public service pensions and Private Finance Initiative contracts.

Source: OBR website: **http://budgetresponsibility.independent.gov.uk/what-we-do.html**

In the spring, usually late March or early April, the Chancellor announces the Budget. This is essentially about the income side of public spending plans—the taxes that will be levied and borrowing required—and it sets the fiscal context or 'spending envelope' within which negotiations over future expenditure are set. Between the spring Budget and the autumn, negotiations take place between the Treasury and the spending departments of government over their allocations and these are generally announced in November. From 1998, Comprehensive Spending Reviews set spending plans for the next three years. In 1998, 2000, 2002, and 2004, announcements were for the subsequent three years, including an overlap with the last year of the previous plan. Thus the final year of the last spending review was open for negotiation in the preparation of the next one. However, in the 2004 review the government decided not to reopen the spending totals for 2005–6, and so the next CPR was in 2007 for spending in 2008–9, 2009–10, and 2010–11. The 2010 review set out expenditure for the next four years, until March 2015, an addition consistent with the coalition government's commitment to five-year parliaments (see Table 8.1).

The Comprehensive Spending Reviews

These three-year plans were designed to break with an older culture of annual spending rounds. By giving departments three-year budgets they set a longer-term horizon for planning, re-prioritization, and investment in delivering services. The weakness of the system of the annual spending rounds that had existed since the early 1960s was that it had led to:

> an annual cycle of year-on-year incremental bids by departments; settlements reached by bargaining over inputs rather than analysis of outputs and efficiency; excessive departmentalism; a split between public and private provision; and a bias towards consumption today rather than investment in our future. (Cm. 3978, 2001: 3)

Under the system of three-year plans the government sought to separate decisions about current and capital spending and encourage investment rather than spending on consumption. In 1998 the government set itself a Code for Fiscal Stability consisting mainly of two fiscal rules designed to constrain political pressures for excessive spending:

- the **golden rule:** over the economic cycle, the government could borrow only to invest and not to fund current spending;
- the **sustainable investment rule**: net public debt as a proportion of GDP would be held over the economic cycle at a stable and prudent level, normally below 40 per cent of GDP over the **economic cycle**. (Cm. 6701, 2005: 15)

Table 8.1 The Comprehensive Spending Reviews (renamed Spending Reviews from 2010)

Year of Spending Review	Years covered by spending plans
1998	1999–2000; 2000–1; 2001–2
2000	2001–2; 2002–3; 2003–4
2002	2003–4; 2004–5; 2005–6
2004	2005–6;*2006–7; 2007–8
2007	2008–9; 2009–10; 2010–11
2010	2011–12; 2012–13; 2013–14;

* plans merely confirmed

These rules were intended to limit expenditure to amounts that a government could afford out of the taxes it collects rather than out of borrowing. In the UK the golden rule meant that while the government could borrow in a year of slower economic growth and therefore lower tax returns, it would have to ensure that over the whole economic cycle, from the beginning of a period of growth to the end of the following period of deflation, it did not fund current spending out of borrowing. The rule worked well until the financial year 2000–1when the stock market fell and economic growth slowed. At the same time the 2000 CSR had planned significant increases in government spending, particularly on education and health. Government spending grew faster than the economy from 2000 and by 2002–3 current spending overtook tax income and the golden rule was in danger of being broken. This led to debate about when an economic cycle begins and ends, something that cannot be finally settled until it is over. In 2005 Gordon Brown, as Chancellor of the Exchequer, twice revised the dates for the economic cycle, first changing its start from 1999 to 1997 and then extending its end from 2006 to 2009 (HC 739 2006: 25–6). In this way the golden rule was adhered to until the financial year 2007–8. The second rule, that net public debt should not exceed 40 per cent of GDP, was also successfully followed until 2008. This measure reached as low as 29.7 per cent of GDP in 2001–2. But as public expenditure began to exceed economic growth and income from taxes, it began to grow, to 35.9 per cent in 2006–7 (ONS 2011: 1–3).

The impact of the banking crisis of 2007–9

In 2008 a combination of the sharp decline in the size of the economy due to the recession and the costs of intervention to support the banking sector and inject demand into the economy forced the then Chancellor of the Exchequer, Alistair Darling, to announce in October the suspension of the Code for Fiscal Stability. By December 2010, the combination of the recession (which raised public expenditure but reduced tax receipts) and the costs of government interventions to support the banks had increased the national debt to 157.9 per cent of GDP. By this time the Treasury had developed a measure of debt that excluded 'exceptional financial interventions' largely involving the support of the banks. Even under this more limited definition, public debt had reached 59.3 per cent of GDP (ONS 2011: 5; see Figure 8.4). It is the government's intention that the costs of nationalizing

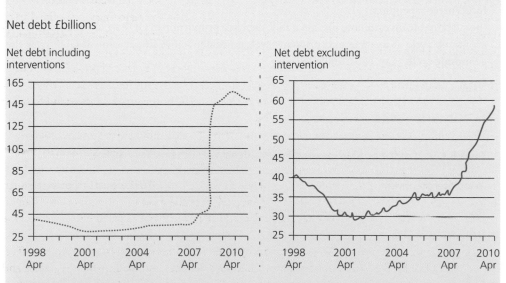

Figure 8.4 UK national debt including and excluding the effects of 'financial interventions' to sustain the banking sector

Source: ONS (2011), *Statistical Bulletin: Public sector finances*, December 2010, Page 2

Northern Rock, Lloyds Banking Group, and the Royal Bank of Scotland will be temporary, and that at some point these assets will be realized by selling the government's share. However, at the point of writing (January 2011) the consequences of the bank 'bail outs' continue to introduce unusual uncertainty into public finances. In addition to the costs of nationalization of key banking groups, the guaranteeing by the state of the liabilities of many other UK banks and building societies, while not adding directly to the national debt, have added contingent liabilities (which may not be called upon should the financial sector recover fully) that have been estimated to exceed £1,500 billion (ONS 2009). These very large financial risks have profoundly changed the context in which politicians make judgements about public expenditure, particularly that on social policy objectives.

The management of public expenditure from 2010

The coalition government set in place new rules for fiscal stability and the management of public expenditure:

- a forward-looking target to achieve cyclically adjusted current balance by the end of the rolling five-year forecast period. This is a commitment to achieve balance in the government budget by 2015–16, i.e. current spending will by then be financed from taxation with no additional requirement for borrowing. In 2010–11 the current budget deficit was about 11 per cent of expenditure and the Spending Review was designed to generate a small surplus by the end of 2014–15.
- a supplementary fiscal target for public sector net debt (PSND) as a percentage of GDP to be falling by 2015–16. In 2010 the Office for Budget Responsibility forecast that PSND (excluding the 'exceptional items' involving the support of the banks), would peak at 69.7 per cent of GDP in 2013–14 and then fall to 67.2 per cent of GDP in 2015. However, this would still be a figure greatly in excess of the low of 29.7 per cent achieved in 2001–2 (HM Treasury 2010: paras 3.2–3).

Ensuring that government departments spend money effectively and efficiently

Historically, the Treasury has faced difficulties in preventing government departments from overspending their budgets. This was particularly a problem in the 1970s when a combination of high inflation and a method of planning that focused on allocating permission to finance a defined set of resources led to unexpectedly high spending in cash terms. Since then the system of Departmental Expenditure Limits (DELs) has tied government departments and local authorities to cash limits in the amount of Treasury funding they will receive. A major part of the task of public expenditure management is ensuring that spending is used effectively and efficiently. In recent years a variety of different controls has been used by the Treasury. All methods, however successful, tend to bring with them disadvantages and unexpected effects.

The Spending Review ties government departments' planned spending to defined outputs and to investments that will improve the efficiency or quality of services. After negotiation, departments are set targets for performance and efficiency that they are expected to meet and upon which the release of further funding is in principle dependent. From 1998 to 2010 these mainly took the form of Public Service Agreements (PSAs) (Box 8.2) and they were the main instrument in a substantial system of audit and inspection to which central and local government departments have become subject in recent years.

The public services are regularly inspected by, amongst others, the National Audit Office, OFSTED (Office for Standards in Education, Children's Services and Skills. which regulates and inspects services for children and young people, as well as schools and colleges), and a range of inspectorates for different parts of the criminal justice system (for each of the police, prisons, probation service, the courts service, and crown prosecution service). Although the use of inspectorates and auditors goes back to Victorian times, their growing use since the election of the Labour

> ## Box 8.2 **Public Service Agreements (PSAs)**
>
> Public Service Agreements were introduced following the 1998 Comprehensive Spending Review. They were abolished by the coalition government in 2010. PSAs were published agreements between the Treasury and spending departments setting out the broad objectives of the policies of the departments and specific measurable targets. They were extended to local government in the form of Local Public Service Agreements (LPSAs) which later developed into a system of Comprehensive Area Assessment. The PSA system was subject to regular changes at both central and local level, but remained essentially a structure under which spending departments and local government were required to produce regular plans and targets that were then audited by bodies such as the Audit Commission. An example of this approach was the star ratings awarded to hospitals for their achievements in reaching PSA targets. The system was both praised for improving performance by public bodies and criticized for costs of regular reporting, and for producing perverse incentives making public bodies engineer the attainment of targets in ways that did not enhance services.

government in 1997 led to criticism which is captured by the concept of an 'audit society' (Power 1999) in which public servants focus on meeting defined targets rather than simply interpreting policies in terms of their professional standards. In 2010 the coalition government abolished a great many of these inspection bodies, including the Audit Commission, which had focused particularly on local government services. At the time of writing (February 2011), the government had begun to set up a system of self-inspection, called the Transparency Framework, which requires all departments and agencies spending public money to publish business plans that they will adhere to. This is supplemented by a system of public accountability under which spending departments and local government must publish all government contracts and details of all spending over £25,000. It remains to be seen how these reforms will work. Progress is reported on the Transparency database at: **http://transparency.number10.gov.uk/**.

The objectives of public expenditure management

Decisions about public spending on social policy account for some 25 per cent of the UK's gross national product or GNP (see Fig. 1.1 in Chapter 1) and even more substantial proportions of the economies of other European Union nations. However, they are much more than decisions about how much should be spent on particular social policies. They fundamentally affect the distribution of resources in a society and the long-term economic health of a country. The decisions are also essentially political, and reflect the priorities of the politicians in power at the time. Four main kinds of judgement are involved:

- *Allocation between different areas of government expenditure.* While it is impossible for governments to raise the overall level of public expenditure faster than the growth of the economy without either increasing borrowing or taxes, they do have discretion over the allocation between policy areas. This is why increased expenditure in a politically sensitive area, such as health, may be accompanied by reductions in less-popular or less-noticed areas such as local government services or housing.
- *Control.* Public expenditure has a tendency to grow faster than planned if not tightly managed. It is much more difficult to contain or reduce public expenditure than it is to increase it. At key

points in the histories of welfare states expenditure has slipped out of control and expanded faster than planned.

- *The balance between consumption and investment.* Public spending on social welfare is necessary to meet the current needs of citizens (expenditure on pensions and income support, for example) but it is also an investment in the future productivity of the society (some aspects of education and training and some healthcare, for example) and of public services themselves (new technologies, more modern methods of using public servants). It is both difficult to assess when spending is investment and when it is consumption (a university education, for example), and tempting to sacrifice the future to satisfying present demands.

- *Efficiency.* Two main forms of efficiency must be managed. Firstly, there is the important question of the effect of public spending on the overall efficiency of the economy in maximizing citizens' welfare. Expenditure by the state is often, though not always, expenditure forgone by the taxpayer. It may be that the taxpayer would have spent the money in a way that added more to social welfare than the choice the state is making. There are also important decisions to be made about the impact of taxes on individuals and families, since these directly affect welfare and inequalities in spending power. The overall effect of public expenditure on the efficiency of an economy is hard to judge (see Box 8.3), but it is critical to the longer-term growth of the economy and the welfare of citizens. Economic criteria involve questions of market failure and opportunity cost, as well as the provision of public goods (such as defence and police) and the management of externalities (such as pollution). Secondly, efficiency within government spending focuses on how cheaply and how effectively policy goals are met. The Public Service Agreements were a key way of doing this. In addition, governments from time to time set up efficiency drives of one sort or another (see Box 8.4).

Box 8.3 **Social policy and economic efficiency**

It is almost a universal axiom of economics that a government should not intervene in an economy unless doing so will produce an efficiency gain or achieve some other goal that is valued above efficiency, such as some criterion of social justice. It follows from this that any proposed or current state activity, such as a social policy, should be carefully evaluated for its likely costs and outcomes. Included in this evaluation should be some estimate of the opportunity cost of the activity. That a social policy achieves its goals is not a sufficient reason to support it. The resources used might have produced even more valued gains in some other area of government policy had they been left to the market to allocate. Economics provides a considerable armoury of concepts and analytical tools that can be used in policy evaluation and it is a source of considerable frustration to economists that these are so rarely or so cavalierly used. For example, Nicholas Barr states firmly at the start of his book on the economics of the welfare state:

The central argument of this book is that the proper place of ideology is in the choice of aims, particularly in the definition of social justice and in its trade-off with economic efficiency; but *once these aims have been agreed* the choice of method should be regarded as a *technical* issue rather than an ideological one. (Barr 1993: 100, emphasis in original)

However, anyone with even only a passing interest in the way in which social policies are initiated or changed will know that this simply does not happen. Technical questions, particularly the evaluations of economists, play very little part in the political processes that change social policy. One reason is to be found in the quotation above. Barr speaks of 'once these aims have been agreed'. Unfortunately, they never are. There are always competing and changing definitions of 'social justice and its trade-off with economic efficiency'.

> ### Box 8.4 **Effectiveness vs. efficiency vs. choice**
>
> The key task of public expenditure management is to achieve a government's desired policy outcomes while at the same time taking as little as possible from taxpayers. As users of public services such as health and education, citizens have high expectations, but as voters they will punish political parties associated with high taxes.
>
> Spending more money on health and education usually generates more activity and intermediate outputs, such as more new hospitals and schools, more treatments, and smaller classes, but it does not necessarily lead to significantly improved final outcomes, less illness, and better educated students. The House of Commons Education and Skills Committee concluded that the big increases in education spending from 1997 to 2003 had not added anything to the rate of improvement in GCSE passes. These seemed to rise irrespective of spending going up. Similarly the Office for National Statistics concluded that the substantial increases in health spending between 1999 and 2006 had added relatively little in more services and better outcomes (Chote et al. 2006: 75–8).
>
> The government's response has been to search for ways to get more per pound spent: to improve efficiency and productivity in public services. The Gershon efficiency review (Gershon 2004) was commissioned to seek savings in the public sector that could be released to add to front-line services. The recommendations were put into the 2004 Comprehensive Spending Review and committed the government to savings worth £21 billion by 2007–8: £5 billion would be saved by reducing the number of civil servants (80,000 in Whitehall and 20,000 in local government), often by replacing them with computer-based methods or 'e-government', £7 billion through procurement reforms (how cheaply the government buys from suppliers), and £9 billion from 'non-cashable' improvements in service quality which required the public sector to raise productivity by 2.5 per cent a year. These figures have been questioned by the House of Commons Treasury Committee (e.g. HC 739 2006, paras. 71–5) and by experts such as Professor Colin Talbot of Manchester University who told the Treasury Committee that 'the efficiency savings set out in the Gershon Review are unrealistic and unachievable, as indeed are many of the alternatives and additions proposed by opposition parties. All parties are playing fantasy efficiency savings'.

How is public expenditure defined and measured?

Public expenditure is the total expenditure of the public sector. In any country, however, what public money is spent on is the outcome of a complex history of values and commitments shaped by political ideology, economic theory, interest group pressure, and changing political and social forces.

Where does the money come from and where does it go? Figure 8.5 shows the variety of sources of UK public expenditure in the financial year from 1 April 2010 to 31 March 2011 and its application to services. Note the relatively low proportion that income tax constitutes of total government revenue, the massive size of the expenditure sums involved, and the dominance in these of welfare payments, the NHS, and education as well as debt interest. Note too the difference between total spending and total receipts. The important questions are how and why these expenditure totals change and, on the revenue side, how the 'burden' of taxation is distributed. First, however, we turn to the problem of defining public expenditure.

Public expenditure can be defined and measured in a great variety of ways (see e.g. Corry 1997; Likierman 1988; Mullard 1993). As Watson notes, 'most of the definitions of public expenditure are biased, in one way or another, to suit the objectives of those who seek to promote them' (Watson 1997: 41–2). To understand the debates over public expenditure we need to know how the government calculates and presents its accounts and what the important features of these are.

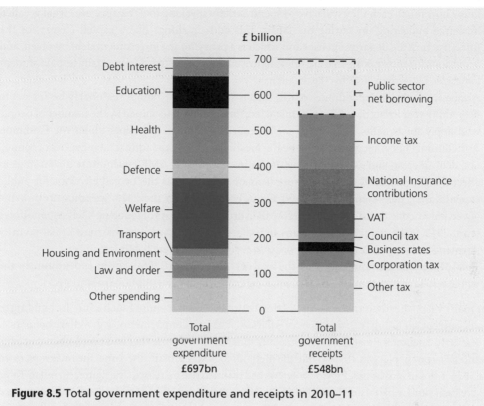

Figure 8.5 Total government expenditure and receipts in 2010–11

Source: Cm. 7942 (2010), Chart 1.3

The UK government's spending plans for 2011 to 2015 are shown in Table 8.2. The important terms are:

● The Departmental Expenditure Limits (DELs): the firm four-year cash spending limits given to departments and within which they plan and prioritize. There are separate limits for current and capital expenditure and departments can carry unspent money from one year over into the next. There is a small centrally held DEL Reserve which is available only for unforeseeable contingencies, which departments cannot be expected to manage within their DEL. Although departments

Table 8.2 Planned total public spending, 2011–15 UK

£ billion	2011–12	2012–13	2013–14	2014–15
Current Expenditure				
Departmental Expenditure Limits (DEL)	343.3	345.0	349.6	348.7
Annually Managed Expenditure (AME)	307.8	319.5	329.1	344.0
Capital Expenditure				
Departmental Expenditure Limits (DEL)	43.5	41.8	39.2	40.2
Annually Managed Expenditure (AME)	7.3	6.7	6.4	6.9
Total Managed Expenditure	**701.8**	**713.0**	**724.2**	**739.8**

Source: Cm. 7942 (2010) Table 1.1

know how much cash they will have to spend, strictly speaking the Treasury uses what is called 'resource budgeting' in setting the DELs. This adds in things like a capital charge for the infrastructure the department uses and which is a proxy for the government debt involved, and provisions for future costs that are relevant to a current year, such as potentially unpaid student loans (see Likierman 2003 for the details).

- Annually Managed Expenditure (AME): this is spending that cannot reasonably be subject to firm multi-year limits because it is demand led, for example determined by the number of people who apply for benefits. It includes social security spending, payments under the Common Agricultural Policy, net payments to the EU, local authorities' expenditure financed out of council tax, debt interest, and expenditure by the national lottery. If AME expenditure grows so as to affect the planned total for expenditure (sometimes known as the 'overall envelope for public expenditure'), then some DELs may have to be reduced. In the 2010 Spending Review the government 'considered' some areas of AME in order to find ways of reducing likely expenditures (Cm. 7942, 2010: para. 1.12). Reforms in welfare were outlined that will limit social security payments, and in public pensions, in order to reduce government liabilities.
- Total Managed Expenditure (TME): the total of DELs and AME. TME covers expenditure by the whole public sector: central government, local government, and public corporations.

For many years, the totals made no distinction between capital spending such as on the building of roads, current spending (e.g. on teachers' salaries), and transfer payments (e.g. welfare benefits).

The 2010 Spending Review was significantly different from those that had taken place since the method was put in place in 1998. While the methodology was broadly the same, the review planned real reductions in most areas. Previous reviews had planned real increases. The figures set out in Table 8.2 are cash sums, unadjusted for inflation. As Figure 8.3 shows, the spending total will require real reductions in spending across most areas of government. As the other chapters in the book explain, in many cases these reductions require big changes in the nature and funding of social provision: for example, in funding for universities and students; the ending of universal access to child benefit; reductions in rate support grants to local authorities and the abolition of Council Tax Benefit by 2013; a cap on total benefit payments to households. The main cuts planned are set out in Figure 8.6.

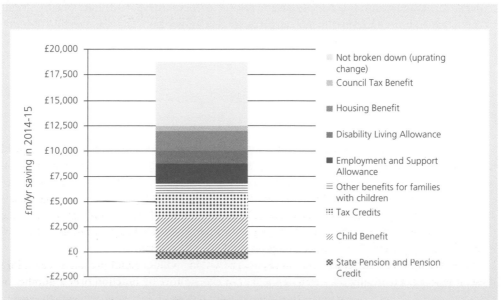

Figure 8.6 The welfare cuts outlined in the 2010 Spending Review

Source: Brewer (2010)

The growth of public expenditure: winners and losers

Is the growth of public expenditure by national governments something to be welcomed or viewed with suspicion? Two economists from the **International Monetary Fund (IMF)** have charted public expenditure growth and its consequences for a selection of industrial economies over a period of 125 years (Tanzi and Schuknecht 1995, 2000). Their findings show similar patterns of development in industrialized countries, especially after 1945. Thus, by 1990, most nations committed over 30 per cent of their gross domestic product to public expenditure, with some (France, Germany) spending in the region of 50 per cent.

Have these increases delivered important social and economic gains, such as declines in infant mortality and increases in life expectancy, educational achievement, and economic growth? Tanzi and Schuknecht argue that before 1960 increased public spending delivered clear results; subsequently, however, achievements have been modest and economies with lower increases have been more innovative. They argue further that smaller-scale government (as in the 'tiger' economies of south-east Asia) does not necessarily perform worse in measures of welfare when compared with nations with larger social programmes. Their analysis needs to be treated with caution, not least because it neglects causation and overlooks the difficulties of comparing different social and political systems. Yet it highlights both the almost inexorable growth in public expenditure in industrial countries (including those with small state welfare systems such as the United States) and some of the puzzles surrounding these developments.

The trend of public expenditure growth in the UK has been steadily upwards. In the twentieth century there was a clear pattern of increasing expenditure up to and including the Second World War and even more so thereafter (Hogwood 1992). In the immediate aftermath of 1945, increases in social expenditure were balanced by declining defence spending, but after 1950 social expenditure began an even more marked rise in absolute terms and relative to GDP under all governments.

The share of public expenditure was low and falling before the First World War, when it rose steeply, only to fall back to a new peacetime level in the 1920s and 1930s. The Second World War was responsible for another sharp rise, followed by a fall after the war to a new and gently rising plateau of public expenditure that is explained by the steadily growing welfare state. The small peaks at the end of the 1970s, the mid 1980s, and the early 1990s were due to the effects of recession and rising expenditures on unemployment benefits and income support.

Competition between spending on social protection, education, and health

To some extent changes in the shares of different areas of social expenditure are not the results of deliberate policy choices but of demographic, economic, technological, and social forces. Social protection spending, for example, has been influenced by the rise in eligible claimants (e.g. pensioners), casualties of downturns in the economic cycle (e.g. the unemployed), and changes to eligibility (e.g. housing benefit). Similarly, health spending until 2002 was mainly affected by the upward pressure of demography (an ageing population), the increased sophistication and cost of medical technology, and greater expectations of and demands for services.

The overall upward trend conceals shifting patterns within public expenditure totals. To explore these, it is worth examining the detail of changes in expenditure by function over a number of years. Figure 8.7 shows how payments to and benefits for older people have grown with the ageing of the population. Expenditure on families and children has been restrained by their relatively stable numbers within the population. NHS expenditure and education expenditure are largely

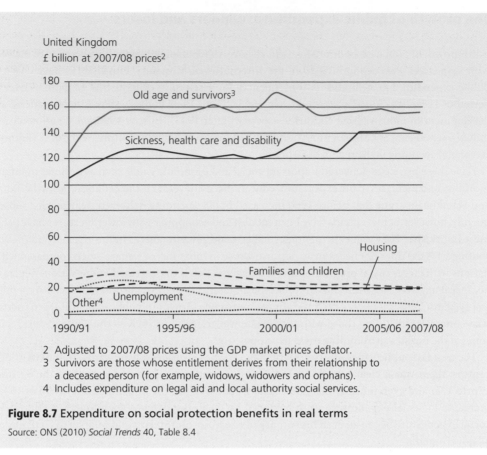

2 Adjusted to 2007/08 prices using the GDP market prices deflator.
3 Survivors are those whose entitlement derives from their relationship to
   a deceased person (for example, widows, widowers and orphans).
4 Includes expenditure on legal aid and local authority social services.

Figure 8.7 Expenditure on social protection benefits in real terms

Source: ONS (2010) *Social Trends* 40, Table 8.4

supply led, governments deciding how much to spend and so growth being a political judgement. Unemployment benefits, on the other hand, are more demand led, and spending rises and falls with the economic cycle.

Very substantial increases in health expenditure were planned in the 2002 Comprehensive Spending Review (Cm. 5570) and these start to become particularly apparent from 2005. A wide-ranging review of health expenditure was undertaken for the government by the former chief of the National Westminster Bank, Derek Wanless, to determine whether the UK should and could match the average for EU spending on health at the time. The review (Wanless 2002) found that no new methods of financing, such as the use of social insurance or private funding, would deliver the required improvements. Only increased public expenditure would be cost effective. As a result, the Chancellor used the 2002 Budget to announce 'the largest ever sustained increase in health resources' of 7.5 per cent in real terms each year for five years.

Conclusion: How the Treasury and the Chancellor determine the future of the welfare state

The object of this chapter has been to explain why it is important to understand the procedures used by governments to decide how much they will spend on social policy objectives. Finding variations in public expenditure between countries is a revealing way of understanding social policy. International comparisons show that nations spent significantly different proportions of their national outputs on public welfare programmes. At the same time, public spending on social welfare programmes has a clear tendency to rise over the long term in all countries. Politicians and governments find it much easier to spend more than to reduce services. The growth can also be un-intended, simply the consequence of the difficulties of managing the expenditure of very large sums. However, global economic competition has made it difficult for governments to raise the costs of their exports through taxation and this has exerted downward pressure on social expenditure. This has meant that the Treasury has become more involved than ever in the details of social policy. In industrial countries, ministers of finance have tended to become the most important ministers of welfare, and this has certainly become true of the role of the Chancellor of the Exchequer in Britain.

FURTHER READING

Before seeking written texts it is best to explore the websites listed below. An excellent introduction to the history of public spending and its management in the UK is **Crawford, Emmerson and Tetlow**'s *A Survey of Public Spending in the UK*, which is available on the IFS website. The best introduction to the management of public expenditure and its significance for social policy is **Howard Glennerster**'s *Understanding the Finance of Welfare: What Welfare Costs and How to Pay for it* (2003, Bristol: The Policy Press). More dated but a good read is **David Lipsey's** *The Secret World of the Treasury* (London: Viking Press, 2000). Not just his reorganization of public spending is described in *Brown's Britain* (**Robert Peston**, 2005, London: Short Books). A reasonably non-technical account of the procedures that the Treasury uses to manage public expenditure can be found on its website, *Public Expenditure Planning and Control in the UK: a Brief Introduction. The Economics of Public Spending* edited by **Miles, Myles, and Preston** (2003, Oxford: OUP) contains good essays on the funding of health, education, crime prevention, and pensions. A much longer-term view of government spending growth, across centuries, is provided by **Peter Lindert**, *Growing Public: Social Spending and Economic Growth Since the Eighteenth Century, Volume 1, The Story* (2004, Cambridge, CUP). A similarly large perspective is **Tanzi and Schuknecht**'s *Public Spending in the 20th Century: a Global Perspective* (2000, Cambridge: CUP). **Francis Castles** explains the growth of government spending in 22 advanced countries in the now classic *Comparative Public Policy: Patterns of Post-war Transformation* (1998, Cheltenham: Edward Elgar). This is a rapidly changing area in which books become out of date quickly, so students should look at recent issues of the journals *Public Administration, Public Money and Management, The Journal of Social Policy* and *Talking Politics*. The weekly magazine, *The Economist*, also often carries short news articles on public expenditure issues.

USEFUL WEBSITES

The Treasury website (**www.hm-treasury.gov.uk**) provides an essential starting place for exploring the most recent documents relevant to public expenditure management in the UK. Most important are the links to the pre-Budget, the Budget, and the Spending Reviews, and to the pages on public spending and services. Alternative and critical assessments of the UK government's economic policies can be found at the website of the Institute of Fiscal Studies (**www.ifs.org.uk**). It is helpful to read their most recent 'Green Budget' reviewing all the issues the Chancellor must consider. The site also includes many useful analyses of public expenditure and social policy questions and a particular strength are analyses of the impact of taxation on people with different incomes. The Office for Budget Responsibility provides quite technical but useful reviews and assessments of expenditure management, fiscal policy and the range of likely outcomes these may have (**http://budgetresponsibility.independent.gov.uk/**). The website of the House of Commons Treasury Committee (linked from **www.parliament.uk**) provides access to their reports on the pre-Budget and the Budget, and it is very useful to read the verbatim evidence of the people called to give evidence. To explore how public expenditure on welfare is managed in other countries excellent sites are the OECD (**http://titania.sourceoecd.org or www.oecd.org**), particularly links to the OECD Economic Outlook and the OECD Economic Surveys of countries. The European Commission homepage (**http://europa.eu.int**) and its publications page (**http://europa.eu.int/comm/publications**) are the gateways to many useful reports and statistics.

Q ESSAY QUESTIONS

1 Outline what is involved in the Autumn Statement, the Budget, and the Spending Review and explain the importance of the fiscal rules within which public expenditure decisions are made in the UK.

2 Obtain the Office for Budget Responsibility's most recent assessment briefing paper forecasting public finances and critically evaluate their implications for social expenditure and social welfare objectives.

3 What are the main objectives of public expenditure management and how far is the current UK government succeeding in achieving them?

4 Why does public expenditure on social policy tend to grow as a proportion of national income over the longer term and what forces moderate that growth?

5 From the website 'SourceOECD', view the most recent OECD Economic Surveys for Britain and two other countries and compare the judgements made about the management of public expenditure and the effects on the welfare of citizens.

@ ONLINE RESOURCE CENTRE

For additional material and resources, please visit the Online Resource Centre at:
www.oxfordtextbooks.co.uk/orc/baldock4e/.

9

Global social policy

Nicola Yeates

Contents

Introduction

The idea that social policy and human welfare can best be understood in terms of what happens 'inside' the borders of the countries in which they live is challenged on a daily basis. Threats to human health in one part of the world spread rapidly to other parts through international travel. The business practices of mortgage lenders in one country have a knock-on effect in other countries because of the international character of the financial services industry. Populations are displaced over wide distances by civil unrest and conflict, military intervention, political discrimination/oppression, and lack of socio-economic opportunity at home. Ideas about what are appropriate approaches to social policy also 'migrate' between countries. Policies are evaluated and benchmarked against international norms, benchmarks, and governmental commitments. Populations respond to human distress and need overseas through charitable giving and voluntary action.

These diverse examples illustrate how the fortunes of social policy in one country are intertwined with those in others. In the UK, we are accustomed to thinking about this in the context of the European Union where member countries are geographically proximate and relatively culturally homogeneous, and where defined supranational institutions coordinate and lead on matters of international cooperation and are closely involved in matters of policy-making on a wide range of issues. But the connectedness or 'enmeshment' of welfare provision and policy formation extends further—geographically, historically—and encompasses a much broader range of supranational institutions than simply those of the EU.

Learning outcomes

In this chapter we shall be looking at how social welfare systems, policies, and practices are connected and interdependent. We shall be considering the implications of thinking 'globally' for social policy as a field of academic study and as a political practice. After reading the chapter you should be able to discuss the following questions:

1 What kinds of transnational processes are involved in social policy?
2 How do these processes impact upon on human welfare?
3 What role do border-spanning organizations play in social policy formation?

Social policy in a globalizing world

At its most basic, globalization is the term that has been given to a range of economic, technological, cultural, social, and political forces and processes that are said to have collectively produced the characteristic conditions of contemporary life. Foremost among these characteristics is a dense, extensive network of interconnections and interdependencies that routinely transcends national borders. The interconnectedness is said not only to be more extensive in scope than in previous periods, but the connections are more intensive and the speed at which such interactions occur increasing (Box 9.1). These interconnections are expressed in ways that appear to 'bring together' geographically distant localities around the world, and events happening in one part of the world are able to quickly reach and produce effects in other parts of it. It is this enmeshment which gives rise to consciousness of the world as a shared place.

> **Box 9.1 Dimensions of enmeshment**
>
> Extensity: the degree to which cultural, political, social, and economic activities are 'stretching' across new frontiers to encompass the world.
> Intensity: changes in magnitude and regularity of interconnectedness.
> Velocity: changes in the speed of global interactions and processes.
>
> Source: Held et al. 1999

There is a vast debate about 'globalization' (see Yeates 2001 and 2007 for further discussion). Whatever one's position on 'globalization', the processes it seeks to capture are significant for social policy. Yeates (2007) discusses the different approaches to globalization and the various approaches and 'schools of thought' that have developed in relation to it—from the 'technological enthusiasts' to 'marxisant pessimists' to 'plural pragmatists' to 'sceptic internationalists'. Even 'sceptic internationalists', who otherwise deny the fundamental precepts of the globalization thesis and argue that the world economy is essentially characterized by transactions between distinct national economies, would agree there is a need to engage with the idea that social structures, institutions, and processes transcend political (i.e. state) borders, and a need to understand social policy formation within a wider global context (Yeates 2007). But what does it mean to do this? What kinds of abstract framing devices (concepts) and explanations (theories) are relevant? What difference does 'thinking globally' about social policy make to the areas and issues examined, the types of questions asked, and ways of going about answering them? One of the immediate ways of beginning to think about this is to rethink the relationship between welfare and the nation-state.

Questioning the national frame

A global perspective 'disrupts' precepts of social policy that have long been taken for granted, namely the idea that the boundaries of welfare are co-terminous with international political borders. The assumption that the 'edges' of welfare coincide with the outer perimeters of the state has been a defining and enduring characteristic of the study of social policy as it has in many other social disciplines. This assumption most obviously manifests itself in country case study approaches (whether of single countries or more than one, as in cross-national comparative analysis) that define the object of analysis by reference to international state borders. Thus, social policy has essentially been concerned with how welfare services are financed, organized, delivered, and accessed within the confines of these political territories as well as with the effects of provision on social structure, social relations, and quality of life of people living within the bounds of a given country. We are used to social policy being discussed as if it had a national ascription and identity—as in British social policy, French social policy, and so on—or as having a more general set of characteristics—as in 'conservative-corporatist' or 'liberal' welfare states—which map onto different countries.

It could be argued that this national framing of social policy simply reflects the fact that most welfare services are funded, regulated, and delivered within the territorial boundaries of individual countries, that welfare goods and services tend to be funded and accessed by resident citizens living in those countries, and that apparently distinct national styles of 'doing' social policy have emerged. But this focuses attention on particular forces, entities, and populations to the neglect of others. For example, it neglects the intended and unintended effects of domestic and foreign policies pursued in and by one country on other parts of the world and populations living outside it. It also obscures border-spanning multilateral economic institutions (MEIs) and fora, such as the World Bank or the World Economic Forum, in social policy formation. It also marginalizes transnational social movements and forms of collective political action in shaping the policies of a country or of supranational institutions. It assumes that social policy develops within an impermeable national 'container space', with little or no reference made to alternative socio-spatial scales of political action, or to countries' actual embeddedness in the wider world and the kinds of connectedness that link them to one another. Nor does it address the influence of developments and events elsewhere in the world on 'domestic' policy formation and collective social action. In what follows we take a closer look at some examples of how social policy transcends state borders.

Historical transnationalization It is possible to argue that it has never, in fact, been appropriate to think of welfare states and social policies as first and foremost the outcomes of national forces or divorced from the dynamics of the wider global geo-political order. During the nineteenth and twentieth centuries, the forces behind welfare state building and the social regulation of capitalism occurred within a world order characterized by extensive international trade and migration, transnational corporations, and developed international monetary and exchange rate regimes (Thompson and Hirst 1996). While much recent critical commentary on welfare in a globalization context focuses on contemporary transnational political mobilization—in the form of the 'anti-globalization movement' for example—there are examples dating back two centuries of political mobilization that were international and extended beyond Europe. Two examples are the Anti-Slave Trade movement (1787–1807) and the Movement Against Congo Colonization (1890–1910).

Colonialism underpinned the development of social policies and welfare states in a range of countries throughout the world. The development of the British welfare system, for example, is intricately tied up with Britain's status as a colonial power; its colonies ranging from Ireland to Australia, Canada, India, Hong Kong, and many African countries sustained its economic foundations, constituted a destination to which criminal classes and other socially deviant groups and individuals could be exported, and formed a labour pool from which Britain drew to staff its welfare services. In turn, these countries' colonial histories impacted upon the development of their social policies, as Britain 'exported' welfare ideologies and systems (the legacy of which these countries still bear today), influenced their social and political structures, and, together with local elites, subsumed their economic development interests to those of Britain. A tangible example of the transnational dimensions of welfare systems is the British social security system. The Commonwealth spawned a global administrative network of offices involved in the processing of war pensions payments not only to British war pensioners living abroad and to residents of former British colonies, but also to those with no connection to the British state, such as Polish soldiers who fought in the Second World War under British command.

The dynamics of colonial ties are further illustrated by the British Colonial Nurses Association (CNA; see Box 9.4 for list of acronyms). Between its foundation in 1896 and 1966, more than 8,400 women applied to join the CNA (renamed the Overseas Nurses Association (ONA) in 1919) to practise nursing in Britain's overseas colonies, looking after British colonists' health and providing training for indigenous women in the colonies in British nursing. This training role would prove enduring, with the CNA/ONA 'creating a workforce capable of contributing to the British National Health Service' (Rafferty 2005). While most of the CNA recruits were drawn from Britain, nearly 6 per cent of applicants had an Irish address. This is a likely underestimation of the number of Irish nurses applying to or employed by the CNA, since Irish nurses based in Britain would have applied directly from there. Nevertheless, although these numbers are modest, we can appreciate that Irish nurses were involved in complex colonization dynamics: as colonial subjects themselves, they also participated in Britain's colonial nursing services that sustained British colonists, shaped the development of nurse training in other British colonies, and laid the foundations for continued out-migration of intending and qualified nurses from the current and former colonies to Britain for generations to come (Yeates 2009).

Not all of these transnational influences were colonial. Japan imported Western models of welfare as early as the 1870s (Goodman 1992), while Western thinking influenced the development of welfare in Taiwan and Korea (Goodman and Peng 1996). Eugenic and population control ideologies have been given particular expressions in a range of different countries. The so-called golden era of welfare statebuilding (1950s to 1970s) in Western Europe was underwritten by economic and development aid from the United States to Europe in the form of the Marshall Plan (Milward 1994). Although much recent critical attention has focused on the influence of the World Bank's approach to social security and poverty reduction in developing countries, similar policy transfer processes between other more 'progressive' international governmental organizations (IGOs) and countries can be discerned. Thus, Western European social democratic approaches to social protection were transmitted through the ILO which was, for most of the twentieth century, the dominant IGO in the social security field and exerted considerable influence on the development of national social security systems around the world, in 'developed' and 'developing' countries alike (Kay 2000). We return to the theme of IGO influence on social policy formation later in the chapter.

Contemporary transnationalization: the case of healthcare The contemporary health sector provides a good example of border-spanning processes in social policy. We focus specifically on health professionals to illustrate the diverse layers of connection involved. This section is derived from Yeates 2009 and 2010.

The most recent estimates put the total global migrant stock at 214 million people, approximately 3 per cent of the world's population. This represents a substantial increase since 1960, when the stock was 75 million, and even more recently 2005, where estimates indicated that the total migrant stock was 191 million (Human Development Report (HDR) 2009). The health sector accounts for one in three international migrants (WHO 2006), and migrants form a sizeable proportion of the contemporary health labour force in many OECD countries, including the UK. Take nurses, for example. In 2000, foreign-born nurses represented 10.7 per cent of the OECD nursing workforce, and nurse migration has significantly increased in many OECD countries since then. Two in three migrant nurses in OECD countries originate from a non-OECD country, with the remaining migrating between OECD countries (OECD 2007, 2010). The extent of this migration plays out in different ways across different countries, but the UK is amongst the most reliant of OECD countries (alongside the United States, New Zealand, Ireland, and Australia) on foreign-trained medical and nursing staff, with about one in three doctors and one in ten nurses being foreign trained or foreign nationals (OECD 2010).

There are many reasons why health professionals migrate. In the case of nurses, many are drawn to working overseas by higher wages, the desire for wider professional experience, better and more specialized training, increased promotional opportunities, and a higher standard of living. The scarcity of people with their skills on the global market means that they can to a certain extent choose the country to which they wish to migrate. This is not to say, however, that such migration is *determined* by economic or market factors; migration also expresses a desire for travel, adventure, a better climate, greater personal autonomy, and security. It may also be prompted by family or kinship obligations to secure socio-economic security and social advancement. The proximity of countries is also relevant—this partly relates to the ease and cost of travel, the existence of a culturally available set of options, and a common language (Yeates 2009). Health professional migration is in response to the increasing demand for healthcare workers in OECD countries, which is a result of rising incomes, new medical technology, increased specialization of health services, and population ageing (OECD/WHO 2010). The size of the nurse workforce has failed to keep pace with this growing demand due to the long-term effects of policies of under investment in nurse education and training together with a deterioration of working conditions so that many trained and qualified nurses leave the profession for another career offering better education and employment prospects (WHO 2006).

Many governments in the Global North are increasingly recruiting abroad to fill nursing labour shortages. International recruitment has been 'sanctioned' and encouraged by international organizations such as the OECD, which regards it as a viable solution to nurse shortages. The impetus for overseas recruitment in part lies with the length of time it takes to train a nurse, which can be up to seven years between commissioning training places to the output of trained staff. Overseas recruitment of already trained and qualified nurses has become an attractive response to 'quickfix' labour gaps. But recruiting overseas nurse labour also provides a significant cost saving. In Britain, for example, the costs of recruiting a foreign nurse are between five and ten per cent of the cost of an experienced home-grown nurse (Padarath et al. no date). Importing labour from abroad helps keep wages from rising, as they would be expected to in a situation of scarce labour supply. The health system is thus able to integrate cheaper and possibly more submissive labour without the costs involved in educating and training that labour. At the same time, many governments across the Caribbean, Africa, Asia, and the Middle East are responding to the global nurse shortage by adopting policies to produce nurses for export. Often these policies are part of a wider strategy to promote labour export as part of economic development, and have been encouraged by international organizations such as the World Bank and others whose policies have supported export-led industrialization strategies. The benefits to exporting countries are many: migrant remittances support families and communities at home, raise the sending state's foreign exchange holdings, help governments pay off debt and obtain loans, and invigorate the economy by supporting consumption, investment, and business (and profits) for educational institutes, recruiters, and travel agents.

There are major concerns about the effects of this migration on source countries. Although most countries simultaneously import and export nurses, poorer countries tend only to export nurses. The problem for these countries is that they have no further countries from which to recruit to make up for the losses of their own nurses and consequently experience nursing shortages. In this regard, both the Philippines and India—two major global nurse exporters—experience chronic nursing shortages (Tan, Sanchez, and Balanon 2005; Hawkes et al. 2009). Such problems are not confined to countries which only export nurses. Jamaica, for example, has been able to make up some of its nursing losses by recruiting from Cuba, Guyana, India, Ghana, Burma, Russia, and Nigeria, but still experiences serious nurse shortages (Salmon et al. 2007). Sub-Saharan Africa has been especially adversely affected by such shortages, with disadvantaged and rural areas being the worst affected (Adepoju 2007; Dovlo 2007; Awases et al. 2004). The emigration of trained health workers from these poorer countries to rich OECD ones has been described as a 'fatal flow' due to its adverse impacts on health outcomes (Chen and Bouffard 2005). In Malawi, for example, where 64 per cent of nursing posts are unfilled, the high maternal mortality ratio and the inability to expand antiretroviral (ARV) therapy are attributed to the lack of trained midwives and nurses (Muula, Panulo, and Masela 2006). The lack of nursing staff is linked to higher rates of death, disability, and morbidity, with this 'widening of the population health gap [resulting] in reduced productivity, loss of national economic investment, and potential damage to economic development' (Ahmad 2005). These examples illustrate why international nurse migration is commonly likened to asset stripping and characterized as regressively redistributive. Indeed, it entails a *net* flow of benefits from poor to rich countries: the economic value of nurse migration from poorer to richer countries exceeds the volume of international medical aid to developing countries. And although migrant remittances provide a significant form of revenue for source countries, remittances are private transfers, so do not flow directly into the public sector or translate into funding health system improvements (Chanda 2003).

In essence, overseas nurse recruitment policies have been developed by richer countries to solve their own (nursing) care shortages but by doing so they are exporting those very shortages to poorer countries, who are much less able to bear them. Not only does this cause a global public health crisis but it also contributes to the distortion and erosion of informal social care provision that nurses (the vast majority of whom are women) would have otherwise sustained in their home countries. This is not to say that those emigrant nurses do not continue to provide informal social care for their families, only that they do so at a distance. Research on migrant workers has shown how they continue to have contact and provide a great deal of care for their families, whether through educational tuition or emotional support for their children by telephone, or through the remittances they send home that are used to support family educational, health, and housing costs in the source country (Yeates 2008a).

From this case study we can see multiple kinds of border-spanning processes and connections at work:

- cross-border movements of people (health professionals);
- internationalized labour markets;
- effects of underinvestment in one country in shaping policies adopted by other countries;
- impacts of domestic policies of international recruitment on the quality of healthcare and the health status of populations overseas;
- the influence of IGO policies on national policy and welfare provision;
- the provision of informal care by migrants for families 'left behind' in the source country;
- financial flows (remittances).

The case study also reveals the extent to which questions of distribution and fairness play out on a global and not only a national scale. In global nurse migration, diverse interests not only coalesce but also conflict. Questions arise as to how the competing interests of state, commercial, professional, labour, and households can be balanced but also whether these interests can be reconciled. Is it possible, for example, to balance—let alone reconcile—the strategies of individual nurses in low-income countries with the need for nursing staff to fill vacancies in middle- and high-income countries with the wider social development impacts? Put another way, the need for nurses to take care of older people in developed countries has to be weighed against the need for nurses in developing countries to help care for people with HIV/AIDS. This goes to the heart of the problem: how can nurse migration be regulated in the interests of global public health, welfare, care, and social development? Several issues arise here. Is it the responsibility of national governments to 'self-regulate' in the wider interest of poorer countries? Is there a role for international organizations in developing an overall set of rules to which all governments should subscribe? How would such rules be developed, agreed, and enforced? Is the answer perhaps not in regulating nurse migration but in addressing the problems of uneven development that underlie migration? What kinds of policies would be needed to address uneven development and global inequalities? And, again, what role might global organizations play in this?

Approaches to global social policy

The examples discussed in the previous section indicate that what we have come to think of as 'national' welfare systems and policies are far more transnational in nature than is commonly thought. They highlight that welfare formations need to be understood in relational terms, with an emphasis on connections and interdependencies which span geographically distant, economically unequal, and culturally heterogeneous territories. Such connections may occur at the level of the individual migrant, who maintains a relationship with her family in the source country and to which she remits funds while living and working abroad. They also occur at the level of welfare systems—in that the healthcare provision in many Northern countries is reliant upon migrants and migrant production policies in the South. Similarly, they occur at the level of welfare outcomes— with the better health outcomes enjoyed by citizens of richer countries adversely related to those in poor countries. Equally, international organizations are key players: they are expressions of collective organization on the part of governments and are global fora in and through which concerns about key social problems are identified and policies articulated.

Thinking 'globally' about social policy, then, involves focusing on activities and processes that link people and places across borders. Two of the most common ways in which the global has been embraced in social policy are:

- Analysing social policy formation in cross-border spheres of governance. These spheres of governance may be world-regional (EU, ASEAN, MERCOSUR) trans-regional, or global (World Bank, United Nations, IMF, etc). In practice, the focus of analysis often falls on intergovernmental fora since these are the clearest institutional expression of a transnational social policy but can also include non-governmental fora such as the World Social Forum or the World Economic Forum.
- Focusing on cross-border flows of people, goods, services, ideas, finance as they relate to the provision, finance, and regulation of social welfare, policy formation, and the impacts of social policies on populations.

These distinctions are sometimes termed 'top-down' globalism and 'bottom-up' globalism, because they relate to formal and informal processes of social policy formation. But these distinctions are not hard and fast ones as the processes involved are closely intertwined. For example, ideas about what makes a 'good' society or 'effective' social policy are circulated and amplified through cross-border policy fora, and cross-border flows of finance and people are regulated by a complex set of regulatory rules involving supranational organizations as well as national governments. What this latter point brings out also is that 'global social policy' is not simply the terrain of supranational organizations operating in a detached way from 'national' social policy or national governments. The two levels of government are closely intertwined in practice, with national governments seeking to influence what IGOs do, and IGOs similarly seeking to influence what policies governments adopt. Also, unilaterally adopted national policies have global impacts—as the case study on healthcare showed. Here, we say that the adoption of policies of underinvestment and policies of overseas labour recruitment have marked global reach and impact. At its core, global social policy emphasizes the transnational, border-spanning formal and informal processes of social policy formation.

A global perspective on social policy opens up to enquiry the ways in which the content of social policy and the distribution of welfare are shaped by: governmental and non-governmental organizations responding not only to domestic issues and sources of pressure but also to circumstances, events, and developments in other countries; the policies of foreign governments, international organizations, and financial institutions; and the decisions and activities of overseas headquarters or branches of transnational corporations. It draws attention to the ways in which societies, economies, and polities—including labour markets and welfare systems—of different countries are deeply interconnected. This appreciation of the extent and dimensions of 'enmeshment' leads us to focus on the 'external' and global sources of what often appear on the face of it to be principally 'domestic' or 'national' social problems and policy issues.

Globalizing social policy is not simply confined to what happens overseas. It involves attending to the domestic policies and practices of rich countries and their governments as they impact upon home and foreign populations. As the example at the beginning of the chapter illustrates, the healthcare crisis in the Global South is attributable to the sustained effects of underdevelopment, combined with Bretton Woods policies aimed at fiscal and social retrenchment, combined with rich countries' recruitment of health workers from poor countries. In recent years the anti-globalization movement and international development campaign groups have done much to raise public awareness of anti-poverty and social development policies pursued by rich countries. They have also drawn attention to the social (policy) dimensions and implications of the UK government's foreign policy and practices (as well as those of other OECD countries) as regards finance, trade, agriculture, and environment, whether pursued bilaterally through aid programmes or multilaterally through world-regional (e.g. EU) or global (e.g. WB, UN, G8) institutions. These groups' campaigns have exposed the adverse social impacts of government policies supportive of, for example, the

> ### Box 9.2 **Global social policy**
>
> - Social policy issues are increasingly being perceived to be global in scope and cause.
> - Transnational flows of goods, services, capital, ideas, people, link different welfare systems around the world.
> - Transnational forms of collective action have emerged.
> - International organizations are tangibly involved in social policy formation.
> - These responses have tangible outcomes and impacts on social groups, policy areas, and on welfare provision in individual countries.
>
> Source: Yeates 2008b

privatization of public utilities (water, energy), the industrialization of agriculture and food production, and international financing and debt relief mechanisms. These campaigns have brought widespread attention to the wider public policy context of and influences on health, social welfare, and livelihoods (or employment), the role of international organizations in perpetuating poverty and widening inequality in rich and poor countries alike, and the responsibilities of richer country governments and populations towards poorer ones.

International organizations and social policy

The study of international organizations' involvement in social policy has become a major focal point for research. What these organizations say and do about particular issues are important because they have been influential in shaping welfare provision and thus people's quality of life and wider life chances. In this part of the chapter we look at the history of international organizations' involvement in social policy matters and then go on to look at their involvement in social policy contemporarily.

International cooperation on social policy: historical aspects

International cooperation and action on social policy issues have a long history. International non-governmental organizations (INGOs) resulting from private initiatives can be traced back to 1863 when the precursor to the Red Cross, the International Committee for the Relief of the Military Wounded, was founded at the initiative of Henry Dunant, shocked by his experiences at the Battle of Solferino in 1859. This led to the signing in 1864 of the Geneva Convention for the Amelioration of the Wounded in Armies in the Field, which is recognized as the beginning of international humanitarian law. War also provided the spur for the foundation of the Oxford Committee for Famine Relief (Oxfam), founded in 1943 and registered as a charity in 1945: its first concern was with famine in Greece caused by the military activities of the German army there during the Second World War and it subsequently developed into a charity concerned with famine relief in developing countries. Another example of an INGO is the International Planned Parenthood Foundation, which was founded in 1952 at the Third International Conference on Planned Parenthood in Bombay and jointly sponsored (with the UN and the New York-based Population Council) the first world conference on family planning in 1981. These INGOs have pursued their objectives by trying to influence government policies and through direct service provision.

There is also a long history of intergovernmental cooperation on social policy issues. The early part of the twentieth century saw the foundation of the International Labour Organization (ILO) as an affiliated agency of the ill-fated League of Nations (1919). Building on the work of the ILO, the establishment of the International Social Security Association (1927) brought together governmental organizations involved in social security and gave further substance to international cooperation in that policy arena by providing a forum for policy dialogue among governmental organizations involved in social security administration throughout the world and promoting appropriate development of social protection adapted to the needs of the population. While this began as an intergovernmental body, over time it included non-governmental bodies involved in social protection, such as Provident Funds and Trust Funds.

During the twentieth century the international institutional and political architecture evolved into a highly complex system involving numerous international agreements, treaties, regulations, and accords agreed and implemented through a wide range of organizations, agencies, and alliances.

The numbers of such international formations have increased dramatically: as Kaul, Grunberg, and Stern note, 'more treaties were signed during the four decades after the Second World War than in the previous four centuries' (1999: 499), while the number of international organizations grew from around seventy in 1940 to over one thousand by 1992 (ibid). With this proliferation, transnational cooperation and coordination have also intensified to the extent that national social policy is now framed to an ever greater extent by a dense web of international legal and political obligations. Currently, the most prominent areas of such cooperation are trade, investment, finance, and macro-economic policy, as well as environmental policies and social policies in employment, migration, social security, education, health and social services, food security, population control, and humanitarian relief. These global institutions and networks play a significant role in directly and indirectly shaping the distribution of resources worldwide through, for example, setting (or attempting to influence) the terms of international trade, overseeing the use of aid funds, setting and monitoring social standards, and influencing the nature of social provision.

International governmental organizations and international non-governmental organizations

There are numerous international organizations currently in existence. These can be divided into governmental organizations and non-governmental organizations. The vast majority of countries in the world are formal members of an international organization of some kind. Some of these organizations operate on a more global scale, while others do so on a more regional scale (Table 9.1). This part of the chapter provides a brief overview of these different organizations and their 'social agendas'.

Global Global agencies vary in terms of their resources, their power to effect policy change at national level, and their degree of autonomy from governments. Some IGOs are little more than political alliances or clubs comprising a minority of the world's governments (OECD, G8, G24). Some have no independent legal force or permanent secretariat (e.g. G8); others have the force of international law behind them (WTO, EU, UN) and/or substantial bureaucracies (ILO, WB). Some aim to achieve their policy goals through powers of persuasion (ILO, OECD), others do so through conditionalities attached to loans (IMF, WB), while others still may impose fines or force governments to compensate other governments should they fail to implement agreements/law (EU, WTO).

Compared with national governments, IGOs' involvement in social policy is quite limited. However, substantial routine cooperation exists in a variety of social policy domains: employment; migration; social security; pensions; education; healthcare; social services; food security; population control; and humanitarian aid and relief. There have been important attempts at regulation through standard-setting efforts at the international level in the UN and its satellite agencies, such as the ILO and WHO, and some recent experimentation in international financing for welfare services (ILO's Global Social Trust, WHO's global health partnerships). The World Bank is also tangibly engaged in social provision through the loans it makes to countries; these loans are used to finance

Table 9.1 Examples of international governmental organization (IGOs) and international non-governmental organizations (INGOs)

IGOs	INGOs
Global	
World Bank	World Economic Forum
International Monetary Fund	World Social Forum
United Nations	World Water Forum
UN social agencies, e.g. International Labour Organization, World Health Organization, Unicef	International Confederation of Free Trade Unions
World Trade Organization	International Planned Parenthood Federation
Organisation for Economic Co-operation and Development	Oxfam, War on Want
G8, G77, G24, etc.	International Pharmaceutical Industries Association
Regional	
European Union	European Services Forum
North American Free Trade Agreement (NAFTA)	European Trade Union Confederation
ASEAN (Association of South East Asian Nations)	European Social Forum
South Asian Area for Regional Cooperation (SAARC)	Asian Social Forum
Mercado Común del Sur (Southern Core Common Market) (Mercosur)	African Social Forum
Caribbean Community and Common Market (CARICOM)	
Southern African Development Community (SADC)	

programmes of aid and relief and through health, social welfare, and population programmes, that are often delivered in 'partnership' with national and international non-governmental organizations (NGOs). Finally, the WTO has emerged as a key actor in global social regulation over the last decade with the inclusion of health and social care, education, and social security in its General Agreement on Trade in Services (GATS). The involvement of IGOs in regulation, financing, and provision of health and welfare services is, then, substantial (Box 9.3).

In addition to international governmental organizations and fora, there are networks of international non-governmental organizations monitoring and lobbying on a variety of social policy issues. INGOs embrace groups from trade unions and professional associations to employers' groups, industry groups, consumer groups, and 'third sector' groups working on issues of poverty, environment, development, and trade. These organizations are involved in both the formulation of social policy (e.g. conducting political campaigns of research and activism, advisory roles) and its implementation through service delivery (emergency and development aid). For example, the main MEIs have formal processes for the consultation of NGOs in decision-making, and many of the social development projects of the World Bank and the UN are delivered through local, national, and international NGOs. Some INGO secretariats have greater numbers of staff than some IGOs (compare, for example, the WTO's 630 staff with Oxfam's 2,800 staff) and command significant budgets and are tangibly involved in policy formation and welfare provision on a range of matters.

Box 9.3 **Key international governmental organizations and their social policy orientations**

The **World Bank** has played the major role in shaping—and damaging—national social policy in developing and transition countries in recent decades. World Bank social policy advocated a safety net policy for people living in poverty and fostered private commercial services for the better off. The World Bank does not enjoy global legitimacy, and is much criticized by political actors in the Global South for serving Northern interests.

The **International Monetary Fund** (IMF) social policy has also been oriented to 'safety nets' comprising targeted subsidies, cash compensation in lieu of subsidies, or improved distribution of essentials such as medicine. Like the WB, the IMF insisted upon these in the process of policy-conditioned structural adjustment lending. Critics of the IMF even after its reforms continue to draw attention to the contradictions between the IMF's short-term concerns with macro-economic stability and longer-term poverty reduction goals. The IMF, too, attracts particular criticism for operating in the interests of rich Northern countries.

The **World Trade Organization** (WTO) is also a key institutional actor in global social policy. It has come under much criticism for its trade treaties that many fear will boost global private (commercial) service providers through its General Agreement on Services (GATS) and in terms of the constraints of the Trade Related Intellectual Property (TRIPs) agreement protecting drug company patents, which impacts upon the cost of drugs in poor countries.

The **Organisation for Economic Co-operation and Development** (OECD) is an international organization of the richest developed countries and its social policy advice occupies a position somewhere between the market-opening and liberalizing push of the World Bank, IMF, and WTO on the one hand and the concern of UN social agencies on the other to protect public services. It has argued that globalizing processes create a need for more, not less, social expenditure but has been criticized for its neo-liberal tendencies.

The **International Labour Organization** (ILO) was a major player in helping developing countries build state pension and social security systems in the period between 1930 and the early 1970s. Although the World Bank took over the global leadership role in the 1980s and 1990s in the social protection domain, arguing for and securing the roll-back of the state system especially in pensions in favour of privatized and individualized forms, the ILO responded by arguing that the European-type schemes are reformable and sustainable. The ILO has been at the forefront of thinking about what kinds of policies are needed to ensure socio-economic security in the context of global labour flexibility.

The **World Health Organization** (WHO) lost its position as the leading global agency concerned with health policy in the 1980s and 1990s with the ascent of the World Bank's influence. It believed it necessary to shift the WHO discourse from a purely normative one about health for all to one which engaged with economists. Health expenditures were to be encouraged not because they were morally desirable but because they were a sound investment in human capital. However, in subsequent work on comparing healthcare systems, the WHO came under heavy criticism for ranking countries and has lost some ground to the OECD where analytical work on health services is expanding rapidly with EU support (see also Chapter 7).

The **United Nations Educational, Scientific and Cultural Organization (UNESCO)** has played a leading role in the formation of global education policy. It is concerned with the content of education, giving emphasis to its social and humanizing purposes, and has issued a set of guidelines to regulate global private education.

> ➡
>
> The **United Nations Children Fund (UNICEF)** is funded in large part by popular donations and operates with a degree of independence from the rest of the UN system. It focuses on the welfare and rights of children and in so doing it addresses a wide range of social policy issues. It has been at the forefront of critiquing the residual social policy approach of the World Bank, and is broadly in favour of universal child support policies.
>
> The **UN Development Programme (UNDP)** operates in countries to support development but has far fewer resources than the World Bank. The UNDP has taken an active role in helping countries shape social protection and development plans, but countries are asked to bring them into line with the World Bank-directed poverty reduction strategy processes (PRSPs), which are still evaluated through the lens of its safety net approach.
>
> The **UN Development Programme (UNDP) United Nations Committee on Economic, Social and Cultural Rights** has responsibility for overseeing and reporting upon violations by countries of the UN's 1966 International Covenant on Economic, Social and Cultural Rights. This covenant states that parties to the covenant must recognize the right of everybody to social security including social insurance and to an adequate standard of living, but there are no enforcement mechanisms, no means of legal redress at the global level, and no individual right of appeal against any failure of governments to protect such rights.
>
> Source: Deacon, 2008

Regional A key aspect of global social policy is the expansion of regional trading blocs in recent decades (Yeates and Deacon 2006; Deacon et al. 2010). Many governments belong to both regional and global IGOs. Regional formations potentially offer a number of advantages. First, regionalist trading strategies are an effective means of protecting, promoting, and reshaping a regional division of labour, trade, and production. Nurturing and protecting internationalizing trade flows enable fiscal resources to be generated for national and regional social policy purposes. Too often global trade comes with tax exemptions for local and global companies that erode such fiscal resources. Second, since regional formations often entail groups of countries with similar (or at least less diverse) cultural, legal, and political characteristics and legacies, agreement on the scope and nature of collaboration may be more feasible and progress can potentially be made more quickly compared with global multilateral negotiations involving a wide diversity of countries. Because of this greater similarity, regional formations can offer countries access to a broader menu of policy alternatives. For smaller and developing countries in particular, regional formations offer enhanced access to and influence over policy developments. In the EU, for example, small countries can have a strong blocking effect on the development of social policy. These national influences on regional formations are not necessarily negative: more socially developed countries can force upwards social standards in the poorer members of that formation. Regional formations offer further advantages to countries within global multilateral negotiations and fora, namely amplifying their voicing of regional circumstances and positions. Finally, given the difficulties involved in coming to an agreement on global multilateral standards, regional formations might give countries (especially those in the South) a stronger voice to advance their own social standards and at a faster rate than would be possible through global fora (Yeates and Deacon 2006).

These regional formations also have a substantial agenda and set of practices in relation to social policy. Table 9.2 summarizes the extent to which different regional formations in Europe, Latin America, Africa, and Asia have adopted policies of social redistribution (where resources are

---

Box 9.4 **Acronyms**

ALBA: Alianza Bolivariana para los Pueblos de Nuestra América (Bolivarian Alternatives for the Americas)

ASEAN: Association of South-East Asian Nations

AU: African Union

CARICOM: Caribbean Community

CNA: Colonial Nurses Association

CoE: Council of Europe

ECOWAS: Economic Community of West African States

EU: European Union

GATS: General Agreement on Trade in Services

IGO: international governmental organization

INGO: international non-governmental organization

ILO: International Labour Organization

IMF: International Monetary Fund

MERCOSUR: Common Market of the South

NAFTA: North American Free Trade Area

NGO: non-governmental organization

OECD: Organisation for Economic Co-operation and Development

ONA: Overseas Nurses Association

OXFAM: Oxford Aid for Famine Relief

SAARC: South Asian Association for Regional Cooperation

SACU: Southern African Customs Union

SADC: Southern African Development Community

UEMOA: Union Economique et Monétaire Ouest Africaine (West African Economic and Monetary Union)

UN: United Nations

UNDP: United Nations Development Programme

UNESCO: United Nations Educational, Scientific and Cultural Organization

UNICEF: United Nations Children's Fund (originally United Nations International Children's Emergency Fund)

USAID: United States Agency for International Development

WB: World Bank

WEF: World Economic Forum

WHO: World Health Organization

WSF: World Social Forum

WTO: World Trade Organization

---

distributed on regional criteria), social regulation (e.g. of markets in the wider interests of social welfare, or to develop common regional social standards), and access to social rights (such as citizens and social charters, and including legal rights of redress). It also summarizes the extent to which each of the formations engages with cooperation in social sectors and cross-border transfers of policy knowledge. The European Union represents the most advanced form of regional integration, having made major advances in social redistribution, social regulation, and social rights. Of all such regional formations the EU has the most extensive involvement through labour and social

Table 9.2 Regional social policies in practice on four continents

Regional association	Redistribution	Social regulation	Social rights	Cooperation in social sectors	Cross-border lesson learning
EUROPE					
EU	Yes	Yes	Yes	Yes	Yes
Council of Europe	No	No	Yes but not force of law	No	Yes
LATIN AMERICA					
MERCOSUR	Yes	Soft law*	Yes but not force of law	Yes	Yes
Andean Community	Yes	Soft law	Yes but not force of law	Yes	Yes
CARICOM	No?	Soft law	Yes but not force of law	Yes	Yes
ALBA	Yes	No	No	Yes	Yes
ASIA					
ASEAN	Yes	Soft law	Yes but not force of law	Yes	Yes
SAARC	Yes	No except trafficking of women and children	Yes but not force of law	Yes	Yes
AFRICA					
AU	No	Soft law	Yes but not force of law	Yes via sub-regions	Yes
ECOWAS	No?	Soft law	Yes	Yes	Yes
UEMOA	Yes	Covered by ECOWAS	As ECOWAS	As ECOWAS	As ECOWAS
SADC	No	Soft law	Yes but not force of law	Yes	Yes
SACU	Yes	Covered by ECOWAS	As SADC	As SADC	As SADC

*Soft law means that regional declarations/agreements on standards are left up to countries to implement with exhortation from the region.

Source: Deacon, Macovei, van Langenhove, and Yeates (2009), Table 10.2

law, the structural funds, and various social programmes. But other regional formations also have advanced social policies to a considerable (though variable) degree (Table 9.2).

Regional formations are, then, a key element of global social policy and look likely to become more so. Here, the UN system generally has welcomed regional integration processes as it needs regional organizations to deliver policy objectives. Questions that arise are to what extent these regionalization processes are simply delivery mechanisms for global agencies and to what extent they will be able to develop their own social policy agenda. This heralds the possibility of potentially undermining the development of common *global* standards and processes even as some regions develop social policy more quickly and to higher standards than others.

Struggles over global social policy

A central question engaging many policy-makers, activists, and scholars is that of how to steer global policy in the interests of social welfare. As we would expect, there is a wide variety of positions and approaches as to what the aims of any reforms should be and how they should be achieved. Regulatory reform issues, for example, boil down to the question of how to maintain or improve social protection, labour, educational, and health standards. Thus, what kinds of controls should be placed on the activities of globalizing corporations in their pursuit of profit—should they be voluntary or mandatory, and who should oversee their implementation? How far should global markets in welfare and other basic services (such as water, food, energy) be permitted to develop? To what extent should social welfare provision be subject to the strictures of international trade agreements? Should there be stronger global and regional mechanisms of social redistribution, and what form(s) might these take? Is it possible to reform the existing international institutional architecture in the interests of global social justice or are more radical courses of action required? What would those entail? What would be the founding principles of such an order and how would these be realized? The range of possible answers to these questions is rendered all the more complicated by the wide variety of countries, actors, and interests involved and the political power struggles between them.

In this part of the chapter we pick up on this idea of policy contestation and struggle in the making of global social policy. The section begins with an overview of what the nature of the struggle over welfare is about. It then moves to look at the area of pensions, which has been a major policy area in which ideological battles have been played out and in relation to which we can examine more closely how successful different IGOs have been in influencing government policies.

IGOs' discourses and policy prescriptions

The international institutional arena has become a key battleground over which political struggle regarding the future of welfare is fought. This struggle has involved a range of IGOs, both regional and global. Table 9.3 maps the nature of this political contestation and the major positions in the debate. The range of welfare futures backed by these institutions is essentially confined to variants of liberalism with its emphasis on individual responsibility and choice, a restricted role for the public sector in finance and provision and a substantial one for the private (commercial) sector; there is a notable absence of any IGO advancing a social democratic or redistributive agenda. Notable also is that these struggles take place within these organizations as well as across them. For example, while some sections of the OECD offer 'welfare as burden' discourses, others promote 'welfare as investment' ones, while the World Bank advances both 'welfare as social cohesion' as well as 'welfare as investment' discourses.

The World Trade Organization is omitted from this schema but for many it is the ultimate institutional manifestation of neo-liberal globalism, extolling as it does the virtues of 'free trade', and—importantly—equipped with legal powers to progress this agenda. The WTO is a relatively 'young' organization (established 1995) but could potentially have considerable effects on social policy through its GATS. Indeed, for some, the inclusion of health, education, financial services, and utilities (water, energy) in the GATS heralds the end of public financing, provision, and regulation of these services where these existed and prevents them from emerging where they do not exist. The fear is that the Agreement contains an inbuilt bias in favour of commercial provision generally and provided by foreign service providers specifically, that it permits only minimal public regulation that would not provide adequate consumer protection, and that it will erode cross-class

Table 9.3 Global social policy discourse

Orientation	Welfare world	Agency promulgating
Existing welfare as:		
Burden	Liberalism (e.g. United States, UK)	IMF, OECD
Social cohesion	Conservative, Corporatist (e.g. France, Germany) (S.E. Asia)	EU, ILO, WB
Investment	Social Democracy (e.g. Nordic)	OECD, WB
Redistributive commitment		—
Emerging welfare as:		
Safety net	Social Liberalism	WB, EU
Work-fare	Social Liberalism	IMF
Citizenship entitlement	Futuristic	ILO, COE
Redistribution		—

Source: Deacon and Hulse 1996: 52

support necessary for the development of public welfare services. Some of these fears have been partially allayed by governments' own reluctance to make specific commitments (especially in health and education) under this agreement but the general concern about the invidious long-term effects of the GATS on public services remains (see Yeates 2005 for a review of this debate in relation to social security). The longer-term effects of this particular agreement on social policy reform are not known.

The struggle that is occurring is essentially about the appropriate welfare mix and social division of welfare and about the appropriate aims of public policy and the role of the state in social and economic development more broadly. It is a conflict between neo-liberal values of individual responsibility, 'choice', self-interest, and enforceable contractual rights, and social democratic ones of collective responsibility, social cohesion, integration, and equity (Dixon 1999).

The case of pensions The ILO and the World Bank represent the principal contrasting positions in this struggle. For most of the twentieth century the ILO's position as premier global authority in matters of social protection was uncontested. Emanating from north European corporatist traditions of social protection, it advocated a major role for publicly funded (tax or insurance), regulated and provided schemes as the means for ensuring access to a minimum standard of living in a context of raising working and living standards. Commercial and informal schemes were to play a minor, supplementary role in this overall approach (Table 9.4). The ILO's approach gained broad international acceptance and influenced the shape of national social security and labour systems in numerous countries, especially among developing countries as a growing number of newly independent states became members of the organization (Kay 2000; Otting 1994).

During the mid 1990s the World Bank (WB), which aggressively promoted a more residualist approach to social protection, openly challenged the ILO's approach and, by extension, its dominant position in the field. Although the WB was not new into this policy field and offered a range of advice, its 1994 publication, *Averting the Old Age Crisis*, represented a clear shift in its position by arguing in favour of pared-down public schemes providing a subsistence income for the 'critically poor' and much greater reliance on informal, occupational, and commercial schemes for everyone else (Table 9.4). Only such an approach would enable countries to become (or remain) fiscally sustainable and economically competitive, as well as address inconsistencies in statutory pension

Table 9.4 World Bank and ILO approaches to pension reform

Feature	World Bank	ILO
Basic state pension	Means tested (tax base)	Universal (tax based)
Second tier	Individualized compulsory defined contribution and privately invested	Solidaristic PAYG defined benefit state pension
Third tier	Voluntary additional private savings/ investment	Voluntary additional private savings/investment

Source: Deacon (2005: 163)

coverage and payment levels. Interestingly, the 'one size fits all' model was not carried over into the health and education domains. For instance, the WB argued that health services could not be handed over to the private sector due to substantial imperfections in the health market, and that the appropriate welfare mix should be decided on a case-by-case basis (Bhatia and Mossialos 2004; Deacon et al. 1997). However, as Mehrotra and Delamonica (2005) point out, the WB consistently encourages private sector involvement in social services.

Although the WB is not the only global actor advocating pension privatization, there is no doubt that it has been instrumental in transforming pension privatization into a mainstream policy idea. It joined an existing transnational coalition that began in Chile in the early 1980s involving economists embedded in a US-based movement to initiate revolution in economic policy-making; through the advice of Chilean reformers to other governments, pension privatization became a template for reform, particularly in Latin America and later also in Central and Eastern Europe (Orenstein 2008). The WB facilitated this international diffusion by applying the model around the world, irrespective of country history, tradition, or circumstances, and providing institutional, human, and financial resources to assist governments—many of which were middle-income developing countries that receive advice and support from international development agencies and that are dependent on the World Bank for development finance—to model pensions reforms and push through WB-preferred reforms. The WB has been assisted in so doing by other global policy actors. Thus, in various regions around the world, the WB and ILO have vied to have countries adopt their particular approach and have been joined by other regional entities such as the EU, USAID, and IMF in Central and Eastern Europe; the IMF, Asian Development Bank, OECD, and APEC in Asia; USAID, UNDP, IMF, and IDB in Latin America (Deacon et al. 1997; Müller 2003; Orenstein 2008).

In terms of the actual impact on national reforms, however, the evidence is more mixed. In Latin America, only Chile's pension system comes close to the World Bank paradigm (and it has most recently embarked on reforms to part renationalize its pension system); Bolivia, El Salvador, and Mexico fit the World Bank paradigm partially; and the remaining countries enacted reforms closer to the ILO paradigm than to the World Bank one (Cruz-Saco and Mesa-Lago 1998). Similarly, Fultz and Ruck (2001) show that most Central and Eastern European countries are reforming their public schemes without establishing a mandatory private pillar. But even if the policy model is not followed to the letter, policies may be consistent with the WB paradigm or adopt particular elements from it (Cruz-Saco 2002; Deacon 2008). None of this is to say that the WB or other IGOs involved in pensions policy are without influence, only that influence is often harder and less straightforward to detect in practice and is mediated by domestic politics and national systems (see Orenstein 2008, for an extended discussion of the influence of WB reforms on pension systems worldwide).

Conclusion

Recent years have witnessed a turn to the 'global' across the social sciences, including in social policy. With this has come an appreciation that social policy formation is more appropriately analysed in relation to the social processes that routinely cut across and transcend international political borders and which link geographically distant people and places. Social policy formation can no longer be analysed solely at the level of the nation state—if it ever could; while health and welfare outcomes are influenced by developments that seem on first sight to have little to do with domestic policy. This openness to alternative socio-spatial scales of welfare and to cross-border spheres of governance casts new light on how welfare is financed, regulated, and delivered beyond the confines of the nation-state.

Global social policy is an area of academic study and research that focuses on the diverse ways in which welfare 'maps' onto different socio-spatial scales other than the nation-state. This field has opened up new questions about the ways in which global and regional actors are actively involved in social policy formation and the ways in which they try to influence domestic policy reform. It has placed under critical scrutiny the policies of international organizations, which had previously focused on evaluating national policies. It has also opened up to view and for discussion the ways in which transnational flows of people, ideas, goods, and services form a routine part of social life and how they are said to be impacting upon the nature of welfare provision. Many examples were used throughout his chapter illustrating these transnational welfare flows—ranging from migration to non-governmental activism to policy ideas about pensions and welfare, and the provision of care and welfare services. One issue that was raised was the extent to which transnational flows meet and fuse with national ones. We discussed this in relation to the relative influence of IGOs' pensions policies on national pensions systems. Here, it was noted that the transnational does not always 'trump' the national and that explanations of social policy reform therefore still need to attend to the balance of political power between diverse forces and actors as well as to welfare histories and traditions of provision. What global social policy does is to argue that there are many more scales and channels through which such balances of power and struggles over welfare are played out than simply in the arena of domestic politics.

FURTHER READING

Students interested in further reading around the subject are directed to **Nicola Yeates** (ed.) (2008) *Understanding Global Social Policy* (The Policy Press, Bristol) and **Nicola Yeates and Chris Holden** (eds) (2009) *The Global Social Policy Reader* (The Policy Press, Bristol). These two volumes are specifically written with students in mind and provide a comprehensive review of debates and issues across a wide range of global social policy areas. Finally, *Global Social Policy: Journal of Public Policy and Social Development* (Sage) publishes a range of full-length and shorter articles on various aspects of global social policy, and a digest highlighting policy developments, events, and publications during the year.

USEFUL WEBSITES

There is an extensive range of online resources covering the issues raised in this chapter. The single most useful portal is **http://www.globalwelfare.net**. This provides a range of learning and teaching resources for students, educators, and researchers interested in issues of global social policy. It includes an extensive range of links to the websites of a wide range of research, policy and activist organizations. The UK social policy Association's *Policy World* also regularly carries articles on matters of international and global social policy. These are available from the SPA website: **www.social-policy.org.uk**.

Q ESSAY QUESTIONS

1 How does 'the global' challenge conventional understandings of social policy?

2 What actors are involved in global social policy, and in what ways?

3 Global social policy is a subject without a history. Discuss.

4 Drawing on this chapter and your own knowledge and experience, identify some possible consequences of global social policy for welfare provision and access to welfare services.

 ## ONLINE RESOURCE CENTRE

For additional material and resources, please visit the Online Resource Centre at:
www.oxfordtextbooks.co.uk/orc/baldock4e/.

Part Four
Delivering welfare

10

Cash transfers

Tony Fitzpatrick

Contents

Introduction

The benefit system arguably attracts more controversy than any other welfare institution. In June 2010, the new government's emergency budget indicated that, even after cuts, expenditure on social protection (including pensions, benefits, and tax credits) would total £192 billion. This represents slightly less than 28 per cent of public expenditure, or about 12 per cent of Gross Domestic Product.

There are two points to bear in mind, though. Firstly, around 43 per cent of the benefits bill is typically spent on the elderly, 16 per cent directly on sick and disabled people, 17 per cent on families with children, and just 1.52 per cent directly on various unemployment benefits. Therefore, we should not over estimate the savings which can be made by pushing the unemployed into jobs, especially low-paid ones where the tax yield is low. Indeed, effective workfare schemes *cost*, rather than save, money. Secondly, the UK's spending on benefits is approximately two-thirds of the West European average. On one level, then, we are required to analyse the economics of the subject, i.e. issues relating to cost and distribution. However, the real controversies concern the moral values driving the benefits system: what it says about us as a society.

Therefore, when we examine services-in-*cash* we are faced with a level of normative and prescriptive commentary that arguably exceeds that of any other welfare scheme. There are several reasons for this but the most significant concerns the fact that a cash transfer can be spent in whatever way the benefit claimant chooses.

Learning outcomes

After reading this chapter you will be able to:

1 describe the history and present configuration of the British social security system;
2 outline New Labour's reforms of cash transfers and their consequences;
3 outline the financial and moral factors relevant to cash transfers;
4 identify the most controversial issues currently debated about the social security system, both in the UK and around the world.

The origins of the British system

By cash transfers we mean the benefits which are paid out by the system of social security, but the meaning of the term 'social security' changes depending upon the context. In the United States a distinction is made between welfare and social security: the former refers to the means-tested assistance for poor households which carries a considerable social stigma; the latter refers to the non-means-tested benefits which are more highly esteemed. In continental Europe, however, social security has a very broad meaning which may encompass healthcare and which sometimes even substitutes for terms such as the 'welfare state' and 'social welfare'. Britain occupies a midway point between these positions. Therefore, we can define social security as referring to the benefits and cash transfers which are provided, financed, and regulated by the state for the purpose of income maintenance in particular and social welfare in general.

Modern social security probably dates back to 1870s Germany. Rimlinger (1971) observed how Chancellor Bismarck responded to the rising influence and importance of the industrial working class by trying to reduce the appeal of socialist ideas. He introduced various benefits inspired by the social insurance principle where people contribute to a collective 'pool' during their periods of economic activity and draw benefits from that pool when they become economically inactive. Social insurance benefits are therefore intended to provide the individual with a collective form of protection. Over the course of time, however, German socialists and social democrats came to adopt the social insurance principle as their own, as something which could protect people from market forces. Therefore, the social insurance principle has been of central importance to welfare systems ever since because it offered conservatives a means of defending the existing order and offered socialists and social democrats a means of changing it.

The German experience convinced the British Liberal government of 1905–15, partly under the influence of William Beveridge, to adopt a scheme of social insurance and so laid the foundations for the benefit system of the interwar years. The Beveridge Report (1942) set the tone for the widespread post-war belief that the welfare state was an essential part of a just society.

The aims and roles of social security

The basic aim of Beveridge's system was the prevention of 'want', or poverty, and he believed that an insurance-based system would do this by guaranteeing a decent minimum income for those who either (a) lost their earning capacity, e.g. due to unemployment, sickness, and accident, or (b) lacked an earning capacity, e.g. due to retirement. However, as well as insuring the incomes of earners, the Beveridge system was concerned to meet the needs of households that depended upon them: in particular, the costs of a family and the important events that might affect it, e.g. birth, death, and marriage. The prevention of poverty, argued Beveridge, would be brought about by reducing to a bare minimum the numbers of people relying upon means-tested assistance and he anticipated that a scheme of compulsory social insurance, in the context of full employment, would achieve this. Keynes was enthusiastic for Beveridge's proposals because he believed that they would assist in the management of the demand for goods and services and so *foster* high levels of employment.

The politicians and policy-makers who followed Beveridge throughout the next few decades held to his expectations. Gradually, however, as unemployment began to rise, the emphasis shifted away from poverty prevention to poverty relief. More and more households either exhausted their rights to insurance benefits or, because of rising unemployment, could not amass the contribution records needed to entitle them to such benefits in the first place. Increasingly, the explicit aim was to keep claimants' heads above water rather than to imagine that social security could free them from poverty altogether. By the 1960s it was admitted that large-scale reliance upon means-tested assistance was not going to disappear. Reliance upon means testing has grown steadily ever since.

Walker (2005: Chapter 2) identifies the following as key aims for the benefit system: poverty alleviation, income maintenance and replacement, promotion of social cohesion, risk protection, redistribution, compensation for contingencies and losses, promotion of economic efficiency, and behavioural change. He also identifies secondary objectives that are relevant to particular programmes, such as raising take-up or tackling fraud. To the above Barr and Coulter (1990: 274–6) add administrative efficiency, equity, and simplicity. But if these are the system's principal aims, what roles does it actually perform in society? The answer to that question is likely to depend upon our political perspective.

Critiques of social security

From the Right, Friedman (1962) attacked social insurance schemes as forms of state compulsion which infringe upon the freedom of individuals and which are less efficient than a market-based system. This last claim is highly controversial, with researchers finding that high social expenditure does not damage, and often assists, growth and employment (Mares 2006; Cichon andHagemejer. 2007: 177–82). As an alternative, Friedman advocated that social security should become a purely means-tested system which aims to relieve the proven need of those whose income falls below a certain level.

By contrast, many on the Left have interpreted social security not so much as a system for addressing poverty but as a system of social control. Marxists have argued that cash transfers function according to wider socio-economic requirements: they help to camouflage the exploitative nature of capitalism and they enforce the values and behavioural norms which enable capitalism to operate more effectively. According to Ginsburg (1979), the social security system can be charged with having three repressive functions. First, it depresses wage levels because benefits are so low that people are effectively forced into low-paid jobs. Second, it maintains the labour supply because in order to claim benefits people are expected to be capable of, and actively looking for, employment, so providing a cheap pool of labour where people can be hired and fired at will. Also, since eligibility for insurance benefits requires the kind of long-term employment histories which women are less likely to have, then they are thrown back onto their domestic roles as carers, 'reproducing' the present and future generations of (male) workers. Finally, the system disciplines claimants and employees alike: the former are rendered powerless, the latter are effectively disciplined into accepting the capitalist labour market since being a wage earner is preferable to being a claimant.

Some feminists have argued that social security reinforces gender divisions. Beveridge assumed that most women would be dependent upon a husband, so their entitlements to benefits could reasonably be determined by the employment records of their spouses. What this has done, feminists argue, is to weaken women's independence within marriage and to restrict their freedom to leave an unwanted partnership. For instance, 22 per cent of women have a 'persistent low income' (compared with 14 per cent of men) while 53 per cent of lone parents (90 per cent of whom are women) are in poverty.

Of the above critiques it was those from the Right which were to be the most influential on policymakers. By the 1980s the Thatcher government was explicit in its belief that social security should aim to:

- relieve the destitution of the genuinely needy, i.e. the deserving poor (contrasted to the 'undeserving poor', who were accused of having brought their poverty on themselves);
- be consistent with the general aims of the economy;
- encourage family life;
- prepare claimants for a return to work;
- be simple to understand and administer.

The benefit reforms of the Thatcher government consequently introduced into the system more means testing, more targeting, more discretion, and greater enforcement of the work ethic. Many of New Labour's reforms were continuous with these assumptions.

Overall, defining basic aims is one thing; creating agreement over what these aims mean, which policies they should inspire, and how those policies (or proposed alternatives) function socially is a much more difficult exercise. In some respects the system seems to have a benign aspect to it (fulfilling basic needs and relieving poverty) whereas in others it may appear less than benign (punishing those who are the victims of circumstance and reproducing underlying social disadvantages).

Direct and indirect forms of transfer

According to Titmuss (1958), the Beveridge system enshrined a 'social division of welfare' where we fail to appreciate the extent and the generosity of an indirect and hidden welfare state.

Firstly, Titmuss distinguished between state welfare and fiscal welfare: the former refers to the attempt to improve well-being by delivering goods and resources *to* people; the latter refers to the well-being which derives from a deliberate failure to collect resources *from* people. Cash transfers may therefore be classified as state welfare whereas tax reliefs, allowances, and credits can be classified as fiscal welfare. Titmuss's distinction is important because the former is defined as expenditure (money that governments pay out) while the latter is merely 'forgone revenue' (money that the government never receives) and so the former tends to attract a level of attention that the latter avoids. Our reactions to state welfare are often different from our reactions to fiscal welfare: we easily become obsessed with the costs and the 'burdens' of the poor because they are seen as draining the public purse, whereas the fiscal welfare state, from which the non-poor mainly benefit, is conveniently overlooked. So, governments seem more obsessed with benefit fraudsters than with the 'tax gap' (the difference between the amount of tax collected and the amount which should be collected). As we see below, New Labour tried to extend the advantages of fiscal welfare to the poorest households also.

Secondly, Titmuss also drew attention to occupational welfare, or the advantages which people may derive from their employment, e.g. subsidized canteens, parking, housing, and gyms, company cars, life assurance policies, and private health insurance. These can be thought of as 'indirect wages' because they help to boost employees' disposable incomes but are more tax efficient for the employer than simply raising salaries. State and occupational provision now interact in ways which are more complex than when Titmuss was writing due to the growth of things such as occupational pension schemes. For millions, the latter have gradually replaced the state pension as the main source of post-retirement income; these schemes are administered by employers but they are also a form of fiscal transfer since people paying into an occupational scheme pay fewer insurance contributions to the state and benefit from certain tax advantages.

Titmuss argued that once all of these forms of provision are taken into account the transfer system is far less redistributive and egalitarian than it might at first appear. Goodin and Le Grand (1987) also confirmed that the non-poor benefit considerably—though they saw this, in a more positive light, as locking the middle classes into the system and so making the latter less vulnerable to right-wing cuts.

According to Rose (1981), Titmuss neglected what she called the 'sexual division of labour'. This sexual division refers to the fact that because it is women who still perform most of the unpaid work in the home, and because it is men who gain the highest wages, as well as the wage-related benefits which go with them, then women could be thought of as being net contributors to the well-being of men by boosting their disposable incomes. Indeed, Sutherland (1997) demonstrated how the distribution of income within the household is skewed in favour of men. Women are more likely to spend their money on their children, whilst men are more likely to spend their money on themselves.

Titmuss's distinctions have been further refined by Mann (2009), who insists that the social division of welfare exists because both policy-makers and the affluent have observed and exploited social divisions within the working class. He finds that the organized labour movement failed to address racial discrimination, and sometimes exacerbated it, ensuring that poverty would have a substantial racial dimension and so giving rise to what Mann calls the 'racial division of welfare', where black people are more likely than their white counterparts to experience the most draconian and least generous aspects of welfare provision. (See Box 10.1.)

The distinctions drawn by Titmuss suggest that any discussion of cash transfers has to be receptive to indirect as well as direct forms of welfare, as illustrated in Figure 10.1.

Throughout the rest of this chapter we shall be mainly discussing the direct cash transfers of the social security system but we will have to make some reference to indirect transfers also since tax credits have become an important element of government policy.

Universalism and selectivism

A debate about the relative merits of universalism and selectivism has shadowed the last fifty years of social policy research, although many authors have come to dismiss it as redundant (Spicker 1993: 94).

> **Box 10.1 The racial division of welfare**
>
> - Two-fifths of people from ethnic minorities live in low-income households, twice the rate for white people.
> - Ethnic minorities are two to four times more likely to be unemployed.
> - Children from ethnic minorities are more at risk of poverty. 'Ethnic minorities make up 12 per cent of the population and 15 per cent of children, but 25 per cent of children who are in poverty' (Platt, 2009: 1).
> - For all ethnic groups, the proportion of people who are in low-income households has fallen at a roughly similar pace over the last decade.
> - More than half of people from Bangladeshi and Pakistani ethnic backgrounds live in low-income households, compared with a quarter of people from an Indian ethnic background.
> - Half of Bangladeshis and Pakistanis earn less than £7 per hour. Bangladeshis and Pakistanis have both the lowest work rates and, once in work, the highest likelihood of low pay.
> - Black Caribbean pupils are three times as likely to be excluded from school as white pupils.
> - Black people are up to twice as likely to be dependent upon means-tested benefits and less likely to claim benefits to which they are entitled in the first place.
>
> Sources:
> http://www.poverty.org.uk/summary/key per cent20facts.shtml
> http://www.statistics.gov.uk/cci/nugget.asp?id=462

According to Titmuss, the principle of universalism refers to:

> the aim of making services available and accessible to the whole population in such ways as would not involve users in any humiliating loss of status, dignity or self-respect. (Titmuss 1968: 129)

This principle therefore seems an admirable one upon which to base a benefit system. However, its critics insist that universalism is not as desirable as it might at first appear.

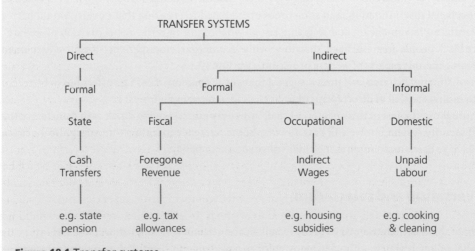

Figure 10.1 Transfer systems

Imagine that we have £1,000 to distribute among 100 people. The universalist might demand either that every person receive the same amount or that if some people are to receive more than others (because their need is greater), then this should be done humanely, i.e. without having to reveal personal details about their income, savings, possessions, and so forth. However, selectivists argue that without tests of income and means, we are not going to target our £1,000 very effectively. We can only identify those who are in genuine need by gathering and examining the kind of personal details from which universalists shy away. As such, universal benefits may fail to help those who need help the most.

The debate does not end there, however, as selectivism works less well in practice than it does in theory. Means-tested targeting implies four basic stages. Firstly, we have to *identify* those to be targeted but since means testing involves a certain amount of stigma, because many may be ignorant about their entitlements, or otherwise reluctant to enter what they see as a bureaucratic, meddlesome system, people may not come forward to be identified in the first place. Secondly, we have to *aim* at our targets but this may not be easy since people's circumstances change rapidly, i.e. the nature of the target may be constantly shifting, and this may put us off our aim, especially where a great deal of discretion is involved. Thirdly, we have to *hit* our target but this may not be easy either since those who receive the benefits (often men) may not be those who need the resources the most (usually women and children). Finally, we have to hit our target *without disabling it* but, as we shall see in the section on unemployment and poverty traps, means testing is often very bad at this.

In short, selectivism implies targeting (effected usually but not always via tests of income and other means) whereas universalism does not. Relatively few commentators believe that you can have one without the other. For universalists, some targeting is warranted so long as this supplements the universalist principle, e.g. combining universal entitlements plus progressive taxes is a way of including everyone in the system, while also withdrawing (clawing back) income from the better-off. Selectivists may acknowledge that universalism brings with it certain cost efficiencies. Titmuss (1968) argued in favour of combining both universalist and selectivist provision.

However, the underlying debate shows no signs of going away, as we see when we explore recent reforms and debates shortly.

Six categories of cash transfer

The six types of benefit are illustrated in Table 10.1 and explained in the following sub-sections.

Social insurance benefits

In order to qualify for insurance benefits in the event of unemployment, sickness, or retirement, employees must previously have paid a certain amount of contributions into a compulsory state-managed fund. Such benefits, therefore, are 'earned entitlements' which go to workers rather than to citizens per se. The state pension, for instance, accounts for approximately one-quarter of benefit expenditure. Social insurance was once the foundation of social security in the form of Unemployment Benefit and the State Pension. However, the former, which was previously payable for twelve months, has been incorporated within Jobseeker's Allowance and is now payable for a maximum of six months, while the relative value of the latter has been steadily eroding because since 1980 it has been uprated annually in line with inflation rather than earnings. The basic state pension will be worth 15 per cent of national average earnings in 2012 (compared with 24 per cent in 1981) and its value will continue to fall unless re-indexed to earnings. In 2008, 60 per cent of women did not qualify for the full amount of the Basic State Pension, though this figure will decrease since the number of 'qualifying years' needed to establish an entitlement to the full amount has been reduced to 30 years (for both men and women). Over 12 million UK people are now of pensionable age and

Table 10.1 Types of benefit

Type of transfer	Principles	Examples
Social insurance benefits	Contributory	Contribution-based Jobseeker's Allowance Retirement Pension
Social assistance benefits	Means tested	Income-based Jobseeker's Allowance Housing Benefit
Categorical benefits	Non-contributory and non-means tested	Child Benefit (but changes announced October 2010) Winter Fuel Allowance (eligibility at age 60, though payments vary)
Discretionary benefits	Rules and judgements	Social Fund
Occupational benefits		
Statutory	Employment status	Statutory Sick Pay
Non-statutory	Employment record	Occupational Pension
Fiscal transfers	Tax concessions	Tax Credits

25 per cent of the population of Western Europe will be 65 years or older by 2025. Social insurance systems therefore have to cope with increasing costs and a lower proportion of working-age adults to fund them. Almost all countries are raising the age at which state pensions can be paid, therefore.

Hills (1997: 44) identifies five problems with an insurance system:

- The link between contributions and entitlement is obscure to most people.
- Beveridge assumed an economy of full-time full (male) employment but women (and other disadvantaged groups) have always been less likely than men to accumulate the necessary contributions and Beveridge's ideal economy no longer exists anyway.
- Insurance benefits have been so low that many more people than Beveridge anticipated have had to rely upon means testing.
- The insurance fund is more symbolic than real since contributions are really a de facto form of taxation.
- Widening the coverage of insurance benefits means that certain groups have to be 'credited' into the system, which undermines the contributory principle.

However, there are also several advantages:

- There is both a real and a perceived link between contributions and entitlements, even if the link is not generally understood.
- Insurance contributions can be thought of as a 'hypothecated tax', i.e. tax revenue which is earmarked for specific purposes.
- The take-up of insurance benefits is high because, as earned entitlements, there is far less stigma than with means-tested benefits.
- Social insurance contributes to the functioning of the labour market, e.g. by reducing the costs associated with risks.

Walker (2005: Chapter 4) adds that the groups who need insurance the most may be at a disadvantage in a market of purely private insurance since the higher the risks the higher the premiums firms will charge. Government compulsion means that coverage can be universal, comparatively cheap, and redistributive from low-risk to high-risk groups.

Social assistance benefits

These benefits provide a residual safety net for those who do not qualify for insurance benefits and they are paid out to those whose income and assets have fallen below a prescribed amount, the level of which depends upon family size and other circumstances. Entitlement to assistance benefits is basically worked out by calculating (a) the amount the claimant is assumed to need, (b) the income, savings, or capital assets which the claimant has access to, and (c) subtracting (b) from (a). The main assistance benefits are: Income-based Jobseeker's Allowance, Income Support (which used to be the main means-tested benefit but can now be claimed only by those who do not need to look for work in order to qualify for benefit), Housing Benefit, and Council Tax Benefit. In 2010:

- 4.75 million people claimed Housing Benefit and 5.78 million claimed Council Tax Benefit.
- Over 1.5 million claimed Jobseeker's Allowance.
- 692,000 lone parents claimed Income Support.
- 479,000 people claimed the Employment and Support Allowance.
- 3.35 million claimed the Pension Credit.

According to Spicker (1993: 141–2), the main arguments for means-tested assistance are that it enables resources to be targeted upon those most in need and that, because it is financed out of taxation, resources are 'vertically' redistributed from rich to poor. However, as already indicated, there are also three problems with means-tested benefits: first, they create a poverty trap where any increase in earnings is largely cancelled out by the withdrawal of benefits; second, they do not reach everyone in need because the take-up of such benefits is typically lower than for insurance benefits; finally, because they are not provided on a universal basis they are complex and expensive to administer.

Categorical benefits

These are paid to specific groups, or categories, so long as certain criteria are met. Prior to the 2010 announcement mentioned above, Child Benefit was provided automatically on behalf of all children under the age of 16. The take-up of Child Benefit is almost 100 per cent of those eligible for it, at a total cost of almost £12 billion. Also, there is a Disability Living Allowance, a tax-free benefit for disabled children and adults who need someone to help look after them, or have walking difficulties, and the Winter Fuel Allowance, a yearly tax-free payment for which those at least 60 years of age are eligible—though the actual amount paid varies according to circumstance.

Discretionary benefits

This refers to the Social Fund which was created in 1988 and provides help for those on means-tested assistance who have urgent or exceptional needs. Strictly speaking, the Social Fund is not entirely discretionary since it contains a regulated element which provides a legal entitlement for funeral payments, maternity grants, crisis loans, budgeting loans, community care grants, and cold-weather payments to those who satisfy the eligibility conditions. However, there is also a substantial discretionary element to the Fund: each benefit office has an annual budget which it must not exceed, there is no legal entitlement to payment as officials decide who receives money and who does not, most payments are in the form of loans which have to be repaid to the Benefits Agency, and there is no right of appeal to an independent tribunal. In 2010–11 the discretionary element of the Social Fund was £802 million.

Occupational benefits

These benefits can be either statutory or non-statutory. The former refers to Statutory Sick Pay and Statutory Maternity Pay, both administered by employers. The category of non-statutory occupational benefits now refers largely to the occupational pension schemes which are run by employers and into which employees contribute a certain percentage of their earnings. Occupational pensions are an increasing source of income for elderly people as the value of the state pension dwindles.

Fiscal transfers

Governments have always used tax allowances and reliefs for this purpose but recent years have seen the increased coordination of fiscal transfers with benefits, to the point where some believe that established terms like 'social security system' or 'benefit system' are becoming redundant. In the United States the Earned Income Tax Credit boosts the income of low-earning families and is generally popular because it is regarded as a hand-up and a reward for work rather than a hand-out. Taking their lead from the United States, New Labour's reforms tried to shift the emphasis away from 'benefits' towards 'tax credits'. In 2010–11 tax credits cost £24 billion; with total spending on both working-age benefits and Tax Credits in 2009–10 amounting to £87 billion.

Unemployment and poverty traps

The unemployment trap and the poverty trap should not be confused, although they both occur because of the ways in which social security interacts with the labour market.

The phenomenon of the unemployment trap was noted by Beveridge:

> ... it is dangerous to allow benefit during unemployment or disability to equal or exceed earnings during work ... To secure this the gap between income during earning and during interruption of earning should be as large as possible for every man. (Beveridge 1942: paras 411–2)

The unemployment trap occurs when income out of work is as high as, or even higher than, income when in work. This is known as a high replacement rate and describes the situation where benefits establish a 'wage floor' below which paid work is either not financially worthwhile or only marginally so. A narrow gap between earnings and non-earnings may provide the unemployed claimant with a significant disincentive against looking for a job.

The unemployment trap became of increasing concern to policy-makers in the 1960s. It was decided to introduce benefits which people could receive whilst in employment in order to tackle the disincentive effect of the unemployment trap. This kind of approach involves a system of earnings disregards, where a person can earn a certain amount without it affecting their benefit entitlement, thus boosting their overall income. A scheme of income-tested rent and rate rebates for the lower paid and Family Income Supplement (FIS) for families with children was implemented. However, while this approach went some way to tackling the unemployment trap it had the additional effect of creating a poverty trap.

This refers to the situation faced by the low-paid worker claiming in-work benefits: as their earnings increase, that person not only has to pay tax and insurance contributions but also experiences a withdrawal of their benefits. For instance, an increase of £1 in earnings might lead to £0.80 of that £1 being effectively taken away again; this would imply a 'marginal tax rate' (the amount of income lost for every extra pound earned) of 80 per cent. We can therefore define the poverty trap as the situation where an increase in earnings leads to no significant increase in overall income due to the combined effect of taxes and transfers (see Box 10.2).

This poverty trap first received an extended analysis by Deacon and Bradshaw (1983). They found that in the early 1980s the low paid could face marginal tax rates of more than 100 per cent so that an increase of earnings could actually leave people worse off than before. Therefore, although those on low wages had slightly higher incomes than they would otherwise have had on benefits alone, they were effectively trapped at this level of income unless their wages rose significantly. The social security reforms of the 1980s were partly designed to address the poverty trap: Housing Benefit was

---

Box 10.2 **The poverty trap in action**

Piachaud (1997) illustrates this disincentive effect by using the example of a married couple with two children who live in council housing. In April 1995 gross earnings of £150 per week would have left this family with a net income of £127 once transfers had been taken into account; however, if their gross earnings were to rise to £210 per week, then, because of the combined effects of taxation and benefit withdrawal, their net income would only be £137, i.e. they would just be £10 better off than previously! In short, they would face a marginal tax rate of 94 per cent and, in 1995, one quarter of all employees were earning less than £210 per week.

---

introduced in 1982 and Family Credit replaced FIS in 1988. The explicit intention of the Conservative government was to improve the incentives of the low paid (without the affluent having to pay more tax) but to what extent did this happen?

According to Adam et al. (2006), this happened to some extent but incentives later worsened under New Labour so that, by 2005, over 2 million workers in Britain stood to lose more than half of any increase in their earnings due to the combination of taxes and benefit withdrawal; 160,000 were able to keep less than 10p of every extra £1 they earned. The increased use of means testing has also introduced a savings trap. Because most means tests now take into account both the capital holdings of claimants and the interest that collects on savings (above a specific amount), then those with savings can either lose their entitlement to means-tested support altogether or have their level of benefit reduced. This savings trap particularly affects those pensioners who are on low incomes but who have saved or invested money 'for a rainy day'.

As we shall see below, governments continue to wrestle with poverty and savings traps.

Stigma, take-up, and fraud

Stigma implies the possession of a low status in the eyes of society: to occupy, and to be seen to occupy, an inferior social rank. According to Spicker (1984), five forms of stigma can be identified. First, there is the stigma engendered by poverty and social exclusion. Second, there is the stigma to which a physical disability or a disease can lead. Third, there are stigmas associated with things such as mental illnesses and drug addictions. Fourth, there are moral stigmas which certain actions or patterns of behaviour can give rise to, e.g. criminal behaviour. Finally, there is the stigma which a dependency upon welfare services can create.

An important question to ask is why this final form of stigma has continued to exist. Is it due to a failure of the welfare state? As we saw above, for those such as Titmuss, universalism was meant to eliminate the stigma that was embodied in the pre-1948 system, enshrined in the Poor Law and institutions like the workhouse. On this reading, the continuance of stigma might be attributed to the failure of modern policy-making. However, such universalism was not the only objective of state welfare. For Marshall (1981) one of the aims of the welfare state should be to eliminate stigma without thereby eliminating social inequality per se, i.e. to create a society of equal citizens who could possess unequal amounts of wealth and income. Yet could this maintenance of social inequality undermine attempts to eliminate stigma? If inequality is needed to make people respond to incentives, then perhaps those who do not respond properly may be legitimately stigmatized. Such was the conclusion of Beveridge himself:

> Assistance . . . must be felt to be something less desirable than insurance benefit…[and] always subject to proof of needs and examination of means; it will be subject also to any

conditions as to behaviour which may seem likely to hasten the restoration of earning capacity. (Beveridge 1942: para 369)

So, although Beveridge desired the gradual reduction of means testing, such arguments suggest that some of the architects of state welfare saw a valuable and continued role for stigma in maintaining people's incentives to better themselves.

One way or another, stigma has always been most closely associated with cash transfers. The association is weakest in the case of insurance benefits, since these are defined as earned entitlements, and strongest in the case of assistance benefits. Carol Walker (1993: 146–68) notes how, as Beveridge's goal of reducing means testing has been abandoned, successive governments have tried to make assistance benefits look more attractive while those who depend upon them have been simultaneously demonized as scroungers. She argues that this mixed message has led to a poor record on the take-up of assistance benefits, with significantly fewer people applying for them than are actually entitled. There are undoubtedly other factors at work with the non-take-up of benefits, e.g. a general lack of knowledge about entitlements, or a wariness at the complexity of the benefit system, but Walker insists that the take-up of assistance benefits is lower than it should be largely because potential claimants can see the stigmatizing effects. These effects can be difficult to quantify, however, though Riphahn (2001) and Walker (2005: 195–9) provide some evidence.

Taken from the Department of Work and Pensions, the most recent figures for the take-up of means-tested benefits are shown in Table 10.2. Somewhere between £6.9 billion and £12.7 billion of means-tested benefits are unclaimed; a take-up rate of just 77 to 85 per cent. Across the entire benefit system it is thought that approximately £16 billion goes unclaimed. These figures are worse than those I reported for the third edition of this book, underlining the difficulty of distributing means-tested benefits and the risk of relying upon them so much.

By and large, governments tend to be more concerned with the amount of benefit being defrauded than they are with the amount going unclaimed. There are two aspects to this issue: the economic and the moral. Firstly, how much is being defrauded? Claim and counter-claim are made in answer to this question. Governments tend to be cavalier when publicizing the extent of benefit fraud. It is easier to court popularity, by proposing to clamp down on stereotypes of the 'workshy', than to acknowledge that few people conform to such caricatures, with most unemployed people struggling in circumstances unfamiliar to most politicians and newspaper columnists (Smith 2005). The Department for Work and Pensions (2010a) estimated that, in 2009–10, fraud and error together accounted for £5.2 billion. How credible are such claims?

Sainsbury (2003: 284) urges us to have a 'healthy degree of caution'. Error (honest mistakes made by administrators or claimants) may itself be a cause for worry but, according to the DWP (2010a), actual fraud accounts for about £1 billion per year and tax credit fraud for £0.5 billion.

Table 10.2 The take-up of income-related benefits, 2008–9

	Percentage by caseload	Percentage by spending	By claimants[1]	Amount unclaimed
Income Support and income-related Employment and Support Allowance	78–90%	85–94%	250,000–600,000	£590m–1.6bn
Pension Credit	62–73%	71–81%	980,000–1.6m	£1.6bn–2.9bn
Housing Benefit	77–86%	82–90%	680,000–1.2m	£1.7bn–3.4bn
Council Tax Benefit	63–70%	65–73%	2.1m–2.9m	£1.4b–2.1bn
Income-based Jobseeker's Allowance	47–59%	49–63%	570,000–940,000	£1.4bn–2.5bn

1 Those not claiming something for which they are entitled.

> ## Box 10.3 **Defrauding whom?**
>
> When asked about it in quite general terms most people condemn benefit fraud. Think of the following vignette, however. Peter is on benefits when his neighbour, Paul, asks him whether he would like to spend some of his spare time mending Paul's garden fence. To make it worth his while, Paul offers to pay £20 to Peter. What should Peter do? Should he do the work and then declare his £20 to the Benefit Agency? But if he does that, the Agency will withdraw some of his benefits so that most of his £20 effectively disappears (remember the poverty trap). Or should he do the work and not declare it? But that would be fraudulent, strictly speaking. Or should he simply decline Paul's offer? Whenever I put this scenario to a classroom of students a surprising number of those who originally condemned fraud end up recommending that Peter should do the work and not declare his earnings. Why? Because they believe that the benefit system should not penalize Peter for doing something of value and improving his income. The object of the exercise is to suggest that benefit fraud is a far more complicated issue than we might gather from hysterical headlines and moralizing politicians.

These are large sums yet also very little compared to the sums lost to tax evasion, about which governments and newspapers are far less vocal. According to unofficial data leaked from HM Revenue and Customs, tax evasion costs the UK anywhere between £97 billion and £150 billion per year (Taylor 2007). Another problem is that government and newspapers tend to roll fraud and error together, giving inflated figures that justify a new wave of crackdowns. In truth, guesswork and wishful thinking still tend to predominate, with officials calculating how much fraud *is* being conducted by estimating how much *would* have been conducted had defrauders not been caught.

Secondly, why do people engage in fraud? The popular image of the defrauder is of a selfish, criminally motivated individual stealing resources from those who genuinely need them. Research by Dean and Melrose (1996), however, found that this image bears little correspondence to reality. People were often motivated out of sheer desperation, genuine confusion (about what they were and were not entitled to), a sense that they had been betrayed by the welfare state, or economic necessity in response to a system which seemed to want to keep them in poverty. Equally, the government could be said to derive an advantage from fraud: because fraud assists the operation of a flexible, low-wage economy, because people who work unofficially in the 'informal' economy are contributing to national output and, finally, because politicians can make political capital out of condemning fraud at periodic intervals. Box 10.3 illustrates why fraud is a more complex issue.

Dependency culture and the underclass

The debate concerning the underclass is a very old one which continually reappears in new guises. Morris (1994: 10–32) traces its roots from the nineteenth century, finding a succession of theorists expressing concern about those, the undeserving poor, who were believed to threaten the stability and prosperity of society: for Malthus they were the 'redundant population', for Marx they were the semi-criminal lumpenproletariat; for Mayhew, Booth, and Stedman-Jones they were the residuum of decent society.

Concerns about the underclass and its supposed 'culture of dependency' revived in the early 1980s. Murray (1984) alleged that overgenerous benefits in the United States had led to the emergence of a significant underclass of several million people. By encouraging neither marriage nor independence within the labour market, the US equivalent of assistance benefits had created a generation of unemployed and unemployable black youths, as well as a generation of lone mothers who expected to be 'married to the state'. Murray's empirical research was subsequently challenged by many but the gist of his argument proved to be highly influential. These kinds of arguments have given a theoretical justification for the expansion of workfare programmes in the United States, in which claimants are compelled to work or train in return for their benefits.

For those such as Murray, therefore, the term 'underclass' does not refer to an extreme of poverty, i.e. the poorest of the poor, but to a different *type* of poverty: the value system (the culture) possessed by those who expect the state to do everything for them without having to contribute anything in return. Murray's thesis has come to wield a certain amount of influence in Britain, including on the Left.

Many projects have thrown sober water on such hyperbole. Dean and Taylor-Gooby (1992) found that terms such as 'underclass' and 'dependency culture' indicate a widespread tendency to blame the victims for the very disadvantages (unemployment, social exclusion) which have been perpetrated against them. Claimants are not culturally separate from 'normal' society: if anything, claimants cope with their situation by adopting and internalizing what they see as the norms and values of non-claimants. Duncan and Irwin (2005) proposed that mothers are often assumed (incorrectly) by policy-makers and administrators to be 'economic agents', motivated by monetary considerations. This leads to misplaced policy responses and, when mothers fail to respond in the expected, 'proper' way, they can be assumed to be acting irresponsibly. Lone mothers who place childcare ahead of wage earning may be especially vulnerable to such misplaced expectations, labelled as having the wrong aspirations, and then subjected to behavioural modification through an increasingly conditional benefit system. Overall, academic research fails to find people conforming to the populist image of a 'couch potato' who expects to be drip-fed by the benefit system.

From New Labour to coalition government

New Labour's principles and strategies

The New Labour government (1997–2010) was committed to three main principles. Firstly, it emphasized merit and the idea that people must be helped to help themselves: 'a hand-up, not a handout'. This assumes that society can be meritocratic, where people rise to whatever position in society they aspire. Secondly, however, this is not to imagine that New Labour ignored the importance of social cohesion. It repeatedly stressed the importance of social inclusion and integration into the norms and mainstream of society. However, New Labour was concerned with the height of the social floor (improving the position of those at the bottom) but not necessarily with the height of the social ceiling. Finally, then, without much of an egalitarian emphasis it spoke more in terms of community and has associated community with notions of desert, duty, and reciprocity. By its motto that 'rights imply responsibilities', New Labour argued that what you put into society must be broadly proportionate to what you take out.

These principles (merit, social inclusion, community) converged around an employment-centred approach with waged work being regarded as the principal means through which people can escape from poverty, hence its slogan: 'Work for those who can, security for those who cannot'. Employment was thought to be the means by which people get on in life and participate in the activities of the social community.

As such, these principles gave rise to some clearly identifiable strategies. New Labour:

- preferred a stick-and-carrot emphasis upon 'labour market activation'. The post-Second World War welfare state was repeatedly (and misleadingly) described as passive, as paying people for doing nothing. An 'active' welfare system is therefore required, one that will help the 'deserving' but will clamp down on those who shirk their social obligations.

- emphasized selectivist reforms and the principle of social insurance was allowed to wither.
- wanted to 'make work pay'. It sought to raise the floor below which wages cannot fall and to improve the system of in-work transfers.
- preferred 'redistribution by stealth' in the hope that affluent households would not notice some of the redistributive measures being introduced.
- repeatedly emphasized the importance of private provision.
- addressed the culture of social security. It introduced tax credits partly to improve in-work incomes but also to signal a discursive shift away from benefits (state handouts and therefore bad) towards credits (fiscal welfare and therefore a deserved reward for hard work).

New Labour's policies

Benefit reform during its period in office was dominated by: the New Deal, tax credits, value-for-money measures, pension reform.

Firstly, the welfare-to-work philosophy of the New Deal stresses that receiving benefits for 'doing nothing' was no longer an option and that to continue receiving benefits claimants must accept one of the following: subsidized employment, full-time education or training, a job in the voluntary sector, work with an environmental taskforce. A range of penalties was introduced for non-compliers, including having their benefit stopped. New Labour hailed the New Deal as a success, especially in reducing youth unemployment. Evidence suggests the effect is positive but fairly modest (Frommand Spross 2009). Activation policies work well in areas of high employment but are less effective where there are few jobs available. Those who find work are more likely to enter low-waged, insecure, part-time jobs with few opportunities and to leave those jobs again in the short term. It may also be that those who find work would have done so anyway (Standing 2011). Dutton et al. (2005) found that the New Deal does not overcome the hurdles facing lone parents, such as employer inflexibility, a lack of affordable childcare, or enough well-paid jobs.

Secondly, the government tried to 'make work pay' by introducing a minimum wage and tax credits. As a fiscal transfer, credits are administered via the tax system and, depending upon entitlement, take the form of either (a) a reduction in the recipient's tax bill, or (b) a reduction plus an additional cash payment.

Thirdly, the government adopted a variety of value-for-money measures that often seemed designed to appease taxpayer anxieties. Disabled people were one group affected by this. Access to benefits has been gradually tightened, including the extension of compulsory measures and a crackdown on fraud that, especially in its early days, was widely perceived as an attack on disabled people; a variety of New Deals have been implemented with the intention of encouraging and facilitating the entry of disabled people into the labour market; finally, measures to combat discrimination were introduced.

Finally, Labour's attempt to reform UK pensions ultimately led nowhere. All welfare states face some hard choices when it comes to pensions due to the rising numbers of those above working age (Taylor-Gooby 2005). Options for defusing the 'demographic timebomb' include raising the retirement age, raising more revenue through higher taxes and/or contributions, or lowering the generosity of pensions. In the early 1980s the Conservative government decided on the third of these options, indexing the state pension to inflation rather than earnings, hamstringing the state's earnings-related scheme and encouraging the growth of occupational and private pension schemes (leading to a massive mis-selling of the latter). But such reforms only delayed the pensions crisis.

Having failed to reform the system effectively, the UK now faces a situation where *all three options* are now being implemented. (The coalition has promised to restore the link between earnings and the state pension; though so did New Labour.) What makes sensible and equitable reform less likely are the conflicts looming between private and public sector workers. With the former facing less generous entitlements, government and employers have argued that fairness only dictates that the public sector undergoes similar pain. Sadly, a politics of 'unfairness for all' is unlikely to create a pensions system that is both sustainable and just. Issues of class and social justice are being neglected in favour of 'phoney wars' (public vs. private; old vs. young).

Coalition government

In May 2010, the UK's first coalition government since the war was established. The Conservative Party had vowed to slash public spending (and pensions) in an effort to significantly reduce Britain's debt over four years and, once in power, the Liberal Democrats agreed with this strategy. The government's argument is that export-led growth in the private sector will soak up job losses in the public one. According to its critics, this strategy is political rather than economic, designed to deliver tax cuts to its middle-class supporters by the next election; there being no need to slash so much so quickly.

Against this background the prospects for benefit reform do not look encouraging, with the Institute for Fiscal Studies (**http://www.ifs.org.uk/projects/346**) warning that the proposed cuts would hurt the poorest most of all. With benefit spending also coming under pressure, it seemed as if the social security system might risk being reduced to a residual, highly conditional, safety net. Arguments broke out between the Treasury (looking for budget reductions) and those within the DWP who are interested in genuine reform.

Within the first six months of the coalition's tenure it was possible to detect several tendencies pulling the government in divergent directions. Firstly, there have been familiar neo-liberal or New Right attempts to demonize 'the undeserving' and treat benefit spending as a sign of failure. New Labour was accused of failing to address the problem of those who could work, but who do not want to, and Chancellor George Osborne fell back on the rhetoric of underclass dependency when he described many families as making a 'lifestyle choice' not to work. Secondly, a kind of 'civic conservatism' has also been apparent. New Labour was criticized for handing too much power to the state and so throttling the space that should be occupied by families, voluntary organizations, and charities. A 'Big Society' agenda, Conservatives argued, would free society from the state, heal 'broken Britain', and ensure social mobility. In this context, an enabling benefits system would facilitate genuine social participation and responsibility, e.g. by using tax allowances to reward marriage. Finally, some have advanced a 'red Tory' politics, which appropriates the Left's emphasis on mutualism, social enterprises, cooperation, and even redistribution and progressivism.

By October 2010, the DWP seemed to have won at least one of its battles with the Treasury. The basic idea is to gradually integrate New Labour's tax credits in order to eliminate poverty traps—so that paid work *always* provides a higher income—and guarantee an income floor below which no one can fall. Across ten years the proposal is to fuse Jobseeker's Allowance, Income Support, and Employment and Support Allowance into a 'universal work credit', while combining Housing Benefit, Council Tax Benefit, Disability Living Allowance, Working Tax Credit, and Child Tax Benefit into a 'universal life credit'. This reform might satisfy neo-liberals (given its emphasis upon incentives and labour market flexibility), civic conservatives (who welcome the emphasis upon marriage and savings) and red Tories (enthusiastic at attempts to plug the benefit gaps and ensure a minimum income floor). Furthermore, since this 'universal credit' reform theoretically lowers rates of benefit withdrawal, no one will be reasonably able to claim that 'work does not pay', which, if anything, might bolster punitive workfare schemes designed to weed out 'the undeserving'.

The essential rationale resembles that for a Negative Income Tax (NIT), an idea that has lingered since the 1940s and was seriously considered in the United States in the 1960s, receiving support from Right (like Milton Friedman) and Left. In Figure 10.2, Alan has a low wage and so a NIT would lift his income from line A to line B; Barry has a higher wage and although he would receive less NIT

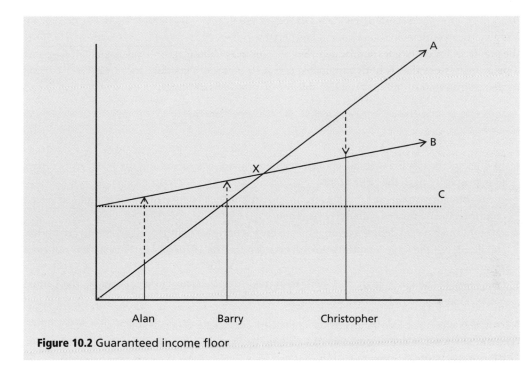

Figure 10.2 Guaranteed income floor

it would still raise his income to line B (at a higher level than Alan's); Christopher has a good wage and so would pay taxes, *reducing* his income to line B. Therefore, the NIT always improves the income of the lowest paid and tapers off towards point X, after which people pay taxes as normal. The scheme can be designed in any number of ways, but the basic idea is that 'work always pays' and, theoretically, no wage earner should fall below line C.

However, whether the universal credit proposal evolves towards a NIT or not, it would need to resolve similar problems. Firstly, a NIT pays money *ex post*, i.e. recipients are moved up to line B after their line A income and needs have been calculated. This means there is a lag between the time they receive their wages and their final income, creating uncertainty for those in insecure employment and meaning that NIT does not necessarily reconcile the aims of encouraging flexibility while ensuring security. Secondly, a NIT supplements wages and says little about those, like carers, whose social contributions lie outside the labour market. Finally, the NIT potentially encourages employers to pay low wages and so effectively becomes a taxpayer-funded supplement for bad employers. Some have argued that if it is to address such difficulties, a universal credit system would need to evolve towards an unconditional Basic Income. With the coalition stating its commitment to the long-term implementation of an additional guaranteed Citizen's Pension, the next few years promise to be an interesting, if somewhat perilous, time for social security reform.

Inequality and poverty

Several important projects researching UK inequalities were published in 2010, including the Marmot Review (2010) and the National Equality Panel (2010). They found:

- The richest 10 per cent own 100 times more wealth than the poorest 10 per cent.
- Among adults in the most deprived 10 per cent of areas in England, 30 per cent have no qualifications at all and fewer than 8 per cent have degrees. In the richest 10 per cent of areas, these figures are reversed.

Table 10.3 UK inequality

	1983	1988	1993–4	1998–9	2008–9
Gini coefficient	28	36	34	34	34

Source: Office for National Statistics: **http://www.statistics.gov.uk/cci/nugget.asp?id=332**

- In England, people living in the poorest neighbourhoods will on average die seven years earlier than people living in the richest ones.
- Inequalities in earnings and incomes are high in Britain, both compared with other industrialized countries and compared with thirty years ago.
- Over the most recent decade, earnings inequality has narrowed a little and income inequality has stabilized, but the large inequality growth between the late 1970s and early 1990s has not been reversed.
- Inequality in the UK is high. Of OECD countries, only Mexico, Turkey, Portugal, the United States, Poland, and Italy demonstrate higher levels.

Statisticians often measure inequality using the Gini coefficient. Basically, the higher the number, the higher the level of inequality. Table 10.3 gives the levels of UK inequality over the last thirty years.

During the 1980s income inequality shot up (New Zealand was the only other country in the world where inequality increased more rapidly), crept down slightly in the early–mid 1990s, decreased to 32 in 2003–4 before rising again. Over the last decade the poorest tenth have seen their income decline by 12 per cent while the richest tenth have experienced improvements of 37 per cent. The poorest tenth now possess just 1.3 per cent of the UK's total income, compared with the 31 per cent possessed by the richest tenth. The income of the richest tenth is more than the combined income of all those living below the median income.

Inequality in the UK is fairly high by comparison with other countries belonging to the UN's 'Very High Human Development' index (UNDP 2009: 195). In 2007, the UK was the sixth most unequal among the 28 European countries for which data were available; only Lithuania, Greece, Latvia, Portugal, and Romania were more unequal.[2] Across the European Union's 24 countries, UK individuals who are unemployed experience the second highest risk of being in poverty; retired people experience the fourth highest risk; and those in work the seventh highest risk.[3]

What explains the UK's performance?

According to Sefton et al. (2009), New Labour's benefits and tax credit policies favoured families with children and pensioners, especially those on low incomes, but progress stalled after 2004. Child and pensioner poverty fell significantly during its period in office; though poverty worsened among working-age adults without children. By contrast, tax policy did little to address inequalities, especially the rise in higher incomes, and was sometimes even regressive. Overall, then, New Labour did not reduce income inequality (despite improvements before 2003–4) but nor did it make things worse.

The implication would seem to be that redistribution through benefits and tax credits can achieve some success, but unless wider economic conditions are also addressed (including extreme high and low earnings, inheritances, bonuses, assets, and housing), then those successes may be offset by entrenched inequalities elsewhere. Sweden does much more through its tax system to transfer income and so reduce 'pre-transfer' inequalities; whereas the UK preference is for lower taxes and targeted support (Stewart 2009). Clark and Leicester (2004) found that post-1979 benefit reforms (which have stressed means testing) account for over 40 per cent of the rise in income inequality

[2] http://www.parliament.uk/briefingpapers/commons/lib/research/briefings/snep-03870.pdf
[3] http://epp.eurostat.ec.europa.eu/cache/ITY_OFFPUB/KS-RA-10-015/EN/KS-RA-10-015-EN.PDF

since then. As we might expect, high-spending nations are more egalitarian than low-spending ones. Compared with some countries, the UK is unusual in achieving a lot from relatively little. This confirms earlier research suggesting that UK social security is reasonably efficient at reducing the levels of inequality and poverty which would otherwise prevail (Kraus 2004). Yet without additional effort (derided by New Labour as old-fashioned 'tax and spend'), there are considerable limits to what any benefits and tax credit system can achieve.

This is unsurprising because social security tends to be horizontally rather than vertically redistributive. That is, it transfers income from those parts of our lives when our earning capacity is greatest to those when it is weakest, though this is less true for those in the bottom deciles. Hills (1997: 19) famously concluded:

> *most* benefits are self-financed over people's lifetimes, rather than being paid for by others ... Nearly three-quarters of what the welfare state does looked at this way is a 'savings bank'; only a quarter is 'Robin Hood' redistribution between different people.

In other words, when we look at the total amount of redistribution effected by the welfare state, 75 per cent is of the life-cycle form and 25 per cent is vertical.

Overall, we can conclude that poverty levels have fallen slightly (for all but working-age adults without children), but income inequality has remained more or less the same. This implies that while improvements have been made at the bottom of the income ladder, those towards the top continued to climb away at a rate that New Labour was extremely reluctant to address. On the plus side, Britain's appalling record in the 1980s and 1990s has been reversed. New Labour's time in office was therefore mixed. For some, it was thirteen years of missed opportunities; for others, the best that could be achieved in a globalizing, capitalist economy. On the one hand, it reduced poverty and inequality to levels lower than might have prevailed otherwise; on the other, it failed to achieve the more traditional social democratic aims which it had (bravely) set itself, e.g. in 1999 Tony Blair set a target of eliminating child poverty within twenty years. Recent data on UK relative poverty are given in Box 10.4.

None of this contradicts international evidence. There is:

> a positive relationship between public social expenditures and income redistribution. Welfare states with higher public social expenditure achieve more income redistribution ... Countries that rely more heavily on private social arrangements achieve less income redistribution. (Goudswaard and Caminada 2010: 17)

European and global dimensions

Benefit systems everywhere face a number of similar challenges and questions (Townsend, 2009a):

- To what extent should benefits be funded through social insurance contributions, taxation, or private insurance schemes?
- Should the emphasis be placed upon targeting and means testing or universalism?
- How can social security entitlements maintain solidarities in the face of various pressures, e.g. ageing populations and migrant workers?
- To what extent can coverage extend to cover more contingencies, e.g. changes to the family and the need for long-term care, and informal, non-waged activities, e.g. caring?
- How can systems cope with changes to economies and labour markets, especially in a global context, in the twenty-first century?

Box 10.4 **Data on relative poverty (1)**

According to the Joseph Rowntree Foundation (MacInnes et al. 2009), in 2007–8:

- 13.4 million people lived in low-income households, up from 12.1 million in 2004–5, but down from the 1996–7 all-time peak of 14.5 million.
- More people are living in households below 40 per cent of median income than ever before.
- 30 per cent of children are at risk of poverty compared with 18 per cent for pensioners.
- New Labour reduced pensioner poverty by around 900,000 and child poverty by around 450,000.
- Inequality in the lower half of the income distribution is now higher than it has been at any time since at least the middle 1990s.
- 40 per cent of the extra income that has been created over the past decade has gone to the richest tenth. The poorest tenth has had no discernible increase at all.
- Between 1998–9 and 2004–5, the 'relative' child poverty rate (before housing costs) fell from 26 per cent to 21 per cent; since then it has risen back to 23 per cent.
- All the progress made in reducing in-work child poverty in the period up to 2003–4 has been wiped out; in-work poverty now accounts for more than half of all child poverty (54 per cent).
- The number of children in low-income, non-working households continued to fall until 2006–7, reaching almost 1.7 million.
- After reaching a peak in 2003–4, the number of households in England presenting as homeless, and the number in temporary accommodation have both declined significantly.
- In 2007, around 2.8 million households in England were in fuel poverty. This was around 1.3 million more than in 2005, but little over half of the number in 1996.
- Infant mortality has fallen slowly, though the rate among the 'manual social classes' is 50 per cent higher than among others.

- How influential will the pressure to liberalize and deregulate be, especially as advocated by institutions like the World Bank and IMF?

Yet nations are likely to answer these questions differently, given the cultural, demographic, political, and institutional diversity which characterizes benefit systems at present. For instance, China constitutes something of a social policy 'laboratory' (Lin and Kangas 2006). The old socialist system has largely been dismantled and there is a battle between those who promote further privatization, marketization, and individualized responsibility and those who would prefer something closer to the European social model.

That said, because European nations are diverse and have themselves embraced the ethos of flexibility, activation, protection through safety-net assistance, and personal responsibility, some query whether there is such a thing as a European social model (Zimmermann 2006: 41–2). Conversely, while there has been a shift towards means testing and greater insecurity, Nelson (2007) finds that targeted benefits are more vulnerable to cutbacks than social insurance benefits in nations with extensive, state corporatist systems. Also:

> . . . social policies more founded on decommodified security in the North mean that people are better integrated by virtue of their entitlements as citizens, and this translates into poverty rates which are lower by half. (Menahem, 2007: 97)

Thus, the ideal and sometimes even the reality of the social model are still apparent.

Overbye (2005: 306) notes that 166 out of the 172 member states of the United Nations now have some kind of work-injury and old age insurance system, though coverage is generally limited in poorer countries to the most privileged workers. Unemployment and family benefits are less widespread. Social insurance continues to be popular but countries such as Argentina, Chile, and Mexico have moved towards fully funded schemes and away from pay-as-you-go (where today's workers pay for today's retirees). Social assistance is also prevalent but across Latin America, Africa, and Asia relatively few countries run tax-financed schemes that provide guaranteed minimum incomes. Indermit et al. (2005) and Feldstein (2005) suggest that a 'multipillar' approach, a combination of individual and social savings to finance pensions, is becoming more widespread as nations shift the emphasis away from social towards individual responsibility. And as the redistributive effects of pension systems fade, those on low incomes will be especially disadvantaged (Queisser and Whitehouse 2006).

According to van Ginneken (2010: 60; also Cichon and Hagemejer 2007: 173–5):

> . . . between 70 and 80 per cent of the global population do not have access to meaningful cash benefits. They live in a state of more or less severe 'social insecurity'.

The problem is particularly acute in sub-Saharan Africa, where only 5 to 10 per cent of the workforce is covered by social insurance schemes. Most countries in sub-Saharan Africa have difficulties in extending pension insurance coverage because of stagnating wages and employment. In Latin America and the Caribbean, social security coverage is very unequal. In the lowest-income countries, fewer than 30 per cent of employed people are affiliated to a social insurance scheme; while the figures for middle-income and high-income countries are 50 per cent and 60 per cent, respectively (van Ginneken 2010: 62–3). Coverage is also fairly low in Eastern Europe.

Against this background, the International Labour Organization has campaigned for all nations to institute a 'social protection floor' which would include a right to income security and which can be raised over time with increasing national affluence (also Townsend 2009b, 2009c). This idea has been supported by the UN.

Conclusion

It may well be that no social security system can achieve all of the aims that benefits are called on to achieve because those aims are themselves often contradictory. Therefore, any system inevitably involves trade-offs of one form or another. If so, then this would indicate that, despite the technical nature of social security and the fact that few are expert in each and every aspect of what is a very complicated system, decisions about those trade-offs are primarily political, cultural, and ethical. For instance, if society decides that it wants a highly targeted system, then it will have to accept the continuance of the poverty trap. If, however, society wants to improve the work incentives of the poorest, then it will have to accept that resources may consequently 'spill over' to those higher up the income ladder who do not need them. In short, as technically complex as the transfer system is, reforming and improving it are ultimately a question of which values and principles we collectively regard as important. To a large extent, cash transfers mirror and reflect the society within which they operate.

KEY LEGISLATION

UK benefit reform will be shaped by the announcements made by the coalition government in its June 2010 budget (**http://www.hm-treasury.gov.uk/2010_june_budget.htm**) and its October 2010 comprehensive spending review (**http://www.hm-treasury.gov.uk/spend_index.htm**). A White Paper was published in November 2010; see **http://www.dwp.gov.uk/policy/welfare-reform/legislation-and-key-documents/universal-credit/**. It is heavily based upon an earlier document entitled '21st century welfare' (**http://www.dwp.gov.uk/docs/21st-century-welfare.pdf**).

FURTHER READING

Beveridge, W. (1942) *Social Insurance and Allied Services* (London: Macmillan).

International Social Security Review.

Journal of Poverty and Social Justice.

Millar, J. (ed.) (2009) *Understanding Social Security* 2nd edn (Bristol: The Policy Press).

Walker, R. (2005) *Social Security and Welfare* (Buckingham: Open University Press).

USEFUL WEBSITES

Child Poverty Action Group: **www.cpag.org.uk**

Department for Work and Pensions: **www.dwp.gov.uk**

HM Treasury: **www.hm-treasury.gov.uk**

Institute for Fiscal Studies: **www.ifs.org.uk**

International Social Security Association: **www.issa.int/engl.homef.htm**

Social Exclusion Unit: **www.socialexclusionunit.gov.uk**

Social Policy Digest: **http://journals.cambridge.org/jid_JSP**

ESSAY QUESTIONS

1 What are the most important aims of the social security system?

2 How effective is means testing?

3 How concerned should we be with benefit fraud?

4 How does the UK system compare with those in other countries?

ONLINE RESOURCE CENTRE

For additional material and resources, please visit the Online Resource Centre at: **www.oxfordtextbooks.co.uk/orc/baldock4e/**.

11

Education, schools, and training

Sarah Vickerstaff

Contents

Introduction

As a universal state service, education has always been a core interest of social policy students and researchers. Inequalities in access to education and variations in educational outcomes, particularly social differences in educational attainment, have been of central concern. It has been much less typical for standard social policy texts to consider the structure of training provision and the policy implications of access to training opportunities. This is largely because training was seen as a labour market or economic issue rather than a social policy issue. However, this is changing: in addition to the traditional concern with the social impact of education, policy debates since the 1970s have focused primarily upon the economic outcomes of education and training provision, namely on their effects on employment, earnings, and economic growth, and hence on welfare.

It has been argued with increasing force since the late 1970s that the quality and capacity of a country's education and training systems (these will be referred to by the acronym ET, the accepted term in the literature) are a critical element in the performance of whole economies. The distinctive differences in ET from one country to the next are thought to be a factor which helps to explain the differential performance and success of national economies. It is argued further that this economic effect of ET may be becoming more significant in the rapidly changing global economic and technological environment that prevails in the new century. The emerging 'knowledge economy' is thought to require improvements in the general level of education and an upskilling of the population.

Learning outcomes

At the end of this chapter you will have an introductory understanding of:

1 the social and economic functions of education;
2 the role of social policy in education and training provision;
3 recent policies on schooling;
4 how youth transitions have changed in the last thirty years;
5 what has been happening in higher education policy.

The social and economic functions of education and training

The fact that governments typically became involved in mass education before the development of other comprehensive services of the welfare state such as healthcare poses the question of why education is thought to be so important. Education is such a natural and taken-for-granted part of all of our early lives that we rarely stand back and pose the question of why it is compulsory. Education has always been seen as providing individual, social, and economic benefits but the primary function of education is much debated (see Box 11.1). For the individual, education is supposed to provide opportunities for personal development and growth, scope to realize potential, and hence the basis for progress into work and careers. On a more social level, education is characterized as a civilizing force, with the potential to reduce social inequality and contribute to social unity. A traditional liberal view of education has tended to stress the value of education for its own sake, eschewing the idea that education should perform an explicitly preparatory function for employment. However, it has always also been argued by some that education should fulfil an explicit role in preparing each generation for employment, by inculcating habits of time keeping and discipline and providing abilities and skills relevant for the world of work.

Box 11.1 **Different views of the purpose of education**

- 'to give intellectual, moral and social instruction to (a pupil, esp. a child) esp. as a formal and prolonged process' (Oxford Dictionary)
- to socialize children into society through the transmission of collective culture
- to provide the skills and attributes necessary for the world of work
- to educate the ruling class for leadership positions and control and discipline the working classes in order to reproduce the conditions for continued capitalist growth

---

What the functions of training should be have been much less debated. Traditionally, there has been both a philosophical and an institutional split between education and training. They have been seen as fulfilling distinct functions, and in Britain, historically, they have been provided by different institutions and agencies. For much of the last century training has been viewed as primarily providing economic benefits for particular employers, and therefore something best left to private individuals to provide. Although training is typically seen in this more instrumental light as providing specific skills and abilities for, or in, employment, it is also recognized as providing advantages to the individual in terms of their employability, their earning potential, and future career prospects, and hence their welfare. More recently it has been argued that a highly skilled workforce is also a more flexible, creative, and innovative one, so that in addition to the immediate benefits of enhancing someone's specific skills there is the broader advantage of a more adaptable pool of labour for the economy as a whole. This is taken one step further in the argument that as society is now subject to a rapid pace of change people must become lifelong learners in a learning society and be willing and able to continue with education and training throughout their lives.

For these reasons it is, in practice, difficult to separate out the individual, social, and economic benefits of access to ET. Levels of ET contribute to an individual's and—it seems—a nation's earning capacity, and hence makes a great contribution to welfare. It is not surprising, therefore, that debates over the 'proper' function of education and the right balance between the individual, social, and economic functions of ET have been a linking thread of policy reform since the 1970s. From that time the view has grown that schools are failing to provide young people with the basic education and kinds of skill they needed for the world of work. As Wolf (2002: 13) has put it:

> For twenty years, British politicians have been obsessed with education—convinced that it is in a uniquely parlous state, and that this matters as never before . . . this passion for education rests on the belief that the world's whole economy has changed. It is now so 'knowledge driven' that only those nations committed to 'lifelong learning' in a 'learning society' can hope to thrive. Lip service may still be paid to learning for personal enrichment and development, but in politicians' speeches the emphasis is unremittingly on what education can do for the economy of the UK.

The role of social and public policy

The key foci for debates on the role of social and public policy in this field are first, to what extent and how should government pay for and provide ET for its citizens and second, in providing ET how much should it try to engineer fair access to education and training opportunities? Much recent debate on ET in Britain (as with other areas of social policy) has been dominated by arguments about the relative roles of the state and the market (or the public and private sectors) in delivering the quantity and quality of services needed. The case for state intervention in ET is usually built around two main lines of argument: economic arguments about market failure and social arguments about equity and equality of opportunity. The economic justification for state involvement in ET revolves around an assessment of the relative benefits that accrue from ET to society as a whole (the public good), to individuals, and to employing organizations (the private good), the argument being that the balance of gains should determine who pays. The question immediately becomes complicated, however, because of course not all education and training have the same benefits or advantages. It is apparent that the more general the education or training, the more difficult it is to apportion the relative benefits to society, to the individual, and to employers. It is now taken for granted that the state should provide access to education in schools, funded through general taxation, and that a basic level of education should be compulsory. Although the individual is the prime beneficiary, the public goods or gains are also clear: the democratic, cultural, and creative benefits of an educated citizenry and the economic advantages, in terms of productivity, flexibility, and innovation, of a well-educated workforce.

The same argument is less transparent for other aspects of ET. Whereas the public good argument is relatively easy to make for compulsory education, it becomes progressively more difficult with further and higher education and training. The more firm specific training is (i.e. the extent to which the training is not transferable to other work situations), the less justifiable it appears to be to finance it from the public purse through general taxation. In response to these issues we can distinguish theoretically between three ideal types of ET finance and regulation: the market model, the social partnership model, and the state model (Sheldrake and Vickerstaff 1987: 55; see also Finegold and Crouch 1994: 276).

Paying for ET

The market model argues that if individuals or firms perceive a commercial advantage in acquiring skills or skilled employees they will undertake training. For example, the return on the investment in adding skills will be recouped either in higher wages for the individual and/or in higher productivity for the employer. The role of policy here is to ensure the smooth operation of the market but to allow the quantity and quality of training provided to be market driven. However, for various reasons the market may produce suboptimal outcomes in terms of the quantity and quality of training desirable for the economy as a whole. For the employing firm, the problem is that in a free labour market the trained employee can take their skills to the highest bidder. This is usually known as the 'poaching' problem, and has often been used by companies as a justification for not investing in training: they spend money on training someone only to see that employee poached by another firm which free-rides on their investment. There are thus incentives for firms either to poach already trained labour or to restrict training to firm-specific skills, which have less value in the labour market. In practice, however, it may be very difficult for training to be sufficiently firm specific. In the case of many vocational and job-specific skills, the obvious beneficiary is the individual whose employment prospects are enhanced. Nonetheless, from the individual's perspective there is a risk that investing in skills, either by not earning or by taking lower wages whilst undergoing education or training, will not be repaid by a better-paid job in the future. There is also an information problem for the individual in knowing which skills would make a sound investment. It may also be the case that the individual cannot currently afford to acquire desirable skills. (For a full discussion of these market incentives and failures see Layard 1994; Finegold 1991.)

Another way of looking at these issues, which has become prominent in higher education policy debates, is by reference to rates of return on spending on ET. By calculating the cost of education and training, for an individual in terms of forgone earnings and for society in respect of public expenditure, we can attempt to determine the rate of return to the individual and to society as a whole in terms of extra earnings and output (see Glennerster 1998a: 54–7). This approach became very significant in the 1990s in the debates about higher education. It was argued that the pay premium for graduates (expected extra earnings as a result of having a degree) justifies asking students to contribute more to the direct costs of their education. This argument has figured large in the most recent review of higher education funding:

> Higher education matters because it transforms the lives of individuals. On graduating, graduates are more likely to be employed, more likely to enjoy higher wages and better job satisfaction … those who benefit directly from higher education as graduates ought to make a contribution to the costs … The public also receives a benefit but this is less than the private benefit…Unlike primary and secondary education which are paid for out of general taxation, higher education is neither compulsory nor universal… As a consequence it is reasonable to ask those who gain private benefits to help fund it rather than rely on public funds collected through taxation from people who may not have participated in higher education themselves. (The Browne Report 2010: 14, 20–1)

These problems of quantifying who benefits from ET, and the market failures and perverse incentives that result, imply that public policy must seek solutions either by providing ET directly (the state model) or by developing mechanisms for sharing the costs of training amongst the main beneficiaries (the social partnership model). In practice, many countries use a combination of approaches depending upon the particular area of ET.

Access to ET?

In addition to the policy issue of who pays for ET there is also the question of whether governments should become involved in determining the structure and content of ET to ensure that its benefits are evenly spread and that the curricula are 'appropriate'. If ET has an impact on an individual's welfare, in terms of earning capacity and participation in the cultural and social life of the society, then public policy faces questions of equality of access to ET opportunities. In practice, evaluations of educational opportunities and outcomes show that the experience of education varies significantly from one social group to another. Rather than being a force for liberation, many writers have argued that schooling reinforces social divisions and serves to perpetuate or reproduce class, race, and gender divisions (see Box 11.2 for further discussion). Access to education and rates of success, as measured by qualifications, are highly correlated with socio-economic background, race, and gender (see Tables 11.1 and 11.2; on gender see discussion later in the chapter). It is also the case that those with the poorest education are least likely to receive substantial post-compulsory education and training, being confined to unskilled work in which little or no training is offered.

Box 11.2 Social class and education

I would argue that a key question that we need to ask is 'What progress has been made towards social justice and equality in education for the working classes over the last hundred years?' The answer has to be remarkably little. The most recent statistical data [2005] show that the educational gap between the classes widened over the last ten years. We are all much more credentialed now than we were then, although there is still a worrying critical mass of the white working class who leave schooling with no qualifications at all. In 2005 ten per cent of students entitled to free school meals, and therefore from the poorest families, were still leaving school with no qualifications at all. The attainment gap between the classes in education is just as great as it was 20, 50 years ago and mirrors the growing material gap between the rich and poor in UK society. Against a policy backdrop of continuous change and endless new initiatives it appears that in relation to social class the more things change the more they stay the same.

(Reay, 2006: 304)

Table 11.1 Percentage of pupils achieving five or more A*–C Grade GCSEs and equivalent by eligibility for free school meals (FSM)

	2002	2003	2004	2005	2006	2007	2008
FSM	23.0	24.2	26.1	29.9	33.0	35.5	40.0
Non-FSM	53.7	55.2	56.1	58.9	61.0	62.8	67.0
All pupils	49.0	50.7	51.9	54.9	57.3	59.3	63.5

Note: not all children are classified.

Source: **http://www.education.gov.uk/rsgateway/DB/TIM/m002021/index.shtml,** accessed 18 November 2010

Table 11.2 Percentage of pupils achieving five or more GCSE grades A*–C or equivalent by ethnic group

	1999	2006
White	50	58
Black	38	50
Asian	48	64
Indian	60	72
Pakistani	29	52
Bangladeshi	29	57
Other Asian	72	77
Other ethnic group	42	56

Source: *Social Trends* (2009), 39, 2009, ONS

In the 1980s the pressures on public expenditure (see Chapter 8 in this volume), the growth and persistence of unemployment, changes in the abilities and skills needed in the economy, and growing fears about the social implications of a poorly educated and increasingly unemployable underclass put all these issues of the role of government in overseeing and providing an 'appropriate' ET system into sharp relief.

The education and training legacy

The capacity of national ET systems to respond to the rapidly changing social and economic conditions in the new century is obviously built, in part, upon the education and training legacy in each country. Britain's education and training system is often seen as inferior to those of its competitors:

> Britain's failure to educate and train its workforce to the same levels as its international competitors has been both a product and a cause of the nation's poor relative economic performance: a product because the ET system evolved to meet the needs of the world's first industrialized economy, whose large, mass-production manufacturing sector required only a small number of skilled workers and university graduates; and a cause, because the absence

of a well educated and trained workforce has made it more difficult for industry to respond to new economic conditions. (Finegold and Soskice 1988: 21–2)

Education policy

A national system of mass schooling developed relatively late in England in comparison with other European countries. The development of education in Scotland followed a different path (see Patterson 2003). Throughout the nineteenth century the development of education was characterized by voluntarism, and provision was neither directed nor coordinated by government. The model for the curriculum was derived from the traditional independent public schools, in which a classical education was prized over science or anything of a vocational or practical bent. As Green comments:

> One of the principal casualties of the tradition of laissez-faire in education was scientific and technical instruction. With the exception of pure science which developed largely independently of formal educational institutions, England was, by the mid [nineteenth] century, incomparably backward in most areas of scientific and technical education. For the working class, elementary education was largely absent. State-organized trade schools for artisans and engineers, which were common in Europe, had not developed in England where received opinion regarded the workshop as the only fit place for learning a trade. (1990: 292)

This tradition of elite education left vocational and practical education and training to industry, and has continued to have effects on the ET system to the present day. With the development, in the last century, of a national education system, the split between education and training was rigidly maintained, and resulted in the failure to develop a comprehensive and integrated system that catered not merely to the needs of an academically oriented minority but also to those of the mass of people destined for skilled and unskilled manual and routine clerical work. The 1944 Education Act recommended the creation of a schooling system composed of three types of secondary school catering for different abilities and aptitudes: the grammar school for a traditional academic curriculum, technical schools for more practical or vocational studies, and secondary modern schools for a less academic route. The aim of the Act was to produce a meritocratic system based on equality of opportunity. The belief was that the testing of 11-year-olds through the 11-plus would allocate children, from whatever backgrounds, to the school most appropriate for their level of ability. The Act also provided for some compulsory education for the post-school 15–18 age group. In practice, the technical schools were never widely introduced and provisions for post-compulsory school education were weak. The failure to create the system outlined in the 1944 Act was due in part to the decentralized nature of education administration in which local government had practical management control over education (Aldcroft 1992: 30–1). In education, over the long period from the end of the Second World War to the mid1970s, change in policy was gradual. The main emerging debate in this period was over the 11-plus as a mechanism of selection and the developing evidence that class background was a strong predictor of success in the test. The movement for all-ability comprehensive schools developed out of discontent with the education that the majority of young people received in the secondary modern schools. The debate about the merits of selection for different kinds of secondary school at 11 remains to the present day, with grammar schools still existing in some local education authority areas such as Kent, and with the development of a diverse range of specialist and Academy schools (see later discussion).

As Taylor-Gooby has argued, the period from 1944 to the mid 1970s can be characterized by four key features: the decentralized nature of education management in the hands of local education authorities; the dominance of teachers and other education professionals in defining and determining the content of education; the gradual replacement of the division between grammar schools and secondary moderns with the extension of the comprehensive schooling model; and lastly, the persistent primacy, culturally and in resource terms, given to academic curricula and

> ## Box 11.3 **Education policy phases**
>
> 1944–early 1960s: secondary education for all, selection at 11 for type of school
> 1960s–1975: the comprehensive vision, the mixed-ability school
> 1976–1979: the Great Debate: Is education meeting the needs of the economy?
> 1980–1997: Conservative reform, tighter central control, the National Curriculum and schools outside local education authority control
> 1997–2010: New Labour 'Education, education, education', a continuation of diversification in types of schools
> 2010: Free schools and the continuing privatization of education

qualifications over more vocational education (1993: 102–3). This pattern met with increasing criticisms from both Left and Right as the 1970s progressed. In the mid1970s, the Labour prime minister, James Callaghan, initiated the Great Debate on education. In the context of a changing economy and the rise in youth unemployment, commentators began to see the education system as failing, especially with regards to standards and preparing young people for the world of work (for an extended discussion see Tomlinson, 2005: 25–6). Some of the blame for this was laid at the teaching profession's door and the relative lack of central control over the school system.

Industrial training policy

Until the end of the 1970s the apprenticeship system was the mainstay of industrial training in Britain. Originally a legally regulated system dating back to the medieval guilds, the apprenticeship had become, over the long haul of industrialization, a self-regulated system administered by the two sides of industry. The apprenticeship system was built on work-based, practical, hands-on learning, as much a process of socialization into a trade as a process of skills acquisition. Divorced from education, this system reinforced the gulf between theoretical learning in education and practical training in industry.

The lack of a national framework for the regulation of training also meant that the apprenticeship model was never systematically extended to cover the broad range of emerging occupations in the new modern industries and services, but remained concentrated in traditional industries and manufacturing such as shipbuilding, construction, and engineering. The apprenticeship system reinforced the split between education and training. A by-product of this differentiation was the higher status and desirability of education, and the identification of vocational education or training as a second-best option.

By the 1960s wider concerns about economic performance, and the pressures of foreign competition put the industrial training issue on the political agenda. Skill shortages and the then current vogue for economic planning and tripartism led to the first major attempt to reform the training system, through the 1964 Industrial Training Act. The French example of an apprenticeship tax was an important model, and the 1964 Act introduced a levy on firms administered by tripartite Industrial Training Boards (ITBs) representing employers and trade unions. Firms paid the levy to the ITBs and could then be reimbursed if they had undertaken appropriate training. The aim was to spread the costs of training more equally across industry (Vickerstaff 1992: 250). Subsequently, the tripartite Manpower Services Commission (MSC) was created in the early 1970s to coordinate policy in the training and employment areas. This was the first time that a single body was commissioned with a strategic capability to oversee and plan policy.

Although these developments were a departure from the voluntarist past, it was still relatively weak regulation by European standards. There was no individual legal entitlement to training as a right; the MSC in practice had very little power to change what happened at the level of the individual firm; and the separation of education and training remained largely intact. With the change of government in Britain in 1979 the previous period of reform towards a more interventionist approach, in which the role of the social partners (trade unions and employers) were institutionalized in agencies like the MSC, began to be challenged.

This potted history of ET in the last century in Britain indicates the specific legacy of institutions and approaches from which current policy reform has had to build. Developments up to the 1970s had resulted in a hybrid system with a bias towards keeping government's role confined to broad overall direction rather than detailed intervention or control. Today ET is offered by five main groups of providers in Britain: the school system (both public and private), further education colleges, higher education in universities, government-sponsored schemes based on work experience and training with employers, and on-the-job training in employment. This mixed system of provision has tended to be poorly integrated, with the status of academic qualifications and routes overshadowing the vocational stream; movement between academic and vocational streams has traditionally been limited.

Recent policy: schooling

Much has been done since the early 1980s to try to upgrade vocational education and provide a coherent system in which the traditional academic routes and the newer vocational schemes are integrated. Governments have taken a far more centralized approach to the development of both the academic and vocational curricula. This has been part of a wider debate about the extent to which schools were accountable for their methods, were delivering acceptable standards, and were meeting the needs of industry (Dale et al. 1990: 13). Thus, the development of government policy had two dimensions: the desire to change the content of education, to focus on the basic skills of literacy and numeracy and to make it more vocational and hence 'relevant' to the world of work; and the urge to change the processes of educational reform by taking tighter centralized control. The key piece of legislation in the process of change was the 1988 Education Reform Act.

The government, through this Act, instituted for the first time a national curriculum for all maintained schools in England and Wales. This continued a trend for more central government control over the school curriculum and the breaking up of the teaching profession's monopoly over curriculum design. An earlier policy, the Technical and Vocational Education Initiative (TVEI), created in 1982, had begun this trend by aiming to involve business people more in the development and delivery of school education. TVEI provided extra funds for schools to develop projects in different subject areas, which gave students experience of how industry worked, and skills relevant to work and new technologies. The 1988 Act also gave the Secretary of State powers to enter into agreements with private sponsors for the creation of City Technology Colleges, with the idea of increasing the role of the business sector further. This began a trend, which continues to the present day, towards privatization of parts of the education system (see Ball 2009).

Box 11.4 The 1988 Education Reform Act at a glance

- introduction of a National Curriculum, monitored through Key Stage tests at 7, 11, 14, and 16
- local management of schools: schools have delegated responsibility for their budget and staffing
- creation of grant-maintained schools: schools could opt out of local education authority control
- open enrolment: designed to give parental choice of school
- league tables of schools' test results

The focus on the curriculum also reflected the growing belief that educational standards in Britain were falling; as has often been the case in the history of ET policy, comparisons with other countries were influential in seeming to prove that Britain was not educating its children as well as some other countries. However, evidence on Britain alone suggests that standards, as measured by examination results, have been improving. Interpretation of such data raised the question of how to define standards in education, which, as we will see, continues to be a major focus of educational policy debate (see Box11.5).

The Education Reform Act of 1988 allowed schools to opt out of local education authority (LEA) control and become grant maintained from central government; those remaining under LEA control moved to local school-level management. The development of local management of schools introduced five new elements to the management of schools: delegated responsibility for the school budget; formula funding, in which most of a school's delegated budget is based on pupil numbers; new admissions regulations; devolved responsibility for staffing matters; and performance indicators

---

Box 11.5 Exercise: school standards

Discussions about school standards as measured by exam results are central to public and policy debate in education, as the following newspaper headlines attest:

- G.C.S.EASY Fears over standards despite record results (*Daily Mirror*, 24 August 2007)
- Schools leave young unfit for work, says Tesco chief (*The Times*, 14 October 2009)
- Dumbed-down GCSEs are a 'scam' to improve league tables, claim critics (*Sunday Telegraph*, 28 August 2005)
- Old and New don't add up; was the maths exam easier than in 1970? (*Derby Evening Telegraph*, 23 August 2002)
- Satnav A levels lead pupils to answers (*Daily Telegraph*, 17 June 2009)
- Science tsar blasts GCSEs for failing to stretch pupils (*Observer*, 23 August 2009)
- GCSEs do not stretch our pupils, independent schools warn after record number of A grades (*Independent*, 3 September 2005)

As the numbers passing GCSEs and A levels have increased, so has the chorus of complaint about standards. Read the article from the *Guardian* below and discuss the following questions:

1 Have GCSEs and A levels got easier?

2 Are school leavers better educated today than their parents were a generation ago?

GCSEs: burdens of success

Whenever examination results are due, Britain seems to go through a bout of euphobia, or fear of hearing good news. We always have to look for the downside, as typified by a headline yesterday stating: 'Language catastrophe blamed for surge in top GCSE grades.' What appears to have happened is that less-able candidates are migrating from learning languages to more practical vocational subjects they are better at, while the more able ones who remain are getting better grades (the A* to C pass rate in French and German improved by seven percentage points).

This is not obviously a catastrophe. Of course, it would be good if more children learned languages (and the government is trying to redress this at primary level), but those without a gift for learning them are not necessarily those who will need languages for a job later in life. Many will be better off doing a vocational course such as information and communication technology (ICT), which is supposed

➜

to be one of the government's aims anyway. At a time when businesses all over the world are making English their corporate language, the downside of being without a language, while regrettable, may not actually affect economic performance.

Indeed the sustained improvement in exam results over many years, both at GCSE and A level, far from being a fix as critics sometimes allege, may be one of the reasons why Britain's economy has been performing better than most of its rivals, particularly compared with the continent of Europe. Education is accepted as one of the prime engines of long-term economic growth. It would have been very surprising if examination results had not improved in recent years, given the sharp increases in spending that the government has allocated to education. There are also signs that students are increasingly studying subjects that create a more flexible response to the skills that the economy may need in future years. Vocational GNVQs attracted over 4 per cent more entries, even though they are due to be phased out.

There was a very encouraging increase in entries for science subjects after years of decline, despite a fall, for demographic reasons, in the total numbers taking GCSEs. Passes at A* to C in maths increased by 1.7 per cent to 53.4 per cent, the sharpest rise for five years, and the English pass rate also got better. Part of the improvement may have been a mild deflation of standards over the years, or the prevalence of coursework not written in stringent examination-hall conditions, but there are plenty of other stronger reasons to explain progress, including better-trained teachers, more resources and a greater determination by government to seek improvements for political as well as economic reasons. There is no logical reason why education should be excluded from the range of activities—from cooking to athletics—in which performance can continuously improve.

Nothing is perfect. The government has been too slow to implement its plans to boost language learning in primary schools and was plain wrong not to adopt the overarching diploma recommended by the Tomlinson commission that would have replaced GCSEs and A levels over the next decade with a more integrated but more challenging set of exams. The employers' organizations, while reluctant to praise the achievements that have been made, are right to point out that illiteracy and innumeracy are still a serious problem for less-advantaged children joining the labour force. But none of this should blind us to the real achievements that have been, and are being, made. There can be no let up. Faced with withering competition from emerging nations such as China and India, which combine high skills with low rates of pay, Britain must lay even more emphasis on education and training. There is simply no alternative.

Guardian leader pages, 26 August 2005: 29

in the form of league tables of pupil performance (Thomas and Bullock 1994: 41). The Act attempted to increase parental choice: by open enrolment, in which parents could 'choose' schools for their children outside their local authority area (some choice had been available before the Act but had been hindered by the operation of LEA quotas on admission numbers). The aim of these reforms was to create a managed market system of education, which encouraged schools to compete for pupils.

The 1988 Act has been a controversial intervention in education, not least for its particular definition of educational standards as something that can be measured primarily by examination results and performance indicators such as rates of truancy. Under the Act such results are published nationally in the form of league tables. This information is supposed to help parents in making a choice of school for their children. Critics of the Act have argued that the league tables merely measure the social class backgrounds of the children and do not give any indication of value added, that is, the extent to which the school has had an impact on individual pupils' progress and achievements during their schooling. The New Labour government which came to power in 1997 remained committed to the publication of league tables, but measures of value added have been incorporated in a limited way.

The 1988 Act has also been challenged for its vision of parental choice. Research by Ball et al. (1997) has indicated that, in practice, the degree of choice may be profoundly circumscribed by parents' social circumstances:

> In the case of the working class respondents, choice of secondary school was a contingent decision rather than an open one . . . School has to be 'fitted' into a set of constraints and expectations related to work roles, family roles, the sexual division of labour and the demands of household organization . . . [I]t is not simply a matter of education being of less importance for working class families, our interviewees were very concerned that their children get a good education. Rather the competing pressures of work and family life made certain possibilities difficult or impossible to contemplate. (Ball et al. 1997: 411)

In addition, the cost of travel and the difficulties of resourcing childcare may make the local school the only real 'choice' for the poor family.

The Labour government which came to power in 1997 fought the election campaign with education policy as one of its main priorities. The first major piece of education legislation of the new government was the School Standards and Framework Act of 1998 which included the following policy developments: the abolition of the assisted places scheme; measures to reduce class sizes for 5–7-year-olds; a new framework of community, foundation, and voluntary schools; and action to raise school standards (Tomlinson, 2005: 95–114). The New Labour government continued the trend towards tighter prescription of the curriculum, introducing the literacy hour and the numeracy strategy in primary schools (Tomlinson 2005: 94–6). The main innovations to the National Curriculum were the introduction of citizenship teaching and a stronger focus on information and communications technology (ICT).

In other respects New Labour policy can be seen as a continuation, even a strengthening, of trends initiated by the 1988 Education Reform Act. New Labour has reinforced earlier arguments about the importance of parental choice and the desirability of business and community interests having a direct role in schools' development. New Labour continued the 'marketization of education' initiated by Conservative governments with the development of the Academies programme, announced in 2000. Academies are conceived as independent semi-privatized schools sponsored by business or voluntary or faith groups and in the first instance were seen as a way of rescuing failing secondary schools. Combined with the specialist schools programme under which many secondary schools rebadged themselves as for example, sports, languages, or IT specialists, the period of new Labour Government witnessed a continuing diversification of types of schools (see Chitty 2009: 58–108). The Conservative–Liberal coalition government, which came to power in 2010, swiftly moved to endorse the Academies programme. The secretary of state for education, Michael Gove, wrote to all schools rated as outstanding by Ofsted to offer a fast track to Academy status, whilst also encouraging all schools to consider going this route. In addition, the new government has announced the parallel programme of encouraging parents, teachers, charities, or voluntary groups to establish 'Free schools', which would also have independence from local authority control.

Over the period 1988–2010 we have seen a major diversification of the types of secondary schools available and along with this development the increasing involvement of business and other private organizations in the provision of schools. The trend towards allowing secondary schools to operate outside local education authority control is one that is likely to be further reinforced by the coalition government.

The transition from school to work

There have been major changes since the late 1970s in the traditional routes from full-time education into work. In the past many school leavers went straight into employment at 15 or 16 (the school leaving age was raised to 16 in 1973) and some into apprenticeships—the latter were mainly young men. In the mid 1970s, youth unemployment began to rise and there was a debate about the role of education, with employers arguing that schools were failing to meet the needs of industry, and many educationalists arguing that schools were still failing the majority of students who were not destined for higher education (Blackman 1992). In addition, during the 1970s the old apprenticeship system was beginning to collapse, through a combination of declining employment in traditional industries and the continuing recession, which was causing a reduction in employers' expenditure on training. Both factors speeded up the decline in apprenticeship that had been apparent for some time.

A contrast is often made between a state-led system of ET provision, such as is found in Sweden where initial vocational education and training are provided in the education system, and the dual systems typical of Germany, Austria, and Switzerland. In the latter, vocational education and training are primarily provided by employer-based apprenticeships, with requirements for off-the-job training and restrictions on firms employing school leavers without providing further ET. In Britain there is a hybrid system. The coalition government has retained the New Labour commitment to raise to 17 by 2012 and then to 18 by 2015 the age to which young people are expected to continue to some degree in education and training.

Britain traditionally had a low rate of 16- and 17-year-olds staying on in full-time education and a low proportion of 16- or 17-year-olds undertaking any further education compared with other advanced capitalist countries. However, the situation has changed substantially over the last two decades for a number of reasons: the introduction of the Youth Training Scheme (YTS) in 1983 meant that a majority of school leavers received some further training and education, and youth unemployment encouraged young people to stay on at school or go to college. The increases in staying-on rates are indicated in Table 11.3. The key enduring legacy of YTS is the breaking of the supposition that young unemployed people are entitled to benefits. Since YTS the policy assumption has been that young people are expected to take up their entitlement to further education or training, as Gordon Brown, Chancellor of the Exchequer, said in 1997: there is 'no option to stay at home in bed watching television' (*Financial Times*, 26 June 1997; see also Chapter 5 in this volume).

Since 1993 successive governments have tried to re-energize the apprenticeship system. The Labour government announced in 2002 the target that one-quarter of school leavers would enter apprenticeships but this target was not achieved. The coalition government has similarly pledged to increase the number of apprenticeships. A major problem with such attempts to persuade people to do apprenticeships has been the simultaneous policy encouraging young people to aspire to degree-level higher education making the training route appear a second-best.

Nevertheless, far fewer British school leavers now go straight into full-time employment or un-employment than was the case in the 1970s. Over three-quarters of 16-year-old school leavers went into work in 1978; for most young people in the new millennium the transition from school (or

Table 11.3 Participation in full-time education of 16-year-olds, females and males: %

1985		1995	2000	2005	2009 Provisional
47.6	59.6	71	71	75.8	84.8

Source: Department for Education, **http://www.education.gov.uk/rsgateway/DB/SFR/s000938/index.shtml**, accessed 15 May 2011

BANX

"GCSEs WERE EASY, 'A' LEVELS WERE EASY, UNIVERSITY WAS EASY, GETTING A JOB WAS HARD."

Cartoon 11.1 GCSEs were easy, A levels were easy, university was easy, getting a job was hard

college) to work has been elongated and no longer typically occurs at 16. This trend for more young people to continue in education after the compulsory school-leaving age, although initially a response to youth unemployment, has become established and there is not the same expectation amongst 16-year-olds and their parents that they will go straight into paid work on leaving school. As Table 11.4 illustrates, it is the further education colleges that have taken a key role in the expansion of full-time staying-on rates. However, the significance of these increased staying-on rates is mitigated by the relatively low levels of qualification of many of these young people. In 2004 the New Labour government introduced the Educational Maintenance Allowance (EMA), which provided weekly payments of up to £30 for young people staying on in education beyond 16 who came from families with an income of £30,000 or less a year. The EMA has been credited with encouraging the increasing participation rates of 16- and 17-year-olds. The coalition government announced in its first comprehensive spending review that EMA entitlement would be severely reduced (HM Treasury 2010a: 41). This is to be combined with a reduction in resources going into further education and as with higher education (see later discussion):

Table 11.4 Participation of 16-year-olds in full-time education by institution type: %

	Maintained schools	Further education colleges	Sixth-form colleges	Independent schools
1985	20.3	17.7	4.6	4.9
1990	24.6	21.8	6.8	6.4
1995	27.4	27.3	9.4	6.7
2000	28.7	26.4	9.4	6.3
2005	29.8	29.3	10.9	6.2

Source: ONS *Social Trends* (2007) 37: 30

Table 11.5 Pupils reaching or exceeding expected standards:[1] by Key Stage and sex; England

	Percentages			
	1990		2009	
	Boys	Girls	Boys	Girls
Key Stage 1[2]				
English				
Reading	78	86	81	89
Writing	75	85	75	87
Mathematics	84	88	88	91
Science	85	88	87	91
Key Stage 2[3]				
English	62	74	75	84
Mathematics	69	70	80	80
Science	75	76	85	87
Key Stage 3[4]				
English	55	73	71	84
Mathematics	63	66	79	80
Science	59	62	76	79

1 By teacher assessment. See Appendix, Part 3: The National Curriculum.
2 Pupils achieving level 2 or above at Key Stage 1.
3 Pupils achieving level 4 or above at Key Stage 2.
4 Pupils achieving level 5 or above at Key Stage 3.

Source: ONS *Social Trends* (2010), 40: 37

the balance of funding will be shifted from the taxpayer towards the individuals and employers who benefit, including though the introduction of student loans, and by exploring mechanisms to increase employer contributions such as voluntary training levies. (HM Treasury 2010a: 53)

The gender debate

In recent years there has been considerable concern about what is typically perceived as the underachievement of boys in the education system. This is a complete reversal of concerns that sociologists of education had in the 1970s and 1980s when the 'gender problem' was thought to be comparative failure of girls. The panic about boys is fuelled by the data, which seem to show that girls outperform boys at school level. However, the gender differences in performance require careful interpretation.

Girls do not outperform boys in all subjects. The gaps in Key Stage performance at 7, 11, and 14 indicated in Table 11.5 are not that significant in maths and science. The greatest differences are for English and literacy but this is true in most other countries as well. The OECD's Pisa study of 42 countries shows that the gap in the UK is smaller than in many countries; only 11 other countries covered by the study had narrower gender gaps in literacy (see Skelton et al. 2007). If we compare the gender gap in performance with that demonstrated in Table 11.1, which compares the class gap as measured by free school meal entitlement, we see that the gender effects are marginal in comparison to class effects. Table 11.2 also demonstrates that the performance gaps between some different ethnic groups are also of a higher magnitude than those for gender.

More girls than boys stay in full-time education after age 16 and more of them achieve two or more A levels, as indicated in Table 11.6. There are, however, big gender differences in the subjects studied at A level and this feeds through into major differences in the degrees that young women and men are likely to study for, as indicated in Table 11.7.

Higher education and training for adults

As with 16–18-year-olds, New Labour had the policy aim of widening and increasing participation in higher education and training for adults. How to fund a major expansion of higher education became a major policy issue in the 1980s and 1990s. An influential committee chaired by Sir Ron Dearing was commissioned in May 1996 to make recommendations on 'how the purposes, shape, structure, size and funding of higher education, including support for students, should develop to meet the needs of the United Kingdom over the next 20 years' (NCIHE 1997: 3). The report indicated that more young people were going into higher education than ever before: 32 per cent of the 18+ age cohort in 1995 compared with just 12.4 per cent in 1980 (p. 40; see also Box 11.5). The target set by the New Labour government in the new century was for 50 per cent of the age cohort to have a higher education experience by 2010.

This expansion in the numbers of people in higher education resulted in a change in intake, with increasing numbers of mature students, growth in the number of part-time students, and a greater diversity of educational background and experience amongst undergraduates. Nonetheless, young people from the upper and middle classes are still far more likely to go on to university than their working-class peers. The Dearing report recommended the continued expansion of higher education and, most contentiously, recommended that students should be expected to contribute more to the cost of their education by paying a proportion of the tuition fees. The report adhered to a traditional liberal view of the functions of education whilst acknowledging the 'rate of return' arguments discussed above:

> Over the next 20 years, the UK must create a society committed to learning throughout life. That commitment will be required from individuals, the state, employers and providers of

Table 11.6 Achievement of two or more GCE A levels or equivalent by sex: %

	Men	Women
1990–1	18.2	20.3
1995–6	26.7	32.7
2000–1	33.4	41.6
2005–6	32.7	42.1

Source: ONS *Social Trends* (2009) 39: 40

Table 11.7 Students in higher education:[1] by subject[2] and sex, 2007/08; UK

	Percentages		
	Men	Women	All
Business and administrative studies	16.1	11.5	13.5
Subjects allied to medicine	5.4	17.7	12.5
Education	4.9	11.7	8.8
Social studies	7.5	9.5	8.6
Biological sciences	5.9	7.8	7.0
Creative arts and design	6.3	7.3	6.9
Engineering and technology	11.8	1.7	6.1
Languages	4.5	6.9	5.9
Historical and philosophical studies	4.5	4.0	4.2
Computer science	7.8	1.4	4.1
Law	3.7	4.0	3.9
Physical sciences	4.9	2.6	3.6
Architecture, building and planning	4.4	1.5	2.7
Medicine and dentistry	2.6	2.7	2.7
Mass communications and documentation	2.1	2.1	2.1
Mathematical sciences	2.1	1.0	1.5
Agriculture and related subjects	0.7	0.8	0.8
Veterinary science	0.1	0.3	0.2
Combined[3]	4.6	5.5	5.1
All subject areas (=100%) (thousands)	988	1,318	2,306

1 Full-time and part-time, undergraduate and postgraduate, and home and overseas students in higher education institutions only. See Appendix, Part 3: Stages of Education.
2 Subject data are classified using the Joint Academic Coding System. See Appendix, Part 3: Joint Academic Coding System.
3 Courses which are a mix of subject groups.
Source: Higher Education Statistics Agency
Source: ONS *Social Trends* (2010) 40: 35

education and training. Education is life enriching and desirable in its own right. It is fundamental to the achievement of an improved quality of life in the UK. (NCIHE 1997: 8)

New Labour accepted the rate of return argument and introduced tuition fees, completing the process of moving from student maintenance grants to student loans started by the Conservatives (Callender 2002: 71–3; for a fuller discussion see Pennell and West 2005). The initial expansion of higher education places was achieved without a proportionate increase in the funding which universities received; this has led to debates about whether universities should be allowed to charge

---

Box 11.6 **Exercise: educational choices**

In comparison with young people leaving compulsory education in the 1950s and 1960s, young people today face a broader range of further education and training opportunities. Government policy has increasingly set targets for certain percentages of young people to take particular routes, e.g. 25 per cent doing apprenticeships, 50 per cent undertaking degrees. It is not always easy, however, for young people, their parents/guardians, teachers, or careers advisers to know which is the best route. This is compounded by the fact that a number of institutions are effectively in competition with each other to attract these young people, so they have a vested interest in selling their route as the best one.

Look at the scenarios below and discuss in groups what your advice to each of the young people would be; give reasons for your recommendations.

Lucy

Lucy is soon to take her GCSEs. She doesn't expect to do brilliantly but hopes to get at least four at grade C or above. She is not sure what sort of work she would like—something in an office environment is where her ideas have gone so far. She is not sure whether to stay on at school as her school suggests and do AS levels, which she thinks will be a struggle, or to go to college and do some more vocational qualifications, perhaps a GNVQ in Business Administration. She has also heard about Modern Apprenticeships and wonders whether this might be an option. On the other hand, she could endeavour to get an office job to try it out for a while and take a bit more time to work out whether she wants to go for more qualifications.

Carl

Carl is about to sit for his A levels and has an offer of a place at university to study fashion design conditional on achieving three Cs. He is expected to achieve these grades without any great effort. However, more recently he has been wondering whether a university degree is really the best route into what he wants to do: bespoke tailoring. He has been thinking about trying to find an apprenticeship, perhaps in Savile Row. Then he could be earning a little, not building up a great debt, and actually getting on with learning and doing the job he really wants to do.

---

top-up fees to students in order to increase their revenue. A further report commissioned by New Labour but delivered during the early days of the coalition government in 2010 took the arguments about rates of return further, arguing that students should pay considerably more for their education and that public finance might be concentrated on only the most significant degree subjects:

> There are clinical and priority courses such as medicine, science, and engineering that are important to the well-being of our society and to our economy. The costs of these courses are high and, if students were asked to meet all of the costs, there is a risk that they would choose to study cheaper courses instead. In our proposals, there will be scope for government to withdraw public investment through HEFCE from many courses to contribute to wider reductions in public spending; there will remain a vital role for public investment to support priority courses and the wider benefits they create. (Browne, 2010:25)

The coalition government accepted the recommendations and made a radical departure from previous policy when it decided to remove public funding from social science and humanities degrees.

Box 11.7 **From an elite to a mass system of higher education**

Percentage of the age group attending university:

- 1938: 3%
- 1962: 7.2%
- 1980: 12.4%
- 1990: 20%
- 1997: 33%
- 2005: 42%
- 2010: 45%
- 2015: ?

The earlier liberal and social rates of return arguments that the Dearing report had endorsed where thus swept aside.

Research on the effects of these changes suggests that lower-income students accumulate the most debt during their undergraduate studies and suffer the greatest financial hardship. As a result it has become widespread for full-time students to work part-time during their studies (Callender 2002; Metcalf 2003). There is also evidence that more students are studying closer to their family home to reduce the cost of a university education (Pennell and West 2005). In many ways the undergraduate experience has changed in the last thirty years and expansion in student numbers has been achieved at the cost of quality, with class sizes increasing and resources per student declining. The impact of top-up fees, to be introduced in 2012, is as yet unknown.

Despite the growth in the number of mature student entrants into universities over the last decade, the wider continuing education and training for adults have traditionally been the weakest area of ET. In Britain there are no specific taxes levied for training. The majority of job-related training is paid for by private industry. Governments have been prepared to intervene with schemes for the long-term unemployed, but continuing training and retraining for employed adults has generally been seen to be industry's responsibility, and has thus been subject to the market failures and perverse incentives described above. One exception to this was the Train to Gain programme introduced by New Labour in 2006. This provided funding to encourage adults in employment to get NVQ level 2 qualifications. It offered advice for employers and some subsidy for training mainly in further education colleges or with private training providers. There is some evidence that it increased the scale of training being undertaken, especially in small and medium-sized enterprises but a National Audit Office report in 2009 concluded that 50 per cent of the employers covered would have done the training anyway even without the public subsidy (NAO 2009) . The coalition government announced in its first Comprehensive Spending Review that the programme would be scrapped.

Most in-work training is of relatively short duration, undertaken either on an employer's premises or at a college of further education (Department of Employment 1993: 23–58). More adults are returning to education and training, either because of unemployment or because of employers' demands for new skills. Nevertheless, there are still concerns about the skills and qualification levels of the British workforce in comparison to other countries. As a recent government strategy document concludes:

We need a more competitive, rebalanced economy, which is environmentally sound and resource efficient, and we need to reduce the deficit. There should be no illusions about the scale of the challenge we face. Our working-age population is less skilled than that of France, Germany and the United States and this contributes to the UK being at least 15 per cent less productive than those countries. We are currently weak in the vital intermediate technical skills that are increasingly important as jobs become more highly skilled and technological change accelerates. Approximately 80 per cent of the people who will be in the workforce in 2020 have already left compulsory education. If we are to achieve a world-class skills base we need to increase the level of their skills and meet the demands of our economy …

Skills are not just important for our global competitiveness, however. Skills have the potential to transform lives by transforming life chances and driving social mobility. Having higher skills also enables people to play a fuller part in society, making it more cohesive, more environmentally friendly, more tolerant and more engaged. (BIS 2010: 4)

This suggests that in the future more and more people will have to learn new skills in order to keep their jobs and that adults will be an increasingly significant group within ET provision. This is heralded as the need for a 'learning society' in which people expect, and are enabled, to continue updating their education throughout life.

Conclusion

This chapter has provided an introduction to some of the key policy issues and debates in the area of education and training (ET). It is clear that the pace of change in British ET has quickened considerably since the early 1980s, and that the state's role in terms of funding, regulation, and provision has come under increasing public scrutiny. At the level of schooling we have seen an increasing trend towards privatization of provision with the development of Academies and other varieties of schools partially funded by business or charities and allowed to operate outside local education authority control. The secondary school landscape has changed fundamentally from that created by the 1944 Education Act. More young people now stay on in education and more school leavers continue in some further education and training than ever before.

In the twenty-first century most young people will continue with some education and training up to 18. With entitlement to compulsory education rising progressively to 18 in 2015, employers taking on school leavers are increasingly required to provide some further ET. There is much rhetoric about the desirability of a 'learning society' in which everyone is enabled to continue with the education and training necessary for work or simply to pursue their own interests and development. It is now much more accepted that ET should be a continuing process throughout life. A key problem for policy debate is how expansion and improvements can be financed, and in particular, how public financing should be spread more evenly across different parts of ET provision. Since the end of the last century there has been a major shift in the arguments about the balance between public and private finance of different aspects of ET. Whilst it is not contested that compulsory schooling is a public good and hence should be funded through general taxation, we are now in a political climate where further and higher education and training are increasingly defined as private goods primarily benefiting the individual and hence it is the individual who should bear the main cost. In respect of university-level education this represents a radical shift in policy.

FURTHER READING

For a history of the British education system, see **A. Green** (1990) *Education and State Formation*. For a detailed account of developments in education since 1945 see **S. Tomlinson**'s (2005) *Education in a Post-Welfare Society* and **C. Chitty** (2009) *Education Policy in Britain*. The Scottish education system has developed along different lines from that of England, Wales, and Northern Ireland; for an introduction to the differences see **L. Patterson** *Scottish Education in the Twentieth Century*. A good edited collection of readings on education, covering the history, sociology, and politics of the educational process, policy, and practice is **A. H. Halsey, H. Lauder, P. Brown, and A. Stuart Wells** (eds) (1997) *Education, Culture, Economy and Society*. Two books which look at the impact of ET on young people, their experiences and the effects of ET on employment prospects are **L. Unwin and J. Wellington** (2001) *Young People's Perspectives on Education, Training and Employment* and **K. Roberts** (1995) *Youth Employment in Modern Britain*. A standard social policy approach to education can be found in **H. Glennerster** (1998) 'Education: reaping the harvest' in **H. Glennerster and J. Hills** (eds) *The State of Welfare*. There is a wide-ranging literature on training policy but an edited volume by **R. Layard, K. Mayhew and G. Owen** (1994) *Britain's Training Deficit* provides a good overview of current issues and the chapter by **D. Finegold and C. Crouch**, 'A comparison of national institutions', introduces some of the key themes in cross-national comparisons of training policy.

USEFUL WEBSITES

http://www.education.gov.uk/ The website for the Department for Education provides considerable information on existing policies, White Papers, and consultation documents. It provides one of the best ways to keep up to date with policy developments.

http://www.bis.gov.uk/ The website of the government department Business, Innovation and Skills covers policy on training, skills, and higher education. It is a good place to look for developments in work-based learning such as apprenticeships.

www.ofsted.gov.uk The website for Ofsted (Office for Standards in Education), a non-ministerial government department which inspects and regulates standards in education and childcare. The site provides access to inspection reports undertaken by Ofsted.

ESSAY QUESTIONS

1 Who should pay for education and training? Give reasons for your answers.

2 'There isn't a problem about different levels of attainment in education. It simply reflects different individual levels of merit.' Explain and discuss this statement. Do you agree?

3 Has the transition into paid employment become more or less difficult for young people leaving education today than it was for their parents?

4 How should we measure school standards?

5 Why did the New Labour government adopt the policy of trying to encourage 50 per cent of the age cohort to go to university? Is it undeniably a good policy objective?

ONLINE RESOURCE CENTRE

For additional material and resources, please visit the Online Resource Centre at:
www.oxfordtextbooks.co.uk/orc/baldock4e/.

Health and health policy

Gillian Pascall

Introduction

Health is very unequal in Britain, related to gender and race, and deeply patterned by socio-economic inequalities. What lies behind these patterns of health and disease in society? It is widely assumed that the National Health Service (NHS) produces health, and that improving health is a result of improving medical care. But what impact does the NHS have on health? The chapter begins with health, examining its social features, to underpin thinking about health services and the needs they may be thought to address. Why has the NHS not produced more equal health? A deeply rooted research tradition, with three key government-commissioned reports, going back to the Black report in 1980 (DHSS 1980), asks why health inequalities persist in the context of an egalitarian healthcare system. By contrast to patterns of inequality in health, the NHS model of healthcare is deeply egalitarian, offering care on the basis of need rather than ability to pay, membership of scheme, or insurance contribution. Health policy in the UK rests on the National Health Service Act of 1946, the key parliamentary Act of the post-war Labour government. The NHS began in July 1948. Health debates even now revolve around the decisions made at that time (see Box 12.1).

The continuing importance of these principles and debate around them do not mean that governments have rested on the legislative laurels of the post-war Labour government. The New Labour governments between 1997 and 2010 published 26 Green and White Papers, and 14 Acts. They doubled spending in real terms, increasing NHS staff, building hospitals and using central government targets to reduce waiting times and increase the quality of care, while developing Primary Care Trusts to plan and commission local services (Thorlby and Maybin 2010: 8–9).

Social, economic, and political change since 1948 has challenged all the ideas and ideals of the post-war era. After its review of health, the chapter will take each of the key policy decisions embedded in the 1946 National Health Service Act, and ask how it has stood up to these changes. How fit is the NHS for the twenty-first century? And how does it compare with other systems of healthcare provision?

Learning outcomes

After reading this chapter students will have an:

1 understanding of the links between health and social inequality;
2 understanding of the principles behind the NHS, as established in the post-war period;
3 the ability to discuss the ways in which these principles have adapted to changing socio-political contexts or remained resilient through social, economic and political changes;
4 ability to debate the merits and demerits of markets in healthcare;
5 understanding of the NHS in an international context.

Box 12.1 The National Health Service 1948

Set up to provide:

- a system of medical care to individuals;
- with ideals of comprehensive services covering all health needs;
- free at the point of use, paid for by general taxation;
- nationally owned and planned from the centre, through regional and local bodies;
- on a universal basis, provided equally to citizens.

Health and health inequalities

> Instead of exposures to toxic materials and mechanical dangers, we are discovering the toxicity of social circumstances and patterns of social organization.

(Wilkinson 1996: 23)

Why study health inequalities?

Health inequalities are a priority in an understanding of health relevant to social policy for three reasons:

1 The intrinsic significance of issues of life, death, health, and disability, and their distribution in society.

2 Relationships of health with social variables—such as socio-economic group and race—give clear evidence of the significance of society, social science, and social policy to health: health does not belong wholly to medicine, however appropriate medicine might be to the sick.

3 A better understanding of how health relates to social disadvantage may provide a basis for better policy. Perhaps the most promising strategies for improving the national health would be to reduce the socio-economic inequalities which underlie poor health.

What are the key social features of health?

Socio-economic group, income, gender, and ethnicity can all be related to people's experience of health, sickness, and disability. Powerful evidence of these inequalities has been collected in the UK for more than thirty years, in three official reports commissioned by Labour governments. Sir Douglas Black (DHSS 1980) collated, analysed, and publicized evidence of health inequalities. His work stimulated research in university departments of public health, deepening our understanding. At the end of the New Labour era, the Department of Health commissioned a new strategic review of health inequalities in England post 2010, published as *Fair Society, Healthy Lives* (Marmot et al. 2010).

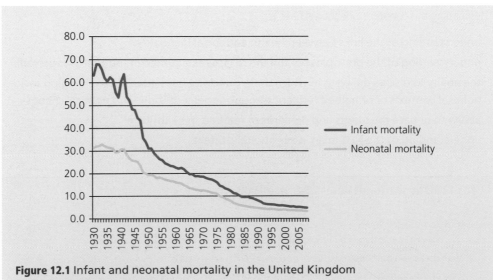

Figure 12.1 Infant and neonatal mortality in the United Kingdom (rates per 1,000 live births)

Source: Office for National Statistics; General Register Office for Scotland; Northern Ireland Statistics and Research Agency

Some measures of health have improved dramatically during the twentieth and twenty-first centuries. Life expectancy increased from around 45 years for men and 49 years for women in 1901 to over 77 and 82 years respectively in 2006. Infant mortality rates (IMRs) have declined: in England and Wales infant deaths declined from 63.1 per thousand in 1930 to 4.7 per thousand in 2008 (ONS 2010a).

But people have not shared equally in this improvement. From the earliest life chances in infancy to old age and disability at the end of life, there are major differences in health and life expectancy. There is a wide gap in infant mortality rates, with the death rate for children with parents in routine manual occupations more than double that for children inside marriage whose parents are managers or higher professionals, with babies born outside marriage at somewhat higher risk (ONS 2009). Figure 12.2 shows these persisting gaps between socio-economic groups.

The Marmot Review shows huge differences in people's life expectancy and disability-free life expectancy in the context of their neighbourhood income levels, showing graded differences between people in different social positions: 'the higher a person's social position, the better his or her health' (see Figure 12.3) (Marmot et al. 2010:37). The life expectancy of people in the poorest neighbourhoods is seven years lower than of people in the richest. The gap in healthy life is much greater: people in the poorest neighbourhoods have, on average, an expectation of healthy life that is 17 years lower than those in the richest. They spend much more of their shorter lives with disability. These differences in the extremes of life and health in the richest and poorest English neighbourhoods are reflected at every point in the income gradient, and are systematic: 'Social inequalities in health arise because of inequalities in the conditions of daily life—the conditions in which people

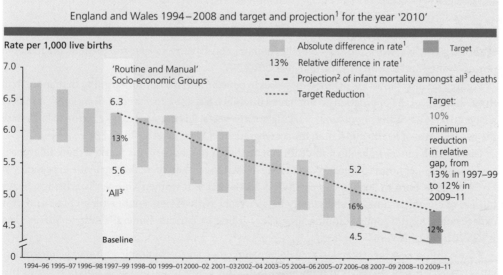

Figure 12.2 Infant mortality by socio-economic group

Source: Office for National Statistics (Department of Health 2009: Figure 12.2)

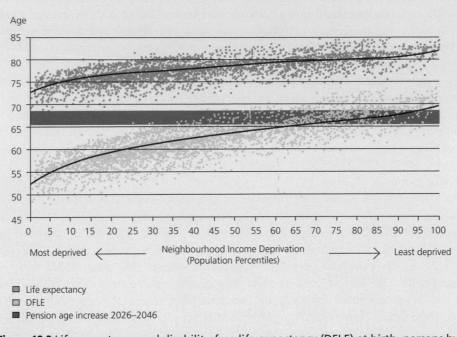

Figure 12.3 Life expectancy and disability-free life expectancy (DFLE) at birth, persons by neighbourhood income level, England, 1999–2003

Source: Marmot et al. 2010, *The Marmot Review: Fair Society, Healthy Lives,* Strategic Review of Health Inequalities in England Post–2010: Figure 1.1, p. 38

are born, grow, live, work and age—and the fundamental drivers that give rise to them: inequities in power, money and resources' (Marmot et al. 2010: 37).

Figure 12.3 also shows the planned increases in pension age, the authors arguing that 'more than three-quarters of the population do not have a disability-free life expectancy as long as 68. If society wishes to have a healthy population, working until 68 years, it is essential to take action to both raise the general level of health and flatten the social gradient' (Marmot et al. 2010: 38).

Gender differences in health and death can be shown too, but are less marked than differences between socio-economic groups. Women tend to live longer than men: the gap in life expectancy at birth for those born in 2008 is 4.1 years (ONS 2010a: 92). But women's longer lives bring a heavy burden of chronic sickness and disability in later years, with 41 per cent of women of 65 and over experiencing limiting long-standing illness, according to current General Lifestyle Survey data (ONS 2010b: Table 7.8).

Ethnic differences have been less well documented than socio-economic group or gender differences. Experience in Britain is that the socio-economic status in particular of different ethnic minority groups, rather than biological or cultural differences, is key to their different experiences of health and death (ONS 1996). Recent infant mortality figures show high rates among the Caribbean (9.8) and Pakistani (9.6) populations, around twice the average among the population as a whole of 4.8 deaths per thousand births (ONS 2009: 98).

The environmental movement has alerted us to man-made risks, produced by nuclear energy, pesticides, and genetically modified food. Such risks may appear to threaten us all. Do these developing environmental threats change the traditional relationship between poverty, ill health, and early death? This evidence suggests not. Patterns of inequality associated with socio-economic inequalities are persistent, even increasing. Indeed, Marmot argues that the close relationship between environmental issues—both impact most on the poor and disadvantaged—means that tackling health inequalities and tackling climate change should go together, with a need for policies towards a 'sustainable economy, food system, transport systems and use of green spaces' (Marmot 2010: 39).

How can health inequalities best be explained?

It is easy to propose reasons for social inequalities in health. Might different patterns of smoking, eating, and exercise bring inequalities between socio-economic groups? Perhaps health services are unequally distributed? Are tobacco and alcohol companies too free to sell damaging products? Perhaps unemployment or low benefits are the problem? It is easier to propose theories than to decide which offer the most powerful explanation. And explanation is a crucial foundation for understanding policy and the failure of policy.

Mapping factors that affect health—and may produce health inequalities—is a first step to unravelling a complex picture. Figure 12.4 aids understanding of how different factors may fit into the picture, fitting individuals into their social and environmental context. In this figure, individuals—with their age, sex, and genetic makeup—are in the centre. A biomedical model of health and disease starts here, with understanding disease processes in individuals. But individuals affect their own health by their lifestyle choices: asking why disease processes start might lead us to behavioural factors such as smoking, food, and drink choices. Asking why people smoke or why they eat unhealthy food might lead to social and community influences. Asking why some social groups smoke, eat, or drink unhealthily might lead us to living and working conditions. But what lies behind living and working conditions? Wider economic and political factors, such as national government policies on benefits and asylum seekers, on food, alcohol, and tobacco companies and markets, as well as international agencies such as the World Bank and International Monetary Fund, are important in the distribution of resources significant to health.

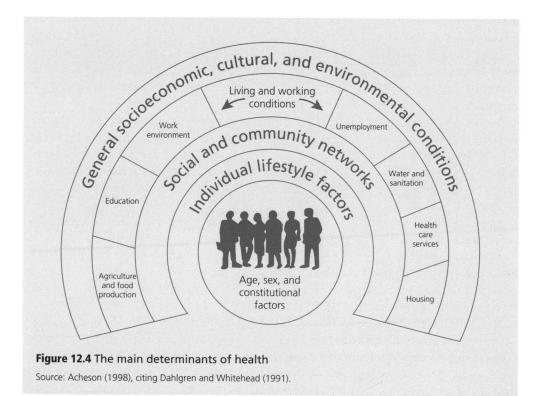

Figure 12.4 The main determinants of health

Source: Acheson (1998), citing Dahlgren and Whitehead (1991).

Three key questions arising from these debates are addressed below. The first is: How important is unequal acccess to medical care in explaining unequal health? The second is: How much people can choose better health by improving lifestyles, following advice about smoking, exercise, drink, and diet, or are the choices and health of poorer people constrained by factors they cannot control? A third is about policy, about which approaches may best improve health and reduce health inequalities.

Medical care and health How important is access to medical care in determining health? McKeown (1976) argued that the biggest improvements in UK health occurred before effective medical interventions existed. Investigating population data from the first registration of deaths in the 1830s, he examined trends for the various causes contributing to the major decline of mortality.Figure 12.5 shows the example of TB.

The graph in Figure 12.5 suggests that TB was already in decline, from the first records. A great reduction in deaths followed during the nineteenth and twentieth centuries, before effective medical or public health interventions. The first scientific understanding of TB came in 1882, with identification of the tubercle bacillis. Effective drug treatment came in the 1940s, and BCG vaccination in the 1950s. Thus medical treatment and prevention came rather late to give assistance to a trend already well established. McKeown showed a similar pattern for most key diseases, arguing that improving health had more to do with improving nutrition and living standards than with medical interventions. McKeown may have understated the importance of public health measures, such as improving water supply and sanitation brought to Britain by the nineteenth-century public health movements (debates discussed in more detail by Gray 2001b: 123–30). We cannot read directly from this account of medicine in the nineteenth and twentieth centuries to the uses of medicine in the twenty-first. But these debates suggest that we should not take the importance of medicine to health for granted.

Access to the NHS not wholly equal: no payment at the time of use and free prescriptions for lower-income groups mean the more obvious obstacles are removed. There are less obvious obstacles: the cost of journeys and time off work. But if equal medical care could produce equal health, we might expect to see greater equality of health in the UK than the data in Figure 12.3 show at present.

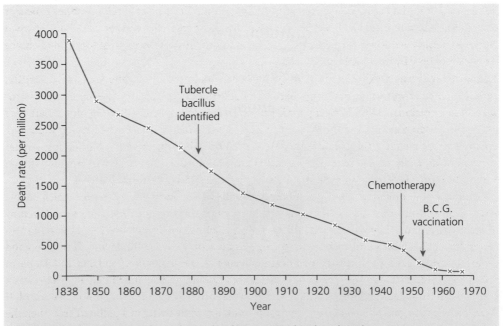

Figure 12.5 Respiratory tuberculosis: death rates, England and Wales

Source: McKeown (1976: 93). Reproduced by Permission of Hodder Arnold.

We might also expect to see more differences between different diseases. The same patterns of inequality show for cancer, heart disease, and accidents: these suggest that something—perhaps to do with living conditions—lies behind the medical situation of people dying from different diseases.

These debates suggest that medicine should take its place as one among many factors that influence health and survival.

Individual behaviour vs. social circumstances? Figure 12.4 may help us to make sense of a complex set of factors and how they fit together. But how do individual choices relate to social circumstances? The clearest evidence relates to smoking, which brings risks of heart disease and cancer and is related to social circumstances, with people in poorer circumstances more likely to smoke. Exercise and healthy eating are also related to socio-economic patterns, with better-off people more likely to exercise and eat a diet rich in fruit and vegetables, following official advice.

How much of the blame for health inequalities lies in poorer people's smoking and food choices? The Whitehall study has been tracking 18,000 government employees in London—from top civil servants to caretakers and other manual workers—since 1967. It shows smoking playing a part in differences between people in different positions. But it also shows that smoking and other known risk factors account for only a third of the difference in mortality between the highest and lowest (a more detailed account of this study and others is given in Gray 2001a: 240).

Have poorer people not understood the official messages? There is research on people's knowledge of health advice. But studies have failed to show major differences in knowledge about food between different socio-economic groups. They do show poor mothers having as much desire as better-off ones for healthy food for their children.

Why have better-off people responded more and more quickly to health warnings? The key to these differences lies in the social context in which people's choices are embedded. There are obvious material constraints on choices when people live in poor environments. Budgeting studies show the difficulty of affording healthy food: 'Far from being able to afford a healthy diet, many members of low-income families frequently go without any food, healthy or unhealthy. Children are less likely to go without food because they are protected by their mothers, but . . . 10 per cent of children said they had gone hungry in the preceding month because of a lack of money (Spencer 1996: 156). Access to fresh food may be improving for those with cars, but car-based out-of-town shopping diminishes access for those who have to add bus fares to the price of food. Food choice may be hampered by inability to risk waste.

Low incomes may also lead to disconnections of essential services of water, gas, and electricity, especially since privatization, making people vulnerable to cold, respiratory infections, and gastro-instestinal infections. Damp housing, poor heating/insulation, traffic pollution, and unsafe play spaces for children are among the problems people on low incomes face when trying to make a healthy environment for their children. These add up to formidable material limitations. Higher incomes bring wider choice of housing, avoiding many kinds of potential environmental threat: traffic pollution, nuclear power stations, electricity pylons, and agricultural chemicals.

A major study compared the impact of healthy living behaviours—lifestyles over which people have some control—and social circumstances, over which they do not. Generally social circumstances were found to be more powerful explanations than personal behaviours. But the study also found differences in what different social groups could achieve by healthy living. People in good social circumstances could improve their health by exercise, non-smoking, good diet. But people in poor social circumstances who made healthy choices did not gain as much benefit. There was a lower return from healthy choices, with health overshadowed by factors they could not control. If there is less health gain to be had from giving up smoking, while living in a polluted area, then the rational choice may be to make less effort (Blaxter 1990).

The damage of social exclusion may go beyond material circumstances. Unemployment and debt create psychological damage; smoking may be used as a—damaging—refuge from social stress. Exclusion from choice in a consumer society is damaging to self-esteem. Wilkinson and Pickett's *The Spirit Level: Why Equality is Better for Everyone* (2010) argues for social equality as the crucial component of health and happiness in more developed societies, drawing on a wide range of international data. In developed societies faith in markets lies behind increasing socio-economic inequalities. These have consequences for our sense of ourselves, our trust in others, community life, mental health, physical health, life expectancy, educational achievement, violence, and social mobility. These are not unavoidable, but can be contained by governments and societies. Social democratic societies such as Sweden and Norway have promoted social equality through high public spending. Japan has promoted it through an egalitarian economy rooted in the post-war period. The social democracies and Japan have high achievements across a range of measures, including life expectancy, health, and child well-being (Wilkinson and Pickett 2010). Swedish infant mortality rates in 2009 were 2.75 per 1,000, with Iceland, France, Finland, and Norway following close behind, compared with 4.85 in the UK. Apart from France, these are social democratic regimes with high levels of government intervention to reduce poverty and social inequality and increase social cohesion. Japan's rather different approach, with lower social spending, but also oriented to equality, brings infant mortality rates of 2.79 per thousand, just below Sweden's. The United States's liberal free-market-based approach to social policy brings IMRs of 6.26 per 1,000, despite high economic development and healthcare spending (CIA World Factbook 2010).

Policies for health and to reduce health inequalities Approaches to understanding health inequalities are clearly connected to policy approaches. Post-war UK governments prioritized access to medical care, giving everyone access to treatment when they became sick. The first official argument for preventing ill health was *Prevention and Health: Everybody's Business* (DHSS 1976), stressing people's ability to look after themselves rather than the conditions that might damage health and make healthy living difficult. Research at the end of the twentieth century found that health advice tended to increase health inequalities: it was more readily adopted by advantaged people than by disadvantaged. These studies preferred policies to improve the conditions under which people lived, which would improve health directly and materially, while making it easier to adopt healthy lifestyles and to lower mental stress. The recommendations from this literature were for changes in housing policy to produce quality social housing and reduce homelessness, raising child benefits, and control over tobacco advertising and sponsorship (Benzeval et al. 1995).

New Labour policy was for 'striking a new balance . . . a third way . . . linking individual and wider action' (Department of Health 1999). This retained—from earlier governments—an emphasis on individuals, but recognized the difficulties arising from poverty, poor housing, pollution, low educational standards, unemployment, and low pay, as well as the link between health inequality and social inequality. Policies across this wide agenda were in practice uneven. But New Labour governments always emphasized individual responsibility, while aiming to reduce and eventually eliminate child poverty. Strategies included higher child benefits, child and childcare tax credits, Sure Start, and supports to mothers' employment. But New Labour's third way was directed more at the bottom of the distribution of income and wealth than at the top. So, while child poverty reduced, socio-economic inequalities increased, especially through very high pay (Hills et al. 2010).

If this New Labour's third way offered one kind of contradiction, between free-market individualism and the social purpose of ending child poverty, coalition government plans suggest another. Public health policy is expressed purely as a matter of individual, personal responsibility:

The Government believes that we need action to promote public health, and encourage behaviour change to help people live healthier lives. We need an ambitious strategy to prevent ill-health, which harnesses innovative techniques to help people take responsibility for their own health (HM Government 2010b: 28).

In contrast, the new government's Equalities policy argues for a fairer society:

> The Government believes that there are many barriers to social mobility and equal opportu-
> nities...We need concerted government action to tear down these barriers and help to build
> a fairer society (HM Government 2010: 18).

A proposal to 'undertake a fair pay review in the public sector to implement our proposed 20 times'
pay multiple' (HM Government 2010: 18) suggests a radical assault on those social inequalities
which are rooted in unequal pay, if only in the public sector. So the coalition may also offer contradiction, between a Conservative individualim in public health, and a more interventionist plan to
reduce socio-economic inequalities through public sector pay.

What is to be learnt from other countries? There are poor countries with good records as well as
rich countries with poor records. Evidence from those poorer countries that have achieved good
health suggests that going for economic growth alone may not be the best way. A UNICEF study
chose ten high-achieving countries which had better health than might be expected given their
levels of national wealth, when infant mortality rates for industrialized countries were 6 per thousand and for low-income countries 80. Chosen countries included Kerala State in India, with an
IMR of 17, Cuba with 7, and Korea with 5. The study emphasized the role of public action and
balanced economic growth, spending on basic services and on education, especially women's education, and fairness in public spending. The overarching principle was that 'these countries did
not give priority to achieving economic growth first, whilst postponing social development'
(Mehrotra 2001).

In more developed economies, if equality is key, waiting for economic growth will not be enough:
we would need to redistribute resources, not simply lift socio-economic levels for everyone. Wilkinson and Pickett argue that we can all develop alternatives to big business: employee ownership in the
manner of the John Lewis Partnership, public ownership, as in universities and hospitals, and rein-
vigorating cooperative and mutual organizations, such as building societies. These would reduce
socio-economic inequalities and the damage they do (Wilkinson and Pickett 2010). Likewise, the
Marmot Review finds roots for health inequalities in the early years of life, in education, work and
lack of work, income and wealth, and in communities. It argues that tackling health inequalities
means tackling social inequalites very broadly. Yes, this will be expensive, but the alternative will be
major loss of life, loss of health, and economic costs resulting from disability, ill health, and healthcare. The Marmot Review calculated the costs of health inequality, in terms of loss of life, health, and
healthcare costs, comparing England in 2010 with a socially equal society, in which all those below
the top 10 per cent could expect the life and experience the health of the top 10 per cent. It found a
loss of 600,000 years of life, and 4.1 million extra years of healthy life. The review—again comparing
a situation in which everyone had the same outcomes as the richest 10 per cent—calculated annual
productivity losses of £31–33 billion, lost taxes and higher welfare payments each year in the range
£20–32 billion, and direct healthcare costs for treating acute illness and mental illness and prescriptions of £5.5 billion per year (Marmot et al. 2010: 82–3). In the context of current government cuts
to public and social expenditure, investment to tackle social inequality may seem unlikely. But it
could be seen as more necessary than ever to avoid loss of life and loss of health, and the economic
costs of disease and disability, with the worst consequences of recession falling on those who can
least afford it.

Health policy

The NHS in 1948

Governments had already intervened in health and health policy, with public health legislation in
the nineteenth century, hospitals under the Poor Law, National Health Insurance early in the

twentieth century, and the Emergency Medical Service during the war. But the Second World War brought a qualitative difference in assumptions about what governments could and should do. It also brought experience of the confusion and inadequacy of existing health services. William Beveridge was commissioned to make plans for social security after the war. His plan assumed that there would be 'comprehensive health and rehabilitation services'. The wartime government planned a major extension of health and medical services. But the first election after the war brought a Labour government to power and Aneurin Bevan to the ministry of health. Reform plans acquired a radical twist. It was already assumed in wartime planning that the new health service would be universal (available to all), comprehensive (including all services, both preventative and curative), and free (involving no payment at the point of delivery) (Webster 1998: 22). Bevan also nationalized the hospitals, reorganizing them into a system that would be managed on a regional basis. He aimed to 'universalize the best' healthcare, in contrast to a Poor Law, minimum-level approach which favoured means-tested services for the poor, and which stigmatized those who used it. The service would not only be free at the point of use; it would also be funded mainly through general taxation, rather than through insurance contributions. People would pay according to how much they could afford, through taxes which Bevan believed should be progressive, taking a higher proportion from higher earnings. Thus the NHS was built on explicitly egalitarian and redistributive principles. The NHS Act was passed in 1946 and the service inaugurated in 1948, with a leaflet, 'The New National Health Service' on everyone's doormat, declaring:

> It will provide you with all medical, dental, and nursing care. Everyone—rich or poor, man, woman or child—can use it or any part of it. There are no charges, except for a few special items. There are no insurance qualifications. But it is not a charity. You are all paying for it, mainly as taxpayers, and it will relieve your money worries in time of illness (quoted in Webster 1998: 24).

While the legislation for the NHS evoked fierce opposition, the service became popular, for the freedom from medical bills and the anxiety surrounding them. The NHS gained loyalty from those who worked in it, and—more surprisingly—from politicians of different colours, including Conservative governments with very different ideals from those of Bevan and the post-war Labour government. There have been opportunities to move from the principles of the NHS, to introduce market-oriented systems of healthcare, but politicians—including Thatcher and Blair—have expressed broad loyalty to NHS ideals. The Conservative–Liberal Democrat coalition's programme for government adds support for NHS values:

> The Government believes that the NHS is an important expression of our national values. We are committed to an NHS that is free at the point of use and available to everyone based on need, not the ability to pay (HM Government 2010: 24).

Bevan's proposals for the NHS can be seen as a 'mixture of audacity and prudence' (Webster 1998: 15). If nationalizing the hospitals, universalizing the best, and funding through taxation were the audacious part, there were prudent elements in the NHS mixture. The NHS held onto pre-existing systems of administration, making a 'tripartite' system whose lack of coherent structure revisited later health ministers. The system was also conservative in the services that it offered. The NHS took over hospitals and general practitioner services and drew local authority public health services under its umbrella. The Appointed Day for starting the NHS brought no chaos of new systems, rather the same services as delivered the previous week, albeit to many more people. 'Comprehensive health and rehabilitation services' dominated by medical services to individuals lay at the centre of this collectivist system of healthcare delivery.

The next sections discuss what has become of these NHS principles over its sixty or so years. Social, political, and economic changes have made a different world. Family change has changed the assumptions we can make about how much we care for each other. Demographic change has brought a much older population, with much heavier healthcare needs. Consumerism brings patients who have more expectations and make more demands than their predecessors. Economic growth brings new resources, but also globalization and less confidence in national government interventions. Technological development brings new possibilities, mainly more expensive possibilities, for all kinds of therapeutic intervention. How has the NHS responded to all these changes? And how well is it placed to adapt to the twenty-first century? Each section takes a key issue deriving from the decisions that established the NHS, asking how it has fared and whether the principles of 1948 are recognizable in today's NHS. The chapter also discusses whether the principles of the NHS are relevant to health and healthcare today.

The NHS in the twenty-first century: contesting medical dominance?

A biomedical model of health was dominant at the beginning of the NHS, rooted in assumptions about the value of medical science in the treatment of individuals. Doctors' authority was central to the operation and management of hospitals, primary care. and community health, including authority over other professionals and health workers. Patients had little role in NHS decision-making, and were seen as having little role in their own healthcare. There were few 'alternative' practices such as chiropractic or acupuncture. As we have seen, medicine's role in health has been challenged by social science. The dominance of medicine in the NHS has been contested from several directions. We may ask whether patients have been turned into consumers, how much doctors' authority has been contested by other professionals in the NHS and outside—lawyers for example— and whether a social or environmental model has gained ground over the medical perspective.

Consumerism is a key social development. If health service users were once assumed to be patients, they may now expect choice and control as consumers of services. Many patients' groups and carers' groups have developed around chronic health conditions, operating as foci for information and support, much enhanced by the internet. People frequently choose alternative therapies rather than medicine or as well as medicine. The transformation of people from patients into medical consumers is partial: illness makes people vulnerable, and they may still be seen as patients needing expertise. But these social changes bring elements of consumerism into relationships between doctors and patients, making the authority of medical decisions less taken for granted.

More politically, new social movements have challenged the assumptions on which medical authority rested. The green movement draws attention to environmental aspects of health in contrast to medical aspects. The women's health movement challenged medicine's masculinity and its relation to other professions, in particular nursing and midwifery. Women were denied access to medical schools in the nineteenth century, and not admitted equally with men until nearly the end of the twentieth. Nursing and midwifery were established as female professions under medical authority. Gender divisions and power relations in health work have been changed—though not wholly transformed—by the women's movement's challenges, which brought legislation including the Sex Discrimination Act 1975. While medicine's relation to other professions was under scrutiny, so was its relation to women patients. Contraception, abortion, childbirth, and new reproductive technologies such as in vitro fertilization bring issues of choice into sharp focus. In the last quarter of the twentieth century the women's movement fought for—and to some extent achieved—more autonomy for women in making decisions about whether, when, and how to have babies (Doyal 1998).

Medical authority has increasingly been challenged in courts and public inquiries. Litigation is increasingly seen as a way for individuals to gain redress when they are dissatisfied with the quality of care. But confidence and trust in medicine have been the subject of high-profile investigations into poor-quality care, the ability of individuals to expose it, and of healthcare systems to deal with it. An increasingly open environment—in which the media play a key role—makes public issues of medical decisions which might earlier have remained within the privacy of doctor–patient relationships.

While medical authority has been challenged, it has not died. The description of the NHS as a national medical service appears in every textbook. NHS spending has always been dominated by spending on hospitals, with primary care and public health lagging behind, currently at four per cent of this NHS spending. Health ministers are always centrally concerned with hospital beds, waiting lists, and standards of care. If these concerns fitted with the 1948 ideas about the role of medical science in health, they are increasingly at odds with research and debates about the sources of this health at the beginning of the twenty-first century. The World Health Organization has encouraged governments to develop strategies to bring health rather than treat disease. Recent national governments have pushed public health up their agenda, with White Papers such as *Saving Lives: Our Healthier Nation* (DoH 1999) and a minister for public health. Ministers of health and government documents refer to the need for prevention and to reduce health inequalities. Old and New Labour governments supported research on health inequalities, culminating in the Marmot Review's *Fair Society, Healthy Lives*, which called for an understanding that health inequalities are rooted in socio-economic inequalities and need sustained policies across a wide range of government departments, not just health departments. It proposed widespread and radical changes to reduce health inequality, from supports to parents, including paid parental leave in the first year of life, to higher-quality early years education, better-quality work, implementing a minimum income for healthy living and greener spaces in all our communities (Marmot et al. 2010). Labour government policies on health inequalities have made some impact. In particular, policies to target child poverty have been a high priority, and 'a revolution in early years provision and parenting support' begins to show results. But 'a second revolution in the early years' is needed to increase investment in the youngest children (Marmot et al. 2010: 94). This seems rather unlikely to be forthcoming from the coalition government.

While the agenda has broadened to include a health perspective as well as a medical one, health service priorities in practice are more persistent. Under a New Labour government the *NHS Plan* set out ten core principles for the NHS (see Box 12.2). These include providing a universal service based on clinical need, shaping the services around the needs and preferences of individual patients, their families, and their carers, and working to improve quality services and minimize errors. The

---

Box 12.2 **NHS core principles, 2000**

1 The NHS will provide a universal service for all based on clinical need, not ability to pay.
2 The NHS will provide a comprehensive range of services.
3 The NHS will shape its services around the needs and preferences of individual patients, their families, and their carers.
4 The NHS will respond to different needs of different populations.
5 The NHS will work continuously to improve quality services and to minimize errors.
6 The NHS will support and value its staff.
7 Public funds for healthcare will be devoted solely to NHS patients.
8 The NHS will work together with others to ensure a seamless service for patients.
9 The NHS will help keep people healthy and work to reduce health inequalities.
10 The NHS will respect the confidentiality of individual patients and provide open access to information about services, treatment, and performance.

(Department of Health 2000: 3–5)

ninth principle is: 'The NHS will help keep people healthy and work to reduce health inequalities.' It is the only principle that reflects the agenda of social change rather than of medical care (DoH 2000: 3–4).

The coalition government goes further down this track, putting medical care at the heart of its priorities, listing thirty under the NHS, and four under public health, with 'encouraging behaviour change' at the heart of public health policy (HM Government 2010: 28).

The medical model of health is no longer unchallenged. Consumerism, the women's and environmental movements, growing litigation and public inquiries, social science research: these diverse changes in society make medicine's authority more open to question than it was at the start of the NHS. But government priorities, expressed through spending and ideals, suggest these have undermined trust in medicine less than may at first appear.

The NHS in the twenty-first century: comprehensive care?

If comprehensive care was part of the 1946 promise, delivering comprehensive health services brings dilemmas. The possibilities of medical intervention already seem limitless, yet they grow all the time. We have not, as a society, decided to spend more than a fraction of our resources on healthcare, and few would wish for a society and economy consumed by meeting healthcare needs. Increasing the resources spent on healthcare would solve some problems, meet more needs, but would not meet them all. Comprehensive care, meeting all health needs, whether defined by professionals or by people as patients, parents, sons, or daughters of patients, may best be seen as an ideal that cannot be realized in practice. These problems emerge internationally in different healthcare systems. The NHS commitment to comprehensive care, free at the time of use, poses the dilemma in a particular form in the UK, but every health system generates debates about rationing and priorities.

Prioritizing or rationing takes place. Some services have been withdrawn from or limited in the NHS in some areas: cosmetic operations, infertility treatment, long-term care of the elderly. Some groups of patients are less likely to receive services than others. There is evidence of discrimination against older patients; drinkers or smokers may be deemed less likely to benefit from treatment. Some rationing mechanisms are in Box 12.3.

More demanding health consumers make these issues more contentious. There was never a golden age in which all possible healthcare needs were met, but patient questioning about priorities defined by professionals has probably grown, as patients have become more ready to complain (Powell 1997: 107). The consequent more overt debates about rationing have raised questions about who should take such decisions and how. Community participation in developing priorities is one kind of solution, scientific calculation of cost–benefit or cost effectiveness another. Public participation in decision-making may bring advantages, but may also tend to exclude unpopular groups/needs from health treatment. The scientific approach—calculating costs and benefits—is more defensible in comparing different treatments for the same problem than in the infinitely complex problem of making systematic comparisons of costs and benefits of treatments to ease multiple sclerosis against those of, say, infertility treatments.

Box 12.3 **Rationing mechanisms**

- waiting lists
- deterrence through charges
- deflecting demand to other services
- diluting (e.g. using cheaper drugs)
- denial of some services

(Hunter 1997: 22)

Central governments have aimed to diffuse the blame attaching to hard decisions, with professionals and health authorities in practice deciding whom to treat and how much, how much to spend, what to leave out. There is therefore variation around the country in these decisions and how they are made. The National Institute for Clinical Excellence (NICE) was established in 1999, aiming to reduce variation between authorities, deciding which treatments are effective and should be provided under the NHS, avoiding the 'postcode lottery'. It aimed 'to provide patients, health professionals and public with authoritative, robust and reliable guidance on current "best practice"'(NICE 2002). NICE has covered specific treatments, such as drugs, techniques, and procedures, and clinical management of specific conditions, reporting on many contentious issues. NICE has approved most of the interventions it has assessed, with 80 per cent receiving a 'yes' or 'partial yes'. NICE has led to greater clarity about what is available on the NHS (Thorlby and Maybin 2010: 20–1). Not all variation has been eliminated, clinical guidance not always being implemented by purchasing authorities, especially when the guidance is expensive. NICE decisions have not been free of criticism, but they have offered guidance based on the best evidence, and more coherence to decisions about what should be included in NHS treatments, drawing necessary limits.

The NHS in the twenty-first century: from state finance to mixed economy?

One idea of UK social welfare during the latter part of the twentieth century is of a transfomation from state domination to a more variegated mix of public, private, voluntary, informal care: a mixed economy of welfare. This section examines the mix of state and private finance in the UK, as well as the mix of state and family care, to ask how true this is in healthcare.

State and private finance Do we spend too much or too little on healthcare? Right-wing critics have argued the need for a price mechanism to regulate demand: people may want more at the point of need than they are prepared to pay for in taxes. NHS defenders have argued for its efficiency in keeping costs down and its humanity in meeting needs. As an experimental system, the NHS overspent in its first two years, an experience which brought a long period of stringency, with spending settling at around 3.5 per cent to 4.1 per cent of GDP during the first twenty-five years (Webster 1998: 30–4).

Afterwards, both public and policy analysts became more concerned about the low levels of NHS spending—and low levels of service—in comparison with other European countries. After long periods in which government policy-makers argued for small government and low taxation, there followed under New Labour support for higher government spending, especially on healthcare. The NHS plan acknowledged that 'in part the NHS is failing to deliver because over the years it has been underfunded (Department of Health 2000:1). The Treasury commissioned a report to quantify 'the financial and other resources required to ensure that the NHS can provide a publicly funded, comprehensive high-quality service available on the basis of clinical need and not ability to pay' (Wanless 2002). This included counting the cost of many years' underinvestment in NHS staff and buildings, to bring them up to contemporary expectations and standards in comparable European countries.

Increasing living standards have tended to bring higher healthcare spending. Most recent figures—for 2007—show Turkey spending 5.7 per cent of GDP, while the United States was spending 16.0 per cent (OECD 2009). At the beginning of the New Labour era, UK spending was seventh from the bottom of this OECD league, between Poland and Hungary. A promise to close the gap with the rest of Europe lifted spending to 8.4 per cent of GDP by 2007 (see Figure 12.6), with spending doubling in real terms over the New Labour period (Thorlby and Maybin 2010: 8–9). Furthermore, the coalition plans—amid all its proposals for cuts—to 'guarantee that health spending increases in real terms in each year of the Parliament' (HM Goverment 2010: 24). So now there is agreement on all sides that NHS spending should go on increasing.

Not only does the coalition plan spending increases, it also plans to maintain the core post-war plan of a public expenditure-based NHS. Bevan's ideal was for a service funded through taxation, reflecting ability to pay, with an element of contribution through national insurance. Private

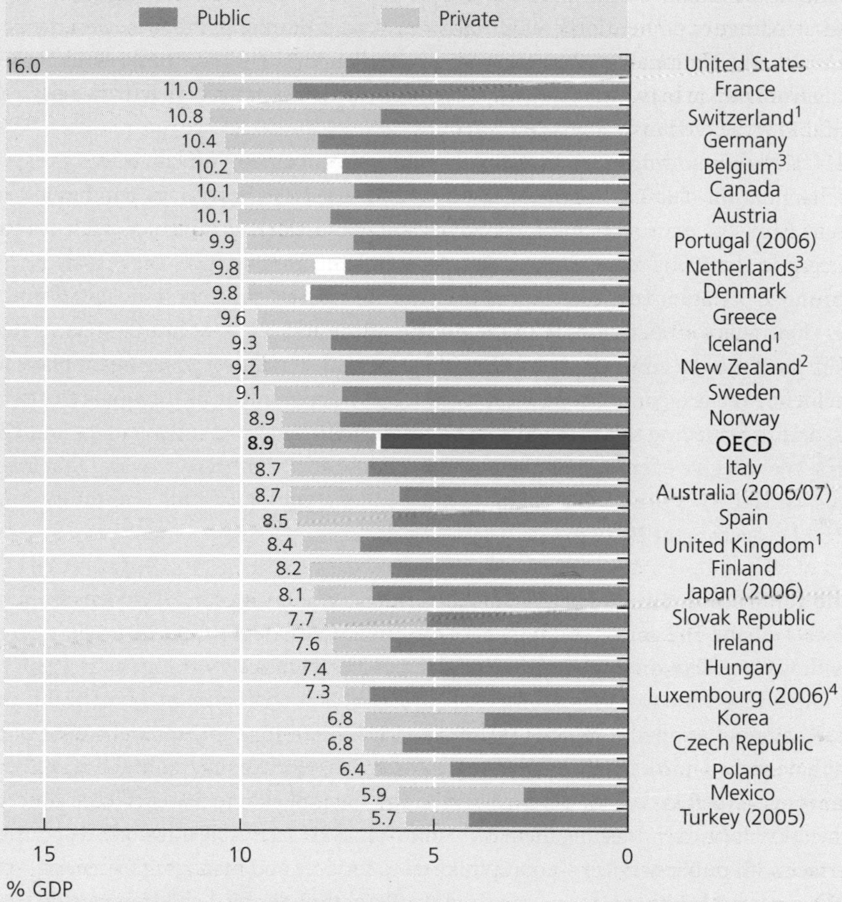

	% GDP
United States	16.0
France	11.0
Switzerland[1]	10.8
Germany	10.4
Belgium[3]	10.2
Canada	10.1
Austria	10.1
Portugal (2006)	9.9
Netherlands[3]	9.8
Denmark	9.8
Greece	9.6
Iceland[1]	9.3
New Zealand[2]	9.2
Sweden	9.1
Norway	8.9
OECD	8.9
Italy	8.7
Australia (2006/07)	8.7
Spain	8.5
United Kingdom[1]	8.4
Finland	8.2
Japan (2006)	8.1
Slovak Republic	7.7
Ireland	7.6
Hungary	7.4
Luxembourg (2006)[4]	7.3
Korea	6.8
Czech Republic	6.8
Poland	6.4
Mexico	5.9
Turkey (2005)	5.7

1 Total expenditure on health

2 Current expenditure on health

3 Public and private expenditures are current expenditures (excluding investments)

4 Health expenditure is for the insured population rather than the resident population

Figure 12.6 Health expenditure in relation to GDP

Source: OECD *Health at a Glance* 2009: Figure 7.2

practice would continue, but universalizing the best in the NHS would give people little incentive to pay privately. Challenges to these ideals started early, with the introduction of prescription charges proving the first crack in the ideal of a service free at the point of use. Political differences around public funding—and political changes from the collectivism of the post-war era—have made more room for charging, as well as for developing alternatives to the NHS. Figure 12.6 shows that the UK's public–private share resembles the Scandinavian social democracies, with very high proportions of spending coming from public sources, rather than resembling the United States, whose public spending was less than half of its total health spending.

The key debate about the merits of public versus private funding is about how redistributive the system is between different income groups. Public funding is mildly 'progressive' with taxation taking a higher proportion from higher-income groups than from lower. The UK's system is less progressive than it seems at first sight because indirect taxes such as VAT hit lower-income groups harder; but overall, public funding means that funding comes disproportionately from higher-income groups. Currently NHS finance comes 80 per cent from taxation, with 12 per cent from National Insurance contributions and 4 per cent from charges. Public funding tends to be associated with better population health outcomes. And, from the point of view of the economy, 'private health spending has no advantages over public health spending. The obvious consequence of shifting from public to private is to shift the burden from the relatively rich to the relatively poor' (Normand 1998, quoted in Wanless 2002: 141).

While UK health funding remains distinctly public, the mixture of private within the system has grown, changing the character of the NHS (Box 12.5). The NHS has always purchased drugs and equipment from the private sector. Hospital cleaning and catering contracts with private companies began in the 1980s, expanding to agencies supplying nursing staff. The Private Finance Initiative brought private investment capital to major investment projects in hospitals and general practice. Contracts for operations with the private sector and overseas health services mean that healthcare itself may be contracted out. This will grow under coalition government plans to diversify providers: 'We are committed to the continuous improvement of the quality of services to patients, and to achieving this through much greater involvement of independent and voluntary providers. We will give every patient the power to choose any healthcare provider that meets NHS standards, within NHS prices. This includes independent, voluntary and community sector providers' (HM Government 2010: 26).

State and family care The idea of a National Health Service taking care of citizens from cradle to grave always missed one crucial component of care: to a large extent people have taken care of each other, without intervention from governments or services. Feminists writing in the 1980s began to identify unpaid care, and women's work as unpaid carers, as crucial components of health and social systems, albeit unquantified components (Pascall 1997). Counting care, understanding who does it and why, have grown into a significant body of research. This work spans cradle and grave, concerned with parenting as well as care for disabled people and the frail elderly. Parents' core concerns with raising healthy children, protecting them from injury, may be seen as health work; responsibility for the interface with public services—taking children to services and managing treatment—puts parents at the centre of healthcare for young children. Parents of disabled children may do specialized nursing work. And older people often meet and manage each others' health and care needs.

Feminist investigation began with the gendering of care work. While parenting has become a fashionable idea, research shows mothering as more common practice. Care for elderly people is more complicated, with spouses often caring for each other, care involving husbands and wives. But women are more likely to take responsibility for heavy nursing care and for a wider range of needs in and beyond the immediate family (Finch 1989). Accounts of time use now include paid and unpaid work, with accumulating evidence across many countries that women's joining the labour market has not been matched by men's joining family work, though there is some convergence between men and women (Gershuny 2000).

If one crucial argument about care work is about its distribution between men and women, another is about its distribution between state and family. Box 12.4 on long-term care looks at the recent history of health and community care for frail elderly people who may need personal and/or nursing care. There is no straighforward way to count a shift from state to family care, but there is evidence to support that shift. First, the reduction in hospital beds suggests that some care has shifted from hospital to home. Second, the elderly population has grown, especially the very elderly, whose healthcare needs are greatest. And third, governments concerned with the numbers of frail elderly and with public finance have shifted policy to ensure that more older people, and more frail older people, live at home.

Does the evidence support the idea of a trend from state provision to a more mixed economy in UK health policy? Increasingly, governments turn to the private sector and to the family. Private insurance outside the NHS has grown, as have private sector contracts in the NHS. While

Box 12.4 **Long-term care**

The policy thread that binds all these official attempts to promote community care has been a concern to shift the responsibility for care from one agency to another—from the NHS to local authorities, from local authorities to families (Lewis and Glennerster 1996: 2).

The issue of long-term care gives an example of changing policy over what should be deemed to be health needs and included as part of the health service. Policy has, in effect, changed, so that people who might once have occupied hospital beds are now more likely to be in nursing homes or residential care, or in their own homes with support from community services. Care that would have been free at the point of need within the NHS may be charged by social services or nursing homes, or may be delivered by relatives without charge or count.

The NHS inherited many long-term beds from the Poor Law, warehouses for older people, some of whom needed hospital or nursing care, but many whose need was for an alternative place to go. Movements in mental health and geriatric medicine towards enabling people to support themselves in their own homes as long as possible have contributed to this decline in long-stay hospital beds. These developments have produced a wider range of community and smaller home provision and enriched the choice for people needing long-term care. But the desire to move costs, from fully funded NHS beds to means-tested local authority responsibility, and from local authority to unpaid care at home, has been a major power behind these changes. An element of privatization has been involved, as the government has fostered development of an industry of care homes, as well as pushing costs onto families and unpaid carers.

At the start of the NHS there were 11 hospital beds per 1,000 population. By 1989–90 this had dropped to 6.2 per 1,000 and by 1999–2000 to 4.1 per 1,000 (Office of Health Economics 2002). There are many reasons for this decline, which affects acute hospital beds as well as long-term ones: the remaining beds are used much more intensively, with quicker patient turnover, shorter hospital stay, and keyhole surgery allowing patients home. But this huge decline in hospital beds, at a time of ageing population, gives some indication of the shift from NHS to local authorities, and from local authorities to families, described above by Lewis and Glennerster.

A Royal Commission on Long Term Care for the Elderly was established by the new Labour government in 1997, and published as a report in 1999. Scotland decided to follow its recommendations for a comprehensive package of care for people with long-term needs. But people in England and Wales have been offered less. There is now agreement to include the costs of nursing care within the NHS. But a new boundary has been created, which may be difficult to defend, between those whose needs are deemed to be for nursing and those whose needs are for personal care. Personal care remains outside the NHS.

there is little quantitative evidence about family care in the post-war period, the implications of changing policy and changing needs are that family healthcare work has been growing, especially for older people. But the UK continues some of its post-war tradition. Its NHS is more collectivist, more dominated by public spending than the more liberal United States, retaining a more social democratic style in healthcare than in other social provisions. And while Conservatives of the Thatcher era contemplated dismantling it, Conservatives now see it as a national treasure to be preserved.

The NHS in the twenty-first century: planning for healthcare—top down or bottom up?

Who should have power over health services? What mix should exist between governments and professionals, service providers and consumers, managers and professionals? And how should

> ## Box 12.5 **Private finance in the NHS**
>
> The Private Finance Initiative (PFI) brought the private sector into public sector developments from 1992, including the design, building, financing, and operation of hospitals and other health facilities. PFI started slowly, with only one major hospital development signed by 1996, to build a district hospital in Norwich.
>
> New Labour governments used private sector capital for funding major projects, arguing that 'private finance might complement public funds, as long as schemes were compatible with NHS priorities' (Baggott 1998: 171). PFI projects enabled a rapid increase in public sector building projects without rapid increases in government borrowing. They were seen as transferring risk to private companies.
>
> PFI grew rapidly under New Labour, with 105 health projects signed by 1 September 2001, worth £2,502 million (Allen 2001: 11). PFI now funds nearly all new major hospital schemes, accounting for 64 of the 68 new projects by 2005. A variant—LIFT (Local Improvement Finance Trusts)—was to build primary care premises (OHE 2005).
>
> Advocates point to the rapid development of new hospital buildings and the modernization of NHS stock. Critics point to longer-run costs, with today's public buildings costing tomorrow's taxpayers, a growing stream of public payments to private companies, and some evidence of risks falling on the public rather than the private sector when costs escalate. Finally, some critics wonder whether this is a route to privatizing the NHS.

power be exercised? Should central government take decisions that apply nationwide? Or should local communities participate in decision-making about local services, even if it brings a so-called postcode lottery? How can health service planning be integrated with social service planning? If governments have tended—ultimately—to take the same line about public funding for a national health service, they have tended to take different lines about how to manage it. The resulting organizations and reorganizations have been many.

Top-down planning for healthcare The 1948 model was top down, with a minister of health in at least theoretical control of a health service managed through regional and local boards with a little local government participation. A new integrated structure delivered hospital services, but the first design for the NHS owed as as much to the need to placate entrenched interests, to get a health service started, as to any ideals about how services should be managed.

The first NHS organization was much criticized for its tripartite nature, with no integration of hospital, general practitioner, or local authority public health services. But the early NHS did develop integrated local services, domiciliary services for health and social care under Medical Officers of Health. Reorganization to make more coherent planning structures for health, implemented in 1974, created a much more difficult environment for integrating local health and social services. It also took the management of health entirely away from local government. Critics see problems of public accountability in health services, with decision-making by non-elected authorities and little public participation in decision-making.

If the 1948 model appeared to critics to be top down, it did not always appear so to ministers of health. Ministers enunciated policies, to move resources to 'Cinderella' services for elderly and mentally ill patients, but spending continued in established patterns, with acute hospitals receiving more money. From the point of view of ministers of health it appeared that medical consultants controlled spending, with resources following medical rather than ministerial decisions.

The NHS came to be criticized as a bureaucratically managed system, lacking flexibility and unresponsive to patients, protecting enrenched interests, especially professional interests. General management was introduced in 1985, as a solution to these problems: managers—never mind whether their background was in industry, financial services, or nursing—would be responsible to government for delivering policy.

This radical change in the management of health services was soon followed by a more radical one. Right-wing critics saw in the NHS a command-and-control management style that bore an uncomfortable resemblance to discredited Soviet systems. Markets were seen as more dynamic, with incentives and freedom to innovate, responsive to consumers, who could take their custom elsewhere if not satisfied. After a brief flirtation with the idea of exchanging the NHS for alternative systems—especially market-based systems—the Thatcher government decided to keep the NHS but import market principles into its management. Hence, the 1989 White Paper, *Working for Patients*, and the NHS and Community Care Act of 1990, which introduced the NHS internal market.

The internal market The government aimed to bring the virtues of markets to the NHS while keeping the promise of public funding for public services. Top-down bureaucracy would be dismantled. Instead of health authorities using government funds to provide services, purchasing authorities would buy services and providing authorities would produce and sell them, competing for market share. Purchasers could pick between providers, and contract for the best services available. General practitioners could become fundholders, purchasing services from hospitals and others. Hospitals could become NHS Trusts, independent from health authorities, with freedom to develop in their own way, subject only to winning enough custom. The internal market offered a very radical reorganization. All provider units in fact became trusts, including hospitals, and ambulance and community health services. GP fundholding also spread widely.

Critics looked for inequalities in the internal market. Would the NHS still offer service on the basis of need, or would some patients get turned off GP lists? Would patients of fundholders get better service than others? Would the high transaction costs of the internal market, the managers, and computers needed to operate it, bring efficiency benefits to outweigh their costs? Perhaps the most politically pressing issue for a new Labour government in 1997 was whether the internal market would generate the kind of inequalities the NHS was founded to eliminate. The incoming government offered a new solution.

Primary Care Trusts: a primary care-led NHS? Primary Care Trusts (PCTs) were New Labour's 'third way' between top-down management and market competition: 'integrated care, based on partnership' (Department of Health 1997: 5). These were to bring key decision-making to local-level groups based on primary care.

PCTs are funded directly from central government according to measures of health need. They provide primary care and community health services and are purchasers for hospital services. They can purchase primary care services such as physiotherapy, counselling, and alternative therapies. New Labour intended to produce a more collaborative arrangement than the internal market. But contracts between one part of the health service and another remain, as well as contracts with outside providers. The development of this PCTs can be seen as softening rather than abolishing the internal market. New Labour's 'third way' shifted between emphasizing the advantages of market competition in NHS management and those of collaboration: 'In the most recent phase, the market-style levers are still in place, but ministerial rhetoric has emphasized collaboration, clinical leadership and favouring the NHS over potential independent competitors' (Thorlby and Maybin (eds) 2010:114–5).

PCTs were designed to be purchasers in an internal market and to devolve power, pushing decision-making to local level. But ideas of local decision-making are in tension with ideas about accountability, quality control, spreading best practice, productivity, efficiency, and performance, which have also been a powerful part of central government rhetoric. Central government has controlled NHS development through targets, and through auditing bodies established to monitor professional standards, reduce waiting lists, and measure the quality of care. Targets and auditing bodies have brought new information, monitoring patient satisfaction, shifting NHS concerns towards patients and away from professionals, and enhancing accountability. There are costs, as managers may become focused on meeting targets rather than on patients. Box 12.6 gives a history of these auditing measures introduced under New Labour, showing them as a considerable policy development.

Under New Labour, local decision-making was ring-fenced by central government control. It aimed to ensure that increased funding—doubling in real terms under New Labour—was well spent to reduce waiting times, enhance patient safety, clinical effectiveness, equity between patients living in different areas, efficiency, and accountability. Quangos and targets had some success in improving patients' experience and NHS quality.

If New Labour governments imposed central control through targets and monitoring, the Conservative–Liberal coalition government plans—expressed through its White Paper *Equity and Excellence: Liberating the NHS*—to revive the bottom-up approach (Department of Health 2010). The coalition will 'strengthen the power of GPs as expert guides through the health system by enabling them to commission care'(HM Government 2010: 24). Reminiscent of earlier Conservative governments' GP fundholding arrangements, which began the 'internal market', these proposals begin another major reorganization. They replace 150 PCTs in England with around 500 GP consortia, putting NHS purchasing power in GPs' hands. The coalition plans a bonfire of quangos and targets, to 'free NHS staff from political micromanagement' (HM Government 2010: 24). A new quango, an NHS Independent Commissioning Board, will allocate and account for NHS resources and distance health ministers from decisions and responsibility.

Box 12.6 Timeline of regulator bodies

1999 A new non-Departmental public body, the Commission for Health Improvement (CHI) is established, to assure local systems of clinical governance.

2002 CHI's role expands to include:
- inspecting NHS organisations and services
- publishing performance reports on trusts including 'star ratings'
- providing annual reports to Parliament on the state of NHS services
- recommending special measures where quality is poor

2004 The Healthcare Commission brings together regulation of the private and public sectors. Its commissioners are appointed by the Appointments Commission rather than government. Its activities are focused on an Annual Health Check of healthcare organisations against core and improvement standards set by the Department of Health, based on inspections.

2005 The Healthcare Commission Annual Healthcheck process starts to be carried out through a system of self-certification, with inspections of only one-fifth of trusts.

2009 The Care Quality Commission is created by merging the Healthcare Commission, the Commission for Social Care Inspection and the Mental Health Act Commission (which monitors services and conditions for patients detained in hospital under the Mental Health Act 1983), in response to pressure for further reductions in the number of regulators

(Office of Public Sector Reform 2003; Department of Health 2004d).

Source: Thorlby and Maybin 2010: Table 17, p. 108

Do GPs want to be at the centre of fundholding? The Royal College of General Practitioners has expressed some reservations. Key doubts are whether another major reorganization, with GPs in key roles, will cost time that might better be spent on clinical practice, whether the cost of making PCTs redundant will outweigh any bureaucratic savings, whether they will lose patients' trust when taking decisions about NHS spending, and whether the more competitive edge of the internal market—including more private providers—will make unequal health more unequal (RCOG 2010).

Market competition is back under the Conservative–Liberal coalition, within a framework of support for the NHS as 'a great national institution' (Department of Health 2010: 1).

A universal NHS in the twenty-first century: do other systems work better?

Is the NHS out of date? Towards the end of the twentieth century it was criticized for everything, from waiting lists to hygiene standards. The argument gained ground that there was something fundamentally wrong with the NHS, a flaw at the centre of its collectivist ideals: a product of the post-war period could not meet the demands of the late twentieth century. Alternatively, NHS ills could be attributed to a hostile climate. The collectivist NHS could not survive without taxation, but taxation was seen only as a burden. All health systems have problems, but the NHS seemed particularly deeply troubled at the end of the twentieth century.

The most contrasting system of healthcare in a developed country is in the United States. A much stronger market operates. Private funding systems tend to be 'inequitable, regressive (those with greater health needs pay the most), have weak incentives for cost control, high administration costs and can deter appropriate use' (Wanless 2002: 141). In the United States three tiers emerged. The best services went to those covered through occupations. Middle tiers of people had 'bare bones' coverage such as Medicaid. A large uninsured population at the bottom had only limited access to public hospital clinic and emergency rooms. Health spending levels far above those of European countries omitted 40 million Americans from health insurance cover.

When the NHS was under great pressure, an American author advised his European readers:

> First, cherish your universal coverage and relatively lower costs. You may not realize how good your systems really are. Second, cherish your commitment to solidarity and equity. Your systems may lack efficiency from the point of view of health economists who are concerned with moral hazard and cross-subsidization from the young and healthy to the old and sick, but that is the price for a sense of community and social justice. Third, be very careful about the creation of a large upper tier of people who purchase all of their care privately . . . Support for the public system could decline, and with it funding for the public system (Kirkman-Liff 1997: 42).

The United States in 2007 spent 16.0 per cent of its GDP on healthcare (Figure 12.6), around half privately, nearly twice the UK's mainly public spending of 8.4 per cent of GDP. After many decades in which vested interests such as insurance companies resisted change, the Obama administration has introduced a more inclusive health insurance system, which will draw in many of the 40 million previously uninsured Americans. It will surely stay a much more expensive system than the NHS, keeping its tiers, with an 'inverse care law' bringing better healthcare to those who need it least.

European systems all use public funding as the main source for healthcare. Some have tax-based systems similar to the NHS, while others use social insurance. Insurance gives a narrower funding base, with contributions during working lives, and countries are shifting from this model. Comparison with European and other countries shows that, despite differences in organization and funding, a number of challenges are shared. These include: 'ensuring equity of access to health services; raising quality; improving health outcomes; sustainable financing; improving efficiency; greater responsiveness; citizen involvement in decision-making; and reducing barriers between health and social care' (Dixon and Mossialos 2002). Not all problems can be put down to the NHS as a system.

Public support for the NHS is strong, with 80 per cent thinking that the NHS is critical to British society and must be maintained (Wanless 2002). Monitoring reveals some weaknesses, but, broadly, satisfaction tends to be high, especially among those who have had recent contact with the NHS, and it has been rising (Thorlby and Maybin 2010). The beginning of the twenty-first century has seen a new commitment to the principles of the NHS from governments. The NHS Plan in 2000 examined other forms of healthcare funding, and concluded that systems used elsewhere do not provide a better route to better healthcare: 'The way the NHS is financed continues to make sense. It meets the tests of efficiency and equity. The principles on which the NHS was constructed in 1948 remain fundamentally sound' (Department of Health 2000: 40). This new commitment was not just to universal principles, but also to a level of funding that would make a universal service work, 'universalizing the best' healthcare. Indeed, such is the national treasure status of the NHS that the Conservative–Liberal coalition has promised to guarantee healthcare spending in real terms each year of the parliament (HM Government 2010: 24). This will mean deeper spending cuts for services and benefits which are arguably more crucial for health.

Conclusion

Looking back to the ideals and ideas of the NHS founders in 1948, there are obvious changes in all the elements identified at the opening of the chapter. The management of the system is the most changed, with top-down planning criticized for bureaucratic inertia and insensitivity to local needs. But perhaps more surprising is how much has survived through to the twenty-first century, through changes of government, economy, and society. Governments have turned to a more mixed economy of care, including markets and families as well as state provision, and charges for some items have increased. But the major part of NHS funding comes from taxation, as it has since 1948. The traditional commitments of the NHS to a universal service based on clinical need, not ability to pay, and a comprehensive range of services have been reasserted by recent governments of different colours. New Labour's radically increased funding has been followed by a coalition promise that it will not only protect the NHS from spending cuts but will increase funding each year. Ideological support for the NHS has been reasserted by New Labour in its NHS Plan and by the coalition's agreement that 'the NHS is an important expression of our national values'.

Social and economic changes reinforce the need for an NHS based on principles of universal service rather than insurance payments by the employed or by charges at the time of use. Increases in the elderly population in proportion to the working population reduce the capacity of workforce-based insurance systems to meet healthcare needs. They also bring an increasing population of vulnerable adults, with large healthcare needs and small incomes. An increasing population of disabled people growing up with significant healthcare needs is another problem that is difficult to meet through any other system. Increasing social inequalities also increase the relevance of a system not related to ability to pay.

Towards the end of the twentieth century the core ideas of the NHS were under attack by critics who preferred a market-based system. But NHS principles began the twenty-first century strengthened. Governments and public opinion value a service that meets healthcare needs mainly through taxation, on the basis of citizenship rather than payment or contribution. These collectivist ideals also continue to support an individualist style of medical care. Medical authority is now more contested by patients, lawyers, and social movements, but public health ideals remain marginal. Perhaps the greatest challenge of the twenty-first century will be to address the problems of health and health inequalities discussed at the beginning of the chapter.

KEY LEGISLATION AND POLICY DOCUMENTS

NHS Act 1946

NHS and Community Care Act 1990

Department of Health and Social Security 1980, *Inequalities in Health: Report of a Working Group* (the Black Report), London: HMSO

Marmot, M. et al. (2010) *Fair Society, Healthy Lives: The Marmot Review*, London: Strategic Review of Health Inequalities in England post-2010

FURTHER READING

Baggott, **R.** (2000) *Public Health: Policy and Politics* (Basingstoke: Macmillan) A wide-ranging text which examines a range of health issues, such as the environment, food, and alcohol, within an account of the politics of public health.

Gray A. and Payne, **P.** (2001) *World Health and Disease* (Buckingham: Open University Press) This Open University text assembles the evidence about health inequalities and their explanations in two accessible chapters: Chapter 9 on 'Contemporary patterns of disease in the UK' and Chapter 10 on 'Explaining inequalities in health in the UK'. Chapter 6 also includes a useful discussion of explanations for the modern decline in mortality.

Ham, **C.** *Health Policy in Britain* (2009) (London: Palgrave Macmillan) An accessible and enlightening study of health policy and policy-making processes.

Marmot, M. et al. (2010) *Fair Society, Healthy Lives: The Marmot Review*, London: Strategic Review of Health Inequalities in England post-2010. The Marmot Review provides a deeply informed and forthright account of health inequalities and the policies to reduce them.

Thorlby, R. and Maybin, J. (eds) (2010) *A High-Performing NHS? A review of progress 1997–2010* (London: the King's Fund). This provides an assessment of NHS achievements under New Labour governments.

Webster, **C.** (1998) *The National Health Service: A Political History* (Oxford: Oxford University Press) An accessible account of the history of the NHS, which covers its implementation and its first fifty years.

Wilkinson, R. and Pickett, K. (2010) *The Spirit Level: Why Equality is Better for Everyone* (London: Penguin Books) This offers a deeply thoughtful, impressive, and readable discussion of equality and health in an international context.

USEFUL WEBSITES

Department of Health: **www.doh.gov.uk**

The King's Fund: **www.kingsfund.org.uk**

National Health Service: **www.nhs.uk**

National Statistics: **www.statistics.gov.uk**

Office for Health Economics: **www.ohe.org.uk**

Organisation for Economic Co-operation and Development (OECD): **www1.oecd.orga/els/health/sof**

World Health Organization (WHO): **www3.who.int/whosis**

Q ESSAY QUESTIONS

1 How can we best understand health inequalities in Britain?

2 How universal was the service introduced in Britain in 1948?

3 How successful have been various challenges to the dominance of medicine in the NHS?

4 Can the NHS provide comprehensive care?

5 What has been the impact of private finance on the NHS?

6 What is the 'internal market' in the NHS?

7 Do other countries have better alternatives to an NHS on universal principles?

@ ONLINE RESOURCE CENTRE

For additional material and resources, please visit the Online Resource Centre at:
www.oxfordtextbooks.co.uk/orc/baldock4e/.

13

Social care

Kezia Scales and Justine Schneider

Contents

Introduction

Most people depend on some level of social care during their adult lives, whether they require assistance after an accident or illness, support for managing a long-term disability, or care in older age. Traditionally, this type of care has been provided by the family and community. In modern welfare systems, however, the organization and delivery of social care have become important policy issues. Considerable variation can be seen across countries regarding how social care is funded, who is eligible for care, and what types of care are provided by whom.

The main recipients of social care are frail older people, physically disabled people, people with mental health problems, and people with learning disabilities. Social care can also refer to services for groups who are covered elsewhere in this book, including children and young people who require state care or protection, young offenders, and ex-offenders in the community. Social care may be provided by the state, by the independent sector, which includes private, voluntary, and not-for-profit agencies, or as informal care by families, neighbours, and friends. It can be delivered in institutional settings such as residential homes, in community facilities such as day centres, or as domiciliary care in individuals' homes.

This chapter outlines the history of social care, discusses recent policy developments, describes the issues which are specific to the main client groups, and explores the different ways that social care is delivered. Throughout the discussion, we introduce key themes in social care policy as well as highlighting cross-cutting issues of demographic change, gender, and social stigma. The focus of this chapter is social care in England, with reference to contrasting examples from the United Kingdom and other welfare states.

Learning outcomes

After reading this chapter you should be ready to:

1 describe the main policy developments in social care since 1948;

2 understand changing perceptions about disability, mental health, and older age, and how these are reflected in policy;

3 discuss the contested boundary between health and social care;

4 understand the impact of social and population change on policy options;

5 critically assess the role of service users and carers in policy and practice development;

6 identify where to find relevant policy documents and further information about social care in England.

Delivering social care in the twentieth and twenty-first centuries

Contemporary social care policy is designed to address the physical and mental health needs and social inclusion of diverse groups through a range of programmes and services. In practice, social care policy can be hard to define as it overlaps considerably with healthcare, housing, transport, and other policy fields. Historically, the development of social care policy in the UK has been characterized by inadequate resourcing, poor-quality services, and stigma towards service users. In recent decades, it has been heavily influenced by the increasing demand for services created by population ageing and demographic change, coupled with decreasing availability of welfare resources due to political and financial pressure. One major theme characterizing the development of social care since the end of the Second World War has been the ongoing revision of the boundary between social care and health policy, leading to a current emphasis on partnership working and joint commissioning. Other broad trends, as we will see in the following sections, have been from institutional to community care, public provision to a mixed economy of care, and paternalism to personalization and choice.

The historical context of social care

Government policy that covers the delivery of social care is also known as 'community care' or 'care in the community'. These terms were once used deliberately to contrast with institutional care in the UK, which derived from the workhouses and poorhouses established under the Poor Laws (see **www.workhouses.org.uk** for a detailed history of the Poor Laws). Recently, however, community care has become synonymous with social care as an umbrella term covering all aspects of non-medical support for people with long-term needs.

The shift towards community care, which was precipitated by scandalous accounts of abuse and neglect in institutional care emerging in the 1950s, was first introduced in the 1962 Hospital Plan. The Hospital Plan emphasized the social and economic advantages of deinstitutionalization, a message which was echoed throughout British policy documents over the next two decades.

The Conservative government which came into power in 1979 stressed that *the family* should be responsible for individual welfare, with the state supplying residual support only to fill major gaps. Associated with this political ideology was the withdrawal of public agencies from service provision in order to save costs. Thus the 1981 White Paper *Growing Older* stated: 'Care *in* the community must increasingly mean care *by* the community' (DHSS 1981: para.1.11). Together, the emphasis on family support and cutbacks in public services contributed to a major overhaul of community care funding and provision in the early 1990s.

The specific trigger for reform was a minor change to social security regulations in 1980 that established a legal entitlement to means-tested assistance with care fees in independent care homes. Between 1978 and 1991, the social security bill for independent sector care homes rose from £6 million to nearly £2 billion per year—a considerable increase in public spending, even allowing for inflation. The Audit Commission (1986) reported that spending cuts and the delayed closure of long-stay hospitals had prompted local authorities to transfer the costs of social care to the social security budget, by placing individuals in residential or nursing care (where their fees were largely covered by social security) rather than paying for their care in the community.

The Audit Commission and other reports prompted the Department of Health to commission a review of public spending on social care in the community. The 1988 Green Paper, *Community Care* (commonly known as the Griffiths Report, after its author), proposed major reforms which reflected the Conservative government's commitment to increasing efficiency through the development of welfare markets. This fed into the 1989 White Paper *Caring for People*, which was followed by the National Health Service and Community Care Act 1990 (Box 13.1). Although the Act itself was relatively thin on community care, detailed policy and practice guidance was also published, constituting a radical reform of the British social care system.

Community care reforms: from institutional care to care management

The reforms gave social service authorities the lead agency role in community care. Care management, rather than direct service provision, was promoted as a new approach which would ensure that resources were used most effectively to meet individuals' needs, while also enhancing choice and self-determination, and encouraging partnership between users, carers, and service providers across sectors (see DH 1991). Shifting the balance of service provision from local authorities to the private and voluntary sectors was criticized as a cost-cutting exercise, however, and prompted warnings about 'welfare for profit' and the 'commercialization of care'.

Contrary to the recommendations of the Griffiths report, no extra public money entered the social care system during the reforms; it was simply transferred from social security (central government) to local authority social service departments (local government). Local authorities were expected to bring the runaway budget for residential and nursing home care under control by establishing eligibility criteria and priority levels for assistance that would balance demand against available resources. In addition, in line with the Conservative government's emphasis on privatization, local authorities were required to spend 85 per cent of the budget transferred from social security on independent sector provision, rather than on local authority residential and home care. In summary, the 1990 Act fundamentally changed the arrangement of social care, with services shifted from institutions to the community, responsibility for service provision transferred from local authorities to independent sector agencies, and funding redirected into a fixed budget administered at the local level.

Although the reform was radical, implementation was slow. The transfer of money from the social security budget to local authorities, which did not start until 1993, was phased in over several years. Local authorities varied in how quickly they devised eligibility criteria, created priorities, and changed social care practice to achieve the desired policy objectives. Three years after the social security budget was first transferred, the Audit Commission (1996) reported that local authorities were still 'spreading their resources too thinly' or 'finding it difficult to refuse services even to the low priority cases' (p.11).

Nonetheless, the reforms eventually took effect. Due to tightened eligibility criteria, the number of people entering residential and nursing home care *and* the provision of home care services fell. The average dependency of those receiving care increased, and lower-level preventive services all but disappeared.

A lasting shift in the balance of service providers towards the independent sector was the other major effect. By 2009, over two-thirds of adult social care jobs (1.21 million jobs) were in the independent sector, with 46 per cent in private agencies and 23 per cent in voluntary organizations. Also, by 2005, the independent sector was providing nearly three-quarters of home care contact hours compared with only 2 per cent in 1992 (CSCI 2008).

Box 13.1 **Main elements of the 1990 community care reforms**

- Local authorities to take lead responsibility for assessing needs and commissioning care services using available resources ('care management').
- Local authorities to make maximum use of the independent sector, stimulating a mixed economy of care.
- Social security funding transferred to local authorities to support costs of residential and nursing home care within a fixed budget.

Enduring issues: beyond the reforms

While transforming UK social care practice and provision, the community care reforms perpetuated rather than resolved several fundamental issues (Lymbery 2009). These issues relate to the system's origins in the Poor Laws, which determined that state support should be means tested rather than free at the point of delivery.

1 *Eligibility*: Variation in eligibility criteria has led to substantial inequalities in access to services across local authorities, an effect known as the postcode lottery (McDaid et al. 2007). In addition, as budgets tighten, local authorities have increasingly restricted eligibility to those with the most acute needs. In 2007, an estimated 74 per cent of local authorities in England and Wales were providing social care only to people with 'substantial' or 'critical' levels of need, though definitions of need varied considerably; and fewer people were receiving home care support in 2006 than in 1997 (CSCI 2008). To address these issues, the government introduced guidance on 'fair access to care services' in 2003. However, after the Audit Commission (2008) reported negligible improvement, this guidance was superseded by the 'whole system approach' (DH 2010b), which requires local authorities to place eligibility decisions in the wider context of all public services so that, where people are not eligible for adult social services, other interventions are made available.

2 *Health versus social care*: The implementation of the NHS and Community Care Act 1990 intensified the division between health and social care, signifying the 'de facto shift in responsibilities away from the health service' for people with long-term needs (Wistow 1995: 86). Since then, the boundary between 'free' NHS continuing care (for those with long-term health needs) and means-tested social care has been subject to ongoing debate and legal challenges. One contentious area has been so-called 'bed blocking', which refers to the delayed discharge of patients who would previously have been discharged directly from NHS hospitals into local authority care. The Community Care (Delayed Discharges) Act 2003 introduced a financial penalty for English local authorities which fail to provide the services needed to ensure timely discharges from acute hospital care. The crux of this issue is coordination (or lack of coordination) between services, which is an ongoing challenge.

3 *Individual payment for care*: The expansion of home ownership initiated by Conservative policies in the 1980s means that more people with modest incomes now enter old age with large capital sums tied up in their property (ONS 2010), and this capital is taken into account when they are assessed to contribute to the costs of their care (through means testing). Having to 'sell the family home' to pay for residential care has been criticized for penalizing those who save for their old age.

'Modernizing social services' under New Labour

When New Labour came to power in 1997 in the UK, the party brought in a discourse of modernization across public services and government departments (Newman et al. 2008). This discourse served rhetorically to justify making changes by casting the 'old way' of doing things as inefficient, unsuccessful, or otherwise inappropriate. Thus the party manifesto for the 1997 election announced that 'community care is in tatters' and committed to reforming the long-term care system (Labour Party 1997), and the new direction for social care was introduced in a White Paper called *Modernising Social Services* the following year (DH 1998a).

The development of social care policy under New Labour saw a major shift towards the personalization of services, designed to improve outcomes for individual service users. Related elements of personalization include flexible, decentralized services which can be tailored to meet individuals' needs; choice between a range of care options; a social care workforce that is trained to support individual service users in choosing their care; and self-directed support, whereby individuals control their own needs assessment and care management.

Self-directed support includes direct payments and individual budgets. Legislated by the Community Care (Direct Payments) Act 1996, which was introduced as a private member's bill backed by disability rights campaigners, direct payments allow individuals to commission their own services from an independent sector agency and/or hire their own staff, rather than being referred into existing services. Direct payments were granted first to younger disabled people and later extended to older people and carers, and it became mandatory for local authorities to offer this option by 2001.

The 2005 Green Paper on adult social care, *Independence, Well-Being and Choice* (DH 2005), introduced individual budgets, which allow service users to choose how and to what extent to manage the explicit amount of funding that is available to meet their assessed needs (Leadbetter et al. 2008). This approach assumes that individuals are the experts on their own needs; that, with appropriate support, they can exercise more control over their own lives; and that this will enhance their social inclusion and overall well-being (Box 13.2).

By 2009, 86,000 adults in England over the age of 18 were receiving direct payments, an increase of 29 per cent from the previous year, while more than 31,000 people had been allocated an individual budget (NHS Information Centre 2010). Recently, the government announced that up to one million adults will be given individual budgets to spend on social care by 2013.

A comparative analysis of direct payments in the four countries of the UK by Riddell and colleagues (2006) identified three barriers to implementation: concern about managing direct payments amongst service users and carers; staff resistance to direct payments; and challenges with the supply of personal assistants (p. 10). Personalization policy has also been criticized for relying on an inadequate evidence base of small-scale research findings and for shifting the burden of risk from the state to individuals, who might not be well-informed or able to exercise as much influence over service quality as large-scale commissioners (Knapp et al. 2001).

Related to the personalization of social services has been increased promotion of user involvement in social care at all levels, from policy development through research and evaluation. Because they were introduced through disabled people's activism, individual budgets are one example of user-led change. The ongoing challenge of user involvement, however, has been to reach a

---

Box 13.2 **Case study of self-directed support**

Elizabeth Brown, who is 69, lives with her husband in an adapted bungalow. She and her husband both have a number of health concerns.

At first, Mrs Brown was reluctant to accept any personal assistance, preferring to rely on her family. After a period in hospital, however, she agreed to have an agency send someone to assist her with self-care tasks in the morning and evening. Then, with help from her social worker, Mrs Brown developed her own comprehensive support plan. Mrs Brown wanted to get the best value for money from her individual budget. She did this by:

- comparison shopping for a smaller, cheaper domiciliary care agency;
- engaging a local gardener at a good rate;
- employing her grandson (at student rates) as her personal assistant for shopping trips;
- hiring another personal assistant to help with household chores;
- finding the best deal on car cleaning.

Mrs Brown can now afford a weekly exercise class as well. She says her individual budget has made her feel more confident and independent as well as improving her relationship with her family.

Further information: www.in-control.org.uk

range of service users rather than only those who are least impaired or most articulate. This means developing specific and appropriate strategies to involve those who have physical or sensory impairments, learning difficulties, experience of mental distress, verbal communication limitations, and/or limited English.

In a review of research findings from the Modernisation of Adult Social Care research programme, Newman et al. (2008) conclude that 'overall, those strands of modernization focused on service user involvement have produced substantial innovation, but the position of users remains one of "now you see them; now you don't". This raises questions about the capacity of service users to influence the future dynamics of social care' (p. 543).

Another plank in New Labour's social care platform was reform of the organizational divide separating health and social care, which has been referred to as a 'Berlin Wall' preventing effective partnership and coordination of services. The most significant policy documents to address this structural problem were the Health Act 1999 and the NHS Plan (DH 2000). The first allowed health and local authorities to pool budgets, delegate commissioning of services to a single lead agency, and integrate service provision. The second encouraged the development of single NHS 'Care Trusts' which would be able to commission and deliver primary and community health and social care, although this route has not proved popular. Only eight Care Trusts have been developed to date, half of which follow the original proposals (Evans and Forbes 2009). The National Service Frameworks, covered later in this chapter, are another example of joint-working initiatives. The Local Government and Public Involvement in Health Act 2007 introduced a statutory duty for health and social care agencies to collaborate in conducting a Joint Strategic Needs Assessment, using the results to plan future services.

Northern Ireland already delivers integrated services through 'Health and Social Service Boards' and Scotland has made significant progress towards partnership. However, a critical analysis suggests that the boundary problem has not been overcome in either country. A review of community care found that 'Northern Ireland still appears to be many years behind in England in terms of achieving the policy aim of providing social services in a community rather than hospital environment wherever possible' (Appleby 2005: 9) and highlighted the problem of social care budgets being spent on acute care. A qualitative comparison between England and Scotland confirmed that structural integration does not necessarily stop acute healthcare from dominating budgets and decision-making (Evans and Forbes 2009). Similar factors appear across these contexts, including the historical primacy of healthcare, scarcity of resources, competing service paradigms (*cure* versus *care*), different accountability mechanisms, and divergent professional affiliations.

Financing long-term care: an ongoing debate

In 1999, a Labour-appointed Royal Commission on long-term care recommended that the state should meet the costs of 'personal care' (encompassing nursing care) for all, regardless of financial means and in private homes as well as long-term care settings. Other aspects of care associated with 'living costs'—such as accommodation or domestic help—would remain the individual's responsibility.

Two of the Commission's members did not agree to the majority report recommendations, however, citing the cost to the public purse and the fact that none of the money would go into the care system. Modest policy developments in England since the Commission suggest that these dissenters' view was more influential. By contrast, Scotland *did* adopt the Royal Commission's majority recommendations. The Community Care and Health (Scotland) Act 2002 requires that free personal care should be available to those aged 65 and over, after an assessment of need by the local authority and irrespective of income, capital, marital status, or level of informal support. However, individuals are still liable for 'hotel costs' including accommodation and everyday living expenses.

In 2006, Sir Derek Wanless (who had already delivered influential reports on the NHS and health) was commissioned to revisit this important issue. The Wanless report, *Securing Good Care for Older People,* proposed a different compromise: a 'partnership model' which would guarantee a basic level of care to everyone while allowing individuals to 'top up' their care through state-matched personal contributions.

Again in 2009, the Green Paper *Shaping the Future of Care Together* (DH 2009a) rekindled the debate on how to provide and pay for long-term care. Following a large consultation process—with input from 70,000 members of the public, carers, and representative organizations—the government then released the *Building the National Care Service* White Paper in 2010 (see Box 13.3 for the options that were considered) (HM Government 2010a). The *National Care Service* proposal was shelved when the coalition government came into power later that year, however. Recommendations from the new government's commission on long-term care are due in 2011.

The debate about how to finance long-term social care can be heard across advanced welfare states, as they face similar demands and constraints (Glendinning and Moran 2009). In most cases, central government plays a lead role in managing resources for social care, which are kept separate from acute health budgets; these arrangements are designed to constrain expenditure. Many countries have also introduced quasi-market mechanisms—with governments, municipalities, or insurance funds commissioning services from the independent sector—but evidence is limited about the extent to which this stimulates competition and offers users a wider range of responsive services. Most systems underpinned by a principle of universal provision have retained that principle; a key exception is Australia, which over the past decade has shifted responsibility for residential care costs from the government to individual users.

In a major overhaul of social care, Germany introduced a system of universal long-term care insurance to replace the means-tested system in 1994. Everyone in paid work is required to contribute. Individuals requiring care can then choose among local services, with priority placed on family care, followed by home-based care, and in the last instance institutional care. Japan has also introduced a mandatory long-term care insurance plan to which everyone over the age of 40 in employment contributes. All those aged 65 and over who are assessed above a minimum level of impairment are eligible for assistance, regardless of income or family situation, although there is currently debate about the inequalities caused by the exclusion of younger people with disabilities.

Box 13.3 Long-term care funding options

The 2009 Green Paper *Shaping the Future of Care Together* considered a number of options for funding long-term care:

1 Pay for Yourself: Each individual is responsible for covering their own basic care costs. The Green Paper ruled this out as fundamentally unfair.

2 Partnership: The state pays a proportion of an individual's basic care and support costs, depending on their means.

3 Insurance: Same as partnership model except individuals can cover additional costs through a voluntary (private or state-run) insurance scheme. Those paying into the scheme receive all basic care and support free.

4 Comprehensive: Everyone over retirement age with sufficient resources is required to pay into a state insurance scheme, based on income, and basic care and support are free.

5 Tax funded: Care is funded through taxes and provided free, like the NHS. The Green Paper also ruled this out for the 'heavy burden' placed on people of working age.

Source: *Community Care* 2009

Adult social care: looking ahead

The coalition government which came into power in 2010 claimed the 'urgency of reforming the system of social care to provide much more control to individuals and their carers, and to ease the cost burden that they and their families face' (Coalition Government 2010). The new government's stated programme includes:

- strengthening the personalization of services, primarily through individual budgets;
- establishing a commission on long-term care;
- breaking down barriers between health and social care.

On the surface, these priorities do not suggest a substantial departure from the policies pursued during the last 15 years in the UK except that a massive reduction of public sector provision is planned. The government's emphasis on the 'Big Society' rather than state support (Box 13.4) signals a new era of welfare reform which will undoubtedly impact social care. Targets for the level of provision by independent sector agencies will likely be introduced, and the new *Equity and Excellence* White Paper (DH 2010a) clearly defines the NHS as the 'senior partner' in health and social care partnership-building. It remains to be seen how these developments interact with demographic changes and funding realities to define the experiences of individuals receiving social care.

Questions for the future include:

- How will successive governments resolve the structural tensions between healthcare and social services?
- How will different welfare states meet the challenge of providing long-term care for growing numbers of older people in generations to come?

Box 13.4 **'Big Society' and social care: the Southwark Circle example**

What will social care look like in the 'Big Society' promoted by the new coalition government (see Chapter 3)?

Given the significant cuts across the welfare budget, the Big Society may simply rely on higher levels of 'compulsory altruism' by family members and other volunteer caregivers to fill gaps in social care provision (Daly and Lewis 2000).

But proponents of the Big Society highlight instead the contribution of new social enterprises such as the Southwark Circle. Designed in cooperation with older people and their families, the Southwark Circle is a membership organization that provides practical support to older people. Members buy £10 tokens which can be used to 'purchase' assistance from registered 'Neighbourhood Helpers'.

The model reflects the Big Society vision in several ways:

- It harnesses older people's capacity to contribute (as 'Helpers') as well as benefit from services;
- As well as meeting specific care needs, it serves as an intergenerational social network that members can draw on for information, recommendations, and social inclusion—thereby contributing to overall well-being and quality of life;
- The model is designed to become financially self-sustaining within three years.

Since the 2009 inception of the Southwark Circle, which now comprises 300 members, two more Circles are under way and nine are in planning.

Further information: **www.southwarkcircle.org.uk.**

● Will the commitment to personalization yield genuine choice and better outcomes for individual users? Will authentic user involvement be achieved?
● How will the expansion of the mixed economy of social care affect the quality of services and who obtains them?

Mental health problems and social care

Definitions and numbers

It is estimated that one in four people will experience some form of mental health problem in their lifetime, which amounts to approximately 450 million people worldwide (WHO 2001). Mental health problems represent five out of the 10 leading causes of disability worldwide, ranking first among ill-nesses that cause disability in the United States, Canada, and Western Europe, and are estimated to cost the English economy alone at least £77 billion every year. Depending on the type and severity of symptoms, mental health problems can affect people's interaction with their social environment, including their relationships, their employment and economic circumstances, their housing, and their quality of life. These broad implications render mental health an issue for social care as well as health policy.

Mental health problems can include anxiety, mood disorders including depression and bipolar disorder, and psychotic disorders such as schizophrenia. All of these may be transient, recurrent, or chronic. There are also degenerative brain disorders collectively known as dementia which mainly affect older people; these are known as 'organic' disorders because they are associated with observable changes in the brain. Dementia affects one in 20 people over the age of 65 and one in five over the age of 80, which will amount to an estimated 115 million people worldwide by 2050 (Alzheimer's Disease International 2010).

Substance misuse, which is the use of alcohol or illicit drugs that injures the user or others, is commonly regarded as a mental health issue and often co-diagnosed with other mental disorders. Although treatment is conventionally led by psychiatric services, health professionals may have an ambivalent attitude towards substance misuse because it 'occurs typically in people who are deemed to be sane' (Pilgrim 2005: 37). Government policy in the past decade suggests a shift away from the medicalization of substance abuse, particularly with regard to alcohol, and toward a broader public health response (Prime Minister's Strategy Unit 2004, 2007).

A good resource for information about mental health in England is the Adult Psychiatric Morbidity Survey series (Table 13.1). Conducted in 1993, 2000, and 2007, the survey is designed to estimate the prevalence of mental health problems according to diagnostic category among

Table 13.1 Prevalence of selected disorders in adults aged 16 and over, according to the Adult Psychiatric Morbidity Survey 2007

Disorder	Total
Depression/anxiety	15.1%
Psychosis	0.4%
Antisocial personality disorder	0.3% (aged 18 and over)
Borderline personality disorder	0.4%
Attention deficit hyperactivity disorder	8.2%
Alcohol dependence	5.8%
Drug dependence	3.4%

Cartoon 13.1

Source: *Private Eye* 'Care home horror' by Colin Wheeler – issue 1260, p.27

individuals aged 16 and over, and yields considerable insight into the associations between gender, age, ethnicity, social factors, and mental health.

Challenging institutional care

At its inception in 1948, over half the inpatient beds in the NHS belonged to psychiatry. Since 1955, when the number of mental hospital beds peaked at 150,000, that number has declined to less than 28,000 (Green 2009). This trend towards deinstitutionalization was underpinned by a number of key factors.

First, public confidence in the treatability of mental illness increased with the discovery of psychotropic medications which treated the recognizable symptoms of psychosis. Introduced in the 1950s, and in widespread use by the 1970s, these medications meant that custodial care was not considered essential for risk management, allowing more people to be treated outside hospital settings.

Another influence was the anti-psychiatry movement, beginning in the 1960s, which held that mental illness is a social construct and critiqued the inhumane treatment of mental patients in institutions. This movement developed against a backdrop of broader civil rights activism across Western society. Influential figures in the movement include David Cooper (*Psychiatry*

mikewiliams.

"OH, THANK GOODNESS YOU'VE ARRIVED, I'D NEARLY
OUTLIVED MY SAVINGS!."

Cartoon 13.2

and Anti-Psychiatry, 1967); Thomas Szasz (*The Myth of Mental Illness*, 1961); and Ronnie Laing (*The Divided Self*, 1960). The movement was also influenced by Foucault (1961), who made the link between institutional care and social control, and Irving Goffman's (1961) work on the effects of institutionalization. In one of the movement's clearest achievements, radical psychiatrist Franco Basaglia and supporters successfully campaigned for the passing of 'Law 180' in Italy in 1978, which prevented new admissions to existing mental hospitals. Italy has been critiqued recently for inadequate mental health service provision in the community and over-reliance on family care, however (McDaid et al. 2007)—perhaps an unintended consequence of Basaglia's reform.

The shift towards community-based treatment has increased the number of people living in group homes and other forms of supported accommodation and has prompted the formation of community mental health teams. These teams typically contain community psychiatric nurses working together with social workers, occupational therapists, psychologists, and psychiatrists. Such multidisciplinary teams have become a common organizational feature of community mental health provision, although a recent Cochrane Review found an 'insubstantial' evidence base for their effectiveness (Malone et al. 2007).

Public safety and policy panic

Beginning in the late 1980s, a series of high-profile violent episodes involving people with mental health problems rekindled fears about mental illness in the community. In 1988, a former patient fatally stabbed Isabel Schwarz, a hospital social worker. The homicide inquiry highlighted the lack of coordinated support for discharged mental health patients (DHSS 1988) and resulted in the 1991 implementation of the Care Programme Approach (CPA). The CPA requires health authorities to collaborate with social services departments and family carers to ensure that people with mental health problems receive appropriate levels of support in the community. Central elements of the CPA include: a named key worker (or care coordinator) for each person; consultation between all agencies involved in that person's care; comprehensive needs assessment; and a care plan that is regularly reviewed.

Three years later, discharged patient Christopher Clunis fatally stabbed a stranger in the London Underground. The inquiry concluded that Jonathan Zito died because Clunis's care and treatment were a 'catalogue of failure and missed opportunity', and held that the CPA systems were inactive or ineffective, with poor coordination and communication between agencies (Ritchie 1994). The inquiry's recommendations set the tone for mental health policy over the following years, focusing on:

- the needs of the most 'dangerous' patients;
- accountability of providers;
- coordination between agencies;
- consistency of provision across the country.

An initial government response was to create supervision registers in 1994, later known as CPA registers. People considered 'at risk of harming themselves or other people' could be placed on a register in order to ensure that they remained under the supervision of the mental health services. Later, the Mental Health (Patients in the Community) Act 1995 extended the scope of healthcare providers' authority over the aftercare of people discharged from hospital. In both cases, the Royal College of Psychiatrists and others expressed concerns about the implications for patients' civil liberties.

Prevailing fears about public safety were reflected in the first strategy for mental health services released by the Labour government, *Modernising Mental Health Services: Safe, Sound and Supportive* (DH 1998b). This White Paper heralded the introduction of the National Service Framework (NSF) for mental health, which established evidence-based national standards, guidelines for developing services, and targets for attainment within set timescales (DH 1999b). The NSF represents a milestone in service development.

Ten years on, annual investment in specialist mental health services in England had increased by over £1.5 billion. The NSF for mental health was updated in 2009 by the policy document *New Horizons* (HM Government 2009), a cross-government programme of action with twin aims to improve the mental health and well-being of the population and improve the quality and accessibility of services for people with poor mental health.

Mental health and human rights

Debate about public safety versus patient rights came to the fore again through the process of reforming the Mental Health Act 1983 in England and Wales. The first draft Mental Health Bill published in 2002 contained provisions for compulsory medication and the possibility of detaining 'dangerous' people with severe personality disorders even if they had not committed a crime. The Royal College of Psychiatrists formed an alliance with voluntary organizations to oppose this overt use of psychiatry as social control. After a second bill also met opposition, the government released a new bill in 2007 which largely left the existing Mental Health Act in place. The Mental Health Alliance claimed this would 'go down in history as a missed opportunity', as it failed to modernize mental health law or promote equality for people with mental health problems (Mental Health Alliance 2007). So far, the revised Mental Health Act has been challenged on several occasions for its compatibility with the Human Rights Act 1998, which enshrines the rights set out in the European Convention on Human Rights into domestic law in England (see MacGregor-Morris et al. 2001).

Another influential piece of legislation is the Mental Capacity Act 2005, which is based on the premise that a person has capacity to make a particular decision unless it is 'proven' that they have sufficient impairment of mental functioning. It is estimated that over two million people in England and Wales lack such capacity, including people with mental health problems, dementia, learning disabilities, or brain injuries. The Act is designed to ensure that a systematic assessment is carried out and that all practicable steps are taken to support a vulnerable person make a decision on their own. When this is impossible, the Act empowers clinicians to make a specific decision on behalf of that person, provided that it is taken in their best interests and that the outcome represents the least restrictive alternative.

An individual's experience receiving social care services may be determined by these important pieces of legislation but is often also influenced by stigmatizing attitudes towards mental illness, which can be perpetuated by staff and professionals as well as members of the general public. Recognition of the magnitude of this stigma has increased in recent years (see Bell and Lindley 2005). Recent anti-stigma campaigns dovetail with early signs of a paradigm shift in the treatment of mental health problems towards the recovery approach (Box 13.5).

Box 13.5 **The recovery approach**

Rather than expecting a 'cure' for mental health problems, the recovery approach focuses on each individual's capacity to build a meaningful life and attain goals regardless of their diagnosis or symptoms (Anthony 2000).

Components of the recovery process include:

1 finding and maintaining hope;

2 re-establishing a positive identity;

3 building a meaningful life;

4 taking responsibility and control.

(From Andresen et al. 2003)

This approach provides a 'new rationale for mental health services' (Shepherd et al. 2008), prioritizing self-determination, social inclusion, and overall health and well-being as well as clinical care. It has been adopted as the organizing principle for mental health services in a number of countries, including New Zealand, parts of the United States, and Australia, as well as in Ireland and Scotland. It was also endorsed in the UK in a position paper released jointly by the Care Services Improvement Partnership, the Royal College of Psychiatrists, and the Social Care Institute for Excellence (2007).

The recovery approach has largely been applied in adult mental health services, but is also relevant to substance misuse, brain disorders, and long-term physical health problems including diabetes, asthma, and cardiac disease.

Learning disability

Definitions and numbers

Learning disability refers to the condition of people whose educational, social, and emotional development is markedly slower than that of others of the same age. The delay may be evident from birth and is often due to congenital anomalies. Learning disability was formerly labelled 'mental handicap'; other terms include mental retardation, intellectual disability, developmental disability, and intellectual impairment. The language used to refer to learning disability often reflects the speaker's ideological position, attitude, and understanding. The first national survey of adults with learning disabilities in England, released in 2005, found that respondents themselves preferred the term 'learning difficulties' (Emerson et al. 2005).

Learning disability is a permanent condition. As adults, people with learning disabilities may lack the skills to lead fully independent lives and they may be vulnerable to abuse or exploitation, which is why social care agencies become involved. Approximately two per cent of the population are affected by some degree of learning disability, although it is estimated that only one in five affected people is known to social services (Emerson and Hatton 2004). The number of people with learning disabilities in England is expected to increase by 11 per cent between 2001 and 2021 to more than a million, while the number of adults over the age of 60 with learning disabilities is expected to increase by 36 per cent (ibid.). Factors for this increase include longer life expectancy and a sharp rise in the reported numbers of children with autism. There is extensive evidence that people with learning disabilities, possibly the most devalued and stigmatized of social care recipients, experience significantly poorer health outcomes, educational and work experiences, socio-economic status, and social inclusion (see for example, Emerson et al. 2005).

Deinstitutionalization, normalization, and beyond

Throughout history, people with learning disabilities have frequently been victims of neglect and abuse. Industrialization brought social changes which reduced the ability of families and communities to support their members with learning disabilities and, like those with mental health problems, they were crowded for life into asylums (which later became 'mental handicap hospitals' under the NHS). Many people with learning disabilities in institutional care had no choice about how they wished to live. The sexes were segregated, patients wore communal clothing or uniforms, and they slept, ate, and bathed according to a rigid timetable. They were also vulnerable to the harmful effects of institutionalization, by which people who are subjected to oppressive organizational regimes can become disempowered, passive, compliant, and even grateful for the apparent security suggested by a lack of choice.

In line with developments in other countries and in response to reports of poor care standards, *Better Services for the Mentally Handicapped* (DHSS 1971) marked the beginning of the deinstitutionalization movement for people with learning disabilities in Britain. The main objectives of the White Paper included:

- coordinating health and social services for people with learning disabilities;
- shifting responsibility for residential care from health to local authorities;
- increasing training provision for people with learning disability.

Then, in 1979, a Committee of Inquiry into Mental Handicap Nursing and Care (known as the Jay Report) recommended that mental handicap nursing be reincorporated as a social profession rather than a separate branch of nursing, to reflect the trend towards care in the community. The report also criticized large institutional forms of care, stating that 'mentally handicapped people have a right to enjoy *normal patterns of life* in the community' (DH 1979).

Normalization (Nirje 1970) and social role valorization (Wolfensberger 1972) were two linked concepts around which proponents of deinstitutionalization rallied in the 1970s and 1980s and which remain influential today. Normalization stresses that people with learning disabilities should enjoy the same range of everyday experiences as other people, from family life through education, sexual relationships, employment, and independent living. Social role valorization, a concept developed in response to the stigma and segregation that prevent normalization, stresses the importance of recognizing the positive contribution that individuals with learning disabilities make to community life. O'Brien (1989) operationalized these concepts in terms of five goals for service delivery, which represent what is required to offer 'normal' opportunities for living, work, and personal relationships to individuals with learning disabilities (Box 13.6).

Valuing people

Influenced by an increasingly vocal disability rights movement (see Brown and Smith 1989), the changes initiated in 1971 developed over time into a more individualized approach towards people with learning disabilities. This approach was enshrined in the 2001 White Paper *Valuing People* (DH 2001b), which establishes four explicit principles for learning disability services:

1 ensuring civil and legal rights of people with learning disabilities;
2 promoting independence rather than dependence;
3 giving people choices about how to live their lives;
4 supporting inclusion in mainstream services and the local community.

The White Paper set out 11 national objectives which were designed to provide a clear direction for local services and increase equity across localities (Box 13.7). A Learning Disability Task Force and Implementation Support Teams were set up at national level, with Learning Disability Partnership Boards to monitor progress at the local level.

Valuing People advocated person-centred planning, a more individualized approach designed to combat problems of disempowerment and social exclusion. Evaluations undertaken by the Institute for Health Research, however, have shown considerable inequalities in the extent to which individuals are likely to receive a person-centred plan and, if they do, the level of benefits they receive, due

---

Box 13.6 **Normalization and social role valorization: service goals**

1 Relationships: Assisting people with disabilities to form and maintain the variety of ties and connections that constitute community life.

2 Contributing to the community: Assisting people to discover and express their gifts and capacities and to develop new skills.

3 Making choices: Assisting people to increase control over their own lives, including by setting goals that are personally meaningful, expressing personal preferences, and managing their assistance.

4 Dignity: Assisting people to experience the dignity and status associated with positively regarded activities, and to be recognized as good neighbours, classmates, friends, home owners, wage earners, and citizens.

5 Community presence: Assisting people to share the ordinary places and activities of community life.

Source: O'Brien 1989

Box 13.7 *Valuing People* objectives

1 Maximizing opportunities for disabled children;

2 Supporting the transition into adult life;

3 Enabling people to have more control over their own lives;

4 Supporting carers;

5 Improving healthcare for people with learning disabilities;

6 Promoting choice and control over housing;

7 Enhancing opportunities to lead fulfilling and purposeful lives;

8 Improving access to employment;

9 Developing high-quality services which promote good outcomes and best value;

10 Strengthening workforce training and planning;

11 Partnership-working between all relevant local agencies.

Source: Department of Health 2001b

---

to individual characteristics and contextual factors (see Robertson et al. 2005, 2007). The White Paper also promoted the involvement of service users in every stage of policy-making, including decision-making, policy development, and evaluation. Although updated in 2009 (DH 2009b), the future of the *Valuing People* programme is uncertain, as it is one of the social programmes slated for review by the Department of Health under the new coalition government.

Choice versus protection?

In contrast to the trend towards increased personalization in social care, a movement to *protect vulnerable adults* has developed in response to evidence that abuse in hospital and community settings remains a significant problem (see the Cornwall example: CSCI and HC 2006). Led by voluntary sector organizations and legal advocates, this movement contributed to the release of the *No Secrets* guidance (DH and Home Office 2000), which put adult protection explicitly on the social care agenda. This was followed in 2004 by the introduction of the Protection of Vulnerable Adults list, which is a national database of people considered unsuitable to work with vulnerable adults.

Now the challenge is to bring together these parallel agendas of choice and protection, in order to promote independence while also recognizing that people with considerable support needs are at risk of exploitation and abuse unless adequately protected. As Fyson and Kitson (2007) note, in the era of personalization it is important to remember 'the possibility that choice and independence are not the only indicators of quality of life' (p. 433).

Adults with physical disability

Definitions and numbers

The causes of physical impairments are diverse and can include:

- conditions that affect a person from birth (e.g. cerebral palsy or spina bifida) or that develop during childhood (e.g. juvenile arthritis);
- accidents or acute illness (e.g. spinal injury, head injury, or the effects of meningitis);

- conditions that develop in adulthood (e.g. multiple sclerosis or Parkinson's disease);
- chronic conditions associated with ageing (e.g. osteoarthritis or heart disease).

Approximately 50 million EU citizens and 650 million people worldwide are living with disabilities. In the UK, the Labour Force Survey estimates that 14 per cent of the working population is disabled, though the incidence rises to 33 per cent for those between 50 and 65 years of age (ONS 2005). In the 2001 Census, one in six people in the UK (10.3 million) living in a private household reported having a disability or 'limiting long-term illness' (ONS 2006). In all cases, these statistics are imprecise because they reflect the numbers of people with mental health problems and learning disability as well as physical impairments.

The first surveys of disability in Great Britain, carried out in 1985 to 1988 by the Office of Population Censuses and Surveys (now the Office for National Statistics), provided detail about type and severity of disability in the population. These surveys had extensive policy impact, for example by directly influencing the introduction of the Disability Living Allowance and the Disability Working Allowance. In future, our understanding of disability will be enhanced by the release of findings from the Longitudinal Life Opportunities Survey, a major new national survey conducted by the Office for Disability Issues (2009a).

A social model of disability

Disability can be conceptualized in various ways, with considerably different implications for policy development and delivery. Two influential models are the medical model of disability and the social model of disability (Box 13.8). The traditional medical model suggests that physical and mental impairments are disabling factors which must be overcome in order for people to participate fully in society. Policy efforts emphasize medical treatment and rehabilitation, along with targeted welfare benefits and service provision for people with disabilities. The social model of disability, by contrast, holds that *social barriers* exclude people with impairments from mainstream society. Such barriers include inaccessible buildings and services; social attitudes such as stereotyping and discrimination; and organizational procedures and practices. Policy efforts stemming from this model emphasize facilitation via support services and an accessible environment.

There has been considerable debate around these models of disability. Whether disability is viewed from a medical or social perspective, however, the prevalence of direct and indirect discrimination against disabled people and resulting social inequality are indisputable. Physical impairment is associated with low levels of employment and income, reduced educational and training opportunities, inadequate housing, and limited access to mainstream facilities and transport systems.

From 'care' to rights

Historically, both disability and age-related frailty were seen as causes of poverty rather than special issues requiring targeted policies. Up until the Second World War, physically disabled people remained at home or were subject to Poor Law provision. After the National Assistance Act was passed in 1948, disabled people continued to be admitted to long-stay care, either in the old workhouses, residential homes intended for older people, or establishments run by the voluntary sector. Local authorities were given the power in 1948 to develop domiciliary services for people with physical or sensory impairments, but this was mandatory only for blind people. It was not until the Chronically Sick and Disabled Persons' Act 1970 that local authorities were obliged to assess the needs of everyone with a disability in their catchment area.

By the 1970s, disabled people had begun campaigning for the right to organize their own housing and assistance outside long-stay hospital settings. The creation in 1972 of the Union of the Physically Impaired Against Segregation (UPIAS) 'marked a turning point in understanding the meaning of disability. This was because for the first time in this country an organization controlled by

Box 13.8 **Impairment and disability**

For many years, disabled people and their organizations have challenged the medical model's assumption that *impairment* is the cause of *disability*. Instead they have argued that social barriers cause disability, by preventing people with impairments from fully integrating into mainstream society.

- Impairment = an injury, illness, or congenital condition that causes or is likely to cause a long-term effect on appearance and/or limitation of function of an individual.
- Disability = the loss or limitation of opportunities to take part in society on an equal level with others due to social and environmental barriers (Office for Disability 2009b).

The following vignettes help illustrate this distinction:

1 A student with cerebral palsy uses a wheelchair. In the supermarket, she cannot reach the top shelf to select her preferred breakfast cereal.
What is preventing her from doing her shopping?

2 A middle-aged man with heart disease can no longer carry out the hard physical work involved in his job. He loses his job and becomes dependent on social security payments.
What is preventing him from working?

3 A young man with multiple sclerosis struggles to help his toddler dress in the morning. His partner replaces all the buttons on the child's clothes with Velcro tape.
Is he less disabled because of his partner's action?

A medical model of disability would say that the student's physical impairment prevented her from doing her shopping, and that heart disease caused the middle-aged man to stop working. A social model, on the other hand, would suggest that the layout of the supermarket disabled the student and that the man stopped working because he did not have the opportunity to retrain for a less physically demanding job. The third example shows how the organization of society can be altered so that an impairment does not become disabling, as a minor modification enables the young man to continue his parenting activities.

disabled people published the view that segregated facilities were a symptom of oppression' (Finklestein 1993: 36). A decade later, the British Council of Organisations of Disabled People (now the UK Disabled People's Council) began campaigning nationally for disabled people's rights to full citizenship and social inclusion.

A more 'rights-based' approach to disability policy took shape in the Disabled People (Services, Consultation and Representation) Act 1986, introduced by a private member's bill, which reinforced and extended local authority duties in relation to disabled people and provided additional rights of representation. However, a review of progress in 1990 showed that only some local authorities had invested money in service development and, overall, disabled people remained a low policy priority compared to other groups (such as children).

Sustained campaigning by the disability rights movement has significantly influenced further developments in disability policy since the 1990 community care reforms. The Disability Discrimination Act 1995, which enshrined the notion of disability rights, was amended in 2005 to include additional groups of people and organizations. Particularly important for protecting disability rights in health and social care, which were not covered by preceding disability legislation, has been the passing of the Human Rights Act 1998 (HRA). Limited progress has been made so far in adopting a human rights strategy in public services, with less than half of local authorities having done so by 2003 (Audit Commission 2003); however, the Commission for Equality and Human Rights (CEHR), which was formed in 2007 to support public authorities in complying with the HRA, may add further impetus. The CEHR brings together three former commissions: the Disability Rights Commission, Commission for Racial Equality, and Equal Opportunities Commission.

On an international scale, the passing in 2008 of the United Nations Convention on the Rights of Persons with Disability has significant implications for social care. The purpose of the Convention is to 'promote, protect and ensure the full and equal enjoyment of all human rights and fundamental freedoms by all persons with disabilities, and to promote respect for their inherent dignity' (UN 2008), and it reflects international recognition that existing human rights treaties have failed to fully protect people with disabilities. Notably, Article 19 sets out the right of disabled people to live in the community. This positive right requires the provision of 'a range of in-home, residential and other community support services, including personal assistance necessary to support living and inclusion in the community, and to prevent isolation or segregation from the community'. This places clear expectations on social care services.

The implementation of direct payments and individual budgets in the UK, which was initially driven by the disability lobby, has the potential to impact immediately on many disabled people's lives. However, as suggested by Article 19 of the UN Convention, cash disbursements may not be enough in themselves—but rather must be seen as part of a network of support and assistance which facilitates independent living in the community.

Older people

Definitions and numbers

Despite common perceptions about ageing, the majority of older people live independently and do not rely on social care. However, it is true that people are more likely to develop physical or mental problems as they age, which means that older people use a higher *proportion* of social care services. In the UK, older people constitute 72 per cent of all social care clients and account for 42 per cent of social care spending (NHS Information Centre 2010). As an example of older people's social care needs, the General Household Survey estimates that 18 per cent of people aged 65 and over living in private households in Great Britain require assistance with at least one activity of daily living (ADL), such as personal care. For those over 85, the proportion increases to almost 40 per cent.

There are currently nearly 12 million people aged over 65 in the UK, which is almost one in five people, and this number is expected to rise to almost 15.8 million by 2031 (Age UK 2010). Other mature welfare states are facing similar or even greater population changes. Help Age International (2010) estimates that worldwide almost one in 10 people are over 60 years old, but by 2050 this ratio is expected to shrink to one in five people. The number of Americans aged 65 and older is projected to be 20.2 per cent by 2050, up from 13 per cent in 2010. Most dramatically, Japan's elderly population is expected to reach 26 per cent of the total population by 2015 (33.8 million)—which means that one in four Japanese people will be 65 or older—and 40.5 per cent by 2055 (36.4 million).

Among those aged over 60, the fastest growing population is that of the 'oldest old', those aged 80 or over. Today, people in this age bracket account for about one in every eight older people but this ratio is expected to increase to approximately two people among every ten by 2050 (UNESA 2007). In the UK, the number of oldest old is projected to reach 3.5 million by 2034, accounting for five per cent of the total population (ONS 2010).

The implications of population ageing can be understood in terms of the support ratio, which is the number of people of working age per person of pension age. The support ratio is affected not only by the growing number of older people but also by falling birth rates, which reduce the absolute and relative sizes of the younger population. The support ratio in the UK is predicted to fall from

3.2 people of working age for each pensioner in 2008 to 2.9 by 2051; without scheduled increases in the state pension age, it could fall as far as 2.0 (ONS 2010).

What does population ageing mean for quality of life in older age? Are we *enjoying* our increased life expectancy, or are we suffering more years of frailty, disability, and ill health? The EU's Healthy Life Years indicator, also known as disability-free life expectancy, has been developed to measure the number of years people might expect to live in a state of good health. Overall, it appears that life expectancy without severe disability has increased at roughly the same rate as life expectancy; in other words, people are as severely disabled (or not) for as long as they have always been, but the age of disability onset is later. There is some variation, however. In 2006, British men at age 65 had 17.2 years of actual life expectancy and 12.9 years of healthy life expectancy, compared with 19.9 years and 14.5 years respectively for British women—but the increases in healthy life expectancy at age 65 from 1981 were *smaller* than increases in actual life expectancy (ONS 2010).

Difference, social change, and older age

These broad figures about age and disability mask considerable variation between different groups. Poor economic circumstances can lead to poorer health outcomes in older age as well as reducing life expectancy; for example, recent figures show that a man living in one of the most deprived areas in Scotland can expect to live in good health for 10.5 years less than the average man in Scotland (Scottish Government 2010). Some minority ethnic groups may experience the biological effects of older age at a younger chronological age than majority groups (or may fail to access the care which would delay onset), and women experience higher levels of disability in older age than men. Also, especially in countries which rely on a means-tested system to underwrite the costs of care, financial circumstances in older age can affect the amount and quality of social care available. This also interacts with gender and ethnicity.

When considering the need for and supply of social care, another important difference between older people is marital status as it interacts with gender. The current generation of older people are 'very married': they experienced a high rate of marriage and, until the law changed in the 1960s, had very little chance of obtaining a divorce. As a result, husbands and wives currently provide the main source of support for each other. However, because women tend to marry older men and men die at a younger average age than women, married women are more likely to experience widowhood and therefore more likely to live alone in older age. Among women over the age of 85 living in private households in 2001 in the UK, 71 per cent lived alone compared to only 42 per cent of men of the same age (ONS 2004). This difference helps explain why older women are more likely to be in residential or nursing home care than older men.

Those with and without children will also have different social care needs, because children are the next most important source of support for older people (after spouses). However, in Britain and many other countries, changing population and family structures suggest that significantly fewer people in future generations may be able to rely on their children for support, as seen in the 'Informal care' section.

From cash to care—and back again

In the past, most older people worked for as long as they were able and then became dependent on family support or subject to the Poor Laws. The introduction of a state pension in 1908 reduced the poverty associated with older age for some people, but others still ended their lives in the workhouse. At the beginning of the Second World War, some 25,000 older people were still in general mixed workhouses or Public Assistance Institutions (Parker 1972) which, after the National Assistance Act 1948, were incorporated wholesale into residential homes provided by local authorities.

Policy from the 1940s to the 1970s continued what Means et al. (2008) call 'the long history of neglect' of older people. Social care services in the community were slow to develop; indeed, until the late 1960s, local authorities were legally prohibited from providing certain services in the community, such as meals on wheels or chiropody. Not until the National Health Service Act 1977 did it become mandatory rather than discretionary for local authorities to provide home care services.

Within the past three decades, older people have become more visible, if intermittently, on the policy agenda. First came the 1981 White Paper, *Growing Older*, which promoted informal care in the community as the only solution to concerns about the costs of an ageing population. Two decades later, the National Service Framework (NSF) for older people brought a national focus back to the needs of older people in health and social care (DH 2001a). This NSF set out eight standards that cover the range of care older people might need, stressing that care should be personalized, preventive, and community based to the extent possible.

Recent evidence, including a review of progress towards the NSF standards (Healthcare Commission 2006), has shown that social services for older people still require considerable improvement. Despite ongoing emphasis on care in the community, the number of older people receiving care in their own homes has almost halved since 1994 as resources have become focused on those most in need (Palmer et al. 2005). Some people with low to moderate needs have had to make do without public support, and others have ended up in hospital or residential care due to inconsistent availability of appropriate community-based services. There has also been ongoing debate about the fairness of the current means-tested system.

Given these concerns, the government commissioned a review of long-term care for older people, as mentioned above (Wanless 2006). Finding that almost 60 per cent of the social services budget for the elderly went to providing residential home placements, the Wanless report recommended the use of individual budgets. According to the principles behind self-directed support, if older people are

Box 13.9 **Dementia: whose problem?**

According to Alzheimer's Disease International (2010), an estimated 35.6 million people around the world currently have dementia, and this number is expected to more than double by 2030. Britain alone may see a million people living with dementia within a generation. Already, the global cost of dementia is almost £400 billion, but this figure is expected to increase by up to 85 per cent within the next two decades.

Dementia is a progressive degenerative brain disorder which affects memory, cognition, behaviour, and emotion. Treatment options are limited and, in advanced stages, individuals with dementia will require assistance with all aspects of daily life—often for years.

The symptoms of dementia are managed largely by social care but, particularly as the majority of those with dementia are older people, healthcare is often required for concurrent medical problems. In care homes, those with advanced dementia depend on higher levels of assistance than many other residents.

For these reasons, dementia exemplifies the challenge of allocating the costs of chronic care across the health sector, social services, and the community. Is it possible (and useful) to distinguish between the health and social care needs of someone with advanced dementia? How much should people with dementia be expected to contribute towards their own long-term care? Is it possible to devise an equitable solution to paying for a disease that is increasingly prevalent across every population? These are the pressing questions faced by governments around the world.

Source: Alzheimer's Disease International 2010

enabled to commission timely and appropriate services in their community, residential care bills should become significantly smaller. To date, older people have been less likely to use individual budgets, with one evaluation suggesting that 'a potentially substantial proportion of older people may experience taking responsibility for their own support as a burden rather than as leading to improved control' (Glendinning et al. 2008). Despite slow uptake and considerable variation between councils, however, an estimated 41 per cent of all individual budgets now go to older people (DH 2010c).

Informal care

Definitions and numbers

Most support and assistance for older and disabled people comes from family members, friends, and neighbours rather than from professional services. This help is described as informal care.

Because informal caregiving takes place largely within personal relationships in the private sphere, it is often a 'hidden process' that is hard to quantify (Glendinning et al. 2009). Also, informal care can be measured in different ways, for example by the needs of disabled people or by carer benefit claims. According to one estimate, up to 19 million people aged 25 and over across the EU provide 20 or more hours of informal care every week to an elderly or disabled person (ibid.). By 2030, this number is expected to increase by 13 per cent to 21.5 million carers, with 10.9 million of those providing at least 35 hours of unpaid care per week. In the UK, according to different estimates, there are up to six million unpaid carers, and the value of their contribution exceeds the budget of the entire NHS (Buckner and Yeandle 2007).

Feminist challenges to community care

As we saw earlier in this chapter, the challenge to institutional care following the Second World War meant that policy-makers began to turn towards 'the community' for the provision of social care. Given that women have traditionally been the primary providers of informal care, feminists highlighted the potentially regressive effect that this policy shift would have on women's employment prospects and well-being. Finch and Groves (1980) expressed the policy shift in terms of the following equation: 'community care = care by the family = care by women'. This equation generated subsequent research into informal care and caregivers which, combined with lobbying by carers' organizations such as Carers UK, eventually led to policy recognition for informal carers.

There are numerous tensions inherent in the discussion and research around informal care. A feminist analysis of women's roles within the family brings to light the important contribution that informal carers make to the delivery of social care. However, recognizing informal carers as a specific policy target can recast older and disabled people as passive, dependent recipients of care. Thus the 'carer' label has been resisted by those in the disability movement—who have long struggled to promote the independence and autonomy of people with impairments—and also by some caregivers who see themselves first and foremost as loving family members, caring friends, or friendly neighbours (not 'carers') (Parker and Clarke 2002). It is also argued that dividing people into those who provide care and those who receive care overlooks the valuable reciprocity inherent in many caring relationships, as well as failing to recognize that individuals may simultaneously be carers and recipients of care, such as parents with disabilities.

The supply of informal care: who cares and why?

Policy discussions around family carers must weigh at least two priorities: first, supporting carers in order to sustain the supply of informal care and, second, saving costs, which is part of what drives the 'care in the community' agenda. How the balance is achieved depends on a range of factors which affect the supply of informal care.

First, family structure affects the availability of informal carers. During the late nineteenth and early twentieth centuries, single women were the primary informal caregivers, especially for parents. Since the 1960s, traditional family structures have been affected by increased rates of divorce and remarriage, delayed age of first marriage, and declining birth rates. Women born in Britain in the 1930s had an average completed family size of 2.45 children, while those born in the 1980s are expected to have an average of 1.74 children. Also, the proportion of women who never have children is increasing. Divorce may affect access to informal care in older age, because spouses are currently the main providers of care for their partners and because 'blended families' can complicate the intergenerational provision of care. The reduction in family size impacts family networks and reduces the number of people who are potentially able to provide care.

Women's increased labour market participation is another important factor. Since 1971, the employment rate for women in the UK has increased from 56 per cent to 70 per cent (ONS 2009). Although paid employment does not necessarily prevent someone becoming a carer, the 'double burden' of professional and personal responsibilities may have negative effects on their health and well-being and thus their ability to care over the longer term. Women's increased labour market participation may also affect the supply of lower-level daily support, such as help with shopping. Geographical mobility has also raised concerns about people's ability to provide informal care when living at a distance from their families.

Why certain people become informal carers is influenced in part by a socio-culturally inscribed 'hierarchy of obligation' (Qureshi and Walker 1989), with those higher up the hierarchy more likely to take on responsibility. For older people in majority white communities, the order tends to be: spouse, daughter, daughter-in-law, and then members of the same household. This shows the importance of gender and marital status in determining who becomes a carer. Different ethnic communities may have slightly different hierarchies, as well as overall rates of caregiving (Young et al. 2006); in South Asian communities, for example, the expectation that sons will look after their parents puts daughters-in-law higher up the hierarchy than daughters. Other factors are involved too, of course, including proximity to the person needing help, the availability of alternative options, personal affection (or not) for the person requiring help, and both physical and financial resources.

The extent to which policy measures support carers in balancing caring responsibilities against their own health, employment, financial stability, and social inclusion needs can also affect the supply of care.

Informal care and policy

In earlier times, policy-makers sometimes saw the family as a problem rather than a solution in the provision of social care. For example, the development of institutional care in the early twentieth century derived in part from the assumption that parents—by dint of heredity or defective parenting—were responsible for causing learning difficulties in their children and therefore unfit to care. However, increasing recognition that the provision of social care relies heavily on unpaid care provided by family and friends has led to the development of policy to support these carers (Box 13.10).

In the UK, the release of the Griffiths Report and the NHS and Community Care Act 1990 marked a significant period for policy recognition of carers. Significantly, the Griffiths report maintained that informal carers would continue to provide the majority of care; they were the 'primary means by which people are enabled to live normal lives in community settings' and this was 'as it should be' (1988: 5).

Despite determined campaigning by the national carers' organization now known as Carers UK, it was not until 1995 that the first carer-specific community care legislation was passed. The 1995 Carers (Recognition and Services) Act gave carers a clear legal status and new rights, primarily the right to their own separate needs assessment, but carried no additional funding. Four years later, the government released a National Carers Strategy (DH 1999a), which further acknowledged carers

> ### Box 13.10 **What do we mean by supporting family carers?**
>
> Although there is increasing recognition that carers require support and services in their own right, there is limited evidence so far about what those support and services should look like. Initiatives with the potential to benefit carers appear to be those that:
>
> - involve a 'package' of complementary interventions or a combination of different approaches;
> - provide synergy (for example, day care combined with psychosocial support and practical help for carers);
> - tailor support to the specific needs of particular groups of carers and care recipients (for example, people with dementia and their carers);
> - consider the needs of both the carer and care recipient;
> - are embedded within existing networks and services;
> - are easily accessible and low cost.
>
> Source: Glendinning et al. 2009

and established their legitimate right to support and services. This was reinforced by subsequent legislation, including the 2000 Carers and Disabled Children Act.

One particular group recognized in the National Carers Strategy is young carers, who are those under the age of 18 caring for a parent who is ill or disabled. According to an analysis of 2001 census data, there are an estimated 150,000 young carers in England and Wales (Dearden and Becker 2004). Research evidence suggests that young people can experience considerable physical, emotional, or social problems related to their responsibility as carers, including difficulty at school and elsewhere (SCIE 2005). Reaching young carers with specific support and services is therefore becoming an increasing priority, but so far only a small proportion of young carers have been identified and assessed for support. One problem is that social service professionals do not always understand young carers' particular needs and concerns; also, young carers often have limited awareness of their entitlements and can be reluctant to seek formal help.

The carers strategy document *Carers at the Heart of 21st Century Families and Communities* sets out a short-term agenda and long-term vision for the care and support of carers (DH 2008). The strategy is underpinned by specific funding for short breaks, job market re-entry assistance, and improved support for young carers. Other schemes include the piloting of annual health checks to help carers stay well, and training GPs to recognize and support carers. One year after the funding for short breaks was doubled, the Princess Royal Trust for Carers surveyed how the £50 million allocated to Primary Care Trusts (PCTs) for this purpose had been spent (Conochie 2009). They found that, because PCTs lacked information about carers in general and did not have to publish how they spent the allocation, it was 'nearly impossible for local carers and communities to hold their PCT to account for how they have used this new money' (p. 2) and only 23 per cent was actually used to increase services for carers. This highlights the importance of monitoring and accountability when putting policy into practice. Campaigning voluntary organizations sometimes adopt this 'watchdog' role (see Useful Websites for specific examples).

Conclusion

This chapter has shown how social care is influenced by a series of boundaries between important policy concerns: the boundary between healthcare and social services; between institutional and community-based care; between the state, the independent sector, the family, and the individual; and between cash and care. These boundaries have shifted over the years, profoundly affecting the ways in which older people and working-age adults living with physical impairments, learning difficulties, or mental health problems experience social care.

We have also reviewed the ways in which British social policy has constructed and responded to the issues of disability, intellectual impairment, mental illness, and frailty in old age. In some instances, policy has responded solely to the poverty associated with disability or older age; in others it has pursued agendas around protection of vulnerable individuals or containment of those considered a social risk; and most recently it has privileged choice above all else. These different policy responses have led to different outcomes for people receiving social care, depending on their circumstances and their generation.

The provision of social care in the community remains a problematic policy issue. The growing population of older people, rising expectations of people living with disabilities, and other demographic and social changes have placed heavy demands on the system. Debates about the appropriate level of state intervention remain polarized along traditional party lines—but actual policy responses on both sides have been largely symbolic and inadequately resourced. As a result, significant responsibility for social care provision continues to fall to families and the community.

By choosing the welfare budget to bear the brunt of spending cuts in the 2010 Comprehensive Spending Review, the coalition government demonstrated commitment to minimizing the role of the state in providing social welfare and re-emphasizing 'care *by* the community'. While statutory duties—such as those outlined in the Mental Health Act—will be retained, the landscape of social care provision is set to change significantly in the next five years, as private and not-for-profit agencies move into the gap created by the reduction in state funding for welfare. The debates and dilemmas reviewed in this chapter are likely to endure, but competing interests in the social care market are bound to generate new issues.

KEY LEGISLATION AND POLICY DOCUMENTS

Poor Law 1601

Poor Law 1834

County Asylums Act 1845

Local Government Act 1929

Mental Treatment Act 1930

National Health Service Act 1946

National Assistance Act 1948

European Convention on Human Rights 1950

Mental Health Act 1959

Hospital Plan 1962, Cmnd. 1604

Seebohm *Report on Local Authority and Allied Social Services* 1968, Cmnd. 3703

Chronically Sick and Disabled Persons Act 1970

Better Services for the Mentally Handicapped 1971, Cmnd. 4683

Better Services for the Mentally Ill 1975, Cmnd. 6233

National Health Service Act 1977

Report of the Committee of Inquiry into Mental Handicap Nursing and Care (The Jay Report) 1979, Cmnd. 7468

Growing Older 1981, Cmnd. 8173

Mental Health (Amendment) Act 1983

Disabled People (Services, Consultation and Representation) Act 1986

Community Care: an Agenda for Action (The Griffiths Report) 1988

Caring for People: Community Care in the Next Decade and Beyond 1989, Cm. 849

National Health Service and Community Care Act 1990

Mental Health (Patients in the Community) Act 1995

Carers (Recognition and Services) Act 1995

Disability Discrimination Act 1995

Community Care (Direct Payments) Act 1996

Human Rights Act 1998

Modernizing Mental Health Services: Safe, Sound and Supportive 1998, LAC (98) 25

Modernizing Social Services 1998

Health Act 1999

Caring about Carers: A National Strategy for Carers 1999

National Service Framework for Mental Health 1999

Care Standards Act 2000

Carers and Disabled Children Act 2000

The NHS Plan: A Plan for Investment, a Plan for Reform 2000, Cm. 4818-I

The NHS Plan: The Government's Response to the Royal Commission on Long-Term Care, 2000,
    Cm. 4818-II

Health and Social Care Act 2001

Valuing People: A New Strategy for Learning Disability for the 21st Century 2001, Cm. 5086

National Service Framework for Older People 2001

Community Care and Health (Scotland) Act 2002

Community Care (Delayed Discharges) Act 2003

Carers (Equal Opportunities) Act 2004

Alcohol Harm Reduction Strategy 2005

Disability Discrimination Act 2005

Independence, Well-being and Choice: Our Vision for the Future of Social Care for Adults in England 2005,
    Cm. 6499

Mental Capacity Act 2005

Mental Health (Patients in the Community) Act 2005

Our Health, Our Care, Our Say: A New Direction for Community Services 2006, Cm. 6737

Local Government and Public Involvement in Health Act 2007

Mental Health Act 2007

Putting People First: A Shared Vision and Commitment to the Transformation of Adult Social Care 2007

Safe. Sensible. Social. The Next Steps in the National Alcohol Strategy 2007

*Carers at the Heart of 21st Century Families and Communities: A Caring System on Your Side, a Life of Your
    Own* 2008

Health and Social Care Act 2008

Transforming Adult Social Care 2008, LAC(DH)(2008)1

United Nations Convention on the Rights of Persons with Disability 2008

New Horizons: A Shared Vision for Mental Health 2009

Shaping the Future of Care Together 2009, Cm. 7673

Valuing People Now: A New Three-Year Strategy for People with Learning Disabilities 2009

Building the National Care Service 2010, Cm. 7854

Equity and Excellence: Liberating the NHS 2010, Cm. 7881

📖 FURTHER READING

Brechin, A., Walmsley, J., Katz, J. and Peace, S. (1998), *Care Matters: Concepts, Practice and Research in Health and Social Care* (London: Sage Publications). This edited collection analyses the concept of care across different contexts and from different perspectives, exploring issues such as empowerment, choice, and the balance between independence, dependence, and interdependence.

British Journal of Learning Disabilities (Blackwell Publishing). This interdisciplinary, international peer-reviewed journal covers debates and developments in research, policy, and practice on learning disability. Topics include current trends in service provision, employment, advocacy and rights, family and carers, and quality of life.

Bytheway, B., Bacigalupo, V., Bornat, J., Johnson, J., and Spurr, S. (eds) (2002), *Understanding Care, Welfare and Community: A Reader* (London: Routledge/Open University). This book explores how care and welfare policies and practice can be developed appropriately and sensitively through an understanding of current issues relevant to a range of populations, including people with mental health problems, homeless people, older people, people with learning difficulties, and people with impairments.

Cameron, C. and Moss, P. (2007),*Care Work in Europe: Current Understandings and Future Directions* (Oxford: Routledge). This cross-national and cross-sectoral comparison of care work in Europe covers policy, provision and practice, as well as exploring how care work is conceptualized and understood.

Glasby, J. and Dickinson, H. (eds) (2009), *International Perspectives on Health and Social Care: Partnership Working in Action* (Oxford: Blackwell-Wiley). With a dual focus on policy and practice, this book examines key topics in partnership-working across health and social care, including boundary management, self-directed support, the impact of technology, and outcomes.

Glendinning, C. and Kemp, P. (2006), *Cash and Care: Policy Challenges in the Welfare State* (Oxford: The Policy Press). This comprehensive text examines and critiques the interrelationship between contemporary cash and care policy in Britain and other advanced welfare states.

Health and Social Care in the Community (Wiley-Blackwell). This interdisciplinary journal promotes critical thinking about the policy, practice, and theoretical issues underpinning all aspects of healthcare and social care in the community.

Means, R., Morbrey, H., and Smith, R. (2002), *From Community Care to Market Care? The Development of Welfare Services for Older People* (Bristol: The Policy Press). Focusing on the interpretation and implementation of national policy at local authority level since 1971, this critical analysis highlights issues such as rationing care, the health and social care divide, the changing role of residential care, and the growing emphasis on provider competition.

Means, R., Richards, S., and Smith, R. (2008), *Community Care: Policy and Practice (4th edn)* (Basingstoke: Palgrave Macmillan). Recently updated, this comprehensive text introduces the historical context of community care before examining current issues, including user and carer empowerment, the changing relationship between health and social care, the restructuring of care delivery, and future challenges.

Morrall, P. and Hazelton, M. (eds) (2004), *Mental Health, Global Policies and Human Rights* (London: Whurr). This book examines the policies and progress in integrating comprehensive mental health services across ten middle- and high-income countries.

Swain, J. French, S., Barnes, C., and Thomas, C. (eds) (2004), *Disabling Barriers—Enabling Environments* (London: Sage Publications). Written by disabled people who are leading academics in the field, this text covers a broad range of disability issues, including gender, sexuality, dependence and independence, ageing, human rights, and service design and delivery.

@ USEFUL WEBSITES

These are the four main sites for healthcare and social care policy in the UK, which are especially useful for accessing up-to-date policy developments and for downloading policy documents:

The Department of Health (England): **http://www.dh.gov.uk/Home/fs/en**

Health and Community Care (Scottish Government): **http://www.scotland.gov.uk/Topics/Health**

Health and Social Care (National Assembly of Wales): **http://new.wales.gov.uk/topics/health**

Department of Health, Social Services and Public Safety (Northern Ireland): **http://www.dhsspsni.gov.uk/**

The following websites provide a useful starting point for specific information about and resources for different populations of social care service users and the social care workforce, although they may change as policies change and services are reorganized:

The British Institute of Learning Disabilities (BILD) **(http://www.bild.org.uk/)**: BILD works in partnership with people with learning disabilities and carers to advance research, training, and policy related to the development of person-centred approaches to learning disability.

Carers' organizations play an important role in supporting and representing informal carers (who are often isolated, overworked, and lacking information); providing policy recommendations and evaluations; and monitoring policy implementation. Examples of UK organizations include:

Carers UK: **www.carersuk.org**
Crossroads Care: **www.crossroads.org.uk/**
Princess Royal Trust for Carers : **www.carers.org**

The English Longitudinal Study of Ageing (ELSA) **(http://www.ifs.org.uk/elsa/)**: ELSA is the first UK study to explore the unfolding dynamic relationships between health, functioning, social networks, and economic position. The survey covers a broad set of topics relevant to a full understanding of quality of life throughout the ageing process. See also the Survey of Health, Ageing and Retirement in Europe (SHARE: **http://www.share-project.org/**) and the University of Michigan Health and Retirement Study (HRS: **http://hrsonline.isr.umich.edu/**).

Joseph Rowntree Foundation (JRF) **(http://www.jrf.org.uk)**: one of the largest social policy research and development charities in the UK, the Joseph Rowntree Foundation (JRF) seeks to understand the causes of social problems, explore ways to overcome them, and show how social needs can be met in practice. Website provides extensive collection of research reports and policy analyses.

National Development Team for Inclusion (NDTi) **(http://www.ndti.org.uk/)**: NDTi is an independent not-for-profit organization that promotes inclusion for three main client groups: older people, individuals with learning disabilities, and those with mental health problems. Work includes policy development, research and evaluation, and training.

Social Care Institute for Excellence (SCIE) **(http://www.scie.org.uk/index.asp)**: an independent charity which seeks to improve the quality of care services by sharing knowledge about what works in all aspects of social care for adults and children throughout the UK, SCIE aims to ensure that all aspects of its work reflect the experience and expertise of service users and carers.

Social Care Online **(http://www.scie-socialcareonline.org.uk/)**: provides a wide range of information and research on all aspects of social care. New content is added daily and is drawn from a range of resources including journal articles, websites, research reviews, legislation and government documents, and service user knowledge. It also has a useful list of links to many other social care sites.

Social Policy Research Unit (SPRU) **(http://www.york.ac.uk/inst/spru/)**: established in 1973 at the University of York, SPRU is concerned with the development of policies and delivery of services to support people made vulnerable by poverty, ageing, disability, or chronic illness. Good source of research reports, papers, and other information.

ESSAY QUESTIONS

1 How have the boundaries between social care and healthcare moved since the 1970s, why, and to what effect?

2 How is long-term care currently funded in the UK, and what are possible options for the future? What are the key issues to consider?

3 What are the arguments for and against the use of individual budgets in social care?

4 Explore the tensions between independence and protection in the design of social care services. What are the issues involved? Can they be reconciled?

5 Can and should social care be delivered without the input of informal carers?

6 Why has physical disability been seen as a social care policy issue? Should it be?

7 What policy measures and other strategies might be effective (or counterproductive) for combating stigma against social care service users?

ONLINE RESOURCE CENTRE

For additional material and resources, please visit the Online Resource Centre at:
www.oxfordtextbooks.co.uk/orc/baldock4e/.

14

The care and protection of children

Derek Kirton

Contents

Introduction

This chapter examines policy and practice in services designed to provide care and protection for children and looks at some of the key factors which help to shape them. The pivot around which the care and protection of children turn is the relationship between state and family. In principle the model is a fairly straightforward one, which sees child-rearing as primarily the responsibility of parents, with the state providing certain supports, setting out particular requirements, and playing a monitoring role. The state is essentially concerned with the question of whether good-enough parenting is being provided. If not, it should intervene, either to ensure adequate care within the family or to provide alternative care for the child.

In terms of service provision, this gives a central role to child protection services and this will be reflected in our coverage of child maltreatment, its prevalence, and the different theoretical perspectives that have attempted to explain it. The chapter will also outline services aimed at providing support for families and the tension that is often perceived between this goal and the protection of children. When the state does intervene to provide alternative care, a number of challenging dilemmas arise, and these will be discussed in greater detail within this chapter. Should the child be allowed to return to her or his family or be found an alternative family, perhaps through adoption? When children are in the care of the state, what form of provision might best meet their needs? What support should be offered to young people leaving care? In recent times, governments have tended to separate the treatment of young offenders from concern with their care and protection. However, for various reasons, this separation is far from complete and so policy relating to young offenders will also be briefly examined within this chapter.

While the model for family–state relationships may appear straightforward, in practice it is rather more complex, not least because the state comprises many different bodies (courts, social care, health, police, etc.), and professional roles in relation to the welfare of children. Who is to make judgements about whether parenting is 'good enough' or when adoption might be in the child's best interests? As we shall see, such matters are strongly influenced by views on the importance of the 'blood tie' between parents and children born to them. In particular, a distinction is often drawn between a 'family support' stance that seeks to sustain biological family relationships wherever possible and an emphasis on 'child rescue' where the removal of children from perceived unsatisfactory circumstances is much more readily endorsed. A related concern is how far the child's interests can be understood as separate from those of their family. Contemporary emphasis on children's rights implies a degree of separation that would have been unthinkable a century ago. It is also important to emphasize the wider political and social policy contexts within which services for the care and protection of children operate. For those who emphasize social causes for child abuse and neglect, highlighting their links with poverty, homelessness, ill health, and school exclusion, the most effective solutions may lie with improving living standards and promoting social inclusion, thereby reducing the stresses that lead to maltreatment. Others, however, argue that the causes are largely individual and should be tackled through targeted intervention to change parental behaviour or to remove the children.

Learning outcomes

On completion of this chapter, the reader should have an understanding of:

1 the prevalence and perceived causes of child maltreatment and a knowledge of the framework for child protection;
2 support services for families and their relationship with child protection;
3 the major issues relating to looked after children (children 'in care');
4 policy and practice in the treatment of young offenders;
5 competing value systems and political ideologies shaping the care and protection of children.

Foundations of the modern childcare system

Although its origins can be traced to the nineteenth-century activities of child-savers such as Thomas Barnardo and Mary Carpenter, the modern childcare system took shape following the Second World War. Responding to material and emotional problems associated with evacuation, and Sir Walter Monckton's report (1945) on the death through neglect and beatings of 13-year-old Dennis O'Neill at the hands of his foster carers, the Curtis Report (1946) led to the Children Act 1948 and the establishment of Children's Departments in local authorities. The new departments were significantly influenced by the work of John Bowlby (1951) on maternal deprivation and attachment, which focused on the importance for children of a consistent relationship with a nurturing figure.

The post-war era saw a growing interest in 'preventive' work (i.e. supporting families in order to avoid children requiring substitute care), but a more immediate effect was the attempt to reform substitute care to ensure that it corresponded as closely as possible to a family model. Fostering became the 'preferred option', while many children's homes were revamped to move away from large 'barrack homes' towards the family group home, with at most ten to 12 children, live-in house-parents, and the twin aims of stability and simulation of family life.

Children's Departments expanded steadily during the post-war years before they were absorbed into the newly created Social Services Departments (SSDs) in 1971 (see Holman 1996 for an interesting historical account of the Children's Departments). SSDs were soon under pressure due to perceived failings in relation to child abuse and the balance struck between family support and child protection. We will return to these issues below, but at this point it is worth noting that the 1980s witnessed a series of conflicting scandals, some portraying social workers as ineffectual, others as over-zealous in their efforts to protect children. The Children Act 1989 represented an attempt to manage these tensions, offering families certain legal protections and the promise of 'partnership' with the state, while also placing children's welfare (and hence protection) centrally and emphasizing their right to be heard (see Box 14.1). Importantly, courts were to become more actively involved in decision-making, thereby placing professional practice under greater scrutiny.

From the 1980s onwards, there was also growing criticism of the care system and the role of the state as a 'corporate parent'. For some, these weaknesses reflected the combined responsibilities of SSDs for both adults' and children's services and the consequent loss of specialized knowledge and

---

Box 14.1 Key features of the Children Act 1989

- More active involvement of courts in decision-making about children
- Welfare of the child to be paramount
- Use of a welfare checklist for decision-making
- Avoidance of delay
- No order to be made unless better than not to do so
- Ascertaining and taking into account child's wishes
- Specific orders to deal with residence and contact
- Parental responsibility to be maximized, even when the child is in care
- Bringing together public (local authority, police powers, etc.) and private (divorce, etc.) law
- Due consideration to be given to child's religious persuasion, racial origin, cultural and linguistic background

---

skills relating to each. Following increasing moves towards separation, services for children underwent a major reorganization following the Children Act 2004. A new post of Director of Children's Services was created within local authorities and in all but a few authorities, education and child social care services were brought together. In line with the New Labour government's emphasis on 'joined-up working', the Act also established children's trusts to facilitate collaboration between relevant agencies working with children.

In 2009, there were 26,800 local authority child and family social workers and a further 8,600 residential childcare staff in England (NHS Information Centre 2010). Local authority expenditure on children and families totalled £5.4 billion in 2007–8, representing 26 per cent of all social services expenditure (NHS Information Centre 2009).

Although the state is the dominant partner, childcare services operate within a 'mixed economy of welfare'. There are many voluntary providers, including long-established national organizations such as the NSPCC (National Society for the Prevention of Cruelty to Children), Barnardo's, or Action for Children, and during the past decade there has been a sharp rise in private providers of foster and residential care.

Child maltreatment: a social construction

The now widely accepted idea that child maltreatment is socially constructed incorporates several linked themes. At its simplest, it acknowledges that understandings of maltreatment are inextricably linked to changing norms of child development and mores regarding discipline, supervision, and nurture. In addition, it draws our attention to the contested nature of child maltreatment. This is apparent both at a macro level, where pressure groups, media organizations, and 'moral entrepreneurs' may seek to influence legislation, policy, and public opinion, and at a micro-level where professionals are gauging harm and formulating appropriate responses, entailing judgements that may frequently be at odds with those of families (and sometimes children) themselves. The domains of child maltreatment and protection are deeply imbued with power, with key interpersonal relationships themselves embedded in wider social divisions.

Over the past three to four decades, child protection has become by far the most prominent activity within child social care, fuelled by a steady stream of negative media coverage. As noted earlier, stories have focused alternately on cases of death or serious injury which might have been prevented by stronger intervention or on the 'unnecessary' removal of children. Beyond creating what can appear to be a no-win situation for social workers, media coverage and public debate have also had important influences over policy and practice, as we shall see.

Constructing child maltreatment: a brief modern history

The origins of modern child protection are often traced to Victorian reformers, such as Thomas Agnew and Benjamin Waugh, the formation of organizations such as the NSPCC in the 1880s, and the first protective legislation dealing directly with parents, the Prevention of Cruelty to and Protection of Children Act 1889. The Act made cruelty, neglect, or abandonment of a child an offence, and gave powers for the court to remove the child and place them with another appropriate adult. Thereafter, there was a steady consolidation of powers, but for over half a century, issues of maltreatment held a generally low public profile. While policy evolved quite gradually and unevenly, it is possible to locate its development within the context of changing views of childhood, notably the growing emphasis on childhood as a period of innocence, vulnerability, and need for protection.

Maltreatment of children re-emerged into the public domain in the 1960s as 'battered child (or baby) syndrome'. Numerous medical research studies, and especially the work of Dr Henry Kempe in the United States, demonstrated (largely through X-ray evidence) that injuries inflicted by parents on children were frequently going undetected. The principal effect of this work was to heighten awareness of physical harm amongst the medical profession and child welfare agencies. In the UK, the NSPCC's Battered Child Research Unit contributed significantly to a higher public profile during the 1970s, described by Moore (1985: 55) as 'the age of child abuse'. Arguably a greater influence arose from the death of Maria Colwell in 1973 and the public reaction to it. Seven-year-old Maria was returned to her mother and stepfather after several years with foster carers, and subsequently suffered extreme neglect before being battered to death by her stepfather. Parton (1985: 69–99) argues that Maria's death coincided with growing concern about violence in society and breakdown in law and order, permissiveness, and perceived decline in the family. Media coverage of the case saw the birth of the 'naive do-gooder' stereotype for social workers—later neatly if cruelly captured in a *Daily Mirror* headline (16 January 1980), 'Malcolm Died as He Lived: Freezing Cold, Starving and Surrounded by Social Workers'—and pressure grew for a more forceful response. Formal measures included: the establishment of committees to coordinate policy and liaison between different agencies (reconstituted as Local Safeguarding Children Boards under the Children Act 2004); a requirement for case conferences bringing all relevant professionals together to discuss individual children; tighter procedures for investigation; and the establishment of a register for children 'at risk' of abuse. Informally, there was pressure towards greater use of legal powers to remove children, and the 1970s saw a significant rise in compulsory removal of children from their homes (Parton 1985: 125).

During the 1980s, child protection was subject to sharpening tensions. On the one hand, there was a steep rise in the number of children on the 'at risk' register, especially in relation to sexual abuse (Corby 2005:89). This 'rediscovery' of child sexual abuse is widely attributed to the influence of the women's movement, whose critical work highlighted the patriarchal family as a site of (sexualized) control and violence over women and children (Frost and Stein 1989). Recognition was also bolstered by the voice given to those who had suffered and survived sexual abuse. Acknowledgement of the particular difficulties for children in telling of sexual abuse and being believed was a significant factor in the establishment of Childline—the free telephone helpline for children experiencing abuse—in 1986. Pressure for greater intervention was also generated by deaths such as those of Jasmine Beckford and Kimberley Carlile.

However, there were countervailing forces, including a growing sense that much state intervention in families had become too heavy-handed, with children being taken into (and remaining in) care unnecessarily. This trend was to receive a powerful boost from events in Cleveland during

1987. When an unexpectedly large number of children were taken into care largely on the basis of a controversial medical diagnosis known as reflex anal dilatation, opinion was sharply divided between those who were inclined to see this as further uncovering of abuse and those, led by the local MP, Stuart Bell, who believed that certain doctors and social workers had 'gone mad' (Campbell 1988). The ensuing inquiry (Department of Health and Social Security (DHSS)1988a) was highly critical of many of the professionals involved, both for their 'kneejerk' reactions to medical diagnosis and for their flawed investigative techniques. Despite this judgment and subsequent similar cases of perceived over-zealousness in Rochdale and Orkney (Social Services Inspectorate 1990; Clyde Report 1992), the climate has remained fairly receptive towards believing children's allegations of sexual abuse. However, there have also been increasing claims that allegations (including those against teachers or care staff) may be malicious, motivated by desire for compensation, or, in the case of so-called false memory syndrome, planted in the mind during therapy (Davies and Dalgleish 2001).

The changing frontiers of child abuse

During the past two decades, while the 'core business' of child protection has continued to focus on dealing with (alleged) maltreatment in families, there have been important shifts in its context and construction, and additionally a broadening of scope to look beyond the family to new 'sites' of abuse. Much of this has been driven by campaigning activities, with children's charities often as key movers.

In the mid 1990s, the 'refocusing debate' drew on a series of research studies to suggest that child protection should move from a narrow focus on investigating 'incidents' towards dealing with more chronic, but equally if not more harmful circumstances, such as long-term neglect or emotional abuse (Department of Health 1995). Subsequently, under the New Labour government, a key phrase from the Children Act 1989, 'safeguarding and promoting the welfare of children', became more central, placing emphasis on realizing potential and optimizing life chances alongside traditional concerns to protect against maltreatment. In an ambitious attempt at 'social investment' in childhood, the government argued that all children's services could thus be seen as having a 'safeguarding' role (Department for Children, Schools and Families 2008).

Domestic violence received increased recognition, both in its connections with child maltreatment and its impact on family dynamics and parenting roles, especially for mothers. Importantly, however, it was also recognized that exposure to domestic violence in the family could itself be seen as abusive to children (Humphreys and Stanley 2006).

Two other long-standing issues that achieved greater recognition and policy responses were the problems of child 'runaways' and those exploited through prostitution. Research on children running away found that many were escaping abusive families and that a disproportionate number were from public care. Policy efforts have focused, with modest but limited success, on providing more 'refuges' for children and ensuring that their concerns are properly addressed on their return to family or care (Macaskill 2006). Campaigning in relation to 'child prostitution' was particularly concerned to reframe it as maltreatment to be dealt with essentially as a welfare matter rather than through the criminal justice system. While this shift was enshrined in government policy in 2000, critics remain concerned about how far welfare agencies are able to provide the necessary protection and support to children and young people involved (Melrose and Barrett 2004).

As one aspect of increasing globalization and migration, trafficking in children into, via, or even from, the UK has emerged as a significant issue. Research by Beddoe (2007) showed that two main purposes behind trafficking were sexual exploitation and domestic servitude, with other pathways including forced labour, marriages, drug smuggling, and benefit fraud. New technologies such as the internet and mobile phones have also introduced new routes for bullying and forms of sexual abuse, including children's involvement (with varying degrees of coercion) in the production of pornography and the potential for perpetrators to 'groom' children for abuse (Gallagher et al. 2006). The Child Exploitation and Online Protection Centre (CEOP) was formed in 2006 to tackle child sexual abuse linked to the internet, both nationally and internationally.

Fuelled by high-profile cases, including murders such as those of Sarah Payne, Holly Wells, and Jessica Chapman, concern about the threat posed by paedophiles has risen dramatically, bringing forth numerous policy initiatives and sparking controversy. These have included the introduction of a sex offenders register under the Sexual Offences Act 2003 and moves towards introducing (scheduled for 2011) a UK version of 'Megan's law' in the United States, which would allow parents to check whether those in contact with their children were sex offenders.

Growing awareness of (risks of) sexual abuse by those in positions of trust (including within churches, sports, and voluntary bodies as well as work roles with children) has led to a progressive extension of vetting and criminal records checks (now codified under the Safeguarding Vulnerable Groups Act 2006). However, this has been criticized from a range of stances, being variously seen as a costly and flawed bureaucracy, as deterring prospective volunteers wishing to work with children, and creating a climate of suspicion around adult–child relationships. At the time of writing, the coalition government is reviewing vetting and barring measures with the expressed aim of looking for ways of scaling back their reach.

Finally on the question of changing frontiers, brief mention should be made of ongoing struggles over recognition of particular forms of abuse. Following the controversy surrounding the Cleveland affair, there were similar 'battles of belief' regarding ritualized and satanic abuse and more recently about fabricated and induced illness (FII), where parents/carers would feign or deliberately induce illness on the part of their children in order to seek attention from medical professionals or play the role of 'concerned parent'. In each instance, battle lines are drawn between those who see such phenomena as extremely rare and others who believe they are more widespread but are under-recognized or suppressed (Gallagher 2001; Sheridan 2003). While these controversies have varied and often changing outcomes, they highlight both the contentious nature of child abuse and the complexity of its diagnosis.

The influence of inquiries

We have earlier outlined how inquiries into the deaths of children, such as those of Dennis O'Neill and Maria Colwell, have influenced child welfare services and how the Cleveland affair helped to shape the Children Act 1989. More recently, the government's response to Lord Laming's (2003) report into the death of Victoria Climbié was to launch the *Every Child Matters* agenda with its five outcomes for children: being healthy; staying safe; enjoying and achieving; making a positive contribution; and economic well-being. Many more inquiries have brought about changes to policy and practice in child protection, though on a less dramatic scale.

In their efforts to 'learn lessons', inquiries can be seen to make a valuable contribution to child protection work. Often well-resourced and thorough in their deliberations, they are able to draw on tragic events to make a powerful impression among professionals and generate pressure for improvements. However, the shaping influence of inquiries has also been questioned on a number of grounds (Corby 2003). First, in their focus on individual errors, inquiries often appear to take little or no account of contextual factors, such as workload pressures, resources, or organizational factors. Second, this may lead to detachment from the routines of child protection work, not least as particular cases may not be representative of practice more generally. Third, there is a danger of hindsight—that *after* a child's death the circumstances leading up to it appear misleadingly 'obvious' (Frost and Stein 1989: 53). Fourth, worries have been expressed about the overwhelmingly bureaucratic measures flowing from inquiries, with for instance the emotional complexities of professional judgement overlooked. 'In the final analysis, when the parents and children are talking alone with the worker, no amount of procedural guidelines will guarantee that the right things are said and done' (Jones et al. 1987: 66). Interestingly, the recently launched review of child protection by Eileen Munro (2010) has the reduction of bureaucracy as one of its main aims, suggesting that this long-running trend may be about to change.

Understanding child maltreatment

The 'knowledge base' for child maltreatment comprises four main areas: measurement, 'causes' of maltreatment, its consequences, and analysing interventions. Beyond academic interest, such knowledge can be valuable in prediction, detection, and prevention of maltreatment, and recovery from its effects. In all these areas, however, there are significant methodological challenges for research, especially those of isolating and measuring particular variables and tracking events over time.

Measuring maltreatment

As for any identified social problem, there is interest in the scale of child maltreatment. Two types of measure are customarily used, namely incidence and prevalence. Incidence refers to the number of new cases in a given time period (usually a year), while prevalence captures exposure at any time during childhood. Information on incidence and prevalence comes from both official statistics and research findings.

In March 2010, there were 39,100 children in England who were subject to a child protection plan (Department for Education (DfE) 2010a). This represented roughly 3.5 per 1,000 children but showed a sharp rise from previous years (almost 50 per cent since 2006), an effect widely attributed to growing risk aversion following the death of Peter Connelly in 2007. Child protection statistics reflect the fourfold official categorization of maltreatment: physical abuse, neglect, sexual abuse, and emotional abuse (for definitions see HM Government (2010c: paras 1.33–6)). Forty-four per cent of registrations were for neglect, 29 per cent emotional abuse, 12 per cent for physical abuse, and 6 per cent sexual abuse, with the remainder registered under more than one category. This balance has shifted dramatically since the 1980s when physical and sexual abuse were the largest categories, but this almost certainly reflects changes in professional practice more than any 'real' changes of incidence.

Thus, while official statistics give crucial insights into the operation of child protection services, their usefulness as a measure of maltreatment is more open to question. Self-report studies (see below) reveal much higher figures. Abuse and neglect may go unrecognized and unreported for a variety of reasons. Referral for investigation, usually from teachers, health workers, neighbours, family members, or police officers, requires both that the alleged maltreatment is known about and that someone regards it as sufficiently important to be reported. Passage through the various filters will then depend on the information available to professionals and on the judgements they make. A study by Dingwall et al., *The Protection of Children* (1983), gives valuable insights into the world of professional judgements. The authors contend that a rule of optimism, in effect the benefit of the doubt, is usually applied to the many situations where maltreatment might be suspected. This rule tends to be suspended mainly for one of two reasons: either where the parents are judged to be behaving inappropriately (including failure to cooperate with the professionals) or where those professionals directly involved feel that they must refer the matter outside their immediate circle, usually to higher authority. More broadly, given the many types of parental behaviour that might potentially be deemed 'abusive', judgements must be made as to their seriousness and regularity, while taking into account overall quality of relationships.

Issues of policy and practice are also important in shaping whether and how (alleged) maltreatment is recorded. As in many areas of social policy, there are wide variations across local authorities (Department of Health 1995: 68). For example, different thresholds or workload pressures may mean that similar cases would be investigated in one authority but not in another. The wider policy context also exerts a powerful influence, especially given the discretion to treat 'concerns' either as a case for family support or child protection (Thorpe and Bilson 1998).

The prevalence of child maltreatment has been explored through longitudinal studies and in the case of physical abuse, surveys of parents. However, the most popular approach has been self-report surveys by young adults reflecting on their childhood experiences, notwithstanding the obvious questions arising regarding the reliability of memory. In the UK, Cawson et al.'s (2000) study of 2,869 young people paints the most comprehensive and detailed portrait of maltreatment, recognizing the importance of family relationships and different 'levels' of abuse and neglect. Cawson and colleagues adjudged seven per cent of their respondents to have suffered serious physical abuse and six per cent to have experienced lack of physical care to a level that might constitute serious neglect. Eleven per cent of respondents indicated sexual abuse involving contact, though perhaps contrary to popular perceptions, a majority of this took place outside the family. Finally, six per cent were regarded as having experienced emotional abuse. Interestingly, respondents were somewhat less likely than the researchers to deem their experiences abusive or neglectful. What is immediately striking, however, is that these figures are far higher than for any officially recorded maltreatment, emphasizing the relatively low levels of reporting and sometimes the filtering out of allegations.

Who abuses whom?

Information drawn from child protection registers indicates that reported child maltreatment (with the partial exception of sexual abuse) is overwhelmingly a phenomenon of poorer working-class families, and closely associated with factors such as unemployment and lone parenthood. Observing also links to incidence of domestic violence, substance misuse, and mental illness in families, a Department of Health report (1995: 25) concluded that 'it is the most vulnerable in our society who are most likely to become the object of [a child protection] enquiry'.

These associations have sparked considerable debate regarding the accuracy of recorded maltreatment. Those who would question the statistics can point to a number of factors which may lead to under-representation of more affluent families. First, such families come to the notice of welfare agencies less frequently, being less likely to seek help or to become objects of professional concern. Second, they are more likely to benefit from the 'rule of optimism' because they are viewed as unlikely abusers and communicate more easily with middle-class professionals. Third, they may be better equipped to contest decisions.

No one would dispute that serious child maltreatment occurs in all social strata, and few would suggest that reporting and processing of cases are entirely without bias. The key question is whether biases can account for the class differences in recorded abuse. One who believes they cannot is Pelton (1985), who attacks what he calls the myth of classlessness. Beyond the weight of evidence from official data and many research studies, Pelton highlights three specific factors in support of his argument: first, that increased awareness and reporting have done nothing to diminish the class gap in recorded abuse; second, that even within classes, levels of abuse correspond with those of deprivation; third, that child abuse fatalities, which are extremely difficult to hide or disguise, also occur mainly in poor families. Gauging the 'real' incidence of abuse is always likely to remain elusive, but, as Pelton has argued, it is difficult to believe that abuse is evenly distributed throughout society. As to why the myth should exist, Pelton suggests that apart from well-meaning concerns not to 'label' poor families, the myth serves the interests of the psychological and helping professions, whose prestige gains from portraying maltreatment as a disease requiring their diagnosis and curative intervention. Recognizing it as a product of poverty would undermine such ambitions and raise awkward questions for politicians and policy-makers. Pelton's broad conclusion is supported by Cawson et al.'s (2000) study, which found higher levels of *self-reported* maltreatment among those growing up in social classes 4 and 5, whilst also noting that maltreatment in families from higher socio-economic groups was more likely to go unreported.

There are relatively few explicit gender differences in relation to child maltreatment, with the stark exception of sexual abuse, where it has been estimated that girls are between two and four times more likely to suffer abuse than boys and where between 80 and 95 per cent of perpetrators are men (Corby 2005). Although it may be that gendered norms lead to some under-reporting of sexual abuse of boys and abuse by women, the broad pattern is fairly clear and has formed the basis for feminist analysis to which we return below. Although women form a small majority of perpetrators of physical abuse, once living arrangements and time spent with children are taken into account, they could be seen as less likely to abuse than men, who moreover are responsible for most of the more serious injuries inflicted on children (Schnitzer and Ewigman 2005). The influence of gender norms is also readily apparent in relation to neglect, where assumptions about mothers' responsibilities tend to place the focus for parenting almost exclusively upon them.

Official child protection figures indicate some over-representation of black children and those of mixed ethnicity, along with some under-representation from those of South Asian backgrounds. However, these categories are notoriously slippery and may hide as much as they reveal (for example, in relation to socio-economic factors, religion, cultural practices, or length of stay in the UK (Chand and Thoburn 2006)). As noted above, official statistics also reflect policy and professional practice and there is some evidence that black and minority ethnic (BME) families may be drawn more deeply into the child protection system than their white counterparts (Brophy et al. 2003). However, 'cultural relativism' may also mean that maltreatment is not always pursued as strongly as it might otherwise be (Channer and Parton1990). Willingness to report maltreatment to official bodies is also important and it has been noted that there is sometimes reluctance in South Asian and to a lesser extent African communities to do so, due to reasons such as family honour, unfamiliarity with the UK child protection system, or fear of racist treatment (Gilligan and Akhtar 2006).

Risk and prediction

Within the professional mainstream, there has been considerable interest in developing profiles of at-risk populations with a view to prediction. Checklists have been developed in order to identify

Box 14.2 Child abuse and neglect high-risk checklist

Parents	Child(ren)
1 Previously abused/neglected as a child	Previously abused/neglected
2 Age 20 or less at birth of first child	Under 5 at time of abuse/neglect
3 Single parent/separated partner not biological parent	Premature/low birth weight
4 History of abuse/neglect or deprivation	Now underweight
5 Socially isolated, frequent moves, poor housing	Birth defect, chronic illness, developmental lag
6 Poverty, unemployed/unskilled worker, inadequate education	Prolonged separation from mother
7 Abuses alcohol and/or drugs	Cries frequently, difficult to comfort
8 History of criminal assault behaviour and/or suicide attempts	Difficulties in feeding and elimination
9 Pregnant, post-partum, or chronic illness	Adopted, foster, or stepchild

parents most likely to abuse and children most likely to suffer maltreatment. A well-known example is provided by Greenland (1987), who lists high-risk factors as shown in Box 14.2.

The quest for prediction is understandably controversial. Checklists clearly have the potential to improve the protection of children by alerting professionals and policy-makers to pertinent risk factors. Yet there are also dangers that listed factors may generate stereotypes, leading to self-fulfilling prophecy, with abuse incorrectly identified among those who score highly on the list ('false positives'), and missed among those who do not ('false negatives'). The challenge for practitioners is therefore to draw on such knowledge without doing so in a mechanistic way (Munro 2002).

Theorizing maltreatment

Whatever its merits, a risk-factor approach offers little in the way of identifying causal links that may facilitate effective interventions. More theoretical efforts have drawn on a range of psychological and sociological perspectives, with Corby (2005: 154–80) providing an excellent review. The main psychological schools of thought have all given rise to explanations of abusive behaviour on the part of individuals and addressed ideas of 'intergenerational transmission' as those subjected to, or witnessing, abuse are themselves more likely to become perpetrators. Psychodynamic, attachment, behavioural, and cognitive perspectives have all used their own frameworks to explain how abusive behaviour may develop and how this may in turn be passed on to children. What is common to all is that they tend to focus on individual pathology, an approach sometimes referred to as a medical model. For its critics, this can be seen as neglecting pressures that arise from relationships, networks, and the wider social and economic context.

Corby identifies a set of middle-range theories rooted in social psychology which address some of these concerns. These include accounts that locate maltreatment in interactions between parents and children, suggesting (though without attaching blame) that the latter's characteristics may trigger abusive behaviours from the former. (This view is implicit in Greenland's model outlined above.) For instance, disabled children have been found to be up to four times more likely to suffer maltreatment than other children, although the reasons for this are complex (Sullivan and Knutson 2000). A second such perspective focuses on family dysfunction, examining communication problems or dynamics that may lead to the scapegoating of children or their use as 'proxies' in adult conflicts. Family dysfunction theories have also been used to explain incest, with (step)fathers 'turning to' their daughters for sexual gratification following the breakdown of relationships with mothers—a view that has understandably drawn fierce criticism from feminists (see below). A third social psychological perspective is the ecological, which places individual and family factors in the wider context of social networks, both as sources of stress (e.g. social isolation) and support (Garbarino et al. 1980).

Finally, there are approaches to understanding child maltreatment which derive from broader sociological theory, which Corby terms the cultural and the structural. In the former, the focus is on understanding maltreatment in a wider cultural context. Thus Straus et al. (1980) have noted the links between high levels of physical abuse and culturally approved use of (lower-level) violence against children. The social structural stance draws attention to the wide range of factors impacting on children's development and well-being, including poverty, unemployment, homelessness, and racism, and how these may be as harmful to children as, or more harmful to them than, those behaviours ordinarily regarded as maltreatment (Gil 1970). This allows a radical redefinition of who is responsible for maltreatment, bringing those in power into the frame. Feminist accounts of child maltreatment find common ground in placing gendered power relations centrally and have been most prominent in relation to sexual abuse. Drawing on the highly gendered nature of both perpetration and victimhood noted earlier, feminists have argued that sexual abuse must be understood as a product of a patriarchal society, where men have 'rights' (including to sex) over women and children (Cox et al. 2000). They have been particularly critical of the family dysfunction model (see above), which is seen as attempting to shift responsibility for sexual abuse away from male perpetrators towards women who are deemed to have failed as partners and as mothers in protecting their children. Feminist perspectives have had some success in advocating that women deal with the aftermath of sexual abuse, whether as police officers, social workers, or carers, and in promoting the removal of perpetrators rather than children from the family home. However, while bringing crucial insights, such perspectives may be seen as reductionist in their focus on gender and as having little to say about maltreatment carried out by women (Ford 2006).

It is widely accepted that no single perspective comes close to offering adequate explanation for maltreatment, and much depends on what type of explanation is being sought. If we are trying to understand abuse and neglect as 'private troubles', then clearly the individual/family-based explanations may have more to offer than a broad-brush social theory. If, however, the aim is to cast light on maltreatment as a 'public issue', its levels, patterns, and trends, then the reverse is likely to be true. Ideally, both psychological and social perspectives can make significant contributions, including informing policy and practice interventions.

Consequences of child maltreatment

Awareness of maltreatment's consequences can be useful in a number of ways: helping to promote public and professional understanding; aiding recognition of 'signs' of maltreatment; increasing knowledge of resilience; and highlighting needs for service provision. As noted earlier, research in this area is difficult, particularly in respect of showing clear links between (types of) maltreatment and later life events and experiences. However, there is a considerable body of evidence to show that maltreatment is correlated with a range of psychological problems, such as anxiety, depression, self-harm, eating disorders, and deviant behaviours (HM Government 2010b). It should be noted, however, that many victims of maltreatment suffer no discernible long-term effects (Collishaw et al. 2007).

Prevention, family support, and early intervention

The adage that 'prevention is better than cure' has been applied to work with children and families since the 1950s and 1960s. Prevention has been applied to a range of possible outcomes, from neglect to children becoming offenders, but perhaps most commonly to preventing the need for entry into care. Prevention can be understood as working at different levels, as shown in Box 14.3.

Under this model, primary preventive services would comprise broader welfare provision available either on a 'universal' basis (e.g. the NHS or state education) or targeted at groups identified as

---

Box 14.3 **Stages of prevention**

- Primary prevention—services providing general support to families and helping to reduce pressures arising from poverty, housing problems, or ill-health.
- Secondary prevention—offering specialized help when children have been identified as 'at risk' or vulnerable.
- Tertiary prevention—avoiding the negative consequences of children spending long periods in substitute care.

Parker (1980)

in need (e.g. social housing or tax credits for lower-income families). Secondary prevention would focus largely on social work and social care services offering family support, such as short breaks for children or attendance at a **family centre**, or attempting to address abusive or neglectful parenting. Tertiary prevention might entail improving the quality of substitute care services or helping children leave public care by returning to their families or adoption.

Traditionally, family support services enshrine a belief that children are best cared for in their families and that when needs arise, assistance should be given to help families carry out this role. Advocates of family support stress that services should be non-stigmatizing, accessible, wide-ranging, and available to all who need them (Frost 2003). However, although they can be managed, tensions can be discerned between family support and child protection, notably through the danger that too strong a focus on the former can lead to over-identification with parents and their needs, and consequently a lack of focus on protecting the child(ren). Over the years, there have been regular pendulum swings between emphases on support and protection respectively. It is worth noting here that the number of children in need is almost ten times greater (375,900 in England in March 2010) (DfE 2010a) than the number for whom there is a child protection plan. However, it is also the case that family support services available under the Children Act 1989 have usually been insufficiently resourced to meet levels of need or demand.

In recent years, the terrain of prevention and family support has increasingly been cast in terms of early intervention, where early may refer to age and/or the genesis of problems. Early intervention has been reflected in ambitious programmes such as Sure Start or family-focused interventions such as the Nurse Family Partnership. While sharing some of the goals of prevention and family support, early intervention tends to be rather harder edged—an expression of 'tough love'. Specifically, it has tended to proactively seek out families whom the state feels should be 'reached' and to heighten expectations of parents (usually mothers) with the threat of more punitive measures in case of parental/maternal 'failure'. Befitting a neo-liberal ideology, early intervention programmes place little emphasis on the effects of poverty, or frame this in terms of parental responsibilities to escape poverty through work (Garrett, 2009).

The state as parent: looked after children

The term 'looked after' was introduced in the Children Act 1989 to describe children formerly (and still often in popular usage) known as 'in care'. Although looked after children are often discussed as a homogeneous group, it is important to recognize that they assume this legal status for different reasons and retain it for varied lengths of time. In recent times, the primary stated reason for children becoming looked after has been maltreatment, accounting for 61 per cent in 2010, with most of the remainder accounted for by various forms of family stress and dysfunction, parental illness, or parental absence (DfE 2010b). The same statistics show that while 49 per cent leave public care in less than six months, 15 per cent do so only after five years or more. Notwithstanding these varied circumstances and careers, most looked after children share the common characteristic of coming from poor families. The looked after population has fallen considerably over the past three decades but most of the reduction took place before the mid 1990s, since when there has been a relatively modest rise (see Table 14.1).

In broad terms, children become looked after by one of two main routes. First, they may do so at the request of a parent (or occasionally, for older children, effectively at their own request). Such voluntary arrangements are known as accommodation and emphasize provision of a service (perhaps to alleviate stress) to children and families, with the parents retaining the key role in decision-making. However, it is not unknown for parents to be pressured into having their children accommodated, with the threat of compulsory measures being taken if they do not (Packman and

Hall 1998). The major such compulsory measure in England is the **care order**, which has the effect of transferring parental responsibility to local authorities, who although in principle sharing this with parents, in practice become the main decision-makers.

Over the past two to three decades, state care has come under regular critical scrutiny for a range of perceived failings. These include maltreatment within its domain, poor support for education, and lack of stability, all of which are discussed below. Such failings are also seen to contribute to a range of other problems for those in or leaving care, such as unemployment, homelessness, mental disorder, young parenthood, and involvement in a range of deviant behaviours. Reforming public care has therefore been seen both as a way of protecting vulnerable children and young people and ameliorating a number of social problems (Sergeant 2006).

Institutional abuse

The term 'institutional abuse' typically describes maltreatment that takes place within the care system, although it may be applied in other settings such as residential schools. In the 1980s and 1990s there were numerous highly publicized cases arising from residential care, often involving many children and occurring over many years (Corby 2005: 55–60). Though less well-publicized, abuse within foster care is not uncommon, shown most clearly in the calls to Childline (Morris and Wheatley 1994). Whatever the setting, the irony of children, often removed from home for their own protection, subsequently being abused by their protectors is a tragic one.

Institutional abuse can take a number of forms. First, it may involve physical, sexual, or emotional abuse or neglect perpetrated by staff or carers. Second, it may entail staff or carers allowing abuse by others through neglectful behaviour or in extreme, though thankfully rare, cases, active collusion with outside perpetrators. Third, other children may be the perpetrators, either through bullying or, in some cases, sexual abuse (Barter et al. 2004). A fourth category, most (in)famously found in the case of 'pindown' (a system of punishment based on isolation and humiliation), can arise where the home's regime itself is deemed abusive (Levy and Kahan 1991). Finally, the wider failings of public care, for instance in providing stability or tending appropriately to educational or health needs, may be regarded as forms of systemic abuse. Recommendations from major reports, including those by Sir William Utting (1997) into safeguards for children living away from home and the Waterhouse (2000) inquiry into abuse in children's homes in North Wales have offered a blueprint to reduce the risks of institutional abuse (see Box 14.4).

Box 14.4 **Measures to counter institutional abuse**

- Emphasis on children's rights (including advocacy), complaints procedures, and participation
- Vetting of staff
- Adequate staffing levels
- Training, especially in the management of behaviour
- Effective supervision
- Good management and leadership
- Openness in communication, both internal and external
- Relationships built on respect rather than authoritarianism
- A strong inspection regime
- Protection for whistleblowers
- Raising the status of public care

Education for looked after children

Over the past two decades or so, increasing attention has been devoted to the education of looked after children, driven by views of the centrality of education for improved life chances and, under the New Labour government especially, a means of escaping social exclusion (Jackson 2001). Studies have revealed a consistent pattern, wherein looked after children were markedly less likely than their peers to achieve benchmark qualifications and proceed to higher education, and conversely more likely to be excluded from school. They also highlighted a range of common weaknesses within the care system that at best did little to counteract previous disadvantage and at worst exacerbated it. These included poor liaison between social care and education personnel, poor recording of educational information on care records, and a culture of low expectations in relation to attainment by looked after children. Moves within care frequently entailed changes of school and consequent disruption to education (Berridge 2008).

Progress over the past decade is open to different interpretations. Undoubtedly, there have been significant improvements, with, for instance, the number of looked after children gaining five GCSEs A*–C rising from 6 to 26 per cent between 2000 and 2010. This still remains low, however, in comparison with a national figure of 70 per cent (DfE 2010c). Yet while this gap is regularly a source of fierce criticism of public care, it must be remembered that it is not a like-for-like comparison. For instance, rates of statemented special educational needs are nine times higher for looked-after children, while (mercifully) far fewer of the wider population have suffered the type of maltreatment and erratic early parenting that are commonplace among those in care.

Care planning

Recognition of the importance of planning can be traced back to Rowe and Lambert's (1973) landmark study of children in long-term care, *Children Who Wait*. The authors identified the problem of drift, where children lived either in foster care or residential homes often for many years, with no clear plan as to whether they would return home to their families, remain in care, or be adopted. The problems highlighted related both to planning for individual children and to planning services for children.

Concerns about planning were also boosted by a wider focus on the importance of long-term security for children, which came to be encapsulated in the term permanence. The philosophy of permanence placed particular emphasis on securing the futures of children both decisively and relatively speedily in order to provide them with 'continuity of relationships with nurturing parents or caretakers and the opportunity to establish lifetime relationships' (Maluccio et al. 1986: 5). If parents could meet the children's needs adequately, without damaging delay and with good long-term prospects, then permanence would be provided by reuniting children with their birth families. If not, then it should be provided through substitute care, most usually adoption, as quickly as possible.

The philosophy of permanence coincided in the 1970s with one of the periodic pendulum swings towards, or in this case away from, the importance of 'blood ties'. The death of Maria Colwell clearly contributed to this, but there were also theoretical influences, notably the emphasis on 'psychological parenting', with parent–child relationships seen to depend much more on the quality of caregiving than on biology (Goldstein et al. 1979). By the late 1970s, with increasing removal of children from their birth families, many critics believed that permanence policies had in effect become adoption policies. Organizations such as the Family Rights Group and later Parents Against Injustice emerged to defend a family rights position, emphasizing both the importance of blood ties and the need to offer more support to (mostly poor) families facing difficulties. The perception that such families received too little help and were often victims of harsh treatment gained ground during the 1980s and underpinned the 'partnership' philosophy of the Children

Act 1989. This shift was helped by research showing that while ongoing contact was important for well-being and prospects for reunification, it was often neglected or even obstructed by social work agencies (DHSS 1985). Meanwhile, studies also showed that the state had a poor record in providing stability for children in care, raising further questions about the benefits of removing them from their birth families.

Reforming public care: the quest for corporate parenting

Responding to increasing concern regarding the quality of state care, the then Conservative government commissioned a working party to consider ways of enhancing the life chances of looked after children (Parker et al. 1991). While not discounting the importance of permanency planning, the working party also drew attention to a more pervasive lack of focus on children's needs. This led to the establishment of a framework for assessing and reviewing children's welfare that has since been adopted throughout the UK and beyond, with children's needs addressed under the following categories:

- health;
- education;
- identity;
- family and social relationships;
- social presentation;
- emotional and behavioural development;
- self-care skills.

This framework has been widely praised for its promotion of rigorous planning, but has also been criticized as unduly bureaucratic and as overemphasizing conformity to 'white middle-class' norms (Garrett 2003).

The term 'corporate parenting' entered the policy lexicon in the early 1990s, attempting to encapsulate the need for cooperation between the various agencies, both governmental and non-governmental, in order to effectively provide for looked after children. Especially under the New Labour government, corporate parenting evolved from a general exhortation to a more finely meshed set of initiatives and organizational developments. These included targets and timescales to increase adoption, improve stability, and raise educational attainment, while a range of designated posts was created within schools, health trusts, and local authorities to heighten a sense of responsibility for looked after children. New Labour's reforms culminated in the *Care Matters* Green Paper (Department for Education and Skills 2006), parts of which were subsequently enacted in the Children and Young Persons Act 2008. Local authorities were encouraged to act as a 'pushy parent' in respect of their looked after charges, seeking the best schools, offering free leisure facilities, and even providing employment opportunities for them. Senior managers and council members were encouraged to take an active interest in the lives of individual children. Looked after children would benefit from dedicated individual budgets for children (including earmarked funding for education) to be held by lead professionals. The most controversial measure, however, was to pilot Social Work Practices (SWPs), the brainchild of academic Julian Le Grand and modelled loosely on GP practices. SWPs are contracted to provide lead professional and other services for looked after children. Working at arm's length from local authorities and paid by results (such as reunification, adoption, or educational qualifications), SWPs are seen by advocates as having the potential to significantly improve social work performance. Sceptics, however, question whether they will weaken corporate parenting and whether a profit motive might deflect attention away from children's welfare. The SWP model does, however, fit well with the coalition government's 'Big Society' model for decentralizing state services and can be expected to spread more widely.

Finding homes for looked after children

Table 14.1 shows changes in the overall looked after population in England and Wales 1980–2010 and the respective levels of placement in foster care and residential care.

In addition to the overall population decline during the period, the most dramatic change has been the precipitous fall in the number of those placed in residential care, with foster care providing for an ever greater proportion of those looked after. Since 1945, foster care has generally been the favoured option for most children, having, according to Packman (1981: 25), 'the blessing of Curtis, Bowlby and the Treasury' but its position became pre-eminent with the contraction of residential care in the 1980s. Although the research evidence is by no means unequivocal, Colton (1988) summarizes the arguments which suggest that foster care typically provides more personal attention, continuity of relationships and familial atmosphere. Despite these factors, and the seemingly greater risk of institutional abuse, many teenagers have expressed a preference for residential care which is seen as affording more interaction with peers and, for some, welcome 'space' away from family relationships (Sinclair and Gibbs 1998). Outcome measures in education or levels of offending also appear to favour foster care, but it must be remembered that residential homes are usually dealing with a more troubled population of young people.

Foster care: the ideal method?

Looking after other people's children on a temporary basis has a long history, both as a formal practice, known as 'boarding out' under the Poor Law, and longer still as an informal one. As noted above, foster care has become increasingly central to public care since 1945 and currently accounts for almost three-quarters of placements. This shift has involved efforts to provide homes for those previously regarded as 'hard to place' (e.g. on grounds of age, disability, or ethnicity) and more specialized forms of care (e.g. children infected with HIV or AIDS, and young offenders on remand). This extension and the growing emphasis on planning brought about a shift from what Holman (1975) referred to as **exclusive** (quasi-adoptive) **fostering** to a more **inclusive** model that involves foster carers working with birth families and (social work) professionals towards particular goals.

Contemporary foster care has been shaped by a steady, if uneven, journey towards professionalization, a term that can be used to describe both particular projects and a broader trend within foster care. The history of professionalization in the UK is usually traced to schemes such as the Kent Family Placement Service which provided placements for troubled teenagers, usually involved in offending. The model rested on foster carers being paid for their work (rather than simply expenses for the child), undertaking training, and receiving intensive support. A 'second wave' of professionalization occurred in the 1980s, led by newly formed independent fostering providers who adopted and extended the Kent model, sometimes introducing additional educational and psychological supports. The independent (mostly private but with some voluntary providers) sector has grown

Table 14.1 Children looked after in England and Wales, 1980–2010 (England only 2010)

	000			
	1980	1990	2000	2010
Children looked after	95.3	60.5	58.1	64.4
Number in foster care	35.2	34.3	37.9	47.2
Number in residential care	32.4	10.7	4.8	6.2

Sources: Department of Health (2001), DfE (2010b)

steadily and accounts for over a quarter of all foster placements (DfE 2010b: Table A3). However, professionalization can also denote the way in which features of the model have become integral to foster care more generally. Training and dedicated support are now mandatory features, while over half of all foster carers now receive some 'reward' payment (usually in the form of a fee). It is possible to identify a number of drivers behind the professionalizing process. Some relate to the demands placed upon foster carers, for example dealing with more 'challenging' children and young people, facing expanded role expectations in respect of work with birth families and the child welfare system, and working within a more regulated environment. Another crucial factor has been the changing role of women, with greater participation in the labour market raising expectations of financial recompense and increasing pressures on agencies to attract and retain foster carers. Finally, support for a more professional model has come from many foster carers themselves as well as representative organizations such as the Fostering Network.

Another important development in recent times has been the increased involvement of family and friends as carers, also known as kinship care (Broad 2001). This is seen by its supporters as offering distinct advantages over foster care by strangers, such as stability and continuity in the child's life, stronger bonds with the carers, and the meeting of identity needs. The treatment of kinship carers, however, has been controversial, with conflict between those who believe they should be treated identically to stranger foster carers, including financially, and others who question their parity with other approved foster carers and hence the case for equal treatment.

Residential care: a positive choice?

Apart from its dramatic reduction in size, residential care has also undergone significant change in its organization and rationale, with homes ceasing to provide long-term care and in principle focusing on achievement of goals such as return to the birth family, preparation for foster care or adoption, provision of a therapeutic environment, or, for older teenagers, transition to life after leaving care. As noted earlier, efforts were made in the post-war era to make children's homes more familial and there has since been an ongoing quest to alleviate their 'institutional' features. Homes, whether run by local authorities, voluntary organizations, or private providers (who now account for around 60 per cent of homes), have tended to reduce steadily in size and are in principle (though not always in practice due to pressure for placements)often specialized around particular functions or modes of treatment (Berridge and Brodie 1998). Despite these developments, the perception of residential care as a 'darkened door at the end of the line' (Department of Health 1998: 39) remains widespread, an option to be considered only when foster care is deemed to have failed or is otherwise

> ### Box 14.5 **Key Factors in high-quality residential care**
>
> - The culture and ethos of residential establishments—underlying values, teamwork, communication
> - Quality of relationships between children and carers—informal, respectful, frank, confidential, reliable
> - Staffing and training—qualifications, training, stability (see below)
> - Leadership—management with clear vision
> - Listening to children
> - Size of home—majority view that smaller homes provider better care
> - Information recording and sharing
>
> Source: Clough et al. (2006)

regarded as inappropriate. Residential care has also suffered from significant staff challenges, characterized by high turnover, while low pay and levels of qualification symbolize a lack of status for its workers compared with field social workers. However, if residential care appears to crystallize many of the difficulties inherent in parenting by the state, it remains both an integral part of the childcare system and appreciated by many of its residents. Box 14.5 sets out some of the requisites for safer and more effective care.

Adoption: a service for children?

Adoption is marked by the legal transfer of parental responsibility from birth parents to adoptive parents and unlike foster care is irrevocable. However, there have also been various legal transfers which are less complete and final, the latest of which is special guardianship. Such transfers tend to be used where a child has a strong connection to birth family members or is opposed to the adoption and sometimes when there is religious or 'cultural' opposition to adoption. Adoption raises profound issues at personal and familial levels—including questions of identity, the meaning(s) of parenting, nature, and nurture—while the scope for accompanying 'secrets and lies' has provided a rich seam for fiction and drama in addition to its 'real life' impact (Novy 2005). At a broader societal level, questions are also raised regarding the efficacy of such transfers. On the one hand, adoption has often received staunch support from the political Right, being seen as a desirable form of social mobility from typically poor, ('undeserving') lone parents to ('deserving') middle-class couples. Once framed as a solution to illegitimacy (and infertility), it has increasingly been recast as a means of reducing welfare dependency (Morgan 1998). Alternatively, however, it may be seen to result from a failure to offer adequate support to poor parents, representing to some critics a form of 'state-sponsored child snatching' (Ryburn 1994). As will be discussed below, the state's role in approving adoptive parents has also proved contentious.

Introduced in England and Wales in 1926 (1930 for Scotland), adoption took on a distinctive form in the post-war era based on the clean break, involving the severance of all legal links with the birth family and identical status to children born to the adopters (with the exception of not being able to inherit aristocratic titles). This was thought to be in the best interests of all members of the adoption triangle—namely birth parent(s), child, adoptive parents. During the 1950s and 1960s this was increasingly questioned, with recognition of the need for adopted people to trace their birth family in order to understand their identity, a possibility (already available in Scotland) that was allowed in England and Wales by the Children Act 1975. Though to a lesser extent, the losses felt by many birth mothers and other relatives also came to be acknowledged (Bouchier et al. 1991). Related research and campaigning combined with changing social attitudes to generate moves towards openness in adoption. Openness can be seen as a continuum, from information and participation of a birth parent in selecting adopters through to continued face-to-face contact between the child and birth family. Research has shown that openness can work (perhaps surprisingly) well in many adoptions (Neil and Howe 2004), though it would perhaps be unwise to extrapolate its value to all.

Table 14.2 Adoption orders, England and Wales 1974–2009

	1974	1980	1990	2000	2009
Number of orders made (thousands)	22.5	10.6	6.5	4.9	4.7
Children under 1	5.2	2.6	1.0	0.3	0.1

Source: Office for National Statistics (2010)

Box 14.6 Adoption and Children Act 2002: key measures

- Establishment of Adoption and Permanency Taskforce
- Setting of timescales for adoption
- National Register of adopters
- Improved support for adopters
- Independent review of approval decisions
- Amendment permitting cohabiting (including lesbian or gay) couples to adopt

---

Moves towards openness reflect and reinforce changes in adoption since the 1960s, with a dramatic fall in adoption especially for babies (see Table 14.2) and increasing concentration on adoption of looked after children. (They may also be seen to fit well with a wider trend towards democratization and management of complex relationships within families.)

The drop in baby adoptions is generally explained as the result of greater use of contraception and termination, and the declining stigma attached to illegitimacy. Adoption is now much more likely to be from public care, which means that the children may be older, be the victims of abuse, and/or have special needs. Importantly, many more adoptions are now contested, i.e. opposed by birth parents, and this has given rise to fierce debates about whether the law should allow adoption in these circumstances (something that happens frequently in the United States and the UK but is rare in most of continental Europe) (Thoburn 2007).

Government policy, however, became progressively more pro-adoption during the 1990s based on its perceived advantages over life in public care (although evidence for this is complex and contested (Biehal et al. 2010)) and a sense that social workers were not pursuing adoption with sufficient rigour. In July 2000, Prime Minister Tony Blair (PIU 2000) launched a review of adoption which led to the Adoption and Children Act 2002. This included a number of measures designed to boost the use of adoption for looked after children (see Box 14.6).

A target to increase adoption from care by at least 40 per cent was almost met by 2004, but having peaked at 3,700, numbers have since fallen back to around 3,200 (in part due to the introduction of special guardianship) (DfE 2010b: Table D1). The setting of targets has always been controversial because of their distorting influence in decision-making, and in an interesting twist, the *Daily Mail*, having vigorously campaigned for greater use of adoption, was within a few years branding the authorities as 'child snatchers' (14 May 2005).

Approving adoptive families: political correctness?

The question of who should be approved as adoptive parents can be an emotive issue, not only for those directly involved, but in wider debates when it touches on politically sensitive issues such as ethnicity or sexuality. Media commentators and politicians have regularly portrayed adoption social workers as 'politically correct' (PC) either for placing 'unwarranted' restrictions on adopters on grounds of age, smoking, or weight, or supporting causes such as adoption by lesbian or gay applicants that offend 'traditional family values' (Hicks and McDermott 1999). Yet nowhere has the debate on PC been as fierce as in the case of adoption of BME children. Since the 1970s, battle lines have regularly been drawn between the supporters of transracial adoption (TRA) and same-race placement, where there is an ethnic match between the child and adoptive parents. Advocates of TRA see it as an ideal solution for BME children, especially where there may be insufficient adoptive families from a similar ethnic background. Some also see TRA as transcending barriers and promoting racial and ethnic integration in society. Opponents, however, have argued that placement in white families has detrimental effects on minority ethnic children's sense of racial identity,

> **Box 14.7 Children (Leaving Care) Act 2000: key provisions**
>
> - A duty on local authorities to assess and meet the needs of care leavers
> - A duty to keep in touch with care leavers until they are at least 21
> - A pathway plan for looked after children aged 16, mapping out a route to their independence
> - A personal adviser to assist care leavers, especially in relation to education, training, or employment
> - Local authorities to provide financial support for care leavers
> - Assistance for care leavers aged 18–21 in education or employment

knowledge of their culture of origin, and ability to cope with racism. They dispute the (extent of) shortage of minority ethnic adopters, blaming this largely on institutional racism within adoption agencies. (For a more detailed discussion see Kirton 2000.)

Services for young people leaving care

Since the pioneering research of Stein and Carey (1986), the difficulties and challenges facing young people leaving care have been more widely recognized. Statistics show that care leavers are significantly over-represented in the homeless and prison populations, among those with drug or alcohol problems, or as teenage parents, although it is important to recognize that a majority of care leavers avoid such outcomes (Stein 2004). Nevertheless, while the figures may exaggerate the influence of care, they highlight wider concerns about both the quality of services for looked after children (see above) and the help that is provided for care leavers, in terms of preparation or after-care support. The challenges facing these young adults are all the more acute because they are leaving care at a rather earlier age (typically 16–18) than for most young people leaving home. Similarly, since the mid 1980s, social policy relating to young adults has been somewhat harsher than previously, with denial or lower rates of benefit, and less access to housing provision.

The Labour government attempted to address the problems faced by care leavers in the Children (Leaving Care) Act 2000, the key provisions of which are set out in Box 14.7.

Research on implementation of the Act by Broad (2005) suggested a mixed picture with many improvements, but continuing difficulties for some in relation to financial support and adequate planning. The Care Matters initiative sought to offer further improvements, including clearer supports for care leavers to enter higher education. More ambitiously, it aimed to move away from the idea of 'leaving care' towards a more phased transition thought to be typical in most families. The necessary reforms (such as remaining longer with foster carers) are not necessarily cheap, however, and it remains to be seen how far they will be implemented in a tough financial climate.

Children, young people, crime, and welfare

During the early twenty-first century, with its more punitive approach to young offenders, it may seem anomalous to include their treatment in a chapter dealing with care and protection of children. This would, however, be to misunderstand the history of what is now termed youth justice and to assume that recent policy swings are irreversible. The last hundred years have seen a continuing debate about whether young offenders are simply criminals deserving punishment or the victims of childhood deprivation in need of social care. (Note: some of the issues covered in this section are also discussed, from a more criminological perspective, in Chapter 18.)

The rise and fall of welfarism

Interest in the 'welfare' of young criminals can be traced to the nineteenth century and the construction of childhood as a period of 'natural innocence', but also of vulnerability to corrupting influences. From the Victorian era through much of the twentieth century, there was a growing belief that children and young people offended because of some form of deprivation which was more appropriately dealt with by kindness than harsh punishment, though discipline remained strict. Reformatory and Industrial Schools were introduced in the mid nineteenth century, and by the early twentieth century the separation of juvenile courts and custodial institutions from those of adults had been enshrined in law. In the post-war years, the focus on welfare continued, supported by Bowlby's work on maternal deprivation (described earlier). The philosophy of welfarism—which treated offending as a symptom of social or psychological deprivation and advocated attention to child welfare as the response—arguably reached its zenith in the late 1960s when the Children and Young Persons Act 1969 introduced measures to decriminalize young people and to give social workers greater influence over their treatment. The rapid demise of welfarism thereafter can be attributed to a political pincer movement, with the emerging New Right attacking it as undermining responsibility and being 'soft on crime', and left-wing critics arguing that it was oppressive in its effects. For instance, taking children into care following relatively minor offences effectively created an 'indeterminate sentence' which might end only on reaching adulthood, while further offences might then lead more quickly to custodial sentences as care was deemed to have 'failed'. During the 1970s, these critiques prompted a change of policy towards what became known as a justice model in which offending was treated as an act of will to be punished according to its seriousness.

Welfare after welfarism

The emergence of the justice model spelt the end of welfare as an overarching philosophy for dealing with young offenders. From that point onwards, interest in children's upbringing and circumstances would be constrained by the need to avoid any hint of 'making excuses'. However, a focus on offending behaviour did allow for identification of certain specific contributory factors such as substance misuse or problems with anger which could justify tailored treatment programmes.

During the 1980s, a new approach developed, based on diversion. Rooted in ideas that offending may well represent a 'passing phase' and that involvement with the criminal justice machinery should be avoided or kept to a minimum, the diversionary approach emphasized the use of cautions and community disposals and introduced innovations such as the making of reparation to victims or to the community (Haines and Drakeford 1998). Thus, paradoxically, despite the strong law-and-order emphasis of the Conservative government, the 1980s witnessed a dramatic fall in the use of custody. In the early 1990s, however, policy on young offenders took a marked 'punitive turn' following a series of moral panics and the controversy that surrounded the murder of toddler James Bulger by two boys barely above the age of criminal responsibility. A range of measures was introduced to increase the use of custody and to toughen its regimes. The Labour Party in opposition also endorsed this approach by pledging to be 'tough on crime' whilst adding the rider that they would also be 'tough on the causes of crime'. Importantly, however, this would not involve any return to welfarist principles.

Following the 1997 election, the New Labour government combined significant use of custody with a community regime based on supervised activities and intensive surveillance using electronic tagging, voice recognition, and police intelligence. A wider agenda of control was also pursued through the use of curfews and antisocial behaviour orders. Being tough on the causes of crime comprised both wider policy to combat poverty and promote social inclusion and a particular focus on parenting, reflecting key 'risk factors' identified in research (Farrington 1996). Emphasis was also placed on principles of restorative justice, whereby the young offender is encouraged to understand the impact of their crime and make restoration to the victim, through apology or community service.

Critics of this approach argue that by emphasizing responsibility and punishment, it is treating young people as 'offenders first, children second'. Children's charities and penal reform groups advocate that youth justice should adhere to the principles of children's rights, notably through decriminalization (by raising the age of criminal responsibility) and opposition to the use of custody (Monaghan et al. 2003). Citing the high levels of mental health problems, self-harm, and even suicide among young inmates, it is argued that young offenders should be treated as vulnerable and entitled to protection, for example by placement in secure accommodation rather than prisons when restraint is necessary (Allen 2006). Campaigning groups such as the Howard League for Penal Reform have enjoyed some success in clarifying that the Children Act 1989 and its protections apply within the 'secure estate'. New social work posts have been created to work in custodial facilities, but the basis and funding for them remain fragile. The approach to young offenders in the UK stands in marked contrast to most of continental Europe, being much closer in style to the United States. The European model remains more rooted in welfarist ideas, with much lower rates of custody, higher ages of criminal responsibility (typically 14–16 against 10 in England and Wales), and an emphasis on investigative enquiry rather than prosecution, though the Scottish hearings system has elements of this approach.

Conclusion: Coalition government: new directions?

Future gazing is always a risky enterprise and, at the time of writing, the coalition government 'elected' in May 2010 is still in its infancy. In addition, its life to date has taught us that we cannot necessarily rely on previous party commitments as an accurate guide to government policy. For the care and protection of children, the big question is how far the government will follow New Labour's emphasis on 'social investment' and its philosophy of 'progressive universalism', with services available to all but with help targeted most towards the disadvantaged. Both post-recession austerity and ideological opposition to 'statism' would suggest a significant retreat from the previous government's approach, and early measures would seem to confirm this.

The new government was quick to scrap Contact Point, a national database of children, on both cost-effectiveness and civil liberties grounds and signal a reduction in target setting. More directly in the field of child protection, the Munro Review (see above) was always premised upon the quest to reduce 'bureaucracy'. In a clear move away from progressive universalism, Sure Start is to be targeted much more closely on the most disadvantaged areas and its universalist aims largely abandoned. Direct spending on schools was largely protected in the autumn 2010 Comprehensive Spending Review, but the wider education budget from which child social care services are funded was subject to a 12 per cent reduction. Local authority budgets suffered much greater reductions and a removal of most ring-fencing, which leaves open the question of how far child social care services will be protected vis-à-vis other local government priorities. Government enthusiasm for early intervention has been translated into a dedicated funding stream but there is great uncertainty about how it will relate to existing projects such as Sure Start and whether it will in practice bring any additional resources. The scale of cuts is undoubtedly severe and it is likely that statutory responsibilities for child protection and looked after children will take priority, calling into question the level of family support services under the Children Act 1989, although some provision, such as short breaks for disabled children, appears to have received protection. However, as the Big Society is pursued, there are likely to more significant changes in the organization and delivery of care and protection services, with greater reliance on private and voluntary provision and further dismantling of local authority services.

KEY LEGISLATION

Prevention of Cruelty to and Protection of Children Act 1889 The Act's two key measures were first to make wilful cruelty or neglect a criminal offence, and second to allow a child victim to be removed and placed with a relative or other 'fit person'.

Children Act 1948 The Act's main measures were the establishment of Children's Departments within local authorities and clarification of circumstances within which children could be received into care voluntarily or where the local authority could assume parental rights. The Act also placed a duty on local authorities to attempt to return children to their families where possible, and to place them in foster families where not.

Children and Young Persons Act 1969 The Act is perhaps best known as the high point of welfare approaches to juvenile crime, with its various measures to decriminalize and to treat crime as a symptom of family problems. The main provision of the Act was the creation of the care order, which could be made by a court where parental care and control were regarded as inadequate and one of a series of conditions was met. These conditions were wide ranging, from being a victim of abuse or being in moral danger, through being beyond parental control, to non school attendance and offending behaviour.

Children Act 1975 The Act aimed to prioritize the welfare of the child, especially where this might be seen to conflict with the interests of their family. Its main measures related to facilitating adoption, allowing children to be legally 'freed' for adoption, strengthening the position of foster carers who wished to adopt, and introducing allowances for those who might not otherwise be able to afford to adopt. Adopted adults were given rights to their original birth certificates and hence a route to tracing their birth parents.

Children Act 1989 Though the term is not used in the Act itself, 'partnership with parents' is widely taken to be its guiding principle. The Act emphasized the importance of parental responsibility, and laid a duty on local authorities to support parents, including maximization of involvement when children are looked after by the state, even when subject of a care order. A greater role for the courts was seen as a way of strengthening the position of parents dealing with social work agencies. The Act also attempted to strengthen the rights of children to be involved in decisions affecting them, and to place greater emphasis on the extended family.

Adoption and Children Act 2002 The clear purpose of the Act was to increase the use of adoption for looked after children. It included measures to widen the pool of potential adopters, to offer them greater support and create a planning infrastructure that would facilitate adoption.

Children Act 2004 This Act sought to improve services for the care and protection of children in the wake of the Victoria Climbié inquiry. Its principal measures were aimed at improving 'joined up' working between professionals and agencies. These included the establishment of Local Safeguarding Children Boards, Directors of Children's Services, a preference for children's trusts to be developed, a common assessment framework to be used by professionals working with children, and databases that would allow for greater sharing of information. The Act also created the post of Children's Commissioner.

FURTHER READING

Kirton, **D.**, *Child Social Work Policy and Practice* (London: Sage, 2009) The author's own text provides more comprehensive coverage of all the issues covered in this chapter, and further detailed guidance on sources.

Frost, N., and Parton, **N.**, *Understanding Children's Social Care* (London: Sage, 2009) This text also provides wide-ranging coverage of child social care and incorporates discussion of wider social policy developments relating to children.

Garrett, **P.**, *'Transforming' Children's Services: Social Work, Neoliberalism and the Modern World* (Maidenhead: Open University Press, 2009). Garrett's most recent book places key reforms of the New Labour government in the wider context of neo-liberalism. Key areas covered include the effects of globalization, use of data gathering and surveillance, reform of the care system and antisocial behaviour on the part of children and families.

Fox Harding, L., *Perspectives in Child Care Policy* (2nd edn) (London: Longman, 1997). Fox Harding provides an excellent analysis of competing value perspectives within child welfare —which she terms laissez-faire, state paternalism, birth family rights, and children's rights—and their impact on policy development.

Corby, B., *Child Abuse: Towards a Knowledge Base* (3rd edn) (Buckingham: Open University Press, 2005). Of the many texts on child abuse and protection, Corby's book offers the clearest and most comprehensive overview of definitions, theory, and research findings as they relate to understanding contexts, causes, and consequences of child maltreatment.

Parton, N., *Safeguarding Childhood: Early Intervention and Surveillance in a Late Modern Society* (Basingstoke: Palgrave, 2006). This text provides an excellent contextualized analysis of developments in relation to safeguarding children.

Thomas, N., *Social Work with Young People in Care* (Basingstoke: Palgrave, 2005). Thomas's book combines theoretical perspectives with policy and practice issues as they relate to looked after children and care leavers.

Smith, M., *Rethinking Residential Care: Positive Perspectives* (Bristol: The Policy Press, 2009). Smith offers a very readable overview of debates relating to residential care and argues a case for its continuing value as a form of provision for looked after children.

Sinclair, I., *Fostering Now: Messages From Research* (London: Jessica Kingsley Publishers, 2005). Part of an ongoing series of 'messages from research', Sinclair's book summarizes findings from a number of recent studies of foster care. The author attempts to look at those factors that make placements successful from the perspectives of foster children, carers, and professionals.

Triseliotis, J., **Shireman**, J., **and Hundleby**, M., *Adoption: Theory, Policy and Practice* (London: Cassell, 1997). Although now quite dated, this book provides a very good overview of research and debates relating to adoption. A useful complement is provided by Department of Health (1999) *Adoption Now: Messages from Research*, (Chichester: Wiley), which summarizes a number of adoption studies carried out in the 1990s.

Muncie, J., *Youth and Crime: a Critical Introduction* (3rd edn) (London: Sage, 2009). This book is probably the most useful of the overview texts in the field of youth crime and youth justice. It provides a good historical account of youth crime and locates discussion in a wider context of theorizing about youth and youth culture(s).

Smith, R., *Youth Justice: Ideas, Policy, Practice* (2nd edn) (Cullompton: Willan, 2007). The main strength of this book is its very detailed analysis of the workings of youth justice, making it complementary to Muncie's book in many respects.

@ USEFUL WEBSITES

For information on current government policy on care and protection of children go to **www.education.gov.uk/**.

Other important government websites include **www.ofsted.gov.uk/** which provides useful information drawn from OFSTED inspections. OFSTED also hosts the office of the Children's Rights Director whose functions including carrying out research on services for looked after children. His reports can be found at **www.rights4me.org/reports.cfm**.

The main role of the Social Care Institute for Excellence **www.scie.org.uk/** is to identify and disseminate good practice in social care. To this end, it provides a range of resources, including practice guidance, reports, and knowledge reviews, the latter being particularly useful. SCIE's online library can be found at **www.scie-socialcareonline.org.uk/**.

Hosted by the National Children's Bureau, the Centre for Excellence and Outcomes in Children's and Young People's Services, **www.c4eo.org.uk/**, seeks to collate and share information to promote 'evidence-based' policy and practice. The website provides information on publications and events and offers some useful research tools such as access to performance data.

The major children's charity websites carry a range of useful information, including news, campaigns, and resources for children and families as well as research reports. The most important are as follows: **www.actionforchildren.org.uk/**; **www.childrenssociety.org.uk/**; **www.nspcc.org.uk/**; **www.barnardos.org.uk/**.

There are various third sector organizations working for looked after children and care leavers, the websites of which contain useful information on services, campaigns, guidance, and research. The main organizations are: **www.thewhocarestrust.org.uk/**; **www.voiceyp.org/**; **www.anationalvoice.org/**; **www.careleavers.com/**.

For information on research, policy analysis, and practice guidance for all 'stakeholders' in family placement, see **www.baaf.org.uk**; **www.fostering.net/**.

The Family Rights Group (FRG) represents families dealing with social care agencies. Information on its work, including guidance to families and professionals, and research can be found at **www.frg.org.uk/**.

Q ESSAY QUESTIONS

1 Is early intervention a good thing?

2 What are the major challenges in conducting research into the causes or consequences of child maltreatment?

3 To what extent is child maltreatment a 'male' problem?

4 What are the most effective ways to provide permanence for looked after children?

5 How far will reforming the care system help to reduce social exclusion?

6 Should the treatment of young offenders be based more closely on children's rights?

ONLINE RESOURCE CENTRE

For additional material and resources, please visit the Online Resource Centre at: **www.oxfordtextbooks.co.uk/orc/baldock4e/**.

15

Housing and housing policy

Chris Pickvance

Contents

Introduction

In this chapter we examine the development of the institutions through which housing is provided in the UK, the changing pattern of housing policy, and the present housing situation. It is shown that historically housing policy responded very slowly to housing conditions, and that it was political changes which were the stimulus to advances in housing policy. Similarly, today housing policy is as much concerned with political goals, such as securing votes and expanding the scope for market activity, as with meeting housing need. It is thus argued that housing policy is only partly a social policy. The distribution of households across the housing stock is discussed and the effects of processes such as the expansion of owner-occupation and the residualization of council housing are outlined.

Learning outcomes

By the end of the chapter you will understand:

1 how the main housing tenures emerged in the UK and what drove this evolution;
2 why housing policy is only partially a social policy;
3 how households with different social characteristics are distributed across the housing stock;
4 how access to owner-occupation and council housing works;
5 how access problems impact on marginal owner-occupiers and homeless people.

What is housing?

Housing patterns and ways of thinking about housing vary between countries, reflecting their different national housing traditions. As every visitor to continental Europe—east or west—knows, flat-dwelling is a much more common pattern than in England and Wales. On the other hand, in Scottish cities in the nineteenth century the 'continental' pattern of flat-dwelling took root rather than the pattern of terraced housing south of the border. The explanation for this is to do with industrialization, wage levels, patterns of land ownership, land prices, the organization of the building industry, and architectural influence. For example, in Scotland in the nineteenth century, working-class wage levels were lower than in England while land prices and building costs were higher, and architects were able to press the flat-dwelling solution more successfully.

A second difference concerns housing tenure, which refers to the legal relationship between household and dwelling. It is widely assumed in the UK that owner-occupation is associated with high income. However, as Table 15.1 shows, Romania, one of the poorest countries in the EU, has the highest level of owner-occupation, and Germany, one of the richest, has the lowest level. Clearly this raises questions about what is owned (flat vs. house), its value and quality, and how it is built (self-built, commercially). It also emphasizes the contrast between agricultural societies, where owner-occupation is the norm, and urban industrial societies, where industrialization leads initially to the growth of rented housing. Tenure, therefore, like any other single characteristic of housing, conceals as much as it reveals.

Table 15.1 also draws attention to contrasts in rented housing between countries. 'Reduced rent housing' varies from 1 per cent to 18.2 per cent; this is usually social housing, i.e. housing allocated by non-market methods to benefit lower-income households. In practice this varies between countries in terms of which social groups it goes to; in France middle-income households are found in

Table 15.1 European housing patterns, 2008

	% owner-occupation	% reduced rent or free	% market rented	Average floor space (m²)
Spain	83.2	8.6	8.1	85.3 (1991)
Greece	76.7	5.4	18.0	79.7 (1991)
UK	72.5	18.2	9.4	85.0 (1991)
France	62.4	18.1	19.5	88.0 (1996)
Sweden	68.8	1.0	30.2	89.8 (1997)
Germany (2006)	50.5	9.5	40.0	86.7 (1998)
Romania	96.5	2.6	0.9	n.a.

Source: Columns 1–3: Eurostat Table ilc-lvh02 accessed 8 October 2010 **http://epp.eurostat.ec.europa.eu/portal/page/ portal/statistics/search_database**; Column 4: Sak, B and Raponi, M. (2002) Table 2.1

this sector too, unlike in the UK. The market rent category refers to housing for which a market rent exists but includes tenants receiving some type of housing subsidy to help them afford the rent, as well as those receiving none. Poorer households can thus be found in both the reduced rent and the market rent sectors. Average dwelling size does not vary greatly between the countries listed.

In the UK, thinking about housing centres on housing tenure, and the following four categories of tenure will be used throughout the chapter:

- owner-occupiers: who own outright or are buying their house or flat with a loan (which is known as a mortgage);
- private tenants: who rent their house or flat from a private landlord;
- council tenants: who rent their dwelling from the local council;
- housing association tenants: who rent from housing associations (which are also known as registered social landlords, or RSLs). Council and housing association housing is often referred to as 'social housing'.

More information on each will be given below. But it should be remembered that tenure gives a partial picture of a housing situation.

Every country, then, has its own way of thinking about housing, which relates to a tradition of housing provision, policy debate, and intervention, and in turn to the country's particular economic, social, and political history. In this chapter we explore these in the UK case. We examine the development of the main types of tenure, and of housing policy, analyse the present housing situation, and show in detail how the owner-occupation and council housing sectors work. The emphasis is on how far housing policy should be seen as social policy and how the housing 'system' works in practice.

The emergence of different housing tenures and the evolution of housing policy up to 1939

We start by examining how and why the four main types of tenure developed and evolved. This historical account will also explain the emergence of housing policy, and will allow us to introduce the question of how far housing policy is about meeting housing need and how far it has other objectives.

In the nineteenth century the vast mass of urban households were private tenants, and their landlords were middle-class business and professional people who invested in housing as a safe way of saving. Low average income levels for most meant that anything beyond renting a room or a house was out of the question. Owner-occupation was restricted to the very well-off. It was in this situation that two types of initiative developed which were to have long-term consequences for housing provision in the UK: building societies and state action. There were others, such as philanthropic housing and employer-provided housing, but these had no lasting effects.

Building societies started as a self-help solution to housing conditions. They developed independently of the state, and subsequently became one of the most important institutions of the UK housing scene.

Building societies were created in the early nineteenth century by people who earned enough to be able to save, and who formed societies to enable them to build houses for themselves. The principle was that the members would commit themselves to making regular savings which would be used to build houses once a sufficient amount had accumulated. This meant that once the first house had been built and the first member obtained a house, the members would continue to make payments into the society until a house had been built for the last member. The society would then 'terminate'. Terminating building societies only worked if members trusted each other to keep up their payments until they all had houses. In practice they were vulnerable to members losing their jobs or falling ill. A second variety was the 'permanent' building society, in which savers did not need to be borrowers, and this became the dominant form of building society, though until the 1930s they lent mainly to private landlords. Unlike public companies owned by their shareholders, building societies were mutual organizations owned by their members.

In the nineteenth century, building societies could not be a widely used solution to housing provision, since they were restricted to the small minority who saved. However, in the interwar period they expanded considerably. They became a convenient place for investors to save—replacing houses in this respect—and as average incomes rose the fraction of the population which could afford to buy a house with a long-term loan increased. The interwar rise in owner-occupation was thus facilitated by the growth of the building societies. As Table 15.2 shows, by the late 1930s owner-occupation was established as a significant form of housing tenure. The growth of building societies

Table 15.2 Housing tenure in Great Britain, 1914–2007

	Owner-occupier	Public rented	Private rented	Registered social landlord	Other tenures
1914	10.0	1.0	80.0	0	9.0
1938	25.0	10.0	56.0	0	9.0
1951	29.6	18.6	51.8	0	
1961	42.7	26.8	30.5	0	
1971	50.1	30.4	19.5	0	
1981	57.7	29.0	11.1	2.2	
1991	66.0	11.4	9.4	3.1	
2001	69.4	14.3	9.8	6.5	
2007	69.4	9.6	12.5	8.5	

Note: 'Public rented' includes new towns as well as local councils. From 1951 'private rented' includes other tenures such as house with job.

Source: Pre-1971: Forrest et al. (1990: 57); 1971–2007: www.clg.gov.uk/housing/statistics, Table 102, accessed 19 October 2010

up to the Second World War happened with minimal government support. Governments established a regulatory framework to prevent fraud and provide security to savers, but did not provide financial support. Today the number of building societies has fallen sharply due to merger, conversion into banks (demutualization), or nationalization (during the 2007–9 financial crisis).

The other main development in the nineteenth century was the gradual growth of pressure for state intervention in housing, which led ultimately to council housing.

As the quotation from Engels in Box 15.1 shows, housing conditions in the nineteenth century were atrocious and aroused moral outrage among observers. If there was a simple connection between housing conditions and housing policy, this would have been a time of dramatic advances in housing policy. In fact it was not. The slow emergence of housing policy shows how ideology, self-interest, and politics are far more important than housing need.

The nineteenth century was a period of laissez-faire in the economic sphere: the market was supposed to work best with minimal state involvement. Those who owned property resented state intrusion into their rights, and in particular central interference in the running of localities. Since only the propertied had the vote until the later nineteenth century, they were able to control local policy. In the early nineteenth century most local councils were made up of landlords who were unlikely to initiate action that would affect the housing they owned or increase the local taxes they paid. They therefore did little—until the 1840s, when cholera struck. The desire of the propertied class for self-preservation overcame their resistance to legislation, and an exception to laissez-faire was allowed. Local and central state action on sanitation and urban infrastructure took place where the benefits to the propertied classes were clear. This paved the way for further state action.

Public health professionals were at the forefront of pressure for reform and had some support from politicians. But landlords defended their right to run their houses as they chose, whatever the resulting housing conditions. The second half of the nineteenth century saw a gradual acquisition of powers by local councils to regulate new and existing housing in their areas. They gained powers to set minimum standards of lighting, ventilation, sanitation, and structural stability in new houses,

---

Box 15.1 Urban housing conditions in 1843

These streets are often so narrow that a person can step from the window of one house into that of its opposite neighbour, while the houses are piled so high, storey upon storey, that the light can scarcely penetrate into the court or alley that lies between. In this part of the city there are neither sewers nor other drains, nor even privies belonging to the houses. In consequence, all refuse, garbage and excrements of at least 50,000 persons are thrown into gutters every night, so that, in spite of all street sweeping, a mass of dried filth and foul vapours are created, which not only offend the sight and smell, but endanger the health of the inhabitants in the highest degree. Is it to be wondered at, that in such localities all considerations of health, morals, and even the most ordinary decency are utterly neglected? On the contrary, all who are intimately acquainted with the condition of the inhabitants will testify to the high degree which disease, wretchedness, and demoralization have here reached. Society in such districts has sunk to a level indescribably low and hopeless. The houses of the poor are generally filthy, and are never cleansed. They consist in most cases of a single room which, while subject to the worst ventilation, is yet usually kept cold by the broken and badly-fitting windows and is sometimes damp and partly below ground level, always badly furnished and thoroughly uncomfortable, a straw heap often serving as a bed, upon which men and women, young and old, sleep in revolting confusion.

(Report in an English magazine, *The Artisan*, 1843, quoted in Engels (1969: 69))

and powers to close and demolish houses unfit for human habitation. They were also obliged to rehouse the tenants and to compensate owners of such housing. These powers were given under public health legislation. It was only in the 1880s that government realized that housing issues needed to be addressed directly. In 1890 councils were allowed to build working-class housing as long as it was sold within ten years—a restriction later removed.

However, the strength of laissez-faire ideology meant that Parliament would not pass **mandatory legislation**, i.e. laws that required action to be taken. Instead it passed permissive legislation, which allowed councils who wished to apply these measures to do so but had no effect on the remainder (Gauldie 1974). Despite these obstacles to public action, a few councils took a pioneering role and built council houses. State intervention in housing became more acceptable in the late nineteenth and early twentieth centuries because of changes in the political situation. The political strength of the working class increased considerably after the vote was given to working-class men in the 1870s, and working-class political parties formed. The embryonic Labour Party made winning control of local councils a first step towards gaining power nationally, and this reinforced the importance of local councils as a means of achieving policy goals. Public mobilization over the state of working-class housing increased and governments were afraid of disorder. Lastly, government grants to local councils increased so that the cost of public action to local ratepayers was reduced.

The culmination of this pressure for a new direction in housing policy did not occur until 1919, when councils became legally obliged to build houses to meet housing need, subject to central government approval, and were given a government subsidy to do so. This dramatic step was partly due to government concern about housebuilding levels: the private sector had been failing to build enough houses before 1914, and war had meant a halt to housebuilding. But again the crucial stimuli were changes in political conditions:

- the continued growth of the labour movement as a political force (and fear that the Russian revolution might incite workers in the UK);
- the Glasgow rent strike in 1915, which caused government to introduce rent control to keep down rent levels;
- the experience of war, with the huge contribution of the mass of the population and the feeling of solidarity that it created, which led the government to believe that a new policy was necessary. Hence the name for the first council housing programme: 'homes fit for heroes' (Gilbert 1970).

It was this policy that gave councils their prominent role as direct providers of housing and helped maintain the tradition of strong local council action. In other countries subsidies were channelled to private building firms or specially created housing organizations.

This historical background reveals the three main types of state intervention in housing:

- The first is state regulation, mostly of private sector activity. This includes the legislation already referred to concerning overcrowding and the closure of unfit housing, building standards, rent controls, and the regulation of building societies. These all remain important, and have been elaborated in the post-war period. For example, detailed planning regulations now exist to improve the appearance and orderliness of the built environment and achieve social goals, and building regulations now reflect the new concern with energy efficiency.
- The second is state subsidization and taxation: the state supports or penalizes private actors such as households, landlords, financial institutions, or building firms in order to encourage or discourage certain behaviours. The tax relief previously paid on mortgage interest was designed to encourage owner-occupation, the cheap government loans paid to housing associations help pay for the social housing they build, and the housing benefits paid to poor households are designed to shield them from the effects of unaffordable rents in the market and social housing sectors. On the other hand, the taxation of capital gains from the sale of a secondary residence is

a form of discouragement of multiple house ownership, though this tax is often avoided due to flexible tax laws.

- The third is direct provision. In the case of housing the clear example of this is council housing where, instead of regulating and subsidizing or taxing private agents to achieve policy aims, government acts directly.

The first and third types of state intervention are mainly the work of local councils (or the 'local state') while the second involves central government and local branches of ministries too. It should be noted that in the case of housing the contrast between 'state' and 'market' provision is particularly unhelpful. Whereas the concept of state provision, i.e. council housing, is clear enough, all private provision, whether by private landlords or owner-occupation, is highly regulated by the state. Hence there is no such thing as a pure market form of housing provision.

Post-war tenure patterns and housing policy

In the post-war period, as Table 15.2 shows, there have been four major tenure trends: the continuing growth in owner-occupation, the continuing decline and recent slight recovery of private renting, the rise and subsequent decline in council renting, and the rise of housing association housing. These changes are connected with changes in housing policy which have made it far more varied in its aims. Housing policy has become an explicit means of winning votes for the main political parties from the better-off as well as a social policy favouring low-income groups. Let us examine policies towards the various housing tenures.

Council housing

From 1945 housing policy concentrated on reconstruction, and council housing played an important role in this task. Subsequently the massive slum clearance programme of the 1950s and 1960s created space for further building of council houses and flats, including the much-criticized high-rise blocks. The council share of the housing stock continued to rise until a peak in 1977–8 in Great Britain, after which it went into a slow decline. We now examine the political and economic reasons for this evolution.

The rationale for council housing is that it is a way of meeting housing need for those who cannot afford a reasonable quality of housing on the private housing market. To achieve this aim, council housing rent levels need to be below market levels. The difficulty of achieving this had emerged in the 1920s, when the rent levels of the first council houses placed them out of reach of the lowest income groups in the working class. Whether council housing is affordable to poor households depends partly on rent levels and partly on social security benefits (such as housing benefits) designed to help with housing costs.

There are three reasons why rent levels have been lower in council housing:

- because the government subsidized the production of council housing. For example, the rate of interest the government pays when it borrows money to build council housing is a special below-market rate;
- because until 1990 councils could subsidize rents from rates (the predecessor of council taxes);
- because council housing operates outside the housing market. This difference between council and private rented housing is explained in Box 15.2.

Policy towards the council housing sector has changed considerably since the Second World War. Initially there was agreement between the Labour and Conservative parties on its importance. But in the mid1960s the Labour government argued that the job of post-war reconstruction was completed and that slum clearance should give way to individual house improvement. Hence the level

---

Box 15.2 Council and private rent levels: how being outside the market helps keep council rents low

Rent levels in council housing depend on original building costs (and also on repair/modernization costs and subsidy levels), whereas rent levels in private rented housing depend on current market values.

In a period of rising house values the current market value of a house may be far higher than its original building cost. In the private sector, successive owners each make a capital gain as the house is sold at successively higher prices, and landlords base their rents on the current value. Council houses do not go through this process, but remain outside the market. (They do have a market value, but this is irrelevant as long as they remain council houses. Only when they are privatized is this market value relevant.) It is because council house rents are based on original building cost, not current value, that they can be much lower than private sector rents. Additionally, since most councils own houses built at different periods, they generally engage in 'rent pooling', which spreads the advantage of the low building costs of the oldest houses over the whole stock.

---

of council house building was reduced. The Conservative Party took this further, and felt it should cater only for a small minority of households, while Labour continued to give it a broad role. These debates fed into conflicting positions about the level of government subsidy, rent levels, and the desirability of selling council housing.

In 1972 the Conservative government's Housing Finance Act reduced the subsidies paid on council housing in order to force councils to raise rents which the government considered excessively low. Its motivation was to encourage households in the council sector to move into private housing, and to discourage demand from new applicants for council housing. The new rents were called 'fair rents', which meant 'closer to private-sector rents'. This major change was an attempt to reverse the traditional advantage of low rents in the council sector by aligning rents with those in the private sector. This measure was reversed by Labour in 1975 but reintroduced by the Conservatives in 1980. The effect was that between 1980 and 1989 average council rents rose from £13 to £20 per week in constant prices. Over the same period, subsidies per council tenant fell by two-thirds, while they increased by one-third per owner-occupier household. By 1995 council rents were at a level which required housing benefit to be paid to two-thirds of tenants in England, which fuelled an increase in spending on housing benefits—see Table 15.3. (The two-thirds figure has changed little since then and in 2008–9, 59 per cent of all social housing tenants in England received housing benefit: CLG 2010.) Paradoxically, therefore, the price of raising council rents to make the sector less attractive was an increase in housing benefit expenditure which more than made up for the reduction in subsidies paid to councils. This example of the dependence of a 'market solution' on increased government spending emphasizes the obstacles to market solutions in the housing of poorer households.

The second major policy change affecting council housing was the right to buy (or council house privatization) policy introduced by the Conservative government in 1980. This policy gave council tenants the right to buy (or 'privatize') their council house or flat at a discount. Whereas previously councils had had the right to sell housing, only a minority of them had used it. The new policy thus gave tenants a new right. The size of the discount was between 33 per cent and 50 per cent initially, the maximum later being raised to 60 per cent for houses and 70 per cent for flats. A maximum discount of £50,000 was set but this was reduced to £38,000 in 1997. In 2001 this figure was reduced to £15,000 in Scotland and in 2003 to £16,000 in forty-two areas of high demand in the south-east.

Table 15.3 Public spending on housing, UK, 1976–2008, at 1995–6 prices (£ million)

	Current spending	Gross capital spending	Capital receipts	Net capital spending	Current and net capital spending	Housing benefits	Total spending	Mortgage interest relief
	a	b	c	d	a+d	e	f	g
1976–7	5,292	12,504	1,152	11,352	16,644	2,947	20,262	4,659
1981–2	3,960	6,277	2,387	3,889	7,850	4,087	12,399	4,569
1986–7	2,321	6,988	3,748	3,250	5,572	5,974	12,063	7,218
1991–2	1,406	7,795	2,658	5,138	6,544	8,513	15,342	6,823
1996–7	–115	4,996	2,279	2,717	2,602	12,423	15,267	2,634
1999–2000	n.a.	n.a.	n.a.	n.a.	3,293	10,358	13,651	1,429
2003–4	n.a.	n.a.	n.a.	n.a.	4,840	10,375	15,215	0
2008–9	n.a.	n.a.	n.a.	n.a.	6,697	14,196	20,89	0

Col. b - col. c = col. d
Col. a + col. d + col. e + N. Ireland spending = col. f
Cols. a–d are for Great Britain; cols. e–g are for the UK.

Source: Hills (1998: Table 5A1; **www.inlandrevenue.gov.uk/statistics,** Table 5.2), HM Treasury (2005a: Table 3.6; 2010, Table 5.2), HM Treasury GDP (market price) deflators

Smaller reductions applied elsewhere. Restrictions were also introduced to penalize resale within three years.

The government had several motivations in introducing this policy:

- the pursuit of a property-owning democracy as a political goal;
- the belief that councils have too much power and too many assets, and are inefficient landlords;
- the belief that the scope for market solutions in housing should be expanded because they are more efficient.

The right to buy policy worked in tandem with the policy mentioned above of reducing subsidies and increasing rents in the council sector to make it less attractive.

The policy achieved its aims. It was the main factor in the 64.6 per cent reduction of the stock of council (and New Town) dwellings in Great Britain from 6.5 million in 1979 to 2.3 million in 2008. As a proportion of all housing, the size of the sector shrank from a peak of 31.7 per cent of all housing in 1977–8 to 8.9 per cent in 2008. At the same time the level of housebuilding by councils fell to below 10,000 houses per year in 1991 and to under 1,000 houses per year after 1996. Councils were only allowed to use a small proportion of the proceeds of the sale of council housing for new building. The result was that the capacity of the council sector to provide housing for the groups most in need in the future has declined.

What were the detailed effects of the right to buy policy? Research by Forrest and Murie (2010) shows that:

- Houses were much more likely to be bought than flats. Between 1981 and 1985 only 5 per cent of sales were of flats whereas they made up 30 per cent of the stock.
- Attractive houses, e.g. post-war houses, with two or more bedrooms and a garden, and houses in attractive areas were most likely to be bought.
- Council housing in areas with higher levels of owner-occupation, higher income levels, and under Conservative control were more likely to be bought. In London, sales levels in outer boroughs were far higher than in inner boroughs.
- The households most likely to purchase were those with a head in employment, with multiple earners, which owned a car, whose adult members were in the 30–59 age group, which had school-age children, and which were white rather than black.

Conversely, there was a low rate of sales in areas with high unemployment and high social deprivation.

This led to two important outcomes:

- Changes in the quality of the council housing stock. As the most attractive council housing was purchased, the housing remaining in the council sector became less attractive, more likely to be in unpopular areas, and more likely to be made up of flats. (40 per cent of social housing is in the 20 per cent of neighborhoods with highest levels of deprivation (Hills 2007: 91)).
- Changes in the social composition of households in the council sector. Council tenants have become more homogeneous and increasingly share characteristics associated with poverty, e.g. having no earners or being female-headed households. This is known as the residualization of council housing. For example, between 1962 and 2005 the proportion of households in council housing in England with no earners (i.e. whose members are unemployed, pensioners, or have long-term illness) rose from 7 per cent to 68 per cent, while in the owner-occupied sector it rose only from 19 per cent to 33 per cent. There is therefore a growing gulf between the two tenure sectors, which is discussed further below.

A third policy was the Decent Homes improvement programme, started in 2000 with the aim of raising the standard of all social housing by 2010. This involved public spending on improvements in the council sector of about £3 billion per annum and allowing RSLs to raise their rents (£1 billion per annum). Typical expenditure was £4,000–£8,000 per dwelling. As 2010 approached, the increase in number of houses that had become non-decent since 2000 meant that the 100 per cent target was not reached but it is estimated that 95 per cent of all council housing and 93 per cent of RSL housing will have benefited from the programme by 2010 (NAO 2010).

Despite these improvements in quality, there is a desperate shortage of council housing and in 2009 there were 1.8 million households on council waiting lists in the England (CLG website, Table 600).

Finally, the 2010 coalition government announced major policy changes affecting council housing. Firstly, funding for all new social housebuilding will be cut by nearly half (from £8.4 billion in 2008–11 to £4.5 billion in 2011–14). The government wants 155,000 houses to be built over the 2011–14 period. Secondly, new council tenants will no longer have secure lifetime tenancies but fixed-term tenancies (possibly for 10 years, with regular reviews of their circumstances) and councils (and RSLs) will be expected to fund new building by raising rents for new tenants to an 'intermediate' level of 80 per cent of market rents. The average rent for a three-bedroom social home is expected to rise from £85 a week to £250 a week. On the other hand, the rent levels and tenure of existing council tenants will remain unchanged, except that housing benefit will rise in line with the Consumer Price Index rather than the Retail Price Index which includes housing costs and generally rises faster than the CPI. The result will be to create two 'classes' of council tenant.

Owner-occupation

The continuing rise of owner-occupation, from 29.6 per cent in 1951 to 69.4 per cent in 2007, has been the most striking trend of the post-war period (see Table 15.2). Successive governments have adopted policies favouring owner-occupation, the type of housing tenure favoured by middle- and high-income groups. In 1963 the tax on imputed rent was abolished, in 1965 principal residence owner-occupied houses were exempted from capital gains tax, and in 1974 tax relief on mortgage interest was left untouched when it was abolished for most other types of borrowing. Additional government support for owner-occupation has taken the form of tax concessions to building societies to enable them to offer higher rates of interest to savers, guarantees to savers in the case of a building society bankruptcy, and the discreet encouragement of takeovers of failing building societies. Support for owner-occupation through mortgage tax relief reached a peak in 1988, after which the value of the relief declined so that its abolition in 2000 was relatively uncontroversial. However, a recent estimate of the value of tax relief on imputed rent and capital gains is £12.7 billion (Wilcox 2010, Table 2.6.1).

After 1991 the proportion of owner-occupied housing rose more slowly than in the previous decade and house prices only recovered their 1989 level in real terms by 1998, and there was a new caution among borrowers and lenders. Eventually confidence in house purchase returned, fuelled by low interest rates and the boom continued until the banking crisis of 2007–9 and consequent economic crisis. The Labour governments of 1997–2010 set regional housing targets to ensure that the planning system allocated enough land for residential purposes, but failed to find a way of increasing the number of houses built. The result was completion of 161,000 new owner-occupied houses in 1997–8, rising to 188,000 in 2007–8 and 139,000 in 2008–9 (CLG website, Table 209).

The coalition government of 2010 announced plans to end regional housing targets under the banner of 'greater localism' and announced a small 'homes bonus incentive' worth six years of council tax to local authorities for each house built in their area (and £350 more for affordable housing).

The strong growth of owner-occupation has led to a debate about whether this growth is entirely due to the government policies outlined which make it more attractive than other tenures. There are two counter-arguments. The first is that in a period of inflation of the type experienced between 1970 and 1990 any asset which provided a hedge against inflation would be very popular. Since the value of houses rose faster than inflation until 1988, there is evidence to support this argument. Calculations by Saunders (1990) based on surveys in three towns in 1986 showed average net capital gains of £20,000 per owner-occupier household at 1986 prices. (Net capital gain is gross capital gain less the value of the outstanding mortgage.) For most households these gains are paper gains in the sense that they are hard to realize; though this can happen, e.g. through inheritance or by over-mortgaging (when a house buyer moves house and takes out a larger mortgage than needed, releasing cash in the process). Capital gains may nevertheless act as incentives to owner-occupation alongside government policies. Interestingly, in Germany, where the level of owner-occupation is low, it is not regarded as a hedge against inflation, and house prices rose only 0.4 per cent per year between 1972 and 1989, compared with 2.2 per cent per year in the UK between 1948 and 1988 (McCrone and Stephens 1995: 53).

The second counter-argument is also put forward by Saunders, who argues that owner-occupation offers greater security and scope for freedom, control, and self-expression than any other type of housing. He goes further and suggests it may be rooted in a 'natural' desire for possession. Others have argued that rented housing can offer the same attractions, and that what is important is that the dwelling is self-contained.

These counter-arguments are not, of course, mutually exclusive. Hence, for example, from Saunders's point of view the different national levels of owner-occupation indicated in Table 15.1 do not imply that there are national differences in the 'natural' desire for owner-occupation. They could equally be due to government policies and to differences in economic incentives to households.

One effect of the rising share of owner-occupation has been the increased significance of owner-occupiers as a bloc of voters. The very success of policies favouring owner-occupation has meant that housing policy is increasingly identified with policy which meets the needs of owner-occupiers.

Private renting

The long-term decline of private renting can be attributed to a number of factors:

- the encouragements to owner-occupation and subsidies for council housing which have not been paralleled by favourable treatment for landlords;
- the attraction to landlords of converting rented housing to owner-occupation;
- the stigma attached to private landlords due to abuses;
- legislation which gave certain tenants security against eviction in the 1960s and discouraged landlords;
- the threat of a return to rent control.

By the late 1980s, however, the size of the sector had shrunk so much that the government introduced new policies such as new types of tenancy with fewer rights for tenants, incentives to householders to rent rooms, and the removal of regulation of rents in new rented housing (1980) and in new rental contracts except where the tenant receives housing benefit (1989). After the collapse of the equity markets in 1987 there was a renewed belief in housing as a safe long-term investment, which led to an upsurge of landlordism via the purchase of houses for rent ('buy-to-let'). These factors, combined with rising house prices and low interest rates on savings, eventually led to an increase in the private rented sector from a low of 2.1 million dwellings in 1989 to 3.2 million by 2007. Nevertheless, there is still a shortage of housing in this sector, rents are high, and tenants cannot always enforce their rights against landlords. The level of rents in the private sector has been a factor in the rise in spending on housing benefits since in 2008–9—19 per cent of private tenants in England received housing benefit.

In 2010, the coalition government announced major changes to housing benefit in the private sector (known since 2008 as Local Housing Allowance). LHA levels will be set at 30 per cent rather than 50 per cent of prevailing rents in an area, the minimum age at which LHA can be claimed for a one person dwelling will rise from 25 to 35 (to encourage sharing), there will be maximum levels (or 'caps') according to house size, and a 10 per cent cut in LHA for people who have received Jobseeker's Allowance for one year (from 2013). There will also be caps on the total benefits received per household of £500 per week from 2013, or £350 per week for out-of-work single people. The aim is to cut the cost of local housing allowances by £1.8 billion per year by forcing landlords to reduce rents, or, where they do not, to force households to move to lower-rent housing or areas (or other regions). This is expected to have very sharp effects in central London and to increase the amount of homelessness.

Housing associations

The 1980s Conservative governments' dislike of council housing was accompanied by support for housing associations. These are non-profit organizations which generally provide rented housing to groups with particular needs, such as elderly people or young people. Originally they were largely funded by government money—on condition that they kept rents below certain levels in order to appeal to low-income households. By 1990 they were building more new housing in the UK than councils (19,300 compared with 16,400 out of a total of 197,900 completions). Their contribution to new building peaked in 1995 (38,600, 19.4 per cent of the total of 198,500), fell to 18,000 in 2003 (9.5 per cent of the 190,600 total) and by 2007 had risen again to 28,500 (13.2 per cent of 216,700). One channel by which the housing association sector increased was 'Section 101'. This is the requirement placed by local authorities on residential developers building say 20 or more houses to set aside a proportion of them (e.g. 20 per cent) which are then sold to housing associations who allocate tenants to them. This was a means of obliging developers to make a contribution to the community and was at the expense of their profits. Section 101 proved not to be a reliable source of social housing since, as private house building declined from 2007, so did this source of social housing.

Housing associations' difficulties increased after 1988 when they came under government pressure to expand but also to rely less on government funding and more on private funding. Under this pressure they have diversified their activities considerably into housing management and urban regeneration, and even into providing market housing. They try to use some of the profits from these activities to subsidize their traditional provision of housing for groups with specific needs, but have had to charge higher rents to pay back the higher interest rates on private sector loans. They are thus less able to provide housing for needy groups than before. This is why, as indicated earlier, a majority of social housing tenants receive higher housing benefit. As mentioned earlier, in 2010 the coalition government announced a cut of funding for new social housebuilding (mostly housing association housing) and wants increased rents to be used to cover more of the cost of building.

Homelessness

The definition of homelessness is a difficult one. The narrowest definition is 'rooflessness'—meaning those sleeping rough. Wider definitions include those who are squatting, those who are staying temporarily with friends and relatives ('sofa surfing'), and those living in hostels for the homeless run by charities or by local councils. Even wider definitions include those living in insecure private housing at risk of eviction, and those who are concealed because they are living as parts of other households. In addition, minorities of homeless people have problems such as drug or alcohol abuse, mental health, or violent behaviour. Clearly the reality is much more complex than the single word 'homeless'.

Government responses have been twofold. In 1977 local councils were given the responsibility of housing **'unintentionally homeless'** people, a label which implies a distinction between the 'deserving' and the 'undeserving'. This was the culmination of a long campaign by squatters drawing attention to empty council housing (Bailey 1973) which finally found support from a Labour government. In 1985 the obligation was redefined, and the **statutory homeless** were defined as those who were unintentionally homeless and who fell into a 'priority need' group, e.g. households with children, pregnant women, or 'vulnerable' persons, and were eligible for housing. Single homeless people and couples without children are generally outside this category (Malpass and Murie 1999). In the early 1990s the government provided funding for a number of shelters for homeless people run by charities. From 1997 councils were no longer required to provide permanent rehousing and were obliged to provide temporary accommodation for two years only; to obtain permanent housing, homeless households had to apply through the council waiting list (Pleace et al. 1997). For those not accepted as statutory homeless, a council's obligation was limited to providing advice on finding accommodation.

In the late 1990s the Labour government gained publicity by appointing a 'homelessness czar' to drive homeless people off the streets. More concretely, in 2002 a new Homelessness Act was passed. This replaced the two-year duty on councils by an indefinite one which ends only when certain types of offer are made. In addition, the list of types of unintentionally homeless persons in priority need was extended to include 16- and 17-year-olds, certain types of care leaver in the 18–20 age group, and vulnerable ex-service people, ex-offenders, and people fleeing all kinds of violence. (Students were generally ineligible.) From 2003 under the Supporting People programme young homeless people became eligible to receive support services which could either be 'floating' or provided via hostels. However, the geographical distribution of such provision depends on where charities and housing associations happen to be located; it was not a coordinated strategy to meet need. From 2008 preventive measures against homelessness were introduced. In 2010 the coalition government announced plans to require councils to place statutory homeless people in priority need in private rented housing for one year rather than in social housing. This more limited provision may have been decided in anticipation of an increase in the number of homeless people following the housing benefit changes for private tenants mentioned earlier, which are expected to mean that many of them are no longer able to afford their current private rented housing and have to move to lower rent housing or become homeless.

Official figures on trends in homelessness are extremely difficult to interpret. They reflect the tightness of criteria used to define statutory homelessness and the types of housing provided or secured for those accepted. The figures for people accepted by councils as statutory homeless rose from 53,000 in 1978 to 170,000 in 1992, fell to 122,000 in 1997, rose to 173,000 in 2003 before falling sharply. Similar numbers were refused because they failed to meet the eligibility criteria. But probably more than half of homeless people never approach a council, so they are never counted in the official figures of requests for assistance; instead they go directly to hostels and support centres. And since half or more of the homeless households who contact councils have their claims rejected, the number of households who are accepted as unintentionally homeless is a considerable underestimate of the failings of the housing 'system'.

Sustainable housing policy

Houses account for 30 per cent of energy consumption and 24 per cent of greenhouse gas emission. Since green issues entered party politics around 1990 these facts have led to a new stream of policy concerning the design and use of housing from a sustainability perspective. It has had four strands. Firstly, domestic energy-saving has been promoted by incentives to households to adopt domestic renewable energy production such as solar panels, by the Warm Front scheme which provides insulation and efficient boilers for households in fuel poverty (i.e. those spending more than 10 per cent of their income on fuel for heating and who are in particular need), and by energy companies which since 2002 have been obliged to promote energy efficiency, e.g. by subsidies for insulation. The latter represents a novel form of public policy since the cost of the measures they provide is paid for by consumers via higher energy bills, rather than from general public expenditure. Secondly, technical measures have been developed for assessing a wide range of housing impacts on sustainability known as EcoHomes, and the Sustainability Code levels 1–6, and for rating home energy efficiency, an EC directive for all houses being sold from 2009. Thirdly, sustainability has been pro-moted via a Code for Sustainable Housing, and a series of steps was announced in 2006 towards the achievement of '100 per cent zero-carbon homes by 2016'. In 2010 these were incorporated into revised building regulations and apply to new houses but not to house extensions. The government used its position as financer of RSL housing to introduce higher standards in that sector earlier than in the private sector. Finally, new Planning Policy Statements have been drafted which tread a fine line between encouraging 'pioneer' local authorities to introduce higher standards than the Building Regulations and discouraging local diversity of standards which the housebuilding industry dis-likes. The largest spending has gone on the social policy, Warm Front, which suggests that political support for environmental initiatives is still limited. In 2010 this policy was halted. The direction of sustainable housing policy is driven by the building supplies and energy industries for whom it represents new markets rather than by the environmental movement itself (Pickvance 2009).

Public spending on housing

One way of understanding the overall character of housing policy is to examine the pattern of public expenditure on housing. Table 15.3 shows the main categories involved. (The figures are at constant prices so they are not affected by inflation.) Column a shows the decline in subsidies on existing social housing. Column b reflects the fall in social housebuilding, and column c the rise and fall of receipts from the sale of social housing. Column d shows the net cost of social housebuilding to the public purse. Column e shows the dramatic growth of spending on housing benefits. Finally, column g shows the rise and fall of mortgage interest relief. In a nutshell one can say that spending on production of social housing (column b) has declined, while spending on consumption (columns e and g) has increased.

Ideally one would like to read each column of figures as a yardstick of policy aims. Whether this is possible depends on whether the spending is under government control or is influenced by factors beyond housing policy. Columns a and c do reflect the explicit policies of reducing subsidies to social housing, and cutting the rate of council housebuilding, which are largely within the government's control. But column b reflects tenants' response to the right to buy social housing, and hence the evolution of spending is partly outside government control. Column e is even less influenced by government policy and hence cannot be read as meaning that the government wanted to devote more and more spending to housing benefits. Rather, the growth of spending on housing benefits is an unintended effect of another housing policy, namely the raising of social housing rents towards market levels and the reduction of regulation of private sector rents. It is also due to continuing low incomes of the tenants concerned. Housing benefit spending has expanded to facilitate the shift to market rent levels, and is critical to the financial stability of housing providers such as councils, RSLs, and private landlords. Finally, the rise and decline of mortgage interest relief in column g are partly due to changing policy but are also influenced by interest rates, which are a matter of general eco-nomic policy. Paradoxically, then, the largest form of public spending on housing in each year since 1986–7—spending on housing benefits—is not the intended result of housing policy but due to the social security 'lifeboat' needed to rescue tenants who could not afford market rents. This is a measure of the obstacles to introducing market mechanisms where people's ability to pay is very low.

In 1997 Labour considered radical plans to reduce the scale of spending on housing benefit. There were a number of reasons for this. As Table 15.3 shows, spending on housing benefit had more than doubled in real terms between 1986 and 1996. In addition, it was believed to be open to abuse, and allegedly created dubious incentives for both landlords (who might be encouraged to impose large rent increases) and tenants (who might be deterred from 'shopping around' for cheaper rents). Proposals included introducing a flat rate or setting a maximum below 100 per cent of the rent charged. In the end the government abandoned its plans. As Kemp (2000) shows, reforming housing benefit would have had knock-on effects for social security, would have disrupted housing suppliers whose financial viability depended on the boost in 'ability to pay' which housing benefit gave tenants, and created many losers, with unpredictable electoral consequences. The way housing benefit was locked into housing finance, social security, and electoral politics thus prevented radical reform. In 2010 the coalition government announced the plans mentioned earlier to reduce spending on housing benefits in the private sector only. This will affect landlords but the effect will vary depending on whether they can find replacements without dropping their rents or not. However, the government's plans to create a new 'intermediate' rent council sub-sector (at 80 per cent of market rents) are likely to require increased spending on housing benefits to enable tenants to pay such rents.

Housing policy and social policy

It has been shown that housing policy is not simply or even primarily aimed at those in greatest housing need. Housing policy was very slow to develop in the nineteenth century, and the driving forces then and since have been political. Only in the 1920s did it gain a strong 'social' strand. For twenty years after 1945 housing policy was the subject of an inter-party consensus and went ahead 'on two legs'—council housing and owner-occupation. Since the 1960s it has increasingly been used to pursue party-political objectives, and has often meant helping the better off more than those in greatest housing need. The promotion of owner-occupation, especially until the mid 1980s, the demotion of council housing, and the attempt to introduce market rents for social tenants are clear illustrations of this. This could happen because the voices of those in housing need and those representing them are weak compared with the voices of financial institutions and builders and the voting strength of the majority.

The present housing situation in the UK

We start by providing a snapshot of the current housing situation. Tables 15.4 to 15.6 show the distribution of households with different social characteristics among the different housing tenure categories.

Table 15.4 can be read by comparing each tenure column with the 'All tenures' column. It shows that outright ownership is concentrated in the middle and older age groups and that under-35s make up one-quarter of owner-occupiers buying with a mortgage, a very high figure by European standards. The age distributions of council tenants and RSL tenants are very similar to those for all tenures, but with an under-representation of 45–64-year-olds. This reflects the fact that young households can enter the sector and once within it are likely to stay—unless they buy the dwelling. Private renting is by far the 'youngest' of the tenures, with over half of private tenants being under 35: this reflects young people's lower incomes, lower priority on housing compared with work, and greater mobility.

Table 15.5 can be read by comparing the row for each tenure with the 'All tenures' row. This reveals whether a tenure group has more or less than the average proportion of households in a particular income group. As might be expected, the table shows that higher-income households are more likely to be buying a house. However, the likelihood of being an outright owner (i.e. having no outstanding loan) is actually higher for lower-income groups. This is partly because on retirement, when most owner-occupiers have paid off their mortgages (see Table 15.4), their household income will fall and they will move to a lower-income decile as they rely on pensions, and partly because of ownership of low-value houses among low-income households.

Conversely, low-income households are more likely to be social tenants. There is no appreciable difference between the incomes of council tenants and RSL tenants. However, neither of the social housing tenures is absolutely restricted to the lowest two income groups. First, social housing is not restricted to the very lowest income groups. On the one hand, council tenants have been increasingly concentrated among the lowest income groups as the size of the tenure category gets smaller, and is

Table 15.4 Age structure of household reference person by tenure category, England, 2007–8 (vertical percentages)

	Outright owner[a]	Owner with mortgage	Council rented	RSL rented	Private rented	All tenures
Under 35	2	23	20	22	52	20
35–44	5	35	19	19	21	20
45–64	39	39	31	30	17	35
65 or over	53	3	31	29	9	25

[a] An outright owner is someone without a mortgage.
Source: CLG website, Table 809

Table 15.5 Annual gross household income of household reference person and partner by housing tenure category, England, 2007–8 (horizontal percentages)

Income	<£5,000	£5,000–10,000	£10,000–15,000	£15,000–20,000	£20,000–30,000	£30,000–40,000	£40,000–50,000	>£50,000
Outright owner	3	16	19	15	19	11	6	11
Buying with mortgage	1	3	4	7	18	19	15	33
Local authority rented	9	38	24	12	12	3	1	1
RSL rented	8	34	23	13	13	5	3	2
Private rented	8	15	13	13	21	14	8	9
All tenures	4	14	14	11	18	13	9	17

Source: CLG website, Table 809

made up increasingly of people without income from employment. On the other hand, while access depends on need, there is no continuing check on household income and no obligation on a household to leave social renting if its income rises. (The 2010 coalition government plans to introduce such checks for new council tenants paying 'intermediate' rents.) In recent decades, as those purchasing have become more heterogeneous in income terms, the council sector has become a more homogeneous and lower-income sector. Finally, the income distribution of private tenants is less skewed towards low incomes than that of social tenants and is close to that for all tenures. Interestingly, because of the high proportion of households in owner-occupation, half of the people living in poverty are either outright owners (18 per cent) or people buying their house with a mortgage (32 per cent) (Burrows 2003). This results directly from the growing economic and social heterogeneity of households in owner-occupation. Burrows points out that current policy measures, for example housing benefit, do not recognize the extent of poverty among owner-occupiers.

Table 15.6 shows the distribution of ethnic groups across tenure categories. Indians and white British tie as most likely to be outright owners or to be buying (73 per cent), followed by Pakistanis (64 per cent), Chinese (53 per cent) and Black Caribbeans (48 per cent) come some way behind, while Bangladeshis (37 per cent) and Black Africans (27 per cent) are least likely to own.

Table 15.6 Housing tenure by ethnic group of household reference person, Q2, 2007 (vertical percentages)

	White British	Other white	Mixed back-ground	Indian	Pakistani	Bangladeshi*	Black Caribbean	Black African	Chinese*	Other ethnic group	Total
Outright owner	33	22	9	28	20	10	15	4	16	10	31
Owner with mortgage	40	30	35	45	44	27	33	27	37	30	39
Council or housing association rented	17	14	35	8	17	49	43	41	7	24	18
Privately rented	10	33	22	19	18	14	9	29	39	35	12

*The data in these columns are not considered reliable due to small numbers.

Source: *Social Trends*, 39 (2009) Table 10.8

These patterns reflect income levels and the differing values of the houses in question. By contrast, Bangladeshis (49 per cent), Black Caribbeans (43 per cent), Black Africans (41 per cent), Mixed background (35 per cent), and Other ethnic group (24 per cent) are over-represented in social housing, where the overall figure is 18 per cent. In private rented housing the overall figure is 12 per cent and the groups most over-represented are Chinese (39 per cent), Other ethnic (35 per cent), Other white (33 per cent), Black African (29 per cent), Mixed background (22 per cent), Indian (19 per cent), and Pakistani (18 per cent). This suggests that the private rented sector houses the most recent immigrant groups and poorest groups. Research on ethnic residential patterns shows that Bangladeshis are the most segregated (in the sense of living in areas whose composition is very different from the average) and that they are followed by Pakistanis and Indians, with Black African, Caribbeans, and other groups coming behind them (Johnston et al. 1992).

Finally, a brief picture of housing conditions can be provided from the English House Condition Survey. Table 15.7 shows that there is a high level of 'non-decent' housing in all tenures but that conditions in the two private sectors, and especially in private rented housing, are worse than in the social housing sector. The situation in the social housing sector reflects the fact that the RSL sector contains relatively newer housing and that the council sector has been the object of the Decent Homes policy introduced in 1997 which sought to ensure that all council homes were decent by 2010. One-fifth of non-decent housing is due to a lack of thermal comfort (mainly lack of insulation) and the rest is due to a lack of repair or modernization or to a high 'housing health and safety rating system' score. The latter score, introduced in 2006, is based on weighting various risks, e.g. excess cold 926, falling on stairs 134, crowding and space 19, fire 17, dampness and mould growth 14, etc. (CLG 2010, Table 5.3). It represents a shift from the previous concepts of 'fit' and 'unfit' housing, and, as can be seen, overcrowding and dampness receive very low scores. Further analyses show that households in the lowest income decile are twice as likely to be in non-decent housing as those in the highest decile, which is perhaps a smaller disproportion than might be expected. No data are published on house condition and ethnicity.

Supply, demand, and affordability

With this descriptive picture of how households are distributed across the housing stock in mind we now address questions of supply, demand, and affordability in a more analytical way. We first need to understand what are meant by a household and the housing stock. This will help answer the question of whether there is a housing shortage.

Table 15.7 Decent and non-decent homes by tenure, England, 2007

	Decent	Non-decent	Total
Owner occupied	65.9	34.1	100
Private rented	54.6	45.4	100
Total private	64.2	35.8	100
Local authority	67.2	32.8	100.0
Registered social Landlord	74.5	25.5	100.0
Total social sector	70.8	29.2	100.0
All tenures	65.4	34.6	100.0

Source: CLG (2009), Table DH1A

The housing stock refers to the available housing in the country. This is partly a physical fact, since there are a certain number of physical dwellings available. This number increases if one includes caravans. However, it is also a social fact which reflects norms about what dwellings are considered habitable and about household space needs. The existence of second homes means that not all the housing stock is available to those seeking housing. Some housing is also necessary to facilitate movement, and to allow repair in both private and social sectors. Some housing is unfit or empty because it is 'hard to let' (e.g. because it lacks lifts or is located in a very unattractive neighbourhood) or is held as an asset.

Turning to households, the census definition refers to 'a single person or group of people who have the address as their only or main residence and who either share one meal a day together or share a living room'. (The pre-1981 definition required that household members were catered for, for at least one meal a day by the same person, a requirement which was abandoned in the face of variability in eating habits.) The number of households depends partly on the size and age structure of the population. But there is no constant relation between the size of the adult population and the number of households. The ratio between the number of households and the adult population is known as the 'headship rate'. This depends on customs regarding young and elderly people living independently, rates of cohabitation, marriage, separation and divorce, women's participation in the labour force, preferences for living alone rather than with partners, etc. For example, in southern Europe it is less common for young people to leave home before marriage or setting up home as a couple. In northern Europe the opposite is the case. Since 1971 there has been an increase in the number of households in England and the mean household size has decreased from 2.9 to 2.3.

However, some households contain other potential households. For example, a single adult or young couple sharing with their parents is known as a concealed household because they would prefer to live as a separate household. Whether they can do so depends on the housing situation itself. When the supply of housing increases, or its affordability improves (either because incomes rise or housing costs fall), the number of households increases as young people leave home earlier, or young couples who are living in the parental home can afford to live on their own. For all these reasons the number of households is not simply a demographic fact. It follows that the quantity of housing needed by the population can never be expressed in a single figure.

In 2006 it was estimated that in the UK there were 25.8 million households and 26.4 million dwellings, a 2.4 per cent crude surplus of dwellings (Wilcox 2010). But the former figure ignores concealed households and the latter ignores second homes, and empty, unfit, or unlettable dwellings, which probably number 750,000 and 230,000. In addition, some empty houses are needed to allow for households to move. It is thus clear that the overall supply of housing is insufficient. The net number of additional dwellings per year in England (new building, conversions and changes of use, fewer demolitions) rose from 132,000 in 2000–1 to 207,000 in 2007–8 and fell to 129,000 in 2009–10 (CLG website, Table 118). This has kept pace with household growth, but only if concealed households are ignored. In addition, local variations in housing supply and demand exacerbate this situation in certain areas. The question of affordability also has to be taken into account in understanding the balance between supply and demand: the ratio of mortgage costs to household incomes for first-time buyers rose from 10.5 per cent to 20.4 per cent between 1994 and 2008, and there was also considerable regional variation (Wilcox 2010, table 2.3.2), so, overall, access came at increasing cost.

Referring back to the trends in public spending on housing, it is clear that government spending on social housebuilding has declined sharply since the 1970s (Table 15.3, columns a and d.) This reflects the choice of successive governments to rely on market providers. The indicators of shortage mentioned above are thus an indicator of the failure of what is very largely a market-based system of provision to meet housing need. To put it another way, increased house prices have not acted as

---

Box 15.3 **The Barker Review and the government's response**

The Barker Review:

1 identified as a main cause of the low level of building the local government planning system which was not supplying sufficient land to builders;

2 proposed:

- increasing building in the private sector from its 2002–3 level of 125,000 completions to 195,000 houses per year to reduce the rate of price increase to 1.8 per cent in real terms (or to 245,000 to reduce it to 1.1 per cent);
- increasing social housing building from 21,000 per year to 38,000 dwellings per year to meet the needs from new households and 47,000 'to make inroads into the backlog of need' (Barker, 2004: 5);
- changes in the planning system to provide more land for development:

  local councils to be allowed to keep some of the council tax receipts generated by new housing; a Planning Gain Supplement by which some of the gains from development accruing to landowners would benefit the community.

The government responded in December 2005 (HM Treasury 2005b) by:

- accepting the Review's lower private sector housebuilding target, and saying it would announce in 2007 its response to the proposed social housing targets;
- putting the Barker Review proposals regarding council tax receipts and a Planning Gain Supplement out for consultation;
- asking Kate Barker to conduct a review of the planning system, to come up with precise recommendations in time for 2007.

---

a signal to housebuilders to produce more housing. Faced with this evidence of market failure, in 2003 the government commissioned an inquiry into how to increase the number of dwellings and how to provide dwellings that are affordable (see Box 15.3).

The Barker Review building targets seem way below the level of need suggested by the prevailing low level of affordability, the level of homelessness, and the level of international migration. However even these levels of production would require radical changes in government policy to encourage private building and finance social housing. Moreover, the proposed levels have aroused environmentalist protest in the south, where much of the new housing would be concentrated. This is turn reflects the fact that the government has no regional policy. Apart from the location of government offices, which are well spread out regionally, the spatial pattern of residence and economic activity is almost entirely market-driven, with the unbalanced results indicated.

The Barker review of the planning system recommended faster decisions (less regulation, faster appeals, and fewer applications called in by the Secretary of State), but otherwise proposed nothing to ensure more houses were built. Overall the Barker Review seems to have delayed action to speed up housebuilding for five years. In 2010 the new government announced plans to abolish the system of regional housing targets which had obliged local authorities to ensure adequate land with planning permission for housing existed but offered a 'homes bonus incentive' of six years of council tax to encourage councils to approve new housebuilding. An exacerbation of the present housing shortage seems the most likely short-term outcome.

Council housing and owner-occupation in practice

As we have seen, the major political debates over housing have concerned the degree to which it should be provided by the state or by the market, and the degree to which it should be subsidized and regulated. To go beyond the ideological debates about market and state alternatives of access to housing, we need to understand how different housing tenures work in practice. The focus here will be on owner-occupation and council housing and how households gain access to them. It will be shown that the normal functioning of both tenures leads to some undesirable results.

It is useful to think of access as controlled by gatekeepers, and to see households as possessing varying characteristics and resources which affect their chances of successful entry. In owner-occupation the gatekeepers are the staff of estate agents and mortgage lenders. In council housing they are council officials. The term 'gatekeeper' is appropriate because these groups operate rules of access which determine the chance that a household will be able to obtain access via the channel concerned. In owner-occupation, access depends on ability to pay and the security of the house as an asset. In council housing, access depends on meeting rules of eligibility which are mostly non-financial.

Owner-occupation in practice

For the vast majority, owner-occupation is possible only with the help of a mortgage. It is true that a small minority of people inherit houses or can afford to buy them for cash. It is also true that the mortgage will not cover the whole cost of purchase, and that some reliance on savings or on a family loan will be necessary. The extent of family financial help and its correlation with social class are discussed in Box 15.4.

The primary concern of banks and building societies—the main sources of mortgages—is profit (or 'surplus'). Originally building societies borrowed only from individuals. Today, like banks, they also borrow on the money markets. As the 2007–9 financial crisis showed, in some cases banks have invested in risky activities or become dependent on flows of short-term funding which dried up, jeopardizing their stability. All of the building societies which demutualized in the 1990s have lost their independence and several major banks are partly nationalized.

To operate effectively, financial institutions need to maintain public confidence and control risk. Their success in doing so until 2007 is a reflection of the prevailing economic environment-which was believed to be benign (with consistent economic growth, low interest rates, and the

---

Box 15.4 **Family help with finance for housing**

It is difficult to research into how much financial help a household has had from its family, since finance may not have been given explicitly for housing. A study of 16–35-year-olds in south-east England in 1991 found that of those who had left home only 29 per cent had received financial help for any purpose since leaving, and only 12 per cent had received help explicitly for housing purposes (Pickvance and Pickvance 1995). This was correlated with parental social class. The average amount received was £1,900. When asked the purpose of the help, 7 per cent (of those who had left home) said it was to help with purchase of a flat or house. As many as 49 per cent of all respondents thought their parents could provide some help—£2,000 being the median figure—but only 20 per cent agreed that parents should provide financial help with housing. This suggests that even in a region where parental incomes are high and house prices are high—so that both the capacity to provide and the need for financial help are great—the extent of actual financial help was very limited.

'end of boom and bust'), the high degree of social stability in the UK, and trust in institutions generally. The government helps by guaranteeing personal savings (up to €100,000 per account from 2011) in the case of a collapse. In practice, banks have been relatively unregulated since the 1990s and have engaged in highly risky activities, while building societies have experienced more constraints.

Since mortgage lenders risk losing their money if borrowers prove unable to maintain their repayments, they are concerned with the security of the loan. This means they examine carefully the capacity of the borrower to repay, and the value of the house. (This is how mortgage lenders should behave. In the UK in 2007 45 per cent of all mortgages were offered without any check on the borrower's income.)

These lending considerations have important consequences:

- *Sub-prime loans* Not all loans for house purchase come from major banks and building societies. Other sources of loans, such as secondary banks and finance houses, are used by borrowers who are rejected by the main lenders. This occurs because the mortgage market is segmented. Secondary banks offer what in the United States are called sub-prime loans, i.e. loans at a higher rate of interest and for a shorter term. In turn they can offer higher rates of interest to savers — who take higher risks in the hope of greater rewards. Each segment of the mortgage market thus involves different types of lender, dealing with different types of borrower and different types of house, and offering different terms. The result is that those who are least creditworthy (including the poorest households) pay most for mortgages or do not get one at all, while the most secure borrower pays least. This is a completely normal effect of market operation. Gatekeepers in market institutions, such as mortgage lenders, create rules of access which have nothing to do with housing need and everything to do with their own solvency. Hence, as a mechanism for ensuring affordable housing for all social groups, one cannot say that the housing market works.

- *Red-lining.* In some cities whole neighbourhoods are considered risky and no loans are obtainable for purchase in them from the main lenders. The term 'red-lining' refers to the line drawn round such neighbourhoods on a map. The refusal to lend in an area by major lenders has inevitable consequences: the area will go 'downhill'. This happens because mortgages are only available from secondary lenders and to meet the repayments the owner has to crowd the house. The result is to worsen the reputation of the district and make the neighbourhood decline feared by the initial risk-averse lender a self-fulfilling prophecy.

- *Unmortgageable dwellings.* Certain types of houses are also judged too risky by lenders and excluded from access to mortgages, for example houses liable to subsidence or flooding, or houses or flats with basements.

- *Risky occupations.* Lenders pay attention to the borrower's occupation and are likely to discriminate against borrowers in 'risky' occupations. These include many self-employed occupations. Cyclical industries such as building are also considered risky.

- *Marginal owner-occupiers* Finally, among those who do obtain mortgages there is a category who are particularly vulnerable to changes in their employment situation. These may be households who felt forced into owner-occupation because of the limited choice of other tenures, or those who have taken on obligations which impose abnormal stresses, e.g. long extra hours, long commuting journeys, squeezing other types of household expenditure. Research showed that the households affected by negative equity (i.e. the value of their house, after deducting the mortgage, was negative) in 1993 following the 15 per cent decline of house prices between 1989 and 1993 were most likely to have purchased in the 1988–91 period, to have been under 25 at the time of purchase, to have purchased a house for under £40,000; to have had an annual joint income of between £20,000 and £30,000, and to have had manual or clerical occupations (Dorling and Cornford 1995). In brief, they were precisely the marginal owner-occupiers attracted into the sector in the 1980s through the right to buy policy and the promotion of owner-occupation among lower income groups.

In sum, mortgage lenders are selective in their lending since their aim is to meet their own financial objectives. They only meet the housing need of those who allow them to do so—in theory. In practice, mortgage lenders have shown a willingness to abandon careful lending criteria in order to pursue their own growth.

Council housing in practice

Turning to the second major housing tenure, to understand how households get access to housing in the council sector it is necessary to be aware of supply as well as demand. Councils own large and diverse stocks of housing. Council housing differs in age from interwar to modern, in type from flats in low- and high-rise blocks to semi-detached houses, in size (e.g. number of bedrooms), in the attractiveness and location of the neighbourhood (from inner city to urban periphery), and in condition from unmodernized to renovated. Councils can also make use of bed-and-breakfast accommodation.

The character of this stock reflects past building policy, modernization policy, and council housing sales. The effect of the latter in removing the more attractive housing from the sector has already been noted. Councils are selective in their modernization efforts, with the effect that some differences in quality are preserved. The heterogeneous stock means that councils are gatekeepers to a variety of housing types.

Turning to how councils allocate their housing, the two main access channels are homelessness (since 1977 councils have been obliged to secure housing for the unintentionally homeless in 'priority need') and the waiting list, which uses an eligibility criterion (e.g. non-UK citizens are unlikely to be eligible, and those with rent arrears are excluded), and a system which awards points for various measures of need. Councils have considerable discretion about the criteria they use. Illness, having young children, living in damp premises are common but so is length of residence in the area. Other less common schemes rely on the date of application (i.e. 'first come, first served') or discretion. Tenancies can be passed on to children, and transferred to or exchanged with other tenants. Normally, moves by existing tenants take priority over tenancies offered to new tenants.

Households with the highest number of points are offered housing. The length of time a household waits is dependent on the number of tenancies becoming available, whether they match the household's characteristics, and the number of households with higher positions on the waiting list. Some households fail to apply for council housing because they think the chance of a tenancy is remote. Likewise, some households give up hope but leave their names on the list, which makes them a poor measure of demand.

In 2002 a new Act allowed councils to abandon single housing registers and widened the groups eligible for council housing. In particular, intentionally homeless people and applicants from outside the area became eligible, but not people 'subject to immigration control'. It might seem surprising that a sector which was shrinking in size should widen the groups eligible to gain access to it. The reason for this was the emergence of large numbers of empty dwellings in certain parts of the country, such as northern England. In such areas councils were under pressure to adopt a marketing mentality ('choice-based letting') rather than a rationing mentality in order to persuade households to occupy these dwellings, a quite new experience on this scale. (Previously there had been 'unlettable blocks' in otherwise popular areas.) The new legislation allowed councils to adopt the appropriate method for their own locality.

Despite the sale of council housing, the number of lettings to new tenants in England remained remarkably constant from 1983 to 1995, after which it fell by 64 per cent in 12 years (from 422,000 in 1996–7 to 151,700 in 2008–9.) Of the latter number, 44,800 lettings (30 per cent) were to existing tenants wishing to move within the sector and 106,900 (70 per cent) to new tenants. Of the latter, 75 per cent were drawn from the waiting list and 25 per cent from among homeless households (CLG website, Table 601, accessed 22 October 2010). Councils can also nominate tenants to housing associations, where they represented 26 per cent of new lettings in 2003–4 (CLG website, Table 602, accessed 22 October 2010). Councils can also nominate tenants to live in housing association tenancies where they have nomination rights.

The allocation of tenancies by councils has been extensively studied, and reveals the importance of the diversity of the housing stock. First, councils give priority in allocating lettings to existing tenants. This allows them to reward tenants for good behaviour and regular rent payments and may also release surplus space. Second, councils see themselves as public landlords with a duty to preserve the value of the stock. To do this they match households to 'appropriate' housing and estates. This is partly a matter of matching household size with dwelling size. More controversially, councils make judgements about both the quality of the dwellings and the 'quality' of the households. 'Good' tenants are offered housing in popular estates or parts of estates with other 'good' tenants, while 'problem' families are placed together in the least attractive housing and estates. Homeless households are allocated unattractive council housing or placed in temporary housing, e.g. low-quality private rented or bed-and-breakfast accommodation.

Thirdly, contrary to what is often believed, the allocation of tenancies has often allowed applicants some choice, though this is much less true today than in the past. The extent of this varies considerably according to demand. A Scottish study by Clapham and Kintrea (1986) showed that applicants could state a preference for an area, and receive several offers. They were not obliged to accept the first offer, but if they did not they could not be sure that a second or third offer would be better, and after three offers they might lose their place on the waiting list. Applicants are more likely to choose the most attractive estates and dwellings, but councils need to let all their dwellings. To find tenants for the least attractive dwellings, they offer the least attractive dwellings as 'first offers' to households in the most desperate need in the hope that they will be accepted. 'Good' households are more likely to be offered attractive dwellings initially. The effect of this is to create and preserve a hierarchy of council estates, and to make it likely that those households in greatest need find themselves in the worst council housing (Pawson and Kintrea 2002). These authors also show that by 2000 the number of offers received had fallen and one was the norm. Council allocation policies are thus concerned with the management of the stock as well as meeting housing need.

***

We have seen that both owner-occupation and council housing operate with rules of access which exclude some households and include but differentially treat others. Two categories of household are excluded from owner-occupation: those whose incomes are too low or too uncertain and those who want to buy 'risky' houses or houses in 'risky' areas. Although the segmentation of the mortgage market means that some households will remain 'included' but have to cope with tough loan terms, others will be totally excluded. The rules of access here are probably resistant to change because they are part of the conventional wisdom of the wider financial system. In council housing the effect of the professional ideologies of council housing managers is to channel households to better or worse housing within the sector. This is differential treatment of the sort normal in a housing market. Exclusion also exists in the council sector. It applied to homeless households who before 2002 did not meet the legal criteria of being unintentionally homeless and in a priority group. But it also occurs because being on the waiting list does not guarantee inclusion, i.e. eventually being offered council housing. This is why some households in housing need do not join the waiting list, while others do so but find their own housing or remain as concealed households. The effects of council housing allocation also depend on the supply situation. In areas of housing surplus, councils may be in the position of desperately seeking households. It is in areas of housing shortage that the phenomenon of exclusion will be most marked.

Thus, whereas the normal functioning of owner-occupation means it cannot meet all housing need, because access depends on ability to pay, council housing too, which is aimed at those unable to pay, in practice is also unable to do so completely. It would be reassuring to think that the private rented sector and housing associations cope with those excluded from these two sectors. Undoubtedly they do so to some extent, but the other options for those who are excluded from the two large sectors are to be homeless and/or to be a concealed household.

Conclusion

In this chapter we have answered the question 'Is housing policy social policy?' by rejecting the idea that it is simply a response to housing need. Rather, we have seen that housing conditions only become a housing problem leading to government action when a successful claim is made following mobilization by interested parties such as residents, political parties, unions, local councils, employers, and housing suppliers and financiers. It is these groups and their mobilization which determine whether state action in response to need takes place, and if so, what form it takes and which groups benefit from it.

The immense level of housing need in the nineteenth century met with minimal response until the century's last decades. What changed then was the rise of the working class as a political actor. This led to housing policy with a 'social' character and, together with the wartime experience of solidarity, to the post-1918 government's major innovation of council housing. After 1945 there was quite a long period when both major political parties supported the building of both council housing and owner-occupied housing. Only in the 1970s did inter-party differences become striking. After that the Conservative government defined council housing as an obstacle to increased owner-occupation and took measures against it. The Labour government passed the 1977 Homelessness Act and briefly reversed the Conservative attack on council housing. But in the 1980s it abandoned its traditional identification with council housing and accepted that there was widespread support among council tenants for the right to buy scheme. By the 1990s, therefore, housing policy was partly 'social' (e.g. council housing, housing associations, housing allowances) and partly support for market provision (assistance to owner-occupiers and private landlords). The explanation of this policy shift is that housing policy became a means of winning votes from the middle-income groups. Since 2000, as state spending on housebuilding has declined and tax relief on mortgages has ended, policy has become weaker in relation to both the private sector and the public sector. Its main (and increasing) financial role has been to help private and social tenants to afford their housing.

Thus in the housing sphere it is not the question of whether state intervention is present or absent which is important but rather what forms it takes and who benefits from it. It is likely that the income groups which benefit from housing policy in the future will depend on the same mix of economic, political, and social need considerations which have been evident in housing policy in the past.

KEY LEGISLATION

1972 Housing Finance Act Introduced 'fair rents' for council tenants and allowed councils to make a surplus on council housing. This initiated the rise in council rents.

1977 Homelessness Act Imposed a duty on councils to rehouse unintentionally homeless families and individuals permanently.

1980 Housing Act The 'right to buy' act, which gave council tenants the right to buy their dwelling at a discount. Previously councils had a right to sell but council tenants had no right to buy.

1988 Housing Act Reduced regulation of private rented sector, and forced housing associations to rely more on private finance. Increased rent levels followed, and helped lead to the increase in housing benefit payments.

1996 Housing Act Required councils to place unintentionally homeless people in temporary accommodation (in either social housing or private rented housing) and said that their access to permanent council accommodation could only be through the waiting list.

2002 Homelessness Act Extended the duty on councils to house unintentionally homeless people, extended the list of applicants in priority need, and gave councils more flexibility in allocating their housing.

FURTHER READING

The References list at the back of this book contains some of the main texts and research monographs in the field. Others include: **G. Bramley, M. Munro, and H. Pawson**, *Key Issues in Housing* (London: Palgrave, 2004); **D. Clapham**, *The Meaning of Housing: a Pathways Approach* (Bristol: The Policy Press, 2005); **D. Cowan and A. Marsh** (eds), *Two Steps Forward: Housing Policy into the New Millennium* (Bristol: The Policy Press, 2001); **Fitzpatrick, S. and Pawson, H.** (2007) Welfare Safety Net or Tenure of Choice? The Dilemma Facing Social Housing Policy in England *Housing Studies* 22: 163–82; **M. Harrison with C. Davis**, *Housing, Social Policy and Difference*, (Bristol: The Policy Press, 2001); **S. Lowe**, *Housing Policy Analysis* (London: Palgrave, 2004); **S. Lowe and D. Hughes** (eds), *The Private Rented Sector in a New Century: Revival or False Dawn?* (Bristol: The Policy Press, 2001); and **A. Marsh and D. Mullins** (eds), *Housing and Public Policy: Citizenship, Choice and Control* (Buckingham: Open University Press, 1998). The most useful journals are *Housing Studies, Journal of Social Policy* and *Urban Studies*.

@ USEFUL WEBSITES

The Communities and Local Government Minister website, **www.clg.gov.uk/housing/statistics/**, includes scores of continuously updated tables of housing statistics, including data on historical trends. Data on spending including on housing is on the Treasury website: **www.hm-treasury.gov.uk/.** Statistical data for the UK or Great Britain such as censuses and surveys is published on the Office for National Statistics website: **www.statistics.gov.uk**. Shelter maintains a useful website on homelessness: **www.homelessnessact.org.uk/.**

ESSAY QUESTIONS

1 Should housing policy be regarded as a social policy?

2 Does meeting housing need drive the evolution of housing policy?

3 Is it true that every household receives adequate housing either through market housing or through social housing?

4 Explain the changing pattern of public spending on housing.

5 To what extent do households choose their housing, and what constraints do they experience?

@ ONLINE RESOURCE CENTRE

For additional material and resources, please visit the Online Resource Centre at:
www.oxfordtextbooks.co.uk/orc/baldock4e/.

Crime, justice, and punishment

Tina Eadie and Rebecca Morley

Contents

Introduction

We are surrounded by crime—as a problem and as entertainment—in the media, in novels, in everyday discussion. We have television programmes which implore us, the public, to assist the police in solving crimes in our communities and to help put right miscarriages of justice. The annual crime statistics for England and Wales make headline news. They are offered as key indicators of the moral condition of society. Periodic rises and falls in crime rates provide ammunition for political debate concerning the successes and failures of social policies in the 'fight against crime', as the main political parties battle for the high ground on 'law and order'. Sensational incidents of crime—the abduction and murder of children, mass killings arising from terrorist attacks, a deranged individual, or even human error—reverberate in the daily conversations of ordinary citizens, filling us with outrage, horror, fear, grief. Less extreme but persistent crime—mobile phone theft, for example—results in anger and indignation that crime is not being controlled. Dramatic rises in recorded crime during the latter half of the twentieth century have only recently begun to show signs of levelling off. Opinion polls show that crime continues to be a major public concern. Many people have a deep sense of the criminal justice system failing them—as victims of crime and as members of communities in which criminal activities and antisocial behaviour are rife. Clearly crime is a central social policy theme.

Learning outcomes

Readers of this chapter will be able to provide preliminary answers to the following questions:

1 What is crime, how much crime is there, and how is it changing?
2 Who are the criminals and how are they dealt with?
3 What are the costs of crime, who are the victims of crime, and can the harm they suffer be prevented?

There are no simple answers to these questions, and debates concerning them are complex and often contradictory. Recognizing that this chapter can only offer a brief overview of some of these questions, we hope that readers will follow up the references and further reading.

What is crime? Measurement, statistics, trends, and politics

The impression often given by politicians and the media is that crime is a physical fact, like the air temperature or rainfall, which, with proper techniques, can be accurately measured and assessed. However, closer examination shows that crime is thoroughly socially produced—that it is a social construction.

The most common and seemingly straightforward and unproblematic definition of crime is violation of the criminal law—'law-breaking'. But laws are 'man-made', in both the generic and specific senses of the word 'man'. Laws change over time and place. We need therefore to ask how and why certain acts are defined and legislated as criminal in certain places and times (and why others are not). Perspectives on this question vary and are underpinned by differing views about the nature of social order: simplistically, whether crime arises from a social consensus about morality and norms of conduct or is the outcome of social conflict and coercion. The first suggests that crime is politically neutral; the second, that we need to examine issues of power and politics—who has the power to define what is criminal, and whose interests do these definitions serve?

Proponents of this second view ask, for example, why property crimes and personal violence are much more likely to be considered crimes than are environmental pollution, unethical business practices, and health and safety hazards in the workplace. Marxist-oriented criminologists argue that the criminal law and its operation are biased towards crimes of the poor and powerless, protecting the economic and political interests of the powerful while ignoring acts which are arguably more socially harmful in terms of financial loss and personal injury or death ('crimes on the streets' as opposed to 'crimes in the suites'). Feminists argue that the law and criminal justice system ignore the bulk of men's physical and sexual violence against women ('private' violence as opposed to street violence), supporting the interests of men or 'patriarchal' power. Domestic violence, for example, was legally sanctioned until the late nineteenth century and is only now—patchily and falteringly—treated as crime by the criminal justice system; rape in marriage was not declared illegal in England and Wales until 1991.

The obvious limitations of legal definitions have led some to argue that crime should be defined as actions which are socially harmful or which violate human rights, whether or not they are legally sanctioned. Such social definitions would include racism, sexism, poverty, and imperialism as crimes. However, in terms of public and policy debate, the most influential definition of crime is clearly law-breaking, and within this, law-breaking that comes to the attention of the police and media.

Measurement

Crime is not just socially constructed in definition, it is socially constructed in measurement. Official crime rates for England and Wales, compiled from police records and notified to the Home Office, have been collated each year since 1857. Comparable statistics are produced for Scotland and Northern Ireland; however, those from England and Wales figure most prominently in policy debates and the media. Police-recorded crime is the endpoint of a complex series of decisions: crime must be recognized by the victim or someone else, reported to the police, classified as an offence, and actually recorded. Some crimes (such as car theft) are far more likely to survive this process than others (such as marital rape).

Further, police record only certain categories of crime, called 'notifiable offences'. Prior to 1998, these broadly corresponded to 'indictable offences'—ostensibly more serious crimes triable only in Crown courts or 'triable either way' in Crown or magistrates' courts—as opposed to supposedly less serious 'summary offences' triable only in magistrates' courts. Thus, for example, violence which the police classified as 'common assault' (a summary offence) rather than 'actual bodily harm' (an indictable offence) was not recorded even though these incidents could be as injurious: Edwards (1989: Chapter 4), for example, found that police routinely 'downcrimed' domestic violence in order to avoid paperwork and further investigation, which they regarded as wasted effort. In 1998 the Home Office expanded the list of notifiable offences to incorporate some closely related summary offences including common assault.

Clearly, then, just as new legislation criminalizes new activities and decriminalizes others, so official views concerning the seriousness of various types of crime change over time, and these changes result in rises or falls in the recorded crime rate. Even within the categories of notifiable offences, different police forces may concentrate their efforts on detecting different sorts of crime at different points in time for a wide variety of reasons. These decisions, too, will affect the volume of recorded crime. More generally, police officers traditionally have had a great deal of discretion in deciding whether and how to record incidents which are reported to them. British Crime Survey (BCS) estimates from 1981 to 2005 indicate that between 25 and 50 per cent of all notifiable offences which are reported to the police each year do not get recorded, though these rates have decreased most years since 1995 and vary significantly according to type of offence (Walker et al. 2006: Table 4.04; these estimates ceased to be published after 2005).

Moreover, rules for counting instances of notifiable offences have changed several times, most recently in 1998 and 2002. The counting changes in 1998, in combination with the expansion of the list of notifiable offences, led to an estimated artificial increase in the total volume of recorded crime in 1998–9 of 14 per cent (Povey and Prime 1999: Table A1). Offences of 'violence against the person' were particularly affected, increasing by a massive 118 per cent, due in large part to the inclusion of common assault in the list of notifiable offences. The changes in 2002 resulted from the introduction of a National Crime Reporting Standard (NCRS) which aimed to take a more victim-centred approach to crime recording—all reports of incidents should be recorded if they amount to notifiable offences in law and there is no evidence to the contrary—and thus to reduce police discretion. This change increased the 2001–2 recorded crime figures overall by 5 per cent. Again, offences of violence against the person were particularly affected (13 per cent increase), as were sexual offences (21 per cent increase), while robbery and vehicle crime were virtually unaffected (Simmons 2002: Table 3b). Overall, violence against the person rose for three years following the introduction of the NCRS, in contrast to British Crime Survey trends which are not influenced by police reporting or recording.

Undeniably, then, recorded crime rates are fragile creatures that require great care in interpretation.

Statistics, trends, and politics

At face value, the overall picture of crime from recorded statistics is startlingly clear. Apart from a small sustained decline in the early 1950s, the total volume of police recorded crime rose steadily from the 1930s to the early 1990s, and particularly dramatically from the mid1950s (see Figure 16.1): in 1950 recorded crime stood at 500,000, or 1 per 100 population; in 1992 it peaked at nearly 5.6 million, or 11 per 100 population, an elevenfold increase (Home Office 1997a). Rates then fell each year until 1998–9, when they rose again—particularly steeply between 2001–2 and 2003–4—due largely to changes in coverage and counting rules which artificially inflated the figures (Osborne 2010: 22). Since 2003–4 rates have fallen every year and, as of 2009–10, are lower than at any time since before 1990.

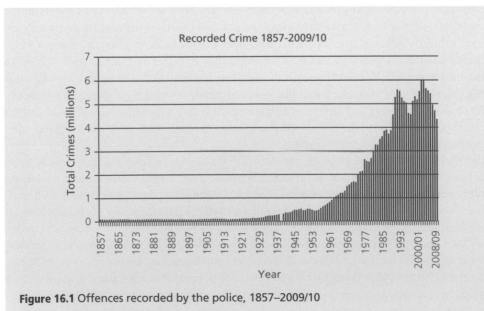

Figure 16.1 Offences recorded by the police, 1857–2009/10

Source: Home Office 1999; 2007; 2010a

The vast majority of recorded crimes are property offences. Of the 4.3 million crimes recorded in 2009–10, 70 per cent were property crimes (burglary, offences against vehicles, other thefts, fraud and forgery, and criminal damage—see Figure 16.2). Despite the considerable impact of changes in coverage and counting on offences of violence, violent crime including robbery accounted for only 22 per cent of total crime. Further, less than 5 per cent of violent crime (less than 1 per cent of total recorded crime) was homicide and other 'most serious' violence (HMIC 2009: 40, Osborne 2010: Table 2.04).

Although recorded crime rates began to rise sharply from the 1960s, it was not until the 1970s that crime started to become a party-political issue. Since that time, crime statistics have become increasingly important weapons in political debate, where they have been selectively and strategically presented to support opposing positions concerning the government's record in tackling the crime problem. The Conservatives were able to celebrate winning the war against crime on the basis of the 1996 figures which revealed the fourth consecutive overall fall in crime, while the Labour Party's 1997 manifesto declared that: 'Under the Conservatives, crime has doubled ... the worst record on crime of any government since the Second World War ... Last year alone, violent crime rose 11 per cent' (Labour Party 1997: 22).

In 2002, New Labour asserted that crime had stabilized after several years of decline, pointing to the impact of the NCRS in inflating a 'real' increase of just 2 per cent from the previous year to a recorded increase of 7 per cent, as well as to the British Crime Survey finding that comparable crime had actually decreased by 2 per cent. The Conservative shadow home secretary responded by accusing the government of 'statistical manipulation' and, alluding to the steep rise in street crime, stated: 'it is the drugs and gangs rather than the forces of law and order that are in charge' (*Independent*, 12 July 2002).

The 2005 manifestos of the two main parties broadcast diametrically opposed pictures of crime trends since New Labour was first elected in 1997. The Conservatives, using official police figures, decreed that: 'Overall crime is up by 16 per cent. Violent crime is up by over 80 per cent. Gun crime has more than doubled.'(Conservative Party 2005: 3), while New Labour proclaimed: '1979–1997: Recorded crime had almost doubled ... Today, there is less chance of being a victim of crime than for more than 20 years ... Overall crime as measured by the authoritative British Crime Survey is

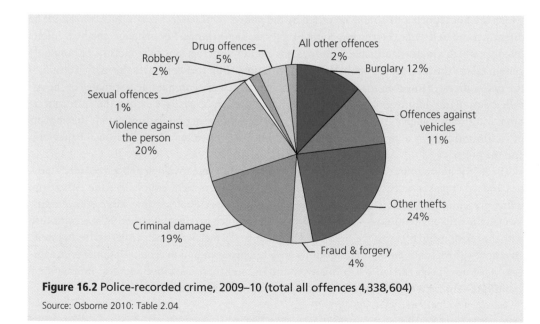

Figure 16.2 Police-recorded crime, 2009–10 (total all offences 4,338,604)

Source: Osborne 2010: Table 2.04

down 30 per cent [since 1997]—the equivalent of almost five million fewer crimes a year' (Labour Party 2005: 42).

Five years later, in a heated exchange in the House of Commons initiated by Labour's attempt to clarify the new coalition government's position on cutting police numbers, Prime Minister David Cameron retorted: 'under the last Government violent crime and gun crime went through the roof … They almost doubled.'(Hansard HC 7 July 2010: Col 364). Protests from Labour prompted a letter from the chair of the UK Statistics Authority pointing out that the introduction of the National Crime Recording Standard in 2002–3 precluded any unqualified comparison of police figures from the late 1990s to the late 2000s, and that, in any case: 'The Authority's view remains that the British Crime Survey (BSC) provides a more reliable measure of the national trend in violent crime. The evidence from the BCS is that there has not been an increase in respondents' experience of violent crime between the late 1990s and 2008–9' (UK Statistics Authority 2010). Indeed, BCS figures released the following day showed that violent crime had decreased by 42 per cent between 1997 and 2009–10 (Osborne 2010: Table 2.01).

Crime surveys and victimology

Issues surrounding the production of official crime statistics raise important questions about the extent to which crime trends represent real changes in criminal behaviour (the realist approach) as opposed to changes in reporting and recording (the institutionalist approach). The development of crime surveys can be seen as one response to these concerns.

Government-sponsored national crime surveys, comprising interviews with random samples of the population who are asked about their experiences of criminal victimization during a specified period, emerged in the United States in the early 1970s with the expressed aim of addressing the problem of interpreting official crime data. By 1980 researchers in the Home Office were arguing for a national crime survey on the grounds that policy-makers needed a better idea of the extent and shape of crime than that provided by official statistics, and that public misconceptions concerning crime levels and risk needed to be challenged (Mayhew and Hough 1988: 157).

The resulting British Crime Survey, first undertaken in 1982 and covering crimes committed in the previous year, claims to allow a more complete count of crime by including incidents which are not reported to and/or recorded by the police. In practice, the two sources cannot be directly compared since they do not count exactly the same things. For instance, the BCS counts offences which are not 'notifiable', but does not count homicide, since the victims of homicide cannot talk to the interviewer about their victimization. (Box 16.1 compares the main features of the two sources.) However, for the subset of crimes which are comparable, estimates of the so-called dark figure of unreported and unrecorded crime can be made. Further, the BCS collects other information such as the distribution of risk across different population groups; the impacts of victimization; fear of crime; and perceptions and experiences of crime, antisocial behaviour, and the police.

The BCS is now a source of major importance to policy-makers, rivalling police-recorded statistics. Indeed, it played a crucial role in the general shift in government policy since the 1980s from crime prevention towards 'victimization prevention'. More generally, crime surveys have transformed the field of victimology—the study of victims—which originated in the 1940s as a concern with the relationship between the victim and offender, and which was much criticized for its preoccupation with victim typologies and notions of victim precipitation of crime. National crime surveys have now been carried out in many countries, and there have been several international victimization surveys producing comparable data across a range of countries.

Box 16.1 Comparison of the British Crime Survey and police-recorded crime

The British Crime Survey	Police-recorded crime
• Starting in 1982, it measures both reported and unreported crime. As such it provides a measure of trends in crime not affected by changes in reporting, or changes in police recording rules or practices	• Collected since 1857. Provides measure of offences both reported to and recorded by the police. As such they are influenced by changes in reporting behaviour and recording rules and practices
• Measured crime mostly every two years until 2001 when it became a continuous survey	• Since 2002, published together with the BCS
• Since 2002, published together with police-recorded crime	• Only includes 'notifiable' offences which the police have to notify to the Home Office for statistical purposes
• Measures based on estimates from a sample of the population. The estimates are therefore subject to sampling error and other methodological limitations	• Provides an indicator of the workload of the police
• Has not measured crime at the small area level well, but more reliable regional information is available from 2001 sweep onwards	• Provides data at the level of 43 police force areas and for Basic Command Units (similar in size to local authorities)
• Does not include crimes against: • those under 16[1] • commercial and public sector establishments • those in group homes and other institutions, and the homeless	• Includes crime against: • those under 16 • commercial and public sector establishments • those in group homes and other institutions, and the homeless
• Does not measure: • victimless crimes • crimes where a victim is no longer available for interview • fraud • sexual offences[2] (due to the small number of incidents reported to the survey and concerns about willingness of respondents to disclose such offences, estimates are not considered reliable) • relatively new crimes[3]	• Measures: • victimless crimes • murder and manslaughter • fraud • sexual offences where these have been reported to the police
• Collects information on what happens in crime (e.g., when crimes occur, and effects in terms of injury and property loss)	• Collects information about the number of arrests, who is arrested, the number of crimes detected, and by what method
• Provides information about how the risks of crime vary for different groups	• Does not show which groups of the population are most at risk of victimization

1 For the first time in January 2009, children aged 10–15 were surveyed but not included in the annual crime count.

2 Surveys in 1996, 2001, and since 2004–5 have included computerized self-interviewing modules on 'intimate violence', including sexual offences, which are published separately.

3 This is to enable comparability across years in the main count. However, questions about new crimes are periodically covered in separate modules.

(Kershaw et al. 2001: Table 1.1, amended to include changes since 2002)

Since 2002, the BCS and police recorded crime figures have been published together in a single volume entitled *Crime in England and Wales* because, it is argued: 'The police-recorded and BCS figures are complementary series that together provide a better picture of crime than could be obtained from either series alone' (Simmons 2002: i).

The picture of crime from the British Crime Survey

As expected, the BCS uncovers many more crimes than recorded statistics—approximately 9.6 million, as compared to 4.3 million, in 2009–10 (Osborne 2010: 13). BCS crime rates rose every year from 1981 until 1995, declining thereafter in most years. In 2009–10, rates were the lowest they have been since the survey began in 1981 (see Figure 16.3). Like police-recorded crime, most BCS crimes in 2009–10 were property offences (78 per cent) with violence, including robbery but excluding sexual offences, accounting for 22 per cent (Osborne 2010: Figure 2.1).

Figure 16.3 compares the BCS and recorded crime from 1981 to 2009–10, clearly illustrating the substantial dark figure of unreported and unrecorded crime. In 2009–10, fewer than half (43 per cent) of all comparable BCS crimes were reported to the police (Osborne 2010: Table 2.11), though reporting rates differed substantially by type of offence (see Figure 16.4). Nonetheless, there is broad similarity in the shape of crime uncovered by the BCS and crime recorded by police—apart from the period between 1998 and 2003–4 when changes in coverage and recording of police crime inflated the numbers. This suggests that changes in police statistics have historically represented more than simply changes in institutional practices.

Although the first BCS, measuring crime in 1981, confirmed the view that much more crime exists than is officially recorded, the tone of the report was overwhelmingly reassuring: 'the real message of the BCS is that it calls into question assumptions about crime upon which people's concern is founded. It emphasizes the petty nature of most law-breaking' (Hough and Mayhew 1983: 33). Indeed, the authors calculated that:

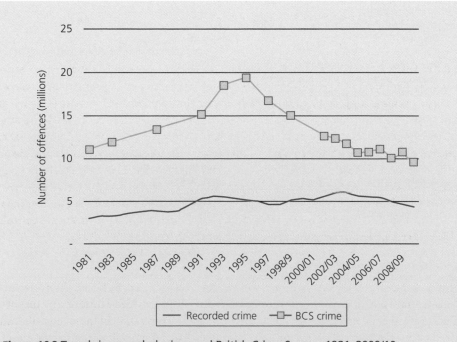

Figure 16.3 Trends in recorded crime and British Crime Survey, 1981–2009/10

Source: Home Office 2007; 2010a; 2010b

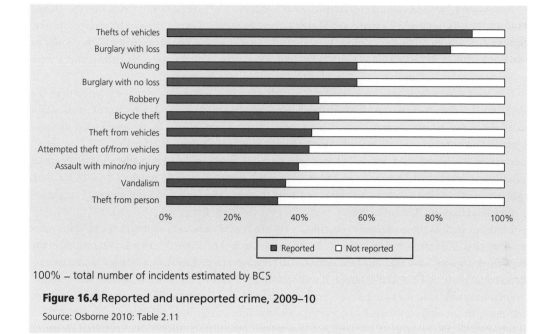

100% – total number of incidents estimated by BCS

Figure 16.4 Reported and unreported crime, 2009–10

Source: Osborne 2010: Table 2.11

assuming that rates remain at 1981 levels ... a 'statistically average' person aged 16 or over can expect:

- a robbery once every five centuries (not attempts)
- an assault resulting in injury (even if slight) once every century
- the family car to be stolen or taken by joyriders once every 60 years
- a burglary in the home once every 40 years
- and a very low rate for rape and other sexual offences.

(Hough and Mayhew 1983: 15)

The authors offered further reassurance through an analysis of the differential risk of serious victimization. For example, the typical victim of assault was found to be a young, single male who spent several evenings a week out, drank heavily, and assaulted others (like himself) (Hough and Mayhew 1983: 21). In contrast, and seemingly paradoxically, fear of crime—measured by questions such as feelings of safety on the street at night—was found to be highest amongst those least at risk of victimization—women and the elderly. In addressing the paradox, the authors hinted at the possibility that fear is in part 'irrational or excessive', and concluded that 'in some areas, fear of crime appears to be a serious problem which needs to be tackled separately from the incidence of crime itself' (Hough and Mayhew 1983: 27). Fear reduction policies, aimed particularly at women and the elderly in the inner cities, were advocated (Maxfield 1984), and a number of policies emerged in the 1980s aimed at educating and reassuring the public concerning the 'reality' of crime.

Critical responses to the BCS

This optimistic picture of the reality of crime was contested, in particular by Left Realists (see Young 1988) and feminists (see Stanko 1988), who argued that the BCS provided a distorted picture of the distribution of risk, failing to uncover the disproportionate victimization of those most disadvantaged in society—the poor, ethnic minorities, and women—and thus misinterpreting the meaning of fear of crime. From the mid 1980s, a number of local crime surveys were conducted in order to elucidate the victimization experiences of these groups.

For example, a survey of an inner-city area of London—the first Islington Crime Survey (Jones et al. 1986)—found that a total of one-third of all households had experienced a burglary, robbery, or sexual violence within the previous year; that women were more likely than men to be victims of assault; and that while older people suffered less crime than younger, assaults against them were more likely to be serious in terms of level of violence, injury, and impact.

Feminist surveys not only uncovered much higher levels of serious violence to women than the BCS, but also documented the pervasiveness of women's experiences of acts which are not classified as crimes—for example, sexual harassment, being touched up, leered at, followed, and so on—which constitute an ever-present climate of threat in women's lives. Radford's (1987) survey of women in Wandsworth, London, for example, found that 89 per cent had suffered some form of assault or harassment during the previous 12 months, covering a wide range of type of incident (see Box 16.2). Most women had experienced more than one incident; some as many as 13 (personal communication, Jill Radford, 1998).

Findings such as these affected the conduct of the BCS, and were undoubtedly crucial to the reassessment by BCS researchers of the relationship of risk to fear of crime. Moreover, alterations in the BCS survey design have been made in response to criticisms regarding its weaknesses in uncovering differential patterns of victimization. For example, in the 1996 survey, a computerized self-completion module was included to improve estimates of domestic violence. In 2001, another computerized self-completion module focused on domestic violence, sexual assault, and stalking; and since 2004–5 this module has become a regular feature of the survey. In addition, the BCS has included an ethnic minority and a youth booster sample—enabling analysis of crime experienced by these groups.

Theories about crime

Theories about the nature and causes of crime are not just academic exercises. They serve both as stimuli to, and as rationalizations of, policy. Theories are thus crucial to understanding policy positions concerning crime control and prevention, although in practice political declarations and

> ### Box 16.2 The Wandsworth Violence against Women survey: proportion of 314 women experiencing various forms of men's violence during previous 12 months
>
> | Type of violence | %[a] |
> | --- | --- |
> | Violent attack | 44 |
> | Threatened in public place | 13 |
> | Threatened/attacked by stranger in their home | 10 |
> | Obscene telephone call | 11 |
> | Sexual harassment at work | 38 |
> | Threatened/attacked by men they were living with | 12 |
> | Total assaulted or harassed | 89 |
>
> [a] Percentages are not additive. Many women experienced more than one type of violence.
>
> (Radford 1987:35)

policy outcomes often represent a—sometimes muddled—coalescence of varying and potentially contradictory theoretical presumptions.

Traditional paradigms of crime

The two competing traditional paradigms of crime are classicism and positivism.

Classicism emerged from eighteenth-century enlightenment thought which views humans as rational, self-interested, and exercising free will. It follows that crime is rationally motivated (freely chosen) by self-interest, and that offenders are fully responsible for their actions. What is required is punishment aimed at deterring (rational) individuals from committing crime. Punishment should be systematically applied, based on the nature and seriousness of the criminal act rather than the characteristics of the offender. In short, criminals should get their just deserts —proportional punishment with determinate (or fixed) sentences.

Positivism is rooted in nineteenth-century empiricist science, searching for the causes of phenomena through objective observation and measurement. In contrast to classicism, positivist theories of crime focus on the offender as determined rather than possessing free will. Crime is thus non-rational, caused by forces beyond the criminal's control. The earliest versions of positivism (still in evidence) focused on individual determinants—defects in the person's biological or psychological make-up which predispose him/her to crime. Because the problem is essentially a pathology or sickness, the appropriate response is treatment (not punishment) aimed at rehabilitation. Since appropriate treatment requires responding to individual needs, sentences should be indeterminate, taking into account not only the seriousness of the crime but the individual's diagnosis and prognosis.

The rise of social positivism

Individual positivism dominated thinking about crime during the first half of the twentieth century. However, by the late 1950s a group of theories—originating in American sociology from the 1920s onwards—were coming to prominence which stressed the social causes of crime. Although these theories can be described as varieties of social positivism (see Box 16.3), most are more accurately viewed as theories which credit humans with certain freedoms within a determined social framework.

One strand focuses on the relationship between the propensity towards criminal behaviour and social norms and values. 'Social disorganization' theory suggests that crime is most likely to occur in specific urban areas where traditional norms and values have broken down due to immigration and migration. Alternatively, in 'strain theory', people at the bottom of the social structure—the working class and poor—are viewed as particularly susceptible to criminal behaviour precisely because they accept dominant norms and values but are denied legitimate means to achieve socially valued goals: crime is a meaningful solution to the disjunction between socially induced goals and the opportunity structures of society. 'Subcultural theory' maintains that these disjunctions are not solved by individuals in isolation, but by groups of people in similar structural positions who form deviant subcultures which may, over time, develop alternative, deviant norms and values. 'Differential association' examines the processes through which criminal behaviour is learned through acquiring skills, meanings, motives, and traditions in association with peer groups involved in criminal activity. All of the above imply that the solution to the problem of crime lies in social programmes designed to alleviate the precipitating social conditions of poverty, deprivation, unemployment, urban decay, and disorganization; in promoting equality of opportunity in education and employment; and through interventions to break up organized criminal groupings.

For labelling theorists, it is not that the poor are more deviant than other people, but that they are more likely to be labelled deviant by those who have the power to label. Once labelled, the person may take on a role or identity commensurate with the label, thus engaging in further deviant activity and seeking out the company of others with similar labels. The impact of labelling is potentially the

---

Box 16.3 **Varieties of 'social positivism' and their policy implications**

Theory	Argument	Policy implications
Social disorganization	Breakdown of moral order of a community	Community development; urban renewal; stamp out extreme criminal elements, e.g. drug pushers
Strain theory	Poverty, deprivation, blocked goals	Anti-poverty programmes; equal opportunity
Subcultural theory	Criminal behaviour socially valued	Social mobility through economic growth; equal opportunity; education policies
Differential association	Local peer/gang cultures	Removal of gang leaders; breakup of peer groups
Labelling	People defined as criminal become criminal	Decriminalization; diversion of first-time offenders to non-penal treatments
Marxist	Inequalities of power and class conflict	Collective ownership of means of production and control; redistribution of resources according to need
Feminist	Patriarchy, women's economic and social subordination	Social empowerment of women through economic, social, and political equality

---

creation of a criminal career, fuelled by a deviancy amplification spiral. Hence, it is argued, criminal justice policy should be geared towards decriminalization and keeping offenders out of formal justice systems as far as possible—radical non-intervention.

While labelling theory begins to question the assumption that there exists a social consensus of norms and values, it does not really challenge fundamental social structures. In contrast, Marxist theories focus centrally on issues of power and conflicts of interest in society: crime arises out of class divisions. The state, including the law and criminal justice system, is viewed as a tool used by those who own and control the means of production—those with power—to protect their interests; hence the criminal justice system targets crimes of the less powerful which threaten the powerful—property crime and public order offences. Unlike the other perspectives discussed so far, Marxist perspectives are interested not only in crimes of the less powerful but also in crimes of the powerful. The latter (such as fraud, environmental destruction, and corruption) are caused by a desire to increase wealth or to gain competitive advantage, while the former are a result of economic necessity—ensuring subsistence—or are acts of alienation. Ultimately the solution of crime requires annihilating inequalities through overthrowing capitalism, collective ownership and control of the means of production, and redistribution of resources according to need. However, lesser demands—for public accountability, for democratization of institutions, and for social programmes to eliminate poverty and deprivation—have all been made in the name of Marxist thinking.

Feminist perspectives are also concerned with power and structural inequalities, but focus primarily on their relation to gender. Feminists argue that women are structurally disadvantaged; society is patriarchal, based on male domination and female subordination. Women's unequal position in society is key to understanding both female offending and victimization. Women who kill men, for example, have often been subject to repeated violence from their victims; female property crime tends to be petty thieving and fraud carried out to support children. Women are vulnerable to sexual violence because of men's power over women, constructed through double standards of masculinity and femininity. The solution to both lies in eradicating patriarchy— empowering women economically, socially, and politically. Feminist perspectives have also raised questions concerning male offending: what is it about men and masculinity that results in their greater involvement in crime?

The theoretical climate from the late 1970s

Many commentators have pointed to a post-war consensus on crime, strongly based on the social positivist notion that improving social conditions and reducing inequalities through social policies would alleviate the crime problem. This consensus had fractured by the end of the 1970s for two interrelated reasons: first, the impact of the recession which resulted in calls for cuts in public expenditure, and second, the apparent failure of rising living standards to halt the rise in crime. Both were accompanied by a questioning of the ability of the welfare state generally, and social programmes specifically, to alleviate social problems held to be, in large part, responsible for crime. A shift in focus began to take place from crime causation and related theorizing to its impact on individuals and communities, and ways in which crime might be prevented, or at least reduced, in order to protect the public from the harm it caused.

'New Right' approaches gained prominence in this climate, the policy implications of which are explored in the following sections. These approaches stress individual responsibility, law and order, and punishment and control of offenders, and include both revitalized classicism and aspects of positivism. They also have historical links with 'control theory', which holds that human nature is not naturally conforming but inherently antisocial, and that all people would commit crime if they were not subject to internalized and/or externalized controls.

'Rational choice theories' suggest that people make decisions to engage in criminal activity, and choose specific times and places, when economic benefits outweigh costs. Rather than focusing on possible causes of crime and motivations of the offender, the solution is deterrence, which requires increasing the cost of criminal behaviour by making it:

- riskier: increase the likelihood of getting caught;
- more difficult to carry out: increase security measures;
- more harshly punished: ensure the costs of getting caught outweigh any benefits gained from the criminal act.

The policy emphasis is on victimization prevention. 'Situational crime prevention' embraced by the Home Office in the 1980s stresses the effectiveness of 'target hardening' (locks and bolts and other devices), surveillance (technology such as CCTV), 'target removal' (for example, not leaving a camera on view in a locked car), and the like in deterring criminal behaviour. At the other extreme are theories which either find biological defects in criminals or imply that human nature is inherently antisocial and blame crime on the 'permissive society', especially lack of discipline in the family (read single parents) and schools (read the liberal 1960s).

Particularly influential on the Right has been the 'bio-social' thinking of James Q. Wilson (Wilson 1975; Wilson and Herrnstein 1985), for whom crime is caused by a combination of constitutional factors which determine the ease with which an individual's conscience can be conditioned, the quality of conditioning of conscience and self-control provided by the family and community, and the costs and benefits of crime. Though the larger constitutional and socialization causes of crime may be difficult to tackle, Wilson suggests that marginal gains can be made. These tend to prioritize enforcing order over social justice. This thinking has fed into zero tolerance policies advocating heavy-handed policing of sub-criminal behaviour at one extreme and calls to get 'tough on criminals' through lengthy prison sentences at the other.

An important challenge to New Right thinking came from Left Realist approaches to crime. These emerged in the mid1980s as an attempt to reclaim the law and order terrain for the Left by acknowledging public anxieties about the rise of crime and disorder in society. A key cause of crime is seen to be relative deprivation—the belief that one's allocation of society's resources is unfair. Thus crime is not confined to those in absolute deprivation—the poor. However, 'it is among the poor, particularly the lower working class and certain ethnic minorities, who are marginalized from the "glittering prizes" of the wider society, that the push towards crime is greatest' (Young 1997: 488). While longer-term social change in the direction of social justice is clearly important in solving the crime problem, Left Realists emphasize the importance of more immediate interventions to control crime—for example, more responsive policing, community involvement, and support of victims.

Somewhat counter-intuitively, New Labour's understanding of crime, underpinned by its central notion of social exclusion, owed as much to the legacy of New Right thinking as to the Left, if not more so (see Muncie 2000). Crime is seen to be concentrated in a minority of the socially excluded underclass populated by inadequate families living in a dependency culture due to excessive welfare provision. The ultimate solution is social inclusion through policies such as welfare to work and neighbourhood regeneration, while controlling crime in the short term through tough criminal justice and zero tolerance policies. While New Labour's more recent interest in restorative justice was viewed by some as signalling a move towards a more rehabilitative, welfare-oriented approach to offending, evidence suggests that it was taken up in an authoritarian and moralizing manner, focusing on individual and family responsibility for offending at the expense of the social contexts of crime and social justice (Gray 2005).

At the time of writing, it is too early to know exactly how the coalition government will construe crime. However, the influence of David Cameron's key idea of the 'broken society' can be detected, perhaps more in policy direction than rhetoric. This idea, loosely developed in a series of speeches and Conservative Party documents (for example, Conservative Party 2007; Cameron 2010a), locates the roots of the broken society in broken families, defined as fatherless or lone-mother families: 'there is a direct link between broken homes (and fatherlessness in particular) and the educational under-achievement, emotional instability and social disengagement which can lead to crime' (Conservative Party 2007: 13); 'Show me an inmate doing time for a violent crime, and I'll show you the man who never knew the love of his father' (Cameron 2010a). Tackling the causes of crime therefore requires supporting the two-parent, married family, welfare reform to eradicate the so-called culture of welfare dependency which allegedly creates and sustains fatherless families, and measures to stop criminal and antisocial behaviour of alcohol-infused youth—the children of broken families. Although the broken society idea was designed as an attack on New Labour, there are striking similarities between the parties in their construction of crime as a problem of the underclass.

Looking overall at the range of theoretical perspectives on crime, we can see that they are underpinned by a variety of contrasting views about human nature, the nature of social order, and resulting policy requirements for dealing with crime. It is also clear that the influence of certain theories and their underlying presumptions at certain historical periods are very much bound up with the larger economic and political climate of the time.

The politics of law and order

As is clear from the discussion so far, crime, justice, and punishment do not exist in a vacuum: political values determine definitions of crime; political beliefs about crime causation are reflected in the criminal justice response to crime and public disorder; and political decision-making determines the social conditions which impact upon crime. An illustration of this is the different strategies towards law and order taken by the Labour and Conservative parties in the 1960s and 1970s—the former citing structural factors such as unemployment and social deprivation as contributing towards crime (social positivism), the latter placing the blame on individuals (classicism). Helping offenders with problems (welfare model) created or at least exacerbated by external causes as opposed to punishing them in proportion to the seriousness of the offence committed (justice model), became the parties' respective responses to crime until the early 1990s. Since then there has been increasing consensus on criminal justice policies as each party has attempted to 'out-tough' the other in the battle to manage—and be seen to be managing—crime effectively. This law and order ideology from New Labour was a far cry from its traditional welfare perspective in the 1960s. More recently the concept of rehabilitation alongside punishment has gained the support of political parties, although whether from conviction or budgetary pressures is debatable.

The rise and demise of the welfare approach

Policy in the mid twentieth century focused on the rehabilitation of the offender. The role of probation officers, social workers, therapists, and counsellors was to provide diagnostic and curative services for wrongdoers. Rehabilitation through treatment embodying the welfare model was at its height in the 1960s in relation to juvenile offenders but began to be challenged from a number of sides during the 1970s. Most damning was research claiming that no penal sanction, method of treatment, or punishment was more successful than any other in reducing reoffending (Martinson 1974). This became known as 'Nothing Works' and a lack of evidence to the contrary, and the fact that the previous 20 years had witnessed steadily increasing crime rates, bolstered the right-wing belief in the justice model and their assertion that it was time to bring back punishment.

The 'party of law and order': Conservative policy

Throughout the 1970s the Conservative Party in opposition linked the continued rise in the crime rate to policy, specifically Labour policy. However, when the Tories, under Margaret Thatcher's leadership, were elected on what was popularly regarded as a 'law and order' ticket in 1979, the New Right ideologues who had criticized the previous government for being 'soft on crime' saw not only prison numbers rise but also crime rates. As Cavadino et al. (1999:17) observed, 'Still "nothing worked", and it cost more.'

Throughout the 1980s and in contradiction to their party's punitive rhetoric, successive Conservative home secretaries began to be persuaded that imprisonment should be reserved for serious offences, and other, less serious, ones should be punished in the community. Box 16.4 shows how this thinking was reflected in both the Green and White Papers preceding the Criminal Justice Act 1991. The legislation contained in the Act set out a 'bifurcation' or 'twin-track' approach to sentencing in which custody was to be reserved for more serious—specifically violent and sexual—crimes, whilst enabling less serious and non-violent offences to be punished in the community.

The 1991 Act was an attempt to introduce a more justice- as opposed to welfare-based sentencing framework in which proportionality between sentence severity and offence seriousness would guide sentencing decisions. Proponents of this 'just deserts' approach argued that imposing a punishment to fit the crime rather than the person would end disparities in sentencing based on welfare considerations. However, sentencers were also able to go *beyond* desert, as set out in the 1990 White Paper (Home Office 1990):

> . . . the legislation which the Government proposes will allow the Crown Court to send [violent offenders] to custody for longer than would otherwise be justified by the seriousness of the offences they have committed, *if this is necessary to protect the public.*

> (1990: 2; our emphasis)

The concept of public protection introduced by the Act began to eclipse both the welfare and justice models as a rationale for sentencing from this point onwards. Capitalizing on the public's concern

> **Box 16.4 Introducing 'Punishment in the Community'**
>
> The Green Paper, *Punishment, Custody and the Community* (Home Office 1988)
>
> - For . . . less serious offenders, a spell in custody is not the most effective punishment. (para. 1.1)
> - Overcrowded local prisons are emphatically not schools of citizenship. (para. 1.6)
> - Imprisonment is not the most effective punishment for most crime. Custody should be reserved as punishment for very serious offences, especially when the offender is violent and a continuing risk to the public. (para. 1.8)
>
> The White Paper, *Crime, Justice and Protecting the Public* (Home Office 1990)
>
> - Nobody now regards imprisonment, in itself, as an effective means of reform for most prisoners. (para. 2.7)
> - Prison is an expensive way of making bad people worse. (para. 2.7)
> - Most crimes are not violent and for many of those who commit them, punishment in the community is likely to be better for the victim, the public and the offender, than a custodial sentence. Imprisonment makes it more difficult for offenders to compensate their victims and allows them to evade their responsibilities. (para. 1.11)

about crime and increasing crime rates, the then home secretary Michael Howard made his infamous 'Prison works' statement outlined in Box 16.5, marking a complete U-turn in the previous decade's penal policy.

From this point onwards the prison population, which had just begun to show signs of decreasing, soared. Further incarcerative measures were introduced in the Criminal Justice and Public Order Act 1994 and legislation planned for mandatory sentencing. Rehabilitative measures lost favour as the policy emphasis shifted to actuarial risk assessment and crime control measures targeted at an underclass of welfare-dependent, socially excluded groups and communities. The fact that the shift went largely unopposed by Labour highlighted the party's own sea change on law and order.

The 'party of law and order': New Labour policy

Tony Blair as shadow home secretary in 1993 stated, 'We will be tough on crime and tough on the causes of crime,' an imaginative compromise of matching the Tory rhetoric of toughness whilst implying a commitment to tackling structural inequalities. The hard-hitting approach helped the Labour Party in opposition to refute its 'soft on crime' label and pave the way towards electoral success.

> **Box 16.5 Prison works**
>
> Prison works. It ensures that we are protected from murderers, muggers and rapists—and it makes many who are tempted to commit crime think twice . . . This may mean that more people go to prison. I do not flinch from that. We shall no longer judge the success of our system of justice by a fall in our prison population.
>
> (Michael Howard, QC, MP, Home Secretary, to the 110th Conservative Party Conference, 6 October 1993)

New Labour's landslide victory in May 1997 saw both public protection and community safety agendas introduced, resulting in measures that would have been unrecognizable as Labour policy 20 years before. These included:

- implementing the Crime (Sentences) Act 1997 drafted by the previous government with mandatory prison sentences for certain types of repeat offending;
- pursuing policies with the potential to criminalize non-criminal populations such as the introduction of antisocial behaviour orders to combat neighbourhood nuisance;
- developing legislation and policies seeking to further restrict, control, and detain immigration and asylum seekers;
- adopting New Right concepts of a 'war' on drugs, and zero tolerance policing;
- piloting proposals such as the suspension of benefits to punish non-compliance with community sentences;
- opening up public sector services for offenders to competition from the private and voluntary sectors, for example prison and probation.

Through three terms in office, Labour policies on law and order included some noteworthy initiatives; one was the introduction of specialist measures to tackle the dramatic increase in illegal drug use and drug related crime whilst at the same time taking the bold step of declassifying cannabis to a Class C drug—the least harmful—and relaxing the law on its possession (although it has since been reclassified to Class B). Another was the pursuit of legislation to tackle racist and racially motivated crime and the acceptance of the Macpherson Inquiry's definition of institutionalized racism in the police force (see Box 16.6). The Inquiry acknowledged that institutionalized racism was likely to be prevalent in other institutions and organizations in society, not just the criminal justice system, and is an important reminder that anti-discriminatory policies must be put into practice in order to be effective. The murder of 19-year-old Zahid Mubarek in Feltham Young Offenders Institution in 2000 by his cellmate, a known violent racist, serves as a powerful and tragic example of the consequences of this not happening.

A further achievement was the introduction of the Human Rights Act 1998, which incorporated the European Convention on Human Rights into UK law and required all institutions to review the impact of policies and practices from a human rights perspective.

However, despite a major programme of reform and investment in tackling crime and its causes, the Labour government left office with a mixed record of success in relation to law and order. Crime rates fell during their 13 years in power but they were already falling when New Labour came into

---

Box 16.6 **Case study: institutionalized racism**

The Macpherson Inquiry (1999) into the racist murder of Stephen Lawrence, an 18-year-old African-Caribbean man, by a gang of young white men in south-east London in 1993 was instigated by Jack Straw in 1997, three months after taking up office. The Inquiry found that institutional racism played a part in the flawed investigation by the Metropolitan Police Service, defining this as:

> The collective failure of an organization to provide an appropriate and professional service to people because of their colour, culture or ethnic origin. It can be seen or detected in processes, attitudes and behaviour which amount to discrimination through unwitting prejudice, ignorance, thoughtlessness and racist stereotyping which disadvantage minority ethnic people.

(Macpherson 1999: 6.34).

office and it could be argued that this downward trend was due to factors besides criminal justice interventions. Crime prevention, crime reduction, and community safety, all high on the government's agenda, resulted in a proliferation of localized multi-agency initiatives such as Crime and Disorder Reduction Partnerships, Drug and Alcohol Action Teams, and Youth Offending Teams. Whilst increasing communication and understanding between agencies, the downside can be increased complexity in working arrangements, leading to confused responsibilities and duplication of effort. Furthermore, despite espousing the benefits of localized decision-making and accountability for crime, the very centralized and target-driven climate created by New Labour worked against this.

Most notably, none of Labour's policies worked to halt the massive increase in the prison population that had begun in the early 1990s, some of which was due to re-conviction within two years of release from prison. A report commissioned by the then prime minister, Tony Blair (Social Exclusion Unit 2002), identified prisoners as a socially excluded group through high levels of family, educational, and health, especially mental health, disadvantage, poor employment prospects, and high levels of debt and homelessness. All of these are known factors in reoffending and with people from black and minority ethnic backgrounds over-represented in almost all of the categories it is not surprising to find them over-represented in the prison population. Recommendations fell short of a robust critique of short-term imprisonment but did call for a rehabilitation strategy, programmes, and support through a sentence and beyond, bringing the concept of rehabilitation back onto the agenda, albeit alongside punishment.

Rehabilitation revisited

The Criminal Justice Act 2003 replaced the sentencing framework introduced by the Criminal Justice Act 1991. The reform and rehabilitation of offenders were given as one of the statutory purposes of sentencing for adults, along with the punishment of offenders, the reduction of crime, protecting the public, and reparation by offenders to those affected by their offences. Amongst its many provisions, the Act replaced all previous community sentences with a single Community Order available to adults and young offenders aged 16 or 17. Courts select one or more of the 12 requirements set out in Box 16.7, some of which are explicitly treatment oriented.

Alongside statutory measures, research evidence from Canada in the 1990s had challenged the 'Nothing works' pessimism of the 1970s and 1980s and suggested that some types of treatment programmes *did* have an impact on recidivism. In the UK the resulting What Works Effective Practice Initiative introduced in the late 1990s and the subsequent roll-out of offending behaviour programmes provided a fresh impetus to the National Probation Service , part of the newly established National Offender Management Service (NOMS) since 2004. The Offender Management Model, a linked initiative introduced in 2005 and designed to ensure the effective management of an offender's 'journey' from the start of a sentence through to its end, combined rehabilitative as well as punitive and restrictive elements, individualized according to an assessment of each offender's risk and need.

NOMS introduced the concept of contestability or competition into the corrections market, making it possible for providers of prison and probation services to come from private and voluntary as well as public sector organizations. This has been taken up by the coalition's justice secretary, Kenneth Clarke, who, as part of David Cameron's 'Big Society' agenda, has stated his intention to make better use of the 'enthusiasm and expertise' of independent organizations to encourage the growth of new approaches to prisons and rehabilitation. Referring to a 'rehabilitation revolution', Clarke outlined plans to stem 'the unsustainable rise in the UK prison population'. Compare what he said about prison (Box 16.8) with what his predecessor said (Box 16.5).

As part of the efficiency savings required by the Spending Review 2010, Clarke also planned to scaleback the massive prison-building programme embarked upon by New Labour, and to discourage the use of short-term sentences for which the rate of reoffending following release is particularly high. To date the justice secretary has said little about young offenders explicitly despite, as

---

Box 16.7 The 12 requirements of the Community Order

Unpaid work	40–300 hours
Specified activities	60 days maximum
Participation in a programme	Programme must be accredited and available.
Prohibited activities	Offender must refrain from a specified activity or activities.
Exclusion	Prohibits offender from entering a specified location for a period of two years maximum.
Curfew	Offender must remain in a specified place for periods of between two and 12 hours per day.
Residence	Offender to reside at a specified place.
Mental health treatment	Offender to submit to treatment by a registered medical practitioner as an in- or outpatient.
Drug rehabilitation	Offender must submit to treatment, including drug testing, for a minimum of six months, and attend regular court reviews if the Order is over 12 months.
Alcohol treatment	Offender must submit to treatment for a minimum of six months.
Supervision	Supervision by a probation officer, the purpose of which is to promote rehabilitation. This is an expected part of each Community Order.
Attendance centre	Available for offenders up to age 25 years: 12 to 36 hours to be completed in sessions of a maximum of three hours.

---

the following section shows, youth crime being the focus of much policy development by both of the major political parties.

Policy implications: young offenders

Nowhere in the criminal justice system are the tensions between competing philosophies and approaches to crime and its control clearer than in relation to young offenders aged 10–17. Disentangling help or treatment from punishment has, in practical terms, never been straightforward, but is particularly difficult when there is a statutory duty to consider the welfare of the child alongside his or her punishment and the protection of the public. Box 16.9 demonstrates care/control tensions in sentencing.

Box 16.8 Prison does not always work

Too often prison has proved a costly and ineffectual approach that fails to turn criminals into law-abiding citizens. Indeed, in all of our experience, in our worst prisons it produces tougher criminals.

(Kenneth Clarke, MP, Justice Secretary, to Centre for Crime and Justice Studies, London, 30 June 2010)

> ### Box 16.9 **Sentencing Jolie**
>
> Jolie experienced years of physical and sexual abuse from her stepfather between the ages of 4 and 11. After repeatedly running away from home, she was accommodated by the local authority. Fostered by a couple with teenage sons, Jolie was bullied and sexually molested by the 15-year-old and began self-harming. She was placed in a residential home for adolescents, where she was introduced to prostitution as a means of obtaining money. Disaffected and rarely attending school, she began to experiment with drugs. Soon she was addicted to crack cocaine, and started shoplifting to fund her habit. At the age of 15 she became involved with a group of lads who used her to solicit men whom they then attacked and robbed at knifepoint. Eventually, following the serious assault of a 40-year-old man, she and two of the group were caught and prosecuted. Tensions in sentencing are highlighted when it is asked whether the sentence imposed should:
>
> - provide help with problems associated with her offending in the hope of reducing or preventing future offending (reductive punishment/rehabilitation);
> - punish her in proportion to the seriousness of the offence to deter her from further offending (retributive punishment/justice);
> - encourage her to make reparation to her victim or to wider society for the harm her behaviour has caused (restorative justice/rehabilitation);
> - protect members of the public from her offending behaviour (incapacitative punishment/justice)

A further layer of complexity is that both criminal and antisocial behaviour by young persons tends to be used as a barometer for the moral climate of the nation. When high, the resulting moral panic—for example, repeat or persistent offending by young people—often leads to policy responses that are tougher or more blaming than are warranted by the original incident. Conflicting attitudes towards young offenders can be traced through several decades of policy responses.

Systems management: diverting young offenders

The election of a Conservative government in 1970, combined with growing right-wing antagonism and legal criticism towards welfarist policies, set the stage for a more punitive, justice-based approach towards young offenders. Throughout the 1970s and 1980s, however, a counter-initiative was developed to divert large numbers from both custody and the criminal justice system, making this one of the most progressive periods in the history of juvenile justice.

The diversionary and decarcerative tactics of this time were based on the belief that youth rather than criminality was the problem and that, with support and encouragement, young offenders would simply 'grow out of' crime. Crucial to this policy, based on theories of labelling and radical non-intervention, was the identification of those young persons demonstrating more serious and persistent delinquent tendencies, and for whom more formal intervention was required. Failure to do this opened the door to the more punitive lobby's accusations that young people were being 'let off' and allowed to continue offending.

Moral panics: punishing young offenders

The deepening of the recession from the late 1980s left an already disillusioned electorate seeking a scapegoat. The publication of official statistics suggesting that crime was on the increase led to tabloid newspapers reflecting (or shaping?) a moral panic relating to inadequate official responses to public disorder, crime, and persistent offending by young people, particularly those termed 'bail bandits', who continued to offend whilst on bail for previous offences. At the height of the media attack, 2-year-old James Bulger was abducted and killed by two truanting 10-year-old boys. The public outrage and 'demonization' of children that followed enabled the Conservative government under John Major to justify an increasingly punitive 'law and order' approach to young offenders to which sentencers responded—predictably—by locking up more young people.

No more excuses: managing young offenders

The shift in New Labour's approach towards young offenders was outlined in the White Paper *No More Excuses* which preceded its flagship legislation, the Crime and Disorder Act 1998:

> An excuse culture has developed within the youth justice system. It excuses itself for its inefficiency, and too often excuses the young offenders before it, implying they cannot help their behaviour because of their social circumstances . . . This White Paper seeks to draw a line under the past and sets out a new approach to tackling youth crime. (Home Office 1997b: 2)

The Crime and Disorder Act 1998 set out to completely reshape the party's agenda in relation to youth crime, shifting it from a discourse of social inequality and disadvantage to one of individual, parental, and community responsibility. Central to the Act was the development of the Youth Justice Board and Youth Offending Teams (YOTs), the latter made up of representatives from probation, social services, police, health, and education to encourage partnership working between the key agencies involved with young people. Their overarching aim was defined as 'preventing offending by children and young persons'. New Labour themes regarding policy towards young offenders aged 10–17 can be traced through some of the measures introduced in the legislation:

- child curfew scheme and child safety order—designed for children under the age of 10 thought to be at risk of becoming involved in crime [early intervention/nipping crime in the bud];
- reprimand and final warning scheme [replacing the much-criticized policy of repeat cautions];
- abolition of the common law presumption of *doli incapax* (literally 'incapable of evil') that had acted as a 'buffer zone' for children aged 10–13 coming to court [young people taking responsibility for their behaviour];
- reparation order [making reparation/recompense to an individual victim or the wider community];
- antisocial behaviour order (ASBO) [seeking to tackle antisocial as well as criminal behaviour];
- parenting order [parents taking responsibility for the socialization and subsequent behaviour of their children];
- action plan order [community penalty combining punishment, reparation, and rehabilitation];
- detention and training order [penalty combining custody and community supervision].

The Crime and Disorder Act 1998 was followed by a raft of further measures focused on young people's behaviour, some more welfare-oriented but many punitive in outcome. The Youth Justice and Criminal Evidence Act 1999 created a new sentence of 'referral to a youth offender panel' or referral order. This was restricted to first convictions and offered a package of interventions designed to prevent reoffending. Referral orders, along with reparation orders, reflected New Labour's interest in restorative justice as a means of holding young people to account in the community whilst also addressing victims' rights. The Intensive Supervision and Surveillance Programme (ISSP), introduced into YOTs to keep more serious and persistent young offenders out of custody, requires daily weekday attendance and strict enforcement by supervising officers in an attempt to make it credible to sentencers. National Standards for Youth Justice, introduced alongside the establishment of YOTs in 2000 and revised in 2004, again focused on making community supervision more robust. The Anti-Social Behaviour Act 2003 extended powers to hold parents to account for children's behaviour and lifted reporting restrictions which had traditionally protected young people from being 'named and shamed' in the media.

Antisocial behaviour: controlling young people

No discussion of New Labour's policies towards youth crime and disorder would be complete without addressing its attempt to 'crack down' on antisocial behaviour as part of its community safety agenda. Not always criminal, and not necessarily caused by young people, antisocial behaviour (ASB) was defined in the Crime and Disorder Act 1998 as behaving in a manner that 'caused or was likely to cause harassment, alarm or distress to one or more persons not of the same household'. Categories of ASB included:

- abandoned or burnt-out cars;
- noisy neighbours or loud parties;
- people being drunk or rowdy in public places;
- people using or dealing drugs;
- rubbish or litter lying around;
- teenagers hanging around on streets;
- vandalism, graffiti, and other deliberate damage to property.

Although the ASBO was introduced as a civil power, any breach results in a criminal conviction. Orders last at least two years and can be imposed on anyone over the age of 10. After a slow start, numbers of orders soared, reaching a peak in 2005. Since then they have declined, partly due to the success of other measures focused on young people, such as parenting contracts and acceptable behaviour contracts (ABCs), but also due to concerns about high breach rates and the criminalizing effect of this on young people in particular. There is a further view that, rather than having any reformative impact on behaviour, an ASBO is regarded by some young people as a 'badge of honour' (see Cartoon 16.1).

Announcing a review of the ASBO and other antisocial behaviour powers in a speech on 28 July 2010, the coalition home secretary Theresa May said it was 'time to move beyond the ASBO' leading to speculation that the ASBO in its current form might be scrapped.

Despite the overwhelming amount of youth justice legislation and measures to prevent youth offending under New Labour, it has been asserted that young offenders 'are today more likely to be criminalized and subject to a greater level of intervention than before the 1998 reforms' (Morgan and Newburn 2007: 1046). This risks bringing already socially disadvantaged children and young people, their families, and communities into a system that has the potential to result in more costs than benefits, as is demonstrated in the following section.

Cartoon 16.1 Teenagers with labels
Source: Grizelda from <http://www.CartoonStock.com>

Implications for policy: costs, numbers, and outcomes

Crime imposes costs on victims, offenders, their families, and society as a whole. Financial costs include the direct loss incurred by victims of acquisitive crime and the 'opportunity costs' to the general public when resources are diverted to making good the damage caused by the criminal act. The highest of these is expenditure on criminal justice system agencies—specifically the police and prison services, but also the Crown Prosecution Service, courts, and probation.

Other financial costs to the general public include crime prevention measures, health services to treat both the physical and emotional scars of violence to the person, and mitigation of victims' losses through insurance and compensation. The Criminal Injuries Compensation Authority (CICA), part of the Ministry of Justice, currently awards amounts between £1,000 and £500,000 for injuries to blameless victims of violent crime, but suffering and distress caused by other offences such as burglary, theft, and vandalism remain more hidden costs.

The punishment of crime also incurs costs, with the financial cost of a custodial sentence far outstripping one served in the community. A popular comparison is that it is more expensive to put someone in prison for a year than it is to send a boy to Eton. There is also a human cost; it was famously stated (Sir Alexander Paterson in Ruck 1951: 13), 'Men [sic] come to prison as a punishment, not for punishment', and yet the experience of prison, in addition to the loss of liberty it imposes, continues to be a punishing one; thousands of prisoners continue to share small cells with a bucket for a toilet and no access to water to wash their hands. Prisoners face bullying and physical attacks, including racist and sexual assaults. Illegal drug use thrives in prison. Even a short sentence of imprisonment can result in the loss of homes, jobs, partners, children, and social ties, militating against successful rehabilitation back into the community on release. Some prisoners lose their lives, although better drug detoxification programmes, mental health services, and the sheer hard work of prison staff in caring for those most at risk of suicide are contributing towards a falling rate of self-inflicted deaths (see **http://www.justice.gov.uk/news/newsrelease010110a.htm**, accessed 12 October 2010). Further costs are incurred to future generations, owing to increased behavioural and mental health problems of children separated from an imprisoned parent.

In the early 1990s, the prison population had actually decreased to 40,000 following the 'talking down' of imprisonment by successive home secretaries in the 1980s and the emphasis on 'punishment in the community' for less serious offenders in the Criminal Justice Act 1991. Following Michael Howard's 'Prison works' speech in 1993, numbers increased steadily, with a slight levelling off between 1999 and 2001 after the introduction of the home detention curfew in January 1999, which allows for the early release of prisoners. In 2007 the prison population rose above 80,000 for the first time in England and Wales, reaching 85,000 in April 2010 and continuing to rise despite falling crime rates. This suggests that more people are being sent to prison, and for longer. With women prisoners continuing to make up less than 5 per cent of the total population, the prison population is primarily affected by the sentencing of males.

Remand prisoners awaiting trial also contribute to the prison population, many unnecessarily so with high numbers acquitted, not proceeded against, or given a non-custodial sentence. Amongst sentenced prisoners, black and minority ethnic (BME) groups accounted for around 27 per cent of the prison population at the end of June 2009, despite making up around 10 per cent of the general population aged 10 years and over (**www.justice.gov.uk/publications/race and cjs.htm**, accessed 18 October 2010). These included foreign nationals, a substantial number being women convicted of drug-trafficking offences who then have to serve their sentence in the UK. BME communities continue to be over-represented at every stage of the criminal justice system, from stop and search practices by the police through to numbers and length of custodial sentences imposed by courts. Reasons are complex and should always be considered within a wider social context as well as specific criminal justice processes that might be contributing towards bias and discrimination.

Predicting the impact of measures introduced by new legislation or any forecast of future outcomes is never straightforward. Home Office statisticians set out different projections of future prison populations in England and Wales in order to aid policy development and monitoring across the criminal justice system, prison capacity planning, and resource bidding and allocation within NOMS. Based on various assumptions, for the period January 2006 to June 2013 (Home Office 2006), these range from a low projected prison population in 2013 of 90,250 to a high one of 106,550.

Criminal justice decision-making, however, is influenced by a multitude of factors, not least pronouncements by ministers about resourcing and political speeches advocating a change in policy towards imprisonment; budget cuts to both the Home Office and Ministry of Justice announced by the coalition Chancellor George Osborne in the October 2010 Comprehensive Spending Review will impact on all criminal justice services, as acknowledged in the justice secretary's 'rehabilitation revolution' speech when outlining ways in which a reduction in the prison population by 2014–15 might be achieved. With community sentences still regarded as the 'poor relation' compared to imprisonment's perceived ability to protect the public, and the tabloid press continuing to talk about offenders 'walking free' from court when a community order is imposed, this is a policy initiative to watch with interest.

European comparisons

Countries throughout Europe have very different historical and cultural experiences of crime control. In France, transportation to the French colonies only ended in 1938. Spain did not begin its transition into democracy until after the death of Franco in 1975. Scandinavian countries' long-standing welfare-based systems have traditionally been reflected in a humane and often radical penal policy; for example, Norway as early as the mid 1970s introduced a 'waiting system' for less serious offenders sentenced to imprisonment. The Netherlands regularly enjoyed the lowest rates of imprisonment for a country of its size for several decades post-war—although this is no longer the case and reflects a general toughening of approach towards crime and criminals in these countries. The opening up of Eastern European countries to the West, and the ending of strict state control, have had, and continue to have, an impact on crime and its management in those countries.

Comparing statistics across national boundaries, each with different legal definitions and measurement of crime rates, is not straightforward. Evidence suggests, however, that rates of recorded crime rose throughout most Western European countries following the Second World War and in Eastern Europe since capitalist economies replaced socialism at the end of the twentieth century, and have generally been falling in the former in the past decade or so. In some Eastern European jurisdictions, prison populations in the early 1990s started to fall from the very high levels of Soviet times but this trend has been reversed and in most European countries prison populations are rising, reflecting the shift to a more punitive criminal justice climate.

As Europe's borders become increasingly permeable, cross-border, transnational crime opportunities abound for organized crime groups which are involved in activities including:

- drug trafficking and people smuggling;
- the smuggling of counterfeit goods, works of art, and illegally trapped endangered species;
- international fraud and money laundering;
- internet-related crime, including financial scams and paedophile rings.

This is leading to more cross-border police activity, including Europol, a Europe-wide intelligence agency which has been operational since the end of the last century.

The eighth edition of Walmsley's (2009) *Prisons Population List* reports that more than 9.8 million people are held in penal institutions throughout the world. Nearly half of these are in the United States, Russia, or China, with the United States having the highest prison population rate in the world (some 756 per 100,000 of the national population). While the United Kingdom's rate of 153 per 100,000 is substantially below this, it is still amongst the two-fifths of countries with the highest rates.

Prison populations are an outcome of criminalization processes as well as wrongdoing. Large numbers of unemployed, poor, homeless, and immigrant persons are routinely incarcerated throughout Europe. Women and minority ethnic groups, both indigenous and from different countries of origin, are being imprisoned at increasingly higher rates. While the conviction and prosecution of women are still far below those of men, there are indications throughout Europe, including the UK, that increasing numbers are being sentenced to imprisonment and for longer. Similar controls are being applied to minority ethnic groups, with heavy policing and imprisoning of those whose lifestyles and ideologies are believed to threaten order and stability—specifically immigrants (legal and illegal), asylum seekers, refugees, guest workers, and foreigners. The terrorist incidents in New York in September 2001 and the London bombings in July 2005 have resulted in young Muslim men being a particular focus of attention.

Many Eastern European countries are looking to the West for ways of reducing high levels of incarceration and are keen to develop alternatives to custody based on those in Western probation organizations. However, high prison populations in the West suggest that so-called 'alternatives' have not made the impact hoped for and there is the added danger that community sentences might be used both for those who would have served only short terms of imprisonment, or others who might have received a fine. In a paper considering the opportunities and challenges of penal policy transfer, Canton (2009) states that countries approaching England and Wales for guidance include Turkey, Bulgaria, Czech Republic, Romania, Croatia, Estonia, Bosnia, Ukraine, and Azerbaijan.

Conclusion

Overall there remains in the UK and Europe, as well as much of the rest of the world, a reliance on imprisonment to deal with those processed through criminal justice systems and found guilty of an offence, whether the purpose of incarceration is essentially punitive or rehabilitative. Rates of imprisonment are not determined by factors wholly beyond government control—they are ultimately a matter of political choice. Policy-makers in Europe, including the UK, must decide whether the huge costs of an incarcerative penal policy for both the most serious *and* less serious but persistent offenders can be sustained. If it cannot, decarcerative strategies must be introduced which are broadly acceptable to voters as ultimately, in a democratic society, it is the electorate who will influence government policy. The challenge for politicians is to ensure that members of the public are aware of the costs—to themselves as taxpayers as well as to victims and offenders—of a continued dependence on imprisonment in the attempt to control crime. A further and equally important challenge is to make clear the benefits to all of the above of identifying and implementing socially inclusive policies which really do work to reduce offending and prevent reoffending, and in doing so also protect the public. While governments continue to avoid the difficult message that no criminal justice sanction can *guarantee* to reduce crime, they also risk ignoring links with other areas of social policy such as the family, education, health, housing, and employment that can have a massive impact on the ability of offenders to desist from further offending.

KEY LEGISLATION

Criminal Justice Act 1991

Criminal Justice Act 1993

The Criminal Justice and Public Order Act 1994

The Crime (Sentences) Act 1997

The Crime and Disorder Act 1998

The Human Rights Act 1998

The Youth Justice and Criminal Evidence Act 1999

Criminal Justice and Court Services Act 2000

The Criminal Justice Police Act 2001

Police Reform Act 2002

The Criminal Justice Act 2003

The Anti-Social Behaviour Act 2003

Criminal Justice and Immigration Act 2008

FURTHER READING

Cavadino, P. and Dignan, J. *The Penal System. An Introduction,* 4th edn (London: Sage, 2006). Highly recommended textbook focusing on England and Wales.

Blackstone Press publishes comprehensive guides to all criminal justice legislation and includes a copy of the relevant Act.

Maguire, M., Morgan, R., and Reiner, R. (eds), *The Oxford Handbook of Criminology* (Oxford: Oxford University Press, 1994, 1997, 2002, 2007). All four editions contain stimulating discussions by leading academic experts on crime, justice, and punishment.

Muncie, J. *Youth and Crime,* 3rd edn (London: Sage, 2009). Provides an integrated and comprehensive analysis of theory, research, policy, and politics.

Flatley, J., Kershaw, C., Smith, K., Chaplin R., and Moon D. (eds) *Crime in England and Wales 2009/10.* (London: Home Office, 2010). Combines the British Crime Survey and police-recorded statistics. (This and other Home Office publications based on the British Crime Survey can be downloaded from: **www. homeoffice.gov.uk/rds/bcs1.html**.)

Reiman, R. *The Rich Get Richer and the Poor Get Prison,* 9th edn (Pearson Education, 2009). This is a classic Marxist-oriented account of the American penal system.

Sim, J. *Punishment and Prisons. Power and the Carceral State* (London: Sage, 2009). The author traces the development of penal strategy since 1974 through a critical analysis of the relationship between penal policy and state power.

USEFUL WEBSITES

Home Office **http://www.homeoffice.gov.uk**

The Home Office is the government department responsible for the police, crime, immigration, drugs policy, and counter-terrorism.

Ministry of Justice **http://www.justice.gov.uk**

A Ministry of Justice was created in May 2007, transferring responsibility for criminal law, sentencing, prisons, probation, parole, and associated matters from the Home Office, with the latter retaining responsibility for policing, immigration, and security.

ESSAY QUESTIONS

1 Crime is a social construction for which there is no accurate measure. Discuss.

2 Is fear of crime rational?

3 How successful was the Labour government's Anti-Social Behaviour Order in addressing public concerns about youth-related crime and disorder?

4 Compare and contrast theoretical perspectives underpinning law and order policy in England and Wales during the Conservative (1979–97) and Labour (1997–2010) governments' periods in office.

5 In what ways does discrimination operate in the Criminal Justice System?

6 Does prison work?

7 Discuss ways in which policy-makers might increase public confidence in community penalties.

ONLINE RESOURCE CENTRE

For additional material and resources, please visit the Online Resource Centre at:
www.oxfordtextbooks.co.uk/orc/baldock4e/.

Comparative social policy and the European Union

Jochen Clasen

Contents

Introduction

Mature welfare states are undergoing similar socio-economic trends, facing common challenges, and tend to respond to social problems such as unemployment or poverty in fairly similar ways. Demographic ageing and low birth rates, for example, are issues which cause financial problems for sustaining national pension systems in most Western countries, albeit to differing extents. Smaller households and less-extensive family networks put pressure on policy-makers to provide more public social care services for older citizens—yet low growth rates and increasing economic internationalization put limits on the financial scope for expansion. In short, studying national social policy in isolation seems increasingly questionable due to the growing impact of external influences on national social policy formation and the increasing interdependence between countries.

Yet what kind of comparisons can be made and what is gained from studying social policy across countries? These two questions are addressed in the first section of this chapter. The second section discusses different interests which researchers bring to the study of cross-national social policy, thereby producing more descriptive, evaluative, or theoretical comparisons. In other words, the first two sections deal with aspects of the academic study of comparative social policy. Subsequently the chapter turns to social policy in Europe. Section three provides a brief discussion of common characteristics and variations in the provision of social policy, as well as the extent of social problems, in selected member states of the European Union. Finally the chapter turns to the role of the EU itself, the causes for the influence of Brussels on national social policy formation, and the question of whether this trend has rendered comparisons of national social policy systems within the EU meaningless.

Learning outcomes

Readers of this chapter will understand and be able to explain the following propositions:

1. Comparative social policy is not necessarily cross-national.
2. Comparative social policy can involve analyses across countries (or societies) and over time.
3. Lesson learning is one motivation for engaging in comparative social policy analysis.
4. Comparative social policy research can be distinguished into primarily descriptive, evaluative, and theoretical studies.
5. The extent of social problems within the EU varies considerably across member states.
6. Social spending varies within member states of the EU but some degree of convergence can be identified.
7. EU social policy is mainly regulatory and the establishment of a European welfare state remains an unlikely prospect.
8. The EU's influence on social policy within member states has economic, political, and legal causes.
9. The aim of social policy harmonization within the EU has been superseded by social policy coordination.

Comparative perspectives and their relevance for the study of social policy

Social policy might broadly be understood as encompassing programmes which are aimed at securing or enhancing the well-being and the life chances of individuals. Conventionally, the study of these policies tended to be confined to Western countries and the ways in which they publicly provide, or regulate, core programmes such as cash benefits, housing, health, and social services. Yet beyond these generally accepted central areas of social welfare, there is a range of other policies which might legitimately be included. Tax allowances, tax credits or exemptions, for example, are in many ways simply alternatives to providing social security (cash) transfers in the sense that they raise the income of certain individuals or households. Education, active labour market policies, occupational health, and health and safety issues impinge on an individual's state of welfare by providing opportunities for, or by directly improving the level of, social and material protection. But also non-public forms of welfare production on the part of voluntary organizations, families, or individuals are important sources for the well-being of large parts of the population. Shifting the focus from a single to more than one country is a powerful reminder of the relevance of such a wider perspective to be applied to the study of social policy. In comparative social policy it is an inherent perspective.

One term, several meanings

Most types of social policy analysis could be regarded as comparative in the sense that observed phenomena, policies, or social problems (such as poverty, homelessness, unemployment, etc.) are compared against a certain point of reference. Often the latter might merely be implicitly assumed rather than openly stated. However, some sort of benchmark is required for assessing, interpreting, or evaluating differences and similarities. Does this mean that there is nothing distinctive about comparative social policy as opposed to other forms of research design? This question has been extensively deliberated in texts on methods of comparative social research generally (Kohn 1989; Øyen 1990; Ragin 1987, 1991; Hantrais and Mangen 1996; Hantrais 2008) as well as comparative social policy in particular (Clasen 1999; Kennett, 2004). Without rehearsing the arguments here, what seems commonly accepted is the fact that a cross-national perspective adds to methodological problems such as generating comparable data, identifying appropriate concepts which can be applied across countries, and achieving a sufficient sensitivity towards the different historical and cultural contexts in which national social policies are embedded.

Treating comparative as synonymous with cross-national is a common shorthand understanding in most contemporary writing on social policy. However, 'nation' is sometimes not the appropriate terminology to be applied in spatial comparisons. Countries belonging to the same nation might be compared, as was the case for studies of divergent forms of social policy delivery in East and West Germany before unification. Nations rather than countries would be the chosen units of comparisons for studying policy differences across Scotland, England, and Wales. Rather than cross-national, the term cross-cultural, or cross-societal, might be preferred for studies with a specific focus or research interest, such as on norms and values towards income redistribution or solidarity, even where the boundaries of different countries are the same as cultures or societies.

A second objection to treating comparative as synonymous with cross-national rests on the fact that the nation (or country) might not be the most useful unit of comparison. The prevalence of a social problem in particular localities within countries (such as forms of social exclusion) might make cross-regional comparisons the more appropriate strategy, covering one or more areas from several countries or within the same country. In other words, countries as units for comparisons might be too large or too small. In the first case, given its cultural diversity, a study of patterns of informal support systems aimed at covering an entire country such as India would generate a wealth of material for intra-country comparisons. In the latter case, a comparison of social policy norms embedded within religious belief systems, for example, might draw on countries for illustrative purposes, but would go beyond nation states as units of comparison.

In short, depending on the particular aim of a comparative study, sub-national entities (local authorities, regions, states in federal countries) or supranational bodies (such as the EU) might be the more appropriate unit of analysis. Indeed, much research which has been labelled cross-national or cross-country is in fact a comparison of particular (and not necessarily representative) regions or towns within different countries. There are often good methodological reasons for such a strategy (e.g. Bradshaw et al. 1993) which should be made explicit.

Finally, comparisons might be inter-temporal rather than (or as well as) cross-national in character. Comparing policy processes during 'critical junctures' in the historical development of particular programmes within a single country (e.g. periods when major legislative changes were made) might be an appropriate research strategy for improving our understanding of the forces which have shaped modern forms of social policy. Combining comparisons over a long time span with those across countries has proved to be a very effective strategy. Ellen Immergut (1992a) applied such an approach to a seminal study in which she suggests that differences in formal political institutions (such as electoral, legislative, and executive systems) explain much cross-national variation in contemporary healthcare provision (see Box17.1).

What is gained from studying social policy across countries?

Potentially there are a number of academic as well as non-academic benefits arising from studying social policy within a comparative perspective (for convenience, from now on understood as synonymous with cross-national). A basic but major justification for looking across borders is associated with what C.W. Mills (1976) called 'the sociological imagination'. While Mills more directly referred to the ability of the possessor of this imagination to grasp history and biography and to place his or her daily experience into a wider structural and historical framework, a similar type of understanding and reflection can be reached by studying and comparing countries or societies. Even a fairly preliminary observation of, in this case, the ways in which other countries respond to similar social problems, organize welfare services, underwrite social rights, or interpret values such as solidarity or equality, tends to lead to reflections about domestic social policy arrangements— and the realization of how much is often taken for granted. Indeed, it might often be some form of 'sociological imagination' which inspires new questions. For example: how do we explain the

Box 17.1 Historical and cross-national comparison on nationalized healthcare

Nearly all West European governments have considered proposals for introducing national healthcare systems at one time or another. In a historical and comparative investigation, Ellen Immergut (1992b) asked why some governments (e.g. Sweden) succeeded while others (e.g. France or Switzerland) failed. She examined these three countries in detail and rejected potential explanatory factors such as different ideologies within national medical associations (all initially objecting to the nationalization of healthcare) or their respective organizational strength. Neither did other factors, such as political demands for national healthcare from unions and leftist political parties in particular, and differences in the relative strength of the latter, explain differences in political outcomes. Instead, Immergut emphasizes political institutions and the ways in which they 'establish the rules of the game' and strongly influence how 'policy conflicts will be played out' (ibid. 1992b: 63). In a careful historical analysis of major decision-making processes during the post-war decades she analysed the impact which different political arenas (executive, legislative, or electoral) exerted on national policy-making. Not the power or influence of particular actors per se was important, she argues, but how the latter were influenced by arenas which provide different 'veto points': constitutional rules in France, the possibilities of popular referendums in Switzerland and the strong position of the political executive vis-à-vis the parliament in Sweden. These veto points heavily impinge on political outcomes, in this case facilitating or hindering the establishment of national healthcare systems.

different emphases which otherwise similar countries place on family policies? Why do unemployed people, pensioners, or lone parents fare considerably better in some countries than in others? Why are some countries able to sustain expensive welfare programmes which require high levels of tax revenue while a similar approach seems to be inconceivable elsewhere? Why have countries with similar average living standards very different levels of homelessness?

While such questions are not new, there has clearly been a growing interest in comparative social policy in recent decades, which might be regarded as a response to political events and processes, as well as economic globalization (see Chapter 9) or social and demographic change. The collapse of the command economies in Central and Eastern European countries after 1989 set in motion a search for social policy models which would accompany the transition towards market economies. The influence of external agencies in this process, such as the World Bank or the IMF, has been considerable. Within the EU, the European Commission has gained in influence not only in economic but also social policy formation, pushing reforms which would allow a stronger level policy coordination across member states (see below). This has spawned comparative social policy research across member states as well as between the so-called European social model and patterns of welfare provision in the United States, for example (e.g. Alber 2010).

But there are also academic reasons why a comparative perspective has become an increasingly common strategy in the study of social policy—even to those who are primarily interested in domestic welfare programmes. At one level, and provided methodological problems of comparisons can be overcome, a comparison of domestic policies with similar arrangements elsewhere can be used as a form of evaluation or test. One way of assessing the effectiveness or efficiency of a particular labour market scheme, a health screening programme, or model of home help services, for example, would be to compare it with analogous policies in one or several other countries. The answer to the question 'what works where and why' is important for both social policy analysts and, potentially at least, policy-makers since learning from other countries might be a step towards improving domestic policy.

On a more abstract level some central enquiries in social policy have always been formulated within cross-national frameworks. For example, the question of why Western countries have developed into welfare states during the twentieth century (measured by, for example, the increase in the rate of GDP spent on social expenditure or the introduction and spread of social rights) has been a major topic of academic debate for many decades (see Pierson 2006 for an excellent overview). Of course, in principle such an investigation can be restricted to the emergence and evolution of social policy within a single country. The impact of the influence of enlightened thinkers and their ideas, the role of increased economic prosperity, growing public demands for welfare, government ideologies, the power of organized labour, and other factors could all be carefully studied in a historically sensitive project on domestic policy trajectory. However, it would seem rather limiting if developments in other countries with similar trends in social policy were to be ignored. Widening the research by including more countries enlarges the empirical basis for testing hypotheses and thus renders potential findings much more robust. In other words, a cross-national rather than single-country research design might be the more theoretically promising strategy. Yet while many comparative studies have been interested in explaining cross-national similarities or variation, others have adopted a more descriptive focus.

Diverse approaches within comparative social policy and the analysis of national welfare states

Many books which discuss social policy instruments, outcomes, and developments, consist of chapters devoted to particular countries. Often such texts lack criteria which would make them explicitly comparative in any analytical sense. For example, disparate country chapters often come without a common analytical framework, systematic structure, or even set of common topics. At times there is little attempt to introduce central concepts or no discussion of how these have been operationalized and, as a consequence, drawing comparative conclusions is difficult. More systematic cross-national analyses can be distinguished in studies primarily aimed at providing descriptive information about other countries, comparative policy evaluations, or theoretical explanations of cross-national variation.

Descriptive accounts

Informative comparisons go back to the 1960s and 1970s, initially concentrating on social administration (Rodgers et al. 1968) and later social policy per se (e.g. Kaim-Caudle 1973; Rodgers et al. 1979). Driven by the idea that considerable knowledge and insight can be gained from looking across countries, these pioneering studies briefly designed an analytical framework and then proceeded with 'constructive descriptions' (Stebbing in Rodgers et al. 1979:xii) and intensive country-by-country discussions of social policy programmes, aims, and forms of delivery. This empirical engagement with social policy in a range of countries was extremely valuable at the time but many aspects were quickly outdated. Also, there were very few in-depth studies which, over and above descriptive purposes, made any claims to theoretical advancement. Heclo's seminal book (1974) on differences and similarities in the development of unemployment insurance and pension programmes in the UK and Sweden was one of the rare exceptions.

Accessing good information about national social policy systems has become much easier since then, not least due to the publication of specialized texts on particular countries, journals which regularly feature articles on comparative social policy (e.g. *Journal of European Social Policy*), the work of international research associations (such as ESPAnet, the European Social Policy Analysis network), and also efforts made by supranational agencies such as the EU or the OECD to harmonize data and thus facilitate cross-national analyses. As a consequence, the value of publications of purely descriptive accounts of national social policy programmes has become somewhat limited when no attempt is made to connect individual country analyses to a wider conceptual framework which would allow inferences about, for example, causes for cross-national convergence or divergence.

Evaluative comparisons in social policy

A second branch of cross-national social policy analysis can be traced back to the early 1980s. It focuses on the evaluation of particular types of social policy intervention (e.g. Bradshaw and Piachaud 1980), or on particular problems such as poverty (Walker, Lawson, and Townsend 1983). Since the 1980s the developments of new and improved datasets, such as the Luxembourg Income Study or the European Community Household Panel (now EU-SILC, European Union Statistics on Income and Living Conditions), have helped to provide a more robust empirical basis for comparative research of this type which is more interested in evaluating the effectiveness of welfare programmes, such as the impact of national income transfer programmes on poverty (Mitchell 1991) or the effect of unemployment on individuals and families (Gallie and Paugam 2000).

Much of this type of analysis produces league tables and rank orders of countries, sometimes with the idea of 'learning' from those countries which seem to be better than others at dealing with social problems or providing social policy in a more effective way. Another more academic value of these types of systematic comparative analyses is to demonstrate how multifaceted and complex social policy interventions can be and thus how superficial and at times misleading country tables in the media appear which arguably show differences in the extent to which countries support particular social groups.

Simple comparisons of child benefit rates, for example, would be rather misrepresenting the overall effort which countries make to help families with the cost of children. While some countries might place an emphasis on universal or means-tested child benefits, others choose tax allowances, or a combination of the two. This has been demonstrated by two projects coordinated by Jonathan

Bradshaw and colleagues (Bradshaw et al. 1993a; 1993b; Bradshaw and Finch 2002). These studies brought together large teams of researchers in order to provide information and data with the aim of identifying the structure of national 'child support packages'. Apart from benefits and tax allowances, other forms of support included in the study were help with the cost of childcare, schooling and healthcare for children, but also housing allowances which can be dependent on the size of a family. Once the structure of these components was identified for each country, the value of child support packages was calculated. Here it is important to recognize that the level of support which countries provide often discriminates between different family types (see Box 17.2). Thus, rather than one child support package, the value of a multitude of packages had to be computed for each country, producing tables with countries ranked in accordance with support levels by income, number, and age of children, family type, and employment status.

Explaining welfare state development and diversity: from welfare effort to welfare regimes

A third branch of comparative social policy is more directly aimed at the generation of theory or theory testing, ranging from two-country comparisons (e.g. Mau 2003; Clasen 2005) to comparisons involving a relatively large number of advanced welfare states. Within the latter group, Peter Flora and colleagues produced landmark publications (Flora and Heidenheimer 1981; Flora 1986). Their main indicator of national social policy development here was the level of spending. Others were the

---

Box 17.2 Evaluating the level of child support across 15 countries

In the early 1990s, Jonathan Bradshaw and colleagues (1993a and 1993b) investigated different ways in which 13 European countries, plus Australia and the United States, help families with the cost of bringing up children and also compared the relative generosity of national support packages. Rather than interviewing families, the research was based on legislation and regulations concerning tax treatment and the entitlement to and level of cash transfers and others forms of support, e.g. with preschool care or healthcare consumption for eight different model families with between one and four children of different ages. National currencies were made comparable by using 'purchasing power parities' which, unlike exchange rates, take account of differences in the cost of living across countries.

The findings show that it is difficult to provide an answer to the question of which country is the most generous in supporting families, because of cross-national variations in outcomes. Comparing countries before or after the cost of housing makes a difference, for example, and there are some significant variations in the level of child support which applies to different families within countries. In the early 1990s, for example, some countries targeted their efforts on families with low income (Germany, the United States, the UK), others favoured large families irrespective of earning levels (France, Belgium, Luxembourg), and some (including Norway, France, and Luxembourg) were particularly generous to lone parents. An 'average rank order' across these and other variations, however, showed that Norway, France, Luxembourg, Denmark, and Belgium were, generally, the most supportive welfare states for families with children. The least generous countries at the time were Spain, Greece, Ireland, Portugal, and the United States. About 10 years later Bradshaw and Finch (2002) repeated the study and extended it to 22 countries. It showed a substantial improvement of the UK's position compared with the early 1990s, and indicated that Austria provided a child support package which was considerably more generous than anywhere else, followed by Luxembourg and Finland.

timing of core social insurance legislation and the growth in programme coverage. The interest in these dependent variables links them to earlier studies conducted in the 1960s and 1970s which, based on statistical observations, argued that the emergence and development of welfare states has to be regarded as a response to socio-economic pressures developed within industrialized societies and growing capacities to meet demands (Cutright 1965; Wilensky 1975). In the 1970s and 1980s, these explanations were questioned in studies which pointed to political factors, and in particular the strength of organized labour, as a crucial variable of welfare state expansion (see Shalev 1983).

The current version of this ongoing debate about causes of welfare state development emphasizes the diversity and the co-existence of several paths towards post-industrialism in accordance with the notion of the existence of different types or welfare regimes around which countries cluster (Esping-Andersen 1990). Gøsta Esping-Andersen's seminal book has impinged on much comparative social policy in the 1990s and beyond.

One of Esping-Andersen's starting points was the argument that the level of social spending is a rather poor 'proxy' variable for social policy (Esping-Andersen 1993). Indeed, a high level of expenditure provides little information as to the degree of redistribution achieved in a particular country or the ways in which welfare programmes ameliorate, perpetuate, or reduce social divisions or income inequality. Instead, an understanding of the impact of welfare states on the social structure of a given country requires a study of the ways in which national welfare programmes are structured and delivered. Applying such a perspective to 18 OECD countries renders, as Esping-Andersen (1990: 80) states, the identification of three distinct 'welfare regimes', defined as:

> institutional arrangements, rules and understandings that guide and shape concurrent social-policy decisions, expenditure developments, problem definitions, and even the response-and-demand structure of citizens and welfare consumers.

Esping-Andersen argues that the provision of social policy and the interaction between markets, states, and families follows a certain logic which differs across the three clusters of welfare states. For example, social policy in 'liberal' welfare states is predominantly aimed at providing support mainly for low-income groups. Consequently, there is an emphasis on means-tested social assistance benefits and only modest universal transfers, and an active encouragement of the use of non-state alternatives such as private forms of social protection. Esping-Andersen regards countries such as the United States, Australia, Canada and, to a lesser extent, also the UK, as belonging to this group. A second regime type, the 'corporatist' or 'conservative' welfare state, aims to preserve status differentials by providing transfers which are closely linked to previous earnings. Since social rights are attached to class and status (e.g. with separate programmes for white- and blue- collar workers, and benefits covering family dependents) private forms of welfare provisions are much less prevalent than in liberal welfare states. Continental European countries such as Germany, France, and Italy belong to this cluster. The third 'social-democratic' type aims to foster cross-class solidarity and equality. Generous benefits, also for the less well-off, and universal forms of support predominate, with the state acting not only as compensator for lost earnings but also as principal provider of care services for children and older people. Social policy in Scandinavian countries such as Sweden, Norway, and Denmark is arguably embedded within such a framework.

Empirically Esping-Andersen distinguished the three clusters by their respective degrees of 'de-commodification' and 'stratification'. The latter indicator refers to the type of social structure which welfare programmes (e.g. pensions) promote and is composed of a measurement consisting of the degree of corporatism (number of distinct public pension schemes), etatism (pension expenditure on government employees), average levels of benefit universalism and benefit equality, and proportions of spending on means-tested social expenditure, private pensions, and private healthcare (see Esping-Andersen 1990: 70–1). 'De-commodification' is understood as the degree to which 'individuals, or families, can uphold a socially acceptable standard of living independently of market participation' (Esping-Andersen 1990: 37). In other words, welfare states differ in the extent to which they allow benefit recipients to withstand the pressure of returning to the labour market (see Box 17.3).

Welfare regimes and beyond

Esping-Andersen's welfare state typology stimulated major debates in comparative social policy. Some commentators questioned the academic value of constructing clusters of welfare states (e.g. Baldwin 1996), others emphasized the need to identify more than three distinct welfare regimes. Stephan Leibfried (1993), for example, argued that southern European ('Latin rim') countries could not simply be regarded as evolving versions of one of the three types but display characteristics which made them different. This has also been claimed by Maurizio Ferrera (1996), who pointed to characteristics such as a fragmented nature of social security, the mix between public and non-public forms of welfare provision, and the role of clientelism and patronage which combined form a distinct southern European welfare state (but critically, see Kastrougalos 1994). Beyond Europe, Castles and Mitchell (1993) pointed to methodological and conceptual problems in Esping-Andersen's typology (such as the treatment of means testing; see Box 17.3). Once taken into account, Esping-Andersen's 'liberal' welfare states arguably consist of two groups, with the UK, Australia,

> ## Box 17.3 De-commodification as a central concept in Esping-Andersen's welfare regimes
>
> One of the two central indicators which Gøsta Esping-Andersen (1990) employs to distinguish between welfare states is the level of 'de-commodification'. With developing capitalism, for the majority of the population the survival outside the labour market became increasingly difficult, work became waged work and labour therefore commodified. Only the gradual establishment of social rights lowered workers' reliance on the labour market somewhat during times of sickness, unemployment, or retirement. The historical expansion of the welfare state can therefore be regarded as a process of de-commodification and countries can be compared in accordance with the degree of de-commodification. Using data from the early and mid 1980s, Esping-Andersen (1990) calculated the degree of de-commodification for pension, sickness, and unemployment programmes in 18 OECD countries. He took account not only of the generosity of transfers but also of benefit duration, access to benefits (eligibility rules), and the ways in which benefits are funded, weighted by the percentage of the relevant population covered. For example, the index for pensions has been constructed as consisting of the levels of both the minimum pension and the standard pension, the number of years to qualify, the proportion of pensions funded by contributors rather than taxation, and the share of people above retirement age who are actually in receipt of a pension. He then scored individual programmes for each country and produced rank orders. These showed the lowest (combined) de-commodification scores for countries such as Australia, the United States, Ireland, and the UK. For average workers in these 'liberal' welfare states the degree of market independence achieved by social policy is therefore low and the pressure to return to paid work high. By contrast, the highest scores were registered for Scandinavia, which means that the same welfare state programmes enable Swedish or Danish workers more easily and for longer periods to survive without participation in the labour market.
>
> The concept of de-commodification has become an important organizing principle in comparative social policy and component in the three-way classification of welfare states it helps to portray. However, it is not free from theoretical, conceptual, and empirical problems. Francis G. Castles and Deborah Mitchell (1993), for example, criticized the somewhat arbitrary low weighting which was ascribed to some programmes simply because they are means tested. Lyle Scruggs (2007) has suggested ways of updating and empirically advancing the measurement of welfare state generosity.

and New Zealand pursuing similar welfare goals as in Scandinavia (poverty reduction, income equalization) but by means of redistributive instruments rather than high social expenditure.

Other criticisms of Esping-Andersen's approach (for reviews see Abrahamson 1999 and Arts and Gelissen 2002), revolved around the actual notion of welfare regimes (are they ideal types or actual systems?), the problem of assigning particular countries to particular clusters, or the dynamic nature of welfare states and the question of regime shifts. The exclusive focus on income transfers has been regarded as another major shortcoming. Placing welfare services such as health and social care at the centre of the analysis would have produced a different clustering of countries (Kautto 2002). The two 'conservative' welfare states of France and Germany, for example, with similar patterns in the provision of social security, differ considerably in the means and the extent to which they provide care for children and support parents (Rostgaard and Fridberg 1998). The inclusion of the role of unpaid care provided by families and networks would help to attain a more adequate understanding of women's relationship with the welfare state which cannot be reduced to that of a paid worker (Lewis 1992).

Despite, or perhaps because of, these various forms of criticism, Esping-Andersen's welfare regime approach has remained a major reference point in the study of comparative social policy to date. Also, his classification has proved to be fairly robust, even though a case can be made for extending the categories to four or even five (with the 'conservative' type as the most heterogeneous) and of repositioning some countries if the focus of analysis is a certain programme or policy fields rather than welfare states per se. If anything, the reference to welfare regimes (implying a certain logic of social policy provision) helps to locate the study of comparative social policy within a wider framework, highlighting national configurations and interdependencies between welfare and other policy areas such as industrial relations, labour market policy, or national production systems (Ebbinghaus and Manow 2001, Bonoli 2003). Indeed, it is difficult to find any macro-level comparisons of European welfare states which does not refer to the 'three worlds of welfare capitalism', critically or otherwise. This is the case even for cross-national comparisons of social policy which concentrate on particular aspects of social policy rather than welfare states, and which are more interested in welfare outcomes rather than configurations of welfare production.

Social policy in the European Union

While it might be argued that national social policy concerns have been superseded by debates which are more international and comparative in nature, criticisms have been made against analyses which remain confined to Western Europe or to economically advanced countries, such as those belonging to the OECD (see Jones Finer 1999). In many cases it is indeed interesting, or sometimes essential, to broaden the scope of cross-national analysis beyond Europe, particularly if social policy variation is a prime interest. In order to capture different value systems underpinning welfare provision or the different roles of families and informal networks in the provision of welfare services, a broad comparative perspective seems appropriate. However, even a 'narrow' European or even European Union perspective can serve the purpose of illustrating some of the similarities and differences in social policy arrangements which have inspired comparative analyses of social policy.

Spending on social policy within the European Union

After its enlargement which extended the membership from 25 to 27 countries in 2004, the EU has become more diverse than ever, with countries differing considerably not only with respect to their population size (between 82 million in Germany and 400,000 in Malta) but also in terms of major national social and economic indicators. This also applies to the structure and level of public funding of social policy. Figure 17.1 provides an overview of social protection spending in eight member states of the European Union, plus the equivalent figures for the United States and Australia. In order to adjust for different population size, social spending is measured as a share of national gross domestic product (GDP). Of course, as always in comparative social policy, there are aspects of comparability which need

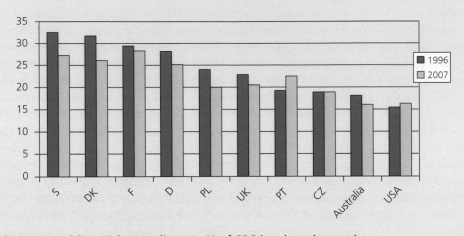

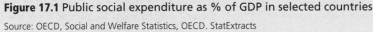

Figure 17.1 Public social expenditure as % of GDP in selected countries

Source: OECD, Social and Welfare Statistics, OECD. StatExtracts

to be taken into account. While some social policy domains (such as education) are excluded, indirect spending (such as tax subsidies) is difficult to identify consistently across countries, as is mandatory employer provision. Recently the OECD has tried to include these elements in a more comprehensive approach of measuring social spending, but empirical and theoretical problems remain (De Deken and Kittel 2007; Castles and Obinger 2007). Also, while taking account of different sizes of national economies, measuring social expenditure as a share of GDP is always liable to fluctuations in national business cycles. Nevertheless, Figure 17.1 provides some indication of differences in public expenditure on social policy, ranging from large welfare state spenders such as France and Sweden to more moderate European welfare state spenders such as the Czech Republic, Poland, and the UK.

The figure invites two further observations. First, while these types of comparisons always depend on the particular years selected, between 1996 and 2008 there seems to have been a decline in social expenditure across most countries. Second, the commitment to publicly funded social protection seems to remain stronger in the EU than in other advanced economies in the world. However, one needs to be somewhat careful here. Other European (but non-EU) countries such as Norway or Switzerland are also large welfare state spenders, while some EU countries not listed here, such as Ireland or the small Baltic states, devote relatively low shares of their GDP to social protection programmes.

A degree of convergence is observable in respect to the ways in which EU countries finance social policy. In principle, there are four forms of revenue: taxation, contributions from protected persons, contributions from their employers, and other forms of receipts from a variety of sources such as interest and dividends, co-payments for prescriptions, and so on. The relative share of the latter has not altered significantly during the 1990s, remaining generally below 10 per cent of all social protection revenue, except for Greece and the Netherlands. By contrast, tax funding (referred to as general government contribution) has lost somewhat in relevance in countries which traditionally put a strong emphasis on taxation, such as Denmark, but has become more important in countries such as Germany, Italy, and France (see Figure 17.2). The background for this convergence is a concomitant reduction of the share of social security contributions in those countries as an attempt to reduce non-wage labour costs which, although contracting, generally remain higher in continental countries.

The extent of social problems: European diversity

Typical problems and risks which social policy spending aims to address include unemployment, poverty, or social exclusion. All of these problems can be defined, and thus measured, in different ways within and across countries. Without rehearsing methodological and theoretical problems

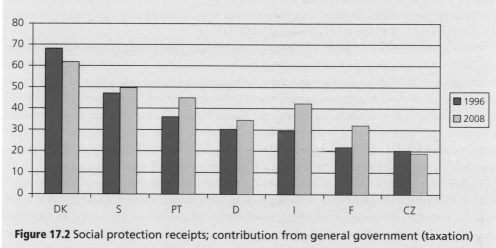

Figure 17.2 Social protection receipts; contribution from general government (taxation)

Source: Eurostat; Statistical database (**http://epp.eurostat.ec.europa.eu/portal/page/portal/statistics/search_database**)

involved, for the purpose of illustrating cross-national variation, Figure 17.3 displays the relative risk of poverty in the nine EU countries and the average for all 27 countries. The risk of poverty is here defined as the share of the population with income below 60 per cent of median disposable income—after the receipt of benefits—adjusted by household size (so-called equivalized income). The data show that poverty rates vary substantially across the EU, but not in accordance with the level of economic development. Some richer countries such as the UK (with per capita income above the EU27 average), have relatively high levels of poverty, while some countries with below-average per capita income (such as Hungary and especially the Czech Republic) have relatively low poverty rates. It is interesting to note that, based on this measure, the 'risk of poverty' has increased in most countries between 2001 and 2009. The two exceptions are the UK and Portugal where it has decreased, and France where there has been no change. As a result, the variation across the nine

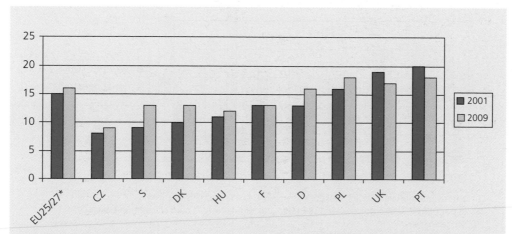

*EU25 in 2001; EU27 in 2009; share of persons with an equivalised disposable income below 60% of the national median equivalised disposable income (after transfers); rounded

Figure 17.3 At-risk-of poverty rates; 2001 and 2009

Source: Eurostat; Statistical database (**http://epp.eurostat.ec.europa.eu/portal/page/portal/statistics/search_database**)

countries selected here has become smaller over time. However, this process of convergence does not hide the fact that the relative positions of countries which had relatively high rates of poverty in 2001, including the UK, remained almost unchanged.

Other aggregate data indicate that different types of social problems are often but not always connected. For example, long-term unemployment is often referred to as a major factor which contributes to poverty. This is certainly true in some countries, as Figure 17.4 indicates. Portugal, for example, has both high levels of long-term unemployment and above-average rates of poverty. The reverse (low unemployment and below-average poverty) holds for countries such as the Czech Republic, Denmark, and Sweden. However, those who have a job can also be at risk of poverty due to low wages or part-time work, for example, especially in households with only one earner. Figure 17.4 indicates that these factors seem to contribute to above-average general poverty rates in Poland and Portugal.

Rather than being in low-paid work or unemployed, people of working age might be involuntarily out of a job for reasons such as disability, long-term illness, training, or caring responsibilities. Labour market inactivity (rather than merely unemployment) might thus be an important indicator of poverty or other social problems, especially at household level. Figure 17.5 underlines this. It depicts the percentage of children who grow up in households with no income from paid work. It suggests that poverty in the UK is at least partly due to a high proportion of households with children where no one is in paid employment.

The European Union and the 'Europeanization' of social policy?

The discussion so far has shown that European countries retain distinctive characteristics in the relative scope of social problems on the one hand, and patterns in which markets, states, and families interact in the provision of social protection on the other. However, at a broad level some of the figures suggest that some degree of convergence has taken place in the areas of social

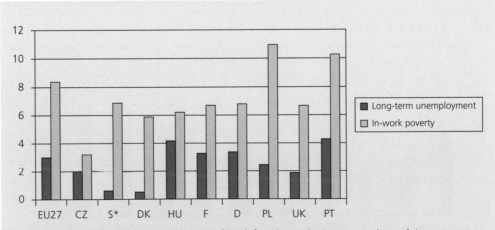

Long-term unemployed are jobseekers out of work for 12 months or more as share of the active population (i.e. employed and unemployed population); * own calculation based on OECD.StatExtracs

The 'in-work poverty' rate is the share of persons who are in paid work and have an equivalised disposable income below the risk-of-poverty threshold, which is set at 60% of the national median equivalised disposable income (after social transfers).

Figure 17.4 Long-term unemployment and 'in-work poverty' rate in selected EU countries, 2009

Source: Eurostat; Statistical database **(http://epp.eurostat.ec.europa.eu/portal/page/portal/statistics/search_database)**

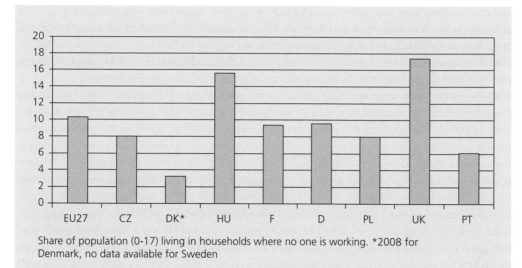

Share of population (0–17) living in households where no one is working. *2008 for Denmark, no data available for Sweden

Figure 17.5 Children aged 0–17 living in jobless households, 2009

Source: Eurostat; Statistical database **(http://epp.eurostat.ec.europa.eu/portal/page/portal/statistics/search_database)**

expenditure, the financing of social policy, and, worryingly, poverty rates. To what extent can this process be attributed to actions at the level of the European Union?

Pushing for a European welfare state?

Most commentators regard the EU influence over national social policy making as limited—and remain sceptical about the prospects of a harmonization of national social policy regimes within the EU. In fact, the EU's reliance on only broadly defined guidelines and flexible forms of implementation leaves sufficient space for further divergence rather than convergence of national social policy provision (see Geyer 2000). But this is not to say that the EU has not had any influence on social policy across its member states. In fact, it can be shown that the degree of social policy activities and intervention has steadily grown since the 1950s (for extensive discussions, see: Geyer 2000; Kleinman 2002; Ferrera 2005; Hantrais 2007; Kvist and Saari 2007).

Essentially a process of creating a common economic sphere, the six founding members of the then EEC (European Economic Community) assumed that a higher level of social welfare would follow from increased economic activity, which was to be achieved via regulations concerning the free movement of workers between member states or the freedom to provide services. Yet even the Rome Treaty, signed in 1957, included some more explicit areas of social policy intervention, such as improved working conditions, equal pay between men and women, and holiday pay. The latter policies were insisted upon by France in order to prevent a potential competitive disadvantage, and can thus be seen not so much as driven by concerns over social welfare but as accompanying elements of economic integration and fostering the mobility of labour.

However, while early social policy activities were rather rudimentary and geared towards mobile workers and creating gender equality in pay and social rights, over the past 30 years or so the EU has become an increasingly influential force in the shaping of social policy regulation within member states. In the 1970s, the Social Action Programme (1974–6) was aimed at improving employment, living and working conditions, and encouraging cooperation between employees and employers. The promotion of the social integration of particular groups in society has been a limited but explicit feature of EU social policy since the 1970s. In 1974 a social action programme fostered the vocational and social rehabilitation of disabled people. This was followed up in the late 1980s with the HELIOS programme, aimed at promoting independent lifestyles for people with disabilities, and other initiatives in the 1990s focusing on the integration of young people with disabilities into ordinary systems of education and training. Other actions have concentrated on older people, including the establishment of an 'Observatory on Ageing and Older People', reporting on the situation in each member state and the policies pursued there. Also, the 1994 White paper on social policy included a particular focus on improving the position of older people in society.

However, the worsening economic context in the mid 1970s contributed to a rather mixed and more modest output than had been anticipated, even though important directives were passed in the areas of equal treatment for men and women and health and safety, as well as the establishment of several European networks and observatories aimed at monitoring social policy developments in the member states. The 1980s were dominated by the preparations towards the completion of the single market. Although social policy was not a major element of the Single European Act of 1986 (the first major revision of the Rome Treaty), the then president of the Commission, Jacques Delors, with the support of the pro-European French President Mitterand and the German Chancellor Kohl, was keen to expand the so-called European 'social dimension' in order to increase public support for further economic and political integration. This became explicit in the growing emphasis which was put on involving social partners in matters of social policy (the so-called 'social dialogue') and the increased use of Structural Funds in order to reduce regional disparities. Another example was the stronger decision-making power of the EU facilitated by the adoption of qualified (rather than unanimous) majority voting in some areas, such as health and safety at work.

Disagreement over the growing European social policy competence in the run-up to the Maastricht European Council in 1991, which formally created the European Union, led to the famous British 'opt-out' from the so-called 'Protocol on Social Policy' which was signed by the other 11 member countries and annexed to the Treaty. It extended the principle of qualified majority voting to further areas, such as working conditions, information and consultation of workers, and equality between men and women. The British opt-out was later rescinded by the incoming Labour government in 1997 and formally incorporated in the Amsterdam Treaty of the same year, paving the way for European directives on areas such as parental leave, atypical forms of employment, working time, and sex discrimination, which now apply across all EU member states. The Amsterdam Treaty also for the first time explicitly mentioned the fight against social exclusion as one of the areas in which the EU was to adopt a more active role.

In 2009 the Lisbon Treaty was adopted, which included a 'horizontal social clause', stipulating that EU policies should aim to ensure that its economic policy objectives should take account of social aspects, such as increasing employment but also fighting against social exclusion, ensuring adequate social protection, improving education, training, and healthcare. This followed on from the so-called Lisbon Strategy which was developed in 2000 and which led to the setting of targets, such as reaching certain employment rates or lowering long-term unemployment and levels of social exclusion. However, within a few years it appeared that these ambitions became overshadowed by a renewed emphasis on the promotion of economic competitiveness and marketization at the expense of public provision.

By the end of the first decade of this century the Lisbon Strategy had failed in reaching most of its targets. This, and the economic crisis in 2008–9, led to the launch of the so-called 'Europe 2020' strategy. In this latest initiative the European Commission set economic, employment, and energy consumption targets for the next 10 years but also reviewed its social policy ambitions, setting itself targets for the year 2020, such as taking at least 20 million people out of being 'at risk of' poverty and improving educational achievements. The ways in which these aims are to be achieved, however, continued to be based on voluntary action of member states, such as the 'open method of coordination' (see below).

European social integration?

The discussion above suggests a growing but still limited and indirect EU influence on social policy across member states. It remains the case that, unlike national welfare states, EU social policy intervention is largely regulatory, and does not guarantee individual entitlements to social benefits paid out of a European social budget. A European welfare state which provides pensions, healthcare, or social services seems as inconceivable now as it has always been, for two main reasons. First, the EU lacks legislative power and financial resources, such as a designated form of tax revenue which would fund these core social policy areas. More importantly, because of their popularity and electoral significance, there is little political will among member states to transfer sovereignty from the national to the EU level to such an extent.

Second, as discussed, the development of European social integration has predominantly been driven by economic rationales. The ambition to create a single European market with free movement of goods, investment, services, and labour continues to be the central driving force, and was cemented by the adoption of the euro as a single currency in 1999, which initially applied in 12 and currently in 17 EU countries. However, as a corollary of economic integration, some social policy intervention was all but inevitable. For example, free movement of labour would be difficult to reconcile with a lack of recognition of pension rights and entitlement to benefits for citizens who work in member countries other than their own. Equal minimum social standards help to put a brake on countries who otherwise might be tempted to gain a competitive advantage over others by lowering the social (non-wage) costs for companies and thus undercut prices (a process which has been referred to as 'social dumping'). As a consequence, there has been some form of social policy legislation at EU level, but characteristically confined to employment-related aspects, such as health and safety at work, working conditions, minimum standards, or regulating the length of the working week.

In short, ever since attempts to harmonize national social policies stalled in the early 1990s, the direct EU influence over social policy has remained limited in the sense that it continues to be restricted to areas which are fairly close to the labour market. In other, more indirect and less legalistic forms, however, EU policy has influenced social policy-making, particularly in areas such as social exclusion (see Ferrera et al. 2002) or the coordination of national employment policies (Goetschy 2001) as part of the 'open method of coordination' (Zeitlin et al. 2005; Büchs 2007; Heidenreich and Bischoff 2008). Originally restricted to the field of employment, this 'method' has subsequently been extended to the areas of social exclusion, pensions, and healthcare. While setting concrete aims and targets, rather than requiring countries to act in a certain fashion is based on fixing common objectives, encouraging cooperation between member states, benchmarking, promoting best practice, conducting evaluations, requesting regular progress reports, and issuing recommendations. It is probably fair to say that the originally high expectations associated with the open method of coordination in terms of attaching more relevance to social protection within the overall EU policy have not been met. Narrowly this might be due to its non-binding voluntaristic approach. More broadly it could be argued that the failure to reach its targets as formulated in the Lisbon Strategy was ultimately due to the EU's primary emphasis of encouraging economic liberalization and competition privatization and consumer choice.

Limited but growing: other forms of EU influence on social policy in Europe

Given the limited direct influence of the EU in social policy fields such as healthcare, social services, family policy, or housing it could be assumed that social policy has remained firmly determined at national level. However, while formally the case, national sovereignty over social policy formation has eroded over the decades while EU influence has grown (see Kvist and Saari 2007). Not that long ago, benefits were largely restricted to citizens of a particular country and their consumption was nation bound. Ever since the 1990s, neither stipulation holds any longer (see Leibfried and Pierson 1995). Even though the extent of loss of national sovereignty differs between types of social benefits, as the result of an ever-increasing number of legal rulings by the European Court of Justice, national governments can no longer exclude non-national EU citizens from social rights or stop the exportability of benefit entitlement to other EU countries. This applies particularly to benefits which can be regarded as providing a minimum level of social protection (such as a minimum pension) but also for family allowances and other long-term, and particularly in-kind, benefits. By contrast, national governments have managed to hold on to sovereignty over transfers which are tightly linked to individual contributions (social insurance), and unemployment insurance transfers especially.

This outcome is not so much the result of a deliberate political move towards a European welfare state but of a conflict between maintaining national autonomy over welfare state matters versus the emphasis on economic liberalization and full European labour mobility including the freedom to provide services in other member states. Public monopolies, such as in healthcare delivery or pension provision, might be interpreted as contravening freedom of enterprise, for example. The arena for this ongoing struggle has been the European Court of Justice in a series of complex legal processes in which, as Leibfried and Pierson (2000: 279) put it, 'supranational efforts to broaden access and national efforts to maintain control go hand in hand, and are calibrated from conflict to conflict and court case by court case'.

In other words, as a form of spill-over and brought about by legal rather than by direct political action, the process of economic or market integration has been accompanied by an incremental process of social policy 'homogenization' (Leibfried and Pierson ibid.). Its driving parameters (exportability of benefits; non-exclusivity; freedom to provide services) have increasingly influenced national welfare state reform processes, as have other policies such as extending the primacy of internal market to the area of social protection, and to social services in particular. Also other measures which accompany the single currency or the enlargement of the EU have contributed to an increasing degree of 'Europeanization' of social policy (Kvist and Saari 2007).

This has consequences for the study of comparative social policy in Europe. On the one hand, abandoning nations as units of comparison seems rather premature because most social policy-making (funding, spending, delivery) is still decided at national rather than at EU level. However, it would be misleading to simply disregard the impact which EU legislation has had on the content and the process of national social policy reforms, or to dismiss the extent to which sovereignty over some social policy fields has been transferred from national governments to supranational EU governance. As discussed, indirect EU action (legal rulings as outcome of market building) as well as direct action in fields relevant to social policy (e.g. European monetary union) or social policy proper (e.g. the open method of coordination) exert some degree of influence on national social policy-making. The lesson for comparative analyses of social policy at European level is to acknowledge that the interaction between the EU and national social policy formation will continue to be a major area of study for some time to come.

Conclusion

The study of social policy has become increasingly comparative in nature, and the comparative analysis of social policy has become firmly embedded within most university courses on the subject. The chapter has covered a number of reasons for this trend, some of which are of an academic nature and others to do with the growing sense of cross-country interdependence and similarities in the challenges which mature, as well as many developing, welfare states face today. The chapter has also illustrated how member states of the European Union continue to display considerable differences both in the extent of social problems, such as poverty, and in the magnitude of national resources devoted to social policy. However, processes of policy convergence within the EU can be identified too.

While there might be many reasons for the latter, the role of the EU as an influencing factor for social policy development in its member states is becoming ever more apparent, which does not mean that national boundaries are no longer relevant for comparative social policy analysis. The prospect of a European welfare state replacing core social policy programmes at national level seems as remote as ever. While this might be good news for those who like to study cross-national social policy, the nature of comparisons will be increasingly influenced by the interface between national and European initiatives, as well as supranational developments beyond Europe.

KEY LEGISLATION

1957: Treaty establishing the European Economic Community (EEC) in Rome.

1992: Treaty on European Union (EU) signed in Maastricht in February 1992. Agreement and protocol on Social Policy which was concluded by all member states with the exception of the UK.

1994: White Paper on European social policy—a way forward for the Union (COM 94 333), an important document setting out the EU's role in social policy.

1997: Amsterdam Treaty is signed (in force in 1999); the UK gives up its opt-out position and signs the Social Chapter.

2000: Lisbon Strategy and the 'Social Policy Agenda 2000–2005'; setting targets in the areas of social protection.

2009: Signing of the Lisbon Treaty (the EU's constitution), which includes a 'horizontal social clause', promoting high employment, adequate social protection, and the fight against social exclusion.

2010: 'Europe 2020' strategy sets new targets for the year 2020.

FURTHER READING

For discussions about applying various methods and approaches in comparative social research, generally good sources are **Hantrais, L. and Mangen, S.** (eds) *Cross-national Research Methods in the Social Sciences* (London: Pinter, 1996), **Ragin, C.**, *The Comparative Method* (Berkeley: University of California Press, 1987) and also **Hantrais, L.**, *International Comparative Research. Theory, Methods and Practice* (London: Palgrave, 2008). More focused on comparative social policy are **Clasen, J.** (ed.) *Comparative Social Policy: Concepts, Theories and Methods* (Oxford: Blackwell, 1999) and **Kennett, P.** (ed.) *Handbook of Comparative Social Policy* (Cheltenham: Edward Elgar Publishers, 2002). Various methodological challenges of comparing welfare states across countries are discussed in **Clasen, J. and Siegel, N. A.** (eds) *Investigating Welfare State Change. The 'Dependent Variable' Problem in Comparative Analysis* (Cheltenham: Edward Elgar, 2007).

Esping-Andersen's *Three Worlds of Welfare Capitalism* (Oxford: Polity Press, 1990) remains the definitive starting point for the discussion of welfare regimes and regime theory. For his response to the debate in the 1990s and a reflection on extending the analysis see **Esping-Andersen, G.**, *Social Foundations of Postindustrial Economies* (Oxford: Oxford University Press, 1999). For overviews of the regime theory and welfare typologies see **Abrahamson, P.**, 'The welfare modelling business', in *Social Policy and Administration*, 33, 4, 394–415, 1999 and also **Arts, W. and Gelissen, J.**, 'Three worlds of welfare capitalism or more? A state-of-the-art report', *Journal of European Social Policy*, 12, 2, 137–58, 2002.

For evaluating the relevance of the EU as influencing social policy in Europe, the collection by **Leibfried, S. and Pierson, P.** (eds) *European Social Policy. Between Fragmentation and Integration* (Washington: The Brookings Institution, 1995) remains a classic source. For more recent reviews and debates about the development of EU social policy and the degree and the ways in which the EU influences social policy formation in member states see **Kvist, J. and Saari, J.** (eds) *The Europeanisation of Social Protection* (Bristol: Policy Press, 2007) and also **Hantrais, L.**, *Social Policy in the European Union* (3rd edn) (London: Palgrave, 2007). For an excellent assessment of the 'open method of coordination' see **Büchs, M.**, *New Governance in European Social Policy. The Open Method of Coordination* (Basingstoke: Palgrave, 2007).

The *Journal of European Social Policy* should perhaps be singled out for the space it devotes to comparative articles and the regular monitoring of social policy initiatives at EU level.

@ USEFUL WEBSITES

For students interested in comparative social policy and European social policy, there are several useful websites:

ESPAnet (the European Social Policy Analysis network) provides good links to relevant national social policy associations and organizations and national research centres within Europe at: **www.espanet.org/**.

EDACwowe (the European Data Center for Work and Welfare) is a web portal with direct links to information on quantitative and qualitative comparative and national data at: **www.edacwowe.eu/**.

For EU social policy involvement and documentation, the Directorate General for Employment, Social Affairs and Equal Opportunities is a good starting point, at the EU webportal: **ec.europa.eu/**.

For social policy data on EU member states EUROSTAT provides a good database; see: **epp.eurostat.ec. europa.eu/portal/page/portal/statistics/search_databaseh**.

The International Labour Organization (ILO) provides information and data on social policy too at: **www.ilo. org**.

For data on various aspects of employment and social policy in economically advanced countries, the OECD provides a very good database: **www.oecd-ilibrary.org/statistics**.

Q ESSAY QUESTIONS

1 What, if any, is the relevance of 'globalization' for comparative social policy?

2 Discuss the methodological challenges in quantitative and qualitative approaches to comparative social policy research.

3 What, if any, is the point in constructing welfare state typologies?

4 Is there a future for social policy at the level of the European Union?

ONLINE RESOURCE CENTRE

For additional material and resources, please visit the Online Resource Centre at: **www.oxfordtextbooks.co.uk/orc/baldock4e/**.

Part Five
Consequences and outcomes of social policy

18

The impact of social policy

Chris Pickvance

Contents

Introduction

Social policy is inextricably linked with the idea of need. In the earlier chapters in this book, and particularly in Part Four, the way in which government action has addressed need in the different fields of social policy has been detailed. In this chapter we examine some of the problems in assessing the effects of these policies. We start by discussing what is meant by social policy, and how to measure it, and in subsequent sections we go on to examine the impact of social policy on individuals and on society as a whole.

Learning outcomes

By the end of the chapter you will have an understanding of:

1   how the volume of social policy can be measured;
2   how the impact of social policy on households can be measured;
3   the impact of social policy on society as a whole.

Measuring social policy

In this chapter we are concerned only with social policy in the form of government policy. This still leaves the question of which policies belong to this category. The first issue is whether social policy should be defined narrowly as policy which seeks to ensure a minimum level of welfare for all, or to reduce inequalities in welfare, or whether broader definitions should be used. For example, is higher education provision part of social policy, and should all policy which seeks to achieve social, as opposed to economic, goals be included? The second issue is whether we should restrict ourselves to what is conventionally labelled as social policy. Some policies are indirectly aimed at helping the poor but are not labelled social policy, such as urban and regional policies to create jobs. On the other hand, labels are not an accurate guide to the purposes of a policy. Social policies may have a mix of objectives and their 'social' content may be limited. Social policies can generally be defined as those policies which seek to meet welfare need irrespective of their label. We will adopt an illustrative approach, and give some examples of the problems of assessing the impact of social policy.

However we define social policy, we must be able to measure its volume in order to establish its impact. To explore this deceptively simple question we examine in turn what is meant by meeting need, since this is the usual description of the purpose of social policy, and how to measure the volume of social policy.

Social policy comes in three forms:

- Regulation, i.e. the establishment of constraints on the actions of individuals and firms so as to increase social welfare. These extend from food standards to pollution controls.
- Taxation, i.e. the differential levying of taxes so as to protect the poorest groups or groups with a particular need. Two examples are income tax, which exempts those with the lowest income, and is set at increasing rates at higher income levels, and the lower rate of VAT on electricity and gas, which recognizes that energy represents a larger proportion of household budgets for poor households.
- Provision, where government spending is used in pursuit of social welfare aims. This takes two main forms:

1 benefits in kind, or services, such as education or personal social services;

2 cash benefits, such as pensions, and housing benefit.

For reasons of space this chapter will mainly be concerned with provision in the form of services. Cash benefits are considered in Chapter 10. In considering what is meant by meeting welfare needs we first examine how welfare needs can be measured.

Measuring welfare needs

The most debated issue concerns how to measure need quantitatively. There are three approaches to measuring need (see also Chapter 4). One can:

- rely on subjective judgements (e.g. by asking service users). This is often referred to as 'felt' or 'expressed' need.
- rely on expert judgements (e.g. by asking the professionals or managers involved in providing a service). This is usually referred to as 'normative need'.
- assume that existing provision meets needs (e.g. by taking the current cost per capita of meeting a particular need for each person in a need category as a measure of need).

Each approach has advantages and drawbacks. The first allows service users to participate in the definition of their needs, which may be seen as desirable in itself. This may lead to different definitions from those currently considered. On the other hand, people may express 'unrealistic' needs which cannot be met. The second approach assumes that specialists in the field are better placed than service users to define their needs, e.g. they may be much more aware of the complexities which affect need and determine appropriate services. On the other hand, professionals and managers may be seen as a 'producer' interest who seek to expand current services. The third approach has the pragmatic advantage of leading to a quantitative measure of need. However, it does not allow for any shortfall in the extent to which need is currently met, and is also crude since it is based on numbers of people in categories rather than individuals and their needs. In practice the second and third approaches overlap, since existing provision is based on both expert opinion and on costs. Most often, calculations of need for a category are based on the third method, by multiplying the cost of existing provision per person and demographic estimates of the number of people in the need category. For example, the need for primary education is based on the number of children of primary school age in an area and the average education spending per child. The fact that need is often calculated in respect of those living in an area, and that there are inter-area variations in need, is central to the idea of territorial justice which is discussed below.

A further useful distinction is between the horizontal and vertical dimensions of need. These are closely related to the concepts of 'breadth' and 'depth' (or 'intensity') of need. The proportion of the population in need is referred to as the 'horizontal' dimension, while the average level of need per person (and hence the level of service provided to each) is referred to as the 'vertical' dimension. A given sum of money could be used to provide a limited service to many or a more adequate service to a minority. The horizontal dimension thus reflects the level of take-up, i.e. the proportion of those eligible who actually receive the service or benefit. This is a misleading term, since it implies that the cause is ignorance, lack of effort or interest, or pride among the potential recipients, rather than poor management or lack of effort by the providers.

The debate about measuring need tends to leave aside the more fundamental question of whether the forms in which education, healthcare, housing, or personal social services are provided do meet people's needs. Policy debates often take for granted that existing forms of provision are largely on the right lines, and that if the right groups are gaining access to a service their needs are being met. But critics would argue that existing forms of provision often represent the interests of providers rather than those of consumers, and that people's expressed needs are highly conditioned by what is available in society. The debate about whether services meet needs is therefore often about who is

CONSEQUENCES AND OUTCOMES OF SOCIAL POLICY

receiving the service, which is a different question. It starts from the expert's view rather than the recipient's view and does not ask what gain recipients derive from the service or benefit. However, innovation in service provision does take place, instigated both by professionals (as in the case of 'community care' for elderly people) or by users, e.g. some forms of 'community care' demanded by disabled people.

Meeting welfare needs

It is easier to ask what is meant by 'meeting need' than to give an answer. A primary school-age child has a need for education. This is a societal value embodied in the state requirement, in the UK, that compulsory education extends from 5 to 16. If state schools were the only way of meeting this need, then we could say that the need for primary-level state education in an area depended on the number of primary-age children. This leads to the principle of uniform service provision, which implies that uniform provision enables uniform meeting of needs. It could, for example, lead to an identical per pupil allocation of funds for primary education in all areas.

An alternative is that primary schools in deprived areas require a greater input of resources to compensate for the disadvantaged situation from which the children come. In other words, to provide equality of opportunity, unequal provision of a particular kind is required to meet needs equally. This is the principle of proportional service provision. It implies that where needs among a population group are unequal, provision should be proportional to need. (The parallel principles in the case of cash benefits are universalism and selectivity—see Chapter 10.)

The two principles may be used together. In education, for example, resources are allocated partly on a per pupil basis and partly in recognition of special situations, e.g. number of children with special educational needs.

Finally it is worth mentioning a closely related idea: the principle of territorial justice. This concept was introduced by Davies (1968; see also Boyne and Powell 1991) in recognition of the fact that most services are provided on an area basis, and need varies from one area to another. Territorial justice refers to a situation where the provision of services (health, personal social services, etc.) in different areas varies in proportion to inter-area differences in need. It should be noted that territorial justice is a relative concept since it does not concern the absolute level of provision. It could mean that need is met equally badly in different areas or that it is met equally well.

Measuring the volume of social policy

Finally, in order to assess the impact of social policy we need to be able to tell whether more or less of it is being provided. Two types of measure of the volume of social policy will be considered here: input measures and output measures. A third type of measure, an outcome measure, is discussed in the next section since it refers to the impact of social policy rather than to its volume.

An input measure of a social policy is a measure of the various resources used to provide a service. The simplest input measure is spending. This covers the wages and salaries of all the staff employed, the goods and services used, and capital spending on facilities and equipment. (The 2000 Labour government commitment to increase total health spending to the EU average by 2005, discussed below, was an input measure.) But what improves the overall state of welfare in a service area is how well services are directed to those in need. This depends on how much of the service is produced and how appropriately it is allocated, which in turn depends partly on the amount of spending on the items listed above and partly on the efficiency with which they are combined and managed. Other input measures are based on the number of direct providers of social services, for example, the number of physicians employed, or more commonly the number of physicians per 10,000 population (see Table 18.1) or the availability of facilities (e.g. the density of acute beds per 10,000 population) (Interestingly the trends in these measures are moving in opposite directions.) Such measures have the advantage that they are 'closer' to service provision than a money measure, but have the weakness that social policy outcomes depend on all inputs and how they are combined.

Table 18.1 Number of physicians per 10,000 people, 2000–7

France	34
Germany	34
Netherlands	37
Sweden	33
UK	23
US	26

Note: The term 'practising physicians' includes practising physicians, GPs, and specialists. The French and Dutch data are not strictly comparable as they use a slightly broader definition that e.g. includes some non-practising staff.

Source: *WHO Statistics 2009*, Table 6

A second type of measure is known as an output measure because it measures the volume of the service itself, e.g. healthcare or personal social services, and hence gets closer to the idea of a measure of the welfare produced by the service. In 2005 the Atkinson Review recommended the replacement of input measures by output measures wherever possible in measuring government output. 'Service-based measures' include the number of 'hospital episodes' (one stay in hospital may include several hospital episodes since the patient may need a series of treatments) or the number of children living in local authority-run children's homes. 'Access-based measures' are not a direct output measure since they refer to delays in accessing a service rather than the service itself. However, in healthcare speed of access can be as important as the service itself, so delays are an aspect of output. In the healthcare area they include maximum list lengths, and average and maximum waiting times for hospital treatment.

Obviously there is some connection between input measures and output measures, since without resources no services could be provided; but output measures have the advantage that they take account of how spending translates into the provision of services. The problem with service-based output measures is that they do not distinguish between more and less appropriate or successful service provision. For example, repeated attempts to treat the same illness would show up as increased healthcare provision even if the treatment failed. The problem with access-based measures such as waiting-list length is that people's need for speedy attention is not equal. Overall welfare may be better served by the proportional than by the uniform principle of provision, i.e. by giving priority in treatment to those with the most urgent need even if they have not waited very long.

Since it would make little sense to spend more on or provide more of a service irrespective of the need for it, both input and output measures are usually calculated *for a region or district* and are considered in conjunction with the need for treatment *in that area*. In other words, territorial justice is sought.

It should be noted that all of the measures (sometimes called 'performance measures' because they are a way of judging welfare providers comparatively) have unintended consequences. Their introduction is likely to have an effect on how the service is organized, how services are provided, and how statistics are collected. In particular, service-providing organizations are likely to take steps to boost their performance on the measures on which they are assessed, possibly by worsening their performance on activities that are not assessed. For example, if hospitals are judged by the length of waiting lists for inpatient treatment but not by waits for outpatient treatment, they may be tempted to shift resources into the measured activity.

In general the problem with these measures is that they do not necessarily measure what service recipients consider important. For example, if the 'waiting time' for an operation is calculated from the time when a consultant decides that a patient needs the operation, this ignores the time that has elapsed between the patient making initial contact with a GP and receiving the decision. Also, if a patient has to be seen by a second consultant, the measure of 'time on the waiting list' starts again. In a period of spending restriction, GPs may limit referrals to consultants but this will not show up in waiting-time measures.

Thus it can be seen that the assumption that more spending on a social policy means more welfare turns out to be questionable. Everything depends on how the spending is used, how it is allocated between areas, how it is targeted on groups in need, and how far measures of performance distort the way organizations work. The idea that 'back office' jobs are intrinsically wasteful and that only 'front-line' jobs are productive is a myth. Good management of resources is as important as having an adequate level of resources.

In the case of social policies which take the form of cash benefits, input measures (spending) are usually used. The main limitation of *total* spending measures of cash benefits as a measure of the volume of social policy is that they are a product of the numbers receiving the benefit (which depends on the number eligible and the level of take-up) and the level of the benefit. A rising trend in spending on a cash benefit may be because of an increase in claimants rather than because of an increase in generosity of benefit levels. Ideally, therefore, both take-up and benefit level need to be known.

In sum, both input and output measures of social policies are either conceptually debatable or difficult to apply in practice, and hence need to be treated with caution.

Measuring the impact of social policy

The question of how to establish the impact of social policy is a particular case of the general issue of how to identify cause–effect relations. This is a thorny problem in all social scientific work. First, society is complex and many possible causes operate simultaneously, which makes it difficult to identify the effect of a single cause (or set of causes) such as a social policy. For example, the number of people experiencing poverty depends on the effectiveness of social policies aimed at eliminating or reducing it, but also on demographic and labour market processes (such as birth rates, household formation and dissolution rates, migration rates, job availability, and wage levels). Second, social science has to find a path through the thicket of claims made by politicians, officials, the media, and pressure groups about the effect of social policy. These claims are more likely to be intended to take credit and avoid blame, or to gather support for a change in policy, than to make a careful assessment.

To claim that social policy has had an impact of some type, three conditions must be met:

- The social policy must occur before the effect claimed for it. This is obvious but it is not uncommon for success to be claimed for a new policy on the basis of trends which had been in existence before it was introduced.
- Variations in the policy must be associated with variations in the claimed effect. This is the familiar point that if two things are causally related they will vary together. However, the reverse is not true. Events or processes which occur together or rise and fall over time together are not necessarily linked by cause–effect relations. Causation is more than correlation. This is not an easy condition to meet, since the presence of multiple causes means that cause–effect relations may be hard to disentangle.
- The nature of the causal process(es) linking the policy with its claimed effect must be identified or hypothesized. This requirement is also difficult to meet. First, causal connections are not

directly observable but are matters of inference. Writers belonging to different theoretical schools disagree both about what causal connections are likely to exist and about what evidence would establish that they do. Second, as mentioned above, many causes are in operation and they may be hard to identify and separate. Comparison with other countries, or with the same country in the past, may be helpful, but only if it is assumed that there are common processes operating and no significant differences—a matter which again may be debated between theoretical schools. Third, we are only aware of some of the causes which operate. Scientific progress involves identifying new causal links and improving our understanding of policy impact.

These complexities can be illustrated when we examine what are known as outcome measures of social policy because they are believed to measure the result of the policy. Examples are the level of morbidity (ill health) in an area, school examination results, or the life expectation of elderly people receiving 'community care'. The attraction of this type of measure is that it comes closest to being an indicator of impact in the sense of additional welfare due to social policy. The drawback is that they measure the outcome of a large number of processes of which the social policy of interest is only one. (The term 'outcome measure' is thus a misnomer.) For example, school exam results reflect the ability of children admitted to a school and the extent of parental support, as well as the efforts of the school; and morbidity reflects nutrition, lifestyles, and living and working conditions, as well as healthcare. Unless the causal influence of these processes can be taken into account, the impact of a social policy cannot be identified. A further issue concerns the timing of outcome measures. While in some cases an immediate measure is appropriate, in others, e.g. preventive healthcare, outcomes need to be measured over a longer period. Social policy can also have wider impacts on society, as shown later in the chapter.

Two more general points about assessing the impact of social policy must be made. First, the effects of a social policy cannot be equated with or deduced from its aims. The concept of policy aim is not straightforward. Policies rarely have single aims: pressure groups outside government may have aims in pressing for a policy, as the policy passes through the government machine it may be shaped by further pressures, and once in operation it will gather suppliers and clients who develop interests in the policy. Any statement of policy aims will be a social construct decided at a particular time, with a particular purpose, and will reflect the relative power of these different groups. Spending programmes may even exist without clear aims or with changing and conflicting aims, as hinted in the book title *The British New Towns: a Programme without a Policy* (Aldridge 1979). Moreover, policy labels may deliberately conceal aims. This was the case of 'urban policy', one of whose hidden aims was to prevent the urban riots experienced in the United States in the mid1960s from occurring in British cities (Cochrane 2007). It may also be the case of the coalition government plans to abolish Primary Care Trusts and make GPs form consortia to administer 80 per cent of health spending, where the stated aim is to cut bureaucracy and save £2 billion. It has been suggested that the real aim is to open a new field of operation for the private sector as GPs who are reluctant to take on this task welcome in private firms. Second, policy aims may not be achieved because the level of funding is inadequate or because of 'unintended effects'. For example, people may respond to the policy in unexpected ways (e.g. people may fail to take up a benefit because it is felt to be stigmatizing; elderly people may divest themselves of assets in order to be eligible for state support for their housing); or countervailing processes are present (a policy aimed at improving housing conditions may result in the displacement of working-class households by middle-class households due to the higher value of the house after the improvements). The effects of a policy can only be assessed in the ways indicated above.

In sum, there are very considerable problems in establishing the effects of social policy, and we need to pay attention to the methods used by those who claim to have identified their effects. Hence any claims made about the impact of social policy need to be regarded with caution.

The impact of social policy on individual households

In this section we present analyses of the impact of one social policy, healthcare, on individual households, and of the combined impact of several services on individuals using the 'social wage' approach. Before doing so it is helpful to break down social policy spending into its component parts, since they affect how policy impacts on individuals. The main difficulty in evaluating the impact of social policy from spending figures is to assess the roles of these five elements:

- The extent of horizontal need. This is easy to estimate in some cases (e.g. the number of school-age children, which can be obtained from statistical sources) but difficult in others (e.g. the number in need of social housing or a particular type of operation). In the latter case, an assessment is made by a professional. This can only take place if the person in need is aware of the existence of services and makes contact with them. Also, as in the case of social housing, in areas where the waiting period to gain access is very long, a person may choose not to register their need.
- The extent of vertical need. Vertical need is generally difficult to estimate because it implies that different people within a need category have different needs (e.g. different children have different intensities of need) and in every case some type of professional assessment is required.
- The cost of salaries and of purchasing goods, services, and equipment, which varies between parts of the country. If salary costs rise, any increase in spending may not translate into increased service provision, so this is a crucial element. Inflation can be taken into account in either of two ways. Actual spending each year (in 'money terms' or 'current prices') will rise simply because of inflation. If allowance is made for the rise in the general price level (i.e. for the increase in prices for *all* goods and services), the result is a figure referred to as real spending. Alternatively, if allowance is made for the rise in prices of those goods and services in the sector concerned (e.g. health or education), which is faster than the general rate of inflation, the result is referred to as 'volume terms spending' or volume spending.[1] Spending in 'real terms' or 'real spending' thus underestimates the rate of inflation in the field of social policy and overestimates the value of social policy inputs. 'Volume spending' allows for inflation experienced in the social services but understates the value of social policy inputs, since it assumes that if the number of, say, teachers remains the same, their productivity remains the same. In practice, through the use of computers or improved management, these teachers may become more productive. Neither real nor volume spending is a perfect measure of inputs and, as Sefton (1997) suggests, the truth lies somewhere in between.
- The quality of the service, and therefore whether, or how well, need is met, Quality is an intuitively simple concept to grasp but a very difficult one to measure. Ideally service quality should be continually improving through the incorporation of the latest knowledge, techniques, and equipment. The implication is that measures of policies which ignore this are missing something essential. In practice quality measures are difficult to obtain, precisely because it is difficult to quantify the qualitative. Quantitative measures tend to predominate because of their availability.
- Efficiency. This reflects how the inputs are combined and how well the service matches users' needs. Efficiency is another difficult element to measure and also one which attracts a lot of political attention. One measure of efficiency is productivity, obtained by dividing an output measure like activities by an input measure like spending or number of staff employed, but unless one can measure service quality, efficiency gains may be achieved at the expense of quality.

---

[1] This is known as the 'relative price effect', and occurs because employees are a crucial part of the service being provided in the social policy sphere, and hence the chance of saving money by substituting employees by machines is very limited. In contrast in manufacturing industry this option is normal: the consumer does not mind if robots rather than workers make cars.

Table 18.2 Total expenditure on health as % of GDP, 2000 and 2006

	2000	2006
France	10.1	11.0
Germany	10.3	10.6
Netherlands	8.0	9.4
Sweden	8.2	9.2
UK	7.1	8.2
US	13.2	15.3

Source: *WHO Statistics 2009*, Table 7

The impact of healthcare on individual households

We now examine the impact of social policy on individual households by using the example of healthcare.

First, it is useful to place healthcare within spending on social policy as a whole. The share of UK social policy spending going on services was greater than the share going on cash benefits. In 2008–9 public spending on health accounted for 7.7 per cent of GDP, on education 5.8 per cent, on personal social services 2.1 per cent, and on housing 1.0 per cent (excluding housing benefits). Spending on cash benefits amounted to 12.1 per cent of GDP (HM Treasury 2010a: Tables 4.4 and 5.2). Table 18.2 shows the UK's comparative position on total healthcare spending (both public and private).

The overall aim of health policy is to improve the nation's health. Secondary aims are to achieve greater equity between groups and places, to use resources efficiently, and to be responsive to changes in need and in medical knowledge. The majority of spending is on hospital care.

What is the volume of healthcare being provided and what is its impact? The simplest input measure of healthcare is health spending. In general, increased spending can only be taken to mean that need is being better met (either horizontally or vertically) if we can be sure that the need for the service has not increased;[2] that costs have not gone up so that the same spending buys less of the service, that service quality has not fallen, and that efficiency has not fallen. If need has increased, costs have risen, or service quality or efficiency has fallen, higher spending will be needed to meet need at the same level.

We consider in turn the periods before and after 1997.

Before 1997 Between 1981 and 1995 real spending on the National Health Service rose 55 per cent, but volume spending rose only 28 per cent (Le Grand and Vizard 1998: Table 4.1).[3] A demographically based estimate of needs suggests that over the 1981–95 period a 10 per cent increase was needed simply to meet the greater demands on healthcare due to people living longer (Le Grand and Vizard 1998: Table 4.4). Hence volume spending on health inputs increased by

[2] Since need for public sector services may reflect the availability of alternatives and also professional judgements, it is misleading to see need as something fixed. For example, Appleby et al. (2004: 19) argue that if hospital waiting lists fall it does not follow that demand remains unaffected. They suggest that for (public) hospitals, treatment may increase, e.g. because some private patients switch to NHS hospitals, because some people will switch from self-treatment or help from a therapist to hospital treatment, or because GPs may start to refer patients to hospital more often.
[3] In places my classification of services as inputs or outputs or my interpretation of the data diverges from that in Glennerster and Hills (1998).

about 1.8 per cent per year faster than needs in this period. The possible effects of changes in quality or efficiency have not been estimated.

How did these inputs vary by region and by social group? The regional distribution of real health spending per capita on all items (e.g. including both hospitals and primary care) between 1985 and 1994 shows an increase in the spread between regions: the 'coefficient of variation', a statistical measure of spread, increased from 0.103 to 0.143 (Le Grand and Vizard 1998: Table 4.8). No data are available to compare this with the changing regional distribution of need for healthcare. But Le Grand and Vizard conclude that 'unless there was also a growing and matching inequality in need, this suggests that regional inequalities may be increasing' (1998: 104). In other words, territorial injustice in this respect is increasing. This trend occurred despite an explicit policy introduced in 1976, following the Resource Allocation Working Party, aimed at reducing regional inequalities. Another measure of variation of inputs by region—the number of GPs per 100,000 population— shows that here too regional variation increased between 1975 and 1995. Thus while the average number of GPs per 100,000 in the UK rose from 48 to 61, it ranged from 43 (Trent) to 58 (Scotland) in 1975, and from 53 (North Western) to 76 (in Scotland) in 1995 (Le Grand and Vizard 1998: Table 4.9).

The variation in input measures of health services received by different social groups has been studied but while research in the 1970s showed that professionals and managers received 40 per cent higher spending per ill person than the semi- and unskilled, later studies found no such bias (quoted in Le Grand and Vizard 1998: 107).

Thus while, overall, inputs may have increased slightly faster than needs in the 1981–95 period, the distribution of these inputs between regions implies considerable and possibly widening territorial injustice. As a result the impact of health service provision on health is likely to have been less than it could have been.

Turning to output measures of healthcare, two types are available: service based and access based. In the case of the former, studies of the use of services suggest that poorer groups visit GP surgeries more than better-off groups (assuming their need is reflected in their age distribution) and are more often hospital inpatients, whereas better-off groups phone their GPs more and make more use of outpatient treatment (Evandrou, referred to in Le Grand and Vizard 1998: 107). On the other hand, South Asians and Caribbeans make less use of both inpatient and outpatient services than their needs would suggest. As far as access-based measures are concerned, waiting lists for inpatient treatment grew from 628,000 in 1981 to 729,000 in 1991, and for all treatment from 948,000 in 1991 to 1,164,000 in 1997 (Le Grand and Vizard 1998: 99). However, the proportion waiting over one year fell from 24 per cent in 1988 to 1 per cent in 1996 (Le Grand and Vizard 1998: Table 4.6). The latter reflects the policy aim of reducing waiting times.

What was the impact of these healthcare inputs and outputs on health? The most commonly used outcome measures are mortality and morbidity rates. There is conflicting evidence about mortality rates. The life expectation for men and women, allowing for differences in the size of each age cohort, increased from 70.4 to 71.5 between 1974 and 1994, and the male–female gap narrowed slightly. On the other hand, class differences for males dying between 20 and 64 have increased: unskilled workers in this age range were 1.8 times more likely to die than professionals in 1970–2 but 2.9 times more likely to do so by 1991–3 (Le Grand and Vizard 1998: Table 4.10).

Evidence on morbidity shows an increase in self-reported chronic and acute illness between 1974 and 1994, even when the effect of the ageing population is taken into account. This may be linked with the increase in waiting lists mentioned earlier. But class differences in chronic and acute illness have not increased over time (Le Grand and Vizard 1998: Figure 4.2 and Table 4.12).

As mentioned earlier, these outcomes reflect many other processes besides the public spending on health. However, if inputs have indeed risen faster than needs in total, then it is likely that it is the maldistribution of inputs and outputs (such as access to hospital and GP care) between need categories (social or spatial) which explains why the effect on morbidity has not been greater. On the other hand, non-health service factors such as lifestyles, and domestic, work, and environmental situations, may have counteracted the positive effects of healthcare provision.

After 1997 The election of the Labour government in 1997 led immediately to strong measures to reduce waiting lists but is probably best known for the prime minister's announcement in January 2000, to the surprise of the Chancellor of the Exchequer, that UK healthcare expenditure (private and public) would be raised to the EU average by 2005. At that time the latest data (for 1998) showed the UK as having 5.7 per cent GDP as public spending on health and 1.1 per cent private, i.e. 6.8 per cent in total (Emmerson et al. 2002), compared with an EU average of between 7.9 and 8.9 per cent depending on how it was calculated. In the event, by 2005 the UK figure reached 8.5 per cent but the EU15 arithmetic average including the UK had risen to 9.4 per cent (OECD 2010). Nevertheless this period was one of rapid spending growth.

A recent publication by Thorlby and Maybin (2010) notes that from 1997 to 2010 expenditure on the NHS doubled in real terms and summarizes the achievements and failures of this period.The main improvements were:

- Reduced waiting lists and waiting times.
- In England inpatient waiting lists fell from 1.1 million in 1997 to 600,000 in 2009, median inpatient waiting times fell from 13 weeks to four, and the goal of 18-week maximum waiting time was achieved for 90 per cent of patients by 2008. 87 per cent were able to see a GP within 48 hours by 2007–8, short of the 100 per cent target, but out of hours access was not satisfactory.[4]
- The creation of NICE in 1999 to assess the value of drugs.
- Patient safety has been recognized as an issue and some progress has been made in eliminating infections such as MRSA.
- Health promotion has been recognized as a key area of policy and progress has been made in some areas (smoking) but not others (obesity).
- Improvements have been made in clinical effectiveness, e.g. in cardiovascular treatment.

However, there has been no change in patient experience of the NHS, cancer survival rates remain below the European average, and class and place inequalities in health remain very significant, reflecting the unequal distribution of services among other factors.

In terms of efficiency, a separate analysis shows that between 1995 and 2008 health outputs grew by 4.1 per cent per annum whereas health inputs grew at 4.4 per cent per annum, a decline in productivity of 0.3 per cent per annum (ONS 2010). The health output figure incorporates a 'quality adjustment' reflecting improved short-term survival rates, health gain following treatment in hospital, and the impact of waiting times. This calculation does not address the question of whether the level of health outputs was sufficient to meet demand.

Thorlby and Maybin provide more detail on the components of productivity. They show that NHS staff numbers increased by 75 per cent between 1998 and 2008 and that 'average staff pay for those working in the hospital and community health services sector increased between 1997–8 and 2007–8 by nearly 75 per cent in cash terms, and by around 36 per cent in real terms: an average real increase each year of around 3.1 per cent' (2010: 93), with consultants gaining the largest increases.They conclude that 'the combination of higher staff numbers and higher pay meant that a significant proportion of the increase in NHS resources after 2000 was absorbed by pay costs' (ibid.). In contrast, the cost of the goods and services used in producing healthcare increased by around 15 per cent over the same period—a real price fall of 10 per cent (2010: 94). This reveals some of the difficulties of converting increased spending into increased outputs and

[4] For a detailed analysis of the access-based targets which were used to achieve these improvements and how they worked in practice, see Appleby et al. (2004) and Harrison and Appleby (2005).

improved outcomes. It also suggests that the coalition government's hopes of making considerable savings in the healthcare budget via productivity increases would mean a departure from the past experience of the NHS.

The impact of all services: the 'social wage' approach

We now turn to an attempt to make a wider assessment of the impact of social policy by looking at three services.

Debates about the overall impact of social policy have centred around two propositions. The first is that social policy helps the poor, and this is because it was set up to do so and because it achieves its aims. The second is that social policy benefits the middle class disproportionately because the middle class is well informed, well organized, and well connected, and (a) ensures the services it benefits from are provided and well funded, and (b) is efficient in taking advantage of the best services that are available. This claim was advanced by Le Grand (1982), who argued that there had been a middle-class 'capture' of the welfare state, preventing it from realizing its aims.

One way to examine these arguments is to assume that the value of the services provided is equal to the cost of providing them and then to measure how these costs are distributed among different social groups. This involves:

- establishing the total cost of a particular service;
- subtracting that part which cannot be allocated to households;
- establishing what use is made of this service by different social groups or categories;
- breaking down the cost of the service among groups in proportion to their usage of it.

This approach is known as the 'social wage' approach since it sees services (along with payments in kind) as increasing people's welfare in the same way as the spending power afforded by a wage. The approach allows us to translate services into quantitative terms and see who receives most and who least. However, it does have disadvantages. It is based on data on expenditure and therefore suffers from the defects of input measures mentioned earlier. Also, since different households have different levels of need, a calculation of who benefits is only an approximate answer to the more interesting question of 'Who benefits and was it in proportion to need?' Ideally we need to take into account different levels of need related to age, gender, ethnicity, etc. The approach thus ignores questions of inefficiency and poor targeting (by need group and spatially), inappropriate service provision, needs which are unmet, etc.

A publication by Sefton (2002) allows us to address the question of who gained more and less from spending on three social services over the period from 1979 to 2000–1. Tables 18.3 and 18.4

Table 18.3 Distribution of value (£ per person) of health, education, and housing services by income quintile, 1979, in 2000–1 prices

Income quintile	Health	Education	Housing	Total
Bottom	632	430	203	1,265
2nd	501	573	167	1,241
3rd	418	585	155	1,158
4th	406	501	119	1,026
Top	406	394	84	883
All	473	496	146	1,115

Source: for Tables 18.3 and 18.4: data supplied by Tom Sefton—see footnote 5.

Table 18.4 Distribution of value (£ per person) of health, education, and housing services by income quintile, 2000/1, in 2000–1 prices

Income quintile	Health	Education	Housing	Total
Bottom	919	819	292	2,030
2nd	1,051	719	262	2,032
3rd	807	671	194	1,672
4th	628	637	134	1,399
Top	545	493	50	1,088
All	790	668	186	1,644

Table 18.5 Ratio of share of spending on services received by bottom quintile divided by share received by top quintile

	Health	Education	Housing	Total
1979	1.56	1.09	2.42	1.43
2000/1	1.69	1.66	5.84	1.86

Source: calculated from Tables 18.3 and 18.4

show the levels of spending per person on the three services—healthcare, education, and housing[5]—for individuals in the five income quintiles in each year. They can be read in several ways. First, the figure for all services and all income groups shows that over the period there has been a 47.4 per cent real increase in spending per individual, from £1,115 to £1,644, on all these services. This is a little less than the real growth of GDP. Secondly, total spending on health per person has risen fastest (£473 to £790, 67 per cent) followed by education (£496 to £668, 34.7 per cent) and housing (£146 to £186, 27.4 per cent).

Thirdly, Table 18.5 presents the ratio of service spending received by the lowest quintile divided by the spending received by the highest quintile. This ratio would be 1 if the richest quintile received the same amount as the poorest, and above 1 if the poorest quintile received more than the richest. It shows that overall this ratio moves up from 1.43 in 1979 to 1.86 in 2000–1. Interestingly, in health the change in the pro-poor direction is least marked (1.56 in 1979 to 1.69 in 2000–1). In education the change is much greater. Finally, in housing the general level of pro-poor policy is strong throughout the period.

To make sense of these patterns and changes it is necessary to look at their components. This is done at length in Sefton (2002). The shares received by particular income groups reflect their need for the service and their use of it. The large size of the pro-poor effect of housing spending is because it refers to subsidies to social housing only. By contrast, education and healthcare are used by all income groups. Widening participation in higher education has the effect of making education spending more pro-poor, as does reliance by higher-income groups on private health-

[5] Housing excludes housing benefit and mortgage interest tax relief. It is mainly made up of the discounts received by tenants buying their council housing and subsidies to social housing rents (economic rent less 'gross rent'). Higher education spending is allocated to parents of students. I would like to acknowledge the kindness of Tom Sefton, Centre for Analysis of Social Exclusion, London School of Economics, in making these tables available to me. They are the tables on which the bar charts in Figure 6 in his report (Sefton 2002) are based, but are not included in the report.

care. There is also evidence that the next-to-lowest income group uses healthcare more than the lowest quintile, which may explain why this quintile receives the most healthcare spending in Table 18.4 .

The relation between age and income plays a key part since 'lower income groups contain a high proportion of children and pensioners, who are the most intensive users of welfare services' (Sefton 2002: 9). The fact that children benefit most from education and older people receive most healthcare therefore also means that lower-income groups receive more of these two services. However, Sefton shows that if the age effect is allowed for, there is still a net pro-poor effect in the distribution of the social wage in 2000–1.

At the end of this discussion of the impact of social policy on households and individuals we can see that the easier data to present are on real and volume spending. Information on efficiency is rarely available and is subject to numerous caveats. However, the major difficulty in estimating the impact of social policy lies in measuring the scope and intensity of need. The eagle-eyed reader will have noticed that statements about need have usually been either statements attributed to unidentified experts or assumptions based on demographic trends which assume that provision at some time in the past was meeting need adequately. This is frustrating given the scale of spending on social policy and the importance of need to measures of the outcome of this spending.

The impact of social policy on society

We now consider the wider social impacts of social policy. This is a very large field and we shall be selective.[6] We examine the following arguments:

- that social policy increases social stability;
- that social policy undermines the market mechanism for allocating resources.

One preliminary point needs to be made. This is that the discussion of wider effects encounters even more problems of identifying cause–effect relations than our discussion of the impact of social policy on different social groups. One reason for this is that 'social stability' is a broad and nebulous concept. The other reason is that in saying that social policy has a wider impact of a particular type, a comparison has to be made with a hypothetical situation in which that social policy was absent, or took a different form—what is known as the 'counterfactual' because it is something that did not happen! This can be done by comparing the UK today either with the UK previously, when the social policy was absent or different in form, or with other advanced capitalist societies. The problem in the first case is to allow for the other changes which will have occurred since the policy was introduced or changed, and in the second to allow for the other relevant differences between the UK and the other societies chosen. These two difficulties mean that there is inevitably greater reliance on the plausibility of the causal inference, and this means that writers of different theoretical persuasions will tend to advance their own interpretations of the wider impact of social policy. Thus the reader needs to be particularly cautious about accepting claims made about the wider impacts of social policy.

Social policy and social stability

One of the most widely held views about social policy is that it contributes to the stability of society. Politicians and reformers have often asserted that by introducing reforms social disorder or even revolution would be avoided. But advocates of reform have a vested interest and are likely to adopt whatever arguments they think will help win support for their case. To establish whether social

[6] For a more extensive discussion of the societal impacts of social policy see George and Wilding (1984: Chapters 4–7). The effects of social policy on the labour force and particularly on women's employment are also very significant.

policy actually has a stabilizing effect, we need to look beyond such statements. We examine the three elements of the claim that social policy has a stabilizing effect: that it reduces the number of deprivations, that it individualizes social problems, and that it reduces conflict.

Social policy reduces the number of deprivations Social policy undoubtedly averts or ameliorates some of the situations which arose before it existed. Cash benefits and services are available to a wide variety of groups in need. Even allowing for a certain degree of mistargeting, incomplete take-up, stigmatization, inappropriate services, and cash benefits which are too low in value, it is undeniable that social policy has the effect of reducing the level of deprivation. However, social policy also has a second effect: to increase the number of deprivations and increase the demands made for policy measures. This is because the number of deprivations is not fixed, but is subject to a 'demonstration effect' by which the success of social policy measures in one sphere triggers pressure for further interventions. For example, the precedent of state intervention in the form of council housing led to subsequent pressure on government to widen the responsibilities of councils to include provision for homeless people. Paradoxically, therefore, social policy can *increase* the number of deprivations which are labelled as social problems, as well as averting or lessening the impact of such problems through remedial action.

Social policy individualizes social problems Typically the individualized mode of dealing with problems in the social policy sphere leads people to experience deprivations as individuals. For example, if a particular job or workplace is hazardous the individual workers may be treated by health services as individuals and no attempt made to discover the common cause of their symptoms. Likewise, if there is a recession, the consequent job losses lead individuals into unemployment and poverty, and they are treated as individuals by the agencies they contact in order to obtain social security benefits and services. The common source of their situation is eclipsed from view. This has an isolating or fragmenting effect, and reduces the probability of group action among those involved. However, it does not rule it out altogether as is shown by the effectiveness of the movement of disabled people (Campbell and Oliver 1996).

Less deprivation means less conflict and greater social stability The third argument is that social policy, by reducing the number of deprivations and individualizing social problems, makes it less likely that groups will demand change, and this strengthens social stability.

The connection between deprivation and social instability is a complex one. Every society generates a wide variety of situations ranging from ill health to unemployment and poverty. There are three factors which determine whether they lead the people in these situations to mobilize and possibly engage in conflict. First, people must define them as deprivations. Second, people must feel they are deprivations that can be changed via mobilization, rather than that they are unalterable. Third, people must believe that the government or other agency is capable of responding to group action.

But is it correct to assume that, in the absence of social policy, deprived groups would engage in social conflict? In fact this is debatable. Research on social movements suggests that the most deprived groups typically lack confidence in themselves and are much less likely to engage in collective action than middle-class groups which are not deprived but have high expectations and are effective in mobilizing themselves (Neidhardt and Rucht 1991).

The further question of whether, if conflict occurs, it is a source of instability is a large one. There are various views about how stable advanced capitalist societies are and what the main sources are of division within them. Orthodox Marxist writers argue that capitalist–worker conflicts have the greatest potential to destabilize society, and that conflicts around consumption issues such as social services are of secondary importance. Others would argue that the consumption sphere is at least as important as a source of conflict (if not more so), and that consumption-based conflicts can be just as destabilizing for society. For example, for owner-occupiers housing is a large investment and the largest monthly expenditure, and hence could generate strong conflicts. Taking the two views together, one might suggest that if the lines of division in consumption conflicts coincide with those in work-based conflicts there is a greater potential for instability, but where consumption divisions cross-cut production divisions the effect is to mitigate the strength of conflict (Castells 1977). There is some evidence that housing and transport consumption do generate different interests (as measured by voting), though this may not lead to conflict (Dunleavy and Husbands 1985). But other writers argue that prior values condition both voting and consumption choices (Heath et al. 1985: 44–57).

Conflict also depends on the types of demand made by those with common interests. One argument is that demands which challenge the way society is organized have a greater destabilizing potential than those which do not. However, in practice this potential is not realized, since only small minorities make radical demands. This leads to a second view that it is demands which do not challenge society, but which have considerable support that give rise to the most conflict, and that these can be destabilizing although they are not demands for radical change. This could be seen in trade union demands in the UK in the late 1970s. Lastly the existence of conflict and whether it has destabilizing effects also depends on the institutions available for reaching compromise. Compared to France, where direct and often violent action is quite usual, government is relatively open in the UK and this encourages negotiation and the channelling of protest into peaceful and less destabilizing forms.

In sum, it has been argued that the likelihood that deprived individuals will engage in collective action and conflict and that any action will be destabilizing is much less than often suggested. In the absence of social policy most deprivations would lead to resignation rather than collective action, and any conflict would not necessarily be destabilizing. It follows that insofar as it reduces deprivation, social policy increases social stability only to a limited extent, contrary to what is often claimed.

We have thus suggested that social policy both expands and reduces deprivations, encourages a view of social problems as something experienced individually, and to a limited extent reduces the amount of collective action that would be taken by deprived groups. It can thus be concluded that social policy on balance helps social stability, but that it encourages forces in both directions.

Social policy and the market mechanism

A second argument about the wider impact of social policy is that it introduces a system of allocating resources which is in contradiction with the market mechanism, and that this is threatening in a capitalist type of society.

The starting point is the idea that markets are the central means of allocating resources in capitalist societies. They allow people to obtain resources according to their ability to pay the current price. This is held to be an efficient mechanism because the price people are willing to pay is taken to be a measure of the value they give to that resource and will hence incentivize them to gain more resources. By contrast, the allocation of services and cash benefits according to need has no place for ability to pay as a principle. Allocation by need is held to be more socially efficient because need is not necessarily indicated by ability to pay, and groups with low incomes would consume less than they need if the market mechanism were the only one operating. Instead, need-based allocation relies on expert judgements about what levels of need people have, and this is claimed to lead to a more efficient allocation of resources. Critics, however, would say that allocation according to need is unsatisfactory because experts are self-interested, because the absence of price as a rationing device leads to over-consumption and over-production, and because it weakens the motivation to work, since the link between reward and effort is broken.

In appearance, therefore, social policy introduces a principle of allocation which threatens the market principle which is central to the operation of capitalism. The reasons for thinking that social policy is incompatible with the market principle are as follows:

- There is a conflict of principle since services and cash benefits in social policy are allocated according to need, not ability to pay. But in practice in advanced capitalist societies it is rare to find groups who are totally opposed to the welfare state. This suggests that in actual advanced capitalist societies the market principle of allocation is combined with values which limit its application.
- Social policy weakens the incentive to work, and is thus threatening to market allocation. This argument is applied particularly to cash benefits paid to those without work and looking for work. It is undermined by the low and declining level of benefits.

The arguments that need-based allocation does not undermine market allocation are as follows:

- Market allocation is not as efficient in resource allocation or as crucial to motivation as is claimed. One example would be to ask whether in the United States, where healthcare spending is double the share of GNP in the UK and mostly takes place through market allocation (e.g. private health insurance), this is a more efficient allocation of resources. Critics argue that the 'market' in healthcare in the United States leads to over-treatment, as hospitals and doctors are paid by insurance companies rather than patients directly and that the NHS discourages over-consumption of health services because of the public spending constraints applying to it.
- Need-based allocation is actually indispensable in advanced capitalist societies. Social policy spending helps to create a productive (i.e. healthy, educated, and disciplined) labour force, and to shield the private sector from direct responsibility for workers who are made redundant. It also embodies values about minimum welfare levels and preferences for greater equality, which are social values that exist within advanced capitalist societies but which cannot be achieved by the market principle.

This relates to a wider debate about the role of the public sector in capitalist societies. The dominant idea is that public spending is unproductive and parasitic on the private sector because it is a burden on taxes which could be either cut or used to benefit the private sector directly. But this is a very one-sided view. Public sector employment is 20 per cent of the total and generates income tax itself, and the private sector is highly dependent on public spending, e.g. on infrastructure, industrial support, public sector contracts, loan guarantees for exports, and bail-outs in case of emergency, and is able to avoid corporation taxes legally. This suggests that the private and public sectors are interdependent. The productivity of each depends on the other.

We would therefore suggest that social policy introduces a principle of allocation which is complementary rather than contradictory with market allocation, as long as values favouring the achievement of minimum levels of welfare for all and some steps towards equality are prevalent in society. If need-based allocation were to become dominant rather than subordinate as a principle, that would undermine the functioning of capitalism. But this is not about to happen.

Conclusion

The two wider impacts of social policy we have discussed show that it contributes to social stability, and that it is not threatening to capitalism despite being based on a principle which contradicts the market principle. Earlier, when looking at the impact on individuals and households, we concluded that on balance social policy distribution is pro-poor, but we found it difficult to be clear about the degree to which social policy raises social welfare, for some people absolutely, or reduces inequality because initial definitions of needs are so varied and so open to question and judgement.

FURTHER READING

Glennerster, H., and Hills, J. (eds) *The State of Welfare* (2nd edn, Oxford: Oxford University Press, 1998) is an indispensable source of data and interpretation on the impact of social policy.

Hills, J., and Stewart, K. (eds), *A More Equal Society: New Labour, poverty, inequality and exclusion* (Policy Press, 2005) is a useful source on the post-1997 period.

Books which explore the role of taxation as a social policy measure are **J. Hills**, *New Inequalities: The Changing Distribution of Income and Wealth in the UK* (Cambridge: Cambridge University Press, 1996) and **J. Hills**, *The Future of Welfare* (2nd edn, York: Joseph Rowntree Foundation, 1997).

John Hills, in the last section of *Inequality and the State* (Oxford: Oxford University Press, 2004), provides an excellent review of the distributional effects of social spending by New Labour.

George, V., and Wilding, P., *The Impact of Social Policy* (London: Routledge, 1984) remains useful for its discussion of societal impacts of social policy. The various websites referred to contain up-to-date publications and data.

USEFUL WEBSITES

A key source of excellent research on the outcomes of social policies can be found at the website of the London School of Economics Centre for the Analysis of Social Exclusion (CASE) at: **http://sticerd.lse.ac.uk/case/publications/**. Look particularly at the 'CASEpapers', to which new reports are regularly added.

Welfare policy outcomes are regularly reported in the Joseph Rowntree Foundation's 'Findings' series of short reports from the research projects it has funded: **http://www.jrf.org.uk/knowledge/findings/**

ESSAY QUESTIONS

1   What is meant by need?

2   Compare the different ways of measuring the volume of social policy.

3   Does increased spending on a policy mean that need is being better met?

4   Does social policy (a) increase social stability and (b) challenge the market mechanism?

5   Explain the difference between the inputs, outputs, and outcomes of social policy.

ONLINE RESOURCE CENTRE

For additional material and resources, please visit the Online Resource Centre at: **www.oxfordtextbooks.co.uk/orc/baldock4e/**.

19

The experience of welfare:
the life course and the welfare state

Hartley Dean

Contents

luction

uncing the components of Britain's post-Second World War reconstruction plan, Prime ister Winston Churchill declared to the nation in a radio broadcast that the welfare state pro- sed by the Beveridge Report (1942) would provide 'for all classes for all purposes from the cradle to the grave' (Barnett 2001: 32). The celebrated expression 'from cradle to grave' (see Cartoon 19.1) captured the extent to which the modern welfare state was to be concerned with everyday human experiences across the whole of the human life course.

The emphasis throughout much of this book has been on social policy as a response to social problems and the ways in which 'personal troubles' may be translated into 'public issues' (see Chap- ter 3). However, social policy is as fundamentally concerned with the nature and substance of every- day life as with its troubles. One definition of academic social policy is that it is the study of human well-being: or, more specifically, 'the study of the social relations necessary for human wellbeing

'Not so much of that Cradle to the Grave stuff, young 'Erbert. Grandpa's sensitive.'

Cartoon 19.1 Smiling through: cradle to grave

Joseph Lee—*Evening News* 5 October 1944

and the systems by which wellbeing may be promoted' (Dean 2006: 1). In this respect, social policy might be regarded as 'the politics of the life course' (Leisering and Leibfried 1999: 24). Importantly, this means everybody's life course.

The welfare state affects all of our lives at a practical and intimate level. As human beings living in an advanced industrialized society, we need many things in the course of our lives (see Chapter 4). We need a means of livelihood, whether through paid employment or through social security or pension provision. At various stages in life we need access to human services: to healthcare, to education, and to housing. There are times when we may be especially vulnerable and require protection: during childhood, in the event of impairment through disease or injury, and during old age.

The welfare state cannot and does not provide for all these needs, many of which are met by our families and communities, or through the market. But the state may yet have a critical role in supporting families and communities or in regulating the market in ways that promote our well-being. Despite this, we should not suppose that the state's intervention in our lives is necessarily benign. The welfare state can function in ways that shape our lives and control what we do. It may treat some social groups differently, or even unfairly. The welfare state has provided a means by which people can share the risks associated with the human life course, although in recent times the nature of those risks and the role of the welfare state have been changing.

Learning outcomes

At the end of this chapter you should have an introductory understanding of:

1 the ways in which the state and different kinds of 'welfare regime' may impact upon our everyday experience as citizens and subjects;

2 the extent to which social policy is concerned with our experiences of human interdependency;

3 different experiences of life and welfare and, in particular, the ability of the welfare state to recognize differences based on gender, ethnicity, age, and disability;

4 the changing nature of the risks we now experience and the ways in which the welfare state may respond.

Experiences of the state

The welfare state shapes our experiences in a variety of ways: it constitutes us as citizens, it structures our lives, and it can control our behaviour. We shall consider each of these influences in turn.

Creating the citizen

Reference has been made in this volume to T. H. Marshall's (1950) classic account of the development of modern citizenship. However, the concept of citizenship and the status and meaning that attach to being a citizen date back to the beginnings of civilization and to the classic city-states of Athens and Rome. Citizenship entailed self-governance by free men. It was a status accorded to a patrician male urban elite. Women, children, slaves, and rural peoples were excluded, since it was supposed they lacked the capacity to participate in self-governance. Citizenship has always been concerned as much with whom to exclude as with defining the rights and responsibilities of those who are included. The citizenship model established in antiquity was adapted to the medieval cities of Western Europe, but by the seventeenth century the idea of citizenship began to be associated not with city governance, but with the governance of sovereign nation states.

The story T. H. Marshall tells is one in which citizenship evolved—becoming increasingly inclusive on the one hand and extensive on the other in terms of the rights it defined—until finally it reached the zenith of its development in the capitalist world with the emergence of the modern welfare state. The citizen has been recast by stages as the holder of civil liberties and legal rights; of democratic freedoms and voting rights; and finally, of welfare entitlements and social rights. We shall return to consider the extent to which, for example, women, minority ethnic groups, and disabled people have or have not been fully included as citizens. And we shall return to consider the ways in which the welfare state may influence the behaviour of its subjects. For now, however, we shall reflect on the different ways in which citizens may come to experience their rights to social welfare provision.

Whereas civil and political rights may easily be understood as being unconditional and inalienable characteristics of modern citizenship, rights to welfare provision are more likely to be partial or conditional in nature (Dean 2002). This is partly, as we have seen above, because many of our welfare needs may legitimately be met without provision by the state; and partly, as we shall see, because provision for human well-being will inevitably be premised on certain normative assumptions about the extent to which people should provide for themselves. A consequence of this is that social citizenship can be more or less exclusionary depending on the degree to which entitlement to welfare is either universal or selective. Universal citizenship entitlements are those to which every citizen has access, by virtue of their citizenship. Selective entitlements are those to which only certain citizens may conditionally have access and such entitlement may signify that some citizens are less equal in status than others. This is diagrammatically illustrated in Figure 19.1.

Conditionality can take a variety of forms:

- Fully universal provision is subject only to the condition that the recipient is a citizen. It is a condition that may nonetheless exclude migrants (Sales 2007).
- Some forms of provision are conditional upon life course contingencies, including age-related contingencies (i.e. childhood and old age) that are universally experienced and contingencies associated with impairment through injury or disease that may be experienced more exceptionally (and where, for example, entitlement may be subject to medical testing).
- Other forms of provision are conditional upon past payment of social insurance contributions. The degree of conditionality varies between schemes, but in general entitlement is subject in some measure to a 'work test': only those who have been in paid employment (or their dependants) qualify.
- Alternatively, provision may be conditional on demonstrable need or a test of means. Citizens may have to prove they have insufficient income or resources for day-to-day survival and/or to pay for essential services.

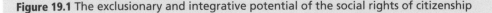

conditional upon	means-testing	'exceptional' contingencies	social insurance payments	'normal' life course contingencies	citizenship status
examples	social assistance (i.e. safety net benefits and services)	disability benefits and services	benefits/pensions during unemployment/ retirement OR (in some countries) healthcare	family allowances/ child benefits and free provision for 'senior citizens'	free health-care/ education

selective ← → universal
exclusionary ← → integrative

Figure 19.1 The exclusionary and integrative potential of the social rights of citizenship

In practice, welfare states may impose a variety of different conditions for different kinds of provision. But conditionality most often involves a test: of whether one has worked enough; of whether one is sick or incapacitated enough; of whether one is poor enough. Entitlement to universal benefits or services may be celebrated as a badge of citizenship and belonging. Entitlement to social insurance-based benefits or services may be celebrated as a just reward for one's industry and social contribution. But the refusal of a benefit or service on the grounds that one has not worked or contributed enough and recourse to means-tested forms of safety net benefits or services can be stigmatizing. Under such circumstances the rights afforded by the welfare state can sometimes be experienced not as a guarantee that one is an accepted member of society, but as confirmation that one is, at best, a second-class citizen or, at worst, beyond the pale of 'normal' citizenship (Dean 1999).

Life course regimes

Esping-Andersen (1990) provides an account of the different kinds of welfare regime that have emerged in the major capitalist countries of the world. One way to understand the differences between these regimes is in terms of the different emphasis that each places upon different kinds of social rights. In the social democratic welfare regimes, the primary emphasis is on universal rights available to all citizens. In the conservative or corporatist welfare regimes, the primary emphasis is on social insurance-based rights available to working citizens. In the liberal welfare regimes the primary emphasis is on selective or means-tested rights targeted to the poorest citizens. Such a generalization may amount to little more than a caricature when applied to the way the welfare state actually works in different countries, since inevitably countries employ a mixture of policies and principles. Nevertheless, it gives us some important clues about the different ways in which the welfare state may be experienced. Welfare regimes may also be interpreted as 'life-course regimes'(Leisering and Leibfried 1999), since each prioritizes different aspects of the life course.

The origins of the life course approach are generally attributed to B. S. Rowntree who, drawing on his study of poverty in York at the turn of the twentieth century, reflected that 'the life of a labourer is marked by five alternating periods of want and comparative plenty' (1901: 169). He produced the diagram shown in Figure 19.2 to illustrate this.

Rowntree's approach had a direct influence on the development of the welfare state, both in the UK and beyond, and Figure 19.2 demonstrates many of the assumptions on which the modern welfare state was premised. Clearly there is nothing 'natural' about the life course it illustrates, since each life stage is a social construct of its day and age. Rowntree and later the founders of the modern welfare state assumed that:

- childhood could be a time of relative hardship, especially in larger households;

- childhood ended when people reached working age, whereafter they would marry and have children;

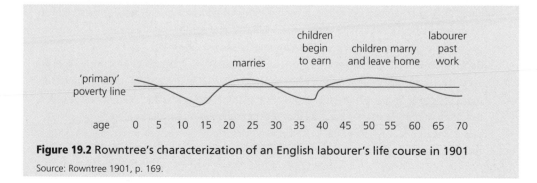

Figure 19.2 Rowntree's characterization of an English labourer's life course in 1901

Source: Rowntree 1901, p. 169.

- married couples with young children could experience relative hardship as they raised their families;
- their children would grow up, go out to work, and themselves get married and leave home;
- eventually people would grow old and infirm and retire from work, whereupon they could once again experience relative hardship.

There is nothing fixed or immutable about these life stages. In the pre-modern era, childhood, as a stage of dependency on parents, would have ended as early as the age of 7, when most young people would be expected to engage in some form of productive work (Gittins 1993). It was the social policies of the nineteenth and twentieth century—factory legislation and the introduction of compulsory education—that curtailed the exploitation of young people's labour and extended our perception of the age at which childhood should end. In a similar way, the separation between work and family that came with industrialization had facilitated the spread of nineteenth-century middle-class ideals of marriage and family and consolidated norms and practices that had not previously applied among the majority of the population. In an age when average life expectancy was much shorter, people did not retire unless or until they became too infirm to work. But the introduction of the first old age pensions at the beginning of the twentieth century made it possible for people to retire and, ever since, the age at which people become eligible for a pension has become widely accepted as the age at which 'old age' begins (Tinker 1997), despite the fact that increasingly in the richer countries of the world, people not only live longer but remain fit and active much longer than in the past.

Social policy is implicated, therefore, in the consolidation and construction of the life course. The different ways in which different welfare regimes structure educational provision for children and young people, in which they manage the social risks for people of working age, and in which they make provision for older people, embody what Leisering and Leibfried refer to as 'tacit life course policies' (1999: chapter 2), which have enduring implications for the everyday experiences of the citizen (see Box 19.1).

As ever, such theoretically modelled 'regimes' do not necessarily exist in a 'pure' form, but this model does help us make sense of everyday experiences in the real world where at any moment in any particular country a mixture of policy assumptions may be at work.

Box 19.1 Leisering and Liebfried's 'life course regimes'

- Regimes centred on *universal* provision model their understanding of the life course upon a work-centred biography in which egalitarian education provision connects with an inclusive labour market with an extensive substantial public sector. The effect is a tendency to standardize the life course, albeit that people's life chances are good and life risks are low.
- Regimes centred on *social insurance* provision model their understanding of the life course upon a 'gendered normal' biography with different trajectories for women and men and for different kinds of worker. Sometimes rigidly streamed forms of educational provision connect with a segmented labour market. The effect once again is to standardize the life course, to structure people's life chances unequally, while minimizing the life risks they face.
- Regimes centred on *residual/selective* provision also model their understanding of the life course upon a work-centred biography, but while educational provision may be formally egalitarian in terms of access, it may be substantively divisive and it connects with labour markets that are less regulated and more volatile than in other regimes, and which are dominated by the private sector. Because such regimes offer limited or minimal security, life courses are more fluidly structured. Life chances are unlimited in theory, but variable in practice, while life risks are high.

The controlling state

The origins of social policy in the Western world lie in the Poor Laws, which in Victorian Britain, for example, were nakedly coercive (Thane 1996). State assistance to people who were destitute required them to enter the workhouse and live under conditions that were deliberately contrived to be a deterrent. Elements of the conditionality associated with current social rights of citizenship are still to some degree coercive. As may be seen from Chapters 5 and 10, unemployed people may have their entitlements withdrawn as a sanction for failing to make themselves available for work or to comply with requirements that they undertake training or work experience.

However, the welfare state is also more subtly implicated in the control of human behaviour. We have seen that it helps to shape the human life course. It can also shape our sense of identity. T. H. Marshall (1950) had supposed that the development of social rights of citizenship would make it possible for old class antagonisms and class identities to wither away since every citizen would be entitled to a basic minimum level of welfare, and each, he believed, could enjoy genuine equality of status. In practice, significant social inequalities have survived (Hills 2010; and see Chapter 4). However, despite the survival of social inequalities, class consciousness and class loyalties, according to some, have eroded (Pakulski and Waters 1996). Post-structuralist theorists, such as Foucault (1977), have claimed that the growth in state administrative power that was associated with the modern state entailed the development of new disciplinary technologies. In place of crude coercion, new ways of controlling behaviour emerged. The very notion that every inhabitant of a welfare state is a 'citizen' has an atomizing and isolating effect. A citizen is an individual juridical subject, whose demands are framed not through shared struggles, but through submission to legal and administrative regulation from above (Garland 1981).

At another level, the welfare state has ushered in new kinds of bureaucratic and professional controls over people's behaviour. Access to social rights may be governed by street-level bureaucrats (Lipsky 1980): receptionists, clerks, and administrators whose conduct and attitudes impact directly on our experiences of welfare provision. Specialist services delivered by welfare professionals entail the exercise of 'normative power'(Clarke and Newman 1997: 63). The superior knowledge of doctors, teachers, and social workers allows them considerable day-to-day power, particularly over those who may be relatively powerless or vulnerable. The power of bureaucrats and professionals within the welfare state may have been diluted through the intervention of managers, but it is through bureaucrats and professionals that people have direct contact with the welfare state. And it is through them that many of the subtler forms of social control may be exercised. For example, it has been argued that whereas the family may once have been an independent mode of patriarchal governance, the supervision by health and welfare professionals of the conduct of children and parents has turned it into an instrument of state governance (Donzelot 1979). Welfare professionals may intervene into the private spaces and intimate details of our lives.

Finally, many of the recent changes to the welfare state—which we shall shortly discuss in greater detail—have entailed a further refinement of disciplinary technologies. Following the 'crisis' of the welfare state in the 1970s (see Chapter 2), there emerged from various quarters of the ideological spectrum a backlash against the concept of social rights and demands for a rebalancing of rights and responsibilities (Roche 1992). What Rose (1999) and others have characterized as an advanced form of liberal governance now envisages that a 'post-social' welfare state is increasingly concerned with facilitating not social protection, but responsible self-provisioning. The process initially entailed attempts to recast the citizen as a consumer, as a responsible customer who would demand efficiency and good value from the public sector in the same way as s/he did from the private sector. Later attempts have sought to recast the citizen as a public service user, who is co-responsible for his/her own welfare and is co-opted into exercising choice about at least certain elements of the services they receive (Le Grand 2003), notwithstanding that vulnerable service users may not wish or may not be able to exercise choices (e.g. Baldock and Ungerson 1996). At the heart of this movement towards self-provisioning is a disciplinary ideal. The immanent purpose is to inculcate prudence and an individualistic ethic of self-responsibility (Rose 1999). Even when it disengages from direct provision, the welfare state bears upon everyday experience.

Experiences of interdependency

With or without the welfare state, the basic condition of the human species is that we are inter-dependent creatures. The welfare state brings particular meaning to our experience of inter-dependency: it creates a particular form of dependency and provides a mechanism by which to organize the way we care for and about one another.

Welfare dependency

It was suggested above that the study of social policy amounts to a study of human well-being. Though 'well-being' may often be regarded as a synonym for 'welfare', there are strategic reasons for preferring the former term. The first is pragmatic: it is quite simply because the term 'welfare' has acquired a pejorative connotation associated with a distinctly downbeat understanding of dependency, whereas 'well-being' has more positive connotations and has lately become something of an upbeat buzzword (Bacon et al. 2010; NEF 2004). The second is that the concept of well-being opens up some critical philosophical distinctions about what it entails to lead a 'good life' and the extent to which this requires our dependency on other people (Dean 2010).

When we speak of the welfare state we are referring throughout this book to a range of policy interventions that includes education, employment policy, healthcare, housing, social security, the personal social services. But in the United States, for example, the term 'welfare' is reserved exclusively for means-tested safety net provision for the poor. And there has been a tendency in recent years in the UK to use the term in the same way (Lister 2001). The expression 'welfare reform' is commonly associated not with developments to social policy provision in general, but with successive reorganizations and the curtailment of cash transfers to non-working people.

Social assistance provision for social groups of working age has in most welfare regimes retained some association with the distinction made under the Poor Laws between the deserving poor (who had managed to sustain themselves without recourse to poor relief) and the undeserving poor (who had resorted to relief from public funds). Despite the fact that social assistance is now provided as a social right of citizenship, it retains an element of stigma. Rather than subsiding, the extent of that stigma has been fuelled since the 1970s by the clamour for a rebalancing of rights and responsibilities. Momentum has been added to such demands by the so called 'underclass' debate (see especially Murray 1990). Murray declared that the welfare state was responsible for the creation of an underclass of lone mothers and workless youths and for the perpetuation of a dependency culture. In most countries, the experience of claiming safety net benefits has always been grim (van-Oorschot 1995), but the popularization of the term 'dependency culture' and the systematic 'othering' (Lister 2004) of those dependent on such benefits have exacerbated the trend.

In the event, research suggests there never was anything amounting to a dependency culture (Dean and Taylor-Gooby 1992). Long-term recipients of social assistance benefits would seem by and large to subscribe to the same aspirations and values as other people. What is more, they do not usually choose, but tend very much to resent, their own dependency on the state. There appears—in England certainly—to be a popular consensus that regards dependency on the state as inherently problematic (Dean and Rodgers 2004). Yet this consensus conceals a number of contradictions. By and large, people are prepared to acknowledge their dependency on others, though they are usually reluctant to do so. Yet even those who deny they are or ever will be in any way dependent will celebrate their own *dependability for* others; their children or near neighbours. Perversely, popular and political discourses alike look upon dependence on an employer for the means of subsistence and on family members for practical and affective support as if were a form of *independence*, while denigrating the receipt of state benefits as welfare dependency. There is more than one paradox here: first, in any human society we are ultimately mutually interdependent; second, insofar as certain kinds of dependency may prove problematic, it is surely to be welcomed that 'dependency' on state welfare provision can, in some circumstances, offer a countervailing degree of independence from labour market exploitation and abusive relationships. One of the justifications for the welfare state is that it can partially de-commodify and de-familialize citizens in order to protect them (Esping-Andersen 1999).

If dominant understandings of dependency seem curiously distorted, then dominant conceptions of well-being are also strikingly one-sided. The classical Socratic philosophical tradition recognized two forms of well-being: one the hedonic, which is associated with the pursuit of pleasure and the avoidance of pain; the other the eudaimonic, which is associated with what some might call spiritual fulfilment, but which entails social participation, civic engagement, and creative reflection. The two understandings have tended to diverge and it is the hedonic conception of well-being that is represented in the modern utilitarian philosophical tradition that has informed key elements of social policy—from the Poor Laws to the present (Jordan 2008). The hedonic-utilitarian tradition is prepared to inflict disutility (i.e. pain) upon the undeserving minority in the interests of the greater happiness of the population as a whole. It assumes that what motivates rational citizens is the pursuit of self-interest and that policy instruments should be designed accordingly. It is this utilitarian understanding of well-being that informs the current vogue for happiness studies and the work of commentators such as Layard, who expressly rejects the validity of the alternative eudaimonic understanding of well-being (2005: 22). Recent suggestions that a nation's progress be adjudged as much in terms of the happiness of its population as the performance of its economy (Stiglitz et al. 2009) represent an important development, but it remains to be seen how meaningfully the implementation of such ideas could accommodate deeper understandings of what constitutes human well-being.

The classical eudaimonic understanding of well-being contended that leading a good life entails the pursuit not of pleasure alone, but of virtue (see Fitzpatrick 2008: Chapter 4). It is a tradition that has found expression in elements, at least, of some quite diverse strands of modern thinking about social justice: ranging from social liberalism to radical communitarianism. These more encompassing understandings tend, nevertheless, to be overshadowed by the hedonic tradition. The enduring significance of the eudaimonic tradition lies in its capacity—most particularly, as we shall shortly see, in its implicit reinterpretation by certain feminists (Kittay et al. 2005) to recognize that human interdependency is axiomatic to the human experience and to our well-being.

A classic justification for a welfare state is that it enables us to define and recognize what Titmuss once called 'states of dependency' which arise 'for the vast majority of the population'(1955: 64).

Caring for and about one another

This leads directly to one of the central concerns of social policy: the question of just how people care for and about each other. There is an important distinction to be made between 'caring for' and 'caring about' (Parker 1981). 'Caring for' people when they are very young or very old, when they are sick, disabled, or frail, is an intensely practical business. 'Caring about' people is different. At a personal level it is what happens when we love somebody, and a great deal of 'caring for' is done because people care about their loved ones (Finch and Groves 1983). At the policy level, however, 'caring about' is more abstractly connected to collective attempts to secure human well-being.

At the policy level, 'caring about' becomes impersonal. It is informed by issues of principle concerning the limits of our interdependency. This we have already seen in our discussion of social rights and citizenship and the question of to whom such rights should extend and on what terms. Williams (1989) has argued that the welfare state has been built around ideological principles concerned with the maintenance of work, family, and nation. These were the institutions that provided the framework in which the practical business of 'caring for' supposedly *should* take place. It is of course possible for caregiving to be stripped of all warmth and compassion. Though the modern welfare state is supposed to have replaced the 'cold charity' once dispensed by judgmental Poor Law officials, the stigma and shame that can still attach to the receipt of certain uncaringly administered forms of means-tested welfare provision can and sometimes do inflict 'hidden injuries' (Frost and Hoggett 2008).

An altogether more optimistic insight into the part played by the welfare state was provided by Titmuss (1970). Having acknowledged that the welfare state may provide for states of dependency—both natural and socially constructed—he drew on social anthropological portrayals of early human societies. Far from being 'primitive', these societies were sustained through elaborate systems of unilateral exchange or 'gift-relationships'. Titmuss argued that gift-relationships have survived in modern capitalist societies through the creation of the welfare state. Capitalist societies are based on the rationality of bilateral market-based exchange, not unilateral gifts. The ostensibly wasteful gift-giving practices customary in earlier societal formations might seem irrational by contemporary standards, but they were essential to sustaining solidarity in social groupings that were highly vulnerable to scarcity and natural disaster. Modern capitalist societies depend on highly complex divisions of labour and require different means of ensuring solidarity. Titmuss suggested that the welfare state meets a basic human need to express altruism; to share, rather than compete. It provides the mechanism through taxes and social insurance to give to others in order to address the inevitable 'diswelfares' to which the capitalist system gives rise. The point here is that the welfare state enables us to care about people, albeit in an impersonal sense. It invites us to have regard not only for whomsoever is our brother/sister or our neighbour, but for strangers; to care not only about intimates and the people we know, but excluded minorities and distant others. It also enables us to envisage modes of collective exchange between generations, whereby we may as voting and taxpaying citizens contribute towards the care of other people's children and other people's elderly relatives (e.g. Walker 1996).

The greater part of practical caregiving or 'caring for' people is undertaken by women: as mothers and daughters (e.g. Ungerson 1987); as *front-line* welfare providers (care assistants, nurses, nursery and primary teachers, social workers), who are predominantly women (e.g. Pascall 1997). But it is men who tend to predominate when it comes to the more impersonal aspects of 'caring about': as male breadwinners; as public sector managers; and as policy-makers. It may be argued (Gilligan 1982) that feminine moral codes of care have been subordinated to masculine codes of moral reasoning. There is a sense in which feminine forms of 'caring for' are rooted in mutual responsibility and relationships, whereas masculine forms of 'caring about' are rooted in rights and rules. However, men and women alike exist within networks of care and are equally capable of both giving and receiving care. We are all constituted not just as the bearers of social rights, but as 'selves in relationship' (Sevenhuijsen 1998). Social policy, it is argued, ought to be informed as much by an ethic of care as by an ethic of justice.

Experiences of difference

This leads in turn to a related normative debate in which it is argued that the pursuit of social justice must embrace a struggle for the recognition of the differences between people and their different needs as much as a struggle for the redistribution of resources (Fraser and Honneth 2003). People's life courses and their experiences of the welfare state differ and are affected by a great variety of factors. Our lives are shaped by differences of class, custom, and culture, and by the particular economic, political, and historical characteristics of the society we inhabit. Here we shall consider how they are affected by gender, ethnicity, and disability. We shall focus on how different identities are socially constructed, how difference may be associated with disadvantage, and how social policy engages with difference.

The social construction of identity

Human beings are not all the same. We are different. Our differences define our identities and affect what we may require for our well-being. Some of those differences are biological. We are born with different sexual characteristics, different skin colours, different physical propensities and abilities. In the course of our lives the differences between us multiply as we grow up and grow old, and as illness, injury, and other vicissitudes may or may not befall us. The complex ways in which societies organize and reproduce themselves result in a further range of differences that are socially determined and can lead to systemic disadvantage or oppression.

So, while sexual difference is biological, gender is socially or culturally constructed. That women have babies and men do not is a biological fact. The prevailing sexual division of labour reflects the extent to which it has characteristically been women who attend to the supposedly 'natural' business of social reproduction in the private sphere of hearth, home, and the ideologically constructed family (see Chapter 6) while men have been free to engage in 'cultural' matters in the public spheres of economic production and political governance. This gendered distribution of roles is not a biological fact; it is a social artefact.

Though it may be argued that women are closer to nature—that they are 'naturally' more caring and less aggressive than men—dominant strands within contemporary feminism are inclined to reject this kind of biological essentialism and contend that the gendered nature of society is a specific outcome of power relations and patriarchy. It is an effect of the dominance of men over women and can be resisted. Patriarchy, as a structural characteristic of human societies, stems from the power that accrues to roles assumed predominantly by men and from the perpetuation and subordination of the dependent roles assumed predominantly by women (Connell 2002). The architects of the modern welfare state were so inured to patriarchal assumptions about the respective roles of male breadwinners and female homemakers that the British national insurance system, for example, was designed on the premise that married women would for the most part be financially dependent on their husbands. While many of the more overtly discriminatory elements of the British system have since been removed, the legacy of the assumptions on which the system was founded remains. In common with other systems in the developed world, British social security provision incorporates a social insurance scheme under which it is predominantly male heads of household who claim entitlements on behalf of predominantly female dependants, and a social assistance system, under which it is predominantly female-headed households—including large numbers of lone parents and single pensioners—that claim stigmatized means-tested benefits: the former have been characterized as 'masculine sub-systems', the latter as 'feminine sub-systems' (Fraser 1989: 111–2). Moves towards systems based on tax credits—which are to be intensified in the UK by proposals from the coalition government (DWP 2010)—portend a continuing shift away from assumptions based on the 'male breadwinner household model' that informed the Beveridgian welfare state, and towards an 'adult worker model'(Lewis 2000) in which men and women alike are expected to sustain themselves through participation in the labour market. In practice, however, such policies take little account of women's preferences or the opportunities available to them and would seem to be privileging paid employment at the expense of unpaid caring. Women's socially constituted roles and identities remain systemically subordinate.

A further kind of systemic subordination may be associated with ethnicity or, more specifically, the racialization of ethnic differences; of phenotypical, linguistic, and cultural diversity. The human species is genetically diverse. We are all born with an observable set of characteristics that we share—albeit in different measures—with our immediate forbears, but which may differentiate us from other members of the species. At the same time, the history of the human species has entailed processes of migration and settlement, of competition as well as cooperation between different social groups, and the building of nations and empires. Human societies have constituted themselves though notions of common identity, through shared languages and customs, but also through the exclusion or subjugation of those who are, or are believed to be, different.

Biological theories about the human species led in the nineteenth and the first part of the twentieth century to what has been called 'scientific' racism, though the term is a misnomer. It was believed that the human species was divided into subspecies or 'races', some of which were physically, intellectually, and morally superior to others. The scientific basis for such understandings has since been widely discredited, but this did not prevent their influence upon the rise of Nazism, for example, nor upon a more general spread of racist thinking. Although the idea that there are biologically distinct races is a myth, racism is a real social phenomenon. Racism may be understood both as an ideology that 'racializes' (Fanon 1967) the relations of power by which social groups and the boundaries between them are defined, and in terms of the outcomes of social and institutional processes that disadvantage racialized social groups. Racism grew out of a mistrust of the 'otherness' of people deemed not to be civilized (Miles 1989). However, racism is more than mere 'heterophobia' (fear of difference), but must be historically situated in relation to processes of economic exploitation: not only slavery in the pre-capitalist era, but specific class conflicts set in train as a result of colonialism, imperialism, and global labour migration (Sivanandan 1990). The welfare state may be implicated in the racialization of the fluid cultural differences through which ethnic identities are defined.

Finally, we should consider how disability may be associated with systemic subordination. Disability is something that may be experienced when people are born with a genetic impairment, if they suffer illness or injury that limits their functioning, or if they suffer from degenerative conditions as they grow older. The impairments associated with disability may be physical or mental and may, for example, include mental health problems or learning difficulties. Disability does not necessarily imply a permanent or static status. Research (Burchardt 2000) has explored how people may become more or less disabled in the course of their lives.

While the impairments or functional limitations to which human beings are subject generally have biological causes or effects, disability—like gender and ethnicity—is socially constructed. Disability can, however, be constructed in different ways. Oliver (1990) has argued that two broad understandings or conceptual models may apply (see also Chapter 13). The first is an individual model, which regards disability as a personal tragedy that has befallen the individual or as an individual medical problem, susceptible to medical explanation and management. The second is the social model, which regards disability in terms of the consequences of a hostile social environment that does not, or will not, accommodate the particular needs, or recognize the particular abilities, of people with impairments or functional limitations.

The application by policy-makers of individual models of disability has led in various directions. On the one hand, during the first part of the twentieth century, according to Williams (1989), elements of the care provided for disabled people were implicitly eugenicist: that is, in order to maintain the genetic purity of the British national 'stock', disabled people—or those adjudged physically, mentally, or morally 'defective'—were maintained in institutions or colonies that segregated them from the 'normal' population and prevented them from having procreative relations. On the other hand, the post-Second World War welfare state developed policies and systems that were intended to ensure that disabled people should no longer be segregated from non-disabled society, but which succeeded nonetheless in excluding disabled people through the creation of dependency. Oliver and Barnes (1998) have argued that provision was shaped by an assumption that people with impairments are not fully competent citizens. Disabled people may no longer have been construed as a threat, but as a burden on society. Their needs were defined for them by welfare professionals and policy-makers.

The penalties of difference

These systemic disadvantages are reflected in substantive penalties. A selection of illustrative indicators drawn from UK statistics may be found in Table 19.1.

Table 19.1 Gender, ethnic and disability 'penalties' in the UK

	Gender			Ethnicity						Disabled people
	men	women	white men	Indian men	Pakistani men	Bangladeshi men	Black Caribbean men	Black African men	
Risk of poverty [1]	19%	21%	20%	29%		60%	32%	48%	24%
Median net individual income [2]	£281 pw	£180 pw	£288 pw	£274 pw	£184 pw	£158 pw	£220 pw	£244 pw	£157 pw
Full-time employment rate [2]	59%	39%	60%	58%	35%	34%	48%	53%	21%
Part-time employment rate [2]	6%	26%	5%	7%	10%	17%	7%	11%	4%
Median gross rate of pay [2]	£11.15 ph	£8.86 ph	£11.35 ph	£11.15 ph	£7.74 ph	£6.90 ph	£10.34 ph	£9.60 ph	£9.04 ph

Sources: (1) DWP (2009) shows percentage of individuals in households with equivalized incomes (after housing costs) of less than 60% of the median in 2008–9.
(2) National Equality Panel (Hills 2010) data relate to 2005/6–2007/8 for net individual incomes and 2006–8 for employment and pay rates.

However, such statistics can only tell a part of the story.

Some commentators have argued that there has been a 'feminization of poverty' (Chant 2008; Scott 1984). Women suffer more poverty than men, because their labour—whether paid and unpaid—is undervalued. There are three principal reasons for the endurance of women's poverty:

- Women are still more likely than men to be 'economically inactive', that is to be excluded from the labour market. They do not have equal access to the 'core' of the labour market and are disproportionately represented within part-time and lower-paid jobs. And not only are they paid less than men, they obtain a smaller proportion of their income from employment and, in retirement, from occupational pensions.
- Women still undertake a disproportionate share of the tasks associated with social reproduction: that is, with unpaid care work and domestic labour. Though it may gradually be changing, the gap between men's and women's contribution to household 'chores' and childcare—at around 40 per cent in the UK—remains considerable (see Figure 19.3).
- The distribution of income and resources within families and households does not necessarily work to the advantage of women. The evidence for this has already been discussed in Chapter 6.

Additionally, women are disadvantaged by other forms of discrimination within the public sphere. Pascall (1997) and others have argued that, although women now make up a high proportion of the public sector workforce—in healthcare, social work, and education—they remain under-represented at senior and managerial levels. As a result, it is largely men who control health and social services, including services that impact particularly on women, such as reproductive health-care and support for informal carers. And although women in Britain have been permitted to vote and to participate in the democratic process on the same terms as men since 1928, following the British General Election in 2010 only 22 per cent of the MPs elected to the House of Commons were women (see **www.parliament.uk**).

Just as some commentators have identified a feminization of poverty, it is also possible to speak of the racialization of poverty. The term 'ethnic penalty' was coined by Heath (Heath and Cheung 2007) and has been shown to apply to minority ethnic groups throughout the developed world. Such groups are especially vulnerable to poverty, and can be especially stigmatized by welfare provision. In Britain a report by the erstwhile Social Exclusion Unit had observed that:

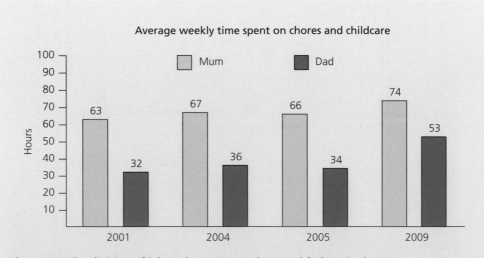

Figure 19.3 The division of labour between mothers and fathers in the UK

Source: Legal and General (2009) *The Value of a Parent 2009*, research report, London

In comparison to their representation in the population, people from minority ethnic communities are more likely than others to live in poor areas; be poor; be unemployed, compared with white people with similar qualifications; suffer ill health and live in overcrowded and unpopular housing. They also experience widespread racial harassment and racial crime and are over-represented in the criminal justice system, from stop and search to prison. (SEU 2000: Chapter 2 summary).

There are nonetheless, in Britain, considerable differences between minority ethnic groups (see Table 19.1). The minority ethnic population of the UK at the time of the last census represented approximately 8 per cent of the total population and was composed as shown in Figure 19.4. Evidence from past and recent studies (Hills 2010; Modood et al. 1997) demonstrated that African-Caribbean and particularly Pakistani and Bangladeshi minorities are particularly prone to unemployment and low pay, to benefit dependency and to income poverty. Indian and other non-white minority ethnic groups (such as Chinese), while often suffering certain disadvantages in relation to the white population, nonetheless fare better than other groups, especially those from professional backgrounds. The overall picture, however, is complex. Crude statistics mask the differences between minority ethnic groups and, for example, between men and women and between younger and older people within ethnic groups.

The household and age structures of different minority ethnic groups are diverse, which can affect the risk of poverty to which they are exposed and the likelihood that they may have to depend on means-tested social security benefits: though the age profile of minority ethnic groups tends to be younger than that of the white population, their older members tend to have had fewer educational qualifications, shorter and less well remunerated working lives, and to be less likely to have access to occupational pension coverage. Minority ethnic groups may also be subject to disadvantage in housing, healthcare, and education. The key issues for minority ethnic groups has been access to the labour market on the one hand, but also access to resources, including the resources of the welfare state, such as public housing (e.g. Dench at al. 2006). Theorists such as Rex and Moore (1967) had argued that it was conflict over such resources, and the unequal outcomes of such

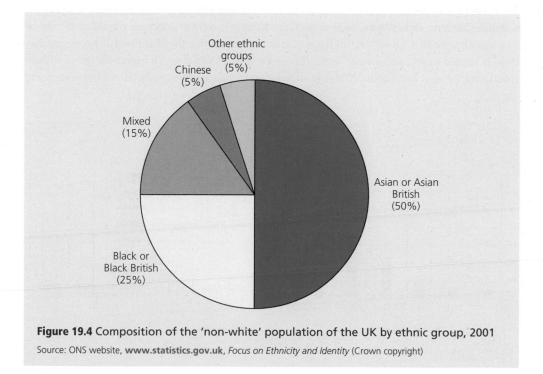

Figure 19.4 Composition of the 'non-white' population of the UK by ethnic group, 2001

Source: ONS website, **www.statistics.gov.uk**, *Focus on Ethnicity and Identity* (Crown copyright)

conflicts, that had constituted minority ethnic groups as an 'underclass'. Though the underclass concept has been challenged, Rex and Moore's analysis was important for the way in which it demonstrated how material, rather than behavioural, factors were implicated in a process that has since been characterized as 'ghettoization'(Wilson 1987). If we are to understand the tendency for minority ethnic groups to be concentrated in poor neighbourhoods and poor housing, we must have regard not simply to discriminatory practices, but the preferences and defensive strategies of minority ethnic groups and the wider social context with regard to competition for scarce resources.

Additionally, there is evidence from a variety of sources that often in the past, minority ethnic social security claimants have received unfavourable treatment by benefits administrators; minority ethnic children have been stereotyped by teachers; the needs of minority ethnic patients have been misinterpreted by health professionals; minority ethnic clients have been treated with cultural insensitivity by social workers (Law 1996). Members of minority ethnic groups are themselves disproportionately represented amongst the lower-paid employees of the welfare state in menial jobs, for example as domestics and catering workers (Williams 1989: 179). Finally, minority ethnic groups are poorly represented in the democratic process. Following the British General Election in 2010, only 4 per cent of the MPs elected to the House of Commons were from minority ethnic groups (see **www.parliament.uk**).

Turning finally in this section to the experiences of disabled people, these have been very directly shaped by the nature of welfare state capitalism. Industrialization and the wage labour system made it more difficult for disabled people to play a productive part in society. Under the Poor Laws, those whose families could not support them became paupers. The modern welfare state has attempted with limited success to promote some measure of labour market participation by disabled people, while sustaining them as benefit and care recipients.

Official disability surveys employ different and contestable definitions but generally rely on self-reporting of long-standing conditions that limit either a person's day-to-day activities or the kind or amount of work they can undertake. The government's Office for Disability Issues (**www. officefordisability.gov.uk**) currently estimates there are more than 10 million people in Great Britain who are disabled: around one in six of the population. Around nine in every ten disabled people were not disabled at birth but became disabled in the course of their lives. If disability is identified with limiting long-term illness, its likelihood predictably increases as people get older, as may be seen from Figure 19.5. However, this figure also demonstrates that the likelihood of becoming disabled is related to socio-economic status. The onset of disability is much higher for those already disadvantaged, and Burchardt (2000) has shown that there are strong associations between being

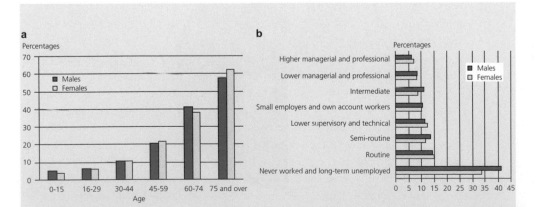

Figure 19.5 Prevalence of limiting long-term illness in UK, 2001 (a) by age and sex (b) by socio-economic status

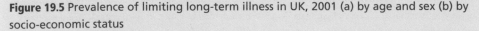

Source: ONS website, **www.statistics.gov.uk**, *Focus on Health*

poor, being out of work, having low educational qualifications, and the risk of developing a long-term health problem or impairment.

As may be seen from Table 19.1, disabled people are less likely to obtain employment, those who are in employment are less likely to work full-time, and, on average, receive lower earnings than non-disabled people. It is hardly surprising, therefore, that household incomes tend to be lower for disabled than for non-disabled adults and that households containing disabled adults or children are more likely than other households to experience below-average incomes (Howard et al. 2001). However, disabled people's poverty—and the difficulty of measuring it—is compounded by the higher costs they face: both the costs of the goods and domestic services required for their personal support, and the additional spending that may be associated with heating, laundry, and transport (Berthoud 1998).

In addition to the difficulties they experience accessing employment and income, disabled people are systematically disadvantaged in a host of other ways. Oliver and Barnes (1998) have argued that disabled people can be systematically disadvantaged (see Box 19.2).

The politics of difference

It was suggested above that the 1970s crisis of the welfare state was associated with a questioning of the social rights of citizenship and a concern for the enforcement of individual responsibilities. The crisis also coincided with other trends, including what is sometimes alluded to as a 'cultural turn' (e.g. Clarke 1999) that included a shift from class politics to identity politics. Identity politics opened the door to demands for the recognition of difference. The concern was that social differences connected to gender, 'race' or ethnicity, and disability—and, just as importantly, to age, sexuality, and religion—should be celebrated and brought to the fore. This was one of the critical

---

Box 19.2 **Oliver and Barnes's critique of the ways in which welfare provision may disadvantage disabled people**

- *Health*. Disadvantage may arise through the complex and often contentious nature of the boundary between healthcare and social care, the effects of which often compromise the quality of the long-term care arrangements that are available (see Chapter 13). Additionally, because healthcare is dominated by a medical model of disability, it is often premised on the idea that disabled patients' 'rehabilitation' must entail their psychological adjustment to impairment, rather than an understanding of the adjustments that may be required to their social and physical environment if patients are to realize or regain their full potential.
- *Education*. Disadvantage may arise through the nature of the education that is made available to disabled children and young people. Although it has been estimated that around 20 per cent of pupils may at some time require special educational assistance, only 2 per cent require separate specialized facilities (DES 1978). In spite of this, over a third of disabled children are educated in segregated environments, such as special schools or special classes. The quality and substance of such education have often been informed by individualistic and stereotypical assumptions about disability and the capacities of disabled people.
- *Housing*. Disadvantage may arise through the poor design and inaccessible nature of most housing provision and much of the built environment. Whereas there are in Britain over four million disabled people with mobility-related impairments, there are fewer than a million accessible homes suitable for their occupation. What is more, partly because of their low incomes, disabled people and their families are twice as likely to live in public housing as their non-disabled peers.

influences upon the growth during the late twentieth century of new social movements (Annetts et al. 2008). As was seen in Chapter 3, the women's, anti-racist, and disability awareness movements were each explicitly critical of the welfare state. The new insights and understandings that they forced on the welfare state have resulted in incremental changes in social policy, but fundamentally, there remains a tension between competing approaches. Should the policy objective be to compensate citizens for the disadvantages that may result from socially constructed differences, or to ensure that all citizens have effective opportunities and equal life chances? In practice, welfare states are likely to adopt a combination of approaches, but the distinction to be drawn between the two types of approach is the subject of critical debate.

The compensatory or social welfare approach is concerned to protect people and promote solidarity. The danger is that such an approach may perpetuate and consolidate social differences, rather than confront their social implications. This is particularly the case if policy implicitly references difference in relation to some notion of a 'normality' that is, by default, male, white, and able-bodied, and which neglects the extent to which masculinity, majority ethnicity, and 'ability' are themselves socially constructed. Compensatory approaches are preoccupied with identifying and meeting substantive human needs, but tend in so doing to prescribe the identity of the welfare subject in a top-down fashion (see Box 19.3).

The second approach may be characterized as the liberal equal opportunities approach and is concerned to promote tolerance and fairness. It has been implemented primarily through various forms of anti-discrimination legislation. The history of recent legislation in the UK is summarized in Box 19.4. However, equal opportunities approaches are preoccupied with observing formal rights, but tend in so doing to ascribe fixed individualized identities. This may fail to address the fundamental causes of disadvantage and underlying relations of power. The focus is on discriminatory attitudes and prejudices, not on social structural factors. Anti-discrimination legislation tends to reduce the problem of discrimination to the level of those individual instances that may be capable of legal remedy by the individual citizen. Feminists may object to the equal opportunities approach when it effectively forces women to compete with men on men's terms. The dilemma attributed to Wollstonecraft (1792)(and see Pateman 1989) is that treating women as the equals of men may fail to recognize that they are different from men. Anti-racists may object to the equal

---

Box 19.3 **Compensatory approaches to difference**

- Benefits and services that support *women* in their role as mothers and carers; policies to make it easier for women and men to combine paid employment and unpaid caring responsibilities; policies to ensure women are better protected from violence or other forms of abuse. Feminists, however, harbour concerns that this may lock women into dependency on men and perpetuate their status as second-class citizens (Lister 2003).
- Urban regeneration and multicultural policy initiatives, assisting *minority ethnic groups* better to celebrate their cultural identities, while integrating with the majority communities in which they live. Anti-racists, however, harbour concerns that this tends either to trivialize ethnic differences or to reify them. Either way the root causes of disadvantage are neglected (Banting and Kymlicka 2006).
- Benefits schemes and domiciliary and residential care services for *disabled people*. Disability movement activists, however, harbour concerns that though such an approach may spare much suffering, it does not confront the extent to which it is society that is to blame for so many of the disadvantages that disabled people face (Shakespeare 2006).

Box 19.4 **British anti-discrimination legislation**

Sex Discrimination Act 1975	Supplemented the Equal Pay Act1970. Outlawed discrimination* on the grounds of sex. Created the Equal Opportunities Commission (EOC)†.
Race Relations Act 1976	Superseded weaker Acts of 1965 and 1968. Outlawed discrimination* on the grounds of 'race', colour, national, or ethnic origins. Created the Commission for Racial Equality (CRE)†. Extended by the Race Relations (Amendment) Act 2000 to apply to the functioning of all public authorities.
Disability Discrimination Act 1995	Outlawed discrimination* on the grounds of disability, but subject to exemptions where, for example, employers can establish a 'justifiable reason' for discriminating. Amending legislation in 1999 created the Disability Rights Commission (DRC)†.
Equality Act 2006	Created a single Equality and Human Rights Commission incorporating the functions of the EOC, CRE, and DRC (see above) and giving it additional powers in relation to the enforcement of newer equality legislation relating to age, religion, or belief, sexual orientation and transgender status, and the encouragement of compliance with the UK's Human Rights Act 1998 and international human rights obligations more generally.
Equality Act 2010	A simplifying measure that replaced all the above laws with a single Act and includes some incremental developments.

* 'Direct' discrimination occurs when a person is treated less favourably than another. 'Indirect' discrimination occurs when conditions are imposed that adversely affect members of a particular social group. Redress in respect of discrimination in employment may be sought before the Employment Tribunal and in respect of discrimination in the provision of goods and services before the civil courts.

† Quangos with power to investigate complaints.

---

opportunities approach because it can promote tactical compliance strategies that leave underlying institutional racism untouched. The disability rights and independent living movement may object to the equal opportunities approach as currently conceived, since it does not positively or pro-actively intervene to ensure that disabled people have autonomy and proper control over their own lives.

If, however, the welfare state is to recognize and accommodate difference, it must nonetheless recognize and accommodate the needs that citizens have in common. Taylor (1998) has suggested that there is a distinction to be made between categorical identity and ontological identity. Categorical identity stems from belonging to a social group or category (or rather a variety of groups and categories); from sameness in difference; from the interests we share with others of the same class, gender, ethnicity, etc. Our ontological identity defines our uniqueness as human beings; it brings coherence and unity to our sense of 'self' in spite of the multiplicity of categorical identities that we have; it is the essential prerequisite of our well-being as individuals. While it is often contended that the function of social policy is to address social problems, Hoggett makes the point that it must also, surely, be about well-being and 'the totality of an individual's social relations'(2000: 145). To put it another way, social policy needs to find ways of addressing simultaneously *particular* claims to recognition by a variety of social groups and *universal* claims to well-being by unique individuals.

This requires a rediscovery of social citizenship as a concept that not only embraces a social rights and redistribution agenda, but also a social recognition agenda. The movement that has endeavoured to suppress social rights in favour of individual responsibilities has also diminished our understanding that citizenship is not an abstract *principle* but a substantive social *practice* and requires us to embrace social diversity (Isin et al. 2008).

Experiences of risk

This chapter has already alluded to the fact that both the welfare state and the nature of the human life course have been subject to change. The workings of the post-Second World War welfare state that endured between the mid1940s and the mid1970s began eventually to lag behind the nature of the risks we face during the life course (Baldwin and Falkingham 1994), as labour markets became more polarized and more flexible; as fertility declined and longevity increased; and as the pattern and diversity of personal and family relationships and household formations began to change. Nevertheless, the welfare state has been adapting and can shape our experiences of life in new ways. In this final section we shall attempt to capture the nature and meaning of the changes that have taken place.

From class society to 'risk society'

The classic welfare state was supposed, according to T. H. Marshall, to achieve a degree of equality 'not so much between classes as between individuals within a population which is now treated for this purpose as though it was one class'(1950: 33). In part at least, the welfare state had been an outcome of demands for greater social equality from the working class and the organized labour movement (Korpi 1983). Though the welfare state has ameliorated social inequality, it has manifestly failed to abate it, especially in the case of liberal welfare regimes. Yet despite this, the advent of the welfare state would seem to have succeeded in weakening the bonds of class. Inglehart (1990), for example, suggests the welfare state was implicated in the coming of a 'post-scarcity' or 'post-materialist' age in which—freed from fears about their everyday survival—people became more introspective and more preoccupied with issues such as those to do with cultural identity, as opposed to class identity.

But the risks that people face under post-industrial capitalism have been changing. Amidst increasing affluence in post-industrial societies, new social risks have been emerging (Taylor-Gooby 2000). The effect of economic globalization has been to diminish the security of livelihoods founded on wage labour. The effect of demographic transition and social change has been to disrupt the security of life course patterns once founded in familial and intergenerational dependencies. The effect of the 'crisis' of the capitalist welfare state has been to diminish the security once guaranteed through social rights of citizenship.

In one sense the risks are not new. The security afforded to wage labourers by industrial capitalism was always tenuous. The security afforded by family and kin was always, potentially, ambiguous. The security afforded by the post-Second World War welfare state was never completely unconditional. Nevertheless, we are led to believe that in today's labour market there is no such thing as a job for life (Doogan 2009; Sennett 1998); that the demands on our personal relationships render them increasingly unstable (Beck and Beck-Gernsheim 2001; Inglehart 1990); that universal healthcare and universal social protection may no longer be sustainable (Mishra 1984; Pierson 1996). Our perceptions of and responses to life's risks are also changing. The coming of what some commentators now refer to as the risk society (Beck 1992; Giddens 1991) has entailed a loss of faith in social citizenship and the institutions of the welfare state.

When Claus Offe claimed 'we no longer live in a class society, but a risk society' (1996: 33), he captured something about the way the changing nature of labour markets has impacted on experiences and understandings of the life course. The principal class division that was assumed to exist when the welfare state was created was between a middle class composed of relatively privileged non-manual workers (whose interests were supposedly associated with those of the capitalist order) and a working class, composed of manual workers (whose interests had historically been opposed to those of the capitalist order). This crude understanding became increasingly outmoded as the middle class expanded and fragmented. On the one hand, a powerful 'service class' of managers and professionals emerged, while on the other large swathes of routine non-manual work in the retail, administration, and public sectors were progressively 'proletarianized' (Braverman 1974). Meanwhile, the effect of new technologies meant the traditional manual working class began to shrink. And as class boundaries became more complex, the nature of labour markets in the more highly developed economies began to change as they became increasingly polarized between a core sector composed of highly skilled, highly paid and relatively secure jobs on the one hand and a peripheral sector composed of lower-skilled, poorly paid and insecure jobs on the other. The demand for new skills and flexible working patterns meant that workers could not necessarily expect to hold on to the same full-time job throughout their working life, as jobs, particularly in the peripheral sector, became increasingly casualized, short-term, and part-time. Commentators such as Hutton (1996) claimed that countries like Britain were turning into '40:30:30 societies', in which maybe 40 per cent of the working-age population were comfortably off, 30 per cent were systemically disadvantaged, while the 30 per cent in between lived with chronic insecurity.

As experiences of work have changed, so have our experiences of family. If labour markets have become more flexible, families have become more fluid (see Chapter 6). Countries like the UK have experienced a long-term decline in first marriage rates, a rise in cohabitation, a rise in divorce rates, and an increase in lone parenthood. There has also been a rising incidence of remarriage, reconstituted families, and stepfamilies, but also of single-person households. In part these changes reflect the extent to which increasing affluence for some has enhanced the scope of the choices available as to how to organize the way they live. In part, however, they reflect an increased riskiness about the nature of familial relationships. The propensity of the welfare state to guarantee support for children and to enable people in some circumstances to live independently of families (to defamilialize) contributes to what is referred to above as post-materialism (Inglehart 1990). Family relationships are no longer pragmatic alliances on which we must depend for our material survival (Gittins 1993) and the value we place on our intimate relationships has much more to do with their affective substance and the emotional support they provide (Beck and Beck-Gernsheim 1995). This makes such relationships more fragile. But if the meaning that families have in our everyday lives has been changing, the demographic context that surrounds such change has another consequence relating to relationships between the generations. The collective interdependency between the generations made possible by the welfare state is affected by the reality that we now have fewer babies, while living longer lives. It is becoming more difficult for an ever more numerous older generation to share risks with an ever shrinking younger generation (see Chapters 12 and 13).

But there is more to the risk society than this. What characterizes that which some refer to as the 'post-modern age' (Lyotard 1984) is a crisis of trust. The modernity that had been associated with the height of industrial capitalism was characterized by certainty that stemmed on the one hand from class solidarities, but on the other from the trust that people placed in science, technology, professional expertise, economic planning, and the political process. The risk society is characterized by uncertainty; by a focus on individualization (Beck and Beck-Gernsheim 2001) as a process by which we must each establish our life course not as an un-reflexive accommodation to established norms, but as a challenging individual project; by scepticism towards the

---

Box 19.5 **Policy responses to new social risks**

- **Education**: emphasis on vocational education and lifelong learning in order to sustain people's ability to update their skills and maintain their earning capacity throughout the life course.
- **Employment**: attempts to maximize labour market participation. Measures include labour market activation, welfare-to-work or 'workfare' policies that in some welfare regimes have been especially focused on lone parents. In several welfare regimes there have been attempts to address the problem of low-wage employment at the labour market periphery through the introduction of tax credits. Additionally, there have been attempts to promote work–family reconciliation or work–life balance arrangements—including provision for maternity and paternity pay, for parental leave and enhanced childcare provision—better to accommodate workers' lives to the demands of a flexible labour market.
- **Social security and pensions**: measures to promote personal savings, asset-based or private insurance provision, and fully funded pension schemes better to meet life course contingencies.
- **Health and social care**: ongoing or unresolved debates in most economically developed countries about how to establish sustainable funding mechanisms for provision for frail elderly people.

---

claims of science, professional wisdom, and regulatory systems. Science and technology have created environmental hazards. Welfare systems are not necessarily benevolent. Economic globalization has fuelled economic insecurity. Political leaders are no longer in control. The world is an uncertain and risky place.

The changing welfare state: the management of risk

In response, the role of the welfare state is evolving. But that evolution is a process at two levels. At one level the welfare state is responding explicitly to newly identified social risks. At another it is implicitly redefining its role in terms not of the provision of welfare, but the *management* of risk.

The welfare state's direct response to new social risks may be seen in a variety of initiatives (Bonoli 2005)—see Box 19.5.

At a deeper level, as has already been suggested, the welfare state is increasingly concerned about promoting individual responsibility and self-provisioning. It is a process that had already begun as a result of the neo-liberal ideological influences exhibited, in the UK for example, in policies that enabled public sector housing tenants to buy their homes and in policies that sought to address health inequalities through health promotion initiatives targeted at individual behaviour and lifestyles. But, especially in the era of public spending austerity that now follows the global financial crisis of 2008–9, it is to be anticipated that governments in all types of welfare regime will seek to shift responsibilities from the state to the individual (Callinicos 2010).

The welfare state will survive. The question is the extent to which its role will focus on the management of the risks its citizens face or on combating those risks. Most of life's hazards are foreseeable and may be commonly understood, but this does not mean that citizens can by themselves do much about them (see Cartoon 19.2).

Notions of risk management have invaded the institutions of the welfare state through the introduction of new managerialist principles which function to manage the organizational risks of those institutions (Hood et al. 2000), but also to promote a culture in which the welfare state citizen is constituted as, or themselves expect to become, a responsible risk manager. The question for social policy is on whose terms they are expected to manage.

Cartoon 19.2 Self-management of risk

Conclusion

This chapter has outlined four different ways in which the welfare state affects our experiences of the life course—from cradle to grave.

First, we have considered the direct influences upon our lives that the welfare state can have as an institution. As a creation of twentieth-century capitalism, the welfare state reinvented the citizen as an individual bearer of social rights: rights to receive such things as education, healthcare, and social security; rights once framed as collective demands, but which now became individual conditional entitlements. The conditions that attach to such rights affect the way in which they are experienced. What is more, the assumptions of policy-makers concerning the nature of the life course and the stages though which it normally progresses are reflected in the way that, on an everyday basis, our lives are supported and implicitly shaped by the welfare state and in which, on occasions, they may be controlled or explicitly directed.

Second, this chapter has considered the extent to which the welfare state provides the very means by which in advanced capitalist societies we now experience the interdependency by which our humanity is defined. The development of the welfare state has created a new kind of social interdependency. This can be experienced and understood in contradictory ways. In certain contexts, dependency on the welfare state is regarded negatively as a stigmatizing experience, despite the fact that the welfare state may actually play an important role in moderating the adverse effects of other forms of dependency, such as dependence on exploitative employers or within abusive family relationships. The welfare state is a vital mechanism by which in a highly complex industrialized society we can manage the ways in which we care for and about one another and by which we can exchange or redistribute resources.

Third, this chapter has considered the extent to which the welfare state has been failing or succeeding in accommodating social difference and the diverse experiences in life that different social groups might have. Biological differences associated with sex, phenotypes, and physical impairment are associated with gendered, racialized, and disabling social divisions that may be reflected in systemic social disadvantages. The welfare state may in some respects have exacerbated or perpetuated such disadvantage, but movements for the recognition of these (and other) forms of diversity are now reflected in critical debates about the way in which the welfare state may compensate for disadvantage and/or promote equality between different social and cultural groups.

Finally, the chapter has considered how changes in society are affecting our experiences of risk and how the welfare state might be changing. On the one hand, our experiences of life are changing as the nature of capitalism and the capitalist labour market evolve. On the other hand, the very achievements of the welfare state are at least partly implicated in fundamental cultural shifts that bear on how we live our lives, what we expect from families and the state, and our perceptions of the risks we face in life. These shifts are mirrored by processes of welfare state reform that increasingly stress not only social rights but also forms of co-responsibility; not just direct state provision, but the self-management of risk.

FURTHER READING

Beresford, P. and Turner, M., *It's Our Welfare* (London: NISW, 1997). The report of a small independent project, the Citizen's Commission on the Future of the Welfare State, that captures some of the everyday experiences of users of welfare state services.

Dean, H., *Understanding Human Need* (Bristol: The Policy Press, 2010). A recent text that addresses several key issues and debates relating to human interdependency and well-being.

Giddens, A., *Modernity and Self-Identity* (Cambridge: Polity Press, 1991). One of several accounts of the challenges posed to the welfare state by the changing significance of identity and perceptions of risk.

Leisering, L. and Leibfried, S., *Time and Poverty in Western Welfare States* (Cambridge: Cambridge University Press, 1999). An important attempt to connect welfare regime theory and understandings of the life course.

Lewis, G., Gewirtz, S., and Clarke, J. (eds), *Rethinking Social Policy* (London: Sage Publications, 2000). A collection of useful chapters addressing a range of issues associated with identity and the life course, including issues of gender, ethnicity, and disability.

USEFUL WEBSITES

Intute: a free online service to help find web resources for studies and research in a wide variety of subjects, including the social sciences: **www.intute.ac.uk/socialsciences/.**

New Economics Foundation: an independent think tank concerned with promoting 'real economic well-being': **www.neweconomics.org.**

Equality and Diversity Forum: a network of national organizations concerned with equal opportunities, social justice, community relations, and human rights: **www.edf.org.uk.**

Equality and Human Rights Commission: the UK's statutory body with responsibility for enforcing and promoting equality in relation to age, disability, gender, race, religion and belief, sexual orientation, and gender reassignment: **http://www.equalityhumanrights.com/.**

Centre for the Analysis of Risk and Regulation: a major interdisciplinary research group concerned with issue of risk and risk management: **www2.lse.ac.uk/researchAndExpertise/units/CARR/home.aspx.**

ESSAY QUESTIONS

1   In what ways might we as citizens be shaped by our experiences of the welfare state?

2   In what ways does the welfare state affect the nature of human dependency?

3   Has the welfare state been good:

- for women?
- for minority ethnic groups?
- for disabled people?

4   How can the welfare state help us to manage the risks we face in an uncertain world?

ONLINE RESOURCE CENTRE

For additional material and resources, please visit the Online Resource Centre at:
www.oxfordtextbooks.co.uk/orc/baldock4e/.

Researching social policy

Lavinia Mitton, Nick Manning, and Sarah Vickerstaff

Contents

Introduction

Study and research in social policy can have an influence on policy-makers and practitioners by monitoring and evaluating the policies of governments and other organizations in civil society. Indeed, it is frequently the link between analysis and practice which draws students to the subject of social policy in the first place. As a student of social policy you might be asked to prepare and present a case study; to undertake a literature review; or to research and write a substantial dissertation. Students can, through their research, contribute to knowledge or make their own recommendations for changes in policy.

In this chapter we shall first discuss research. We shall then discuss how to choose research topics and the kinds of approaches and methods which might be appropriate. We will also be concerned with the ethical considerations which apply when doing social policy research. Finally, we shall consider how to present the findings of research.

Learning outcomes

At the end of this chapter students should have familiarity with:

1 the nature of social research;
2 how to conduct a literature review and evaluate different sources of information;
3 some examples of qualitative and quantitative research methods and when it is appropriate to use them;
4 how to present their own research.

What is research?

To be defined as 'research', a piece of work must be carried out in a systematic, disciplined, and rigorous way using research methods appropriate to answering the specific research question posed.

Research in social policy is concerned with understanding social problems and what leads us to label an issue as a social problem. It is also concerned with the responses of governments, civil society, and individuals to social problems. It aims to provide evidence which can inform future policy or practice by influencing research 'users' such as academics, policy-makers, professionals (for example social workers and health workers), organized groups, the users of welfare services, and the general public.

Interest in evidence-based policy rests on the argument that we should be confident of successful outcomes before wasting public funds and has been particularly prominent in the fields of medicine and healthcare. This interest has led to pressures for researchers to make their work more useful and relevant, and for practitioners to undertake research (Locock and Boaz 2004). However, frequently it is not research findings alone that impact on policy and practice; the media and campaign groups also play a part in raising awareness and bringing about change, as does the political context (Wright et al. 2007). As Becker and Bryman (2004) explain, the relationship between research, policy-making, implementation, and practice is a complex one.

The direct influence of research evidence on decision-making can be tempered by factors such as financial constraints and decision makers' own experiential knowledge, and instead impact on policy in indirect ways, including shaping policy debate, as Elliott and Popay's (2000) study of local NHS policy-making found. Sometimes research of high quality will be ignored or fail to have influence if there is strong political resistance to its particular findings. In addition, policy researchers may be restricted from publishing as controversial reports are 'shelved' (Blackmore and Lauder 2005). Nevertheless, Bloor (2004) concludes that the addressing of social problems is a legitimate objective of social research and that, although the effectiveness of social research as an agency of social change may be somewhat limited, it is certainly not entirely ineffective.

Choosing a research question

Formulating research questions is the most critical, and, perhaps, the most difficult, part of any research design (Blaikie 2000: 58). One source of research questions in social policy is new legislation, or growing awareness of the problems facing a particular group in society. A second source of research questions is to look to our existing knowledge and understanding of a topic and identify gaps. Some research may be designed specifically to test a theory or proposition. Other research may set out to evaluate the outcomes or likely outcomes of specific policies or policy proposals. The following are important in deciding what you want to study:

1   First, choose a topic that interests you. Your research may involve many hours of work and you need motivation to stay committed to it.

2   Second, you should investigate what is already known in connection with a topic. Even apparently un-researched topics need to be assessed in the context of what we already know.

3   Third, you must be clearly focused. You need to move from a general topic of interest to formulating a particular research question.

4   Fourth, the research must be achievable. Although a research project is a substantial piece of work for a student, you are limited in the time and resources you have available, so your research will have to be small scale.

Literature reviews

A literature review is an assessment of our current state of knowledge about a topic. Conducting a literature review is necessary to familiarize yourself with the conceptual, theoretical, historical, and factual background to a subject and the gaps in existing knowledge. Projects similar or identical to yours may have already been undertaken and the findings published. You will have to take a different angle and justify why your research question is different from, or similar to, research already undertaken. A literature review will also provide you with an overview of the research methods that have been used to examine research questions similar to yours.

The skills required for undertaking literature reviews include the use of online literature searches and citation indices. Systematically reviewing and interpreting the existing literature on a subject is a form of research activity in its own right.

How to conduct a literature review

You will have to decide on keywords which you will use to search online databases. If you are a student you may have access to bibliographic databases of published literature through your college or university. Databases that are specifically focused on social policy and are freely accessible are listed at the end of this chapter.

When writing a literature review it is important to keep with your notes a full and accurate record of what you have read. This is crucial for referencing in your write-up. It is also inevitable that you will have to go back and recheck a particular point. Software exists to make the storing of your references and managing of your bibliography easier. Such a computer application simplifies the task of writing up your research as it can be used with MS Word to insert references into the text and automatically create a correctly formatted bibliography. It will also allow you to search your references by keyword and in some cases, import reference information directly from an online database during a literature search. Widely used applications include Endnote and Refworks.

Writing the literature review

As Silverman (2000) points out, it is a misconception of a literature review that it is a boring thing to be got out of the way at the start of your research. Instead, it should combine knowledge and critical thought and be interesting to read. It is necessary not to simply summarize each item, but to adopt a critical narrative by comparing them and constructing an overall story.

When writing a literature review you need to make judgements about what to include and what to exclude. You also need to reflect on the strengths and weaknesses of what you have read. A literature review has to demonstrate that all the main concepts, theories, theorists, and methodological approaches relevant to the topic have been identified, understood, and critically evaluated (Hart 1998).

You will have to evaluate your sources, showing sensitivity to their quality, as you will be dealing with materials that have a variety of purposes. Articles in academic journals are the outcome of rigorous quality control, usually having been blind peer-reviewed by two or more referees who do not know who the author is. Many articles submitted are not published because they are not considered good enough. Books by academic authors are also highly regarded, but it should be borne in mind that they are not always blind refereed. Professional periodicals, such as those in community care or social work, will give you an insight into the perspective of practitioners but articles are not strictly peer-reviewed and rarely address academic matters.

Much literature is available online, but when accessing an online resource it is imperative to critically assess its academic rigour. Online reports listed by *Social Policy Digest*, for instance, are likely to be authoritative because experts have put together that database. On the other hand, sites such as Wikipedia should not be taken at face value as a source of information because the identity of the authors is unknown. If you want to use Wikipedia, or other sites like it, you should also look at the sources cited in the articles to check the accuracy of the site's content. Babbie (2008) suggests questions you should ask yourself in evaluating quality of internet materials, such as: Who is the author? Does the site advocate a particular point of view? Do the data seem consistent with data from other sites?

Other sources of information on social policy issues

Publications from outside the academic mainstream are also accessible. They are often written by people who are grappling with practical policy issues on a daily basis. They often contribute greatly to the study of social policy. This chapter provides an introduction to the main sources of information on social policy issues outside those produced by government and commercial publishers. Instead, it focuses on voluntary organizations, think tanks, and foundations.

Such material has a contribution to make to the social policy debate. Compared with academic publications, it is likely to be much more up to date. However, it may not display much awareness of ongoing academic debates. It is more likely to be practical than theoretical in orientation. In addition, a publication will also have been written with a particular purpose in view; a pressure group may want to persuade the government for or against a certain policy, and think tanks are often linked to particular political parties or ideologies. This should be kept in mind when using such material for an essay or dissertation. Always ask yourself the question: Who wrote this and do they have a particular agenda?

At the end of this chapter there is a list of research organizations which are particularly useful sources.

If your research extends beyond a literature review, you will need to choose methods for gathering and analysing data. The term 'data' can apply to any type of information resulting from counting, measuring, and observing. A project may be based on data gathered using several research methods. Data can exist or be recorded in quantitative or numerical form, or be qualitative or discursive (either written or spoken).

Qualitative research methods

Interviews

Interviews are a commonly used qualitative method in social research and we are all used to seeing or hearing people being interviewed on the media. We may also have some experience of being interviewed ourselves to check our eligibility for a service or benefit or for a job. An interview is a conversation with a purpose and it seems obvious that if we want to find out about how a social policy is working or whether someone is struggling with an unmet need, then talking to them about it seems a logical place to start. Although apparently easy and natural, interviews can vary considerably and in a research context it is important to think about the purpose of the research and whether an interview is likely to elicit the kind of information that will answer our research question.

Different types of interview Interviews can vary from the relatively formal structured interviews in which a respondent is asked a set of predetermined questions, through semi-structured interviews with a looser question guide, through to oral history interviews where the person being interviewed is allowed to talk at length and in their own way about the topic at hand. We will concentrate here on semi-structured interviews, the most common type used in social policy research.

Semi-structured interviews involve: asking the same questions of all those involved; putting the kind and form of questions through a process of development to ensure their topic focus; prompting interviewees if they have not dealt spontaneously with one of the areas of interest (Gillham 2005).

Why use semi-structured interviews? They are a good method when you want to get in-depth information on a particular subject from the perspective of the individual being interviewed. As a technique, they assume that the individual has a privileged and interesting perspective on the subject in hand. They allow you to get behind a topic that perhaps has been revealed by other research

> ## Box 20.1 **Steps for in-depth interviewing**
>
> - Selection of research topic and consideration of available research methods: choose interviewing if you want to focus on the relationship of individuals to particular social and cultural contexts.
> - Prepare an interview guide or interview schedule: a list of questions or topics that will be covered in the interview.
> - It is desirable to pilot the schedule by doing some test interviews to see if the questions 'work'. Fowler (2002) summarizes some of the problems which might arise.
> - Select respondents: think about the numbers and types of interviewees that you want. For example, is it important to balance female and male respondents? Is age, race, or class a factor that needs to be included? How will you find your respondents?
> - Arrange the time and location of the interview; have a recorder ready to tape the interview if the respondent is happy to be recorded.
> - Make sure that respondents can give informed consent, that they understand what the interview is about, that the contents will be confidential, and that they are at liberty to terminate the process at any point (see ethical considerations below).
> - Transcribe the interview and develop a strategy for data analysis.

methods, to reach a deeper understanding of the processes affecting the issue. To give an example, we know from statistical data that the take-up of means-tested benefits is always lower than the take-up of universal benefits in the sense that some people who are entitled to the benefit do not claim it. To understand this more fully, a study based on interviewing claimants and potential claimants might give us an insight into why people do not claim when they are entitled to. Of course, there are always practical constraints on the number of people who can be interviewed and therefore it is very important to select our respondents carefully.

Question design In any interview you are likely to use a mixture of closed and open-ended questions. What you want to do is balance the need for information with trying to allow the interview to develop naturally into a useful and interesting conversation for both sides. You need background information about the respondent and you also want to put their answers about your particular issue of concern in a broader context. You need to use the skills of interviewing, which include: probing, clarification, showing appreciation and understanding, asking for examples, and carrying the narrative forward (Gillham 2005).

You must use language that is easy to understand without being patronizing, and avoid asking leading questions such as:

I expect you didn't claim your benefit because you didn't know about it, is that right?

Although in many ways an interview is a very natural situation, you must be aware that power differentials and social position can play a part and distort the answers you get. You may be seen as powerful or of a particular class or gender, and therefore the respondent may defer to you or otherwise react less to your questions and more to who they perceive you to be. Your respondent does not owe you anything and if they do not want to answer a question or answer it in a way that obscures what they really think, there is little that you can do about it. If you are dealing with sensitive issues, you have a duty to make sure that the respondent knows where to go for help or guidance if the interview raises difficult issues for them.

As with any social science research method, there are disadvantages to interviews. As noted earlier, there is a limit to the number of people who can be interviewed and this can reduce the

---

Box 20.2 **Different types of questions**

Most questions used in semi-structured and unstructured interviewing tend to be open rather than closed. Closed questions are those in which the respondent is offered a predetermined list of answers. An example is:

How would you describe the state of your health over the past 12 months? a) Good; b) Fairly good; c) Not very good.

This gives the respondent three options and the interviewer will record answer a, b, or c as appropriate. This same question could easily be posed as an open question:

How would you describe the state of your health over the past 12 months?

In this case no options are offered to the respondent and the interviewer records exactly what the interviewee said. Oppenhiem (1992) sums up the advantages and disadvantages of closed and open questions, while Dillman, Smyth, and Christian (2009) provide many examples of well-constructed questions.

---

representativeness and generalizability of what you find out. You have to take into account that those being interviewed may have forgotten things or simply invented what they said to you; they may not be reliable witnesses. It is only by doing a number of interviews that you can begin to situate individual responses into a wider social frame. The responses you get will only be as good as the questions you ask, so preparation and pilot testing beforehand are very important.

The final stage is analysing the interviews and making sense of them: what do they tell you? Your analysis can be inductive (theory developing) or deductive (theory testing) (see Blaikie 2000: 102–7).

Focus groups

A focus group is comprised of preselected individuals who have similar characteristics or who share some experience of the research topic. The original application of this method was market research, but it has since been used extensively as a technique in public consultation. Focus groups typically involve the groups meeting for an hour and a half to two hours. They usually meet once, but can reconvene again, especially if the topic area is unfamiliar to the participants. The discussion is led by a moderator or facilitator. There will be variation in how far the discussion is structured, depending on how strongly the researcher has a sense of the issues to be explored.

When to use focus groups The use of focus groups is a research technique that collects data through group *interaction* on a topic determined by the researcher. What is key is that participants contribute their own views and experience, but they also hear from other people. Participants prompt others to reveal more. Multiple views can be elicited and this can help to explain what lies behind apparently contradictory views. The interaction in a group discussion is the source of the data as well as the individual responses to questions. This is different from a group interview, where responses are directed to the interviewer (Morgan 1998a).

Focus group participants are less influenced by the researcher than might be the case in a one-to-one interview, and in that sense it is a more natural environment. Focus groups can be distinguished from procedures that use multiple participants but do not allow interactive discussions, and

> Box 20.3 **Some applications of focus groups**
>
> - To explore ideas, opinions, views, feelings, attitudes, experiences. and reactions
> - To explore new topics about which there is not an existing body of knowledge
> - To see how people respond to views other than their own
> - To elicit a multiplicity of views and discover the range of views
> - To reduce power differences between researcher and respondents
> - To find out how much respondents know about a topic
> - To gain information about a wider range of individuals in a shorter time
> - To feed back the results of surveys, to assess the impact of results, and to consider implementation

methods that collect data from naturally occurring group discussions where no one acts as a moderator.

Advantages and limitations Advantages of using focus groups are that they enable the researcher to elicit respondents' answers in a way which would not be possible with other methods, such as observation, one-to-one interviews, or postal questionnaires, and they provide insights into the sources of complex behaviours and motivations. Further, a large amount of data can be collected in a short time and group discussion is always something more than just the sum of separate individual interviews. Finally, people may find it interesting and empowering to be involved in a focus group.

On the other hand, the limitations of focus groups are that the range of topics that can be researched effectively in groups is limited. They are time consuming and require a great deal of preparation. In addition, who is present in the group may affect what people say. A focus group will not achieve the research aims if what are needed are detailed personal accounts and if individuals are not comfortable saying what they think in a group. Interaction between the participants may produce false levels of consensus, or people may profess to hold views which in reality they do not hold and which do not correspond to what they do in practice. Shy or inarticulate people may not be able to express their views, so a focus group may be dominated by a small number of individuals. Lastly, another limitation is that contributions to such a discussion are not confidential, so some topics have to be avoided.

Selecting focus group participants The ideal size of group depends on the sensitivity of issues to be discussed and the amount participants are likely to have to say. Usually there are five to eight participants, although there can be from four to 15. A large group discussion is harder to transcribe (although videoing the discussion or having an observer take notes are also options). In a large group, participation is more likely to be uneven.

The composition of a group will be critical in shaping the group dynamic. Some diversity aids the discussion but too much can inhibit it. In choosing the participants you will have to take account of factors known to have a bearing on the subject. Typically the researcher considers the ethnic group, age, gender, and income of the participants. It is also important that participants know sufficient about the topic.

Practical considerations Running focus groups involves a substantial amount of forward planning (Morgan 1998b). For example, you will have to think about how participants should be contacted and recruited. How can the research be presented to them as valid and responsible? Where and at what time should the group take place? You will also have to think about practical issues such as refreshments and how to accommodate other people who come with the participants.

Moderating a focus group Moderating a focus group is a very skilled job and whole books have been written on the subject (e.g. Krueger 1998a). It is important to be non-judgemental, and to draw out less confident people. You need to keep the discussion moving along, but to allow time for a topic when it is going well.

In guiding the discussion, the basic principles are to:

- use simple, *open* questions;
- avoid leading questions;
- pose questions which get people talking to each other;
- address questions to the group rather than individuals;
- give the clear message that there are no right or wrong answers;
- avoid expressing points of view, or showing surprise or shock;
- not intervene too much, thereby disrupting the interaction that was the point of the group.

In other words, the questions should elicit discussion, debate, and dialogue, not yes/no answers (Krueger 1998b). You should also pay attention to non-verbal responses such as shaking heads or muttering, which will not be picked up on the recording. To avoid an abrupt finish, you should signal when the group is on its final topic. You should always conclude by thanking the participants and stressing how helpful the discussion has been.

Observational methods

Ethnography means literally the 'mapping of culture'. It was developed in the early twentieth century by social anthropologists. Early examples include Malinowski's work in the Trobriand Islands, published in 1922 as *Argonauts of the Western Pacific*. This was the first study to be based on a sustained pattern of fieldwork in which the anthropologist gained an understanding of the totality of a culture through a fully 'lived experience' of it. This idea of field-based observation retained an association with indigenous cultures as being not only culturally and symbolically more straightforward, and hence amenable to observation, but also as a blueprint for the subsequent evolution of more 'complex' Western societies. In the 1950s, bolstered by Emile Durkheim's theories of the 'functionality' of society (Durkheim 1964)—in which all human activities, even those considered 'deviant', are bound together in maintaining the social whole—ethnographers became more adventurous in their choice of subject.

Observation could range from the passive recording of public social actions of all kinds, to the adoption of a particular role in a small society to gain entry to less public places. This is richly illustrated in the work of Erving Goffman, who became the first ethnographer to study a modern Western institution in depth: the mental hospital 'asylum' (1961). Goffman posed as a physical education assistant whilst collecting fieldnotes: a tactic which has subsequently been termed 'covert' research, as it involves the ethnographer being present in the chosen culture under a pretence. He investigated strategies for coping with institutional life on the part of both staff and inmates; he looked at the 'ceremonies' which brought the two groups together and the consequences of this mixing; he developed the idea of a 'moral career' of the inmate/patient as they progressed from lack of repentance, to guilt and remorse, and ultimately discharge as responsibility was accepted for past actions; and he depicted the 'hospital underlife': the way in which official rules and regulations were subtly altered, undermined, and bypassed by internal regimes of the exchange of goods both physical (tobacco) or symbolic (prestige, a reputation for 'honesty' or as 'a grass').

In more recent years, the ethnographic method has been applied to all kinds of modern social settings, including the fields of health and medicine (the ceremonial order of the clinic), education (classroom teacher–pupil interactions), social care (life in old people's homes), and social security (poverty survival strategies). The general approach has been to use this method to explore the structures and processes in complex situations where the researcher is uncertain of the way in which those in the field, both clients and professions, typically interact, make decisions, and so on. This kind of study continues to dig out the hidden processes in such settings that more formal data collection (for example, through financial transactions or psychological scales) can miss. In addition, observational methods can lead to the development of new 'grounded theory' (Glaser and Strauss 1967), which could in principle be tested out more widely through quantitative methods. The commissioning of contemporary policy-related research by government ministries and research councils has shown growing enthusiasm for this method.

However, there are limitations to this method. The obvious one is that it is difficult to generalize from the specific circumstances of the observation to other settings and circumstances that we might wish to know about. How far do other doctors, patients, teachers, pupils, old people, carers, poor people, and so on act, think, and talk in the ways observed? How can the research observer be sure that what they see is in some sense typical? To what extent do the observer's own preconceptions bias the things that are recorded or the sense that is made of them? One way of dealing with this issue is for the observer to be more active in their participation, so that they can explore the realities that they think they are seeing by, for example, changing what they see, which might then expose the hidden assumptions of the other participants. This was famously used by Harold Garfinkel (1967) in his creation of an approach he called 'ethnomethodology'. In it he violated unstated but assumed norms, such as the social distance between individuals in public places, to see how other people reacted and thereby revealed the norms of public order. These norms are regularly violated in, for example, medical practice, but under a special set of rules which gives doctors dispensation from their normal application. A further addition widely used in observation methods is to supplement them with interviews, to explore further, and to check the significance of the observations gathered.

Documentary and archive research

It is easy to assume that social policy researchers are solely concerned with current and future policies. However, political actors are often constrained in the policies they can implement by the institutions they inherit, and therefore much policy-making is incremental in nature. Often history matters in explaining and understanding contemporary social policy.

Published and unpublished documents There are many different types of document, published and unpublished, historical and contemporary. Published documents include books, government reports, and policy documents. Researchers can also analyse newspaper coverage for information on the debates surrounding how a policy was implemented. A newspaper indexing service, which may be available through your college or university, will help this type of research.

Unpublished sources include personal documents, government records, and the archives of voluntary organizations. For example, there exist archives of the papers of political figures, such as those of Margaret Thatcher, held at Churchill College, Cambridge. It is harder to research the perspective of ordinary people, but Mass Observation has collected the views of a large number of people on many subjects for much of the post-war period in an archive held at the University of Sussex. Increasingly, researchers are finding the internet a rich source of information on people's views as they write about themselves in their blogs and on digital networking sites. The unpublished records of government departments such as memos, correspondence, and meetings of minutes, are held at the UK government's official archive, the National Archives. Local record offices may also hold personal papers and local government archival materials. Usually there is a rule that government records are only made publicly available after 30 years has elapsed. Voluntary organizations and pressure groups may keep their own archives or have them deposited elsewhere. For example, the Trades Union Congress (TUC) archive is housed at Warwick University.

Reading the documents You will need to think about the order in which you will tackle reading documents. You can start with the most general and accessible published documents, many of which are available on the internet, so that you are prepared with full background knowledge of the larger picture and are able to interpret the historical context before visiting an archive. On the other hand, if you already have a tightly focused research question, it may be better to begin with the documents that seem most relevant to your specific topic and from that identify the further reading you need to do. As Denscombe (2007) remarks, for the purposes of research, documentary sources should never be accepted at face value. You will need to consider how to weigh the evidence by reflecting on who wrote the document, with what purpose, and how they constructed the policy problem.

Archival documents can be very time consuming to read. However, they can provide insights into how a policy decision was reached. In writing up the history of social policy it is easy to get absorbed in detail and produce a chronology of events. However, the contribution of historical research must be to explain events, and the researcher must be clear as to how history matters in their analysis of the documents.

Methods of analysis

Qualitative data may be analysed either by coding them in ways which make it possible to apply quantitative techniques, or by a variety of techniques for interpreting the content and the themes which emerge within discursive material. The procedures involved in analysing qualitative data are to collate the data, such as field notes and transcripts. You have to identify key themes, phrases, or ideas. This is usually called coding the data. Boyatzis (1998) discusses of the features of 'good' code.

Coding the data can be done manually or by using software developed for the analysis of textual material, such as NVivo, which makes the process of marking the (frequently voluminous) data with codes and later searching the documents by code easier than by using a paper-based method (Bryman 2008, provides an introduction to NVivo). Whatever the method of managing the data, it is important that the researcher works from the data, drawing conclusions supported by them, rather than picking out material which supports their own pre-existing beliefs.

Quantitative research methods

Quantitative methods are ones which involve numbers and measuring. A quantitative data set is a collection of observations or measurements (variables) from a study of cases (e.g. individuals, households, businesses). The data set contains the variables for each case. The most typical data set contains data collected from a survey. Researchers using quantitative methods need to consider issues such as the reliability of their measurements and to what groups or populations the findings can be generalized.

Cross-sectional and longitudinal surveys

Surveys can be designed in several ways. Two common designs are cross-sectional and longitudinal. In a cross-sectional survey design, data are collected from respondents at a single point in time; this is the typical design for a large-scale social survey. Unlike a cross-sectional survey, the aim of a longitudinal survey is usually to deepen understanding of change over time. There is a basic distinction between the panel design and the cohort design. In a panel design a survey is carried out with the same respondents at least twice, and sometimes many more times. Rose (2000) provides an overview of the methods used in panel studies and examples of panel study findings. A cohort design, on the other hand, takes people born in a particular period and follows them up at intervals. Longitudinal studies suffer from the problem of attrition, that is, drop-outs, as former respondents decline to continue their involvement, die, or move away, and cannot be traced.

Sampling

Quantitative researchers typically want to be able to generalize their findings beyond the group surveyed. This involves surveying a sample that is representative of the population from which the sample was selected. Researchers therefore have to pay attention to how to draw their sample. There are two broad sampling methods: probability and non-probability sampling.

Probability sampling In probability sampling each member of the population from which the sample is drawn has an equal chance of being included. Conveniently, when probability sampling has been used, statistical theory can allow us to say with a specific degree of confidence that, based on the survey result, the true figure (for example, the average value) lies within a range of values. The variability of the population will affect the precision of the estimate of the true figure, as will the sample size: the larger the sample, the more accurate the estimate (see Blaikie 2008: 208–13 for a discussion of how large a sample needs to be).

In simple random sampling each unit in the population (such as individuals or businesses) has an equal probability of being selected for the survey. It requires a list of the members of the population, known as the sampling frame. There are various methods available for randomly selecting a sample from this list. For example, a computer can be used to randomly generate a sample.

In stratified sampling the population is split into subgroups known as strata. Within each subgroup, selection is still made at random. This sampling method can be used to ensure that certain groups are represented in the sample. For example, stratification by ethnic group can ensure that there are sufficient numbers of black respondents for robust statistical analysis of this subgroup. Since black individuals will have a higher chance of being selected under this method, weighting adjustments are made to take this into account in the analysis.

The last method of probability sampling that will be considered here is cluster sampling. For example, in a survey of pupils, a sample of schools might be selected. This involves the notion that the population units (pupils) can be aggregated into higher units (schools). Carrying out the survey at a limited number of school sites would minimize fieldwork costs. Such a survey might also employ multi-stage sampling, in which pupils to be invited to take part in the survey are chosen at random once schools have been selected.

Non-probability sampling Sometimes probability samples cannot be used, for example where no sampling frame is available. In these cases the sample has to be drawn using non-probability sampling procedures in which the researcher exercises judgement about the units to include. In non-probability sampling each member of the population from which the sample is drawn does not have an equal chance of being included in the sample. The credibility of research based on these methods depends very much on its objectives. Four main types of non-probability sampling will be considered here: convenience sampling, purposive sampling, snowball sampling and quota sampling. Convenience sampling and snowball sampling are mainly used in qualitative research in which the ability to generalize is less of a concern than in quantitative research

A convenience sample is one that happens to be available to the researcher. The problem with such a sampling strategy is that it is impossible to generalize the findings, as the researcher does not know whether the sample is representative of the population. The element of deliberate selection by the researcher and the fact of his or her association with the chosen respondents, or their accessibility, can seriously compromise the research (Aldridge and Levine 2001). However, sometimes a convenience sample is the only one available. It may also be an appropriate technique to use when piloting a questionnaire.

Purposive sampling is a technique in which researchers purposely choose respondents who, in their opinion, are relevant to the project because of their knowledge. For example, 'key informants' who have expertise or can offer useful information might be interviewed.

Snowball sampling is an approach in which the researcher approaches a small group of respondents initially, and asks them to suggest other potential respondents within their social network. These respondents are next asked whether they can recommend further contacts to the researcher, and so on, until the desired sample size is reached. As with convenience sampling, it is impossible to generalize from such a sample (Aldridge and Levine 2001). Therefore, this technique is particularly used for exploratory studies, or when researching very specific or small groups that would be hard to reach or difficult to identify otherwise because of the absence of a sampling frame (Babbie 2008).

Quota sampling aims to achieve a sample that reflects the target population in terms of categories such as gender, ethnicity, age group, socio-economic group, and so on. However, unlike a stratified sample, once the numbers to be surveyed in each of these combinations of categories (strata) are decided, respondents are not selected randomly but by the interviewer. For example, the interviewer may be told to find 10 white females aged 25–34. The interviewer could do this by standing in a town centre and approaching people who seem superficially to fit that category, and this is a technique often used in market research. This will plainly not achieve a representative sample. Nevertheless, this technique may be justified when carrying out exploratory work or testing a questionnaire. It can also be used when the focus is on gaining understanding by surveying respondents with a range of characteristics.

Questionnaires and structured interviews

There are several elements involved in designing a survey. For example, decisions have to be made about whether a questionnaire will be administered by an interviewer or by self-completion, how the survey questions will be designed, and how the data collected will be coded and edited. This section explores these tasks.

Interviewer-administered and self-completion questionnaires A questionnaire administered by an interviewer can either take place face to face or over the telephone. In either case the interviewer can record the interviewees' responses on a paper questionnaire or into a computer-based questionnaire. An advantage of face to face interviewing is that often the response rate is higher than when carrying out a telephone survey. It is easier to encourage an individual to take part and to engage a respondent in a longer interview face to face. Telephone interviews tend to be shorter. Further, a face-to-face interview may be called for if the interviewer needs to use visual aids. On the other hand, the advantage of telephone interviews is that they are cheaper to carry out because the interviewer does not have to travel.

A self-completion questionnaire is another option. This involves the respondent completing a questionnaire on their own. This is cheaper than employing interviewers. Self-completion questionnaires can be distributed in paper format, as a program on a laptop computer, or as an e-mail or internet-based survey. A drawback of paper-based methods is that there is potential for more errors in filling in the questionnaire than if it were done by an interviewer. In consequence, the questionnaire design must be as simple as possible. The strengths and weaknesses of both methods are usefully summarized in de Vaus (2002: 132).

Internet surveys Self-completion internet surveys can consist of an online questionnaire accessible via a web page, sent as e-mail, or sent as an e-mail attachment. Responses from a large number of people can be collected relatively cheaply (Denscombe 2007). Another advantage of online surveys is that questions can automatically be asked only of a subgroup (usually determined by answers to previous filter questions). This is quite complicated to do on a paper questionnaire in which there is a risk of respondents being confused about which questions they should answer. With an online survey, automatic checks for respondent errors can also be built in, and with some software, preliminary analysis of the data can be conducted. The principal drawback of internet-based surveys is the uncertainty over whether a survey of internet users can be used for generalization (Sarantakos

contemporary. Its website is **www.data-archive.ac.uk**. Registration and an undertaking to use the data responsibly are normally conditions for obtaining access.

A disadvantage of this research method is that, inevitably, the data were collected for a different purpose from the one the researcher has. Therefore, the questions asked in the survey may not elicit the information the researcher ideally would like to know, or the sample may not be ideal for their purposes. You also need access to a computer with software suitable for analysing large data sets and some skill in how to use the software. It is very important to know well the data you wish to use, and understanding the structure of the data can be time consuming, particularly when it is supplied as several files.

However, secondary analysis of large-scale surveys has the advantage that it is cheap, as access to the data from the UK Data Archive can be provided free. Where a survey has been in place for several years, the researcher has the opportunity to analyse change over time. It can also enable the researcher to carry out analysis on a representative sample, which it would be impossible to survey themselves.

Methods of analysis

Once gathered, data must be analysed. The patterns and relationships within quantitative data may be analysed using statistical techniques, be they simple or complex. With software such as SPSS, the statistical manipulation of quantitative data is relatively straightforward (see Bryman 2008 for a guide to getting started in SPSS).

There is not space in this book to illustrate the different types of statistical analysis which can be performed on quantitative data using computer software, and there are many textbooks and websites available that go into far more detail than is possible here. This section will provide a brief overview of the initial techniques that a researcher might use, without delving into the statistical theories underlying these methods and their more technical aspects. It is possible to make a preliminary exploration of patterns and trends using the relatively simple techniques described here. In any case, it is always a good idea to start with simple analysis to avoid wasting time on more sophisticated analysis than may be necessary.

The types of statistics that are discussed in this section are often referred to as descriptive statistics, meaning that they just summarize the results and no attempt is made to draw inferences from them.

First, simple averages can be calculated, such as arithmetic means, medians, and modes. The spread of the data can be determined by looking at the range between maximum and minimum values. Any outliers should be investigated in case they are a coding error. Variation in the data can be measured using the standard deviation for differences about the means. If the data are a time series it is relatively simple to produce a graph showing trends over time, which enables the researcher to identify peaks and troughs.

Data can be collated into groups, such as social class or ethnic group, so that the magnitude of the numbers can be understood and the groups with the lowest and highest values can be identified. These figures may be displayed in the form of a frequency table, as in Table 20.1, which shows some hypothetical data.

Cross-tabulating data shows the results of two or more methods of classification in a table also known as a contingency table. One variable (for example, economic activity status) is tabulated across the other variable (for example, sex), as shown in Table 20.2.

However, it is difficult to judge the extent to which males have a higher employment rate than females because there are so many more males than females in the data set. It is therefore desirable to express the numbers as percentages, as shown in Table 20.3. In this case the numbers are *column* percentages, which show the breakdown of economic activity for males and for females. A cross-tabulation giving *row* percentages would, in this instance, give the breakdown by sex for each economic activity category. Figures in tables can be presented in charts, which can make the information easier to understand.

Table 20.1 Frequency of economic activity status of adults aged 16+

Economic activity status	Frequency	Percentage (%)
In employment	817	59.5
Unemployed	54	3.9
Inactive	503	36.6
Total	1374	100.0

Table 20.2 Frequency of economic activity status of adults aged 16+, by sex

Economic activity status	Sex		Total
	Male	Female	
In employment	563	254	817
Unemployed	38	16	54
Inactive	285	218	503
Total	886	488	1374

Table 20.3 Frequency of economic activity status of adults aged 16+, by sex

Economic activity status	Sex		Total (%)
	Male (%)	Female (%)	
In employment	63.5	52.0	59.5
Unemployed	4.3	3.3	3.9
Inactive	32.2	44.7	36.6
Total	100.0	100.0	100.0

A key concern can be to determine the strength of any association between variables. A basic technique for initial exploration of relationships is to draw a scatter diagram. This will show whether there are any interesting patterns which deserve further investigation. The strength of an association can be measured using a correlation coefficient. Another gauge of strength of association is the chi-squared test. This calculation shows whether there is any statistical association between the answers given to a pair of questions and is particularly useful for analysing results from opinion surveys. A good source of further information on basic statistics for social research is Denscombe (2007).

It is important to note that the statistical techniques outlined in this section do not tell us about the direction of causality. In other words, the researcher may find an association between two variables, but this does not imply that one variable is the cause of change in the other. For example, there may be an association between poor health and low income in survey data, but we cannot infer from this whether poor health is the cause of low income, or the other way round. Indeed, there may be a third factor that influences them both.

Research ethics

All social research involves ethical considerations, and social policy research is often concerned with particularly vulnerable people. Your research may raise ethical issues, especially if you are dealing with sensitive or stressful subject matter or are seeking access to children or users of welfare services.

Universities will have ethical guidelines or codes of practice which staff and students are required to follow, and they usually have ethics committees to which research proposals must be submitted for approval. Some of kinds of project may require ethical approval from other bodies. For example, any project which collects data from or about NHS patients must be considered by a local research ethics committee.

If your research involves respondents directly answering questionnaires, taking part in interviews, or allowing themselves to be observed, it is essential that their participation should be on the basis of their informed consent (Israel and Hay 2006). Not only should they agree to take part, but they should understand the purposes of the project and that participation is voluntary (de Vaus 2002). You will need to prepare a leaflet or letter explaining your research. Denscombe (2007) provides an example. Wiles et al. (2007) discuss the factors that make the issue of obtaining informed consent problematic, especially in research involving members of groups that are commonly characterized as 'vulnerable', such as children and people with learning disabilities.

It is often important to undertake to protect the confidentiality of people or organizations taking part, to make sure that you do not pass on information about them which they would wish to keep confidential, or disclose their identity in any report or publication if they wish to remain anonymous (de Vaus 2002; Israel and Hay 2006).

At a more general level, all students have a responsibility to act ethically at all times. Students must also be responsible for the way they represent their college or university as they go about doing their research. They must take into account their own welfare and not place themselves in dangerous situations.

Writing up your findings

'Writing up' is an integral part of the research process, not something tagged on at the end (Denscombe 2007). The skills involved in presenting findings are among the most important you will learn. The ability to provide clear, concise, and relevant information is required well beyond college or university. Research that does not come to the attention of policy-makers and practitioners cannot inform decision-making. How research is communicated to target audiences is therefore critical to whether it can have an influence.

Your report should:

- explain how you first identified and defined the question or problem which the dissertation addresses;
- set out the conceptual or theoretical framework you decided to use and why;
- outline the background provided by the literature review, the issues raised, and any conclusions you may have drawn from the literature or from other secondary sources.

If your project entailed an original empirical investigation, it should:

- describe the research design and methods used, and the way you analysed the resulting data: readers should be given all the information they need to evaluate the research;
- explain any limitations or constraints on the dissertation, and the implications these might have for the reliability or validity of the findings;

- not make too many claims for the data;
- set out and discuss your findings;
- provide conclusions and, if appropriate, recommendations for action.

You will also need to decide the form of the 'story' you want to tell about your research, and structure your data chapters accordingly, as Silverman (2000: 248) explains. If you are presenting the results of analysis of quantitative data, you should use tables when readers need actual numbers or when you wish to show three or more data series together. It is desirable to have explanatory text relating to a table, but you should also ensure that it is independently intelligible by specifying the:

- full title;
- table number;
- column headings and row labels;
- units;
- descriptive statistics, for example totals, averages;
- sources.

Tables should also be simplified by rounding numbers and only specifying figures to the number of decimal places necessary. Numbers should be in meaningful ranges, so very big numbers and fractions of 1 should be avoided. It is possible to express very large numbers as numbers of thousands, for example. If you wish to use charts, it is important to choose the right type of chart for the data. For example, a pie chart looks crowded with more than six segments; it would be better to use a bar chart in such a case. You can add numbers and text to your charts to strengthen your message. Denscombe (2007) provides a more detailed checklist for the presentation of quantitative data.

Conclusion

The opportunity to undertake extended essays or research is an important component of study at college or university. The value of doing research lies in the experience it offers in independent study, the application of theory to real-world situations, the use of research and analysis skills, and report writing. It should be an enjoyable opportunity to investigate in depth a topic which really interests you.

📖 FURTHER READING

There are a vast number of books on social research methods, but one specifically aimed at social policy students is **Becker, S. and Bryman, A.** (eds) (2004), *Understanding Research for Social Policy and Practice: Themes, Methods and Approaches*, Policy Press.

Other excellent texts are **Bryman, A.** (2008), *Social Research Methods*, 3rd edn, Oxford University Press and **Gilbert, N.** (ed.) (2008), *Researching Social Life*, 3rd edition, Sage.

@ USEFUL WEBSITES

www.socscidiss.bham.ac.uk: a companion site for undergraduate dissertations in sociology, anthropology, politics, social policy, social work, and criminology.

Databases focused on social policy

The following databases are freely accessible:

- Welfare Reform on the Web. This is produced by the British Library. The library scans the press, social science books, and government publications, and trade and academic journals to identify relevant material. It then produces detailed abstracts to give an overview of the research literature. **www.bl.uk/collections/social/sswelfare.html**.
- Social Policy Digest. This is a fully searchable source of information about current events across the whole social policy field. The Digest provides a commentary on changes in social welfare legislation and a review of the major reports and surveys published by government departments, leading think tanks, and voluntary bodies. Go to the Cambridge University Press page for *Journal of Social Policy* and look for the link.
- Social Care Online. This is a searchable database of literature on social care: **www.scie-socialcareonline.org.uk**.
- The King's Fund Library Database. This is a searchable database of literature on policy and management of health and social care services: **www.kingsfund.org.uk/library/index.html**.

Further sources of information on social policy issues

- National Centre for Social Research (NatCen). This is the largest independent social research institute in Britain. It carries out research into all areas of social policy on behalf of a range of public bodies. Publications are mainly policy evaluations. **www.natcen.ac.uk**
- Joseph Rowntree Foundation (JRF). The JRF is one of the largest social policy research and development charities in the UK. Its website has four-page summaries ('Findings') of research projects and reports, some of which can be downloaded free of charge. **www.jrf.org.uk**
- Institute for Public Policy Research (IPPR). This is a prominent independent think tank on the centre left. It publishes reports on a wide range of social policy issues. **www.ippr.org.uk**
- Compass. This is an ideas-based political pressure group aiming to develop a more coherent and radical programme for a progressive left government. **www.compassonline.org.uk**
- Fabian Society. This is a left-of-centre think tank, affiliated to the Labour Party. **www.fabian-society.org.uk**
- Institute of Economic Affairs (IEA). This is a free market think tank. Its stated goal is to explain free market ideas to anyone interested in public policy. **www.iea.org.uk**
- Centre for Policy Studies (CPS). Think tank founded by Sir Keith Joseph and Margaret Thatcher in 1974 to champion economic liberalism in Britain, which has since played a pivotal role in the dissemination of free market economics. It promotes rolling back of the state. **www.cps.org.uk**
- Adam Smith Institute (ASI). Think tank which promotes free market policies and 'researches practical ways to inject choice and competition into public services, extend personal freedom, reduce taxes, prune back regulation, and cut government waste'. **www.adamsmith.org**
- Social Market Foundation (SMF). Think tank which promotes market-based reform of state healthcare, education, and welfare provision. **www.smf.co.uk/site/smf**
- Institute for the Study of Civil Society (CIVITAS). Right-wing group seeking to promote a 'better' division of responsibilities between government and civil society (i.e. mutual, church, and charitable organizations, informal support of neighbours and the family). **www.civitas.org.uk**
- Policy Exchange. Official network for promoting new ideas for Conservative public policy, including social policy. **www.policyexchange.org.uk**
- The Smith Institute. Independent think tank. Its work centres on the policy implications arising from the interactions of equality, enterprise, and equity. **www.smith-institute.org.uk**
- Centre for the Analysis of Social Exclusion, LSE. Useful sources from influential and leading academic analysts of poverty and social exclusion. **http://sticerd.lse.ac.uk/case/**
- King's Fund. Independent healthcare charity. **www.kingsfund.org.uk**
- Child Poverty Action Group (CPAG). Its website has a guide to poverty in the UK that includes key facts and statistics from the government and elsewhere. The CPAG also publishes a journal, Poverty, and selected articles are available free on its website. **www.cpag.org.uk/povertyfacts**
- The Poverty Site. This site monitors what is happening to poverty and social exclusion in the UK. The material is organized around 100 statistical indicators covering all aspects of the subject, from income and work to health and education. **www.poverty.org.uk**

- New Policy Institute. The NPI is a left-of-centre think tank. Its mission is to advance social justice in a market economy and its focus is mainly on poverty and social exclusion. **www.npi.org.uk**
- Institute for Fiscal Studies (IFS). The IFS is an independent research organization which produces reports on taxes, benefits, and public spending. **www.ifs.org.uk**

Sources of statistical data

Surveys are used by governments to help inform policy-making and evaluation. They are also sources of evidence for researchers and students. Many government surveys are conducted by the Office for National Statistics (ONS), which is responsible for collecting and disseminating UK statistics. In addition, government departments conduct their own surveys, and report and produce their own statistics, the majority of which are published online:

- Social Trends, published online, draws together social and economic data from a wide range of government departments and other organizations to provide a comprehensive guide to UK society. **www.statistics. gov.uk/socialtrends**
- The neighbourhood statistics site allows you to find detailed statistics within specific geographic areas, for example by local authority or ward. **www.neighbourhood.statistics.gov.uk/dissemination**
- Nomis is a service provided by ONS to give free access to UK labour market statistics from official sources. **www.nomisweb.co.uk**

Q   ESSAY QUESTIONS

1 What are the merits and limits of different forms of interviewing?

2 What are the unique features of focus groups as a research method?

3 What are the practical problems associated with ethnographic methods?

4 What are the problems associated with evaluating and interpreting documentary sources?

5 What ethical issues might arise in research with the following groups: asylum seekers; people with learning disabilities; drug users; young children?

6 To what degree should the divide between qualitative and quantitative research be regarded as hard and fast?

ONLINE RESOURCE CENTRE

For additional material and resources, please visit the Online Resource Centre at:
www.oxfordtextbooks.co.uk/orc/baldock4e/.

absolute poverty Poverty defined and measured in terms of the minimum requirements necessary for basic subsistence and survival. Those deemed to be in absolute poverty are unable to afford even the basic necessities in life. They exist below even 'subsistence poverty', the level at which people can just continue to survive.

accommodation This term, originating in the Children Act 1989, refers to children becoming looked after with the agreement of their parents. (See also **care order**.)

accountability structures the formal and informal controls surrounding management which support goals such as effective service-delivery outcomes.

Activities of Daily Living (ADL) Term used in health and social care to refer to functional tasks such as washing, dressing, feeding, and so on. Ability to perform ADLs is often used to assess someone's support needs, particularly for older persons and those with physical or mental impairments.

actuarial risk assessment Statistical calculations which are used to predict the likelihood of an offender being reconvicted within a defined period based on reconviction rates for offenders with similar characteristics in similar circumstances.

adoption triangle This term, coined by Sorosky and colleagues in the United States, refers to the relationships between child, birth parent(s), and adoptive parent(s). It serves as a reminder that adoption is always a triangular affair, and can aid understanding of the relationships involved.

affordable housing Housing whose cost is below some threshold considered socially acceptable, for example 20 per cent of household income. A measure of the affordability of owner-occupied housing is the ratio of the average price paid by first-time buyers to average incomes in an area. Though apparently clear, this is a highly confusing concept since a) household income itself can be measured in many ways, especially when incomes in an area are of interest, b) the sacrifices made by households in order to achieve a given income are excluded from consideration, and c) the subjectivity of the term 'affordability' opens the way for all housing providers to claim that their housing is affordable.

age structure This term is used to describe populations in terms of the relative numbers of people of different ages. The age structure of the population reflects variations in the past number of births, together with increased longevity and changes arising from migration (National Statistics 2010).

ageing population A change in the age structure of the population, whereby the proportion of older people increases relative to the numbers of younger people. The term is often used to describe a population in which the proportion over pensionable age is increasing, which in turn may imply more social spending on pensions and healthcare, and less revenue.

altruism Means acting selflessly, for example in donating blood, or giving to a charity.

amateurism When things are done without self-interest or for pay.

Annually Managed Expenditure (AME) Government spending on programmes which are volatile and demand-led, and are not subject to firm multi-year limits in the same way as DEL. The biggest single element is social security spending. Other items include tax credits, Local Authority Self-Financed Expenditure, and debt interest.

anti-globalization movement Transnational movement against neo-liberal globalization which unites a variety of international and national movements, such as the environmental, development, labour, and consumer movements. Has received most publicity for attempts to disrupt summits of MEIs and IGOs. Also known as the global justice movement.

anti-psychiatry movement A socio-political movement emerging in the 1960s, based on the premises that 'mental illness is a myth' and that institutional treatment is more harmful than therapeutic.

antisocial behaviour order (ASBO) Introduced in the Crime and Disorder Act 1998 and implemented in April 1999, these are civil orders which can be applied for by the police or local authorities against an individual aged 10 or over whose behaviour is deemed to be 'antisocial'.

arithmetic mean Also known simply as the mean, this is the total of a distribution of values divided by the number of values.

assisted places scheme Under the 1980 Education Act, local education authorities could give financial assistance on a means-tested basis to enable young people who would otherwise be unable to, to attend private schools.

asylums Large-scale long-stay accommodation and treatment facility for people with mental health problems, learning disabilities, or other impairments.

asymmetric information Describes a situation in which some relevant information is known to some but not all parties involved. Information asymmetry causes markets to become inefficient, since all the market participants do not have access to the information they need for their decision-making processes.

benefits in kind are social policy provisions which are administered as services (rather than cash transfers), e.g. healthcare, education, home helps, foster care, etc.

biomedical model An understanding of health rooted in the biological and medical sciences, oriented towards treating illness in individuals.

bonding social capital Refers to those relationships between individuals which are based on reciprocity and trust rather than contract and payment where the emphasis is on close, dense relationships usually within a locality, such as immediate family, close friends and neighbours. See also **bridging social capital**.

bridging social capital Refers to those relationships between individuals which are based on reciprocity and trust rather than contract and payment where the emphasis is on extended, thinner relationships between localities or groups rather than bonding social capital, such as loose friendships and workmates. See also **bonding social capital**.

British Crime Survey (BCS) A series of large household surveys of people's experiences and perceptions of crime in England and Wales.

Budget The most important financial and economic statement made each year by the Chancellor of the Exchequer to Parliament. It is best known for announcing changes in taxation required to finance the government's spending plans.

building society Financial institution which attracts money from savers and lends it to house purchasers. Today most have been privatized and have become banks.

business groups Representative organizations for employers whose major allegiance is to further their members' economic interests.

care management A system of social care which gives a named person (the 'care manager') responsibility for looking after the interests of a vulnerable person; this may entail providing, commissioning, and/or coordinating services.

care order A court order which transfers parental responsibility to the local authority, although it does not entirely extinguish the responsibility held by the child's parent. Care orders are made where the court believes this necessary to prevent significant harm to the child.

Care Programme Approach (CPA) Introduced as a guideline in 1991, this structured approach to care has become mandatory for people with severe mental health problems, as well as being used with other groups. It features a named 'care coordinator', linked-up services, and regular reviews.

carers' organizations Charities and other voluntary sector organizations set up to publicize carers' issues, to provide information and support, and sometimes to lobby for change.

case The unit of analysis. A case can be an individual, or a group of individuals such as a family or business. A case could also be a school, a country or an event.

cash benefits Where the state provides welfare in the form of money (rather than services in kind) such as unemployment benefits (called Job Seeker's Allowance in the UK), pensions, disability benefits, and a minimum income (Income Support in the UK).

cash limits Term used in central and local government budgeting to indicate the monetary ceiling on expenditure for particular activities or categories of expenditure in any one financial year.

cash planning Linked with a system of cash limits, this is a system of planning (brought in by UK governments in the 1980s) where public expenditure planning is done in cash terms; e.g. service level is determined by money available (how many books can we get for £10,000) rather than the previously used volume planning system (we will plan to purchase 1,000 books whatever they cost).

cash transfers An expression for all types of social policy provision which, in contrast to benefits in kind, are made as monetary support to individuals or families. In Britain (but not the United States) cash transfers have become synonymous with social security.

categorical variable A **variable** in which that the numbers used to name the different answers do not represent size or rank order.

census The enumeration of an entire **population**. Unlike a **sample**, a census counts all units in a population.

charity The state defines, registers, and monitors charitable organizations. Charitable status is granted to organizations promoting the relief of poverty, the advancement of education, the advancement of religion, and other purposes beneficial to the community. Such status brings advantages (e.g. significant tax exemptions and privileges) and disadvantages (e.g. limitations on political activity).

child benefit Until 2011 this was a universal benefit, paid to the mother of a child under 16, or under 19 if the child was still in full-time education. At the time of writing there are higher rates of benefit for the first child and even higher rates for the first child of a lone parent (Child Poverty Action Group 2010). However, the coalition government plans to take the benefit away from higher earners.

child rescue An approach to child welfare that holds high expectations of parents in attending to their children's needs and advocates strong and decisive intervention (including the children's removal) when this does not occur.

childcare This term is used to refer to the paid help used by families to assist in caring for dependent children. It includes day nurseries and playgroups, as well as care by childminders and nannies, some of whom may come to the child's house.

children's rights The term is used both to describe formal and substantive legal rights held by children and, more broadly, a philosophy which seeks to maximize the involvement of children in decision-making. There are different approaches to children's rights, most notably those which see rights in a more paternalistic way, i.e. as rights to a certain treatment by adults, and those tending more towards 'liberation', emphasizing that children should have greater powers.

children's trusts Introduced under the Children Act 2004, children's trusts are intended to promote integrated services by bringing together social care, education and health provision for children. Youth offending teams and the Connexions service may also be brought under the trust umbrella.

child-savers A term coined by Platt to describe nineteenth-century reformers who sought to rescue children from life on the streets and its attendant deviance, and to provide homes which would offer a more constructive upbringing. In effect, this represented an early form of child rescue (see above).

chi-square test The chi-square (χ^2) is a test of statistical significance, which is typically used to establish how confident we can be that the findings displayed in a **contingency table** can be generalized from a **probability sample** to a **population**.

choice Choice over goods and services can be established in markets through the act of buying. However, where these are distributed through administrative and professional means, the question of clients exercising choice can challenge received wisdoms about accepted welfare arrangements. It is difficult to increase choice for everyone, since the choices of some may restrict the choices of others.

citizen(ship) This is the formal status conferred on a member of a national community. With it normally come a set of rights to equal treatment under the law, to vote, and to social support. It has famously been used by Marshall to analyse the twentieth-century welfare state.

citizenship A term denoting legitimate membership of a political community, most usually that delineated by a nation-state. The term may refer to the status of a citizen on the one hand, but also to the attendant rights and responsibilities that are enjoyed by or demanded of a citizen.

citizenship Legal membership of a nation-state, together with political and social rights and obligations; often there are social categories (e.g. women, ethnic minorities) excluded from full citizenship.

civil servants Permanent salaried administrators available to a government whose duty it is to undertake to develop and implement policies determined by government ministers, and who take a neutral stance to the ideological position of the government.

civil society The 'spaces' between the market and the state where individuals and institutions can campaign for, and further develop, social and political rights.

classicism A traditional, punishment-oriented approach to crime emphasizing clarity in the law and due process in criminal procedure, combined with certainty and regularity of punishment. Classicists see human beings, including offenders, as having free choice and as individuals who will therefore be deterred from certain acts prohibited by the law by the anticipation of swift and certain punishment.

clean break An approach to adoption which involves complete severance of ties between the child and birth family, with its proponents arguing that this is in the best interests of the child, adopters, and usually, birth parents. See also **openness in adoption**.

closed question Interview of self-completion survey question in which the respondent is offered a predetermined list of answers. For example, 'How would you describe the state of your health over the past 12 months? a) Good; b) Fairly good; c) Not very good'. See also **open question**.

cluster sampling A **sampling** procedure in which at an initial stage the researcher samples areas (known as clusters), usually using a **probability sampling** method. For example, a **sample** of schools might be selected for a survey of pupils.

Cochrane Review Systematic review of evidence about the effects of interventions for prevention, treatment, and rehabilitation in healthcare settings.

codebook A document that lists the information about the **variables** in a data file, such as the variable names and the value labels for the **coding** of responses.

coding In quantitative research methods, the process by which numbers are assigned to responses to a survey questionnaire in preparation for computer analysis. In qualitative analysis, coding is the process by which segments of text are labelled with code words or phrases.

coding frame A list used in the analysis of survey data that shows the number allocated to each possible response to a survey question.

cognitive interviewing A technique in which qualitative techniques are applied to explore interviewees' responses to the questions.

cohort survey design A **longitudinal survey** that takes people born in a particular period and follows them up at intervals. See also **panel survey design.**

collective goods (or social goods) are defined goods that are usually delivered by the government for various reasons.

collectivism A system that favours collective or common provision and ownership in contrast to a system of individual provision and reliance on free markets.

command economies One of many terms which describes the former communist Central and East European countries, highlighting the fact that their economies did not function on a free market basis but were, to a large extent, politically planned.

community mental health team A group of health and social care professionals who share responsibility for a defined group of service users and communicate on a regular basis.

community order A community sentence introduced by the Criminal Justice Act 2003 and implemented in April 2005 which has a 'menu' of 12 possible requirements of which one or more can be included in the sentence.

compact A formal agreement about the principles that should govern relationships between government and the private or voluntary sectors; established since 1998 at both central and local government levels, with both general and specific (black and minority ethnic groups, volunteering and community groups) publications.

comparative need Need established by comparing the standards achieved by similar groups within one society—for example those living in different parts of the country—or in different societies—for example a comparison of the incomes of, or provision for, retired people in one nation compared with those in another. In other words, need is seen as an inherently relative concept, and any debate about need must be related

to the wider context within which the debates are taking place.

Comprehensive Spending Reviews (CSRs) Introduced by the 1997 Labour government, these Treasury reviews consider public provision item by item, asking whether any particular service needs to be provided by the state and, if the answer to this is yes, explores whether it might be possible to deliver it in alternative ways (e.g. more economically, efficiently, and effectively). The review then sets fixed three-year Departmental Expenditure Limits and, through **Public Service Agreements** (PSAs), defines the key improvements that the public can expect from these resources. The CSR was also a mechanism through which public expenditure could be redistributed between spending departments in line with the government's priorities (see further Cm. 4011, 1998).

concealed household A single person or group of people who share a meal a day together or a living room with another single person or group of people. Typically it refers to single persons or couples who are living with their parents but who would like to live independently, i.e. form separate households.

conditionalities Attached to loans by MEIs, include requirements to open economic sectors to foreign investment, privatization of state-owned enterprises and welfare services, removal of tariff barriers, food and fuel subsidies.

conditionality With respect to state benefits conditionality refers to eligibility for a benefit being tied to other actions on the part of the claimant, for example to be eligible for out of work benefits such as Job Seeker's Allowance claimants must actively be seeking work or work related support.

consensual approach to poverty Attempting to establish a consensus about what the population consider to be necessities in that particular society, at that particular period in time, without which one could be defined as being in poverty.

consent Uncoerced agreement to a course of action.

constitution Basic rules formulating the structure of and procedures for government, either written or customary.

contested adoption Adoption applications where the birth parent(s) does not consent to the child's adoption. In this situation, courts can dispense with parental consent if they think the child's welfare requires it.

contingency table A table, comprising rows and columns, that shows the relationship between two variables. Each cell in the table shows the frequency of occurrence of that combination of categories.

continuing care Care provided over an extended period of time to meet physical or mental health needs arising from accident, illness, or impairment. In the UK, continuing care is provided by the NHS.

contract culture The supposition that quasi-legal agreements ('contracts'), between local authorities (purchasers) and service-delivery voluntary organizations (providers), promote better procedures in the latter. Advocates of such approaches welcome the specificity and cost effectiveness of such an approach, whereas critics point to a loss of agency independence and the marginalization of volunteers.

contracting out When the public sector contracts the provision of social services to an independent for-profit or a not-for-profit organization.

contracting out When the responsible (state) organization contracts out the performance of a task (e.g. refuse collection) or the provision of a service (e.g. nursing home care) to another, often private or voluntary, agency.

convenience sampling When a **sample** is selected because it is one that happens to be available to the researcher.

corporatist Describes a welfare state which is work-oriented and based on individual contribution. State welfare maintains existing class and status differentials, thus encouraging political and social stability. The state is important in the delivery of welfare, but redistribution and equalization are not encouraged.

correlation An approach to the analysis of relationships between **variables** that seeks to assess the strength and direction of the relationship between those variables.

cost–benefit and cost effectiveness analysis Economic tools for assessing the merits of policies or practices. Both involve a broad assessment of the full costs of a decision to individuals, to the health service and to society more broadly. Cost–benefit analysis also attempts to make a full assessment of the benefits, in order to compare treatments for different kinds of problem.

criminal justice system A collective term for agencies responsible for various aspects of maintaining law and order and the administration of justice: most commonly the Police, Crown Prosecution, Court, Prison and Probation Services.

critical junctures Are brief historical periods of intense policy debates and changes in policy direction are likely.

cross-sectional survey A survey design in which data are collected from respondents at a single point in time. This is the typical design for a large-scale social survey.

cultural relativism The idea that norms and behaviour can only be judged in the context of their own culture and that those of different cultures are equally valid.

dark figure (of crime) refers to the amount of actual crime that does not appear in criminal statistics. It is often used to denote the volume of crime uncovered by the British Crime Survey that is not reported and/or recorded by the police.

decarcertative An approach to sentencing which deliberately moves away from the use of imprisonment as the 'first option' penal sanction.

de-commodification A central concept in Esping-Andersen (1990). Welfare states (or particular social policy programmes) differ in the degree of de-commodification, i.e. the extent to which they allow benefit recipients to withstand the pressure of returning to the labour market.

decontestation The process of finding consensus and agreement over political ideas, values or policy options which might otherwise have been neglected or remained the subject of contention and conflict.

deductive Describes an approach to the relationship between theory and research in which research is conducted with reference to hypotheses inferred from theory. In general, deductive research is theory-testing. See also **inductive**.

deinstitutionalization The process of replacing long-stay psychiatric hospitals with less isolated community mental health services for those diagnosed with mental health problems or learning disabilities.

dementia A degenerative brain condition, attributable to a range of causes, which is most prevalent in elderly people. The leading cause of dementia is Alzheimer's disease, which accounts for up to 60 per cent of all cases.

demographic change Measurable shift in the characteristics of a geographically defined population (e.g. change in age profile, racial/ethnic composition, family patterns).

Departmental Expenditure Limits (DEL) The total spending limits for government departments over a fixed period of time, excluding demand led and exceptionally volatile items. DELs are planned and set at Spending Reviews. They are split into resource and capital budgets.

dependency A state of needing support from another. All human beings are to an extent interdependent, but dependency is relative. The extent of a person's dependency will be greater at some times than at others, depending on their circumstances and the nature of their needs.

dependency culture Used to describe a situation where individuals are believed to be passive recipients of welfare and dependent on benefits.

dependency ratio This term was coined by economists to describe the ratio between those who are 'economically active', in that they earn their own living in the labour market, and those who depend on other earners for their financial support. The definition does not, of course, recognize the fact that those who are economically active are often dependent on those who are 'economically inactive' for the provision of domestic services, childcare, and other supports, and that 'economically inactive' people can be contributing valuable unpaid work to their family or community.

dependency ratio Usually the ratio of those outside the labour force (for example 0–15 and 65 and over) to those defined as in the labour force or of working age.

dependent population The section of the population economically supported by those in employment.

depoliticization Where a contested issue is reduced to a technical problem, about which there are no fundamental disagreements.

deprivation index A list of items defined as essential to being a full member of society, without which one could be deemed to be experiencing deprivation.

descriptive statistics When statistics summarize results and no attempt is made to draw inferences from them.

deviancy amplification spiral A process whereby a certain type of deviance arouses public attention and is focused on by, for example, the police and the media. The activity then appears to increase (and may actually increase) through heightened awareness, reporting, recording, and research.

direct payments Introduced by the Community Care (Direct Payments) Act 1996, direct payments are provided by local authorities to individuals to commission their own services from independent sector agencies and/or to hire personal care staff. It is now mandatory for all local authorities to offer direct payments to social care service users in England.

direct provision Where a social service is organized, financed, and provided by permanent government employees.

direct taxation When government levies taxes on people's incomes and not on goods that they purchase (indirect taxation). Income tax is the main form and is usually progressive, taking proportionately more the more people earn.

dirigiste Describes an economy controlled or guided by a central authority.

disability The condition of being prevented from doing or achieving something. Disability may be associated with impairment (see below) but people may be disabled by

particular features of their social context or physical environment that do not accommodate their particular needs or requirements.

diversion A strategy in youth justice which seeks to avoid or minimize contact with the courts and custody.

division of labour 'One of the most distinctive characteristics of the economic system of modern societies is the development of a highly complex and diverse division of labour. In other words, work is divided into an enormous number of different occupations, in which people specialize.' (Giddens 1993: 491.)

domiciliary care Services provided in a person's own home, such as home help, meals on wheels, or a bathing service.

drift Describes a situation where there is either no clear long-term plan regarding a child's future or where the plan is not being effectively implemented.

dual systems This is a system of vocational ET which combines work-based training with school- or college-based education. The German apprenticeship system is one example.

early intervention An approach to policy that emphasizes tackling problems early (this can mean early in children's lives and/or early in relation to the onset of problems). Early intervention is seen as a way of improving outcomes for deprived children and thereby improving their life chances and reducing the likelihood of later involvement in deviant behaviour.

economic cycle Also known as the business cycle. The tendency of an economy to move in waves between periods of growing output and employment and lower or falling output and greater unemployment. More strictly refers to the movement of an economy's growth around the core long-run trend determined by labour supply, productivity, and technical change. Economies typically move from years where they grow above the trend, creating inflationary pressures, to years where they grow below the trend, implying deflation and wasted resources. A cycle takes place between two points where output moves above the long-run trend. It is a task of economic policy to keep economic activity as close to the trend as possible, avoiding large and disruptive vacillations.

education This can refer both to the institutions, e.g. schools, colleges, universities, and to the process—that is, what is learnt in educational institutions or indeed in other contexts. The issues of what education is for or what it should contain are much debated.

empowerment Recent developments in welfare debate have acknowledged that under the original 1948 arrangements, many clients of the welfare state were expected to be passive and grateful recipients of state handouts. There has now been a common criticism of this assumption on all sides, in favour of clients having more power, dignity, respect, and autonomy through a process of empowerment.

equality of opportunity This means that citizens will be given an equal start in life, but thereafter will be allowed to make what they can of their talents and opportunities.

equality of outcome This means that those with equal needs receive equal treatment. This may mean that some disadvantaged people might receive more support than others.

ethnicity A term used to describe the specific but shared historical, linguistic, and cultural context that defines a human being's identity, the society from which they come, and/or the community to which they belong.

ethnography A research method in which an organization, small society, or social setting is observed. Observation can range from the passive recording of public social actions of all kinds, to the adoption of a particular role in a small society, to gain entry to less public places. Ethnographic researchers gather data by seeking to immerse themselves in participants' activities, while keeping careful records of what they experience.

ethnomethodology A sociological perspective concerned with understanding the social orders people use to make sense of the world through analysing their accounts and descriptions of their day-to-day experiences.

European Anti-Poverty Network (EAPN) An independent network of non-governmental organizations (NGOs) and groups involved in the fight against poverty and social exclusion in the member states of the European Union, established in 1990.

European Community Household Panel A large-scale comparative survey involving interviews with the same representative households and individuals over a number of years. Covering initially twelve European countries (in 1994), the ECHP was superseded by EU-SILC, the European Union Statistics on Income and Living Conditions, in 2004. It provides cross-sectional and longitudinal data on aspects such as income, poverty and social exclusion in EU member states as well as other European countries (e.g. Norway, Switzerland, Iceland and Turkey).

European Social Model Defined somewhat vaguely, this term has been used by the EU as an expression of common values in member states, including democracy, individual rights, free collective bargaining, equality of opportunity, market economy as well as social welfare and social solidarity. Essentially it emphasizes that economic competitiveness and social progress are not in conflict but go hand in hand.

European Union (EU) Social Chapter An initiative taken by European Community members in 1989 to begin to harmonize social policy in particular in the area of labour market and employment relations, due to a concern that workplace conditions and arrangements might suffer as a result of the competitive single market. The Conservative government of John Major secured the UK an 'opt-out' from this arrangement; however, one of the first acts in the EU of Tony Blair's Labour government in 1997 was to waive this 'opt-out' and accept the Social Chapter's terms.

evidence-based policy Public policy informed by the evidence of research studies. It was popularized by the Blair governments.

exclusive and inclusive foster care Terms used to describe foster care, depending on whether the birth family (and sometimes professionals) tend to be excluded from or included in the foster family and actively involved in the foster child's life.

expressed need Need that has become a demand. There is a close relationship between need and demand, but simply because someone demands or wants something does not necessarily mean that they need it.

extended family This term was coined by sociologists to describe the wider kin group, in contrast to the 'nuclear family'. An extended family may link three or more generations and will include people whose relationship is that of grandparent and grandchild, brothers and sisters, uncles and aunts, nephews and nieces and cousins.

externalities (external costs and external benefits) Either the costs or the benefits that economic behaviour bestows on those who are not parties to the bargain; for example, the damage done to a house by passing lorries or the 'gain' from living close to a perfume factory.

fabricated and induced illness A form of abuse where a parent or carer fakes or creates symptoms in a child in order to gain attention from medical personnel. Previously known as Munchausen Syndrome by Proxy.

false memory syndrome A memory which is objectively false but strongly believed to be true by the person concerned. The 'syndrome' connotes a situation in which this false memory has a profound influence on personality and lifestyle. In relation to sexual abuse, it has been claimed that false memories can be 'planted' during therapy, leading to false accusations being made.

family The official definition of the family, used in all government censuses and surveys, is that a family is a married or cohabiting couple, either with or without their never-married children (of any age), including childless couples or a lone parent together with his or her never-married child or children (ONS 2010).

family centres Provided either by voluntary organizations or local authorities, family centres are usually based in deprived areas and offer a range of services from supervised contact or family therapy to support for young mothers and play facilities. Historically, they have striven to provide non-stigmatizing support services. Many have recently converted to become children's centres.

family group home A residential home modelled on 'family life' with relatively small numbers of residents and consistent parental figures among the staff.

family policy For a social policy to be described as family policy the family would need to be the deliberate target of specific actions by central or local government, and the measures should be designed so as to have an impact on family resources and, ultimately, on family well-being (Hantrais and Letablier 1996: 139).

family rights An approach to childcare issues which emphasizes the importance of birth family ties (or blood relationships). It advocates state support for families and is critical of 'oppressive' state intervention in families.

family support Describes both a set of services designed to help families meet their children's needs but also a philosophy that whenever possible children should be brought up within their family of origin and that the state should facilitate this in its policies.

felt need An individual's or group's belief that they need something. This relies heavily upon an individual's own perception of their need, and their perception of any discrepancy between what their situation may be and what their situation should be. This definition is very similar to a 'want'.

feminization A process through which women, women's roles, women's disadvantages, and/or women's perspectives may acquire more particular salience.

feminization The idea that in education, jobs, and economic life men are progressively losing out to women.

field notes Descriptions of events observed during fieldwork in a social setting and recorded at the time of observation, or shortly thereafter.

Financial Management Initiative (FMI) Initiative introduced into UK government departments by the Treasury in 1982 aimed at improving the management of resources by a variety of strategies, including delegated budgeting and increasing the accountability of individual managers for the management of resources.

financial support Where a social service is financed by government but organized and provided by non-government organizations.

fiscal crisis Term used to indicate a projected crisis for states with large public expenditure programmes, especially in areas such as health, welfare benefits, and pensions, where it is argued (but also disputed) that a combination of rising public demand, entitlements, and falling tax revenue will place governments under an increasing, if not intolerable, economic strain.

fiscal policy A general term covering all of a government's decisions about taxation and spending and borrowing. Fiscal policy is important not only because it determines the size and nature of the welfare state but because it affects the distribution of incomes and the performance of the economy. Currently fiscal policy is constrained by two fiscal rules the government has set itself: the **golden rule** and the **sustainable investment rule**.

fiscal welfare The distribution of welfare which derives from not collecting revenue from people, e.g. tax allowances.

flexible or casual work This refers to jobs which are not full-time and permanent but rather temporary, on short-term contract, variable hours, or one-off contracts for a particular piece of work. Labour flexibility is the ability of a firm to modify the employment and utilization of its labour force in the face of changing labour and product market conditions (Pass et al. 1991: 328).

focus group A group interview or discussion led by a moderator with individuals who have similar characteristics or who share some experience of the research topic. Focus groups are used when the researcher wants to collect data through group interaction on a topic.

Fordist regime Referring back to Henry Ford's car factory as the archetype of factory production, the notion of a Fordist regime is that for much of the last century the economic growth and development of Western societies was based on mass production, mass labour, and mass consumption. People's work and life experiences, like the products they bought, were standardized.

full employment Usually defined either as more jobs available than people seeking employment or as a job available for anyone seeking one.

further education Refers to post-16 and mainly pre-degree level education offered at further education colleges.

gatekeeper In the housing context, the owner or financier whose rules of access control who is able to gain access to a particular type of housing. It applies to mortgage lenders, councils, housing associations, private landlords, etc.

GDP Stands for Gross Domestic Product and is an expression of the total value of goods and services produced within a given period (normally a year) within a given country. The increase (or decrease) of GDP is a conventional indicator of the growth (or decline) of the domestic economy.

gender A term relating to the socially constructed differences in the characteristics and roles associated with sexual difference. While sexual differences are biological, gender is socially determined.

gender pay gap The Equal Opportunities Commission (1996: 2) offers a definition: 'The gender pay gap is defined as women's earnings as a percentage of men's earnings. The pay gap is said to be narrow as this figure approaches 100 per cent.'

General Government Spending (or Expenditure) The international definition of general government expenditure (or public expenditure) includes the spending of central government, of local authorities and in the case of most counties, regional government.

generalizability A concern with the question of whether the results of a study can be generalized beyond the specific context in which it was conducted.

globalization In its economic sense, the tendency for the world to become one market in which goods will be produced where costs are lowest and sold where prices are highest.

GNP and GDP Gross national product is all of a country's output of goods and services (usually in a calendar year) plus income from assets abroad but with no deduction (i.e. gross, not net) for depreciation in the value of the country's assets. Gross domestic product is GNP minus income from assets abroad.

golden rule The self-imposed rule, followed by Gordon Brown as Chancellor of the Exchequer, that over the economic cycle the government will borrow only to invest and not to fund current spending.

good enough parenting Phrase used to indicate a threshold below which action must be taken to ensure that the child is able to receive appropriate parenting.

government department A major branch of central government responsible for a significant section of state activity, such as healthcare or social security.

GP fundholders As part of the internal market within the NHS created by the Conservatives in the 1990s, GP practices were able to opt to receive a budget (become fundholders) with which they could establish contracts with their chosen healthcare providers.

grant-maintained school Under the 1988 Education Reform Act, schools were enabled to opt out of local authority control and become self-governing schools run by their head teachers and governors funded (grant-maintained) directly by central government. Under the New Labour government's 1998 School Standards and Framework Act many of these schools will become Foundation Schools.

grievance-claims This refers to the process whereby individuals or groups express their concerns (grievances) about a social issue to an agency that they feel should deal with it—usually a government department.

Gross Domestic Product (GDP) is gross national product, but excludes income from assets abroad.

Gross Domestic Product The value of all goods and services which are produced by those British citizens who are resident in Britain.

Gross National Product (GNP) All of a country's output or goods and services (usually measured in a calendar year) plus income from assets abroad, but with no deduction (i.e. gross, not net) for depreciation in the country's assets.

grounded theory A form of analysis of qualitative data used when instead of testing pre-formed hypotheses, **inductive** researchers attempt to develop new theory from their empirical observations of the social world.

high demand stakeholder An actor so strongly committed to providing a public service in line with his or her individual, or communities', needs and preferences, that they are willing to establish and implement that service themselves, thus simultaneously operating on both the demand and the supply side of a market.

higher education This refers to degree-level and post-degree-level education.

Home Detention Curfew (HDC) Introduced in the Crime and Disorder Act 1998, the scheme began operating on 28 January 1999. It allows prisoners serving sentences of between three months and four years to be considered for early release subject to a home curfew enforced by electronic monitoring.

horizontal dimension of need Number of people with a given level of need.

horizontal redistribution Contrasts particularly with vertical redistribution and is where resources are taken from some (usually in the form of tax) and given to others no worse off but who have particular characteristics or needs (such as children in state schools or who are ill or disabled).

household A person living alone or a group of people who have the address as their only or main residence and who either share one meal a day or share the living accommodation (ONS 2010).

household A single person or group of people who have the address as their only or main residence and who either share one meal a day together or share a living room (definition used in the UK census from 1981).

housing association A non-profit organization set up to build and manage social housing.

housing stock The number of available housing units in the country. There are a certain number of physical dwellings available, though the convertibility of buildings between residential and other uses means the size of the stock is not absolute. However, not all units are available to those seeking housing. For example, some housing is unfit or 'hard to let', some are second homes.

housing tenure The legal relationship between household and dwelling. The main types of tenure—owning and renting—involve sets of rights and obligations which depend partly on national legislation and partly on rules applied by mortgage lenders, councils, etc. Hence, for example, the rights of private tenants vary between countries and over time.

hyphenated society Marshall (1963) argued that industrial society in the UK had by the middle of the twentieth century developed to a balanced point that included a strong but not uncontrolled capitalist economy, and a comprehensive but not too intrusive welfare state brought about by democratic means. This balance, which he felt was a good one, was a mixture, or hybrid, whereby the various parts kept each other in check in a hyphenated society of democratic-welfare-capitalism.

Ideal types Central to the sociology of Max Weber. For Weber ideal types do not exist in empirical reality but as conceptual thought figures which highlight characteristics of phenomena to be analysed. In comparative welfare state research. Esping-Andersen's three worlds of welfare capitalism (1990) can be regarded as ideal types in the sense that the Swedish welfare state, for example, is an empirical reality which can be measured against Esping-Andersen's ideal type of a social democratic welfare state.

identity An important concept in modern adoption, which recognizes the importance of 'origins' or heritage (e.g. familial, social, cultural, racial, religious) in the adoptee's sense of self and well-being.

identity/identities The sense(s) of self by which individuals define who they are—both in terms of belonging to a society or social group and in terms of having integrity as a unique being.

ideology Sets of ideas, assumptions, and images, by which people make sense of society, which give a clear social identity, and which serve in some way to legitimize power relations in society (McLennan 1991: 114).

IMF stands for International Monetary Fund. The Fund promotes international monetary cooperation, exchange stability, and orderly exchange arrangements. It provides temporary financial assistance to countries to help ease balance of payments adjustment—and can therefore play an important role in the of social policy decision-making processes.

impairment The absence of, limitation of, or damage to a bodily organ or physical or mental function, that may (or may not—depending on the nature of the social context and physical environment) result in disability.

imputed rent An imputed rent is an attempt to value the housing services owner-occupiers enjoy as they live in their house. In private rented housing, tenants pay rent for the housing services they receive and governments tax landlords on this income. As owner-occupation progressively displaced private landlordism governments lost access to a source of taxation. The taxation of the imputed rents of owner-occupiers was an attempt to preserve it. In practice it was difficult to understand and hence lacked legitimacy.

incapacitative Punishment which attempts to remove an offender's ability to commit further crime(s). The ultimate form of this type of punishment is the death penalty.

incarcerative Punishment which ensures an individual is unable to reoffend through some form of constraint—for example the physical constraint of the prison walls or a form of electronic tagging or tracking.

income quintiles The division of a population, such as individuals or households, into a hierarchy of five parts each containing equal numbers. The bottom quintile would contain the fifth with the lowest incomes, and so on to the top fifth, containing those with the highest incomes. The income of each quintile is usually given in the form of the average income of all the units in it.

independent sector In social care, the independent sector includes private enterprises and voluntary and not-for-profit agencies which provide services such as home care, residential homes, etc.

indirect taxation When government raises money by adding taxes to other things that people do (drive cars) or to goods and services that they buy (value added taxes, duties on fuel, liquor, and cigarettes). Indirect taxes tend to be regressive and to hit the poor harder as a proportion of their incomes.

individual budget Refers to the amount of money that is available to fund a person's care and support costs, which is calculated by assessing the person's needs and spent according to a plan developed by the individual and approved by the local authority. This term is used interchangeably with 'personal budget', although personal budgets refer specifically to social care funds while individual budgets also include other sources of funding, such as disability living allowance.

individual welfare The good of the individual citizen.

individualism In contrast to **collectivism**, a set of beliefs that puts paramount importance on the rights and freedoms of individuals and the power of free-market mechanisms.

individualization The socially contingent process by which personal identities are established and conceptualized. It is a process that may, arguably, be changing in nature.

individualization This term refers to the process by which the individual, rather than the group, becomes the key unit in society. The idea implies the breaking down of the structures of class, occupation, locality, age and gender.

inductive An approach to the relationship between theory and research in which theory is generated out of research. In general, deductive research is theory-testing and inductive research is theory-generating. See also **deductive**.

Industrial Revolution A period from the eighteenth to the nineteenth century when, starting in the United Kingdom, major changes in agriculture, manufacturing, mining, transport, and technology had a profound effect on the socio-economic and cultural conditions.

industrialization The process by which economies change from an agricultural to an industrial base, and the ongoing development of that process.

Infant Mortality Rates (IMRs) These count the deaths of children under one year old, measuring them over time, or in comparison with other countries. They are expressed per 1,000 live births, and are regarded as an indicator of comparative health.

informal care Unpaid care provided to people with disabilities or older people by family members, friends, neighbours, or volunteers.

informed consent A principle in social research ethics that implies that research participants should be given the information they need to make an informed decision about whether or not they wish to participate in a study.

input measure Measure of resources used in providing a service or benefit, e.g. spending, number of staff employed.

institutional care Care provided away from a person's home in a group setting such as a long-stay hospital or asylum or a residential or nursing home.

institutionalist approach An approach to interpreting crime statistics which suggests that they are more a product of the institutions that define and measure crime than 'real' phenomena.

institutionalization Term given to the negative psychological effects of living in impersonal settings which feature disempowerment and lack of personal choice.

intermediate needs Needs which are not ends in themselves, but rather a means to an end. For example, we may need some things, such as a basic education, in order to fulfil other needs, such as finding employment, which in turn may answer the more ultimate need for income.

internal market A reform to the organization of the NHS brought about by the Conservatives in the 1990s, based on separating the functions of purchasing and providing healthcare.

internal market A structure for providing health (or other public services) in which the authorities responsible for purchasing services are separate from organizations which produce and deliver services to patients. They introduce competitive market forces into public services.

internal markets Pseudo- or **quasi-markets** within an organization or a service system where one part plays the part of purchaser and the other of provider. Real money transfers or merely shadow prices may be used.

International Governmental Organizations (IGOs) Organizations formed by governments and operated by international civil servants. Includes the United Nations, MEIs such as the IMF and the World Bank, and regional formations such as the EU.

International Labour Organization (ILO) Founded in 1919 and became the first UN specialized agency in 1946. The ILO produces international labour standards in the form of conventions and recommendations, provides technical assistance, and promotes the development of employers' and workers' organizations. It is governed by a tripartite structure in which workers, employers, and governments cooperate as equal partners.

International Monetary Fund (IMF) International body established (together with the **World Bank**) as a result of the 1942 Bretton Woods meeting of 44 countries to create and stabilize the world monetary order, including exchange rates, balance of payments deficits, and the operation of the system as a whole. The IMF can advance credit to countries with serious balance of payments deficits, but has the right to demand economic compliance with its suggestions. Hence it has the power to intervene in the domestic policy-making of countries it assists.

International Monetary Fund (IMF) Set up in 1944 to promote international monetary stability by supervising monetary and exchange rate policies. Provides loans to countries with balance of payment difficulties.

International Non-Governmental Organizations (INGOs) Part of the international voluntary sector, INGOs are non-governmental organizations based mainly in Western countries which operate in a variety of countries, sometimes in cooperation with local and national NGOs, often delivering government aid in emergency situations.

Recent decades have seen the growth of super INGOs such as Oxfam and Save the Children, which dominate their areas of operation.

interview guide Refers to a list of the general areas to be covered in an **unstructured interview** or to the more structured list of issues to be raised or questions asked in **semi-structured interviewing**.

interview schedule A list of questions to be asked by an interviewer. It is used in a **structured interview**.

joint commissioning Designed to result in services that are well-coordinated, efficient, and non-duplicative, joint commissioning involves more than one agency (such as health and social care) working together to assess needs, identify available resources, and arrange service delivery.

just desserts The classical notion that wrongdoers should be punished in proportion to the harm done, and in accordance with what the act deserves. Dessert-based sentencing is based on this principle.

justice Social justice is a fair action in accordance with rules that prescribe our rights. Increasingly social policies are seen as fulfilling social rights that citizens possess. In complex societies it may be that an unequal distribution of services can increase the capacity of the whole system to fulfil social rights, and simple egalitarian social justice is thus difficult to operationalize.

justice model An approach to youth crime which stresses the responsibility of young offenders for their crimes, that punishment is important, and that it should be proportionate to the seriousness of the crime.

justice model An approach which seeks to reduce official discretion in the justice system, and to ensure that like cases are treated alike—punishment to fit the crime, not the criminal.

key worker housing Affordable housing provided for specified groups of workers, usually in the public sector and on a small scale. It is a response to the successful definition of these groups' problems as deserving special treatment and allows governments to gain a 'responsive' image.

Keynesian economic policies Economic policies based on the ideas of the twentieth century British economist John Maynard Keynes. Keynesian economics advocates active policy responses by the government to mitigate the adverse effects of economic recessions and depressions.

Keynesian economics An approach to national economic management named after the British economist and political adviser John Maynard Keynes that places strong emphasis on governmental intervention in economic management and, traditionally, on an associated goal of full employment.

knowledge economy This refers to the fact that as the economy moves from one based on manufacturing to one based on services, the kinds of skills that people need to get jobs changes from manual to mental skills.

l'économie sociale et solidaire Sometimes translated as 'social economy', this French term collectively embraces associations, mutuals and cooperatives, and emphasizes their contributions to community development and citizenship. These organizations all have an economic role, but differ from orthodox for-profit enterprise because they are run for the benefit of members, or of wider society, rather than private shareholders or owners.

labour intensification Increasing the intensity of work means that people have to work harder and expend more mental or manual effort in a given period of work.

labour market Refers to the process whereby firms look for employees (the demand side of the market) and people offer their labour power in return for a wage/salary (the supply side of the market). In practice, there can be said to be many different labour markets, for example local labour markets: the supply and demand for labour in a local area; or skilled and specialist labour markets.

leading question Survey question that pushes the respondent to give a particular answer. For example, 'I expect you didn't claim your benefit because you didn't know about it, is that right?'

lean production The original idea of lean production is usually associated with the 1990 book by J. Womack and colleagues, *The Machine that Changed the World* (New York, Maxwell Macmillan), in which they advocated the need for organizations to restructure to reduce staffing and waste in order to survive in harsher competitive conditions.

legal definitions (of crime) The definition of a crime simply as an act defined as criminal by the law, irrespective of how current social values define the act.

liberal Describes a welfare system with predominantly market-based social insurance and means-testing of state benefits, which are stigmatized and largely for the poor.

liberal democracy The system of government based on the universal right to vote for candidates chosen from a range of alternatives to represent the interests of sections of the community, combined with the freedom to organize and propose policies on issues of the day.

liberal, free-market-based approach An approach to social policy built on the assumption that individuals should be free to choose their own welfare, buying through markets, rather than having the state providing services.

life course A holistic term used to describe the development and experiences of an individual, cohort, or social group though a lifetime. (Unlike the term 'lifecycle', it does not imply that the processes of a human life are necessarily fixed or recurring.)

lifelong learners Traditionally, education and schooling were associated with learning at the outset of life. It is argued that to face the fast pace of change in contemporary society, and especially in the world of work, individuals will have to continue to learn and update their knowledge and skills throughout their lives.

lifetime redistribution An understanding of state provision of benefits and services which interprets it in terms of taking resources from people at points in their lives when they are well off (usually through taxes and social insurance contributions paid by the employed) and returning them when they are less well off or in need (when they are unemployed, ill, or retired, for example).

linking social capital Social capital that reaches out to unlike people in dissimilar situations, such as those who are entirely outside of the community, thus enabling members to leverage a far wider range of resources than are available in the community.

literature review A text that assesses the current state of knowledge about a research topic.

local authority In the UK, the level of local government responsible for providing or commissioning a range of services, including social care services.

local management of schools Under the 1988 Education Reform Act, the budgets for schools were devolved from the local authority to individual schools. The board of governors for each school became responsible for managing the budget.

lone-parent family Consists of a lone parent living with his or her never-married dependent children, provided these children have no children of their own (ONS 2010).

longitudinal survey Unlike a **cross-sectional survey**, the aim of a longitudinal survey is usually to deepen understanding of change over time. There is a basic distinction between the **panel design** and the **cohort design**.

long-run efficiency Obtaining economic efficiency over a variously specified longer term, usually several years, and contrasted with **short-run efficiency**. Long-run efficiency usually requires saving, investment, and innovation.

long-term care insurance Policy taken out by individuals against the possibility of requiring residential or nursing home provision.

lumpy goods Those products that cannot be bought in small amounts, for example a house or primary education. This means that many people may not be able to afford them.

macroeconomic management The management by a government of the overall performance of the economy using such controls as interest rates, taxes, and government spending.

male breadwinner model Traditional nuclear family structure in which the man goes out to work and earns a family wage (enough for himself and his dependants) and the woman stays at home and works in the domestic sphere.

mandatory legislation Legislation which imposes a duty on, for example, a council to undertake certain actions.

marginal benefit The satisfaction or utility gained by the consumption of the last unit of a product, for example the last mouthful in a meal or the last day of a holiday.

marginal cost The cost, measured either in money spent or the effort of work, required to obtain or produce the last unit of output, for example the last car off the production line or the last working hour of the week.

market failure An imperfection in the market mechanism that prevents the achievement of economic efficiency.

market failure When the market fails to produce what is most wanted at the lowest possible price: usually reflected in unemployed resources, unconsumed output, or unmet demands.

market model The market model of training provision is where government provides little or no direct training provision nor imposes any requirement on companies to train. The amount of training is left to the market to decide. In theory, if the company needs a particular skill in order to compete, it will acquire it through either training or recruitment. An individual may invest in their own training because they can see a future labour market advantage in doing so.

Marxisant pessimism Sees globalization as the latest stage of capitalism, driven by constant search for increased profitability, leading to homogenization of culture through commodification. Claims transnational corporations' increasing control of the world economy leads to decline in the power of the state and organized labour.

material deprivation Having insufficient physical resources—food, shelter, and clothing—necessary to sustain life either in an absolute sense or relative to some prescribed standard.

maternal deprivation and attachment A theoretical perspective deriving from the work of John Bowlby, which emphasizes the importance of secure attachments between children and their parental figures, and explores the consequences of attachment problems.

maternity leave This term refers to the right of women to take paid leave from employment around the time of the birth of a baby.

means-tested Benefits or services that are allocated on the basis of financial need following an assessment of the individual's income and savings.

means-tested Type of welfare benefit for which entitlement is conditional on having an income and/or capital below a specific threshold.

median The mid-point in a distribution of values.

medical model An approach to understanding child maltreatment which treats it as a disease, with abusive and neglectful behaviour the visible symptoms.

medical model of disability Theoretical approach which regards disability as a consequence of impairment. This approach, which is often implicit, locates the problem of disability and hence the need for change with the individual, not society.

medicalization Refers to the way in which social issues can be re-defined as amenable to medical intervention, even if they have not been in the past.
For example naughty children can be defined as having a disorder such as ADHD (Attention Deficit Hyperactivity Disorder).

merit Means that under the rules an individual receives what they deserve. For some writers this is an essential incentive for individuals to produce effectively for the whole system, and to deter others from non-production. For other writers, the rules are seen to be devices for exclusion, such that the term 'merit' camouflages the systematic reproduction of inequalities.

merit goods Goods and services where individual consumption also produces a more general community benefit, e.g. a child's consumption of education.

ministry See **government department.**

mixed economy of care Refers to a social care system in which services are provided by a variety of providers from the public, private and voluntary sectors. Based on the principle that competition between services will provide greater choice for individuals and drive up the quality of care.

mixed economy of welfare A description of the diverse sources of welfare, in state, private, voluntary, and informal family sectors. From the latter part of the twentieth century governments aimed to stimulate and support a wider range of sources of provision, beyond the state.

mixed economy of welfare A term used to indicate that social welfare is produced not just by the state but also by families, communities, for-profit, and not-for-profit (charitable) sources.

mode The value that occurs most often in a distribution of values.

moderator The person who guides the questioning in a focus group. Also called a facilitator.

modernization A theme running throughout New Labour's policy discourse around public services in the UK. Features of the modernization agenda in social care include a focus on personalization, independence, and choice; increased user involvement; strengthened coordination and statutory regulation of services; and greater emphasis on staff training and development.

moral panic Introduced by Stanley Cohen (1972) to indicate a process of collective over-reaction to a form of apparently widespread deviance. The media initially 'identify' the 'crisis', and the inevitable societal reaction is to demand greater control through increased policing and more retributive law.

mortgage, mortgage arrears Households buying dwellings normally take out loans, or mortgages. The mortgage allows the purchaser to pay the whole cost of the dwelling to the seller, and in exchange the household undertakes to make monthly repayments of the loan to the mortgage lender. When the household fails to maintain these payments the mortgage is said to be in arrears.

multilateral economic institutions (MEIs) Exemplified by the IMF and the WB, these are believed to have increasing influence on national economic and social policy formation, in particular through conditionalities attached to loan programmes.

myth of classlessness A phrase coined by Pelton which attacks the view that child abuse occurs equally across all social classes, and which highlights the importance of poverty and inequality in generating abuse.

National Assistance (In Britain, successively called Supplementary Benefit and Income Support.) Social security that individuals are entitled to on the basis of need, for instance when they do not qualify for sufficient social insurance benefits for subsistence.

national curriculum This was introduced by the 1988 Education Reform Act; it applies to all children of compulsory school age in state schools, with a few exceptions such as hospital schools. The curriculum specifies subjects to be taken and levels of attainment to be achieved at different ages.

National Health Service (NHS) The system of health service provision established by the NHS Act in 1946. Its system of public funding, with no charges at the time of use, made it a model of the collectivist ideals of the post-war era, when the emphasis was on collective, state action to meet human needs and to regenerate society.

National Insurance In social security, entitlement to social insurance benefits based on having made financial contributions.

National Offender Management Service (NOMS) Aims to reduce re-offending through closer working between prison and probation staff and ensuring end-to-end management of offenders in which contact with a probation officer is maintained from start to finish of each sentence.

National Probation Service (NPS) The Criminal Justice and Courts Services Act 2000 renamed the Probation Service for England and Wales 'the National Probation Service for England and Wales', and set out its aims as being to protect the public, to reduce offending, and to provide for the proper punishment of offending.

national standards Introduced into legislation by the Criminal Justice Act 1991 and updated regularly since then, the standards prescribe how probation officers are to supervize and manage offenders in the community, including under what circumstances an offender should be returned to court for breach of an order. Standards for Youth Justice were introduced alongside Youth Offending Teams in April 2000.

National Vocational Qualifications (NVQs) In 1986, the National Council for Vocational Qualifications (NCVQ) was set up to establish a system of national vocational qualifications (NVQs). These NVQs are work-based assessments of competence and skill at five levels. The standards for each level were developed by leading bodies in industry, the public sector, and commerce.

needs The most central concept to social policy debate. Where goods and services are distributed outside the market, in which we can express our preferences through the act of buying, it is difficult to identify who should have what. What people need is established in relation to administratively or professionally defined norms, but these are inherently open to debate and challenge. In particular, beyond very basic needs for food and shelter, there is considerable cultural variation in socially defined needs.

negative equity Equity refers to the value of a household's investment in a dwelling. This value is calculated by estimating the value of the dwelling and then deducting the value of outstanding loans. If the result is positive, the household has positive equity; if it is negative, the household has negative equity.

neo-liberalism A political philosophy of competitive individualism which calls for minimal state involvement in economic and social regulation, associated with the emergence of the New Right (Reagan and Thatcher) in the 1980s and exemplified in the **'Washington consensus'**.

neo-liberals People whose political ideology is to promote economic liberalism that has its roots in classical liberalism.

new managerialism Also sometimes referred to as 'new public management'. This is an approach to the management of government bureaucracies that has been borrowed from the private sector. Broadly it gives managers freedom to attain specific policy targets within devolved budgets. This can lead to significant changes to how a traditional public sector organization goes about its work.

New Right A school of thought combining economic neo-liberalism and social conservatism. The former gives a high value to a reduced role for the state. The latter emphasizes the value of traditional family forms.

New Right Term used in the 1980s to describe the intellectual and political influences on conservative-inclined governments such as those of Margaret Thatcher in the UK and Ronald Reagan in the USA. The intellectual basis of New Right thinking is often associated with writers such as the political economist and philosopher Friedrich Hayek and the economist Milton Friedman and the development of free market or 'public choice' economics. New Right thinking is also heavily influenced by ideas of **individualism**, and advocates social and governmental systems based on this.

new social movements Collective protests, aiming to work through public opinion and civil society. The women's movement and environmental movements have influenced social policy widely, including health policy.

new social movements Social movements are collective attempts to change social arrangements through public campaigns. Traditional movements included the labour movement and the suffragette movement. Since the 1960s a number of new social movements have developed or renewed themselves as part of the general liberalization of social values at that time. These include movements focused on environmentalism, women, and anti-racism.

new social movements The term is usually applied to the kind of globally oriented campaigns—such as second-wave feminism, pacifism, and environmentalism (but including the anti-racist and disability awareness movements)—that developed during the last half of the twentieth century and challenged the existing boundaries of institutional politics.

NGO (Non-Governmental Organization) Term traditionally used to identify those agencies dedicated to economic and social development in the Third World.

nominal variable Also known as a **categorical variable**, this is a **variable** in which the numbers used to name the different answers do not represent size or rank order.

non-probability sampling In this type of **sampling** the **sample** is not selected using **random sampling**. This means that some units in the **population** are more likely to be selected than others. See also **probability sampling.**

normalization The principle that people with learning disabilities or other impairments should lead a life which resembles, as far as possible, the rest of society, with equal opportunities to live independently, study, work, enjoy close relationships, and pursue leisure activities.

normative concepts Much debate in social policy between different major ideological positions, such as Left and Right, takes place at a middle range, or intermediate level, over particular concepts that are prescriptive—that is, they say what ought to be or should be the case. The case for more or less state intervention, or equality, for example, is often made through appeal to these middle-range normative concepts, such as needs, choices, justice, merit, rights, and obligations.

normative need How an expert, such as a doctor or welfare professional, may define need in a given situation or circumstance. It is important because welfare professionals are closely involved in the identification of need, and the determining of how this may best be met within the confines of existing resources.

not-for-profit organizations Those that seek only to cover the costs of providing services, as do most charitable welfare organizations, and not to make a profit.

nuclear family This term was coined by sociologists to describe the social group consisting of parents and their children; it is particularly contrasted with the extended family, which includes members of the wider kin group, such as grandparents, uncles and aunts, cousins, nephews and nieces, and grandchildren (McCarthy and Edwards, 2011).

obligations In recent years most shades of ideological opinion have come to place increasing emphasis on the obligations that go along with the rights that individuals can acquire. This is in part a recognition of the anthropological observation of the central place of reciprocity in social life: exchanges are usually balanced, and in the case of a right the balance is an obligation. Thus an individual is expected to work hard, get better, or take employment in exchange for education, healthcare, and income support.

occupational identity In the past a lot of men, especially skilled workers, could expect to stay in their industry or craft throughout their working lives, and as a result there were often strong occupational identities, for example in shipbuilding, mining, and the steel industry.

occupational welfare The benefits which a person receives by virtue of their occupation or career.

offending behaviour programmes Groupwork (and sometimes individual) intervention based on a synthesis of methods from behavioural and cognitive psychology which aim to change how offenders think and feel about themselves, their victims, and their environment in order to encourage behavioural change which reduces or halts further offending.

Office for Budget Responsibility (OBR) Created in 2010 the office produces an independent assessment of the public finances and the economy before each Budget and regular assessments of the health of public finances.

Office for Civil Society Created in the Cabinet Office in May 2010, to take a lead across government on Big Society policies.

official inquiry Government-sponsored review of the operations of a particular area of policy.

Open Method of Co-ordination (OMC) a form of policy coordination at the EU level. Agreed upon at the Lisbon Summit of March 2000, the OMC has become a means of spreading best practice within the EU and thereby achieving greater convergence. Its mechanisms include fixing guidelines at the EU level and translating them into national and regional policies by setting specific targets, adopting quantitative and qualitative indicators and benchmarks, and monitoring and evaluating policy development. The OMC has become a central tool for the European Employment Strategy and the EU 'social inclusion' process.

open question Survey question in which the respondent is asked to answer in their own words. See also **closed question**.

openness in adoption Adoptions where contact (which may take a variety of forms) is continued between the adopted child and the birth family.

opportunity cost Refers to the value of all possible lost opportunities to consume resources in other ways from the current or proposed one.

oral history A process of collecting, usually by means of an **unstructured interview**, recollections, accounts, and personal experience narratives of individuals for the purpose of understanding historical events.

Organization for Economic Cooperation and Development (OECD) A Paris-based international organization financed mainly by the leading international industrial countries set up in the wake of the US Marshall Plan of the 1940s. The OECD is engaged in a variety of research and similar activities in areas ranging from economic forecasting and studies of comparative economic performance to science policy, environmental policy, and the growing importance and effects of information technology.

outcome measure Type of measure (of social policy) which looks at final impact, e.g. level of illness, examination results. It is usually affected by non-policy influences too.

outdoor relief Following the 1601 Poor Law, this was provision (such as money, food or clothing) given to help individuals avoid poverty without the need to enter an institution—the workhouse.

output measure Measure of volume of service produced, e.g. number of patients treated, number of council houses built, number of people receiving home help. An intermediate measure between input measures and outcome measures.

panel survey design A type of **longitudinal survey** that is carried out with the same respondents at least twice, and sometimes many more times. See also **cohort survey design.**

paradigm shift Term used by Thomas Kuhn (1962) to explain scientific advancement; later applied to social sciences, the humanities, and other fields. A paradigm shift occurs when one collective set of beliefs about how things work is replaced, given new evidence or arguments, by another.

parental responsibility The Children Act 1989 used this term to sum up the collection of duties, rights, and authority which a parent has in respect of a child. The aim was to stress that parents, rather than the state, have the prime responsibility for children. Mothers, and the fathers of legitimate children, automatically have parental responsibility, while fathers who are not married to the mother of the child can acquire parental responsibility in a number of different ways (Department of Health 1989: 1).

parish An administrative subdivision of a county.

participation rates This refers to the percentage of a particular group, for example women, who are in or seeking paid employment.

particularism An excessive focus on a particular group.

paternalism A person or a government that behaves in a benevolent and yet intrusive manner towards subordinates.

path dependency A situation in which the set of policy options one faces is limited by the decisions made in the past, even though past circumstances may no longer be relevant.

pensioner states A term used by the OECD to describe countries that spend 10 per cent or more of their GDP on income payments to retired people.

permanence A principle of childcare which seeks to avoid **drift** and to resolve the long-term futures of children both decisively and fairly speedily.

permissive legislation Legislation which allows but does not require, for example, a council to undertake certain actions.

personality disorder An enduring pattern of inner experience and behaviour that deviates markedly from cultural expectations, is pervasive and inflexible, has an onset in adolescence or early adulthood, is stable over time, and leads to distress or impairment (APA 1994). Some argue that personality disorder is not a treatable mental health problem, being an enduring feature of an individual's character. Yet the public outcry over violence perpetrated by people labelled with 'dangerous and severe personality disorder' has made it an important issue in the development of mental health policy and practice.

personalization In UK social care policy, personalization refers to the trend towards decentralized, flexible service packages which can be tailored to meet individuals' needs. A key element is self-directed support, whereby individuals control their own needs assessment and care management.

person-centred planning An approach to personal support developed within learning disability services which seeks to realize the aspirations of individuals by giving them control over the planning process, recognizing them as experts with respect to their own lives.

philanthropy Practical efforts to promote the happiness and well-being of others, especially by the generous donation of money to good causes.

platform of european social NGOs An alliance of European federations and networks of non-governmental organizations active in the social sector. It promotes social justice and participatory democracy by voicing the concerns of its member organizations.

plural pragmatism Sees globalization as a long-term process, resulting in greater interdependence of national economies, driven by a variety of forces, including technological, ideological, and cultural ones. In this view local and national factors continue to be of importance in mediating the impact of global forces.

points system System of allocating council housing in which applicants are given points based on criteria of housing need.

policies Plans of action formulated in general terms by political parties, and their representatives in government, especially ministers, and often developed in detail by civil servants.

policy networks Informal affiliations of actors with a conscious interest in shaping policies and their outcomes.

political legitimacy Term used to indicate the likely necessity that policy initiatives and spending decisions should match the values and expectations both of voters and of those making such proposals. For example, while the economic case for reforming the welfare state may be strong, the political legitimacy of many proposals for this may be challenged by the public.

Poor Law The law in England under which provision was made for the destitute from the seventeenth to the early twentieth century.

population ageing Refers to the shift in the distribution of a country's population towards older ages, usually reflected in an increase in the population's mean and median ages, which is caused by declining birth rates and increasing life expectancy. Occurring across most countries in the world.

population In research methods, the collection of all the people belonging to a particular group. Usually, in order to find out about a population one selects a **sample** to study and then infers from the sample to the population.

positional goods Some goods and services are valuable to us in part because they are not available to everyone. For example, not everyone can enjoy a beautiful country-side view from a commanding height above the potential viewing points of others. Some social services, such as higher education, can be thought of in this way. While there is a limited technical solution to the problem of mass viewing (as in football stadia and theatres), in the end there will have to be an unequal distribution of the view. We can describe these goods and services as 'positional goods'.

positive rights Economic and social rights, such as the right to health, education, or housing, which require redistribution of resources across society. Positive rights are more politically contentious than negative rights, which are political and civil rights that imply autonomy/non-interference, such as the right to freedom of speech.

positivism Most commonly associated with the Italian Cesare Lombroso (2006), the positivist school of crimi-nology views crime as caused by factors and processes that can be discovered by observation and scientific investiga-tion. Positivists often subscribe to the doctrine of determinism: that human beings, including criminals, do not act from their own free will but are impelled to act by forces beyond their control.

positivist Social science that proceeds on the model of the natural sciences, and that assumes that the more it resembles them the better—the more rigorous, more valid, more useful and so on—it will be.

postcode lottery Refers to the way that local budgets and decision-making can lead to unequal access to public services, particularly health and social services, across different localities in the UK.

post-industrial As the share of employment in industry has declined and advanced capitalist economies such as Britain are dominated by non-industrial employment, the term 'post-industrial' has been used to denote a new phase for these economies.

post-war settlement The political consensus, accepted by most major political parties in Britain and elsewhere, that the welfare state institutions established after the Second World War should be maintained.

poverty trap The situation where an increase in earnings leaves an employed individual not much better off due to the combined effects of taxes and benefit withdrawal.

pre-Budget report A report to Parliament by the Chancellor of the Exchequer. First introduced in 1997 it provides a progress report on the outcomes of government spending and outlines government economic policy that will inform the **Budget** the following spring.

pressure groups Organized groups aiming to develop or influence government policies.

Primary Care Trusts (PCTs) PCTs in England and Local Health Groups in Wales are the main purchasers of healthcare services. They receive money from central government, mainly according to their population size. PCTs provide primary care services, but purchase hospital and other services from other providers. They are being replaced by commissioning based on GP consortia. In Scotland the system of purchasing and providing is more integrated.

principle of proportional service provision Principle according to which provision varies in proportion to need.

principle of uniform service provision Principle according to which provision is equal per member of group in need.

Private Finance Initiative (PFI) A scheme introduced by John Major's Conservative government and continued by Tony Blair's Labour government that seeks to finance public sector projects (e.g. bridges, hospitals, student accommodation) by schemes that involve the injection of private-sector capital in return for an income stream from such investments to the financing organization (e.g. through tolls or rents).

private member's bill A proposed law introduced by a Member of Parliament (MP) or peer, from government or opposition parties, but without government support.

private social expenditure The definition used here is that developed by the OECD. It is expenditure by organizations separate from government, such as health insurance funds, or pension funds, to which people have been required by law to pay premiums and which subsequently provide individuals or households with payments or services in order to support them during circumstances that adversely affect their welfare.

private-for-profit organizations Organizations which, in the context of social policy, provide welfare services, such as social care or nursing home care, but seek not only to cover their costs but also to make a profit for their owners.

privatization When publicly owned resources are transferred to the independent sector. Government may retain some control over privatized resources, such as limiting prices or controlling quality through commissioning mechanisms.

privatization When publicly owned service providers are transferred into the for-profit sector and run by private owners.

probability sampling In this type of **sampling** each member of the **population** from which the **sample** is drawn has an equal chance of being included in the sample.

producer capture This occurs where the producer of a service is able to 'capture' and dictate the preferences of consumers and terms of service delivery. Professional groups such as doctors are accused of this control from time to time. Where consumer representatives or advocates have been set up, there is concern that in a more narrow sense they may also be captured and come to espouse the interests of the producers rather than the consumers.

professional associations Representative organizations for different professions, sometimes with a legal monopoly over the interests of a particular profession.

progressive taxation Taxation, usually of income, that takes a larger proportion of whatever is taxed the more someone has of it; e.g. a tax rate that starts at 10 per cent of income and rises in stages to a higher rate such as 40 per cent.

progressive taxes Taxes that take a growing proportion of people's incomes as their incomes go up. Income tax is usually progressive, the percentage rate of tax going up as particular income thresholds are passed. Taxes that do not rise in this way are said to be regressive.

Protocol on Social Policy Allowed eleven EU member states to proceed in implementing their 'agreement on social policy' in 1991. Impossible to reach agreement among the then twelve EU members, a solution was found in the form of an 'opt-out' for the UK from the social policy provisions of the Maastricht Treaty to which the Protocol was annexed in December 1991.

public and private spheres The separation of public and private has a long history in Western European thought, deriving from the Ancient Greek distinction between the *polis*, meaning the sphere of public life, and the *oikos*, meaning the private household. The involvement of the state in the private life of the family has been criticized as interference and control, or it has been welcomed as a support to the work done in this sphere and as a check on the tyranny which the strong can exercise over weaker members of families.

Public Expenditure Survey (PES) Annual system of public expenditure planning in UK government involving bilateral bargaining between the major Whitehall spending departments and the Treasury, culminating in Cabinet agreement on public expenditure objectives over the next (and subsequent) financial years. Formerly conducted on an annual basis, this process was moved to a three-year cycle from 1998/9 (see further Cm. 3978, 1998).

public goods Products from which people cannot be excluded from consumption (e.g. fresh air) and where one person's consumption does not reduce what is available to another. There is no possible profit in the production and marketing of such goods.

public health A branch of medicine concerned with the health of communities and populations considered as a whole and the measures that can be taken to enhance it. It was central to social policy in the nineteenth century.

public schools These are independent schools, which charge fees; they do not have to provide the national curriculum.

public sector This is the share of the whole economy under the control of the government. It includes both central and local government, and the institutions of the welfare state, such as the health and education services and a growing number of government agencies.

Public Sector Net Borrowing (PSNB) Measures total managed expenditure (TME) less current receipts. PSNBex excludes the effects of financial interventions to support the banks and other forms of financial support to the private sector after 2007 (see: ONS 2010).

Public Sector Net Cash Requirement/Public Sector Borrowing Requirement (PSBR) The amount the government needs to borrow at any one time to bridge the gap between income and expenditure. In 1998 this was retitled the Public Sector Net Cash Requirement in line with other changes to the organization and operation of the public expenditure planning system introduced by the Labour government (Cm. 3978, 1998).

Public Sector Net Debt (PSND) Is a measure of the stock of debt that includes the government's financial liabilities (such as gilts and National Savings) less liquid assets. PSNDex excludes the value of liabilities due to the financial interventions to support the banking sector that are classified as temporary in the national accounts.

Public Service Agreements These were written agreements between the Treasury and government spending departments negotiated as part of the **Comprehensive Spending Reviews** between 1998 and 2007 and published with the reviews. They set out the main performance outcomes the departments were expected to achieve over the next three years, how they were measured and who was responsible for achieving them. In 2010 they were replaced with the Transparency Framework.

public social expenditure The definition used here is that developed by the OECD. It is expenditure by governments on services or payments provided to households and individuals in order to support them during circumstances that adversely affect their welfare.

purchaser–provider splits The separation of a state welfare bureaucracy into one part that commissions the provision and another part that 'contracts' to provide it.

purposive sampling A **sampling** technique in which researchers purposely choose respondents who, in their opinion, are relevant to the project because of their knowledge and expertise.

qualitative methods Research methods which involve words rather than quantification. See also **quantitative methods.**

quality of life The basis for one attempt at measuring medical need, and hence distinguishing between different medical cases where resources are limited and have to be rationed. The argument is that medical care should be used to maximize the number of years and the quality of life of the patient. In principle this allows a rational choice to be made, for example between a case where the quality of life will only be increased modestly, but over many years, and a case where quality may be increased substantially but for a short period only. This might favour the treatment of children over the treatment of older people, for example.

quango A quasi-autonomous non-governmental organization, operating at arm's length from the central state and local authority, but authorized to oversee aspects of public administration such as health service trusts.

quangos Quasi non-governmental organizations; that is, only partly independent of government influence, often appointed by government, but supposedly free to pursue policies independently.

quantitative methods Research methods which involve numbers and measuring. See also **qualitative methods.**

quasi-market A public sector institutional structure that is designed to lead to the efficiency gains of free markets without losing the social goals of traditional systems of public administration and financing.

quasi-markets Markets in social services, such as schools and healthcare, set up administratively to encourage different providers to compete with each other in the hope that this will motivate them to increase quality, or at least cut costs, and that consumers will get greater choice as a result. They are not full markets, since there are many areas where natural monopolies operate, where real prices are difficult to set for complex services, or where it is not politically acceptable for services to be driven out of business. Experience to date suggests that the costs of inter-unit contractual development have been high, and that choice has not been greatly increased.

quasi-markets Where internal markets or contracting out are limited by regulations that mean the arrangements are not fully exposed to market competition.

quota sampling A **sampling** strategy that aims to achieve a **sample** that reflects the population in terms of categories such as gender, ethnicity, age group, socio-economic group and so on. However, unlike a **stratified sample**, once the numbers to be surveyed in each of these combinations of categories (strata) are decided, respondents are not selected randomly but by the interviewer.

racialization A process through which racial definitions and racist ideologies are actively promoted or may acquire particular salience.

random sampling **Sampling** in which each unit in the **population** has an equal chance of being included in the **sample** drawn.

rates of return This refers to extra earnings gained by an individual who invests in extended education. For example, a university student may forgo some earnings now in expectation that a degree will subsequently increase earnings. This is a private rate of return, but there can also be social rates of return, although there is more debate about these. In the latter case it is argued that, for example, the extra earnings accruing from extended education translate into a measure of the society's economic gain overall.

rationing Decisions about allocating resources: which services to provide as part of the NHS and which not and who should be treated and who not.

real spending Spending which has been adjusted for the effect of the general level of inflation in the economy.

realist approach An approach to interpreting crime data which suggests that they reflect 'real' trends in criminal behaviour, as opposed to the practices of the institutions that produce the data.

recognition The acknowledgement of personal identities and social differences in relation to people's needs and the claims they make upon each other.

recorded crime Crime which is recorded by the police and notified to the Home Office. Includes all 'indictable' and 'triable either way' offences together with some closely related 'summary offences'.

recovery approach An approach to the treatment of mental health problems and other long-term conditions which emphasizes hope, self-determination, and the potential for individuals to fulfil their chosen life goals despite their diagnoses or symptoms.

redistributive A system which reduces inequality by taking a higher proportion of taxes from higher-income groups and giving a higher proportion of services and benefits to poorer households.

reductive Punishment which seeks to reduce the incidence of the types of behaviour prohibited by the criminal law, whether committed by the person punished (individual deterrence) or by others (general deterrence).

registered social landlord Another term for housing association.

regulation Achieving social policy objectives by requiring people or organizations to do things such as wear seatbelts, send their children to school, or abide by health and safety standards and practices.

regulation Where social service provision, whether by government or by other organizations, is monitored carefully in accordance with legally enforceable rules and standards.

relative deprivation Deprivation measured by comparing one's situation to that of relevant others, or to standards accepted in a particular society at a particular time.

relative income standard of poverty A measure of poverty which relates it to average income levels within society. For instance, those found to be living at or below incomes which are 50 per cent of the average may be defined as being in poverty.

reliability Data are reliable when repeated measurements of the same thing are consistent.

remand prisoners Unconvicted persons committed to custody rather than released on bail pending a further stage of criminal proceedings. The defendant is said to be 'on remand' during the adjournment.

rent control Controls imposed by legislation on the level of rents which landlords can charge tenants.

replacement rate The difference between earnings and benefits when out of work.

replacement ratio The ratio between the total income of an unemployed person (including benefits) and the income they could earn if employed. If the ratio is high, then it acts as a disincentive to seeking employment.

residualization Process of social change in council housing in which the composition of households changes to include more households in great housing need. This happens because households leaving council housing are less deprived than those entering, due for example to the right to buy and to homelessness legislation.

resources Capacities for action, often financial, but also personal, cultural, scientific, or political.

response rate The percentage of respondents invited to take part in a survey who agree to take part in the research and return a usable questionnaire.

restorative justice A new way of thinking about responding to crime, aiming to make offenders aware of the harm they have caused and encouraging them, in consultation with victims and members of their community, to seek to make reparation (direct or indirect) for the harm.

retributive Punishment which sets out to impose an amount of pain proportionate to that caused by the criminal act. The criminal receives his or her **just desserts**.

right to buy The council house privatization policy introduced by the Conservative government in 1980 under which council tenants were given the right to buy their council house or flat at a discount. This replaced the previous policy under which councils had the 'right to sell' housing, a right which was little used.

rights Constitutionally or legally defined capacities, such as the capacity to vote, usually conferred on members of the relevant community or society, often through the acquisition of citizenship. Where these involve freedom from constraint, such as the capacity to engage in religious worship, they are relatively simple to define and cheap to guarantee. Where they involve capacities that depend on the provision of services such as education or healthcare or income maintenance, they are difficult to define and expensive to guarantee. The Right has tended to argue for rights to freedom from constraint; the Left has tended to argue for rights to services.

risk regime The risk regime or risk society is usually counterposed to the earlier **Fordist regime** as being a society, economy, and polity in which insecurity, uncertainty, and loss of boundaries prevail. The life course is individualized and people can no longer rely on standard experiences and assumptions; they must chart their own paths.

risk society A term coined by Ulrich Beck to refer to the way in which complex industrial societies present individuals, and even whole populations, with a range of risks created by technology, the economic market, and powerful organizations and institutions.

risk society A term that has been coined to characterize the increasing insecurity to which the inhabitants of post-industrialized societies are, supposedly, exposed, having regard to the effects of global economic, demographic, cultural, ecological and other changes.

Royal Commission A major inquiry into an important or controversial issue, which usually involves research and consultation with a range of experts and sometimes the general public.

rule of optimism A term used by Dingwall and colleagues which suggests that professionals generally give parents the benefit of the doubt where there might be suspicions of child abuse.

rules Agreed course of action, established in law or by custom and practice.

rules of access Criteria applied by owners and financiers of housing governing who gains access to housing and under what conditions.

same-race placements A policy under which children from particular racial or ethnic groups will be fostered or adopted by families from the same group.

sample In research methods, a subset of members of a **population** selected for research. Statistics collected from a sample can be used to make inferences to the population. The process of selecting a sample is referred to as **sampling**. The method of selection may be based on **probability sampling** or **non-probability sampling**.

sampling frame In research methods, a list of the members of the **population** from which the **sample** is selected.

sampling In research methods, the process of selecting a **sample**.

sceptic internationalism Rejects globalization, believing international economy is best described as involving transactions between distinct national economies. Accepts the state's control has diminished in some areas but argues that it has increased in others.

secondary data analysis Analysis of data that the researcher did not collect themselves.

selectivism Allocating benefits or services on the basis of income or a means test.

self-completion questionnaire A questionnaire that the respondent answers without the help of an interviewer.

self-directed support Originating in social care services but now extending to health, education, and other services, this term refers to a system in which service users are enabled to control their own support. Covers direct payments and individual budgets.

semi-structured interview A type of interview in which the interviewer asks questions in the **interview guide** in the same way to all respondents but may alter their sequencing and may probe for more information.

sentenced prisoners Persons committed to custody following conviction of a criminal offence in a law court.

service sector It is typical to characterize the economy as divided into three main sectors: the primary sector, which includes activities such as agriculture, mining, and fishing; the industrial sector, which includes manufacture and construction; and the service sector, which includes retail, banking, teaching, and health and personal services.

services in kind Social services which are provided to users directly, such as education, healthcare, or housing, rather than money (cash benefits) for them to purchase the benefits themselves.

short breaks A service involving short breaks when children are looked after by another family or in a residential unit in order to give parents (and sometimes children) respite. Most commonly used for children with disabilities but also available as a support service for families under stress. Previously known as respite care.

short-run efficiency Obtaining the maximum satisfaction at the lowest cost in the very immediate term. Unlike **long-run efficiency**, this is usually obtained by using up all resources as fast as possible, for example in a war.

simple random sampling In this method of **sampling** each unit in the **population** (such as individuals or businesses) has an equal probability of being selected for the survey.

snowball sampling A sampling strategy in which the researcher approaches a small group of respondents initially and asks them to suggest other potential respondents within their social network. Those respondents and then asked if they have any contacts who would be willing to participate in the research, and so on, until sufficient respondents have been found.

social administration The management of the production and distribution of social services in general. It was used to define the academic discipline of social administration from the late 1940s, when the first chair in the subject was established at the University of Nottingham, and the national association which dealt with the subject, the Social Administration Association. In 1988 the title was changed to the Social Policy Association to reflect a wider academic interest in the sociological and political science analysis of the welfare state. 'Social administration' now connotes a rather limited and uncritical approach to the subject, dominant between the 1940s and the 1970s.

social and environmental models A social model of health stresses inequalities between socio-economic groups as key determinants of health. Environmentalists share the concern with factors beyond the individual, but are more focused on health hazards which may affect everyone: nuclear fallout, agricultural chemicals, air pollution.

social capital Refers to those relationships between individuals which are based on reciprocity and trust rather than contract and payment. It is further conceptualized as of various types: bonding, bridging and linking social capital.

social construction The notion that a phenomenon—in this case crime—is not an objective, observable entity in the world waiting to be discovered, but rather is created (constructed) by social values and preconceptions.

social constructionist A sociological approach to knowledge that considers how social phenomena develop in social contexts, how they are created and institutionalized by people.

social contructivist An approach to a social issue that has been created subjectively by a group of people that may bear little connection to objective facts or circumstances

social Darwinism In the nineteenth century the revolutionary biological ideas of Charles Darwin were applied to society and social relations by writers such as Spencer in the UK and Sumner in the United States. The main point taken from Darwin was the idea of the survival of the fittest, suggesting that state intervention to protect or support the weak was not only self-defeating but might be positively harmful if it allowed the weak to flourish at the expense of the strong.

social definitions (of crime) Definitions which are based not on whether or not an act is against the law (legal definitions) but on broader social criteria; for example, social values and norms or social justice.

social democratic Describes a welfare state with universal benefits, high standards in state provision and which promotes equality.

social democratic regimes The social democratic belief that capitalism can be reformed by state intervention lies behind the welfare strategies of Scandinavian countries. Social policies are based on government intervention to produce social cohesion, with higher taxation, income redistribution, labour market policies to bring people into work, and more equal outcomes than in most western European countries or the USA.

social dialogue Became a central institution in EU social policy making after the Social Agreement of the Maastricht Treaty in 1992. It seeks to involve the social partners in matters of EU social policy and requires the Commission to consult social partners before initiating policy in the area related to employment. Within the remit of the social dialogue, the Commission's role is to provide relevant information for policy making and to facilitate negotiations between the social partners. Social partners can initiate and formulate policy and determine which form of legislative instrument should be chosen for policy implementation, including collective agreements rather than formal adoption by the European Council Structural Funds.

social dimension Refers to areas of social policy competence where minimal standards are set at the EU rather than national level, e.g. in matters concerning workers residing in a member state other than their own, or moving between member states and in labour market related areas such as equal treatment, health and safety measures and working conditions.

social dumping A term which has been used to denote one possible outcome of economic and political integration between the member states of the EU. It refers to companies which might decide to move to countries where wages and wage related social contributions are low.

social enterprise Refers to organizations that apply market-based strategies to achieve a social purpose. Their aim is to accomplish targets that are social as well as financial. The movement includes both non-profits that use business models to pursue their mission and for-profits whose primary purposes are social.

social exclusion The processes by which people become disconnected from the wider society and the communities they live in because of characteristics they have (low incomes, age, poor education) or because of the ways in which they are discriminated against by other people or institutions.

social exclusion A term, first developed in continental Europe, for the conditions and causal processes which characterize a broader range than income poverty; so social and political exclusion are included as well as limited financial resources. The term can be applied to individuals, groups and localities.

social inclusion policies Those that seek to combat the processes of **social exclusion**.

social insurance contributions Also known as National Insurance contributions in the UK. These are the payments that people make out of their wage packets in addition to direct taxation in order to pay for and build entitlements to state-financed pensions, healthcare, and unemployment insurance benefits. In some cases the money is paid into special funds but often it is simply an addition to general government revenues.

social insurance principle The principle that individuals should be collectively insured against the risks, e.g. unemployment, which they face within the labour market, through the payment of contributions into a fund during periods of employment.

social model of disability Theoretical approach that distinguishes between impairment and disability, regarding disability as caused by material, attitudinal, and structural barriers within society. The locus of change lies in society, not the individual, according to this model.

social movements Collective non-parliamentary attempts to change substantial areas of social life, major social institutions, prevailing ideologies and identities, or government policies. Often split between 'old' social movements, such as the labour movement, and 'new' social movements, such as environmentalism, feminism, or anti-racism.

social need A judgement that someone is lacking something (income, education, housing, or social care for example) that they ought to have, or has fallen below some minimum level in some area. The term can be given more precision by unpacking it into felt need, expressed need, normative need, comparative need, and technical need.

social origins framework A theoretical approach to explaining patterns of non-profit development among countries that focuses on broad social, political, and economic relationships.

social partners A term which is used in some European countries, and also by the EU, as a description of employer and employee (e.g. trade union) organizations. Within the EU social partners have adopted an increasingly important role as policy initiators in the area of social policy. They are free to initiate and formulate policy and determine which form of legislative instrument should be chosen for policy implementation, including collective agreements rather than formal adoption by the European Council.

social partnership model This refers to joint public and private funding of training provision through tripartite (government, industry, trade unions) delivery systems within a framework of nationally agreed procedures and standards.

social policy The principles and practice of state activity—including state policy for private or voluntary action—relating to redistribution in pursuit of, or leading to, welfare outcomes.

social positivism The positivist belief that the main cause of crime is to be found in social conditions rather than in the biological or psychological make-up of the individual.

social reproduction The idea that in addition to the biological reproduction of human beings, there is an equally important activity of reproducing the fundamental social relationships necessary to the continuity of human society. These include the capacity for relating to a group and responding appropriately to emotions, mostly learnt in families, and the capacity to learn and to work cooperatively, mostly learnt in schools.

social role valorization The principle that certain populations that are labelled as 'different' and devalued by society, such as people with learning disabilities, should have opportunities to contribute to society and receive acknowledgement for their contribution.

social security The system of benefits and transfers for income maintenance.

social stigma Refers to negative attitudes towards and/or discrimination against groups of people who share certain characteristics that are labelled as 'different', such as those with mental health problems, learning difficulties, or physical impairments.

social wage If public spending is treated as a source of benefits to individuals, then the value of the services and cash payments received per household can be termed a 'social wage' since it is like a form of income.

social wage The social wage is the income value of all the benefits in kind and in cash that individuals and households obtain from state welfare, such as free education and healthcare, income credits, and children's allowances. In some countries and for some households they constitute substantial proportions of total incomes.

social wage The value of welfare services which are provided in kind, rather than as cash benefits, such as the NHS, state education, personal social services, and subsidized social housing.

social welfare The well-being of individuals or of families, households, and whole communities, in both material but also non-material terms such as education and health, which is produced through the provision of goods and services by families, the community, the voluntary sector, the market, and the state.

sociological imagination A term which has been coined by C.W. Mills (1976). Mills referred to the ability of the possessor of this imagination to grasp history and biography and to place his or her daily experience into a wider structural and historical framework. A similar type of understanding and reflection can be reached by studying and comparing countries or societies.

special guardianship Introduced under the Adoption and Children Act 2002 as a form of permanence without the finality and complete severance of ties characteristic of adoption. Typically used when the child does not wish to be adopted, or there are very strong connections with the birth family or cultural/religious opposition to adoption.

state model This model of training is when public funding via taxation and delivery through public institutions predominates, within a context of legal training rights and duties.

statist A welfare system that supports the use of the state to achieve goals.

status The esteem in which we are held in a community in relation to some of the central values cherished in that community. Max Weber argued that it was the third basic dimension that stratified societies alongside class and power. The new social movements have increasingly drawn attention to the way in which social values can divide people by esteem. Where maleness, whiteness, and physical and mental dexterity are esteemed, this can lower the status of women and of black and disabled people.

statutory homeless Those who are unintentionally homeless and in priority need.

stepfamilies Families in which one or both parents have been married before, so at least one parent–child relationship involves a step-parent and a stepchild.

stigma Is the mark or signal that someone has an identifiable condition or is in a recognized situation which attracts public disrespect, disgrace, discomfort, disgust and so on, and who consequently experiences personal shame.

stigma The feeling of shame and rejection which accompanies low status.

stratification A central concept in Esping-Andersen (1990) who refers to it as the type of social structure which welfare programmes help to promote. In Esping-Andersen (1990) it is a composite measurement consisting of the degree of corporatism (e.g. number of distinct public pension schemes), etatism (pension expenditure on government employees), average levels of benefit universalism and benefit equality, plus spending on means-tested social expenditure, private pensions and private health care.

Stratified sampling In this method of **sampling,** the **population** is split into subgroups known as strata. Within each subgroup selection is made at random.

structural deficit A gap between government expenditure and tax receipts that is growing faster than the economy and will continue to do so unless either expenditure is reduced or taxes increased. A risk attached to reducing public expenditure or increasing taxes is that doing so will reduce growth even further. If a public expenditure deficit is not tackled a point may be reached where the government can no longer finance the borrowing required because interest rates demanded by lenders rise too high.

Structured interviews A type of research interview in which the interviewer asks questions with the same wording and the same order in each interview using an **interview schedule**.

subsidiarity This idea originated within the Roman Catholic Church and has been adopted as a central principle of the European Community. It expresses the idea that actions should be taken at the lowest appropriate administrative level. So actions should not be undertaken by nation-states if they can be carried out by regional bodies, and public agencies should not take on responsibilities which can be undertaken within the family (Hantrais and Letablier 1996: 45).

subsistence level The level of income that will purchase only basic necessities, and often used to refer to the lowest level at which benefits should be set.

supervision order Requires a young person aged 17 years or under to be supervized by a member of a youth offending team for between three months and three years. Specified activities to help them address their offending behaviour can be attached as a condition of the order.

supply side Refers to the goods and services people produce (supply) in the economy. Typical policy recommendations of supply-side economics are lower marginal tax rates and less regulation. According to the theory, consumers will then benefit from a greater supply of goods and services at lower prices.

support ratio Refers to the number of people of working age per person of pension age; affected by birth rates and changing life expectancy.

supramedian demand The demand of the non-majority of voters for collective goods.

sustainable investment rule The self-imposed fiscal rule followed by Gordon Brown when Chancellor of the Exchequer that public sector net debt as a proportion of GDP will be maintained below 40 per cent of GDP over the **economic cycle**.

take-up Refers to the percentage of those who receive the benefits to which they are entitled.

take-up The extent to which all those entitled to a service or benefit receive it.

tax credits Instead of taking from incomes as they rise, the tax authorities add to people's incomes as they fall below a defined amount. Tax credits are an alternative to a separate system of means-tested cash benefits.

technical change Inventions and innovations that allow cheaper ways of producing existing goods or which create new goods.

technical need Need arising when some new provision is invented or existing provision is made much more effective, creating a need for a solution that was not previously available.

technological enthusiasm Conceives of globalization as transnationalization of world economy, driven by developments of information and communication technologies, resulting in the creation of a borderless world as **transnational corporations (TNCs)** and **multilateral economic institutions** (MEIs) grow in influence relative to declining state power.

territorial injustice Where social service provision in relation to need is unequal between different geographical areas.

territorial justice A situation where the provision of services in different areas varies in proportion to inter-area differences in need.

Thatcherism The ideas and policies of Margaret Thatcher, the British Prime Minister 1979–1990.

think tanks Groups relatively autonomous from government which specialize in policy innovation and advice.

third sector This term attempts to avoid debate about the relevance of 'voluntary', 'non-profit', and 'independent' as alternative labels; it does not imply lower rank or status in relation to other sectors.

third way A term adopted by New Labour to describe policy initiatives combining state, for-profit, and voluntary sector values and institutions rather than reflecting any single sector.

third way The approach of the New Labour government which came to power in 1997. It looked for a route between two political traditions, based on the central state (old Labour) and the market (new Right), using a mixture of state and market, according to 'what works'.

top-up fees Fees that higher education institutions may charge above the standard fee paid by the state for lower income families (£1,100 in 2003). From 2006 up to £3,000 may be charged.

Total Managed Expenditure The sum of Departmental Expenditure Limits (DEL) and Annually Managed Expenditure (AME).

trade unions Representative organizations for working people whose major allegiance is to further the interests of their members, in terms of working conditions and wages.

training There is no single agreed definition of training. A definition used by the Department of Employment in 1993 is not untypical: training is an 'intentional intervention to help the individual (or the organization) to become competent, or more competent, at work' (Department of Employment, 1993: 8).

transcript The written version of the recording of an interview or **focus group** session.

Transnational Corporations (TNCs) (also known as Multinational Corporations, or MNCs). Large business enterprises which have operations in a variety of countries. They increasingly dominate the world economy and international trade and are seen as operating outside the control of national governments. A small number of them have annual turnovers greater than the GDP of many nations.

Transparency Framework This is the overall name for the systems of accountability that replaced the Public Service Agreements from 2010. It consists mainly of a requirement that government departments and other publicly funded agencies produce business plans that include indicators of performance. Departments are required to produce monthly reports on progress to meeting targets. The Framework places considerable emphasis on publication on the web for public scrutiny of expenditures by public bodies

transracial adoption The adoption of a child from one racial group by a family from another; in practice, almost invariably the adoption of minority ethnic children by white families.

ultimate needs Needs which are seen as ends in themselves, and to which other activities and needs are directed: for example, survival, autonomy, and self-fulfilment may be defined as ultimate human needs.

underclass 'A social group or class of people located at the bottom of the class structure who, over time, have become structurally separate and culturally distinct from the regularly employed working class and society in general through processes of social and economic change (particularly de-industrialization) and/or through patterns of cultural behaviour, who are now persistently reliant on state benefits and almost permanently confined to living in poorer conditions and neighbourhood.' (Macdonald 1997: 3–4.)

unemployment trap Due to a combination of benefit withdrawal, taxation, and low wages, the earnings received while in work are hardly greater than the income received while out of work.

unintended consequences Occur where policy actions over time may not bring about the changes intended, through ignorance, error, ideological commitment, or self-contradiction.

unintentionally homeless Not homeless by their own choice. A concept introduced in the 1977 Homelessness Act which obliged local councils to provide housing only for those who were 'unintentionally' homeless (and who had a local connection), as opposed to those who were considered to have made themselves homeless by their own choice.

universal service, universalizing the best The NHS was founded on the principle of providing to the whole population, according to need rather than ability to pay. The stigma attached to means-tested provision and the poorer quality of services for poorer people which characterized Poor Law systems were to be avoided by providing the highest-quality care for everyone, 'universalizing the best'.

universalism Allocating benefits or services to all who fall into certain categories irrespective of their income.

unstructured interview An interview in which the interviewer typically has only a list of areas to be covered (an **interview guide**). The phrasing and sequencing of questions will vary from interview to interview.

urbanization The process by which populations become concentrated in towns.

user involvement Refers to participation of service users in some or all stages of the policy-making process, including needs assessment, policy development, and evaluation.

value added In relation to education, this refers to the extent to which schooling has affected the rate of learning or improvement of an individual child. Whereas league tables measure outcome in terms of examination or test performance, a value-added measure would need to assess how much a child had progressed, regardless of whether or not they achieved a particular test outcome.

variable An observation, characteristic or measurement from a study of **cases**.

vertical dimension of need Need defined in terms of its hierarchical distribution amongst similar units, such as individuals or households, such that some are said to have higher needs than others.

vertical redistribution The taking away of resources (usually in the from of taxation) from those who have more and the distribution of them to others who have less (usually in the form of cash benefits or services in kind).

victimology The study of the relationship between victims and offenders. The academic 'discipline' of victimology was founded in the late 1940s.

volume spending Spending which has been adjusted for the effect of the level of inflation experienced in a particular sector, e.g. healthcare.

voluntarism This is the belief that society and industry are best left to manage their own social and employment affairs free of government intervention or legislation.

voluntarism Voluntary action not directly constrained by state coercion or driven essentially by market imperatives, and also outside the informal sector.

voluntary and community sector (VCS) A generic term for the total field of non-profit distributing organizations, which have varying numbers of volunteers on their management and in their workforce. The term is used to underline the inclusion of small and volunteer-led groups as well as larger organizations, with significant numbers of paid employees. Use of 'sector' does not imply a particular degree of common identity and organization.

volunteer Person who feels they are freely contributing their time to help an individual or group outside the immediate circle of family, neighbours, and friends.

volunteerism A subcategory of voluntarism, referring specifically to uncoerced giving of time, as opposed to money

vulnerable adults Someone aged 18 or over who is, or may be, in need of community care services because of mental or physical disability, age or illness; and who may be at risk of significant harm or exploitation (see *No Secrets* guidance, DH 2000).

'Washington consensus' Neo-liberal consensus which emphasizes privatization, economic and social deregulation, public sector reform, and residualized welfare provision as the formula for economic growth. There are claims that this has given way to a 'post-Washington consensus' which emphasizes the need for limited regulation, targeted poverty reduction, and 'smart' conditionalities.

welfare markets Refers to provision of public services, including social care, by independent sector agencies according to market principles.

welfare mix approach Refers to understanding welfare as derived not only from the state, but also from the market, and civil society.

welfare model Most commonly referred to in the context of juvenile justice to describe a 'positivistic' approach which holds that young offenders should be helped rather than punished. Transferable to the young adult offender and adult context.

welfare regime A term used to characterize or categorize the different kinds of welfare state arrangements that pertain in different countries or parts of the world. Categorization may be based on a variety of different criteria.

welfare regime Implies the existence of a certain logic of social policy provision, and specific configurations in which markets, states and family (or households) interact in the provision of welfare in a given country.

welfare state Refers to the governmental and/or administrative apparatus by or through which human services—including health and social care, education, housing and social security—may be provided, funded or regulated. In Britain the term was coined towards the end of the Second World War by those who urged that the administrative might of the warfare state be turned in peacetime to serve the cause of social welfare.

welfare state The institutional arrangements through which the state provides money, goods, and services to its citizens. This concept is usually used to refer to main institutions of the post-war welfare settlement: the National Health Service, the social security system, the state-funded education system, the state role in the provision and funding of housing, and state personal and social work services. Some observers insist that a welfare state, as distinct from some welfare services, can only be said to exist where the state guarantees that citizens will not fall below defined minima in terms of income and possibly health and education.

welfare states Those that have a self-conscious commitment to the provision of adequate minimal access to income, healthcare, education, and housing for all citizens.

welfare system The organizations and mechanisms primarily concerned with providing or guaranteeing the social welfare of citizens. These may include non-state organizations such as those in the voluntary sector and those in the private (for-profit) sector. This is a wider definition than the more traditional one of 'the welfare state'.

welfare to work An umbrella term for policies focused on getting people off benefits and back into paid employment.

welfarism An approach to youth crime which sees offending as a symptom of deprivation, whether psychological or social, and hence in need of social work intervention rather than punishment.

well-being A contestable term that refers to the state of being well or of having a good life. The term is contestable because there are different accounts of what might constitute a good life, but discussions of well-being have gained prominence as a possible alternative to the term 'welfare'.

what works A research-led agenda leading to increased optimism about the ability of community sentences to rehabilitate offenders and demonstrate reduced reconviction rates. As the latter are not an accurate measure of reoffending (measuring only those who get caught), measures of attitude and behavioural change are also used to evaluate the effectiveness of different sentences.

workfare Claimants are required to engage in some form of employment or training scheme in order to qualify for benefits.

workfare This can be defined as any social policy in which participation in job search, training, or work, is a condition of receiving benefits.

workhouse A form of institutional care in sixteenth to twentieth century Britain, paid for by local taxation, which housed destitute people of all ages in basic, communal lodgings in return for their labour. Workhouses could also accommodate those too elderly, infirm, impaired, or mentally unfit to work in 'sick wards' or similar facilities.

World Bank (WB) (The International Bank for Reconstruction and Development) Set up in 1944 to promote economic development in the developing world through providing loans for programmes and projects which assist economic development but for which no private finance can be found.

World Bank or International Bank for Reconstruction and Development, is one of the world's largest sources of development assistance. It works with government agencies, non-governmental organizations, and the private sector to formulate assistance strategies mainly to developing countries. As a consequence, it can have a considerable impact on social policy debates.

World Bank An agency of the United Nations, based in Washington. It has 184 member countries and its main function is to manage a large trust fund, made up of contributions from the richer nations, which is used to lend money, interest-free, over long periods to poorer countries for specific programmes, including poverty reduction, social services, protection of the environment, and promotion of economic growth. In 2002 the Bank provided loans totalling $11.5 billion in support of 96 projects in 40 countries.

World Health Organization (WHO) Established in 1948 as the UN specialist agency on health whose objective is the highest possible level of health for all peoples. It is governed by its 192 member states through the World Health Assembly.

World Trade Organization (WTO) Set up in 1995 to promote international trade, with executive and legal powers recognized in international law to enforce international trade and investment law and to adjudicate in international trade disputes.

zero tolerance A form of high-profile, proactive, maximum enforcement street policing that requires police officers to pursue minor offences with the same vigour as more serious ones in an attempt to reassure the public that all forms of crime and antisocial behaviour are under control.

REFERENCES

Abbott, P. and Wallace, C. (1997), *An Introduction to Sociology: Feminist Perspectives*. London: Routledge.

Abel-Smith, B. and Townsend, P. (1965), *The Poor and the Poorest*. Occasional Paper in Social Administration No. 17. London: Bell.

Abrahamson, P. (1999), 'The welfare modelling business', *Social Policy and Administration*, 33, 4, 394–415.

Abrahmson, P. (2000), 'The welfare modelling business'. In N. Manning and I. Shaw (eds), *New Risks, New Welfare: Signposts for Social Policy*. Oxford: Blackwell, 57–78.

Adam, S., Brewer, M. and Shephard, A. (2006), *The Poverty Trade-Off: Work Incentives and Income Redistribution In Britain*. Bristol: The Policy Press.

Addison, P. (1975), *The Road to 1945: British Politics and the Second World War*. London: Cape.

Adepoju, A. (2007), *Migration in sub-saharan Africa. A background paper commissioned by the Nordic Africa Institute for the Swedish Government White Paper on Africa*. [Online] Available at: http://www.sweden.gov.se/content/1/c6/08/88/66/730473a9.pdf (accessed 9 April 2010).

Age UK (2010), *Proportion of Over 65s Set to Soar*. Available online: http://www.ageuk.org.uk/latest-news/archive/over-65s-rise/?paging=false (accessed 28 October 2010).

Ahmad, O. B. (2005), Managing medical migration from poor countries. *British Medical Journal*, 331: 43–5. [Online] Available at: http://www.bmj.com/cgi/content/full/331/7507/43 (accessed 18 November 2006).

Alber, J. (1995), 'A framework for the comparative study of social services', *Journal of European Social Policy* 5, 2, 131–49.

—— (2010), 'What the European and American welfare states have in common and where they differ: facts and fiction in comparisons of the European Social Model and the United States', *Journal of European Social Policy* 20, 2, 102–25.

Alcock, P. (2010), 'Building the Big Society: a new policy environment for the third sector in England', *Voluntary Sector Review* 1, 3, 379–89.

—— (2011), 'Unpacking the Big Society discourse: Old political rhetoric or new policy programme', paper given at TSRC seminar, University of Southampton, 10th February, presentation forthcoming at http://www.tsrc.ac.uk/

—— and Kendall, J. (2011), 'Constituting the third sector: processes of decontestation and contention under the UK New Labour government in England', *Voluntas*, forthcoming.

Alcock, P., Beatty, C., Fothergill, P., Macmillan R. and Yeandle, S. (2003), *Work to Welfare: How Men Become Detached from the Labour Market*. Cambridge: Cambridge University Press.

Alcohol Strategy. London: Cabinet Office.

Aldcroft, D. H. (1992), *Education, Training and Economic Performance*. Manchester: Manchester University Press.

Aldridge, A. and Levine, K. (2001), *Surveying the Social World: Principles and Practice in Survey Research*. Buckingham: Open University Press.

Aldridge, M. (1979), *The British New Towns: a Programme Without a Policy*. London: Routledge.

Allen, G. (2001), *The Private Finance Initiative (PFI)*. Research paper 01/117. London: House of Commons Library.

Allen, R. (2006), *From Punishment to Problem Solving: A New Approach to Children in Trouble*. London: Centre for Criminal Justice Studies.

Alzheimer's Disease International (2010), *World Alzheimer Report 2010*. Available online: http://www.alz.co.uk/research/worldreport/ (accessed 20 October 2010).

American Psychiatric Association (APA) (1994), *Diagnostic and Statistical Manual of Mental Disorders (DSM-IV)*. Washington, DC: APA.

Andresen, R., Oades, L. and Caputi, P. (2003), 'The experience of recovery from schizophrenia: Towards an empirically validated stage model. Australian and New Zealand'. *Journal of Psychiatry* 37, 586–94.

Anheier, H.K. (2005), *Nonprofit Sector Organisation: Theory, Management, Policy*. London: Routledge.

Annetts, J., Law, A., McNeish, W. and Mooney, G. (eds) (2008), *Understanding Social Movements and Social Welfare*. Bristol: The Policy Press.

Anthony, W.A. (2000), 'A recovery-oriented service system: Setting some system level standards', *Psychiatric Rehabilitation Journal* 24, 2, 159–68.

Appleby, J. (2005), *Independent Review of Health and Social Care Services in Northern Ireland*. Available online: http://www.dhsspsni.gov.uk/publications/2005/appleby/appleby-contents.pdf (accessed 17 October 2010).

—— Boyle, S., Devlin, N., Harley, M., Harrison, A., Locock, L. and Thorlby, R. (2004), *Sustaining Reductions in Waiting Times: Identifying Successful Strategies. Final report to the Department of Health*. London: King's Fund (www.kingsfund.org.uk).

Arber, S. and Ginn, J. (1995), 'Gender differences in the relationship between paid employment and informal care', *Work, Employment and Society* 9, 3, 445–71.

Arts, W. and Gelissen, J. (2002), 'Three worlds of welfare capitalism or more? A state-of-the-art report', *Journal of European Social Policy* 12, 2, 137–58.

Ashdown, C. (2000), 'The Position of Older Workers in the Labour Market', *Labour Market Trends*, September: 397–400.

Ashton, D. (1992), 'The restructuring of the labour market and youth training', in Brown and Lauder (1992: 180–202).

Atkinson, A. B. (2005), *Measurement of Government Output and Productivity for the National Accounts Final Report*. London: Palgrave and HMSO. (Also at www.statistics.gov.uk)

—— Cantillon, B., Marlier, E. and Nolan, B. (2005), *Taking Forward the EU Social Exclusion Process*. Luxembourg: Ministere de la Famille et de L'Integration (available at: http://www.ceps.lu/eu2005%5Flu/inclusion/).

Audit Commission (1986), *Making a Reality of Community Care*. London: HMSO.

Audit Commission (1996), *Balancing the Care Equation: Progress with Community Care, Community Care Bulletin 3*. London: Audit Commission.

Audit Commission (2003), *Human Rights: Improving Public Service Delivery*. London: Audit Commission.

Audit Commission (2008), *The Effect of Fair Access to Care Services Bands on Expenditure and Service Provision*. London: Audit Commission.

Awases, M., Gbary, A., Nyoni J., and Chatora, R. 2004. *Migration of Health Professionals in Six Countries: A Synthesis Report*. Brazzaville: World HealthOrganization, Regional Office for Africa. [Online] Available at: http://www.afro.who.int/dsd/migration6countriesfinal.pdf (accessed 19 November 2006).

Babbie, E. (2008), *The Basics of Social Research*, 4th edn. Belmont, Ca.: Thomson.

Bacon, N., Brophy, M., Mguni, N., Mulgan, G. and Shandro, A. (2010), *The State of Happiness: Can Public Policy Shape People's Wellbeing and Resilience?* London: The Young Foundation.

Baggott, R. (1998), *Health and Health Care in Britain*. Basingstoke: Macmillan.

Bailey, R. (1973), *The Squatters*. Harmondsworth: Penguin.

Baldock, J. and Ungerson, C. (1996), 'Money, care and consumption', in H. Jones and J. Millar (eds), *The Politics of the Family*. Aldershot: Avebury.

Baldwin, S., Godfrey, C., and Propper, G. (1990), *Quality of Life: Perspectives and Policies*. London: Routledge.

Baldwin, P. (1996), 'Can we define a European welfare state model?', in B. Greve, *Comparative Welfare Systems* London: Macmillan.

Baldwin, S. and Falkingham, J. (eds) (1994), *Social Security and Social Change*. Hemel Hempstead: Harvester Wheatsheaf.

Ball, S. J. (2009), 'Privatising education, privatising education policy, privatising education research: network governance and the 'competition state' *Journal of Education Policy* Vol 24 (1), pp. 83–99.

—— Bowe, R. and Gewirtz, S. (1997), 'Circuits of schooling: a sociological exploration of parental choice of school in social-class contexts', in Halsey et al. (1997: 409–21).

Balls, E. (1993), 'Danger: men not at work: unemployment and non-employment in the UK and beyond'. In Balls, E.

and Gregg, P. (1993) *Work and Welfare. Tackling the Jobs Deficit*. London: Institute for Public Policy Research.

—— and Gregg, P. (1993), *Work and Welfare: Tackling the Jobs Deficit*. London: Institute for Public Policy Research.

Banting, K. and Kymlicka, W. (2006), *Multiculturalism and the Welfare State*. Oxford: Oxford University Press.

—— (2001), *The Audit of War: The Illusion and Reality of Britain as a Great Nation* London: Pan.

Barker, K. (2004), *Review of Housing Supply: Final report*. London: HMSO.

Barnes, G., Thompson, P., Daniel, G. and Burchardt, N. (1998), *Growing up in Stepfamilies*. Oxford: Clarendon Press.

Barnett, C. (1986), *The Audit of War*. London: Macmillan.

Barr, N. (1993), *The Economics of the Welfare State*, 2nd edn. Oxford: Oxford University Press.

—— and Coulter, F. (1990), 'Social Security: solution or problem?', in N. Barr, J. Hills, and J. Le Grand, (eds), *The State of Welfare*. Oxford: Oxford University Press. pp. 274–337.

Barry, N. (1990), *Welfare*. Milton Keynes: Open University Press.

Barter, C., Renold, E., Berridge, D. and Cawson, P. (2004), *Peer Violence in Children's Residential Care*. Basingstoke: Palgrave.

Beatty, C. and Forthergill, S. (forthcoming) 'The Changing Profile of Incapacity Claimants, in S. Vickerstaff, C. Phillipson and R. Wilkie (eds) *Work, Health and Wellbeing: The Challenges of Managing Health at Work*, Bristol: The Policy Press.

Beck, U. (1992), *Risk Society: Towards a new modernity* (London: Sage).

—— (2000), *The Brave New World of Work*. Cambridge: Polity Press.

—— and Beck-Gernsheim, E. (1995), *The Normal Chaos of Love*. Cambridge: Cambridge University Press.

—— and Beck-Gernsheim, E. (2001), *Individualization*. London: Sage Publications.

Becker, F. and Becker, S. (2008), *Young Adult Carers in the UK: Experiences, Needs and Services for Carers aged 16–24*. London: Princess Royal Trust for Carers.

Becker, S. (2007), 'Global perspectives on children's unpaid care-giving in the family: research and policy on young carers in the UK, Australia, the USA and sub-Saharan Africa'. *Global Social Policy*, 7, 1, 23–50.

—— and Bryman, A. (eds) (2004), *Understanding Research for Social Policy and Practice: Themes, Methods and Approaches* Bristol: The Policy Press.

Beckford, J. (1991), 'Great Britain: Voluntarism and sectoral interests', in R. Wuthnow (ed) *Between States and Markets: The Voluntary Sector in Comparative Perspective*. New Jersey: Princeton University Press.

Beddoe, C. (2007), *Missing Out: A Study of Child Trafficking in the North-West, North-East and West Midlands*. London: ECPAT UK.

Bell, A. and Lindley, P. (2005), *Beyond the Water Towers: The Unfinished Revolution in Mental Health Services*. London: The Sainsbury Centre for Mental Health.

Benzeval, M., Judge, K. and Whitehead, M. (1995), *Tackling Inequalities in Health: An Agenda for Action*. London: King's Fund.

Bernard, J. (1982), *The Future of Marriage*. New Haven: Yale University Press.

Berridge, D. (2008), 'Theory and explanation in child welfare: education and looked after children', *Child and Family Social Work* 12(1): 1–10.

—— and Brodie, I.(1998), *Children's Homes Revisited*. London: Jessica Kingsley.

Berridge, V. (2008), 'History Matters? History's Role in Health Policy Making', *Medical History* 52(3): 311–26.

Berthoud, R. and Gershuny, J. (2000), *Seven Years in the Lives of British Families*. Colchester: University of Essex.

Beveridge, W. (1942), *Social Insurance and Allied Services: A Report by Sir William Beveridge*. Cmd. 6404, London: HMSO.

Bhatia, M. and Mossialos, E. (2004), 'Health Systems in Developed Countries',in A. Hall and J. Midgely (eds) *Social Policy For Development*. London: Sage, pp. 168–204.

Biehal, N., Ellison, S., Baker, C. and Sinclair, I. (2010), *Belonging and Permanence: Outcomes in Long-Term Foster Care and Adoption*. London: British Association for Adoption and Fostering.

Billis, D. (ed) (2010), *Hybrid Organizations and the Third Sector: Challenges for Practice, Theory and Policy*. Palgrave Macmillan: Basingstoke.

—— and Glennerster, H. (1998), 'Human services and the voluntary sector: towards a theory of comparative advantage', *Journal of Social Policy* 27, 1, 79–98.

Bird, R. and Cretney, S. (1997), *Divorce: the New Law*. London: Bristol Family Law.

Black, C. (2008) *Working for a Healthier Tomorrow*. London: HMSO.

Blackman, S. (1992), 'Beyond vocationalism'. In P. Brown and H. Lauder (eds), *Education for Economic Survival*. London: Routledge, 203–25.

Blackmore, J. and Lauder, H. (2005), 'Researching Policy'. In B. Somekh and C. Lewin, *Research Methods in the Social Sciences*. London: Sage.

Blaikie, N. (2000), *Designing Social Research*. Cambridge: Polity Press.

Blair, T. (2010), *A Journey*. London: Hutchinson.

Blaxter, M. (1990), *Health and Lifestyles*. London: Routledge.

Bloor, M. (2004), 'Addressing Social Problems through Qualitative Research'. In D. Silverman, (ed) *Qualitative Research: Theory, Method and Practice*, 2nd edn. London: Sage.

Bonoli, G. (2003), 'Social policy through labour markets. Understanding national differences in the provision of economic security to wage earners', *Comparative Political Studies* 36 1007–30.

——(2005), 'The politics of the new social policies: Providing coverage for new social risks in mature welfare states', *Policy and Politics,* 33/3: 431–49.

Booth, C. (1891), *Labour and Life of the People*. London: Williams and Nargate.

Bouchier, P., Lambert, L. and Triseliotis, J. (1991), *Parting with a Child for Adoption: the Mother's Perspective*. British Agencies for Adoption and Fostering.

Bowlby, J. (1951), *Child Care and the Growth of Love*. Harmondsworth: Penguin.

Boyatzis, R.E. (1998), *Transforming Qualitative Information: Thematic Analysis and Code Development*. Thousand Oaks, Ca: Sage.

Boyne, G. and Powell, M. (1991), 'Territorial justice: a review of theory and evidence', *Political Geography* 10: 263–81.

Bradley, H., Erikson, M., Stephenson, C. and Williams, S. (2000), *Myths at Work*. Cambridge: Polity Press.

Bradshaw, J. (1972), 'A taxonomy of social need', *New Society* No. 496 (30 Mar.): 640–3.

—— and Finch, N. (2002), *A comparison of child benefit packages in 22 countries*, DWP Research report No. 174 (CDS: Leeds); research.dwp.gov.uk/asd/asd5/174summ.pdf.

—— and Mayhew, E. (eds) (2005), *The Well-being of Children in the United Kingdom*. London: Save the Children.

—— and Piachaud, D. (1980), *Child support in the European Community*. London: Bedford Square Press.

—— Ditch, J. Holmes, H. and Whiteford, P. (1993a), *Support for Children. A comparison of arrangements in fifteen countries*, DSS Research Report No. 21. London: HMSO.

—— Ditch, J. Holmes, H. and Whiteford, P. (1993b), 'A comparative study of child support in fifteen countries', *Journal of European Social Policy* 3, 4, 255–72.

Brandsen, T, van der Donk, W. and Putters, K. (2005), Griffins or chameleons: Hybridity as a permanent and inevitable characteristic of the third sector, *International Journal of Public Administration* 28, 9, 749–65.

Braverman, H. (1974), *Labor and Monopoly Capital*. New York: Monthly Review Press.

Breeze, B. (2010), 'How donors choose charities', Centre for Charitable Giving and Philanthropy Occasional Paper 1, http://www.kent.ac.uk/sspssr/cphsj/documents/How%20Donors%20Choose%20Charities%2018%20June%202010.pdf, (last accessed 13 February 2011).

Brewer, M. (2010), *Cuts to Welfare Spending: Take 2*. London: Institute of Fiscal Studies.

Bridge, S., Murtagh, S. and O'Neill, K. (2009),*Understanding the Social Economy and the Third Sector*. Basingstoke: Palgrave Macmillan.

Broad, B. (ed) (2001), *Kinship Care: The Placement Choice for Children and Young People*. Lyme Regis: Russell House.

—— (2005), *Improving the Health and Well-Being of Young People Leaving Care*. Lyme Regis: Russell House.

Brophy, J., Jhutti-Johal, J. and Owen, C. (2003), *Significant Harm: Child Protection Litigation in a Multi-Cultural Setting*. London: Department for Constitutional Affairs.

Brown, H. and Smith, H. (1989), 'Whose "ordinary life" is it anyway?' *Disability, Handicap and Society* 4, 2, 105–19.

Brown, P. and Lauder, H. (eds) (1992), *Education For Economic Survival*. London: Routledge.

—— Halsey, A. H., Lauder, H. and Stuart Wells, A. (1997), 'The transformation of education and society: an introduction', in Halsey et al. (1997: 1–44).

Browne, Lord (2010),Securing a Sustainable Future for Higher Education, An independent review of higher education and student finance in England.

Bryman, A. (2008), *Social Research Methods*, 3rd edn. Oxford: Oxford University Press.

Buchan, J. and Sochalski, J. (2004), 'The migration of nurses: trends and policies', *Bulletin of the World Health Organization*, Vol. 82, No. 8, pp. 587–94.

Büchs, M. (2007), *New Governance in European Social Policy. The Open Method of Coordination*. Basingstoke: Palgrave.

Buckner, L. and Yeandle, S. (2007), *Valuing Carers— Calculating the Value of Unpaid Care*. London: Carers UK.

Burchardt, T. (2000), 'The dynamics of being disabled', *Journal of Social Policy* 29/4: 645–68.

Burrows, R. (2003), *Poverty and Home Ownership in Contemporary Britain*. Bristol: The Policy Press.

Business, Innovation and Skills (BIS) (2010), *Skills for Sustainable Growth*, strategy document, Executive Summary. London: BIS.

C. 7872 (2010), *The Spending Revew Framework*. London: HMSO.

Cahill, M. (1994), *The New Social Policy*. Oxford: Blackwell.

—— and Fitzpatrick, T. (eds) (2002), *Environmental Issues and Social Welfare*. Oxford: Blackwell.

Callender, C. (2002), 'Fair Funding for Higher Education; The Way Forward' in A. Hayton and A. Paczuska (eds) *Access, Participation and Higher Education*. London: Kogan Page.

Callinicos, A. (2010), *Bonfire of Illusions: The Twin Crises of the Liberal World*. Cambridge: Polity Press.

Cameron, D. (2010), 'Families and relationships', Speech to Leeds Relate, 10 December.

—— (2010a), 'Let's mend our broken society'. Speech, 27 April. (www.conservatives.com/News/Speeches/2010/04/David_Cameron_Lets_mend_our_broken_society.aspx;accessed October 2010).

Campbell, B. (1988), *Unofficial Secrets*. London: Virago.

Campbell, J. and Oliver, M. (1996), *Disability Politics*. London: Routledge.

Canton, R. (2009), 'Taking Probation Abroad' *European Journal of Probation* 1/1: 66–78.

Care Quality Commission (CQC) (2010), *The State of Health Care and Adult Social Care: A Look at the Quality of Care in England in 2009*. London: CQC.

Care Services Improvement Partnership, the Royal College of Psychiatrists, and the Social Care Institute for Excellence (2007), SCIE Position Paper 08: A Common Purpose: Recovery in future Mental Health Services. Leeds: SCIE.

Castells, M. (1977), *The Urban Question: a Marxist Approach*. London: Edward Arnold.

Castles, F. G. and Mitchell, D. (1993), 'The Worlds of welfare and families of nations', in F. G. Castles, *Families of Nations: Patterns of Public Policy in Western Democracies*. Aldershot: Dartmouth.

—— and Obinger, H. (2007), 'Social expenditure and the politics of redistribution', in *Journal of European Social Policy* 17 3, 206–22.

Cavadino, M., Crow, I. and Dignan, J. (1999), *Criminal Justice 2000. Strategies for a New Century*.Winchester: Waterside Press.

Cawson, P., Wattam, C., Brooker, S. and Kelly, G. (2000), *Child Maltreatment in the United Kingdom: A Study of the Prevalence of Child Abuse and Neglect*. London: NSPCC.

Chand, A. and Thoburn, J. (2006), 'Research review: child protection referrals and minority ethnic children and families', *Child and Family Social Work* 11(4): 368–77.

Chanda, R. (2003),*Trade in services—movement of natural persons and development(IT and health). Country case study, India*. UNDP, Asia Pacific Initiativeon Trade, Economic Governance and Human Development.

Channer, Y. and Parton, N. (1990), 'Racism, cultural relativism and child protection', in Violence Against Children Study Group, *Taking Child Abuse Seriously: Contemporary Issues in Child Protection Theory and Practice*. London: Unwin Hyman.

Chant, S. (2008), 'The feminization of poverty and the feminization of anti-poverty programmes', *Journal of Development Studies* 44/2: 165–97.

Charity Commission (2010), Facts and figures, available at http://www.charitycommission.gov.uk/About_us/About_charities/factfigures.aspx (last accessed 13 February 2011).

Charles, N. (2000), *Feminism, the State and Social Policy*. Basingstoke: Macmillan.

Chen, L. C. and Boufford, J. L. (2005), 'Fatal flows— doctors on the move', *New England Journal of Medicine*, No. 353, pp. 1850–2.

Cherry, S. (1996), 'Accountability, Entitlement, and Control Issues and Voluntary Hospital Funding c1860–1939', *Social History of Medicine* 9(2): 215–33.

Child Poverty Action Group (2005), 'Ending child poverty must be centrepiece of PBR', press release produced on 17.11.05. London: Child Poverty Action Group.

—— (2010), *Welfare Benefits Handbook*. London: Child Poverty Action Group.

Chitty, C. (2009) *Education Policy in* Britain 2nd edn. Basingstoke: Palgrave Macmillan.

Chote, R., Emmerson, C., Harrison, R. and Miles, D. (eds) (2006), *The IFS Green Budget 2006*. London: Institute of Fiscal Studies.

Cichon, M. and Hagemejer. K. (2007), 'Changing the Development Policy Paradigm: Investing in a social security floor for all', *International Social Security Review*, Vol. 60, No. 2–3, pp. 169–96.

Clapham, D. and Kintrea, K. (1986), 'Rationing, choice and constraint: the allocation of public housing in Glasgow', *Journal of Social Policy* 15: 51–67.

Clark, J. Cane, D. Clifford, K. and Wilton, J. (2010), *The UK Civil Society Almanac 2010*. London: National Council for Voluntary Organisations.

Clark, T. and Leicester, A. (2004), 'Inequality and Two Decades of British Tax and Benefit Reform', *Fiscal Studies* Vol. 25, No. 2, pp. 129–58.

—— and Dilnot, A. (2002), *Long-term Trends in British Taxation and Spending*. London: Institute of Fiscal Studies.

Clarke, J. (1999), 'Coming to terms with culture', in H. Dean and R. Woods (eds), *Social Policy Review 11*. Luton: Social Policy Association.

—— and Newman, J. (1997), *The Managerial State*. London: Sage.

Clasen, J. (1992), 'Unemployment insurance in two countries: a comparative analysis of Great Britain and West Germany in the 1980s', *Journal of European Social Policy* 2(4): 279–300.

—— (2002),'Modern Social Democracy and European Welfare State Reform', *Social Policy and Society* 1(1): 67–76.

—— (ed) (1999), *Comparative Social Policy: Concepts, Theories and Methods*. Oxford: Blackwell.

—— (2003), 'Towards a New Welfare State or Reverting to Type? Some Major Trends in British Social Policy since the Early 1980s', *The European Legacy* 8(5): 573–86.

—— (2005), *Reforming European Welfare States. Germany and the United Kingdom Compared*. Oxford: Oxford University Press.

—— and Freeman, R. (eds) (1994), *Social Policy in Germany*. London: Harvester Wheatsheaf.

—— and Siegel, N. A. (eds) (2007), *Investigating Welfare State Change. The 'dependent variable' problem in comparative analysis*. Cheltenham: Edward Elgar.

Clifford, D. and Backus, P. (2010), Are big charities becoming increasingly dominant? Tracking charitable income growth 1997–2008 by initial size, TSRC Working Paper 38, http://www.tsrc.ac.uk/LinkClick.aspx?fileticket=ROx6x3orD1o%3D&tabid=500 (last accessed 13 February 2011).

Clyde Report (1992), *The Orkney Inquiry: Report of Inquiry into the Removal of Children from Orkney in February 1991*. Edinburgh: HMSO.

Cm. 3901 (1998), *Public Expenditure: Statistical Analysis, 1998–9*. London: HMSO.

Cm. 3978 (1998), *Stability and Investment for the Long Term: Economic and Fiscal Strategy Report 1998*. London: HMSO.

Cm. 4011 (1998), *Modern Public Services for Britain: Investing in Reform: Comprehensive Spending Review and New Public Spending Plans 1999–2002*. London: HMSO.

Cm. 5570 (2002), *Opportunity and Security for All: Investing in an Enterprising, Fairer Britain: New Public Spending Plans 2003–6*. London: HMSO.

Cm. 5571 (2002), *Public Service Agreements White Paper*. London: HMSO.

Cm. 6237 (2004), *Stability, Security and Opportunity for All: Investing in Britain's Long-term Future. The 2004 Spending Review*. London: HMSO.

Cm. 6238 (2004), *Public Service Agreements 2005–8*. London: HMSO.

Cm. 6673 (2005), *Opportunity for All, Seventh Annual Report*. London: HMSO.

Cm. 6701 (2005), *Britain Meeting the Global Challenge: Enterprise, Fairness and Responsibility. Pre-Budget Report, November 2005*. London: HMSO.

Cm. 7942 (2010), *The Spending Review 2010*. London: HMSO.

Coalition Government (2010), 'The Coalition: Our programme for government—Social care and disability'. Available online: http://webarchive.nationalarchives.gov.uk/20100526084809/http://programmeforgovernment.hmg.gov.uk/social-care-and-disability/ (accessed 26 October 2010).

Cochrane, A. (2007), *Understanding Urban Policy: a Critical Approach*. Oxford: Blackwell.

Cohen, S. (1972), *Folk Devils and Moral Panics: The Creation of the Mods and Rockers*. Oxford: Martin Robertson.

Coleman, D. and Salt, J. (1992), *The British Population: Patterns, Trends and Processes*. Oxford: Oxford University Press.

Collishaw, S., Pickles, A., Messer, J., Rutter, M., Shearer, C. and Maughan, B. (2007), 'Resilience to adult psychopathology following childhood maltreatment: evidence from a community sample', *Child Abuse and Neglect* 31(3): 211–29.

Colton, M. (1988), *Dimensions of Substitute Child Care*. Aldershot: Avebury.

Commission for Social Care Inspection (CSCI) (2008), *The State of Social Care in England 2006–7*. London: CSCI.

Commission for Social Care Inspection and Healthcare Commission (CSCI and HC) (2006), *Joint Investigation into the Provision of Services for People with Learning Disabilities at Cornwall Partnership NHS Trust*. London: Commission for Healthcare Audit and Inspection.

Commission on Social Justice (1994), *Social Justice: Strategies for National Renewal*. London: Vintage.

Communities and Local Government (2010), *English House Condition Survey 2007, Technical Report,* London: CLG.

Community Care (2009), 'Social care leaders' verdicts on the adult care green paper July 2009'. Available online: http://www.communitycare.co.uk/Articles/2009/07/21/112144/Social-care-leaders39-verdicts-on-the-adult-care-green-paper-July.htm (accessed 15 October 2010).

Community Organising Foundation (2007), Reweaving the Fabric of Society : Position statement of the Citizens Organising Foundation. COF, London.

Connell, R. (2002), *Gender*. Cambridge: Polity Press.

Conochie, G. (2009), *Primary Care Trusts and The Carers Strategy*. Essex: The Princess Royal Trust for Carers and Crossroads Care.

Conrad, F. G. and Schober, M. F. (2000), 'Clarifying question meaning in a household telephone survey'. *Public Opinion Quarterly* 64(1): 1–28.

Conservative Party (2001), *Time for Common Sense*. London: Conservative Party.Conservative Party (2001), *Time for Common Sense*. London: Conservative Party.

—— (2005), *Action on Crime. Conservative Manifesto 2005*. London: Conservative Party.

—— (2007), *It's Time to Fight Back: How a Conservative Government Will Tackle Britain's Crime Crisis*. London: Conservative Party.

—— (2008), *A Stronger Society : Voluntary Action in the 21*st *Century*, Responsibility Agenda Policy Green Paper No. 5. Conservative Party, London.

Corby, B. (2003), 'Towards a new means of inquiry into child abuse cases', *Journal of Social Welfare and Family Law* 25(3): 229–41.

—— (2005), *Child Abuse: Towards a Knowledge Base*, 3rd edn. Buckingham: Open University Press.

Corry, D. (ed) (1997), 'The role of the public sector and public expenditure', in D. Corry (ed), *Public Expenditure: Effective Management and Control*. London: Dryden Press.

Council on Social Action (2008), Side by Side and Implications for Public Services, CoSA paper no. 3. London: Community Links.

Cox, P., Kershaw, S. and Trotter, J. (eds) (2000), *Child Sexual Assault: Feminist Perspectives*. Basingstoke: Palgrave.

Crawford, R. (2010), Where did the axe fall? Presentation delivered at the IFS 2010 Spending Review briefing, 21 October 2010, http://www.ifs.org.uk/publications/5311.

—— Emmerson, C. and Tetlow, G. (2009), *A Survey of Public Spending in the UK*. London: Institute of Fiscal Studies.

Crompton, R. (2003), *Organisations, Careers and Caring*. Bristol: Policy Press.

—— Brockman, M. and Wiggins, R. (2003), 'A woman's place: employment and family life for men and women'. In A. Park, J. Curtice, K. Thomson, L. Jarvis, and C. Bromley (eds), *British Social Attitudes: the 20th Report*. London: Sage.

—— Gallie, D. and Purcell, K. (eds) (1996), *Changing Forms of Employment: Organisations, Skills and Gender*. London: Routledge.

—— Lewis, S. and Lyonette, C. (2010), *Women, Men, Work and Family in Europe*. Basingstoke: Macmillan.

Cruz-Saco, M.A. and Mesa-Lago, C. (eds) (1998), *The Reform of Pension and Health Care systems in Latin America: do options exist?* Pittsburgh: University of Pittsburgh.

Cullen, P. (2010), 'The Platform of European Social NGOs: ideology, division and coalition', *Journal of Political Ideologies* 15, 3, 317–31.

Curtis, M. (1946), *Report of the Care of Children Committee*. Cmnd. 6922. London: HMSO.

Cutler, T. (2003), 'Dangerous yardstick? Early cost estimates and the politics of financial management in the first decade of the National Health Service'. *Medical History* 47(2): 217–38.

Cutright, P. (1965), 'Political structure, economic development, and national social security programs'. *American Journal of Sociology* 70, 537–50.

Dahlgren, P. and Whitehead, M. (1991), *Policies and Strategies to Promote Social Equity in Health*. Stockholm: Institute of Futures Studies.

—— (2000), *The NHS Plan: A Plan for Investment, a Plan for Reform*. Cm. 4818-1. London: HMSO.

Dale, R., Bowe, R., Harris, D., Loveys, M., Moore, R., Silling, C., Sikes, P., Trevitt, J. and Valsecchi, V. (1990), *The TVEI Story*. Milton Keynes: Open University Press.

Daly, M. and Lewis, J. (2000), 'The concept of social care and the analysis of contemporary welfare states'. *British Journal of Sociology* 1, 51, 2, 281–98.

—— and Rake, K. (2003), *Gender and the Welfare State: Care, Work and Welfare in Europe and the USA*. Cambridge: Polity Press.

Davies, B. P. (1968), *Social Needs and Resources in Social Services*. London: Michael Joseph.

—— (1978), *Universality, Selectivity and Effectiveness in Social Policy*. London: Heineman.

Davies, G. and Dalgleish, T. (eds) (2001), *Recovered Memories: Seeking the Middle Ground*. Chichester: Wiley.

Daycare Trust (2003), *Towards Universal Childcare*. London: Daycare Trust.

De Deken, J. and Kittel, B. (2007), 'Social expenditure under scrutiny: the problems of using aggregate spending data for assessing welfare state dynamics', in J. Clasen and N. A. Siegel (eds) *Investigating Welfare State Change. The 'dependent variable' problem in comparative analysis*. Cheltenham: Edward Elgar pp. 72–105.

De La Porte, C. and Pochet, P. (2003), *Building Social Europe through the Open Method of Coordination*. Brussels: Peter Lang.

De Vaus, D. (2002), *Surveys in Social Research*, 5th edn. London: Routledge.

Deacon, A. (2002), *Perspectives on Welfare*. London: Palgrave.

—— and Bradshaw, J. (1983), *Reserved for the Poor: The Means-Test in British Social Policy*. Oxford: Basil Blackwell and Martin Robertson.

Deacon, B. (2005), 'Global Social Policy: From Neo-Liberalism to Social Democracy', in B. Cantillon and I. Marx (eds)*International Cooperation in Social Security: How to Cope with Globalisation?*. Antwerp: Intersentia.

—— (2008), 'Global and regional social governance', in N. Yeates (ed) *Understanding Global Social Policy*. Bristol: The Policy Press.

—— and Hulse, M. (1996), *The Globalisation of Social Policy*. Leeds: Leeds Metropolitan University.

—— with Hulse, M. and Stubbs, P. (1997), *Global Social Policy: International Organisations and the Future of Welfare*. London: Sage.

—— Macovei, M. van Langenhove, L. and Yeates, N. (2009), 'Global Social Governance and World Regional Social Policy' in B. Deacon, L. van Langenhove, M. Macovei and N. Yeates (eds)*World-Regional Social Policy and Global Governance: New Research and Policy Agendas in Africa, Asia, Europe and Latin America*. London: Routledge.

Dean, H. (2002), *Welfare Rights and Social Policy*. Harlow: Prentice Hall.

—— (2006), *Social Policy*. Cambridge: Polity Press.

—— (2010), *Understanding Human Need*. Bristol: The Policy Press.

—— and Melrose, M. (1996), 'Unravelling Citizenship: the significance of social security benefit fraud', *Critical Social Policy* Vol. 16, No. 1, pp. 3–31.

—— with Melrose, M. (1999), *Poverty, Riches and Social Citizenship*. Basingstoke: Macmillan.

—— and Taylor-Gooby, P. (1992), *Dependency Culture: The Explosion of a Myth*. Hemel Hempstead: Harvester Wheatsheaf.

—— and Rodgers, R. (2004), 'Popular discourses of dependency, responsibility and rights', in H. Dean (ed), *The Ethics of Welfare*. Bristol: The Policy Press.

Dearden C. and Becker S. (2004), *Young Carers in the UK. The 2004 Report*. London: Carers UK.

Delphy, C. and Leonard, D. (1992), *Familiar Exploitation: a New Analysis of Marriage in Contemporary Western Societies*. Cambridge: Polity Press.

Dench, G., Gavron, K. and Young, M. (2006), *The New East End*. London: Profile Books.

Denscombe, M. (2007), *The Good Research Guide*, 3rd edn. Maidenhead: Open University Press.

Department for Children, Schools and Families (2008), *Staying Safe: Action Plan*. London: DCSF.

Department for Education (2010a), *Children In Need in England, Including their Characteristics and Further Information on Children Who Were the Subject of a Child Protection Plan*. London: DfE.

—— (2010b), *Children Looked After by Local Authorities in England (including Adoption and Care Leavers)—Year Ending 31 March 2010*. London: DfE.

—— (2010c), *Outcomes for Children Looked After by Local Authorities in England, as at 31 March 2010*. London: DfE.

Department for Education and Skills (2006), *Care Matters: Transforming the Lives of Children and Young People in Care*. Cm. 6932. London: DfES.

Department for Work and Pensions (2002), *Opportunity for All. Fourth Annual Report 2002*. Cm. 5598. London: HMSO.

—— (2002a), *Pathways to Work: Helping people into employment*. Cm. 5690. London: HMSO.

—— (2005), *Department for Work and Pensions Five Year Strategy*. Cm. 6447. London: HMSO.

—— (2009), *Households Below Average Income 1994/95 to 2008/09*. London: HMSO.

—— (2010), *Universal Credit: welfare that works*. Cm. 7957. London: HMSO.

—— (2010a), *Fraud and Error in the Benefit System: October 2008 to September 2009*, London: DWP. Available at: http://research.dwp.gov.uk/asd/asd2/fraud_error.asp.

—— (2010b), *Households Below Average Income Statistics*, London: DWP.

Department of Education and Science (DES) (1978), *Special Educational Needs (The Warnock Report)*. London: HMSO.

Department of Employment (1993), *Training Statistics 1993*. London: HMSO.

Department of Health (1979), *Committee of Inquiry into Medical Handicap Nursing and Care (Jay Report),* Vol. 1. Cmnd. 7468-1. London: HMSO.

—— (1989), *Caring for People: Community Care in the Next Decade and Beyond*. London: HMSO.

—— (1989a), *An Introduction to the Children Act 1989*. London: HMSO.

—— (1990), *Community Care in the Next Decade and Beyond: Policy Guidance*. London: HMSO.

—— (1995), *Child Protection: Messages from Research*. London: HMSO.

—— (1998), *Caring for Children away from Home: Message from Research*. Chichester: Wiley.

—— (1997), *The new NHS: modern, dependable*. Cm. 3807. London: DoH.

—— (1998a), *Modernising Social Services: Promoting Independence, Improving Protection, Raising Standards*. Cm. 4169. London: HMSO.

—— (1998b), *Modernising Mental Health Services: Safe, Sound and Supportive*. London: HMSO.

—— (1999a), *Caring about Carers: A National Strategy for Carers*. London: HMSO.

—— (1999b), *National Service Framework for Mental Health*. London: HMSO.

—— (2000), *NHS Plan: A Plan for Investment, a Plan for Reform*. Cm. 4818-I. London: HMSO.

—— (2001), *Health and Personal Social Services Statistics 2000*. London: DoH.

—— (2001a), *National Service Framework for Older People*. London: HMSO.

—— (2001b), *Valuing People: A New Strategy for Learning Disability for the 21st Century*. Cm. 5086. London: HMSO.

—— (2005), *Independence, Well-Being and Choice: Our Vision for the Future of Social Care for Adults in England*. Cm. 6499. London: HMSO.

—— (2008), *Carers at the Heart of 21st Century Families and Communities: A Caring System on your Side, a Life of your Own*. London: HMSO.

—— (2009), *Mortality Target Monitoring (Infant Mortality, inequalities)*, London: DoH.

—— (2009a), *Shaping the Future of Care Together*. Cm. 7673. London: HMSO.

—— (2009b), *Valuing People Now: A New Three-Year Strategy for People with Learning Disabilities*. London: HMSO.

—— (2010), *Equity and Excellence: Liberating the NHS*. Cm7881, HMSO.

—— (2010a), *Equity and Excellence: Liberating the NHS*. Cm. 7881. London: HMSO.

—— (2010b), *Prioritising Need in the Context of Putting People First: A Whole System Approach to Eligibility for Social Care—Guidance on Eligibility Criteria for Adult Social Care, England 2010*. Available online: http://www.dh.gov.uk/en/Publicationsandstatistics/Publications/PublicationsPolicyAndGuidance/DH_113154 (accessed 26 October 2010).

—— (2010c), *Putting People First: Personal Budgets for OlderPeople—Making it Happen*. London: Putting People First.

Department of Health (2010), *Equity and excellence: Liberating the NHS* Cm 7881, HMSO.

Department of Health and Home Office (2000), *No Secrets—Guidance on Developing and Implementing Multi-Agency Policies and Procedures to Protect Vulnerable Adults from Abuse*. London: HMSO.

Department of Health and Social Security (DHSS) (1976), *Prevention and Health—Everybody's Business: A Reassessment of Public and Personal Health*. London: HMSO.

—— (1980), *Inequalities in Health: Report of a Working Group* (the Black Report). London: HMSO.

—— (1981), *Growing Older*. Cmnd. 8173. London: HMSO.

—— (1985), *Social Work Decisions in Child Care*. London: HMSO.

—— (1988), *Report of the Committee of Inquiry into the Care and After Care of Sharon Campbell* (Chairman: J. Spokes). London: HMSO.

—— (1988a), *Report of the Inquiry into Child Abuse in Cleveland* (Butler-Sloss). Cm. 412. London: HMSO.

—— (1998). *New ambitions for our country: A new contract for welfare*. London: HMSO.

Department of Health and Social Security (DHSS)/ Welsh Office (1971), *Better Services for the Mentally Handicapped*. Cmnd. 4683. London: HMSO.

Department of Health Social Services Inspectorate/Scottish Office Social Work Services Group (1991), *Care Management and Assessment: Managers' Guide*. London: HMSO.

Dillman, D. A., Smyth, J. D. and Christian, L. M. (2009), *Internet, Mail, and Mixed-Mode Surveys: The Tailored Design Method*, 3rd edn. Hoboken, NJ: John Wiley & Sons.

Dingwall, R., Eekelaar, J. and Murray, T. (1983), *The Protection of Children: State Intervention and Family Life*. Oxford: Blackwell.

Dixon, A. and Mossialos, E. (2002), *Health Care Systems in Eight Countries: Trends and Challenges*. London: European Observatory on Health Systems, LSE.

Dixon, J. (1999), *Social Security in Global Perspective*. Westport, CT: Praeger.

Donnison, D. V. (1975), *An Approach to Social Policy*. Dublin: National Economic and Social Council and Republic of Ireland Stationery Office.

Donzelot, J. (1979), *The Policing of Families: Welfare Versus the State*. London: Hutchinson.

Doogan, K. (2009), *New Capitalism? The Transformation of Work*. Cambridge: Polity Press.

Dorling, D. and Cornford, J. (1995), 'Who has negative equity? How house price falls in Britain have hit different groups of home buyers', *Housing Studies* 10: 151–78.

Douglas, M. (1999),Four cultures: the evolution of a parsimonious model, *GeoJournal* 47: 411–15.

Dovlo, D. 2007. 'Migration of nurses from sub-Saharan Africa: a review of issues and challenges', *Health Services Research,* Vol. 42, No. 3 pt 2, pp 1373–88.

Doyal, L. (1998), *Women and Health Services*. Buckingham: Open University Press.

—— and Gough, I. (1984), 'A theory of human needs', *Critical Social Policy* No. 10: 6–33.

—— (1991), *A Theory of Human Need*. Basingstoke: Macmillan.

Duncan, S. and Irwin, S. (2004), 'The Social Patterning of Values and Rationalities: mothers' choices in combining caring and employment', *Social Policy and Society*, Vol. 3, No. 4, pp. 391–400.

Dunleavy, P. and Husbands, C. T. (1985), *British Democracy at the Crossroads*. London: Allen & Unwin.

Durkheim, E. (1964), *The Division of Labour in Society*. London: Houndmills.

Dutton, D. (1991), *British Politics since 1945: The Rise and Fall of Consensus*, Oxford: Blackwell.

Dutton, E., Warhurst, C., Nickson, D. and Lockyer, C. (2005), 'Lone Parents, the New Deal and the Opportunities and Barriers to Retail Employment', *Policy Studies* Vol. 26, No. 1, pp. 85–101.

DWP (Department for Work and Pensions) (2010), *Households Below Average Income (HBAI) 1994/95–2008/09*. Department for Work and Pensions.

Dyer, O. (2006), 'Private group wins Derbyshire GP contract', *British Medical Journal* 332: 194.

Ebbinghaus, B. and Manow, P. (eds) (2001), *Comparing Welfare Capitalism*. London: Routledge.

EC (2000), *Social Protection in Europe*. Luxembourg: Office for Official Publications of the European Communities.

EC (2001), *Joint Report on Social Inclusion—Part I: The European Union*. Brussels: COM.

Economic and Social Research Council (2010), Note from the ESRC/Birkbeck/IVR public policy seminar 'Volunteering and Democratic engagement', 10 October, http://www.esrc.ac.uk/_images/Seminar_%20notes_18_Oct_2010_tcm8-3832.pdf (last accessed 13 February 2011).

Edwards, M. (2009), *Civil Society*, 2nd edn. Cambridge: Polity Press.

Edwards, P. and Wajcman, J. (2005), *The Politics of Working Life*. Oxford: Oxford University Press.

Edwards, R. and Duncan, S. (1997), 'Supporting the Family: lone mothers, paid work and the underclass debate', *Critical Social Policy* Vol. 17, No. 4, pp. 29–49.

Edwards, S. S. M. (1989), *Policing 'Domestic' Violence: Women, the Law and the State*. London: Sage.

Elliot, H. and Popay, J. (2000), 'How are policy makers using evidence? Models of research utilisation and local NHS policy making', *Journal of Epidemiology and Community Health* 54(6): 461–8.

Ely, M., Richards, P., Wadsworth, M. and Elliott, B. (1999), 'Changes in the association of parental divorce and children's educational attainment', *Journal of Social Policy* 28, 3, 437–56.

Emerson, E., Malam, S., Davies, I. and Spencer, K. (2005), *Adults with Learning Difficulties in England 2003/04*. London: Department of Health.

Emmerson, C., Frayne, C. and Goodman, A. (2002), *How Much Would it Cost to Increase UK Health Spending to the European Union Average?* London: Institute of Fiscal Studies (www.ifs.org.uk).

—— (2010), *Public Expenditure Statistical Analysis 2010*. Cm. 7890. London: HMSO (www.hm-treasury.gov.uk)

Engels, F. (1969), *The Condition of the Working Class in England* (1845). London: Panther.

Equal Opportunities Commission (1996), *Briefings on Women and Men in Britain: Pay*. Manchester: EOC.

Ermisch, J. (1990), *Fewer Babies, Longer Lives*. York: Joseph Rowntree Foundation.

Esping-Andersen, G. (1990), *The Three Worlds of Welfare Capitalism*. Cambridge: Polity Press.

—— (1993), 'The comparative macro-sociology of welfare states', in Moreno, L., *Social Exchange and Welfare Development*. Madrid: Consejo superior de investigaciones cientificas.

—— (1996a), 'After the golden age? Welfare state dilemmas in a global economy'. In Esping-Andersen (1996b: 1–31).

—— (ed) (1996b), *Welfare States in Transition: National Adaptations in Global Economies*. London: Sage.

—— (1999), *the Social Foundations of Post-Industrial Economies*. Oxford: Oxford University Press.

—— (2002), 'A child-centred social investment strategy'. In G. Esping-Andersen (ed), *Why We Need a New Welfare State*. Oxford: Oxford University Press, 26–67.

—— and Korpi, W. (1987), 'From poor relief to institutional welfare states: the development of Scandinavian social policy', in R. Erikson, E. J. Hansen, S. Ringen and H. Uusitalo (eds), *The Scandinavian Model*. Armonk, NY: Sharpe.

European Commission (2004), Commission staff working paper: Analysis of replies of Member States of the European Union and the acceding countries to the Commission questionnaire on voluntary activities of young people, SEC(2004) 628, http://ec.europa.eu/youth/archive/whitepaper/post-launch/sec%282004%29628_en.pdf, (last accessed 13 February 2011).

Eurostat (1994), *Detailed Tables European Social Statistics: Expenditure and receipts, 1980–92*. Luxembourg: Office for Official Publications of the European Communities.

—— (2001), *Detailed Tables European Social Statistics: Expenditure and Receipts, 1980–99*. Luxembourg: Office for Official Publications of the European Communities.

—— (2009), News Release *Youth Unemployment*, http://epp.eurostat.ec.europa.eu/cache/ITY_PUBLIC/3-23072009-BP/EN/3-23072009-BP-EN.PDF accessed 4.2.11.

Evans, D. and Forbes, T. (2009), 'Partnerships in health and social care: England and Scotland compared'. *Public Policy and Administration* 24, 1, 67–83.

Evans, M. (1998), 'Social Security: Dismantling the Pyramids?', in: H. Glennerster, and J. Hills, *The State of Welfare*, 2nd edn. Oxford: Oxford University Press.

Evans, R. J. (1988), 'Epidemics and Revolutions: Cholera in Nineteenth Century Europe', *Past and Present* 120: 124.

Evers, A. (1988), 'Shifts in the welfare mix: introducing a new approach for the study of transformations in welfare and social policy', in A. Evers and H. Wintersberger (eds), *Shifts in the Welfare Mix: Their Impact on Work, Social Services and Welfare Policies*. Vienna: European Centre for Social Welfare.

—— (1995), 'Part of the welfare mix: the third sector as an intermediate area', *Voluntas* 6, 2, 159–82.

Falkingham, J. (1989), 'Britain's ageing population: the engine behind increased dependency ratios', *Journal of Social Policy* 18 (2): 211–33.

Fanon, F. (1967), *The Wretched of the Earth*. Harmondsworth: Penguin.

Farrington, D. (1996), *Understanding and Preventing Youth Crime*. York: York Publishing Services.

Feldstein, M. (2005), 'Structural Reform of Social Security', *Journal of Economic Perspectives* Vol. 19, No. 2, pp. 33–55.

Ferrera, M. (1996), 'The southern model of welfare in Europe', *Journal of European Social Policy* 6, 1, 17–37.

—— (2005), *The Boundaries of Welfare—European Integration and the New Spatial Politics of Social Protection*. Oxford: Oxford University Press.

—— Matsaganis, M. and Sacchi, S. (2002), 'Open coordination against poverty: the new EU 'social inclusion process', *Journal of European Social Policy* 12, 2, 227–39.

Ferri, E. and Smith, K. (1998), *Step-parenting in the 1990s*. London: Family Policy Studies Centre.

Finch, J. (1989), *Family Obligations and Social Change*. Cambridge: Polity Press.

—— and Groves, D. (1980), 'Community care and the family: a case for equal opportunities', *Journal of Social Policy* 9, 4, 487–511.

—— (eds) (1983), *A Labour of Love: Women, Work and Caring*. London: Routledge and Kegan Paul.

—— and Mason, J. (1993), *Negotiating Family Responsibilities*. London: Routledge.

Finegold, D. (1991), 'Institutional incentives and skill creation: preconditions for a high skill equilibrium', in Ryan (1991: 93–116).

—— and Crouch, C. (1994), 'A comparison of national institutions', in Layard et al. (1994: 251–81).

—— and Soskice, D. (1988), 'The failure of training in Britain: analysis and prescription', *Oxford Review of Economic Policy* 4(3): 21–50.

Finklestein, V. (1993), 'Disability: A social challenge or an administrative responsibility?' in J. Swain, V. Finkelstein, S. French, and M. Oliver, (eds), *Disabling Barriers—Enabling Environments*. London: Sage Publications in association with the Open University.

Finlayson, G. (1990), 'A Moving Frontier: Voluntarism and the State in British Social Welfare 1911–49', *Twentieth Century British History* 1(2):183–206.

Fitzpatrick, T. (2008), *Applied Ethics and Social Problems*. Bristol: The Policy Press.

Fitzpatrick, T. and Cahill, M. (eds) (2003), *Environment and Welfare: Towards a Green Social Policy*. London: Palgrave Macmillan.

Flaherty, J., Veit-Wilson, J. and Dornan, P. (2004), *Poverty: the Facts*. London: Child Poverty Action Group.

Flora, P. (ed) (1986), *Growth to Limits*. Berlin: De Gruyter.

—— and Heidenheimer, A. J. (eds) (1981), *The Development of Welfare States in Europe and America*. New Brunswick: Transaction Books.

Ford, H. (2006), *Women Who Sexually Abuse Children*. Chichester: Wiley.

Forder, A. (1974), *Concepts in Social Administration: A Framework for Analysis*. London: Routledge and Kegan Paul.

Forrest, R. and Murie, A. (2010), *Selling the Welfare State*. London: Routledge.

—— Murie, A. and Williams, P. (1990), *Home Ownership: Differentiation and Fragmentation*. London: Unwin Hyman.

Foucault, M. (1961), *Madness and Civilisation: A History of Insanity in the Age of Reason*, translated by R. Howard (1967). London: Tavistock.

—— (1977), *Discipline and Punish*. Harmondsworth: Penguin.

Fowler, F.J.(1995), *Improving Survey Questions: Design and Evaluation*. Thousand Oaks, Ca.: Sage.

—— (2002), *Survey Research Methods*, 3rd edn. Thousand Oaks, Ca.: Sage.

Fraisse, L. (2009), 'The third sector and the policy process in France: the centralized horizontal third sector community faced with the reconfiguration of the state-centred republican model', in J. Kendall (ed) *Handbook on Third Sector Policy in Europe: Multi-Level Processes and Organized Civil Society*. Edward Elgar: Cheltenham.

Fraser, D. (2003),*The Evolution of the British Welfare State : a History of Social Policy since the Industrial Revolution*, 3rd edn. Basingstoke: Palgrave Macmillan.

Fraser, N. (1989), *Unruly Practices: Power, Discourse and Gender in Contemporary Social Theory*. Minneapolis: University of Minnesota Press.

—— and Honneth, A. (2003), *Redistribution or Recognition?* London: Verso.

Freeden, M. (1996), *Ideologies and Political Theory*. Oxford: Oxford University Press.

—— (1992), *Children, their Families and the Law: Working with the Children Act*. Basingstoke: Macmillan.

Friedman, M. (1962), *Capitalism and Freedom*. Chicago: University of Chicago Press.

Frohman, L. (2008), 'The Break-Up of the Poor Laws—German Style: Progressivism and the Origins of the Welfare State, 1900–18', *Comparative Studies in Society and History* 50(4): 981–1009.

Fromm, S. and Spross, C. (2009), 'A standardized review of activation programmes for needy welfare recipients: A comparison of four different welfare states'. Institut für Arbeitsmarkt—und Berufsforschung.

Frost, L. and Hoggett, P. (2008), 'Human agency and social suffering', *Critical Social Policy* 28/4: 438–60.

Frost, N. (2003), 'Understanding family support: theories, concepts and issues', in N. Frost, A. Lloyd and L. Jeffrey (eds) *The RHP Companion to Family Support*. Lyme Regis: Russell House.

—— and Stein, M. (1989), *The Politics of Child Welfare: Inequality, Power and Change*. Hemel Hempstead: Harvester Wheatsheaf.

Fultz, E. and Ruck, M. (2001), 'Pension reform in central and eastern Europe: Emerging issues and patterns, *International Labour Review*, Vol 140, No 1, pp :19–43.

Fyson, R. and Kitson, D. (2007), 'Independence or protection—does it have to be a choice? Reflections on the abuse of people with learning disabilities in Cornwall'. *Critical Social Policy* 27, 3, 426–36.

Gallagher, B. (2001), 'Assessment and intervention in cases of suspected ritual child sexual abuse', *Child Abuse Review* 10(4): 227–42.

—— Fraser, C., Christmann, K. and Hodgson, B. (2006), *International and Internet Child Sexual Abuse and Exploitation. Research Report*. Huddersfield: University of Huddersfield.

Gallie, D. (1991), 'Patterns of skill change: upskilling, deskilling or the polarisation of skills?', *Work, Employment and Society* 5(3): 319–51.

—— (1996), 'Skill, gender and the quality of employment', in Crompton et al. (1996: 133–59).

—— and Paugam, S. (eds) (2000), *Welfare Regimes and the Experience of Unemployment in Europe*. Oxford: Oxford University Press.

—— Paugam, S. and Jacobs, S. (2001), *Unemployment, poverty and social isolation: is there a vicious circle of social exclusion?*, paper presented at Euresco conference on Labour Market Change, Unemployment and Citizenship in Europe, Helsinki.

Garbarino, J., Stocking, H. and Collins, A. (1980), *Protecting Children from Abuse and Neglect: Developing and Maintaining Effective Support Systems for Families*. San Francisco: Jossey-Bass.

Garfinkel, H. (1967), *Studies in Ethnomethodology*. Englewood Cliffs, N.J.: Prentice-Hall.

Garland, D. (1981), 'The birth of the welfare sanction', *British Journal of Law and Society* 8/1: 29–45.

Garrett, P. (2003), *Remaking Social Work with Children and Families*. London: Routledge.

—— (2009), *'Transforming' Children's Services: Social Work, Neoliberalism and the Modern World*. Maidenhead: Open University Press.

Gauldie, E. (1974), *Cruel Habitations*. London: Allen & Unwin.

George, V. and Wilding, P. (1994), *Welfare and Ideology*. Hemel Hempstead: Harvester Wheatsheaf.

—— (1984), *The Impact of Social Policy*. London: Routledge.

Gershon, P. (2004), *Releasing Resources to the Front Line: independent review of public sector efficiency*. London: HMSO and http://www.hmtreasury.gov.uk/spending_review/spend_sr04/associated_documents/spending_sr04_efficiency.cfm.

Gershuny, J. (2000), *Changing Times: Work and Leisure in Post-Industrial Society*. Oxford: Oxford University Press.

Geyer, R. (2000), *Exploring European Social Policy*. Oxford: Oxford University Press.

Giddens, A. (1991), *Modernity and Self-Identity*. Cambridge: Polity Press.

—— (1992), *The Transformation of Intimacy*. Cambridge: Polity Press.

—— (1993), *Sociology*. Oxford: Oxford University Press.

—— (2006), *Sociology*. Cambridge: Polity Press.

Gil, D. (1970), *Violence against Children*. Cambridge, Mass.: Harvard University Press.

Gilbert, B. B. (1970), *British Social Policy 1914–39*. London: Batsford.

Gillham, B. (2005), *Research Interviewing: The Range of Techniques*. Maidenhead: Open University Press.

Gilligan, C. (1982), *In a Different Voice: Psychological theory and women's development*. Cambridge, MA: Harvard University Press.

Gilligan, P. and Akhtar, S. (2006), 'Cultural barriers to the disclosure of child sexual abuse in Asian communities: listening to what women say', *British Journal of Social Work* 36(8): 1361–77.

Ginn, J. and Arber, S. (1993), 'Pension penalties: the gendered division of occupational welfare', *Work, Employment and Society* 7(1): 47–70.

Ginsburg, N. (1979), *Class, Capital and Social Policy*. London: Macmillan.

Gittins, D. (1993), *The Family in Question: Changing Households and Familiar Ideologies*, 2nd edn. Basingstoke: Macmillan.

Gladstone, F. (1979), *Voluntary Action in a Changing World*. London: Bedford Square Press.

Glaser B.G. and Strauss, A. (1967), *Discovery of Grounded Theory. Strategies for Qualitative Research*. Sociology Press.

Glendinning, C. and Moran, N. (2009), 'Reforming long-term care: Recent lessons from other countries'. *Research Works*, 2009–06, Social Policy Research Unit, University of York.

—— Challis, D., Fernandez, J., Jacobs, S., Jones, K., Knapp, M., Manthorpe, J., Moran, N., Netten, A., Stevens, M. and Wilberforce, M. (2008), *Evaluation of the Individual Budgets Pilot Programme: Final Report*. York: Social Policy Research Unit.

—— Tjadens, F., Arksey, H., Morée, M., and Moran, N. (2009), *Care Provision within Families and its Socio-Economic Impact on Care Providers*. York: Social Policy Research Unit.

Glennerster, H. (1998), 'New Beginnings and Old Continuities', in: H. Glennerster, and J. Hills, *The State of Welfare*, 2nd edn. Oxford: Oxford University Press.

—— (1998a), 'Education: reaping the harvest', in H. Glennerster and J. Hills (eds), *The State of Welfare*. Oxford: Oxford University Press, 27–74.

—— (2000), *British Social Policy since 1945*, 2nd edn. Oxford: Blackwell.

—— (2003), *Understanding the Finance of Welfare: What Welfare Costs and How to Pay for it*. Bristol: The Policy Press.

—— (2007), *British Social Policy Since 1945*, 3rd edn. Wiley-Blackwell.

—— and Hills, J. (eds) (1998), *The State of Welfare*, 2nd edn. Oxford: Oxford University Press.

Glucksmann, M. (1995), 'Why Work? Gender and the total social organisation of labour', *Gender Work and Organization* 2(2): 63–75.

Goetschy, J. (2001), 'The European employment strategy from Amsterdam to Stockholm: has it reached its cruising speed?', *Industrial Relations Journal* 32, 5, 401–18.

Goffman, E. (1961), *Asylums: Essays on the Social Situation of Mental Patients and Other Inmates*. Garden City, N.Y: Anchor Books.

—— (1963), *Asylums: Essays on the Social Situation of Mental Patients and Other Inmates*. New York: Doubleday.

Goldstein, J., Freud, A. and Solnit, A. (1979), *Beyond the Best Interests of the Child*. New York: Free Press.

Goode, J., Callender, C. and Lister, R. (1998), *Purse or Wallet: Gender Inequalities and Income Distribution within Families*. London: Policy Studies Institute.

Goodin, R. (1988), *Reasons for Welfare: The Political Theory of the Welfare State*. Princeton: Princeton University Press.

—— and Le Grand, J. (eds) (1987), *Not Only the Poor*. London: Allen & Unwin.

Goodman, R. (1992), 'Japan: pupil turned teacher?' *Oxford Studies in Comparative Education* 1: 155–73.

—— and Peng, I. (1996), 'The East Asian Welfare States: Peripatetic Learning, Adaptive Change, and Nation-Building', in G. Esping-Andersen (ed), *Welfare States in Transition: National Adaptation in Global Economies*. London: Sage.

Gordon, D. and Pantazis, C. (eds) (1997), *Breadline Britain in the 1990s: The Full Report of a Major National Survey on Poverty*. Bristol: University of Bristol.

—— Adelman, L., Ashworth, K., Bradshaw, J., Levitas, R., Middleton, S., Pantazis, C., Patsios, D., Payne, S., Townsend, P. and Williams, J. (2000), *Poverty and Social Exclusion in Britain*. York: Joseph Rowntree Foundation.

Gorsky, M. (2008), 'The British National Health Service 1948–2008: A Review of the Historiography', *Social History of Medicine* 21(3): 437–60.

Goudswaard, K. and Caminada, K. (2010), 'The Redistributive Effect of Public and Private Social Programmes: A cross-country empirical analysis, *International Social Security Review* Vol. 63, No. 1, pp. 1–19.

Gough, I. (1979), *The Political Economy of the Welfare State*. London: Macmillan.

Graeff, P. (2009), 'Social capital: the dark side', in G. T. Svendsen, and G. L. H. Svendsen (eds) *Handbook of Social Capital: the Troika of Sociology, Political Science and Economics*. Cheltenham: Edward Elgar.

Graham, H. (1983), 'Caring: a labour of love', in Finch, J. and Groves, D. (eds), *A Labour of Love: Women, Work and Caring*. London: Routledge.

Gray, A. (2001a), 'Explaining inequalities in health in the United Kingdom', in A. Gray and P. Payne, *World Health and Disease*. Buckingham: Open University Press.

—— (2001b), 'The decline of infectious disease: the case of England', in A. Gray and P. Payne, *World Health and Disease*. Buckingham: Open University Press.

—— (2005), 'The changing availability of grandparents as carers and its implications for childcare policy in the UK', *Journal of Social Policy* 34, 4, 557–78.

Gray, P. (2005), The politics of risk and young offenders' experiences of social exclusion and restorative justice. *British Journal of Criminology* 45: 938–57.

Green party (undated), 'Citizen's Income an end to the poverty trap' http://policy.greenparty.org.uk/policy-pointers/ppcitizensincome.pdf; (accessed 4 Febuary 2011).

Green, A. (1990), *Education and State Formation*. Basingstoke: Macmillan.

Green, B. (2009), 'The Decline of NHS Inpatient Psychiatry in England'. *Psychiatry On-Line*: http://priory.com/psychiatry/Decline_NHS_Inpatient_Psychiatry.htm (accessed 14 October 2010).

Green, F. (2001), 'It's been a hard day's night: the concentration and intensification of work in late twentieth-century Britain', *British Journal of Industrial Relations* 39(1): 53–80.

Green, H. (1988), *Informal Carers*. London: HMSO.

Greenland, C. (1987), *Preventing CAN Death: An International Study of Deaths due to Child Abuse and Neglect*. London: Tavistock.

Gregory, A. and O'Reilly, J. (1996), 'Checking out and cashing up: the prospects and paradoxes of regulating part-time work in Europe', in Crompton et al. (1996: 207–34).

Grenier, P. (2009), 'Social entrepreneurship in the UK: from rhetoric to reality?' in R. Zigler (ed) *An Introduction to Social Entrepreneurship: Voices, Preconditions, Contexts*. Cheltenham: Eldward Elgar.

Griffiths, R. (1988), *Community Care: Agenda for Action*. London: HMSO.

Hacker, J. S. (2002), *The Divided Welfare State: The Battle over Public and Private Social Benefits in the United States*. Cambridge: Cambridge University Press.

—— and Pierson, P. (2002), 'Business Power and Social Policy: Employers and the Formation of the American Welfare State,' *Politics and Society* 30, 2, pp. 277–325.

Hague, G. and Malos, E. (1998), *Domestic Violence: Action for Change*. Cheltenham: New Clarion Press.

Haines, H. H. (1979), 'Cognitive claims-making, enclosure and the depoliticization of social problems', *The Sociological Quarterly* 20: 119–30.

Haines, K. and Drakeford, M. (1998), *Young People and Youth Justice*. Basingstoke: Macmillan.

Halpern, D. (2005), *Social Capital*. Cambridge: Polity Press.

Halsey, A. H. et al. (eds) (1997), *Education, Culture, Economy, and Society*. Oxford: Oxford University Press.

Hampton, P. (2005), *Reducing Administrative Burdens: effective inspection and enforcement*. London: HM Treasury.

Hansmann, H. (1987), 'Economic theories of nonprofit organisation', in W.W. Powell (ed)*The Nonprofit Sector: A Research Handbook*. New Haven: Yale University Press.

Hantrais, L. (2004), *Family Policy Matters: Responding to Family Change in Europe*. Bristol: The Policy Press.

—— (2007), *Social Policy in the European Union*. 3rd edn. London: Palgrave.

—— (2008), *International Comparative Research. Theory, Methods and Practice*. Basingstoke: Palgrave.

—— and Letablier, M. (1996), *Families and Family Policies in Europe*. London: Longman.

—— and Mangen, S. (eds) (1996), *Cross-National Research Methods in the Social Sciences*. London: Pinter.

Harris, B. (2004),*The Origins of the British Welfare State: Society, State and Social Welfare in England and Wales, 1800–1945*. Basingstoke: Palgrave Macmillan.

Harrison, A. and Appleby, J. (2005), *The War on Waiting for Hospital Treatment: What has Labour Achieved and What Challenges Remain. Summary*. London: King's Fund.

Harrison, S. and Ahmad W. (2000), 'Medical Autonomy and the UK State 1975 to 2025', *Sociology* 34: 129.

Hart, C. (1998), *Doing a Literature Review: Releasing the Social Science Research Imagination*. London: Sage.

Harvey, D. (1973), *Social Justice and the City*. London: Arnold.

Haskey, J. (1996), 'Population review: families and households in Great Britain', *Population Trends* 85, Autumn, 7, 13.

Hawkes, M., Kolenko, M., Shockness, M. and Diwaker, K. (2009), 'Nursing brain drain from India', *Human resources for health: overcoming the crisis*, Vol. 7, No. 5. [online] Available at: http://www.human-resources-health.com/content/7/1/5 (accessed 9 April 2010).

Hay, J. R. (1983),*The Origins of the Liberal Welfare Reforms 1906–14*. London: Macmillan.

HC 739 (2006), *The 2005 Pre-Budget Report*, House of Commons Treasury Committee. London: HMSO.

HC 633-1 (2006), *The Schools White Paper: Higher Standards, Better Schools for All*, Vol.1: Report and Minutes, Education and Skills Committee. London: HMSO.

HDR UN Human Development Report (2009), *Human Mobility and Development*.

Healthcare Commission (2006), Living Well in Later Life: A Review of Progress Againstthe National Service Framework for Older People. London: Commission for Healthcare Audit and Inspection.

Heath, A. and Cheung, S. (2007), *Unequal Chances: Ethnic Minorities in Western Labour Markets*. Oxford: British Academy/Oxford University Press.

——Jowell, R. and Curtice, J. (1985), *How Britain Votes*. Oxford: Pergamon.

Heclo, H. (1974), *Modern Social Politics in Britain and Sweden: From Relief to Income Maintenance*. New Haven: Yale University Press.

Heidenreich, M. and Bischoff, G. (2008), 'The open method of coordination: a way to the Europeanization of social and employment policies', *Journal of Common Market Studies* 46, 3, 497–532.

Held, D., McGrew, A., Goldblatt, D. and Perraton, J. (1999), *Global Transformations,* Cambridge: Polity Press.

Help Age International (2010), *Ageing Data*. Available online: http://www.helpage.org/resources/ageing-data/ (accessed 28 October 2010).

Hemerijck, A. (2002), 'The self-transformation of the European social model(s)', in G. Esping-Andersen, D. Gallie, A. Hemerijck, and J. Myles (eds), *Why We Need a New Welfare State*. Oxford: Oxford University Press.

Hennessy, P. (1992), *Never Again: Britain 1945–51*. London: Cape.

Hewitt, P. (1996), 'The place of part-time employment', in Meadows (1996: 39–58).

Heywood, A. (2003), *Political Ideologies: an Introduction,* 3rd edn. London: Palgrave Macmillan.

Hicks, S. and McDermott, J. (1999), *Lesbian and Gay Fostering and Adoption: Extraordinary but Ordinary*. London: Jessica Kingsley.

Hills, J. (1993), *The Future of Welfare: A Guide to the Debate*. York: Joseph Rowntree Foundation.

—— (1995) *Inquiry into Income and Wealth*. York: Joseph Rowntree Foundation.

—— (1998), 'Housing'. In H. Glennerster and J. Hills (eds), *The State of Welfare*, 2nd edn. Oxford: Oxford University Press.

—— (2004), *Inequality and the State*. Oxford: Oxford University Press.

—— (2007), *Ends and Means: the future roles of social housing in England* (CASE Report 34) London: STICERD, LSE http://sticerd.lse.ac.uk/case/_new/publications/.

—— et al. (2010) *An Anatomy of Economic Inequality in the UK: Report of the National Equality Panel*. London: Government Equalities Office.

—— with K. Gardiner and the LSE Welfare Programme (1997), *The Future of Welfare: A Guide to the Debate*, revised edition. York: Joseph Rowntree Foundation.

Hirsch, F. (1977), *Social Limits to Growth*. London: Routledge and Kegan Paul.

Hirschman, A. O. (1970), *Exit, Voice, and Loyalty: Responses to Decline in Firms, Organisations, and States*. Cambridge, Mass: Harvard University Press.

Hirst, P. and Thompson, G., (1996), *Globalization in Question: the International Economy and the Possibilities of Governance*. Cambridge: Polity Press.

HM Government (2009), *New Horizons: A Shared Vision for Mental Health*. London: HMSO.

—— (2010), *The Coalition: our programme for government*. London: Cabinet Office.

—— (2010a), *Building the National Care Service*. Cm. 7854. London: HMSO.

—— (2010b), *Working Together to Safeguard Children: A guide to Inter-Agency Working to Safeguard and Promote the Welfare of Children*. London: HMSO.

HM Treasury (2004), *Choice for Parents, the Best Start for Children: a Ten Year Strategy for Childcare*. London: HMSO.

—— (2005), *Public Expenditure Statistical Analysis 2005*. Cm. 6521. London: HMSO (www.hm-treasury.gov.uk)

—— (2005a), *Public Expenditure Statistical Analysis 2005*. Cm. 6521. London: HMSO (www.hm-treasury.gov.uk)

—— (2005b), *The Government's response to Kate Barker's review of housing supply*. (www.hm-treasury.gov.uk)

—— (2010), *Public Expenditure Statistical Analysis 2010*. Cm. 7890. London: HMSO (www.hm-treasury.gov.uk)

—— (2010a), *Draft: Charter for Budgetary Responsibility*, November 2010. London: HM Treasury.

—— (2010b), *The Comprehensive Spending Review*, Cm. 7942, London: TSO.

HMIC (Her Majesty's Inspectorate of Constabulary) (2009), *Crime Counts: A Review of Data Quality for Offences of the Most Serious Violence—Technical Report*. London: HMIC.

Hoggett, P. (2000), 'Social Policy and the emotions', in G. Lewis, S. Gewirtz and J. Clarke (eds), *Rethinking Social Policy*. London: Sage.

Hogwood, B. (1992), *Trends in British Public Policy*. Buckingham: Open University Press.

Holman, B. (1996), *The Corporate Parent: Manchester Children's Department 1948–71*. London: National Institute of Social Work.

Holman, R. (1975), 'The place of fostering in social work', *British Journal of Social Work* 5(1): 3–29.

Home Office (1988), *Punishment, Custody and the Community*, Cm. 424. London: HMSO.

—— (1990), *Crime, Justice and Protecting the Public: The Government's Proposals for Legislation*, Cm. 965. London: HMSO.

—— (1997a), *Criminal Statistics England and Wales 1996*, Cm. 3764. London: HMSO.

—— (1997b), *No More Excuses: A New Approach to Tackling Youth Crime in England and Wales*. London: Home Office.

—— (1999), *Crimes Recorded by the Police 1857–1999*. London: Home Office www.homeoffice.gov.uk/rds/digest4/chapter1.xls; (accessed October 2010).

—— (2005), *Domestic Violence: A National Report*, London: Home Office.

—— (2006), *Prison Population Projections 2006–13, England and Wales*. London: Home Office.

—— (2007), *Recorded Crime Statistics 1898–2001/02*. London: Home Office www.homeoffice.gov.uk/rds/pdfs07/recorded-crime-1898-2002.xls; (accessed October 2010).

—— (2009), *Homicides, Firearm Offences and Intimate Violence*, London: Home Office

—— (2010a), *Recorded Crime Statistics 2002/03–2009/10*. London: Home Office www.homeoffice.gov.uk/rds/pdfs10/recorded-crime-2002-2010.xls; (accessed October 2010).

—— (2010b), *Trends in BCS incidents of crime from 1981 to 2009/10*. London: Home Office www.homeoffice.gov.uk/rds/pdfs10/hosb1210tab201.xls; (accessed October 2010).

Hood, C., Rothstein, H. and Baldwin, R. (2000), *The Government of Risk: Understanding Risk Regulation Regimes*. Oxford: Oxford University Press.

Hough, M. and Mayhew, P. (1983), *The British Crime Survey: First Report*. Home Office Research Study No. 76. London: HMSO.

House of Commons (2000), *The BSE Inquiry: report, evidence and supporting papers of the inquiry into the emergence and identification of bovine spongiform encephalopathy (BSE) and variant Creutzfeldt-Jakob disease (vCJD) and the action taken in response to it up to 20 March 1996*. London: HMSO; also available at www.bseinquiry.gov.uk.

Howard, M., Garnham, A., Fimister, G., and Veit-Wilson, J. (2001), *Poverty: The Facts*, 4th edn. London: CPAG.

Humphreys, C. and Stanley, N. (eds) (2006), *Domestic Violence and Child Protection: Directions for Good Practice*. London: Jessica Kingsley.

Hunter, D. J. (1997), *Desperately Seeking Solutions: Rationing Health Care*. London: Longman.

Hutton, W. (1996), *The State We're In* revised edn. London: Vintage.

Hyman, P. (1994), *Women and Economics*. Wellington, New Zealand: Bridget Williams Books.

—— (1992), 'The cost of caring', in C. Glendinning and J. Millar (eds), *Women and Poverty in Britain: the 1990s*. Hemel Hempstead: Wheatsheaf.

Immergut, E. (1992a), *Health Politics. Interests and Institutions in Western Europe*. Cambridge: Cambridge University Press.

—— (1992b), 'The rules of the game: the logic of health policy-making in France, Switzerland and Sweden', in S. Steinmo, K. Thelen, and F. Longstreth. (1992 57–89).

In Control (2009), *Introduction to Self-Directed Support, Factsheet 1*. Available online: http://www.in-control.org.uk/site/INCO/Templates/General.aspx?pageid=539&cc=GB (accessed 15 October 2010).

Indermit, G., Packard, T., Pugatch, T. and Termo, J. (2005), 'Rethinking Social Security in Latin America', *International Social Security Review* Vol. 58, No. 2–3, pp. 71–96.

Inglehart, R. (1990), *Culture Shift in Advanced Industrial Society*. Princeton NJ: Princeton University Press.

Isin, E., Brodie, J., Juteau, D. and Stasilius, D. (2008), 'Recasting the Social in Citizenship', in E. Isin (ed), *Recasting the Social in Citizenship*. Toronto: University of Toronto Press.

Israel, M. and Hay, I. (2006), *Research Ethics for Social Scientists*. London: Sage.

Jackson, S. (ed) (2001), *Nobody Ever Told Us School Mattered: Raising the Educational Attainments of Children in Care*. London: British Agencies for Adoption and Fostering.

Jefferys, K. (1987), 'British Politics and Social Policy During The Second World War', *Historical Journal* 30(1): 123–44.

Jochum, V. (2010), NCVO/TSRC Big Society evidence seminar, 11 October, https://docs.google.com/leaf?id=0Bzmr36kJY6jwZWJmYjQ1MDctOWZmZC00NDAxLWFlMTItMjlmODAzMmEwZGVh&hl=en, (last accessed 13 February 2011).

Johnston, R. J., Forrest, J. and Poulsen, M. (2002), 'Are there ethnic enclaves/ghettos in English cities?' *Urban Studies* 39: 591–618.

Jones, D., Pickett, J., Oates, M. and Barbor, P. (1987), *Understanding Child Abuse*. Basingstoke: Macmillan.

Jones, K., Brown, J. and Bradshaw, J. (1983), *Issues in Social Policy*, 2nd edn. London: Routledge and Kegan Paul.

Jones, M. A. (1990), *The Australian Welfare State*. London: Allen & Unwin.

Jones, T., MacLean, B. and Young, J. (1986), *The Islington Crime Survey: Crime, Victimization and Policing in Inner-City London*. Aldershot: Gower.

Jones Finer, C. (1999), 'Trends and Developments in Welfare States', in Clasen, J. (ed), *Comparative Social Policy: Concepts, Theories and Methods*. Oxford: Blackwell, 15–33.

Jordan, B. (2008), *Welfare and Well-Being: Social Value in Public Policy*. Bristol: The Policy Press.

Joseph Rowntree Foundation (1995), *Inquiry into Income and Wealth* (2 vols). York: Joseph Rowntree Foundation.

Joshi, H. (1989), *The Changing Population of Britain*. Oxford: Blackwell.

—— (1992), 'The cost of caring', in C. Glendinning and J. Millar (eds), *Women and Poverty in Britain: the 1990s*. Hemel Hempstead: Wheatsheaf.

Kaim-Caudle, P. R. (1973), *Comparative Social Policy and Social Security: a Ten-Country Study*. London: Martin Robertson.

Kastrougalos, G. (1996), 'The Greek welfare state: in search of an identity', *Journal of European Social Policy* 6, 1, 39–60.

Kaul, I., Grunberg, I. and Stern, A. (1999), 'Global Public Goods: Concepts, Policies and Strategies', in I. Kaul, I. Grunberg and M. Stern (eds), *Global Public Goods: International Cooperation in the 21st Century*. Oxford: Oxford University Press.

Kautto, M. (2002), 'Investing in services in West European welfare states', *Journal of European Social Policy* 12, 1, 53–65.

Kavanagh, D. (1992), 'The Postwar Consensus', *Twentieth Century British History* 3(2): 175–90.

Kay, S. (2000), 'Recent changes in Latin American welfare states: is there social dumping?' *Journal of European Social Policy* 10(2): 185–203.

—— and Delamonica, E. (2005), 'The Private Sector and Privatisation in Social Services: Is the Washington Consensus 'Dead'?', *Global Social Policy* Vol 5, No 2, pp. 141–74.

Kemp, P. (2000), 'Housing benefit and welfare retrenchment in Britain', *Journal of Social Policy* 29: 263–79.

Kendall, J. (2003), *The Voluntary Sector: Comparative Perspectives in the UK*. London: Routledge.

—— and Knapp, M. (1999), 'Evaluation and the voluntary (non-profit) sector: Emerging issues', in D. Lewis (ed) *International Perspectives on Voluntary Action: Reshaping the Third Sector*. Oxford: Earthscan/Taylor and Francis.

—— and Knapp. M. (1996), *The Voluntary Sector in the UK*. Manchester: MUP.

—— (2009a), Handbook on Third Sector Policy in Europe: Multi-Level Processes and Organized Civil Society. Edward Elgar: Cheltenham.

—— (2009b), 'The UK: Ingredients in a hyperactive policy environment', in J. Kendall (ed) *Handbook on Third Sector Policy in Europe: Multi-Level Processes and Organized Civil Society*. Edward Elgar: Cheltenham.

—— (2009c), Valuing volunteering in the noughties: what would Beveridge have thought? paper presented at joint ESRC-Community Service Volunteers public policy seminar, 2 November, text published as TSRC Working Paper 37, http://www.tsrc.ac.uk/LinkClick.aspx?fileticket=yStY%2F2IeyHM%3D&tabid=596, (last accessed 13 February 2011).

—— (2010a), 'Bringing ideology back in: the erosion of political innocence in English third sector policy', *Journal of Political Ideologies* 2010, 15, 3, 241–58.

—— (2010b), 'The limits and possibilities of third sector Europeanisation', *Journal of Civil Society* 6, 1, 39–65.

—— Will, C. and Brandsen, T. (2009), 'The third sector and the Brussels dimension: trans-EU governance work progress', in J. Kendall (ed) *Handbook on Third Sector*

Policy in Europe: Multi-Level Processes and Organized Civil Society. Cheltenham: Edward Elgar.

Kennett, P. (ed) (2004), *Handbook of Comparative Social Policy*. Cheltenham: Edward Elgar.

Kershaw, C., Chivite-Matthews, N., Thomas, C, and Aust, R. (2001), *The 2001 British Crime Survery*. London: Home Office.

Kiernan, K. and Wicks, M. (1990), *Family Change and Future Policy*. York: Joseph Rowntree Foundation.

Kirby, J. (2002), *Broken Hearts: Family Decline and the Consequences for Society*. London: Centre for Policy Studies.

—— (2005), *The Price of Parenthood*. London: Centre for Policy Studies.

Kirkman-Liff, B. (1997), 'The United States', in C. Ham (ed), *Health Care Reform: Learning from International Experience*. Buckingham: Open University Press.

Kirton, D. (2000), *'Race', Ethnicity and Adoption*. Buckingham: Open University Press.

Kittay, E., Jennings, B. and Wasunna, A. (2005), 'Dependency, difference and the global ethic of long term care', *The Journal of Political Philosophy* 13/4: 443–69.

Klein R. (2006),*The New Politics of the NHS: From Creation to Reinvention*. Oxford: Radcliffe Publishing.

Kleinman, M. (2002), *A European Welfare State? European Union Social Policy in Context*. Houndmills: Palgrave.

Knapp, M., Hardy, B. and Forder, J. (2001), 'Commissioning for quality: Ten years of social care markets in England'. *Journal of Social Policy* 30, 2, 283–306.

Knight, B. (1993), *Voluntary Action*. CENTRIS: Ovingham.

Kohn, M. L. (ed) (1989), *Cross-National Research in Sociology*. Newbury Park: Sage.

Korpi, W. (1983), *The Democratic Class Struggle*. London: Routledge and Kegan Paul.

Kramer, R. (2000), 'A Third Sector in the third millenium?' *Voluntas* 11, 2, 1–24.

Kraus, M. (2004), 'Social Security Strategies and Redistributive Effects in European Social Transfer Systems', *The Review of Income and Wealth* Vol. 50, No. 3, pp. 431–57.

Krueger, R. A. (1998a), *Moderating Focus Groups*. Thousand Oaks, Ca.: Sage.

—— (1998b), *Developing Questions for Focus Groups*. Thousand Oaks, Ca.: Sage.

Kuhn, T. (1962), *The Structure of Scientific Revolutions*. Chicago: University of Chicago Press.

Kvist, J. and Saari, J. (eds) (2007), *The Europeanisation of Social Protection*. Bristol: The Policy Press.

Labour Party (1997), *New Labour: Because Britain Deserves Better*. London: The Labour Party.

—— (2005), *The Labour Party Manifesto 2005: Britain Forward Not Back.*London: The Labour Party.

Laming, Lord (2003), *The Victoria Climbié Inquiry: Report of an Inquiry by Lord Laming*. Cm. 5730. London: HMSO.

Law, I. (1996), *Racism, Ethnicity and Social Policy*. Hemel Hempstead: Harvester Wheatsheaf.

Layard, R. (1994), 'The welfare economics of training', in Layard et al. (1994: 31–49).

—— (2005), *Happiness: Lessons from a New Science*. London: Penguin.

—— Mayhew, K. and Owen, G. (eds) (1994), *Britain's Training Deficit*. Aldershot: Avebury.

Le Grand, J. (1982), *The Strategy of Equality*. London: Allen & Unwin.

—— (1993). 'Paying for or providing welfare', in N. Deakin and R. Page (eds), *The Costs of Welfare*. London: Avebury.

—— (2003), *Motivation, Agency and Public Policy: Of Knights, Knaves, Pawns and Queens*. Oxford: Oxford University Press.

—— and Vizard, P. (1998), 'The National Health Service: Crisis, Change or Continuity?', in: H. Glennerster and J. Hills, *The State of Welfare*, 2nd edn. Oxford: Oxford University Press.

Leadbeater, C., Bartlett, J. and Gallagher, N. (2008), *Making it Personal*. London: Demos.

Leete, L. (2006), 'Work in the non-profit sector', in W.W. Powell and R. Steinberg (eds) *The Nonprofit Sector: A Research Handbook*, 2nd edn, 2006, especially pp. 166–76.

Leibfried, S. (1993), 'Towards a European welfare state?' in C. Jones, *New Perspectives on the Welfare State in Europe*. London: Routledge, 133–56.

—— and Pierson, P. (eds) (1995), 'Semisovereign Welfare States: Social Policy in a Multitiered Europe', in *European Social Policy. Between Fragmentation and Integration*. Washington: The Brookings Institution.

—— and Pierson, P. (2000). 'Social Policy', in H. Wallace and W. Wallace (eds), *Policy-Making in the European Union*, 4th edn. Oxford: Oxford University Press pp. 267–92.

Leisering, L. and Leibfried, S. (1999), *Time and Poverty in Western Welfare States*. Cambridge: Cambridge University Press.

Levin, E., Moriarty, J. and Gorbach, P. (1994), *Better for the Break*. London: HMSO.

Levitas, R. (2000), 'What is Social Exclusion', in D. Gordon and P. Townsend (eds), *Breadline Europe: The Measurement of Poverty*. Bristol: The Policy Press, pp. 357–83.

Levy, A. and Kahan, B. (1991), *The Pindown Experience and the Protection of Children*. Stafford: Staffordshire County Council.

Lewis, D. (2008), 'Using life histories in social policy research: the case of third sector/public sector boundary crossing', *Journal of Social Policy* 37, 4, 559–78.

Lewis, G. (ed) (2004), *Citizenship: Personal Lives and Social Policy*. Bristol: The Policy Press.

Lewis, J. (1992), 'Gender and the development of welfare regimes', *Journal of European Social Policy*, 2,3, 159–73.

—— (2000), 'Work and care', in H. Dean, R. Sykes and R. Woods (eds), *Social Policy Review 12*. Newcastle: Social Policy Association.

—— and Glennerster, H. (1996), *Implementing the New Community Care*. Buckingham: Open University Press.

—— and Maclean, M. (1997), 'Recent developments in family policy in the UK', in M. May, E. Brunsdon, and G. Craig (eds), *Social Policy Review 9*. London: Social Policy Association.

—— (2003), 'Developing early years childcare in England, 1997–2002: the choices for (working) mothers', *Social Policy and Administration* 37(3): 219–38.

Likierman, A. (1988), *Public Expenditure: Who Really Controls it and How?* London: Penguin.

—— (2003), 'Planning and Controlling UK Public Expenditure on a Resource Cost Basis', *Public Money and Management*, January 2003: 45–50.

Lin, K. and Kangas, O. (2006), 'Social Policymaking and its Institutional Basis: Transition of the Chinese social security system', *International Social Security Review* Vol. 59, No. 2, pp. 61–76.

Lindert, P. (2004), *Growing Public: Social Spending and Economic Growth since the Eighteenth Century, volume 1, The Story*. Cambridge: Cambridge University Press.

Lipsey, D. (2000), *The Secret World of the Treasury*. London: Viking Press.

Lipsky, M. (1980), *Street-level Bureaucracy: Dilemmas of the Individual in Public Services*. New York: Russell Sage Foundation.

Lister, R. (1990), 'Women, economic dependency and citizenship', *Journal of Social Policy* 19(4): 445–68.

—— (2001), 'New Labour: A study in ambiguity from a position of ambivalence', *Critical Social Policy* 21/4: 425–47.

—— (2003), *Citizenship: Feminist Perspectives*, 2nd edn. Basingstoke: Macmillan

—— (2004), *Poverty*. Cambridge: Polity Press.

Lloyd, K. and Devine, P. (2010), 'Using the internet to give children a voice: an online survey of 10- and 11-year-old children in Northern Ireland'. *Field methods* 22(3): 270–89.

Locock, L. and Boaz, A. (2004), 'Research, policy and practice: worlds apart?', *Social Policy and Society* 3(4): 375–84.

Lombroso, C. (2006), *The Criminal Man* (1876). Durham NC: Duke University Press.

Loretto, W., Vickerstaff, S. and White, P. (2005), *Older workers and options for flexible work*, Working Paper series No. 31, Manchester: Equal Opportunities Commission.

Lowe, R. (1990), 'The Second World War, Consensus, and the Foundation of the Welfare State', *Twentieth Century British History* 1(2): 152–82.

—— (1993), *The Welfare State in Britain since 1945*. London: Macmillan.

—— (2005), *The Welfare State in Britain Since 1945*, 3rd edn. London: Palgrave Macmillan.

Lymberry, M. (2009), 'A new vision for adult social care? Continuities and change in the care of older people', *Critical Social Policy* 30, 1, 677–702.

Lyotard, J. (1984), *The Postmodern Condition: A Report on Knowledge*. Manchester: Manchester University Press.

Macaskill, C. (2006), *Beyond Refuge: Supporting Young Runaways*. London: NSPCC.

Macdonald, R. (ed) (1997), *Youth, the 'Underclass' and Social Exclusion*. London: Routledge.

Macgregor-Morris, R., Ewbank, J. and Birmingham, L. (2001), 'Potential impact of the Human Rights Act on psychiatric practice: The best of British values?'. *British Medical Journal* 322, 7290, 848–50.

MacInnes, T., Kenway, P. and Parekh, A. (2009), *Monitoring Poverty and Social Exclusion 2009*. York: Joseph Rowntree Foundation.

Mack, J. and Lansley, S. (1985), *Poor Britain*. London: Allen & Unwin.

—— (1991), *Breadline Britain*. London: Unwin Hyman.

Maclennan, D. and Gibb, K. (1990), 'Housing Finance and Subsidies in Britain after a Decade of "Thatcherism"', *Urban Studies* 27(6): 905–18.

Macmillan, R. (2010), The third sector delivering public services: an evidence review, TSRC Working Paper 20, Third Sector Research Centre, University of Birmingham, http://www.tsrc.ac.uk/LinkClick.aspx?fileticket=l9qruXn%2FBN8%3D&tabid=712; (accessed 13 February 2011).

Macpherson, Sir W. (1999), *The Stephen Lawrence Inquiry* Cm. 4262-1.London: HMSO.

Malinowski, B. (1922), *Argonauts of the Western Pacific: an Account of Native Enterprise and Adventure in the Archipelagoes of Helanesian New Guinea*. London: Routledge.

Malone, D., Marriott, S., Newton-Howes, G., Simmonds, S. and Tyrer, P. (2007), 'Community mental health teams (CMHTs) for people with severe mental illnesses and disordered personality', *Cochrane Database of Systematic Reviews* 3, CD000270.

Malpass, P. and Murie, A. (1999), *Housing Policy and Practice*, 5th edn. London: Macmillan.

Maluccio, A., Fein, E. and Olmstead, K. (1986), *Permanency Planning for Children: Concepts and Methods*. London: Tavistock.

Mann, K. (2009), 'Remembering and Rethinking the Social Divisions of Welfare: 50 years on', *Journal of Social Policy* Vol. 38, No. 1, pp. 1–18.

Manning, N. (ed) (1991), *Social Policy Review 1990–1*. Harlow: Longman.

Mares, I. (2006), 'The Economic Consequences of the Welfare State', *International Social Security Review* Vol. 60, No. 2–3, pp. 65–81.

Marmot, M. (2010), *Fair Society, Healthy Lives*, The Marmot Review Executive Summary. London: The Marmot Review. See www.ucl.ac.uk/marmotreview

Marsh, C. (1991), 'The right to work: justice in the distribution of employment', in Manning (1991: 223–42).

Marshall, T. H. (1950), 'Citizenship and social class', in T. Marshall and T. Bottomore (eds), *Citizenship and Social Class*, 1992 edn. London: Pluto Press.

—— (1963), *Sociology at the Crossroads*. London: Heinemann.

—— (1967), *Social Policy*, 2nd edn. London: Hutchinson.

—— (1981), *The Right to Welfare*. London: Heinemann Educational Books.

Martinson, R. (1974), 'What works? Questions and answers about prison reform', *Public Interest* 35: 22–54.

Marx, K. and Engels, F. (1976), *The German Ideology*. Moscow: Progress.

Masefield, J. (1946), *Poems*. London: Heinemann.

Maslow, A. (1954), *Motivation and Personality*. New York: Harper.

Mathias, P. (2001), *The First Industrial Nation: The Economic History of Britain 1700–1914*. London: Routledge, Taylor & Francis.

Mau, S. (2003), *The Moral Economy of Welfare States. Britain and Germany compared.* London: Routledge.

Mauss, M. (1967), *The Gift: Forms and Functions of Exchange in Archaic Societies*. New York: Norton.

Maxfield, M. G. (1984), *Fear of Crime in England and Wales*. Home Office Research Study No. 78. London: HMSO.

Mayhew, P. and Hough, M. (1988), 'The British Crime Survey: origins and impact', in M. Maguire and J. Pointing (eds), *Victims of Crime: A New Deal?* Milton Keynes: Open University Press.

Mayo, E. (1996), 'Dreaming of work', in Meadows (1996: 143–64).

McCabe, A. (2011), Below the radar in a Big Society? Reflections on community engagement, empowerment and social action in a changing policy context, TSRC Working Paper 51, Third Sector Research Centre, University of Birmingham. http://www.tsrc.ac.uk/LinkClick.aspx?fileticket=OMbpEZaAMKI%3d&tabid=500; (accessed 13 February 2011).

McCarthy, J. and Edwards, R. (2011), *Key Concepts in Family Studies*. London: Sage.

McCrone, G. and Stephens, M. (1995), *Housing Policy in Britain and Europe*. London: UCL Press.

McDaid, D., Oliveira, M., Jurczak, K., Knapp, M. and the MHEEN Group (2007), 'Moving beyond the mental health care system: An exploration of the interfaces between health and non-health sectors'. *Journal of Mental Health* 16, 2, 181–94.

McKeown, T. (1976), *The Modern Rise of Population*. London: Arnold.

McKnight, A. (2005), 'Employment: tackling poverty through "work for those who can"', in J. Hills and K. Stewart (eds), *A More Equal Society? New Labour, Poverty, Inequality and Social Exclusion*. Bristol: The Policy Press.

McLennan, G. (1991), *The Power of Ideology, Society and the Social Sciences*. Milton Keynes: Open University.

Mead, L. (1986), *Beyond Entitlement: The Social Obligations of Citizenship*. New York: Free Press.

Mead, L. M. (1997), *From Welfare to Work: Lessons from America*. London: Institute for Economic Affairs.

Meadows, P. (ed) (1996), *Work Out—or Work In?* Layerthorpe: Joseph Rowntree Foundation.

Means, R., Richards, S. and Smith, R. (2008), *Community Care: Policy and Practice,* 4th edn. Basingstoke: Palgrave Macmillan.

Mehrotra, S. (2000), *Integrating Economic and Social Policy: Good Practices from High Achieving Countries*. Florence: UNICEF.

—— and Delamonica, E. (2005), 'The Private Sector and Privatisation in Social Services: Is the Washington Consensus 'Dead'?', *Global Social Policy* Vol 5, No 2, pp. 141–74.

Melrose, M. and Barrett, D. (eds) (2004), *Anchors In Floating Lives: Interventions with Young People Sexually Abused Through Prostitution*. Lyme Regis: Russell House.

Menahem, G. (2007), 'The decommodified security ratio: A tool for assessing European social protection systems', *International Social Security Review* Vol. 60, No. 4, pp. 69–103.

Mental Health Alliance (2007), *Mental Health Alliance Gives Final Verdict on 2007 Mental Health Act (Press Release)*. Available online: http://www.mentalhealthalliance.org.uk/news/prfinalreport.html (accessed 14 October 2010).

Merton, R. K. (1936), 'The Unanticipated Consequences of Purposive Social Action', *American Sociological Review* 1, 6: 894–904.

Metcalf, H. (2003), 'Increasing Inequality in Higher Education: The Role of Term-Time Working', *Oxford Review of Education* 29(3): 315–29.

Middleton, S., Ashworth, K. and Braithwaite, I. (1997), *Small Fortunes: Spending on Children, Childhood Poverty and Parental Sacrifice*. York: Joseph Rowntree Foundation.

Miles, D., Myles, G. and Preston, I. (eds) (2003), *The Economics of Public Spending*. Oxford: Oxford University Press.

Miles, J. and Probert, R. (2009) *Sharing Lives, Dividing Assets*. Oxford: Hart Publishing.

Miles, R. (1989), *Racism*. London: Routledge.

Miliband, R. (1961), *Parliamentary Socialism*. London: Allen & Unwin.

Mills, C. W. (1976), *The Sociological Imagination*. Oxford: Oxford University Press.

Milward, A. (1994), *The European Rescue of the Nation-State*. London: Routledge.

Ministry of Health (1962), *A Hospital Plan for England and Wales*. Cmnd. 1604. London: HMSO.

Mishra, R. (1984), *The Welfare State in Crisis*. Hemel Hempstead: Harvester Wheatsheaf.

Mitchell, D. (1991), *Income transfers in Ten Welfare States*. Aldershot: Avebury.

Modood, T., Berthoud, R., Lakey, J., Nazran, J., Smith, P. and Beishon, S. (1997), *Ethnic Minorities in Britain*. London: Policy Studies Institute.

Monaghan, G., Hibbert, P. and Moore, S. (2003), *Children in Trouble: Time for Change*. Ilford: Barnardo's.

Monckton, Sir W. (1945), *Report on the Circumstances which Led to the Boarding Out of Dennis and Terence O'Neill at Bank Farm and the Steps Taken to Supervise their Welfare*. Cmd. 6636. London: HMSO.

Mooney, J. (2000), *Gender, Violence and the Social Order*. Basingstoke: Macmillan.

Moore, J. (1985), *The ABC of Child Abuse Work*. Aldershot: Gower.

Morgan, D. L. (1998a), *The Focus Group Guidebook*. Thousand Oaks, Ca.: Sage.

—— (1998b), *Planning Focus Groups*. Thousand Oaks, Ca.: Sage.

Morgan, P. (1995), *Farewell to the Family?* London: Institute of Economic Affairs.

—— (1998), *Adoption and the Care of Children*. London: Institute of Economic Affairs.

—— (2000), *Marriage-lite: the Rise of Cohabitation and its Consequences*. London: Institute for the Study of Civil Society.

Morgan, R. and Newburn, T. (2007), 'Youth Justice', in M. Maguire, R. Morgan and R. Reiner (eds) *The Oxford Handbook of Criminology*, 4th edn. Oxford: Oxford University Press, 1024–60.

Morison, J. (2000), 'The government-voluntary sector compacts: governance, governmentability and civil society', *Journal of Law and Society* 27, 1, 98–132.

Morris, J. (1993), *Community Care or Independent Living?* York: Joseph Rowntree Foundation.

Morris, L. (1994), *Dangerous Classes: The Underclass and Social Citizenship*. London: Routledge.

Morris, S. and Wheatley, H. (1994), *Time to Listen: The Experiences of Young People in Foster and Residential Care*. London: Childline.

Mullard, M. (1993), *The Politics of Public Expenditure*. London: Routledge.

—— (2001), 'New Labour, New Public Expenditure: The Case of Cake Tomorrow', *The Political Quarterly* 72 (3), 310–21.

Müller, K. (2003), *Privatising Old-Age Security: Latin America and Eastern Europe Compared*. Aldershot: Edward Elgar.

Muncie, J. (2000), 'Pragmatic realism? Searching for criminology in the new youth justice', in B. Goldson (ed) *The New Youth Justice*. Lyme Regis: Russell House Publishing.

Munro, E. (2002), *Effective Child Protection*. London: Sage.

—— (2010), *The Munro Review of Child Protection: Part One: A Systems Analysis*. London: DfE.

Murray, C. (1984), *Losing Ground: American Social Policy 1950–80*. New York: Basic Books.

—— (1990), *The Emerging British Underclass* (London: Institute of Economic Affairs).

Muula, A. S., Panulo, B. and Masela, F. C. (2006), 'The financial losses from the migration of nurses from Malawi', *BMC Nursing* Vol. 5, No. 9. [Online] Available at: http://www.biomedcentral.com/1472-6955/5/9 (accessed 28 June 2010).

National Audit Office (NAO) (2004), *Welfare to Work: Tackling the Barriers to the Employment of Older People*. House of Commons HC 1026. London: HMSO.

—— (2009), *Train to Gain. Developing the Skills of the Workforce*, London: NAO.

—— (2010), *The Decent Homes Programme*. London: NAO.

National Commission on Education (1993), *Learning to Succeed*. London: HMSO.

National Equality Panel (2010), *An Anatomy of Economic Inequality in the UK*, London: Government Equalities Office.

National Statistics Online (2002), www.statistics.gov.uk/Census2001/default.asp.

NCIHE (National Committee of Inquiry into Higher Education) (1997), *Summary Report*.

NCVO (no date), Briefing on the Charities Act 2006, http://www.ncvo-vol.org.uk/policy-research-analysis/policy/charity-law-regulation/charities-act-2006-briefing, (last accessed 13 February 2011).

Neidhardt, F. and Rucht, D. (1991), 'The analysis of social movements: the state of the art and some perspectives for further research', in D. Rucht (ed), *Research on Social Movements*. Frankfurt: Campus/Boulder, Colo.: Westview Press.

Neil, E. and Howe, D. (eds) (2004), *Contact in Adoption and Permanent Foster Care: Research, Theory and Practice*. London: British Association for Adoption and Fostering.

Nelson, K. (2007), 'Universalism versus Targeting: the vulnerability of social insurance and means-tested minimum income protection in 18 countries, 1990–2002', *International Social Security Review* Vol. 60, No. 1, pp. 33–58.

New Economics Foundation (NEF) (2004), *A Well-being Manifesto for a Flourishing Society*. London: NEF.

Newman, J, Glendinning, C. and Hughes, M. (2008), 'Beyond modernization? Social care and the transformation of welfare governance'. *Journal of Social Policy* 37, 4, 531–57.

NHS (National Health Service) (2000),The NHS Plan: A plan for investment, a plan for reform. Cm. 4818-I.

NHS Information Centre (2009), *Personal Social Services Expenditure and Unit Costs: England 2007–8.* London: HMSO.

NHS Information Centre (2009), *Personal Social Services Staff of Social Services Departments at 30 September 2009, England.* London: HMSO.

NHS Information Centre, Social Care Statistics (2010), *Personal Social Services Expenditure and Unit Costs, England 2007–8.* London: The Health and Social Care Information Centre.

Nirje, B. (1970), 'Symposium on "normalization": The normalization principle: Implications and comments'. *Journal of Mental Subnormality* 16: 62–70.

Novak, T. (1997), 'Hounding delinquents: the introduction of the Jobseeker's Allowance', *Critical Social Policy* 17(1): 99–110.

Novy, M. (2005), *Reading Adoption: Family and Difference in Fiction and Drama.* Ann Arbor: University of Michigan Press.

O'Brien, J. (1989), *What's Worth Working For? Leadership for Better Quality Human Services.* Lithonia, Georgia: Responsive Systems Associates.

O'Reilly, J. and Fagan C. (1998), *Part-time Prospects: An International Comparison of Part-time Work in Europe, North America and the Pacific Rim.* London: Routledge.

Oakley, A. (1974), *The Sociology of Housework.* London: Martin Robertson.

—— (1997), *Social Trends* 27. London: HMSO.

OECD (Organization for Economic Cooperation and Development) (1994), *New Orientations for Social Policy.* Brussels: OECD.

(OECD), Organisation for Economic Cooperation and Development. 2007. *International Migration Outlook.* OECD: Paris.

—— *Health at a Glance 2009 OECD Indicators.* OECD iLibrary.

—— (2005), *OECD Economic Surveys: United Kingdom*, Volume 2005/20, Supplement No 2. Paris: OECD.

—— (2005a), *OECD Outlook No 78.* Paris: OECD.

—— (2005b), *Net Social Expenditure, 2005 Edition: more comprehensive measures of social support*, OECD Social, Employment and Migration Working Papers No. 29, compiled by Willem Adema and Maxime Ladaique. Paris: OECD.

Offe, C. (1996), *Modernity and the State: East, West,* Cambridge: Polity Press.

Office for Disability Issues (2009a), *Life Opportunities Survey.* Available: http://www.officefordisability.gov.uk/research/survey.php (accessed 18 October 2010).

—— (2009b), *Models of Disability.* Available online: http://www.officefordisability.gov.uk/resources/models-of-disability.php (accessed 28 October 2010).

—— (2010), *Historic Adoption Tables (1974–2009).* London: ONS.

—— (2010), *Public Service Output, Inputs and Productivity: Healthcare* http://www.statistics.gov.uk/articles/nojournal/healthcare-productivity-2010.pdf.

—— (ONS) (1997). *Social Trends* 27. London: HMSO.

—— (2004), *Focus on Older People.* London: HMSO.

—— (2005), *Labour Force Survey.* Available online: http://www.statistics.gov.uk/statbase/Source.asp?vlnk=358 (accessed 14 October 2010).

—— (2006), *Limiting Illness.* Available online: http://www.statistics.gov.uk/cci/nugget.asp?id=1326 (accessed 18 October 2010).

—— (2009), *Social Trends* 39, London: ONS.

—— (2009), *Women in the Labour Market.* Available online: http://www.statistics.gov.uk/cci/nugget.asp?id=2145 (accessed 28 October 2010).

—— (2010), *Pension Trends.* Available online: http://www.statistics.gov.uk/downloads/theme_compendia/pensiontrends/Pension_Trends_ch02.pdf (accessed 26 October 2010).

—— (2010), *Social Trends* 40, London: HMSO.

Oliver, M. (1990), *The Politics of Disablement: A Sociological Approach.* Basingstoke: Macmillan.

Oliver, M. and Barnes, M. (1998), *Disabled People and Social Policy: From exclusion to inclusion.* Harlow: Longman.

Olsson, S. E. (1990), *Social Policy and the Welfare State in Sweden.* Stockholm: Arkiv.

—— (2002), *Social Trends* 32. London: HMSO.

—— (2005), *Social Trends* 35. London: HMSO.

—— (2010), 'Earnings Full-time gender pay gap narrows':http://www.statistics.gov.uk/cci/nugget.asp?id=167 (accessed 3 February 2011).

—— (Office for National Statistics) (1996), *Social Focus on Ethnic Minorities.* London: ONS.

—— (2010a), *Social Trends* 40. London: HMSO.

—— (Office for National Statistics) (2010b), *Results from the 2008 General Lifestyle Survey.* London: ONS.

—— (2006), *Social Trends* 36. London: HMSO.

—— (2007), *Social Trends* 37. London: HMSO.

—— (2009), *Social Trends* 39. London: HMSO.

—— (2010a), *The effects of taxes and benefits on household income, 2008/09.* ONS.

—— (2010b), *Social Trends* 40. ONS.

—— (2010c), *Births in England and Wales by characteristics of mother 2009, Statistical Bulletin.* Office for National Statistics. www.statistics.gov.uk/pdfdir/birth1010.pdf

—— (2010d), *Historic marriage tables.* Office for National Statistics. www.statistics.gov.uk/downloads/theme_population/historic_marriage_tables.zip.

—— (2010e), *Historic divorce tables.* Office for National Statistics. www.statistics.gov.uk/downloads/theme_population/historic-divorce-tables.xls.

—— (2010f), Interactive Population Pyramid. Office for National Statistics www.statistics.gov.uk/populationestimates/flash_pyramid/default.htm

—— (2010g), Estimates of the very elderly (including centenarians)(experimental). Office for National Statistics www.statistics.gov.uk/statbase/Product.asp?vlnk=15003

—— (2010h), Summary of key live birth statistics: *Population Trends* 116 . Office for National Statistics http://www.statistics.gov.uk/StatBase/ssdataset.asp?vlnk=8393&More=Y

—— (2010i) Non-married people cohabiting: by sex and age, 2001/02: *Social Trends* 34. Office for National Statistics http://www.statistics.gov.uk/StatBase/ssdataset.asp?vlnk=7266&More=Y.

—— (2009), *Public Sector Interventions in the Financial Crisis:decisions on the National Accounts classification of the financial crisis interventions by public sector authorities between 2007 and August 2009,* (author: Martin Kellaway). London: ONS (http://www.statistics.gov.uk/cci/article.asp?ID=2301).

—— (2011), *Statistical Bulletin: public sector finances, December 2010*. London: ONS (http://www.statistics.gov.uk/pdfdir/psf0111.pdf).

ONS Labour statistics accessible from: http://www.statistics.gov.uk/default.asp

ONS (Office for National Statistics) (2010), *Social Trends No. 40*. London: The Stationery Office.

Oppenhiem, A. N. (1992), *Questionnaire Design, Interviewing and Attitude Measurement*, London: Continuum.

Orenstein, M. (2008), 'Global Pensions Policy', in N. Yeates (ed) *Understanding Global Social Policy*. Bristol: The Policy Press.

Organisation for Economic Cooperation and Development (2007), *International Migration Outlook*. OECD: Paris.

Organisation for Economic Cooperation and Development (OECD) and World Health Organisation(WHO)(2010), International Migration of Health Workers: improving international co-operation to address the global health workforce crisis. Policy Brief, February. Paris: OECD.

Osborne, S. (2010), Extent and trends, in J. Flatley, C. Kershaw, K. Smith, R. Chaplin and D. Moon (eds) *Crime in England and Wales 2009/10*. London: Home Office.

Otting, A. (1994), 'The International Labour Organization and its standard-setting activity in the area of social security', *Journal of European Social Policy*. Vol. 4, No. 1, pp. 51–7.

Overbye, E. (2005), 'Extending Social Security in Developing Countries: a review of three main strategies', *International Journal of Social Welfare* Vol. 14, No. 4, pp. 305–14.

Øyen, E. (ed) (1990), *Comparative Methodology: Theory and Practice in International Social Research*. London: Sage.

Packman, J. (1981), *The Child's Generation: Child Care Policy in Britain*, 2nd edn. Oxford: Blackwell.

—— and Hall, C. (1998), *From Care to Accommodation: Support, Protection and Control in Child Care Services*. London: HMSO.

Padarath, A., Chamberlain, C., McCoy, D., Ntuli, A., Rowson, M. and Loewenson, R. (nd), *Health Personnel in South Africa: Confronting Maldistribution and Brain Drain*. Regional Network for Equity in Health in South Africa. Equinet Discussion Paper No. 3.

Page, R. M. (2007), *Revisiting the Welfare State*. Milton Keynes: Open University Press.

Pahl, J. (1989), *Money and Marriage*. Basingstoke: Macmillan.

—— (1995), 'His money, her money: recent research on financial organisation in marriage', *Journal of Economic Psychology* 16, 3, 361–76.

—— (2005), 'Individualisation in couple finances: who pays for the children?' *Social Policy and Society* 4, 4, 381–91.

—— (2006), 'The costs of caring for a disabled child'. In C. Glendinning and P. Kemp (eds), *Cash and Care: Policy Challenges in the Welfare State*. Bristol: Policy Press.

—— Hasanbegovic, C. and Yu, M. (2004), 'Globalisation and family violence', in V. George and R. Page (eds), *Global Social Problems*. London: Polity Press.

—— Kendall, J. and Baglioni, S.(2009), 'The United Nations International Year of Volunteers: a significant non-EU transnational initiative for European countries?' in J. Kendall (ed) *Handbook on Third Sector Policy in Europe: Multi-Level Processes and Organized Civil Society*. Edward Elgard: Cheltenham.

Pakulski, J. and Waters, M. (1996), *The Death of Class*. London: Sage.

Palmer, G. (2010), The Poverty Site. [internet site] www.poverty.org.uk.

—— Carr, J. and Kenway. P. (2005), *Monitoring Poverty and Social Exclusion 2005*. York: Joseph Rowntree Foundation.

Park, K., Curtis, J., Thomson, K., Jarvis, L. and Bromley, C. (2001), *British Social Attitudes: the 18th report*. London: Sage.

Parker, G. and Clarke, H. (2002), 'Making the ends meet: Do carers and disabled people have a common agenda?' *Policy & Politics* 30, 3, 347–59.

Parker, J. (1972), 'Welfare', in Halsey, A. H. (ed), *Trends in British Society since 1900*. London: Macmillan.

Parker, R.(1980), *Caring for Separated Children*. London: Macmillan.

—— (1981), 'Tending and Social Policy', in E. Goldberg and S. Hatch (eds), *A New Look at the Personal Social Services*. London: Policy Studies Institute.

—— Ward, H., Jackson, S., Aldgate, J. and Wedge, P. (1991), *Looking After Children: Assessing Outcomes in Child Care*. London: HMSO.

Parsons, T. and Bales, R. (1956), *Family, Socialisation and Interaction Process*. London: Routledge.

Parton, N. (1985), *The Politics of Child Abuse*. Basingstoke: Macmillan.

Pascall, G. (1997), *Social Policy: A New Feminist Analysis*. London: Routledge.

Pass, C., Lowes, B., Pendleton, A. and Chadwick, L. (eds) (1991), *Collins Dictionary of Business*. Glasgow: Collins.

Pateman, C. (1989), *The Disorder of Women*. Cambridge: Polity Press.

Patterson, L. (2003), *Scottish Education in the Twentieth Century*. Edinburgh: Edinburgh University Press.

Pawson, H. and Kintrea, K. (2002), 'Part of the problem or part of the solution? Allocation policies and social exclusion in Britain', *Journal of Social Policy* 31: 643–67.

Peattie, K. and Morley, A. (2007), *Social Enterprises: Diversity and Dynamics, Contexts and Contributions*. Social Enterprise Coalition and Economic and Social Research Council, Cardiff and Swindon.

Pelton, L. (1985), 'Child abuse and neglect: the myth of classlessness', in L. Pelton (ed), *The Social Context of Child Abuse and Neglect*. New York: Human Sciences Press.

Pennell, H. and West, A. (2005), 'The Impact of Increased Fees on Participation in Higher Education in England', *Higher Education Quarterly* 59(2): 127–37.

Peston, R. (2005), *Brown's Britain*. London: Short Books.

Phillips, M. (2004), 'Teenagers on family values', in A. Park, J. Curtice, K. Thomson, C. Bromley and M. Phillips (eds), *British Social Attitudes: the 21st Report*. London: Sage.

Philpott, J. (1997a), 'Looking forward to full employment: an overview', in Philpott (1997b: 1–29).

—— (ed) (1997b), *Working for Full Employment*. London: Routledge.

Piachaud, D. (1981), 'Peter Townsend and the Holy Grail', *New Society* 57 (10 Sept): 419–22.

—— (1997), 'The Growth of Means-Testing', in A. Walker, and C. Walker, (eds), *Britain Divided*. London: CPAG, pp. 75–83.

—— and Sutherland, H. (2002), 'Child poverty', in J. Hills, J. Le Grand and D. Piachaud (eds), *Understanding Social Exclusion*. Oxford: Oxford University Press.

—— and Sutherland, H. (2002), *Changing Poverty Post-1997*. London: London School of Economics.

Pickvance, C. G. (2009), 'The construction of UK sustainable housing policy and the role of pressure groups' *Local Environment* 14:329–45.

Pickvance, C. G. and Pickvance, K. (1995), 'The role of family help in the housing decisions of young people', *Sociological Review* 43: 123–49.

Pierson, C. (2006), *Beyond the Welfare State? The New Political Economy of Welfare*, 3rd edn. Cambridge: Polity Press.

Pierson, P. (1994), *Dismantling the Welfare State? Reagan, Thatcher and the Politics of Retrenchment*. Cambridge: Cambridge University Press.

—— (1996), 'The new politics of the welfare state', *World Politics*, 48/2: 143–79.

—— (1998), 'Irresistible forces, immovable objects: post-industrial welfare states confront permanent austerity,' *Journal of European Public Plicy* 5(4): 539–60.

Pilgrim, D. (2005), *Key Concepts in Mental Health*. London: Sage Publications.

PIU (Performance and Innovation Unit) (2000), Adoption: Prime Minister's Review. London: Cabinet Office.

Pixley, J. (1993), *Citizenship and Employment*. Cambridge: Cambridge University Press.

Plant, R. (1985), 'The very idea of a welfare state', in P. Bean, J. Ferris, and D. Whynes (eds), *In Defence of Welfare*. London: Tavistock.

Platt, L. (2009), *Ethnicity and Child Poverty*, Research Report No 576. Department for Work and Pensions.

Pleace, N., Burrows, R. and Quilgars, D. (1997), 'Homeless-ness in contemporary Britain: conceptualization and measurement', in R. Burrows, N. Pleace, and D. Quilgars (eds), *Homelessness and Social Policy*. London: Routledge.

Pol, L. G. (1992), 'A Method to Increase Response When External Interference and Time Constraints Reduce Interview Quality'. *Public Opinion Quarterly* 56(3): 356–9.

Povey, D. and Prime, J. (1999), *Recorded Crime Statistics England and Wales, April 1998 to March 1999*. Home Office Statistical Bulletin 18/99. London: Home Office.

Powell, M. (1997), *Evaluating the National Health Service*. Buckingham: Open University Press.

Power, M. (1999), *The Audit Society: Rituals of Verification*. Oxford: Oxford University Press.

Preston, G. (2005), *At Greatest Risk: the Children Most Likely to be Poor*. London: Child Poverty Action Group.

Priestley, M. (2003), *Disability: A Life Course Approach*. Cambridge: Polity Press.

Prime Minister and Minister for the Cabinet Office (1999), *Modernising Government*. Cm. 4310.

Prime Minister's Strategy Unit (2004), *Alcohol Harm Reduction Strategy for England*. London: Cabinet Office.

—— (2007), *Safe, Sensible, Social: The Next Steps in the National Alcohol Strategy*. London: Cabinet Office.

Propper, C., Burgess, S. and Gossage, D. (2008), 'Competi-tion and Quality: Evidence from the NHS Internal Market 1991–9', *Economic Journal* 118(525): 138–70.

Putnam, R. (1993), *Making Democracy Work*. New Jersy: Princeton University Press.

—— (2000), *Bowling Alone?* New York: Sinion and Schuster.

—— (2002), *Democracies in Flux?* Oxford: Oxford University Press.

Quality Assurance Agency for Higher Education (2007), *Social Policy and Administration*. Benchmark statement

http://www.qaa.ac.uk/academicinfrastructure/
benchmark/statements/SocialPolicy07.pdf (accessed
12 February 2011).

Queisser, M. & Whitehouse, E. (2006), 'Comparing the
Pension Promises of 30 OECD Countries', *International
Social Security Review* Vol. 59, No. 3, pp. 49–77.

Qureshi, H. and Walker, A. (1989), *The Caring Relationship: Elderly People and their Families*. London:
Macmillan.

Radford, J. (1987), 'Policing male violence: policing men',
in M. Maynard and J. Hanmer (eds), *Women, Violence
and Social Control*. London: Macmillan.

Ragin, C. (1987), *The Comparative Method*. Berkeley,
CA: University of California Press.

—— (1991), *Issues and Alternatives in Comparative Social
Research*. Leiden: Brill.

Rawls, J. (1972), *A Theory of Justice*. Oxford: Clarendon
Press.

Reay, D. (2006), 'The Zombie Stalking English Schools:
Social Class and Educational Inequality' *British Journal of
Educational Studies* 54 (3): 288–307.

Rex, J. and Moore, R. (1967), *Race, Community and
Conflict*. Oxford: Institute for Race Relations/Oxford
University Press.

Rhodes, R. A. W. (1988), *Beyond Westminster and
Whitehall*. London: Unwin Hyman.

—— and Marsh, D. (1992), 'New directions in the study of
policy networks', *European Journal of Political Research*
21: 181–205.

Riddell, S., Priestley, M., Pearson, C., Mercer, G., Barnes,
C., Jolly, D. and Williams, V. (2006), Disabled People and
Direct Payments: A UK Comparative Study. ESRC End
of Award Report (RES-000-23-0263). Available online:
http://www.leeds.ac.uk/disability-studies/projects/
UKdirectpayments/UKDPfinal.pdf (accessed 26 October
2010).

Ridge, T. (2005), 'Supporting children: the impact of child
support policies on children's wellbeing in the UK and
Australia', *Journal of Social Policy* 34, 1, 121–42.

Rimlinger, G. (1971), *Welfare Policy and Industrialization
in Europe*. New York: John Wiley & Sons.

Riphahn, R. (2001), 'Rational Poverty or Poor Rationality?
The Take-up of Social Assistance Benefits', *Review of
Income and Wealth* Vol. 47, No. 3, pp. 379–98.

Ritchie, J. (1994), *Report of the Inquiry into the Care and
Treatment of Christopher Clunis*, presented to the
Chairmen of North East Thames and South East Thames
Regional Health Authority. London: HMSO.

Ritter, G. A. (1986), *Social Welfare in Germany and
Britain. Origins and Development*. Leamington
Spa: Berg.

Ritzer, G. (1993), *The McDonaldization of Society*.
Newbury Park, Calif.: Pine Forge Press.

Roberts, K. (1995), *Youth Employment in Modern Britain*.
Oxford: Oxford University Press.

—— (1997), 'Is there an emerging British "underclass"? The
evidence from youth research', in Macdonald (1997:
39–54).

Robertson, J., Emerson, E., Hatton, C. et al. (2005), *The
Impact of Person Centred Planning*. Lancaster: Institute
for Health Research, Lancaster University.

—— Hatton, C., Emerson, E., Elliott, J., McIntosh, B., Swift,
P. et al. (2007), 'Reported barriers to the implementation
of person-centred planning for people with intellectual
disabilities in the UK', *Journal of Applied Research in
Intellectual Disabilities 20*, 4, 297–307.

Robins, T. and Lucas, P. C. (eds) (2004), *New Religious
Movements in the 21st Century: Legal, Political, and
Social Challenges in Global Perspective*. London:
Routledge.

Roche, M. (1992), *Re-thinking Citizenship*. Cambridge:
Polity Press.

Rodgers, B., Greve, J. and Morgan, J. S. (1968), *Comparative Social Administration*. London: Allen & Unwin.

—— with Doron, A. and Jones, M. (1979), *The Study of
Social Policy: a Comparative Approach*. London:
Allen & Unwin.

—— and Pryor, J. (1998), *Separation and Divorce: the
Outcomes for Children*. York: Joseph Rowntree
Foundation.

Rose, D. (ed) (2000), *Researching Social and Economic
Change: The Uses of Household Panel Studies*, London:
Routledge.

Rose, H. (1981), 'Re-reading Titmuss: the sexual division of
welfare', *Journal of Social Policy* Vol. 10, No. 4, pp.
477–502.

Rose, N. (1999), *Powers of Freedom: Reframing Political
Thought*. Cambridge: Cambridge University Press.

Rose, R. (1989), *Ordinary People in Social Policy: a
Behavioural Analysis*. London: Sage.

Rostgaard, T. and Fridberg, T. (1998), *Caring for Children
and Older People in Europe—A Comparison of European
Policies and Practices*. Copenhagen: Danish National
Institute of Social Research.

Rothstein, B. and Stolle, D. (2003), 'Social capital,
impartiality and the welfare state: an institutional
approach', in M. Hooghe and D. Stolle (eds) *Generating
Social Capital: Civil Society and Institutions in Comparative Perspective*. Palgrave: Basingstoke.

Rowe, J. and Lambert, L. (1973), *Children Who Wait*.
London: Association of British Adoption Agencies.

Rowntree, B. S. (1901), *Poverty: A Study of Town Life*.
London: Macmillan.

Royal College of General Practitioners (2010), *Department
of Health Consultation on Equity and Excellence:
Liberating the NHS*. London: Royal College of General
Practitioners.

Royal Commission on Long-Term Care (1999), *With
Respect to Old Age: Long-Term Care—Rights and
Responsibilities*. Cm. 4192. London: HMSO.

Rubery, J. (1997), 'What do women want from full employment?', in Philpott (1997b: 63–80).

Rubington, E. and Weinberg, M. S. (2010), *The Study of Social Problems.* New York: Oxford University Press.

Ruck, S. K. (ed) (1951), *Paterson on Prisons.* London: Muller.

Ryan, P. (ed) (1991), *International Comparisons of Vocational Education and Training for Intermediate Skills.* London: Falmer Press.

Ryan, W. (1971), *Blaming the Victim: Ideology Serves the Establishment.* New York: Pantheon.

Ryburn, M. (ed) (1994), *Contested Adoptions: Research, Law, Policy, and Practice.* Aldershot: Arena.

Sainsbury, R. (2003), 'Understanding Social Security Fraud', in Millar, J. (ed) (2003), *Understanding Social Security.* Bristol: The Policy Press, pp. 277–96.

Sak, B. and Raponi, M. (2002), *Housing Statistics in the European Union.* Liège: Université de Liège.

—— Hills, J. & Sutherland, H. (2009), 'Poverty, Inequality and Redistribution', in Hills, J. Sefton, T. & Stewart, K. (eds) *Towards a More Equal Society?* Bristol: Policy Press, pp. 21–45.

Salamon, L. M. (1987), 'Partners in public service: the scope and theory of Government-nonprofit relations', in W.W. Powell (ed) *The Nonprofit Sector: A Research Handbook*, New Haven: Yale University Press, 1st edn.

—— and Anheier, H.K. (1997), *Defining the No profit Sector: A Cross national analysis.*

Sales, R. (2007), *Understanding Immigration and Refugee Policy.* Bristol: The Policy Press.

Salmon, M. E., Yan, J., Hewitt, H. and Guisinger, V. 2007. 'Managed migration: the Caribbean approach to addressing nursing services capacity', *Health Services Research,* June. [Online] Available at: http://findarticles.com/p/articles/mi_m4149/is_3_42/ai_n27260228/?tag=content;col1. (accessed 28 June 2010).

Salter, F. K. (2004), *Welfare, Ethnicity and Altruism: New Data and Evolutionary Theory.* London: Frank Cass.

Sarantakos, S. (2005), *Social Research*, 3rd edn. Basingstoke: Palgrave Macmillan.

Saunders, P. (1990), *A Nation of Home Owners.* London: Unwin Hyman.

Schnitzer, P. and Ewigman, B. (2005), 'Child deaths resulting from inflicted injuries: household risk factors and perpetrator characteristics'. *Pediatrics* 116(5): 687–93.

Schwartz, P., Kelly, E. and Boyer, N. (1999), 'The Emerging Global Knowledge Economy', in OECD, *The Future of the Global Economy: Towards a Long Boom?*, Paris: OECD.

Scott, D. (2007), 'The role of the voluntary and community sectors', in J. Baldock, N. Manning and S. Vickerstaff (eds) *Social Policy*, 3rd edn. Oxford: Oxford University Press.

Scott, H. (1984), *Working your Way to the Bottom: The Feminization of Poverty.* London: Pandora.

Scottish Government (2010), *Increase Healthy Life Expectancy at Birth in the Most Deprived Areas.* Available online: http://www.scotland.gov.uk/About/scotPerforms/indicators/lifeExpectancy (accessed 17 October 2010).

Scruggs, L. (2007), 'Welfare state generosity across space and time', in J. Clasen and N. A. Siegel (eds) *Investigating Welfare State Change. The 'dependent variable' problem.* Cheltenham: Edward Elgar, 133–66.

Secretary of State for Social Security (1995), *Improving Child Support.* London: HMSO.

Seelos, C., Mair, J., Battilana, J. and Dacin, M.T. (2010), The embeddedness of social entrepreneurship: understanding variation across local communities, IESE Business School Working Paper WP-858, IESE Business School, University of Navarra.

Sefton, T. (1997), *The Changing Distribution of the Social Wage.* STICERD Occasional Paper 21. London: London School of Economics.

—— (2002), *Recent Changes in the Distribution of the Social Wage.* London: London School of Economics.

Sennett, R. (1998), *The Corrosion of Character: The Personal Consequences of Work in the New Capitalism.* New York: Norton.

Sergeant, H. (2006), *Handle With Care: An Investigation into the Care System.* London: Centre for Young Policy Studies.

Sevenhuijsen, S. (1998), *Citizenship and the Ethics of Care.* London: Routledge.

Shakespeare, T. (2006), *Disability Rights and Wrongs.* London: Routledge.

Shalev, M. (1983), 'The Social Democratic Model and Beyond', *Comparative Social Research* 6, 315–51.

Sheldrake, J. and Vickerstaff, S. (1987), *The History of Industrial Training in Britain.* Aldershot: Gower.

Shepherd, G., Boardman, J. and Slade, M. (2008), *Making Recovery a Reality. Policy Paper.* London: Sainsbury Centre for Mental Health.

Sheridan, M. (2003), 'The deceit continues: an updated literature review of Munchausen Syndrome by Proxy', *Child Abuse and Neglect* 27(4): 431–51.

Silverman, G. (2000), *Doing Qualitative Research: A Practical Handbook.* London: Sage.

Simmons, J. (2002), *Crime in England and Wales 2001/2002.* London: Home Office.

Sinclair, I. and Gibbs, I. (1998), *Children's Homes: A Study in Diversity.* Chichester: Wiley.

Sivanandan, A. (1990), *Communities of Resistance: Writings on Black Struggles for Soialism.* London: Verso.

6, P. and Leat, D. (1997), 'Inventing the British Voluntary Sector by Committee: From Wolfenden to Deakin', *Non-profit Studies* 1, 2, 33–47.

Smart, C. (2005), 'Texture of family life: further thoughts on change and commitment', *Journal of Social Policy* 34, 4, 541–56.

Smith, D. (2005), *On the Margins of Exclusion*. Bristol: The Policy Press.

Smith, G. (1988), *Social Needs: Policy Practice and Research*. London: Routledge.

Social Care Institute for Excellence (SCIE) (2005), *SCIE Research Briefing 11: The Health and Well-Being of Young Carers*. London: SCIE.

Social Exclusion Unit (SEU) (2000), *Minority Ethnic Issues in Social Exclusion and Neighbourhood Renewal*. London: Cabinet Office.

Social Exclusion Unit (SEU) (2002), *Reducing Re-offending by Ex-prisoners*. London: Office of the Deputy Prime Minister.

Social Services Inspectorate (1990), *Inspection of Child Protection Services in Rochdale*. London: HMSO.

Spector, M. and Kitsuse, J. I. (1977), *Constructing Social Problems*. Menlo Park, CA: Benjamin-Cummings.

Spencer, N. (1996), *Poverty and Child Health*. Oxford: Radcliffe.

Spicker, P. (1984), *Stigma and Social Welfare*. Beckenham: Croom Helm.

—— (1993), *Poverty and Social Security*. London: Routledge.

Spross, C. (ed) (2006), *Beschäftigungsförderung älterer Arbeitnehmer in Europa*. Beiträge zur Arbeitsmarkt— und Berufsforschung: Nürnberg.

Standing, G. (2011), 'Responding to the Crisis: Economic Stabilisation Grants', *Policy and Politics* Vol. 39, No. 1.

Stanko, E. A. (1988), 'Hidden violence against women', in M. Maguire and J. Ponting (eds), *Victims of Crime: A New Deal?* Milton Keynes: Open University Press.

Stein, M. (2004), *What Works for Young People Leaving Care*, 2nd edn. Ilford: Barnardo's.

Stein, M. and Carey, K. (1986), *Leaving Care*. Oxford: Basil Blackwell.

Steinmo, S., Thelen, K. and Longstreth, F. (eds) (1992), *Structuring Politics. Historical Institutionalism in Comparative Analysis*. Cambridge: Cambridge University Press.

Stewart, K. (2009), 'Poverty, Inequality and Child Well-being in International Context: still bottom of the pack?' in J. Hills, T. Sefton, and K. Stewart, (eds) *Towards a More Equal Society?* Bristol: The Policy Press, pp 267–90.

—— and Hills, J. (2005), 'Introduction', in J. Hills and K. Stewart (eds), *A More Equal Society?: New Labour, poverty, inequality and exclusion*. Bristol: The Policy Press, pp. 1–19.

Stiglitz, J., Sen, A. and Fitoussi, J.-P. (2009), *Report by the Commission on the Measurement of Economic Performance and Social Progress*: see www.stiglitz-sen-firoussi.fr.

Stocks, J., Diaz, C. and Hallerod, B. (2007), *Modern Couples Sharing Money, Sharing Life*. Basingstoke: Palgrave Macmillan.

Straus, M., Gelles, R. and Steinmetz, S. (1980), *Behind Closed Doors: Violence in the American Family*. New York: Anchor.

Sullivan, P. and Knutson, J. (2000), 'Maltreatment and disabilities: a population-based epidemiological study', *Child Abuse and Neglect* 24(10): 1257–73.

Sutherland, H. (1997), 'Women, Men and the Redistribution of Income', *Fiscal Studies* Vol. 18, No. 1, pp. 1–22.

Svendsen, G. T. and Svendsen, G. L. H. (eds) (2009), *Handbook of Social Capital: the Troika of Sociology, Political Science and Economics*. Cheltenham: Edward Elgar.

Tamas, P. (2010), Civil Society 'industries' in Eastern Europe. Paper given at conference 'Civil Society and NGOs in Europe and Russia: Responding to New Challenges and Opportunities' in St. Petersburg, Russia, available at http://www.zdes.spb.ru/index.php?option=com_content&task=view&id=316&Itemid=57, (last accessed 13 February 2011).

Tan, J. Z. G., Sanchez, F. S. and Balanon V. L. (2005), 'The Brain Drain Phenomenon and Its Implications for Health'. Paper presented at the University of the Philippines Alumni Council Meeting, 24 June. [Online] Available at: www.up.edu.ph/forum/2005/Jul-Aug05/brain_drain.htm (accessed 10 February 10 2006).

Tanzi, V. and Schuknecht, I. (1995), *The Growth of Government and the Reform of the State in Industrial Countries*. Washington, DC: IMF.

—— and Schuknecht, I. (2000), *Public Spending in the 20th Century: A Global Perspective*. Cambridge: Cambridge University Press.

Taylor-Gooby, P.(1991), 'Social change, Sociel Welfare and Sociel Science. London: Harvester Wheat sheaf.

—— P. (1993), 'The new educational settlement: National Curriculum and local management', in P. Taylor-Gooby and R. Lawson, *Markets and Managers*. Buckingham: Open University Press, 102–16.

—— (ed) (2000), *Risk, Trust and Welfare*. Basingstoke: Macmillan.

—— (2005), 'UK Pension Reform: A Test Case for a Liberal Welfare State?', in Bonoli, G. and Shinkawa, T. (eds) (2005), *Ageing and Pension Reform Around the World*. Aldershot: Edward Elgar, pp. 116–36.

Taylor, A. (2007), 'A Taxing Problem', *The Guardian*, January 10th.

Taylor, D. (1998), 'Social identity and social policy: Engagements with post-modern theory', *Journal of Social Policy* 27/3: 329–50.

Taylor, G. (2007), *Ideology and Welfare*. London: Palgrave Macmillan.

Thane, P. (1984), 'The Working Class and State 'Welfare' in Britain, 1880–1914', *The Historical Journal* 27(4): 877–900.

—— (1996), *Foundations of the Welfare State*, 2nd edn. Harlow: Longman.

Taylor-Gooby, P. (1991), '*Social Change, Social Welfare and Social Science*. London: Harvester Wheat sheaf.

Thoburn, J. (2007), *Globalisation and Child Welfare: Some Lessons from a Cross-National Study of Children in Out-of-Home Care*. Norwich: University of East Anglia.

Thomas, H. and Bullock, A. (1994), 'The political economy of local management of schools', in S. Tomlinson (ed), *Educational Reform and its Consequences*. London: IPPR/ Rivers Oram Press, 41–52.

Thorlby, R. and Maybin, J. (eds) (2010), *A High-Performing NHS? A Review of Progress 1997–2010*. London: King's Fund. http://www.kingsfund.org.uk/ publications/a_highperforming_nh.html.

Thornton, S. (2006), 'A Case of Confusion and Incoherence: Social Security under Wilson, 1964–70', *Contemporary British History* 20(3): 441–59.

Thorpe, D. and Bilson, A. (1998), 'From protection to concern: child protection careers without apologies', *Children and Society* 12(5): 373–86.

Tinker, A. (1997), *Older People in Modern Society*, 4th edn. Harlow: Longman.

Titmuss, R. (1955), 'Lecture at the University of Birmingham in honour of Eleanor Rathbone', in P. Alcock, H. Glennerster, A. Oakley and A. Sinfield (eds), *Welfare and Wellbeing: Richard Titmuss' contribution to Social Policy*, 2001 edn. Bristol: The Policy Press.

—— (1958), *Essays on the Welfare State*. London: Allen & Unwin.

—— (1968), *Commitment to Welfare*. London: Allen & Unwin.

—— (1970), *The Gift Relationship*. London: Allen and Unwin.

—— (1974), *Social Policy: An Introduction*. London: Allen & Unwin.

—— (1976), *Essays on the Welfare State*, 3rd edn. London: Allen & Unwin.

Tomlinson, S. (2005), *Education in a Post-Welfare Society*. 2nd edn. Buckingham: Open University Press.

Townsend, P. (1957), *The Family Life of Old People*. Routledge and Kegan Paul.

—— (ed) (1970), *The Concept of Poverty*. London: Heinemann.

—— (1979), *Poverty in the United Kingdom: A Survey of Household Resources and Standards of Living*. Harmondsworth: Penguin.

—— P. (ed) (2009a), *Building Decent Societies*, Basingstoke: Palgrave Macmillan.

—— (2009b), 'Social Security and Human Rights', in Townsend, P. (ed) (2009a), *Building Decent Societies*, Basingstoke: Palgrave Macmillan, pp. 29–59.

—— (2009c), 'Investment in Social Security: a possible UN model for Child Benefit?', in Townsend, P. (ed) (2009a), *Building Decent Societies*, Basingstoke: Palgrave Macmillan, pp. 151–66.

Trades Union Congress (nd), *Jobs, Unemployment and Exclusion*. London: TUC.

UK Statistics Authority (2010), Letter from Sir Michael Scholar to Rt Hon Alan Johnson MP 14072010(http:// www.statisticsauthority.gov.uk/reports-correspondence/ correspondence/letter-from-sir-michael-scholar-to-rt- hon-alan-johnson-mp-14072010.pdf; (accessed October 2010).

Ungerson, C. (1987), *Policy is Personal: Sex, Gender and Informal Care*. London: Tavistock.

—— (2000), 'Cash in care', in M. Harrington Meyer (ed), *Care Work: Gender, Labour and the Welfare State*. London: Routledge.

—— (2006), 'Gender, care and the welfare state', in K. Davis, M. Evans and J. Lorber(eds), *Handbook of Gender and Women's Studies*. London: Sage.

United Nations (2008), *United Nations Convention on the Rights of Persons with Disability*. New York: United Nations.

United Nations Department of Economic and Social Affairs, Population Division (UN ESA) (2007), *World Population Ageing 2007*. New York: United Nations.

Unwin, L. and Wellington, J. (2001), *Young People's Perspectives on Education, Training and Employment*. London: Kogan Page.

Utting, W. (1997), *People Like Us: The Review of the Safeguards for Children Living Away from Home*. London: HMSO.

van Ginneken, W. (2010), 'Social Security Coverage Extension: a review of recent evidence', *International Social Security Review* Vol. 63, No. 1, pp. 57–76.

van-Oorschot, W. (1995), *Realizing Rights: A Multi-Level Approach to Non-Take-Up of Means-Tested Benefits*. Aldershot: Avebury.

Vickerstaff, S. (1992), 'Training for economic survival', in P. Brown and H. Lauder (eds), *Education for Economic Survival*. London: Routledge, pp. 244–67.

—— (2006), 'Work and Welfare for Older Workers: A British review', in C. Spross, (ed), *Beschäftigungsförder- ung älterer Arbeitnehmer in Europa*. Beiträge zur Arbeitsmarkt- und Berufsforschung: Nürnberg.

W.W. Powell and R. Steinberg (eds) (2006), *The Nonprofit Sector: A Research Handbook*, 2nd edn. New Haven: Yale University Press.

Waddell, G. and Burton, A. K. (2006), *Is Work Good for your Health and Well-being?* Norwich: HMSO.

Walker, A. (1996), *The New Generational Contract: Intergenerational Relations, Old Age and Welfare*. London: UCL Pres.

—— Kershaw, C. and Nicholas, S. (2006), Crime in England and Wales 2005/06.

Walker, C. (1993), *Managing Poverty*. London: Routledge.

Walker, R. (2005), *Social Security and Welfare.* Buckinghamshire: Open University Press.

—— Lawson, R. and Townsend, P. (1983), *Responses to poverty in Europe.* London: Heineman.

Wallace, H. and Wallace, W. (eds) (2000), *Policy-Making in the European Union* 4th edn. Oxford: Oxford University Press.

Walmsley, R. (2003), *World Prison Population List,* 5th edn. London: Home Office.

Wanless, D. (2002), *Securing our Future Health: Taking a Long-Term View.* London: HM Treasury.

Wasoff, F. and Dey, I. (2000), *Family Policy.* Eastbourne: Gildredge Press.

Waterhouse, R. (2000), *Lost in Care: Report of the Tribunal of Inquiry into the Abuse of Children in the Former County Council Areas of Gwynedd and Clwyd since 1974.* Cm. 4776. London: HMSO.

Watson, S. (1997), 'What should count as public expenditure?', in D. Corry (ed) (1997), *Public Expenditure: Effective Management and Control.* London: Dryden Press.

Weber, M. (1947), *The Theory of Social and Economic Organization.* Oxford: Oxford University Press.

Webster, C. (1998), *The National Health Service: A Political History.* Oxford: Oxford University Press.

Wedderburn, D. (1965), 'Facts and theories of the welfare state', in R. Miliband and J. Saville (eds), *The Socialist Register.* London: Merlin Press.

WHO (World Health Organization) (2010), *Global Health Indicators:Part II.* Geneva: WHO.

Wilcox, S. (2010), *UK Housing Review 2010.* York: University of York. http://www.york.ac.uk/res/ukhr/ukhr0910/index.htm.

Wilensky, H. L. (1975), *The Welfare State and Equality: Structural and Ideological Roots of Public Expenditures.* Berkeley: University of California Press.

—— (1981), 'Leftism, Catholicism, and democratic corporatism: the role of political parties in recent welfare state development', in P. Flora and A. J. Heidenheimer (eds), *The Development of Welfare States in Europe and America.* London: Transaction.

Wiles, R., Crow, G., Charles, V. and Heath, S. (2007), 'Informed consent and the research process: following rules or striking balances?' *Sociological Research Online,* 12(2).

Wilkinson, R. G. (1996), *Unhealthy Societies: The Afflictions of Inequality.* London: Routledge.

—— (2000), *Mind the Gap: Hierarchies, Health and Human Evolution.* London: Weidenfeld & Nicolson.

—— and Pickett, K. (2010), *The Spirit Level: Why Equality is Better for Everyone.* London: Penguin Books.

—— and Pickett, K. (2010a), *The Spirit Level: Why More Equal Societies Almost Always Do Better.* Harmondsworth: Penguin Press.

Williams, F. (1989), *Social Policy: A Critical Introduction: Issues of Race, Gender and Class.* Cambridge: Polity Press.

Williams, S. (2002), 'Individual agency and the experience of new deal', *Journal of Education and Work* 15(1): 53–74.

Wilson, J. Q. (1975), *Thinking About Crime.* New York: Basic Books.

—— and Herrnstein, R. (1985), *Crime and Human Nature.* New York: Simon and Schuster.

Wilson, W. (1987), *The Truly Disadvantaged.* Chicago: Chicago University Press.

Wincott, D. (2003), 'Slippery concepts, shifting context: (national) states and welfare in the Veit-Wilson/ Atherton Debate', *Social Policy and Administration* 37(3): 305–15.

Wistow, G. (1995), 'Long-term care: Who is responsible?' in A. Harrison, and S. Bruscini, (eds) *Health Care UK 1994/5.* London: King's Fund Policy Institute.

Wolch, J. (1990), *The Shadow State: Government and Voluntary Sector in Transition.* Foundation Center: New York.

Wolf, A. (2002), *Does Education Matter?* London: Penguin.

Wolfensberger, W. (1972), *The Principle of Normalisation in Human Services.* Toronto: National Institute on Mental Retardation.

Wollstonecraft, M. (1792), *A Vindication of the Rights of Women,* 1982 edn. Harmondsworth: Penguin.

Womack, J. (1999), *The Machine that Changed the World.* New York: Maxwell Macmillan International.

World Health Organisztion (WHO) (2001), *International Classification of Functioning, Disability and Health.* Geneva: WHO.

—— (2005), *Multi-Country Study on Women's Health and Domestic Violence Against Women.* Geneva: WHO.

—— (2006),*World Health Report 2006.* Geneva: WHO.

World Health Statistics (2009), Fact Sheet no. 290, Tables 6 and 7 (http://www.who.int/whosis/whostat/2009/en/index.html).

Wright Mills, C. (1959), *The Sociological Imagination.* London: Oxford University Press.

Wright, J. S. F., Parry, J. and Mathers, J. (2007), 'What to do about political context?' Evidence synthesis, the New Deal for communities and the possibilities for evidence-based policy'. *Evidence and Policy* 3(2): 253–70.

www. justice.gov. uk/news/news released 010110a.htm: accessed 12.10.10.

Yeates, N. (2001), *Globalisation and Social Policy.* London: Sage.

—— (2005), 'The General Agreement on Trade in Services: What's in it for social security?', *International Social Security Review* Vol 58, No 1, pp. 3–22.

—— (2007), *Globalisation and Social Policy,* in J. Baldock, et al. (2007) *Social Policy,* 3rd edn. Oxford: Oxford University Press.

—— (2008a), 'Global Migration Policy', in N. Yeates (ed) *Understanding Global Social Policy*. Bristol: The Policy Press.

—— (2008b), 'The idea of global social policy', in N. Yeates (ed) *Understanding Global Social Policy*. Bristol: The Policy Press.

—— (2009), *Globalising Care Economies and Migrant Workers: Explorations in Global Care Chains*. Basingstoke: Palgrave.

—— (2010), 'The globalization of care–labour migration: Policy issues and responses', *International Labour Review* Vol. 149, No. 4.

—— and Deacon, B. (2006), *Globalism, regionalism and social policy: framing the debate*, United Nations University Centre for Comparative Regional Integration Studies (UNU-CRIS) Working Paper 0-2006/6, Bruges, Belgium [available online].

Young, H. Grundy, E. and Jitlal, M. (2006), *Characteristics of Care Providers and Care Receivers over Time*. York: Joseph Rowntree Foundation.

Young, J. (1988), 'Risk of crime and fear of crime: a realist critique of survey-based assumptions', in M. Maguire and J. Ponting (eds), *Victims of Crime: A New Deal?* Milton Keynes: Open University Press.

—— (1997), 'Left realist criminology: radical in its analysis, realist in its policy', in Maguire, R. Morgan and R. Reiner (eds), *The Oxford Handbook of Criminology*, 2nd edn. Oxford: Oxford University Press.

Zeitlin, J., Pochet, P. and Magnusson, L. (eds) (2005), *The Open Method of Coordination in Action: the European Employment and Social Inclusion Strategies,* Brussels: Peter Lang.

Zimmeck, M. (2010), 'The Compact 10 Years on: Government's approach to partnership with the voluntary and community sector in England', *Voluntary Sector Review* 1, 1, 125–33.

Zimmermann, B. (2006), 'Changes in Work and Social Protection: France, Germany and Europe', *International Social Security Review* Vol. 59, No. 4, pp. 29–45.

Office for Budget Responsibility (OBR) 180, 183
Office for Civil Society 156
Office for Disability Issues 452
Office for National Statistics (ONS) 186
Office of Population Censuses and Surveys 302
Office for Standards in Education, Children's Services and Skills (OFSTED) 183, 250
Office for the Third Sector 156
official inquiries 63
official poverty 86–7
oil crisis (1970s) 38
old age pensions
    introduction of 31
older people 22, 304–7
    definition 304
    increasing numbers of 304–5
    intermediate care 13
one-person households
    increase in 133
O'Neill, Dennis [1932–45]
    effects of murder of 321
online searching
    keywords 465
Open Method of Co-ordination 171, 411
open-ended questions 467
openness
    in adoption 333
operations
    waiting times 424
opportunity
    equality of 72
opportunity cost 185
oral history interviews 466
Organisation for Economic Co-operation and Development (OECD) 10–1, 66, 208, 210
    role of 204
organized crime 379
organized labour
    power of 400
Orkney child abuse case 320
Osborne, George 232, 392
outcome measures
    social policy 425
outcomes
    equality of 72
    social policy 19–20
outdoor relief 29
output measures
    healthcare 428
    social policy 423
Overseas Nurses Association (formerly Colonial Nurses Association) 196
owner-occupation 362–4
    housing 342–3

rise of 351–2
Oxford Committee for Famine Relief (Oxfam) 203
    foundation of 201

P

Pakistani ethnicity
    incomes of people of 89
panel doctors 32
parent
    state as 327–30
parental choice
    education 249
Parental Leave Directive 140
parental responsibilities 137
parenting
    quality of 316
Parents Against Injustice 329
parishes
    responsibility for poor 29
part-time work
    increase of 104
    pros and cons of 104
Part-Time Work Directive 140
participatory democracy 158
particularism
    voluntary and community sector 167
paternalism
    voluntary and community sector 167
Paterson, Sir Alexander Henry [1884–1947] 391
path dependence 33
Pathways to Work 119–20
patient safety 429
patriarchy 447
pay gap
    gender 110
Payne, Sarah
    murder of 321
Pelton, Leroy H. 323
penal reform groups 337
pension age
    raising for women 107
pension costs
    rising 105
Pension Credit 225
pension reform
    World Bank and 210
Pensioner States 12
pensioners
    poverty among 37
pensions 11, 34
    privatization 210
pensions age 33
'People's Budget' (1909) 31–2
performance measures 423
permanence
    children 329
'permanent austerity' 49
permanent building societies 344

permissive society
    crime blamed on 381
Perri 6 159
person-centred planning
    learning disability 300
personal care
    older people 22
personal documents 471
personal savings
    government guaranteeing 363
personal social services 10
    effects of demographic changes 97–8
personality disorders 297
personality stabilization 128
pesticides
    risks produced by 264
philanthropy
    welfare support from 29
Philippines
    nursing shortage in 198
physical abuse
    category of child abuse 322
physical disability
    adults with 301
    model of 302
    social barriers caused by 302
physical impairment
    causes of 301–2
physicians
    per 10,000 people 423
planning
    healthcare 277–81
Plant, Raymond 85
Platform of European social NGOs 171
plural pragmatists
    globalization 195
pluralism 48–9
Poland
    healthcare spending 274
    public expenditure on welfare 406
police
    institutionalized racism 385
    reducing number of 374
policing
    zero-tolerance 385
policy community 60
policy documents 471
policy goals
    ambiguous 13
policy networks 60
    social policy 60
political alliances
    international non-governmental organizations 202
political competition
    welfare state as consequence of 23
political figures
    papers of 471